Thank you for purchasing *The Science of Digital Media,* by Jennifer Burg. The information below provides instruction on how to access the activeBook site which brings the world of digital media alive.

This textbook is delivered as an *integrated learning system*. Students can learn from the printed text and/or by using the *first-time free* access code to access the **activeBook** and associated **online learning aids**.

*The Science of Digital Media* activeBook is embedded with numerous active examples, programming exercises, problem-solving and concept-testing worksheets, interactive tutorials, mathematical modeling exercises, and video tutorials which makes learning about digital media fun and interactive.

– Margin icons in your textbook let you know that an online learning aid is available for a particular concept or technique.

Access to the Digital Media Community site is free with the activeBook subscription.

**To access the activeBook for The Science of Digital Media:**

1. Go to *www.prenhall.com/digitalmedia*
2. Click on the title *The Science of Digital Media,* by Jennifer Burg.
3. Click on the link to Burg activeBook. There you can register as a First-Time User and Returning User.
4. Use a coin to scratch off the coating below and reveal your student access code.
   **\*\*Do not use a knife or other sharp object as it may damage the code.*

5. On the registration page, enter your student access code. Do not type the dashes. You can use lower or uppercase letters.
6. Follow the on-screen instructions. If you need help during the online registration process, simply click on Need Help?
7. Once your personal Login Name and Password are confirmed, you can begin using the integrated digital content.

**To login to the Burg activeBook for the first time after you've registered:**
Follow steps 1 and 2 to return to the Burg activeBook link. Then, follow the prompts for "Returning Users" to enter your Login Name and Password.
**Note to Instructors:** For access to the Instructor Resource Center, contact your local International Pearson Representative.

**PEARSON**
Prentice
Hall

Upper Saddle River, NJ 07458
www.prenhall.com

*To get help with registration, visit http://247.prenhall.com*

# The Science of Digital Media

# The Science of Digital Media

## Jennifer Burg

Wake Forest University

PEARSON

Prentice
Hall

Pearson Education International

Vice President and Editorial Director, ECS: *Marcia J. Horton*
Executive Editor: *Tracy Dunkelberger*
Editorial Assistant: *Melinda Haggerty*
Senior Managing Editor: *Scott Disanno*
Production Editor: *Rose Kernan*
Cover Designer: *Kenny Beck*
Art Editor: *Gregory Dulles*
Director, Image Resource Center: *Melinda Reo*
Manager, Rights and Permissions: *Zina Arabia*
Manager, Visual Research: *Beth Brenzel*
Manager, Cover Visual Research and Permissions: *Karen Sanatar*
Manufacturing Buyer: *Lisa McDowell*
Marketing Manager: *Mack Patterson*

© 2009 Pearson Education, Inc.
Pearson Prentice Hall
Pearson Education, Inc.
Upper Saddle River, NJ 07458

Printed in the United States of America
10 9 8 7 6 5 4 3 2 1

ISBN-(10): 0-13-506222-5
ISBN-(13): 978-0-13-506222-7

Pearson Education Ltd., London
Pearson Education Singapore, Pte. Ltd
Pearson Education, Canada, Inc.
Pearson Education–Japan
Pearson Education Australia PTY, Limited

Pearson Education North Asia Ltd., Hong Kong
Pearson Educación de Mexico, S.A. de C.V.
Pearson Education Malaysia, Pte. Ltd.
Pearson Education, Upper Saddle River, New Jersey

To Jim, who smoothes my way with his love

# Brief Table of Contents

# Table of Contents

# Preface

## Welcome

Welcome to *The Science of Digital Media*. This book is intended for anyone interested in the essential mathematics, algorithms, and technology that are the foundation of digital media tools. What do we mean by *digital media*? This is a broad term used in different ways in different contexts. In our view, the term describes itself. *Digital media* is defined as media—images, sound, and video—that are represented and manipulated digitally. By *digital media tools*, we mean application programs for manipulating digital images, audio, and video—for example, Photoshop, GIMP, Illustrator, Audition, Audacity, Sound Forge, Pro Tools, Reason, Max/MSP/Jitter, Premiere, Final Cut, and MATLAB®. We also mean the programming languages and authoring tools that make it possible for you to put together your images, audio, and video in a dynamic, interactive production—for example, Director, Flash, Processing, Python, and Java.

## Text Organization

This book begins with a chapter on fundamentals, covering topics that are relevant across media; it continues with chapters on digital imaging, digital audio, digital video; and it concludes with a chapter on multimedia authoring. There are two chapters on each medium. The first introduces basic concepts. The second discusses what you can do with images, sound, and video from the scientific, mathematical, and algorithmic perspective.

Digital media application programs are the basis for the topics chosen in *The Science of Digital Media*. This is not to say that the book is about how to use specific application programs. To choose topics for the book, I looked at the features of application programs and the activities you do when you use these features. In digital image processing, you decide on a color mode, shift to indexed color, change resolution, choose a file type, and decide whether or not to compress. In digital audio processing, you choose a sampling rate and bit depth, dither if necessary, look at spectral views of your audio file, adjust the dynamic range, and equalize frequencies. In digital video, you shoot and capture video footage, edit it and apply special effects, compress, and prepare the video appropriately for distribution. But the question is not "what's the right button to click or menu item to select?" The question is "what makes these features work?"

## Level of Material

The mathematics for digital media ranges from high school to college level. Some of the material in *The Science of Digital Media* is not beyond the reach of high school students with sufficient background in mathematics and computer programming. The book would be most appropriate for a junior or senior level elective course for computer science majors, a course like graphics or image processing, but with the difference that this course would bring together three media—images, sound, and video—examining their mathematical and algorithmic basis. At the other end of the spectrum, graduate students could use this book as an introduction to digital media, image processing, or digital signal processing, going into more depth in the mathematical and algorithmic complexities.

The essential mathematical foundation for the book includes numeric bases (particularly base 2), exponents, logarithms, summations, functions, graphs of functions, and matrices. (See Table 1.) A few sections assume some knowledge of calculus—for example, the sections on transforms. However, mathematics beyond the level of students in a course could be skipped without loss of continuity. For example, the section on FIR and IIR filters and Z-transforms could be omitted, or the essential concepts could be explained without the details, and Chapter 5 would still be useful and understandable.

The presentation of algorithms in the book assumes that students have some programming experience. At a minimum, they should understand procedural problem solving and be able to read pseudocode. Chapter 8 focuses on a comparison of multimedia authoring environments and thus assumes some programming experience. However, instructors can use this book for a course without requiring students to write any programs.

| Mathematical concept | Where it is applied in the book |
| --- | --- |
| discrete and continuous number systems<br>discrete and continuous functions | analog vs. discrete phenomena throughout |
| 1D and 2D arrays (i.e., vectors and matrices)<br>functions and graphs<br>Cartesian coordinates<br>polar coordinates<br>trigonometric functions<br>radians and degrees | bitmaps and audio files;<br>sinusoidal waveforms throughout |
| base 2<br>conversion between bases<br>bits and bytes<br>exponents<br>square roots | digitization process and algorithms throughout |
| logarithms<br>natural logarithms<br>e (the base of the natural logarithm) | decibels (Chapters 1 and 4); data rate (Chapter 1); non-linear quantization (Chapter 4); Q-factor (Chapter 5) and throughout |
| round, floor, and ceiling functions<br>mod operator | algorithms throughout |
| integrals (basic understanding only) | Fourier transform (Chapters 4 and 5) |
| inverse of a function | discrete cosine transform (Chapter 2)<br>Fourier transform (Chapter 4) |
| 3D graphs<br>linear transforms through matrix multiplication<br>algorithmic non-linear transforms<br>normalization of values<br>projection of a function to a plane | color models, color model conversions, and CIE chromaticity diagram (Chapter 2) |

| Mathematical concept | Where it is applied in the book |
|---|---|
| implicit and explicit forms of function<br>parametric functions<br>matrix operations<br>derivatives<br>tangents | vector graphics and curves (Chapter 2) |
| complex numbers<br>imaginary numbers | fractals (Chapter 2)<br>Fourier transform (Chapters 4 and 5)<br>z-transform (Chapter 5) |
| tree data structure | Huffman encoding; indexed color (Chapter 3) |
| convolutions and convolution masks<br>matrix operations | image dithering and filtering (Chapter 3)<br>audio filtering (Chapter 5) |
| histograms<br>mean, median, mode, standard deviation | pixel point processing (Chapter 3) |
| root mean square | root mean square amplitude of an audio file<br>(Chapter 4) |
| nth root | octaves and frequency of notes (Chapter 5) |

## Features and Elements Found in the Textbook

A number of features help to guide you through the textbook:

- **Key terms**: Key terms are boldfaced. When a key term appears in several places, it is boldface where it is first introduced and explained.

- **Key equations**: Equations that are likely to be used in later computations, exercises, or applications are marked as key equations.

- **Learning aids**: There are several types of learning aids in the text. (See the subsection below.) They are marked with icons in the margin. These learning aids are available at this book's activeBook site and can be accessed by entering the access code found on the card in the front of this book.

- **Asides**: Asides contain additional information about scientists or additional discussion of a concept. As "extras," this information is placed to the side of the main text so as not to interrupt the flow of the related discussion.

## activeBook and Online Learning Aids

This textbook is delivered as an *integrated learning system*. Students can learn from the printed text and/or by using the *first-time free* access code to access the **activeBook** and associated **online learning aids resources**. The interactive multimedia resources and activeBook can be accessed at www.prenhall.com/digitalmedia.

**The activeBook and online learning aids provide a more exciting learning experience**—the activeBook touches students on multiple levels. It is embedded with numerous active examples, programming exercises, problem-solving and concept-testing worksheets, interactive tutorials, mathematical modeling exercises, and video tutorials throughout the online text to stimulate student learning by making them active participants in the learning process. Because activeBook marries print content with dynamic online resources, content is brought to life and available anytime, from anywhere.

The activeBook experience is customizable by faculty and students. Students can annotate their activeBook and customize their view of the book's dynamic resources.

The diagnostic tools within the activeBook can create custom study plans tailored to the student's or the class's weaknesses and strengths in the subject matter.

An activeBook can contain course management tools, exist only as a linked resource from an external course management system, or it can be used as a help link with no navigation between online pages.

The availability of online learning aids is marked in the margins of the book in the sections to which the learning aids apply. The online learning aids available for this textbook include:

- **Interactive tutorials** that demonstrate concepts, activities, mathematical operations, and algorithms in a way that makes the concepts easier to grasp.

- **Problem-solving and concept-testing worksheets** that reinforce concepts and check the student understanding.

- **Mathematical modeling exercises** that can be completed by students in MATLAB® or Octave (open source freeware) or can be used by the instructor as the basis for an in-class demonstration.

- **Programming exercises** that challenge students to implement algorithms "from scratch."

- **Hands-on exercises** and **suggestions for projects** that tie science to application.

- **Pre- and post-tests** provide a means of assessing student progress.

## Digital Media Community Forum

The ability to exchange ideas and experiences make every learning experience more meaningful. Access to the Digital Media Community site is free with the activeBook subscription. Students and instructors can share ideas and learning materials, make contributions, participate in discussion forums, and connect with other students and faculty teaching digital media.

## Instructors Resources

Protected instructors resources are available at the Prentice Instructor Resource Center (IRC). Contact your local Prentice Hall Sales Representative to gain access to this site. Instructors will find solutions to worksheets, programming solutions, and pre- and post-tests with solutions at this site.

## A Three Book Digital Media Series

Digital media is an inherently interdisciplinary area, of interest to both artists and scientists. A growing number of colleges and universities are introducing digital media courses to their curriculum in art, communication, computer science, or independent departments. In response to the need for new interdisciplinary curriculum material, Prentice Hall is publishing *The Science of Digital Media* as part of a three book set:

- *Digital Media Primer*, by Yue-Ling Wong, covering the fundamentals of digital media, relevant to both artists and scientists
- *The Science of Digital Media*, by Jennifer Burg, focusing on the mathematics, science, and algorithms which underlie digital media applications
- *Digital Arts: Its Arts and Science*, by Yue-Ling Wong, focusing on digital media from the perspective of creating art

The three books have parallel chapters—one on background, two on each of the media (images, audio, and video), and concluding chapters on multimedia authoring.

The primer creates a bridge between the art and science disciplines. In a computer science course that uses *The Science of Digital Media* as a textbook, the *Primer* could be recommended to students as reference on fundamentals. In an art or interdisciplinary course that uses the *Primer* or *Art* volumes as their basic textbook, *The Science of Digital Media* could be recommended as a source for additional information. The parallel organization of the chapters facilitates moving from one to the other.

## How to Use This Book
### Computer Science Courses

*The Science of Digital Media* was written particularly as a textbook for computer science or interdisciplinary courses that view digital media as a combination of science and applications. The book contains more than enough material for a single course. My goal in writing the book was to make it possible for instructors to select topics relevant to their courses, with the remainder available as reference.

Here are four ways that *The Science of Digital Media* could be used as a textbook.

- A course that emphasizes breadth would make a pass over the entire book, with the instructor focusing only on the topics of most interest to him or her.
- If a course covers only one medium, only the chapters on that medium would be used and covered in detail. For example, a course on digital imaging would include Chapters 1, 2, 3, and 8. A course in digital audio would include Chapters 1, 4, and 5. Such a course would leave ample time for the students to apply concepts to practice and to solve problems at various levels of abstractions—through low-level programming, MATLAB® signal processing toolkits, MAX/MSP, or audio processing tools like Audacity, for example.
- The book could be used over two semesters, one semester emphasizing algorithms and one semester emphasizing mathematics.
- The book could be used over two semesters, each semester making a pass over the entire book. The first semester would focus on basic concepts and high level tools; the second semester would go into more depth on the mathematics and problem-solving at a lower level of abstraction.

It's possible to teach an interesting and relevant digital media course that focuses entirely on science, mathematics, and algorithms and includes no hands-on practice in using digital media tools. On the other hand, students are often attracted to the study of digital media because it relates to *doing things* and *making things*: pictures, sound, video, interactive games, educational software, and the like. Applying concepts to practice is an exciting way to learn. I've found that a good way to organize a digital media course is to focus classroom instruction on science and mathematics, while assigning projects and exercises that require the use of application programs. For example, I often have my students implement game programs for their final projects, pulling together digital images, sound, interactivity, and possibly video by means of a multimedia programming language.

In a course that combines science with hands-on practice, students will need access to software for the media covered. Below is a table of relevant software for each medium. Some of this software is open source and free. Commercial software comes in varying levels and prices ranges. An alternative to purchasing the software is to download trial versions, many of which are usable for 30 days.

| Digital Imaging and Vector Graphics | | | |
|---|---|---|---|
| **software** | **platform** | **availability** | **use** |
| Adobe Photoshop | Mac, Windows | commercial | bitmap images |
| Adobe Photoshop Elements | Mac, Windows | | bitmap images |
| GIMP | Linux, Mac, Windows, Unix | free | bitmap images and vector graphics |
| Inkscape | Linux, Mac, Windows, Unix | free | vector graphics |
| Adobe Illustrator | Mac, Windows | commercial | vector graphics |
| CorelDraw | Windows | commercial | bitmap images and vector graphics |
| Corel PaintShop Pro | Windows | commercial | bitmap images |
| Ulead Photoimpact | Windows | commercial | Bitmap images |
| **Digital Audio Processing and MIDI** | | | |
| **software** | **platform** | **availability** | **use** |
| Audacity | Linux, Mac, Windows, Unix | free | digital audio |
| Adobe Audition | Windows | commercial | digital audio |
| Ardour | Linux, Mac | free | digital audio |
| Apple Logic Pro | Mac | commercial | digital audio and MIDI |
| Apple Logic Express | Mac | commercial | digital audio |
| Sony Sound Forge | Windows | commercial | digital audio |
| Digidesign Pro Tools | Mac, Windows | commercial | digital audio and MIDI |
| Cakewalk Sonar | Windows | commercial | digital audio and MIDI |
| Cakewalk Music Creator | Windows | commercial | digital audio and MIDI |
| Cycling 74 Max/MSP | Mac, Windows | commercial | digital audio and MIDI |
| ChucK | Mac, Windows, Linus | free | digital audio and MIDI |

| Digital Video Processing | | | |
|---|---|---|---|
| software | platform | availability | use |
| Adobe Premiere Pro | Windows | commercial | digital video |
| Adobe Premiere Elements | Windows | commercial | digital video |
| Ulead VideoStudio | Windows | commercial | digital video |
| Windows Movie Maker | Windows | comes with Windows | digital video |
| Apple iMovie | Mac | comes with Mac | digital video |
| Cinelerra | Linux, Mac | free | digital video |
| Apple Final Cut Pro | Mac | commercial | digital video |
| Apple Final Cut Express | Mac | commercial | digital video |
| Cycling 74 Jitter | Mac, Windows | commercial | digital video |
| Multimedia Authoring | | | |
| software | platform | availability | use |
| Adobe Flash | Mac, Windows | commercial | multimedia authoring, 2D animation, optimized for vector graphics |
| Adobe Director | Mac, Windows | commercial | multimedia authoring, optimized for bitmap images, 2D and 3D |
| Java | Linux, Mac, Windows, Unix | free | multipurpose language |
| Processing | Linux, Mac, Windows | free | bitmap images (art inspired) |
| Python | Linux, Mac, Windows, Unix | free | Multipurpose language |
| Mathematical Modeling of Digital Images and Sound | | | |
| software | platform | availability | use |
| MATLAB | Mac, Windows, Linux, Unix | commercial | modeling images and sound and operations on them |
| Octave | Linux, Unix, Mac, Windows | free | modeling images and sound and operations on them |

## Using the Book Outside of a Course

*The Science of Digital Media* could be of interest to anyone working in digital media—not just those taking a course. There are people who just like to know how things work. If you're this type, it isn't enough to poke around on menu items and click buttons by trial and error until you get the effect you're looking for. You want to know what's *really* going on. Understanding the mathematics and science behind digital media tools gives you a mastery over the tools that is hard to achieve by hands-on experience alone. For practitioners of digital media curious enough to "look under the hood," *The Science of Digital Media* can be a helpful and, we hope, even an interesting reference book.

Whatever your reason for reading this book, I encourage you to dig in, find answers to questions that have always puzzled you, and realize there are questions that never even occurred to you. The practice of digital media can fascinate the eyes and ears with images, sound, motion, and interactivity. The science, mathematics, and technical ingenuity of digital media can equally dazzle the mind.

## Acknowledgments

I'd like to acknowledge the help of the students, colleagues, and friends who contributed to the writing and editing of this book and its supplements:

- Donna Williams, Professor of Computer Science at Stetson University, who served as proofreader and mathematics consultant
- Jason Romney, instructor of digital sound design at North Carolina School of the Arts, who served as consultant on the audio chapters
- Todd Martin, Wake Forest student, who created many of the online tutorials and worksheets
- Michael Boger, Wake Forest student, who contributed greatly to the proofreading process with his eagle-eye and mathematical acumen
- Angelique Lausier and Grey Ballard, Wake Forest students, who contributed online tutorials and worksheets
- Chris Thomas, Wake Forest student, who proofread and created exercises for the video chapters
- Ching-Wan Yip, who proofread Chapters 6 and 7
- Jonathan Burg-Grigsby and Trevor Laurence, who proofread early chapters and provided a student's perspective
- Tyson Badders, who did a final proofreading of the pre- and post-tests

I'd also like to thank the professors who participated in the pilot-testing of my book:

- Julie Carrington of Rollins College
- Edward A. Fox of Virginia Polytechnic Institute and State University
- Kristian Damkjer of the University of Florida
- Robert Kenny and Steve Teicher of the University of Central Florida
- Glenn Chance, Rochester Institute of Technology
- Lloyd Smith, Missouri State University

## Support

This material is based on work supported by the National Science Foundation under grants No. DUE-0127280 and DUE-0340969. Any opinions, findings, and conclusions or recommendations expressed in this material are those of the author(s) and do not necessarily reflect the views of the National Science Foundation. The PI and co-PI of the two grants were Yue-Ling Wong and Jennifer Burg, respectively. Professor Leah McCoy was the assessment expert in the second grant.

JENNIFER BURG
*Wake Forest University*

# Prentice Hall's
# Digital Media
## Series

## AN INTEGRATED LEARNING SYSTEM

Textbook, *activeBook*, dynamic multimedia learning aids, collaborative online community portal

At the section level, the textbook contains margin icons that indicate the availability of online learning aids.

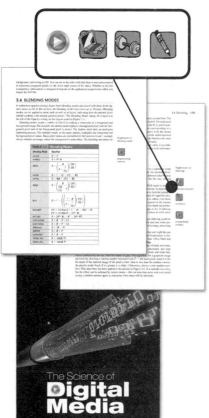

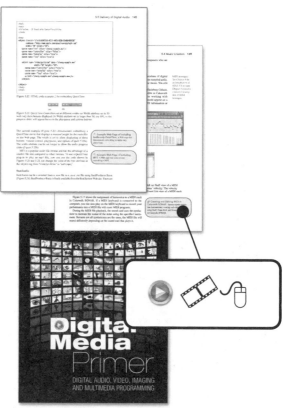

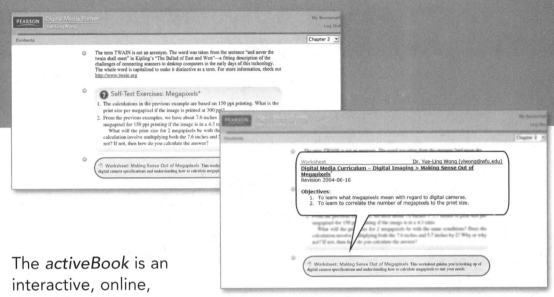

The *activeBook* is an interactive, online, digital book that integrates robust multimedia resources with the textbook to enhance the learning experience. *activeBooks* are embedded with:

- active examples
- programming exercises
- problem-solving and concept-testing worksheets
- interactive tutorials and demos
- mathematical modeling exercises
- video tutorials

The authors and Prentice Hall have worked together to integrate the textbook, the *activeBook* and the dynamic multimedia learning aids to make teaching and learning easier!

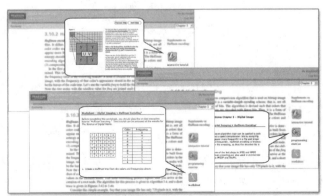

Everything works together for a unified teaching and learning experience!

# STUDENTS BECOME PARTICIPANTS IN THE LEARNING PROCESS!

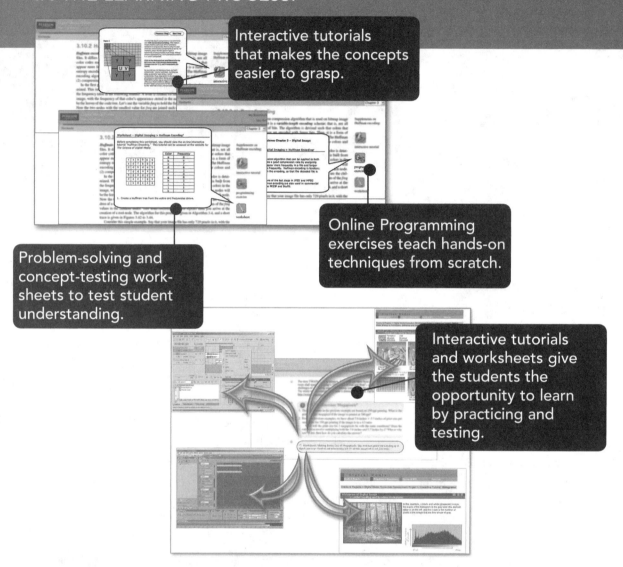

Interactive tutorials that makes the concepts easier to grasp.

Online Programming exercises teach hands-on techniques from scratch.

Problem-solving and concept-testing work-sheets to test student understanding.

Interactive tutorials and worksheets give the students the opportunity to learn by practicing and testing.

To gain access to the *activeBook*, the community portal and the dynamic and interactive media that accompanies this product, visit www.prenhall.com/digitalmedia and enter the access code printed on the card in the front of this book. If your book does not include an access card, you can purchase access at www.prenhall.com/digitalmedia.

## Digital Media Series

We heard the cry! In response to the need for new interdisciplinary curriculum material, Prentice Hall is publishing a three-book set of interactive digital media products:

- *Digital Media Primer*, by Yue-Ling Wong, fundamentals of digital media that are relevant to both artists and scientists

- *The Science of Digital Media*, by Jennifer Burg, the mathematics, science, and algorithms that underlie digital media applications

- *Digital Arts: Its Arts and Science*, by Yue-Ling Wong, digital media from the perspective of making art

# Digital Data Representation and Communication

# 1

*I am an instrument in the shape of a woman*
*trying to translate pulsations into images....*
—Adrienne Rich, "Planetarium"

## OBJECTIVES FOR CHAPTER 1

- Understand the difference between analog and discrete phenomena.
- Understand how images and sound can be represented as sinusoidal waveforms.
- Understand how sinusoidal waveforms model sound waves of a given frequency.
- Understand how sinusoidal functions can be summed to create more complex waveforms.
- Understand how undersampling leads to aliasing.
- Understand how quantization leads to quantization error.
- Understand and be able to apply the equation for signal-to-noise ratio.
- Be able to calculate the storage space needed for digital images, audio, and video files given basic parameters.
- Know the storage capacity of common storage media.
- Understand basic concepts of digital data communication.
- Understand the various usages of the term *bandwidth*.
- Know how to compute maximum data rate given bandwidth and number of different signal values that can be communicated.
- Understand the relationship between bit rate and baud rate.
- Be able to perform run-length encoding, entropy encoding, and arithmetic encoding.
- Be familiar with common compression algorithms and codecs.

## 1.1 INTRODUCTION

### 1.1.1 The Approach of this Book

Something caused you to open this book. Maybe this book is the required text for a course you're taking, a course such as Digital Media or Multimedia Systems. Maybe you've been dabbling in photographic, sound, or video processing on your own and have gotten curious about how your tools actually work. Maybe you're a mathematician, engineer, or physicist who finds digital media a fascinating arena in which to apply your discipline. Maybe you're a musician, a graphic artist, or a professional in some field that requires the support of digital media, and you want to know more. If science and mathematics have always interested you, you may be curious to look behind the scenes, expecting that a deeper understanding of your digital media tools will enhance your creative powers.

Whatever your reason for opening this book, we assume that the greatest motivation for most people interested in digital media is the excitement of creation. Digital media is multimedia driven by computers. You can see it, hear it, maybe even touch it, and certainly interact with it. It becomes even more exciting when the images, sound, and motion are the work of your own hands and brain. What draws most people to a study of digital media is the satisfaction of making something that communicates, entertains, or teaches.

With this goal in mind, we've chosen the topics in this book by considering the specific activities undertaken in digital media work—choosing color modes, compressing files, identifying aliased frequencies, filtering, transforming, and creatively editing. However, rather than present step-by-step methods related to specific application programs, we present the mathematical and algorithmic procedures upon which the tools are built. We attempt to make the explanations simple, straightforward, and relevant to hands-on activity. Procedures and algorithms are illustrated with interactive demos and mathematical modeling exercises that reinforce the text. We believe that the science behind digital media can be just as fascinating as the end product, and that understanding the science not only will increase your creative powers but also will make the creative process more intellectually satisfying. Dig in and see what you discover.

### 1.1.2 Where to Begin

So where do we begin? This book is organized around three main media—digital imaging, audio, and video—woven together at the end with multimedia programming. Topics in each chapter are motivated by activities done in digital media application programs such as Photoshop, Premiere, Final Cut, Audition, Sound Forge, Logic, Reason, Illustrator, Flash, and Director, but they are presented from a mathematical or conceptual perspective.

Chapter 1 covers concepts that are relevant to more than one medium. In particular, the digitization process of sampling and quantization is introduced, to be revisited in the context of image and sound in later chapters. Analog-to-digital conversion is where it all begins. We then move on to fundamentals of data communication and data storage. A survey of compression methods covers concepts relevant to all media. We conclude the chapter with an overview of standards and standardization organizations. Accompanying the chapter are interactive tutorials introducing you to mathematical modeling tools that will help you visualize and experiment with concepts.

There's a lot of material in this chapter. You'll probably find some of it easy and you'll be able to skim through it quickly. Some you can note as reference material to look back at later when you need the information. Some of the material is more challenging and may not sink in entirely until you read on and work more with your tools. A lot of the material is reinforced in later chapters, as it applies to a particular medium—images, sound, and video. Focus on what interests you most, and don't forget to look at the interactive tutorials and learning supplements online.

## 1.2 ANALOG TO DIGITAL CONVERSION

### 1.2.1 Analog versus Discrete Phenomena

*Analog phenomena* are continuous—like a steady stream of water, a line on a graph, or a continuously rotating dial on a radio. With analog phenomena, there is no clear separation between one point and the next; in fact, between any two points, an infinite number of other points exist. *Discrete phenomena*, on the other hand, *are* clearly separated. There's a point (in space or time), and then there's a neighboring point, and there's nothing between the two. A dripping faucet is a discrete phenomenon, whereas the water in a running tap is continuous and thus analog. Many of our sensory perceptions come to us in analog form (although some may consider this debatable, perhaps even a philosophical question). A live orchestra presents music to us in analog form, as continuous sound waves. A standard microphone is an analog device, detecting and recording sounds over time and transmitting them as a continuous wave of varying voltages.

Converting the continuous phenomena of images, sound, and motion into a discrete representation that can be handled by a computer is called *analog-to-digital conversion*. You may wonder what the advantages are of digital over analog data. Photographs, music recordings, and television have been around for a long time without the benefit of being digitized, so why should we change now? Why did the consumer market switch so willingly from vinyl record albums to compact disks? Why should you buy a digital camera if you have a perfectly good analog one? What could motivate you to switch to digital television?

There are, in fact, quite a few advantages to digital media. It may seem that analog data—with infinite values that can run smoothly and continuously from one to the next—would be more precise and give better quality in photographs, music, and videos. But as storage media have increased in size and communication channels have increased in data rate, it has become possible to increase the resolution of digital images, audio, and video. This means that a digitized picture and sound can now be captured in fine detail. Digital data also has an advantage in the way that images and sound are communicated. Analog data communication is more vulnerable to noise than is digital, so it loses some of its quality in transmission. With digital data, which is communicated entirely as a sequence of 0s and 1s, error-correcting strategies can be employed to ensure that the data is received and interpreted correctly. Moreover, digital data can be communicated more compactly than analog. This may seem counter-intuitive. You might think that a digitally encoded television program, for example—in the primitive language of 0s and 1s—would require much more data than the same program broadcast in analog form. However, excellent compression algorithms exist for digital data that significantly reduce the amount of data without sacrificing quality. The result is that digital cable television transmissions are actually able to divide their bandwidth among numerous broadcasts, offering the consumer both a variety of programming and high quality picture and sound. How this all happens should become clearer to you as you learn more about analog-to-digital conversion, digital data communication, and compression algorithms.

## 1.2.2 Image and Sound Data Represented as Functions and Waveforms

The two primary media in digital media are images and sound. They are primary in the sense that the two are combined to produce video. Haptic output—based on the sense of touch—is sometimes present in digital media but is not yet common. Both images and sound can be represented as functions, and we can visualize these functions by means of their corresponding graphs. (If you don't need this refresher on the basic physics and mathematics of sinusoidal functions and waves, you can skip this section.)

Sound, for example, is a one-dimensional function—that is, a function with one variable as input. If we think of sound as a continuous phenomenon, then we can model it as a continuous function $y = f(x)$ where $x$ is time and $y$ is the air pressure amplitude.

The essential form of the function representing sound is sinusoidal, which means that it has the shape of a sine wave. In this book, we assume that you have some background in trigonometry, but let's review the sine function briefly. Assume you have a triangle with vertices A, B, and C. We give the name $\angle V$ to the angle at vertex V, for any vertex V. An angle can be measured in degrees, abbreviated as °, or radians, abbreviated as rad. The relationship between radians and degrees is as follows:

## KEY EQUATION

Let $r$ be the size of an angle measured in radians, and let $d$ be this size measured in degrees. Then

$$\frac{r}{d} = \frac{\pi}{180}$$

In this book, we will assume all angles are in radians.

Assume $\angle B$ is a *right angle*, which means that it is of size $\pi/2$, as pictured in Figure 1.1. A triangle that contains an angle of size $\pi/2$ is called a *right triangle*. The side opposite the right angle is called the *hypotenuse*, whose length we call $h$. Consider either of the two non-right-angles in the triangle—say, for our example, $\angle C$, which has size $\alpha$. The side opposite $\angle C$ is called the *opposite side* with regard to $\angle C$. Say that this side has length $c$. The other side is the *adjacent side* with regard to $\angle C$. Assume that the side adjacent has size $a$. Then the sine and cosine of $\angle C$ are defined by the angle's size as follows:

$$\sin(\alpha) = c/h$$
$$\cos(\alpha) = a/h$$

We call sines and cosines *sinusoidal functions*.

The previous definition defines the sine and cosine functions for angles that are less than $\pi/2$. We can generalize this definition for angles of any size by looking at angles at the center of a Cartesian coordinate system. In a Cartesian coordinate system, values increase horizontally from left to right across the $x$-axis and vertically from bottom to top up the $y$-axis. $(x, y)$ denotes a point in this Cartesian space. $x$ and $y$ are called the *coordinates* of the point. The place where the two axes cross is called the *origin*, at point $(0, 0)$. Consider a circle of radius 1 around the origin, called a *unit circle* (Figure 1.2). Note that by the Pythagorean

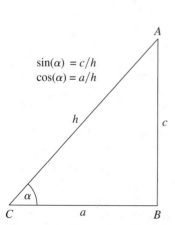

**Figure 1.1** Sine and cosine functions defined within a right triangle

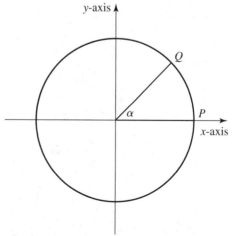

**Figure 1.2** Sine and cosine functions defined within a unit circle

theorem, the equation for a unit circle is $x^2 + y^2 = 1$. Let point $P$ be at position (1, 0), which is located on the $x$-axis. For every point $Q$ on the unit circle, you have an angle connecting $P$ to the origin and then to $Q$. Let the size of the angle be $\alpha$. As you move $Q$ around the unit circle counterclockwise, $\alpha$ goes from 0 to $2\pi$. Notice that when $Q$ returns to its initial position on the $x$-axis, the angle can be considered to be of size 0 or $2\pi$. In fact, it is angle $2\pi k$, $k$ being the number of times you have gone around the unit circle. ($k$ is positive if you move counterclockwise and negative otherwise.) Because $Q$ lies on the unit circle, $Q$'s $x$ and $y$ coordinates give the sine and cosine, respectively, of the angle created by $P$, the origin, and $Q$. That is, $\sin(\alpha) = y$ and $\cos(\alpha) = x$. For angles of size $\theta$ where $\theta$ is greater than $2\pi$ or less than 0 and $\theta = \alpha + 2\pi k$, the definitions of the sine and cosine functions generalize as follows:

$$\text{If } \theta = \alpha + 2\pi k \text{ and } k \text{ is an integer then}$$
$$\sin(\theta) = \sin(\alpha + 2\pi k) = \sin(\alpha)$$
$$\cos(\theta) = \cos(\alpha + 2\pi k) = \cos(\alpha)$$

Thus, the sine and cosine functions are considered periodic functions in the sense that their values cycle in a regular pattern, as shown in Table 1.1.

| TABLE 1.1 | Sine Function | |
|---|---|---|
| **Angle in Radians** | **Angle in Degrees** | **Sine of Angle** |
| 0 | 0 | 0 |
| $\pi/6$ | 30 | 1/2 |
| $\pi/4$ | 45 | $\sqrt{2}/2$ |
| $\pi/3$ | 60 | $\sqrt{3}/2$ |
| $\pi/2$ | 90 | 1 |
| $2\pi/3$ | 120 | $\sqrt{3}/2$ |
| $3\pi/4$ | 135 | $\sqrt{2}/2$ |
| $5\pi/6$ | 150 | 1/2 |
| $\pi$ | 180 | 0 |
| $7\pi/6$ | 210 | $-1/2$ |
| $5\pi/4$ | 225 | $-\sqrt{2}/2$ |
| $4\pi/3$ | 240 | $-\sqrt{3}/2$ |
| $3\pi/2$ | 270 | $-1$ |
| $5\pi/3$ | 300 | $-\sqrt{3}/2$ |
| $7\pi/4$ | 315 | $-\sqrt{2}/2$ |
| $11\pi/6$ | 330 | $-1/2$ |
| $2\pi$ | 360 | 0 |

We can visualize this pattern through a graph of the values. In this graph, the $x$-axis represents the size of the angle and the $y$-axis represents the sine of the angle. This shape is referred to as a sine wave, as shown in Figure 1.3. (The graph of the cosine is also shown in the figure.) We refer to this as a *simple sine wave* when we wish to emphasize that it is a single sine function rather than the sum of two or more.

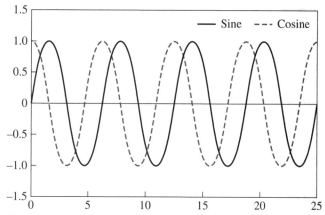

**Figure 1.3** Graphs of sine and cosine waves

Now let's see how sinusoidal functions relate to waves and thus to sound and images. Sound is a good medium with which to begin this discussion because it is easy to understand as an analog phenomenon and to think of as a wave.

You're probably familiar with the concept of sound waves as a physical phenomenon, but this review may be useful since sinusoidal waves are an important abstraction in digital media, relevant to images as well. First, sound is a *mechanical wave*, which means that it results from the motion of particles through a transmission medium—for example, the motion of molecules in air. Because sound is a mechanical wave, it has to have something to move through; sound cannot be transmitted through a vacuum.

The movement associated with a sound wave is initiated by a vibration. Imagine one of the strings inside a piano vibrating after one of the piano's soft hammers hits it. The air molecules next to the string are set in motion, radiating energy out from the vibrating string. For simplicity, let's just picture a single "wave" moving from left to right. As the string vibrates to the right, the molecules closest to the string are pushed to the right, moving closer to the molecules next to them, which in a chain reaction move closer to the molecules next to them, and so forth. When molecules are pressed closer to their neighbors, air pressure rises. When the piano string moves back to the left, the molecules next to the string have space to spread out and move to the left as well, so the pressure between these molecules and the molecules to their right is reduced. This periodic changing of air pressure—high to low, high to low, etc.—radiates out from the string from left to right. (See Figure 1.4.)

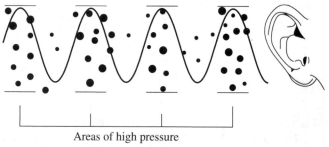

Areas of high pressure

**Figure 1.4** Changing air pressure caused by vibration of air molecules

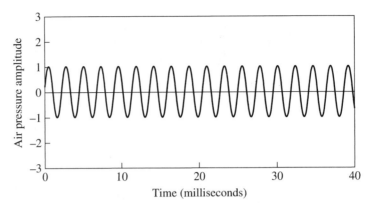

**Figure 1.5** A single-frequency (440 Hz) tone with no overtones, represented as a waveform

If you can visualize a sound wave as we just described it above, you can see that the motion of the air molecules is back and forth from left to right, the same direction in which the wave is radiating out from the string. A wave of this type is called a ***longitudinal wave***, defined as a wave in which the motion of individual particles is parallel to the direction in which energy is being transported. Sound is a longitudinal mechanical wave.

The sound wave in Figure 1.5. is a graphical and mathematical abstraction of the physical phenomenon of sound. Prefix definitions for units are given in the table below. The graph represents represents the periodic change of air pressure. First the pressure increases as molecules are pushed closer together, shown by the upward arc in the graph. Then the pressure decreases as the molecules move apart, shown by the downward arc. These changes happen over time, so the $x$-axis in the graph represents time, while the $y$-axis represents air pressure.

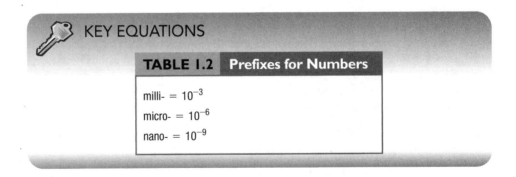

### KEY EQUATIONS

| TABLE 1.2 | Prefixes for Numbers |
|---|---|
| milli- = $10^{-3}$ | |
| micro- = $10^{-6}$ | |
| nano- = $10^{-9}$ | |

A wave is said to be ***periodic*** if it repeats a pattern over time. The pattern that is repeated constitutes one ***cycle*** of the wave. A ***wavelength*** is the length (in distance) of one complete cycle. The ***frequency*** of a wave is the number of times a cycle repeats per unit time, which in the case of sound corresponds to the rate at which the air molecules are vibrating. The frequency of a sound wave is measured in cycles per second, or Hertz. Common prefixes and frequency measurements are summarized in Tables 1.2 and 1.3.

KEY EQUATIONS

| TABLE 1.3 | Abbreviations for Frequency or Sampling Rate |
|-----------|---------------------------------------------|

Assume the following abbreviations:

| | |
|---|---|
| Hertz | Hz |
| kilohertz | kHz |
| megahertz | MHz |
| second | s |
| millisecond | ms |
| microsecond | μs |
| nanosecond | ns |

1 Hz = 1 cycle/s
1 kHz = 1000 Hz
1 MHz = 1,000,000 Hz

The *period* of a wave is the amount of time it takes for one cycle to complete. Period and frequency are reciprocals of each other.

KEY EQUATION

Let $T$ be the period and $f$ be the frequency of a sinusoidal wave. Then

$$T = 1/f \text{ and}$$
$$f = 1/T$$

The height of a wave is called its *amplitude.*

To create a sine function representing a sound wave of frequency $f$ Hz, you must convert $f$ to angular frequency first. The relationship between the two is as follows:

KEY EQUATION

Let $f$ be the frequency of a sine wave measured in Hz. Let $\omega$ be the equivalent *angular frequency* measured in radians/s. Then

$$\omega = 2\pi f$$

Thus, the sine function representing a sound wave with a frequency of 440 Hz is $\sin(880\pi)$. This sine wave is pictured in Figure 1.5.

A graphical representation of sound in the form of a wave tells us something about the sound without our having to hear it. If the wave is completely regular like the one in Figure 1.5, then the sound is a single-pitch tone, like a single musical note with no overtones. The amplitude of a wave corresponds to how loud the sound is; the larger the amplitude, the louder the sound. The frequency of a wave corresponds to the pitch of the sound; the higher the frequency, the higher-pitched the sound.

Figure 1.5 shows a simple waveform corresponding to an idealized musical tone at a single frequency. A single-frequency tone takes the form of a sine function; that is, it is a *sinusoidal waveform*. Few sounds in nature are this pure in form. Then how are more complex sounds created and represented? It is possible to add a number of simple waveforms to get a more complex one. Figure 1.6 shows the result of adding the musical notes C, E, and G together. The sum of the three sound waves creates the harmony of the three notes played simultaneously.

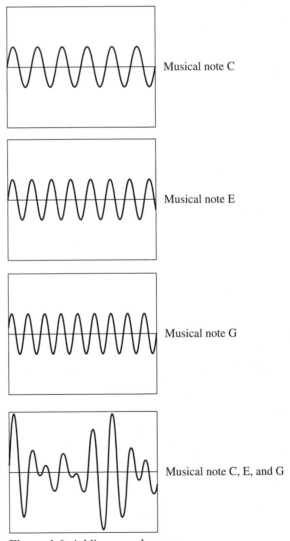

Musical note C

Musical note E

Musical note G

Musical note C, E, and G

**Figure 1.6** Adding sound waves

We can do this process in reverse. That is, we can take a complex waveform and break it down mathematically into its frequency components. The method for doing this is called the *Fourier transform*. Fourier analysis shows that any periodic signal can be decomposed into an infinite sum of sinusoidal waveforms. The simple sinusoidal waves are called the *frequency components* of the more complex wave. The Fourier transform makes it possible to store a complex sound wave in digital form, determine the wave's frequency components, and filter out components that are not wanted. Filtering can be done in order to improve audio quality or to compress a digital audio file. These concepts and procedures will be discussed in more detail in Chapter 4.

> **ASIDE:** Jean Baptiste Joseph Fourier was an 18th century French mathematician whose analyses of periodic functions (*i.e.*, sines and cosines) have been fundamental to advances in engineering and digital signal processing.

In Chapter 2, you will see that sinusoidal waveforms can also be used to represent changing color amplitudes in a digital image. Look at the image in Figure 1.7. Imagine that each point in the picture can be represented by a number—its *grayscale* value. Grayscale values range from 0 to 255 and correspond to shades of gray, black, and white. (We could also think of 256 different colors. The point is that they are simply represented as numbers.) For the moment, assume that the image is continuous, with an infinite number of points in each row and column of the image. We'll worry about digitization later. Assume that the grayscale values vary smoothly from left to right, increasing and decreasing in a regular pattern. Now take just one horizontal line of grayscale values from that image. If the grayscale values are graphed over space, we get the sine wave pictured in Figure 1.8. The values in the vertical direction could be graphed similarly, as a one-dimensional waveform. By extension, we could graph the values taken from both the $x$ and $y$ directions on the image, representing the grayscale values as amplitudes—that is, representing them by their height above the image plane. In this sense, the values in the image, when graphed over the spatial domain, define a two-dimensional waveform, as pictured in Figure 1.9. (The shading of the waveform in this figure is only to help you see its contour better. It is the shape that is significant.) We'll return to the concept of images as waveforms in more detail in Chapter 2.

Viewing a sound or an image as a waveform underlines the continuous nature of the data. The wave varies smoothly across time or space. There are an infinite number of points between every two points we might choose. How, then, do we capture this information in a computer? We have an infinite number of points of information to deal with, and that's too much data for a computer to handle. Thus, the first problem to be tackled in digital media is transforming analog information to a discrete form by means of analog-to-digital conversion.

**Figure 1.7** Grayscale image, smooth gradient

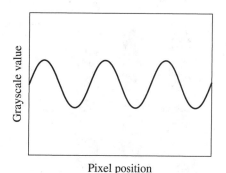

Pixel position

**Figure 1.8** Sine wave corresponding to one line of grayscale values across the image to the left

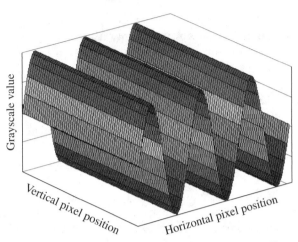

**Figure 1.9** Two-dimensional waveform corresponding
to the grayscale image in Figure 1.7.

Regardless of the medium, analog-to-digital conversion requires the same two steps: *sampling* and *quantization*. The first step, sampling, chooses discrete points at which to measure a continuous phenomenon (which we will also call a *signal*). In the case of images, the sample points are evenly separated in space. In the case of sound, the sample points are evenly separated in time. The number of samples taken per unit time or unit space is called the *sampling rate* or, alternatively, the *resolution*. The second step, quantization, requires that each sample be represented in a fixed number of bits, called the *sample size*, or, equivalently, the *bit depth*. The bit depth limits the precision with which each sample can be represented. We will give simple examples of sampling and quantization in digital imaging and sound in this chapter, and more detailed explanations in Chapters 2 and 4.

### 1.2.3 Sampling and Aliasing

What if you had a simple picture like the one in Figure 1.10 and you wanted to record it digitally by taking a sample of the color at evenly spaced places in the horizontal and vertical directions? In Figure 1.11, the sample areas are designated by rectangles which we call *sample blocks*. At each sample block, a digital camera detects the color of the object

**Figure 1.10** An image with
a regular pattern

**Figure 1.11** Squares denote areas where
samples are taken, called *sample blocks*.
(They are not part of the original image.)

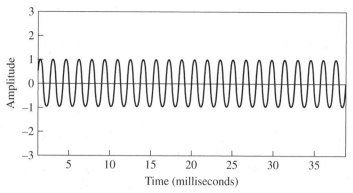

**Figure 1.12**  Audio wave at 637 Hz

being photographed, recording the information in a *pixel*, short for picture element. To recreate the scene from the samples taken in each sample block, by extrapolation you could assume that the whole block was the color of the sample. If you took your samples in the center of the blocks shown in Figure 1.11, you could recreate your picture correctly. However, what if you sampled only every other block in a row, beginning on the left? Reconstructing from those samples, you'd mistakenly think your entire picture was black. This is a simple example of *undersampling*. Your sampling rate did not keep up with the rate of change of the pattern in the image. *Aliasing* in a digital image arises from undersampling and results in an image that does not match the original source—it may be blurred or have a false pattern.

A similar situation can occur when you sample an audio wave. A sound wave can be represented by a sine wave such as the one shown in Figure 1.12. This is a pure tone with a frequency of 637 Hz. Say that you sample this wave at a rate of 770 samples per second. That would be a rate of 770 Hz. (Note that with regard to sampling rate, Hz means *samples per second*, whereas with regard to a sound wave Hz means *cycles per second*.) Extrapolation could be used to reconstruct a sine wave from the samples, resulting in the lower-frequency wave shown in Figure 1.13. The circles represent the sample points. The lower-frequency wave connected through the circles is the aliased frequency that results from reconstructing the wave from too few samples. This is obviously not the original wave, and because the

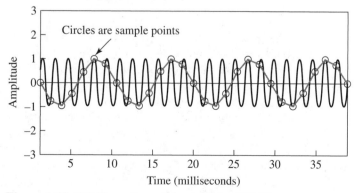

**Figure 1.13**  637 Hz audio wave sampled at 770 Hz

wave reconstructed from the samples has a different frequency from the original, it won't sound the same.

Both these examples illustrate how aliasing occurs as a result of undersampling. In general, aliasing is a situation where one thing takes the form or identity of another. Aliasing in digital images manifests itself as a lack of clarity, or a pattern in the digital image that did not exist in the original; in text, it shows up as jagged edges on letters that ought to be smooth; and in digital audio, it results in sound frequencies that did not exist in the original.

The precise cause and nature of aliasing is captured in the *Nyquist theorem,* which specifies the sampling rate needed for a given spatial or temporal frequency. In simple terms, the Nyquist theorem states that to guarantee that no aliasing will occur, you must use a sampling rate that is greater than twice the frequency of the signal being sampled. The theorem is most easily understood as it relates to audio sampling, since we are already accustomed to thinking of sound in terms of frequency. In the example above, the sound wave being sampled has a frequency of 637 Hz. Thus, according to the Nyquist theorem, we need to sample at more than twice this rate; that is, the sampling rate must be greater than 1274 Hz. This makes sense if we consider that we want to be able to extrapolate the maximum and minimum amplitudes of the wave from our samples. If we sampled exactly twice per cycle and the samples were taken at the maximum and minimum points, this would suffice for the extrapolation. (But notice that if we sampled twice per cycle but always at the 0 points, we would not be able to recreate the wave from the samples.) Thus, intuitively it makes sense that sampling more than twice per cycle should be enough. Anything less than twice per cycle results in audio aliasing—that is, the digitized audio sounds different from the original.

The Nyquist theorem applied to a single-frequency, one-dimensional wave is summarized in the following equation:

## 🗝 KEY EQUATION

Let $f$ be the frequency of a sine wave. Let $r$ be the minimum sampling rate that can be used in the digitization process such that the resulting digitized wave is not aliased. Then

$$r = 2f$$

$r$ is called the *Nyquist frequency.*

ASIDE: Harry Nyquist was a physicist and electrical and communications engineer. He was born in Sweden and educated in the United States, where he worked at Bell Laboratories. He formulated his theorem regarding sampling rate in 1928. The theorem was later proven and extended by Claude Shannon in 1949. For this reason, the theorem is sometimes referred to as the Nyquist-Shannon theorem.

The Nyquist theorem applies equally to digital images, and is illustrated by the image shown in Figure 1.10. This image has a simple pattern with a regular frequency of repetition. If the sampling rate does not keep pace with this rate of repetition, the pattern cannot be reproduced faithfully. Most images are much more complex than this simple pattern, but they have a spatial frequency. The concept of spatial frequency and its relationship to the Nyquist theorem and aliasing will be explained in more detail in Chapter 2. In both digital imaging and digital sound, undersampling creates aliasing and results in a digital reproduction of the image or sound that does not look or sound exactly like the original analog version.

## 1.2.4 Quantization, Quantization Error, and Signal-to-Noise Ratio

The second step in analog-to-digital conversion is quantization. We have seen that samples must be taken at discrete points in time or space, but we haven't yet considered how each sample is represented in a computer.

For digital images, each sample represents a color at a discrete point in a two-dimensional image. How many colors can we possibly represent in a digital image? The number of colors possible is determined by the number of bits used to represent each sample—that is, the sample size or bit depth (which, in the case of an image file, can also be called the *color depth*). If only one bit is used per sample, then only two colors are possible because one bit can take on only two values—0 or 1. If eight bits are used, then $2^8 = 256$ colors are possible. (Eight bits are also used for grayscale.) If 24 bits are used, then $2^{24} = 16,777,216$ colors are possible. In general

---

### 🔑 KEY EQUATION

Let $n$ be the number of bits used to quantize a digital sample. Then the maximum number of different values that can be represented, $m$, is

$$m = 2^n$$

---

The "different values" in the definition above correspond to color levels or sound amplitudes. In an image processing program, you are offered a choice of color modes with implicit bit depths. Clearly, the larger the bit depth, the more subtle the color changes can be in a digitized image, but the file size also increases as the bit depth increases.

For digital audio, each sample represents the amplitude of a sound wave at a discrete point in time. Common sample sizes are eight or 16 bits. Stereo CD-quality digital audio uses 16 bits per sample in each of the two stereo channels, for a total of 32 bits per sample.

Sample size affects how precisely the value of a sample can be represented. In digital sound, sample size affects how much you have to round off the amplitude of the wave when it is sampled at various points in time. In digital images, this corresponds to how close the digital image's colors are to the original colors that it is supposed to represent. In digital sound, sample size affects how much you have to round off the amplitude of the wave when it is sampled at points in time. This is shown in Figure 1.14. The samples, which are taken at evenly spaced points in time, can take on the values only at the discrete quantization levels on the y-axis. A sample must be rounded to the closest discrete level. The difference between its actual value and its rounded value (represented by pairs of points parallel to the y-axis in the figure) is the quantization error.

The amount of error implicit in a chosen bit depth can be measured in terms of the *signal-to-noise ratio* (*SNR*). Before looking at SNR specifically in the context of digital imaging and sound, let's consider the general definition.

Signal-to-noise ratio can generally be defined as the ratio of the meaningful content of a signal versus the associated noise. A signal is any type of communication—something a person says to you, a digital signal sending an image file across a network, a message posted on an electronic bulletin board, a piece of music being played from a cassette, etc. The noise is the part of the message that is not meaningful; in fact, it gets in the way of the message intended in the communication. You could use the term signal-to-noise ratio to

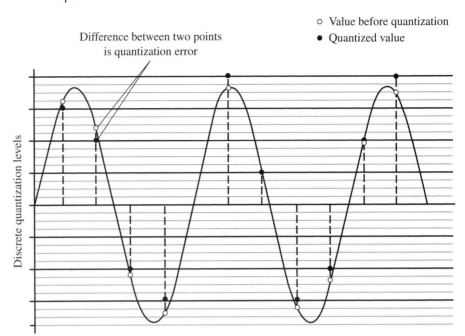

**Figure 1.14**  Quantization error

describe communications in your everyday life. If you know someone who talks a lot but doesn't really convey a lot of meaning, you could say that he or she has a low signal-to-noise ratio. Web-based bulletin board and chat groups are sometimes described as having a low SNR—there may be quite a few postings, but not very much meaningful content. In these first two examples, the noise consists of all the empty filler words. In the case of a digital signal sent across a network, the noise is the electronic degradation of the signal. On a piece of music played from cassette, the noise could be caused by damage to the tape or mechanical imperfections in the cassette player.

More precise definitions of signal-to-noise ratio vary according to context. This might be confusing if you see the term used differently in different places, so let's differentiate between the two main usages.

- In analog data communication, the signal-to-noise ratio is defined as the ratio of the average power in the signal versus the power in the noise level. In this context, think of a signal being sent over a network connection compared to the extent to which the signal is corrupted. This is related to the general usage of the term described above. This usage of the term SNR applies to particular signals. The SNR depends on real-time conditions.

- For a digitized image or sound, the signal-to-noise ratio is defined as the ratio of the maximum sample value versus the maximum quantization error. In this usage of the term, the ratio depends on the bit depth chosen for the signal, not upon real-time conditions. Any signal encoded with a given bit depth will have the same ratio. This can also be called **signal-to-quantization-noise ratio** (**SQNR**), but you should be aware that in many sources the term signal-to-noise ratio is used with this meaning as well. Let's look at this more closely. (Henceforth, we'll use the term SQNR to distinguish this measurement from SNR.)

SQNR is measured in terms of decibels. A **decibel** is a dimensionless unit that is used to describe the relative power or intensity of two phenomena. The definition of a decibel, abbreviated **dB**, is as follows:

$$1\ dB = 10 \log_{10}\left(\frac{I}{I_0}\right)$$

> **ASIDE:** A decibel is 1/10th of a **bel**, named after Alexander Graham Bell. For two signals with power $I$ and $I_0$, a bel is defined as follows: If $\log_{10}(I/I_0) = 1$, then the ratio is 1 bel. This is to say that $I$ has 10 times the power of $I_0$, since $\log_{10}(10) = 1$. A bel turned out to be too coarse a measurement for its purposes, so the decibel came into common usage.

where $I$ and $I_0$ are the intensities (also called **power** across a surface area) of two signals, which can be measured in watts. So, you might ask, intensity of *what*? Once again, that depends on what you're interested in. Decibels are often used to measure sound intensity, and this is the use of the word that you're probably the most familiar with. But decibels can also measure the intensity of a data signal on a communication network, the optical power output of lasers, or anything that can be measured in watts. Notice that decibels are a dimensionless unit. Since both $I$ and $I_0$ are measured in watts, the units are canceled in the division, and you are left with just the number representing the ratio.

You may often see another definition for decibels, that is:

$$1\ dB = 20 \log\left(\frac{E}{E_0}\right)$$

where $E$ and $E_0$ are amplitude, potential, or pressure, measured in volts. You can see that the two definitions for a decibel are equivalent if you consider the relationship between power $I$, potential $E$, and resistance $R$.

$$I = \frac{E^2}{R}$$

Assuming that $R$ is constant for the two signals, then

$$10 \log_{10}\left(\frac{I}{I_0}\right) = 10 \log_{10}\left(\frac{\dfrac{E^2}{R}}{\dfrac{E_0^2}{R}}\right) = 10 \log_{10}\left(\frac{E^2}{E_0^2}\right)$$

$$= 10 \log_{10}\left(\left(\frac{E}{E_0}\right)^2\right) = 20 \log_{10}\left(\frac{E}{E_0}\right)$$

(Recall that $\log_{10}(x^2) = 2 \log_{10}(x)$.)

Because SQNR is just a ratio, it is measured in decibels. Using the second definition of decibels from above (because we are measuring amplitudes), we can now explain SQNR as it applies to linearly quantized samples. First, we define max(*quantization value*) as the magnitude of the maximum sample value. With $n$ bits for quantization, the samples values range from $-2^{n-1}$ to $2^{n-1} - 1$. (Audio signals are represented as sine waves that go from positive to negative values.) Thus, the maximum sample value in magnitude is $2^{n-1}$. On the scale of sample values, the maximum quantization error is half a quantization level, which is where we get the denominator of ½ (assuming rounding is used in quantization.) Then

$$SQNR = 20 \log_{10}\left(\frac{\text{max}(\textit{quantization value})}{\text{max}(\textit{quantization error})}\right) = 20 \log_{10}\left(\frac{2^{n-1}}{1/2}\right)$$

The above explanation is intended to give you an intuitive sense of SQNR, defined more simply as follows:

> ### 🗝 KEY EQUATION
>
> Let $n$ be the bit depth of a digitized media file (e.g., digital audio). Then the signal-to-quantization noise ratio **SQNR** is
>
> $$SQNR = 20 \log_{10}(2^n)$$

Signal-to-quantization-noise ratio is directly related to **dynamic range**. In fact, we will see that mathematically, they are the same value. Let's look at the concept intuitively. Dynamic range, informally defined, is the ratio of the largest-amplitude sound (or color, for digital images) and the smallest that can be represented with a given bit depth. (Doesn't that sound like the definition of SQNR above?) The idea is that the fewer bits you have to represent a range of colors or a range of sound samples, and the wider the range of colors or sound you want to represent, the less ability you have to represent subtle differences between values. Say that you use three bits to represent colors, so you can represent only $2^3 = 8$ colors. Because of the small bit depth, you have a limited dynamic range in the palette you can use in digitizing an image. Think about the implications of being restricted to a palette with such a small dynamic range. What if the original image has many colors and these colors are widely ranged? You may need some blues, greens, reds, yellows, oranges, purples, and white and black. Since you can use only eight colors, you can use only one shade of each of the colors mentioned. Thus, the difference between one color and another is relatively large. If you take a photograph that has thousands of colors ranging widely across the spectrum but you have to reproduce these with only eight colors, you're going to have a large rounding error. Alternatively, if you want subtle differences between one color and the next, you can have only a narrow range of colors. These two alternatives are shown in Figure 1.15. Notice that the rounding error, which is relative to the narrow range of colors in this second example, will be the same. That is, the dynamic range, as dictated by the bit depth, is the same.

The situation is similar when measuring dynamic range in digital audio. A small bit depth for an audio file limits the range of amplitudes in the digitized sound. A small bit depth is not good for a digital recording of a symphony orchestra playing a piece of music that has very loud and very soft passages. In order to be able to represent sound amplitudes that are so far apart in value, but using a small bit depth, you are forced to have quantization intervals of a large size, and this increases the amount of error relative to the true signal. With a small bit depth, more values will round to 0 than with a higher bit depth. We will revisit the concept of SQNR and dynamic range related to digital audio in more detail in Chapter 4.

## 1.3 DATA STORAGE

Working with digital media requires that you handle large amounts of data. Let's first consider the size of typical image, audio, and video files (leaving aside, for the moment, the possibility of compressing them). We'll return to the details of how each medium is represented in later chapters, but for now Table 1.4 gives you an overview of digital media file sizes. The examples assume that RGB color is used, with three bytes per pixel. (RGB will be

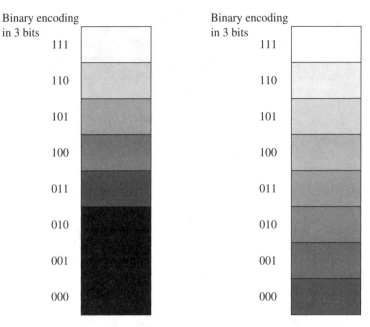

With three bits, you have eight colors. You can spread these colors out over a wide range, with big differences between one and the next, or spread them out over a narrow range, with small differences between one and the next. In either case, the dynamic range is the same, dictated by the bit depth, which determines the maximum error possible (resulting from rounding to available colors) relative to the range of colors represented.

**Figure 1.15** Dynamic range of colors

| TABLE 1.4 | Example File Sizes for Digital Image, Audio, And Video | |
|---|---|---|
| **Example Digital Image File Size (without compression):** | **Example Digital Audio File Size (without compression):** | **Example Digital Video File Size (without compression):** |
| **Resolution:** 1024 pixels × 768 pixels | **Sampling rate:** 44.1 kHz (44,100 samples per second) | **Frame size:** 720 pixels × 480 pixels |
| **Total number of pixels:** 786,432 | **Bit depth:** 32 bits per sample (16 for each of two stereo channels) (*i.e.*, 4 bytes) | **Bits per pixel:** 24 |
| **Color mode:** RGB | | **Frame rate:** ~30 frames/s |
| **Bits per pixel:** 24 (*i.e.*, 3 bytes) | | **Number of minutes:** one minute |
| **Total number of bits:** 18,874,368 (=2,359,296 bytes) | **Number of minutes:** one minute | **Total image requirement:** 14,929,920,000 bits |
| **File size:** 2.25 MB | **Total number of bits:** 84,672,000 (=10,584,000 bytes) | **Audio requirement:** 84,672,000 (See column 2.) |
| | **File size:** 10.09 MB for one minute | **Total number of bits:** 15,014,592,000 (=1,876,824,000 bytes) |
| | **Data rate of the file:** 1.35 Mb/s | **File size:** >1.7 GB |
| | | **Data rate of the file:** 238.65 Mb/s (This calculation doesn't take chrominance subsampling into account. See Chapter 6 for a discussion of subsampling.) |

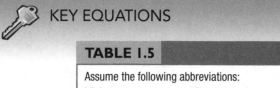

## KEY EQUATIONS

### TABLE 1.5

Assume the following abbreviations:

| | |
|---|---|
| kilobyte | kB |
| megabyte | MB |
| gigabyte | GB |
| kilobit | kb |
| megabit | Mb |
| gigabit | Gb |
| terabit | Tb |
| terabyte | TB |

For memory and file sizes, assume the following equivalences:

1 byte = 8 bits
1 kB = $2^{10}$ bytes = 1024 bytes
1 MB = $2^{20}$ bytes = 1,048,576 bytes
1 GB = $2^{30}$ bytes = 1,073,741,824 bytes
1 TB = $2^{40}$ bytes = 1,099,511,627,776 bytes
kb, Mb, Gb and Tb are defined analogously.

explained in more detail in Chapter 2.) The video example assumes a frame rate of about 30 frames/s. Each frame is like a still image. Frame shown in quick succession create the effect of motion. (This will be explained in more detail in Chapter 6.)

Common abbreviations for data sizes are given in Table 1.5. The prefixes *kilo-*, *mega-*, and *giga-* can lead to confusion because they are used inconsistently. You have seen that with regard to Hertz, *kilo-* means $10^3 = 1000$, *mega-* means $10^6 = 1,000,000$, and *giga-* means $10^9 = 1,000,000,000$. However, with regard to data storage, *kilo-* is sometimes defined as $10^3$ and sometimes as $2^{10}$, *mega-* is sometimes $10^6$ and sometimes $2^{20}$, and *giga-* is sometimes $10^9$ and sometimes $2^{30}$. It depends on the source. Manufacturers want to make their storage media look larger, so they generally use powers of 10. On the other hand, many computers will give file sizes defining terms with powers of 2. For example, on your computer you may be able to click on a file to see its properties, which could be listed as 3,686,456 bytes in one place, 3,600 kB in another place, and 3.52 MB in another. Clearly, powers of two are being used for the definitions, since $3,686,456/1024 \approx 3600$ and $3,686,456/1,048,576 \approx 3.52$. Although usage is inconsistent in the computer industry with regard to the prefixes *kilo-*, *mega-* and *giga-*, the most common convention is to use powers of 2 for memory and file sizes and powers of 10 for data rates. We will adopt this convention in this book, unless indicated otherwise. You should note, however, that manufacturers sometimes use kilobyte to mean 1000 bytes, megabyte to mean 1,000,000 bytes, gigabyte to mean 1,000,000,000.

Table 1.6 lists the reported capacity of the storage media at the time of the writing of this chapter. Since the definitions of *kilo-*, *mega-*, and *giga-* depend on the manufacturer, you can take these values to be approximate.

A little arithmetic will show how quickly computer storage can be taken up with uncompressed digital media files, especially audio and video. The audio requires more than about

| TABLE 1.6 | Storage Media and Their Capacity |
|---|---|
| **Storage medium** | **Maximum capacity** |
| **Portable Media** ||
| CD (Compact Disk) | 700 MB |
| DVD (Digital Versatile Disc or Digital Video Disk), standard one sided | 4.7 GB standard; 8.5 GB dual-layered |
| DVD video or high capacity | 17–27 GB |
| Memory stick or card | 8 GB |
| HD-DVD (High Definition DVD), standard one-sided | 15 GB standard; 30 GB dual-layered |
| Blu-ray Disk | 25 GB standard; 50 GB dual-layered |
| Flash drive | 64 GB |
| **Permanent Media** ||
| Hard disk drive | 1 terabyte (1000 GB) |

10 MB per minute, so about 70 minutes would fit on a CD. The situation is worse for digital video. Let's just take a rough estimate. One minute of digital video takes about 1.5 GB. So on a DVD that holds 17 GB, you'd be able to store just a little over 11 minutes of uncompressed video. Clearly, digital media files can be very large, and consequently, compression is crucial to reducing the file size. But before moving on to compression, let's consider an issue related to data storage, and that is data communication.

# 1.4 DATA COMMUNICATION

## 1.4.1 The Importance of Data Communication in the Study of Digital Media

Data communication is a broad and deep field of study that straddles the disciplines of computer science and electrical engineering. We can only scratch the surface in this introduction and give superficial treatment to issues that are technically quite complex. Before we begin tackling this topic, you may find it helpful to know the ways in which data communication is relevant to your study of digital media. Here are our motivations for looking at issues of data communication:

- Digital media files are typically very large, and rarely do you keep them to yourself. You store them on CDs and DVDs, send them in email, and post them on web pages. Thus, you need to consider transmission media and communication methods for digital data.
- Sound and video are time-based media that require large amounts of data. Both capturing and transmitting sound and video in real-time require that the data transmission keep up with the rate at which the data is played. Thus, issues of bandwidth and data rate are crucial in the capturing and transmitting of digital audio and video.
- Communication media in our homes and offices are "going digital." We are surrounded by cellular phones, digital cable, digital television, HDTV, and more. To be knowledgeable in the field of digital media, you need to understand the difference between analog and digital modes of communication as they appear in your home and work environments.

## 1.4.2 Analog Compared with Digital Data Communication

Whether data are in analog or digital form, information needs a channel of communication to get from sender to receiver. You use these communication channels every day—land-based or cellular telephones; shortwave or regular radios; cable, terrestrial, or satellite television; and wired or wireless computer networks. You hear that some of these are digital, though you don't have to think about this to use them. So how do you know which communications are being sent digitally?

An important thing to keep in mind is that the transmission medium does not determine whether the data is communicated in analog or digital form. Both analog and digital data can be communicated across copper wire (e.g., telephone or computer networks), coaxial cable (e.g., television), optical fiber (e.g., high-speed computer networks), and free space (e.g., radio or television). Copper wire, coaxial cable, and optical fiber all require a physical line between sender and receiver. Across copper wire or coaxial cable, data can be transmitted by changing voltages. Through optical fiber, data can be communicated by a fluctuating beam of light. Data can also be communicated through free space via electromagnetic waves sent by satellite or radio transmission. All of these transmissions methods use some type of analog waveform, but it is important to note that they all can be adapted to carry data in both analog and digital form. It is the representation of the data, not the transmission medium, which determines if the communication is analog or digital.

Then what is the difference between the ways analog and digital data are transmitted across a network? Analog telephone transmissions through wire are a good starting point for understanding how analog data are communicated. When sound is captured electronically, the changes in air pressure are translated to changes in voltage. In an analog telephone, a microphone picks up the changes in air pressure and translates them into voltage changes on an electrical wire. For the spoken word "boo," the voltages rise and fall in a pattern like the one in Figure 1.16. The voltage changes are continuous in the same way that the waveform representing the word "boo" is continuous.

If the word "boo" is digitized, on the other hand, it is sampled and quantized such that the data are transformed into a sequence of 0s and 1s. Over copper wire, these 0s and 1s are sent by means of an electrical current and can be represented as two discrete voltage levels. For example, a voltage of $-V$ can represent a 0 bit, and a voltage of $+V$ can represent a 1 bit. Communication begins with some initial synchronization between sender and receiver. Then to send each bit, the sending device maintains a steady voltage for a fixed amount of time. The receiving device, in turn, samples the transmission at evenly-spaced points in time to interpret whether a 0 or a 1 has been sent. Figure 1.17. illustrates this type of discrete transmission. Varying the voltage in two levels in the manner just described is called

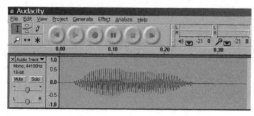

**Figure 1.16** Waveform for part of the spoken word "boo"

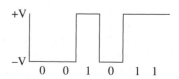

**Figure 1.17** Baseband digital transmission. Bits are transmitted by discretely changing voltages.

*baseband transmission*, and the line of communication between sender and receiver is called a *baseband channel*.

Baseband transmission is used across wire and coaxial cable, but it works well only across relatively short distances. Noise and attenuation cause the signal to degrade as it travels over the communication channel. Attentuation is the weakening of a signal over time and/or space. Baseband transmission is not the only nor even the most common method of data communication. An alternative, called *modulated data transmission* (or sometimes *bandpass transmission*), is based on the observation that a continuously oscillating signal degrades more slowly and thus is better for long distance communication. Modulated transmission makes use of a *carrier signal* on which data are "written."

Here again in digital media, sinusoidal waveforms become an important abstraction. A carrier wave is a signal—for example, a beam of light passing through optical fiber or radio waves across free space—that is made to oscillate in a regular sinusoidal pattern at a certain frequency, as shown in Figure 1.18. This carrier wave is transmitted and oscillates at its characteristic frequency even when no data are being sent. Data are written on the carrier signal by means of *modulation* techniques.

The three basic methods for modulating a carrier wave are *amplitude modulation*, *frequency modulation*, or *phase modulation*. In amplitude modulation, the amplitude of the carrier signal is increased by a fixed amount each time a digital 1 is communicated; in frequency modulation, the frequency is changed; and in phase modulation, the phase is shifted. These modulation methods are shown in Figure 1.18, where the digital signal 101 is being sent. You should note, however, that modulated signals are not necessarily digital. Carrier frequencies and modulation have long been used to transmit analog radio and television signals as well.

The name bandpass transmission arises from the fact that in this method of data communication, the carrier signal lies in the center of a *frequency band*, called a *channel*, that is allocated for communication. The sender and receiver both know the channel assigned to them. The sender sends information using only those frequencies that lie within its channel, and the receiver listens for communications only within that channel.

Communication across optical fiber or via electromagnetic waves in free space lends itself to bandpass transmission using carrier signals. Different colors of light actually have different frequencies that can be divided into bands or channels when communicated along optical fiber. The spectrum of light is shown in Figure 1.19. This figure shows colors by their wavelength. Wavelength $\lambda$ and frequency $f$ are related by the equation $\lambda = \dfrac{c}{f}$ where $c$ is the speed of light in a vacuum. Electromagnetic waves also can be divided into frequency bands, as shown in Figure 1.20. Both analog and digital messages can be encoded using carrier signals in the form of light or other electromagnetic waves modulated to contain the information being sent.

A continuously oscillating electrical voltage can also be used as a carrier signal. This fact has made it possible for the telephone system to handle digital data. Telephone systems were originally designed to communicate data in analog form. With the proliferation of computers in homes and offices, the need arose for network communication among them. The telephone system was already in place to accommodate this need, as long as a way could be found to send the digital signal along the analog telephone line. This is the role of a modem. The word *modem* stands for *modulator and demodulator*. A modem takes the data given to it by a computer and writes the 0s and 1s onto a continuously oscillating voltage using one of the modulation methods described above. Then at the other end of the call, another modem *demodulates* the signal for delivery to another computer.

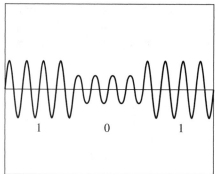

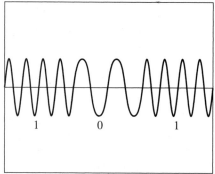

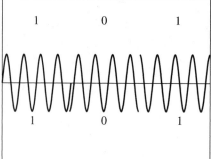

**Figure 1.18** Modulation methods

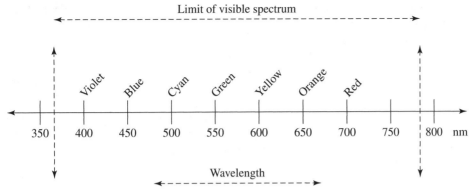

**Figure 1.19** The spectrum of visible light

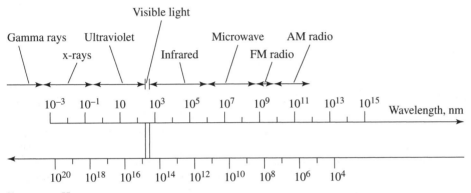

Frequency, Hz

**Figure 1.20** The electromagnetic spectrum

Technical details for baseband and bandpass (modulated) communications have been studied and refined by engineers for many years. Standards have been developed so that data can be communicated around the world. The main organizations for developing standards are the International Telecommunications Union (ITU), the Institute for Electrical and Electronic Engineers (IEEE), and the Electronic Industries Association (EIA). Many variations of communication methods exist, but the details are beyond the scope of this book. For the study of digital media, the important concepts to grasp are the essential differences between analog and digital data and the ways they are transmitted. We will discuss more details of data communication in the chapter on digital video, since the data-intensive, time-based nature of video makes data communication an important issue.

The discussion in this section has moved back and forth between analog and digital modes of communication, so it may help to summarize the key points:

- Both analog and digital data can be transmitted by means of copper wire, coaxial cable, optical fiber, and free space. The medium of transmission does not determine whether the communication is analog or digital. The form of the data does.
- Digital data can be transmitted by means of a baseband signal or a bandpass (*i.e.*, modulated) signal. The baseband signal uses discrete pulses representing 0s and 1s.

The modulated signal uses a carrier frequency and an encoding of data based on periodically altering the frequency, amplitude, or phase of the signal.

*   Both analog and digital data can be communicated by means of a modulated signal. A carrier signal can be modulated to contain either analog or digital data.

We began this discussion by comparing how analog and digital data are communicated as a way of approaching the issue of bandwidth. The term *bandwidth* is one that you will hear frequently in different contexts and with slightly different meanings. Bandwidth is important to the study of digital media because image, audio, and video files are large, and in the case of audio and video they are time-based. Thus, the rate at which these files can be created and transmitted is crucial.

In the next sections we'll discuss three definitions of bandwidth used in three different contexts. These usages are closely related, but not exactly the same, and the overloading of the term can lead to confusion. Separating the discussion into three different definitions should help to clarify the usage.

## 1.4.3 Bandwidth

### 1.4.3.1 Bandwidth as Maximum Rate of Change in Digital Data Communication

The first and perhaps most important usage of the term bandwidth (for our purposes) relates to digital data communication. In this context, keep in mind that we are talking about the transmission of discrete 0s and 1s. This transmission can be done by discrete pulses—that is, discrete changes of voltages in baseband data transmission. Alternatively, in the case of modulated communication, the data can be communicated by discrete changes in the frequency, amplitude, or phase of a carrier signal. The question with regard to bandwidth in this context is this: How fast can the signal be changed? That is, how fast can the sender change the signal from a voltage of V to a voltage of $-$V and back again? Or, in the case of modulated communication, how fast can the sender change the amplitude of the carrier signal (or the frequency or the phase)? This is not a matter of the sender only. Keep in mind that the receiver must be able to understand the changing signal as well.

An example from everyday life might help to clarify the concept of bandwidth used in this context. What if you wanted to tell a friend something *really fast*? How fast can you talk and still speak clearly? Don't forget that your friend has to be able to keep up with your talking; he or she has to be able to understand. The maximum rate at which you can talk and your friend can understand is the bandwidth of the communication. Notice that this has nothing to do with the speed of sound. Try another example. What if you had to send Morse code by means of a blinking flashlight? How fast could you send the code? The speed at which you can send the code is limited by how fast the hardware (your flashlight) can be operated and how fast your hand can click it. Even if you could flash the flashlight as fast as you wanted, at some point the person looking at it wouldn't be able to distinguish one signal from the next. Again, the bandwidth has nothing to do with the speed of light. It's a matter of the sending and receiving devices.

In digital data communication, there's a limit on the rate at which digital signals can be changed—whether it is voltages across copper wire or coaxial cable, light across optical fiber, or an electromagnetic wave changing frequency or amplitude from a satellite transmission. Just as we can move our vocal cords only so fast, the sending device can change its signal only so fast. The physical properties of the transmission medium also have an impact on the way the signal degrades and errors are introduced. At the receiving end of the transmission, there are limits on how fast the receiver can read and distinguish the signal correctly. Whatever the transmission medium and the engineering of the sending and receiving devices, there is a maximum rate of change for that communication system. This is the system's bandwidth.

Bandwidth is measured in cycles per second or Hz. Think about what this implies. A baseband transmission system with a bandwidth of 5000 Hz can *cycle* through its signal—that is, it can change its signal from one voltage level to a different one and then back again—at a maximum rate of 5000 times per second. We can say this another way: Every 1/5000th of a second, this system can communicate two things. If one voltage represents a 0 and another represents a 1, then the system can transmit a 0 and a 1 every 1/5000th of a second. This means that it can transmit 10,000 bits every second. Thus, we have the following definition:

## KEY EQUATION

Assume that a signal is sent with two possible signal levels and a bandwidth of $b$ Hz. Then the data rate, $d$, in bits/s is

$$d = 2b$$

It makes sense that to get the data rate, you multiply the bandwidth by two. Bandwidth is defined by how fast the signal can change. Change implies that first there must be one thing, and then another—two different pieces of information. Those pieces of information, in this context, are bits.

What if more than one signal level is permitted? What if four instead of two voltages are possible? Instead of having one voltage represent 0 and the other represent 1, we could have one voltage represent 00, the second represent 01, the third represent 10, and the fourth represent 11. In this way, each change of voltage would transmit two bits instead of one. Allowing more than two signal levels such that more than one bit can be communicated at a time is called **multilevel coding.** To generalize,

## KEY EQUATION

Assume that a signal is sent with $k$ possible signal levels and a bandwidth of $b$ Hz. Then the data rate, $d$, in bits/s is

$$d = 2b \log_2(k)$$

An example of this is shown in Figure 1.21. Four possible voltage levels are transmitted. If the lowest level is transmitted, it is meant to communicate 00. The second lowest level communicates 01, the third 10, and the highest level 11. Thus, two bits are communicated at a time.

If you can increase the data rate simply by increasing the number of voltage levels allowed, then why not have hundreds of voltage levels? The reason has to do with the engineering of the hardware. The more voltage levels, the more complex the hardware must be to be able to read and interpret the different levels, and the more chance there is for error. Thus, the number of voltage levels used is generally not very high.

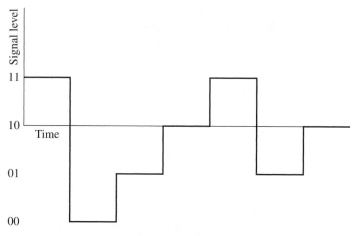

With k signal levels, $\log_2 k$ bits are transmitted with each signal.

**Figure 1.21** Data rate as determined by number of signal levels

### 1.4.3.2 Bandwidth of a Signal in Terms of Frequency

The *bandwidth of a signal* is easier to define. In this context, we are talking about a signal that is sent in the form of a wave. As discussed in Section 1.2.2, any complex *periodic waveform* can be decomposed—both mathematically and physically—into frequency components that are simple sine waves. These frequency components range from some minimum to some maximum. Then the bandwidth of a signal is the difference between the maximum and minimum frequency components. We will use the term *width of a signal* to avoid confusion with the other use of the term bandwidth.

>  **KEY EQUATION**
>
> For a signal that can be represented as a periodic waveform, let $f_{max}$ be the frequency of the highest-frequency component and let $f_{min}$ be the frequency of the lowest-frequency component. Then the width of the signal, $w$, is
>
> $$w = f_{max} - f_{min}$$

For example, the complex waveform at the bottom of Figure 1.6 is composed of three frequencies: the notes C (262 Hz), E (330 Hz) and G (392 Hz). The difference between the maximum and minimum frequency components—in this case, 130 Hz— is the width of the signal. (Note that in this definition, we make no assumption about the nature of the data communicated by the signal. It could be either analog or digital.)

This use of the term bandwidth differs from the one in the previous section in that we are no longer dealing with the maximum rate that a signal can change on a transmission medium. Instead, we are talking about the frequency range for a particular signal, assuming that the signal is sent as a waveform. In this case, the signal in question may be transmitted on a carrier signal that lies in the center of a frequency band, called a channel. The significance of this usage lies in the fact that the width of the signal must fit within the width of the channel on which it is transmitted. Otherwise, some information will be lost. For example, high definition television (HDTV) requires a large bandwidth so that the television frames can be transmitted at a rate of 30 per second. For this to be possible, the bandwidth of the channel on which HDTV is broadcast must be large enough to accommodate the bandwidth of the HDTV signal. This leads us to another use of the term bandwidth, as it relates to channels.

### 1.4.3.3 Bandwidth of a Communication Channel in Terms of Frequency

When data are communicated across the airwaves, they are sent along some particular channel, which is a band of frequencies. The sender communicates within its designated frequency band, and the receiver tunes to that band to receive the communication. The range of frequencies allocated to a band constitutes the *bandwidth of a channel*. (We could also call this simply the *width of a channel*, since it correlates with the width of a signal.) In the case of the airwaves for television and radio, the Federal Communications Commission allocates channels of an appropriate bandwidth large enough to accommodate the type of communication (Table 1.7). For example, each AM radio station is allocated a bandwidth of 10 kHz. FM radio stations have bandwidths of 200 kHz. Analog television has a bandwidth of about 6 MHz. Digital high definition television (HDTV) requires a bandwidth of approximately 20 MHz. Again in this usage of the term bandwidth, we are talking about data that are transmitted by means of a carrier signal of a given frequency that lies at the center of channel, but we make no assumptions about the nature of the data being communicated. Both analog and digital data can be sent by means of a carrier signal. However, there are repercussions to modulating the carrier signal so that it contains data, regardless of whether it is analog or digital. Modulation adds frequency components called *sidebands* to the original carrier signal, and these sidebands must lie within the designated channel. Thus, the bandwidth of a channel affects the amount of information that can be communicated.

This definition of bandwidth raises a number of relevant questions. How is an appropriate bandwidth determined for AM radio, FM radio, television, and digital HDTV? What makes 10 kHz, 200 kHz, and 6 MHz, and 20 MHz, respectively, the right size? How does modulation of a carrier signal give rise to sidebands? What are the frequencies of these sidebands, and how do they affect the bandwidth requirements for channels? These questions will be examined in more detail in Chapter 6.

## 1.4.4 Data Rate

### 1.4.4.1 Bit Rate

The main goal in this section is to give you a basic understanding of the terminology used to compare data communication systems and the rates at which they transmit data. Let's return to the first definition of bandwidth: the maximum rate of change of a signal, as a

| TABLE 1.7 | Frequency Bands for Radio and Television | |
|---|---|
| **Radio** | **Television** |
| AM, 535 kHz to 1.7 MHz | 54 to 88 MHz for channels 2 to 6 |
| shortwave radio, 5.9 MHz to 26.1 MHz | 174 to 216 MHz for channels 7 to 13 |
| CB radio, 26.96 MHz to 27.41 MHz | 470 to 890 MHz for UHF channels 14 to 83 |
| FM radio, 88 MHz to 108 MHz, allocated in 200 kHz channels | |

property of the communication system on which the signal is being sent. This definition is closely related to *data rate* or *bit rate*. In fact, bandwidth is often loosely used as a synonym for data rate or bit rate, and this has become widely accepted. However, in our discussion, we distinguish between the terms. Bandwidth is measured in cycles per second—Hertz. Data rate is measured in bits per second—more precisely, in kilobits per second (kb/s), kilobytes per second (kB/s), megabits per second (Mb/s), megabytes per second (MB/s), gigabits per second (Gb/s), or gigabytes per second (GB/s). If measured in bits per second, data rate is synonymous with bit rate. (The inconsistency in the definitions of *kilo-*, *mega-*, and *giga-* that we noted in the section on data storage carries over here. Generally, powers of ten define these terms when they are associated with data rate, and that's the convention adopted in this book.)

Recall that bandwidth and data rate are related by the equation $d = 2b \log_2(k)$. where $k$ is the number of different signal values that can be transmitted. What we did not mention earlier is that in this equation, $d$ is a theoretical data rate—a maximum that is not achievable in reality. The actual amount of data that can be sent per unit time is limited by the noise that is present in any communication system. No signal can be sent with perfect clarity over an indefinite span of space and time. Some amount of noise is introduced by electromagnetic interference. If too much noise is introduced, the receiver cannot always interpret the signal correctly. Some transmission systems are more susceptible to noise than others, and this lowers their actual achievable data rate.

A refinement of the relationship between data rate and bandwidth is given by *Shannon's theorem*, which quantifies the achievable data rate for a transmission system that introduces noise. According to Shannon's theorem, $c = b \log_2(1 + s/p)$. $s$ is a measure of the signal power, and $p$ is a measure of the noise power. (Note that $s/p$ is another application of the signal-to-noise ratio discussed above.) For our purposes, we don't need to do precise measurements of signal and noise and calculations of data rates, but this theorem helps us to understand the origin of data rates reported for certain digital communication systems. These data rates arise from the rate at which a signal can be changed on the given transmission medium coupled with the amount of noise typically introduced in proportion to the actual signal.

**ASIDE:** Claude Shannon (1916–2001) was an American mathematician and electrical engineer educated at the Massachusetts Institute of Technology and later employed at Bell Labs. His work has been seminal in information theory.

Data rate is important in three aspects of digital media—not only in communicating the data, but also in capturing it, and, in the case of audio and video, playing it. Data rate is important in digital data communication because no one wants to wait an unreasonable length of time to transfer pictures, sound, and video from one place to another.

Refer back to Table 1.4, which gives typical file sizes for digital images, audio, and video. With these file sizes in mind, consider the situations in which you might want to send a digital picture, sound, or movie from one computer to another. You may have posted an image on your web page, and someone at another location has gone to your page and is downloading the image. How long will this take? It depends on the image size and the type of network connection. Table 1.8 lists some common network types and their typical data transfer rates as of the writing of this chapter. With this information, you can estimate the time it would take to download, for example, a 2.25 MB digital image (from the example in Table 1.4). Over a network connected by means of a 28.8 kb/s telephone modem, the file would take over ten minutes—far too long for the patience of most web users. In contrast, a cable modem achieving a data transfer rate of 20 Mb/s can download the image file in under a second.

| TABLE 1.8 | Data Transfer Rates for Common Communication Links |
|---|---|

| Wide Area Network | |
|---|---|
| Type of Data Connection | Data Rate |
| telephone modem | 28.8–56 kb/s |
| ISDN (Integrated Services Digital Network) | 64–128 kb/s |
| ADSL (Asymmetric Digital Subscriber Line) | 1.544–8.448 Mb/s (downstream) 16–640 kb/s (upstream) |
| ADSL2 | 0.8–3.5 Mb/s up, 5–12 Mb/s down |
| ADSL2+ | 1–3.5 Mb/s up, 24 Mb/s down |
| VDSL (Very High Bit DSL) | 12.96–55.2 Mb/s ($\sim$12 Mb/s down and 52 Mb/s up, or $\sim$26 Mb/s symmetrical at 1000 feet, 10 Mb/s at 4000 feet ) |
| Cable modem | 20–40 Mb/s |
| VDSL2 | 50–250 Mb/s |

| Local Area Network | |
|---|---|
| Type of Data Connection | Data Rate |
| Token ring | 16 Mb/s |
| Ethernet (10base-X) | 10 Mb/s |
| Fast ethernet (100base-X) | 100 Mb/s |
| FDDI | 100 Mb/s |
| Gigabit ethernet | 1 Gb/s |
| Wireless 802.11b | 11 Mb/s |
| Wireless 802.11g | 54 Mb/s |

| Computer Interfaces | |
|---|---|
| Type of Data Connection | Data Rate |
| Serial | 10–230 kb/s |
| Parallel | 8 Mb/s |
| SCSI 1 | 12 Mb/s |
| SCSI 2 | 80 Mb/s |
| Fast wide SCSI | 160 Mb/s |
| SCSI (various ultra versions) | 320–2560 Mb/s |
| USB, USB2 | 12–480 Mb/s |
| SDI (serial digital interface) | 143–360 Mb/s |
| Firewire (IEEE 1394) | 400–800 Mb/s |
| DMA ATA | 264–1064 Mb/s |

It's even more important to have a high-speed connection for the transfer of digital audio and video files. First of all, video files are larger than still images, containing thousands of images in the form of frames, along with sound. If you want to download a DVD-formatted video so that you can play it later, you have a very large file to deal with. Secondly, digital audio and video are both time-based media. What if you want to play an audio or video transmission in real-time, as it downloads? If this is the case, the communication link must

| TABLE 1.9 | Data Transfer Rates for Common Storage Devices. (Not all generations are listed.) |
|---|---|
| **CD Drives (Compact Disc)** | |
| 1X | 150 kB/s (1200 kb/s or 1.2 Mb/s) |
| 2X | 300 kB/s |
| 8X | 1200 kB/s |
| 52X | 7.8 MB/s |
| **DVD Drives (Digital Versatile Disc or Digital Video Disc)** | |
| 1X | 1.32 MB/s |
| 16X | 21.09 MB/s |

be fast enough to deliver the data so that it can be played at the appropriate speed. For the example audio file in Table 1.4, it would be necessary to transmit data at a rate of 1,411 kb/s. For the example video file, the rate would be 222,595 kb/s. None of the data connection types in Table 1.8 can accommodate such a data rate. This is why compression becomes so important in digital media applications.

Data rate is important in capturing digital video, since video is time-based and the most data-intensive of the media. When digital video is captured, motion and sound are happening in real time. Motion is captured as a sequence of frames, with a common frame rate of 30 frames per second. Each frame is a digital image composed of pixels defined by their color values, often three bytes per pixel. Sound is captured in a sequence of audio samples, often four bytes per sample at a sampling rate of 44.1 kHz. Sound and image together generate a large amount of data, on the order of 30 MB per second or more if uncompressed. This data must move from the digital camera to the computer and be stored at a rate that keeps up with the live motion that is being captured. Thus, the data rate of the connection from camera to computer and the storage rate on the hard disk are crucial. Table 1.8 gives the data transfer rates of commonly used camera-to-computer connections as of the writing of this chapter. Firewire (IEEE 1394) is a commonly used physical connection between a digital video camera and a computer for live video capture because of its high data transfer rate.

Data rate is also an issue when you play a digital *CD* or *DVD* (*compact disc* and *digital versatile disk*, respectively). In this case, you don't have to transfer the data over a network. You already have it on a CD or DVD in your possession. But the CD or DVD player needs to have a data transfer rate that is adequate for your medium. Consider, for example, a music CD. Each strain of music is composed of audio samples. If the CD player cannot play the data fast enough, it will not be possible to play the music at the correct speed. CD player speeds have evolved steadily since the 1980s. The first CDs were playable at a rate of 1200 kb/s. The next generation could play at twice the rate—which is 2400 kb/s—and were called 2X speed. Each subsequent generation was based on the speed of the original CD players. The current 8X to 52X CD players now range from 1200 kB/s to 7800 kB/s. Similarly, the first generation of DVD-ROMs had a data transfer rate of 1.32 MB/s, and all subsequent generations have been measured as multiples of this original benchmark.

#### 1.4.4.2 Baud Rate

A term close in meaning to bandwidth and bit rate is **baud rate**. As is the case with bandwidth, there is some confusion—or at least lack of agreement—about the definition of **baud**. The most precise definition of baud rate is "the number of changes in the signal per second, as a property of sending and receiving devices." This would

**ASIDE:** Baud rate is named for J.M.E. Baudot (1845–1903), a French engineer who invented the Baudot telegraph code and the first successful teleprinter.

be a property measured in cycles per second, Hertz. Under this definition, baud rate is synonymous with bandwidth, not bit rate. As you saw earlier in this chapter, if the sending device uses more than one signal level—say, $k$ signal levels—then the bit rate, $d$, is given by the equation $d = 2b \log_2(k)$. Thus, to convert from baud rate to bit rate, you have to consider how many different signal levels are possible. However, just like bandwidth, the term baud rate is used loosely. Baud rates for telephone modems are commonly reported in bits per second rather than cycles per second. For example, current telephone modems are often described as having a baud rate of 56 kb/s (although this is actually their bit rate). In light of this confusion, here are the main points to understand:

- Baud rate is close in meaning to bandwidth as bandwidth relates to digital data communication. The main difference is that baud rate is usually used to refer to sending and receiving devices, whereas bandwidth has other meanings related to frequencies over the airwaves.
- A device like a modem can have a maximum baud rate as well as an actual baud rate. The actual baud rate is the rate agreed upon between sender and receiver for a particular communication.
- What is often reported as a baud rate is really a bit rate. (But bit rate is generally what you want to know anyway, so no harm done.) To be precise, baud rate and bit rate are related by the equation $d = 2b \log_2(k)$.

## 1.5 COMPRESSION METHODS

### 1.5.1 Types of Compression

For good fidelity to the original source, it is necessary that image, sound, and motion be digitized at a fine degree of resolution and with quantization levels covering a wide dynamic range. This typically translates to thousands or millions of samples, each of which is, say, two to four bytes in size—sometimes larger. In short, digital media files are usually very large, and they need to be made smaller—compressed, that is. Without compression, you probably won't have the storage capacity to save as many files as you'd like to, and you won't be able to communicate them across networks without overly taxing the patience of the recipients. On the other hand, you don't want to sacrifice the quality of your digital images, audio files, and videos in the compression process. Fortunately, the size of digital media files can be reduced significantly with little or no perceivable loss of quality.

Compression algorithms can be divided into two basic types: **lossless compression** and **lossy compression**. In lossless compression, as the name implies, no information is lost between the compression and decompression steps. Compression reduces the file size to fewer bits. Then decompression restores the data values to exactly what they were before the compression. Lossy compression methods, on the other hand, sacrifice some information. However, these algorithms are designed so that the information lost is generally not important to human perception. In image files, it could be subtle changes in color that the eye cannot detect. In sound files, it could be frequencies that are imperceptible to the human ear.

Aside from the broad categories of lossy and lossless compression, you will see other labels given to types of compression algorithms, including *dictionary-based, entropy, arithmetic, adaptive, perceptual* and *differential compression methods.* Dictionary-based methods (e.g. LZW compression) use a look-up table of fixed-length codes, where one code word may correspond to a string of symbols rather than to a single symbol in the file being compressed. Entropy compression uses a statistical analysis of the frequency of symbols and achieves compression by encoding more frequently-occurring symbols with shorter code words, with one code word assigned to each symbol. Shannon-Fano and Huffman encoding are examples of entropy compression. Arithmetic encoding benefits from a similar statistical analysis, but encodes an entire file in a single code word rather than creating a separate code for each symbol. Adaptive methods gain information about the nature of the file in the process of compressing it, and adapt the encoding to reflect what has been learned at each step. LZW compression is by nature adaptive because the code table is created "on the fly" during compression and decompression. Huffman encoding can be made adaptive if frequency counts are updated as compression proceeds rather than being collected beforehand; the method adapts to the nature of the data as the data are read. Differential encoding is a form of lossless compression that reduces file size by recording the difference between neighboring values rather than recording the values themselves. Differential encoding can be applied to digital images, audio, or video. In the sections that follow, we will look more closely at three algorithmic approaches to lossless compression. Other methods will be examined in detail in the chapters on digital image, audio, and video.

The *compression rate* of a compression algorithm is the ratio of the original file size $a$ to the size of the compressed file $b$, expressed as $a:b$. Alternatively, you can speak of the ratio of $b$ to $a$ as a percentage. For example, for a file that is reduced by compression to half its original size, you could say that 50% compression is achieved, or alternatively, that the compression rate is 2:1.

## 1.5.2 Run-Length Encoding

*Run-length encoding* (*RLE*) is a simple example of lossless compression. It is used in image compression. For example, files that you see with the *.bmp* suffix—a Microsoft version of bitmap image files—optionally use run-length encoding. Here's how it works. An image file is stored as a sequence of color values for consecutive pixel locations across rows and down columns. If the file is in RGB color mode, there are three bytes per pixel, one for each of the red, green, and blue color channels. If the file is grayscale, there is one byte per pixel. For simplicity, let's use a grayscale file in this example. (Extending the algorithm to three bytes per pixel is straightforward.) Since each pixel position is encoded in one byte, it represents one of 256 grayscale values. (You recall that $2^8 = 256$, so eight bits can encode 256 different things.) Thus, a grayscale image file consists of a string of numbers, each of them between 0 and 255. Assume that the image has dimensions $100 \times 100$, for a total of 10,000 pixels. Assume also that the pixels are stored in row-major order, which means that the values from a whole row are stored from left to right, then the next row from left to right, and so forth.

You can easily imagine that in many images, there could be rows with strings of repeated grayscale values. The simple idea in run-length encoding is that instead of storing each of the 10,000 pixels as an individual value, it can be more concise to store number pairs $(c, n)$, where  indicates the grayscale value and  indicates how many consecutive pixels have that value. For example, say that in a 10,000-pixel grayscale image, the first 20 pixels are:

255 255 255 255 255 255 242 242 242 242 238 238 238 238 238 238 255 255 255 255

The run-length encoding of this sequence would be

$$(255, 6), (242, 4), (238, 6), (255, 4)$$

Let's compare the number of bytes needed to store the run-length encoded version of this line of pixels versus the number of bytes needed to store it originally. For this example, we'll assume that everything has to be rounded to units of bytes. (We could compute how many bits are needed, but working with bytes suffices to make the point in this example.) Without RLE, 20 pixels require

$$20\,pixels * 1\,byte/pixel = 20\,bytes$$

To determine the number of bytes required with RLE, we first need to figure out how many bytes are needed to store $n$ in each $(c, n)$ pair. Clearly, $c$ can be stored in one byte since its values range from 0 to 255. Now we have to consider how large $n$ could possibly be. In our example, the image has 10,000 pixels in it. It is possible that all 10,000 pixels have the same color, in which case $n = 10{,}000$. To store 10,000, we'd need 14 bits. ($10{,}000_{10} = 10011100010000_2$.) Since we're assuming we allocate memory only in byte increments, this means we need two bytes.

Say that the run-length encoding algorithm scans the image file in a preprocessing step to determine the size of the largest run of colors, where a run is a contiguous sequence of the same color. Let the size of this largest run be $r$. Try some examples values for $r$. What if the largest run is 300—that is, $r = 300$? Then how many bits would you need to store the second value in each $(c, n)$ pair? You can represent the numbers 0 through 255 with eight bits, right? So eight bits is not enough, because you can't represent a number as big as 300. You can represent the values 0 through 511 with nine bits, so nine bits is enough. If you round this up to the nearest byte, that's two bytes. If you think this through intuitively, you should be able to see that the formula for figuring out how many bytes you need to represent a number that can be anywhere between 0 and $r$ is $b = \left\lceil \dfrac{\log_2(r + 1)}{8} \right\rceil$. If you need two bytes to store $n$ in the $(c,n)$ pair, then in the example above, the RLE encoded string of values would require 12 bytes rather than 20.

Now, what if you have a sequence like the following?

255 255 255 255 243 240 242 242 242 241 238 238 237 237 237 237 255 255 255 255

The run-length encoding of this sequence would be

$$(255, 4), (243, 1), (240, 1), (242, 3), (241, 1), (238, 2), (237, 4), (255, 4)$$

In this case, run-length encoding actually requires more rather than fewer bytes than the original uncompressed image—24 rather than 20.

The actual implementation of this might be different. Rather than determining the largest $n$ in advance and then setting the bit depth of $n$ accordingly, it makes sense to choose a bit depth of $n$ in advance. Then if more than $n$ consecutive pixels of the same color are encountered, the runs are divided into blocks. For example, if one byte is used to represent each $n$, then the largest value for $n$ is 255. If 1000 consecutive whites exist in the file (with color value 255), they would be represented as

$$(255, 255), (255, 255), (255, 255), (255, 235)$$

**Figure 1.22** Simple image
that is a good candidate for
run-length encoding

The image in Figure 1.22 is a good example of an image where run-length encoding is beneficial. Disregarding heading information on the image file, the image contains $100 \times 100 = 10{,}000$ pixels. With run-length encoding, again disregarding the size of the header on the file, the file requires 1084 bytes. The compression rate is $\dfrac{10000}{1084}$, or about 9:1. This is an excellent compression rate, but obviously most images will not have such clearly defined color areas, and so few of these areas. (The encoded file size was obtained by saving the file as a BMP image in an application program and then looking at the file properties.)

Run-length encoding is a simple algorithm that gives acceptable results on some types of images, with no risk of loss of quality. It should be clear that no information is lost in the encoding process. We still have precisely the same values for the pixels after the file is encoded and then decoded. The encoded values are just represented in a way that is potentially more concise. In practice, RLE algorithms are fine-tuned and do not operate in precisely the way shown here, but the main principle is always the same.

The second example of run-length encoding given above illustrates a case where the encoding did not result in a smaller file. You should note that for *any lossless compression algorithm and for any length file, there will always exist at least one case where the algorithm does not reduce the size of an input file of that length.* Why is this necessarily so? You should be able to prove this to yourself with what is called a ***counting argument***. Let's walk through the argument together.

- Consider an arbitrary file that you want to compress. Whether it is an image, audio, or video file, it is just a sequence of bits.
- Consider all the files that have $n$ bits in them. How many different files of length $n$ are there? Each bit can have a value of 0 or 1. That's $2^n$ files with length $n$.
- Assume that we have a lossless compression algorithm that can reduce the size of any file given to it as input. If the algorithm is given a file of length $n$, it will produce a compressed file of length $\le n - 1$. How many different files are there of length $\le n - 1$? There's 1 zero-bit file, 2 one-bit files, 4 two-bit files, etc. Thus, there are $1 + 2 + 4 + \cdots + 2^{n-1} = 2^n - 1$ such files.
- A key to this argument is that we are talking about *lossless* compression algorithms. Since the algorithm we are considering is lossless, it cannot be the case that two files of length $n$ compress to yield the same file (some file of length $\le n - 1$). If two files did compress to yield the same file, then in decompression, how would it be determined which of the two original files was the source? In such a case, some information

would be lost, and the algorithm could not be lossless. Thus, we want to map each of the input files of length $n$ to exactly one compressed file of length $\leq n - 1$.

- We've discovered a contradiction. There are fewer files of length $\leq n - 1$ than there are files of length $n$. This argument shows that for any lossless algorithm and for any length of input file, there will exist cases where the algorithm does not reduce the size of the input file.

Lossless compression algorithms are applied in situations where loss of data cannot be tolerated. This is the case in the compression of both text and of binary-encoded computer programs, for example, and thus lossless algorithms are used in tools such as *gzip* and *compress* (on the Unix platform) or *pkzip* and *winzip* (on the Windows platform). Sound files do not lend themselves well to lossless compression. Consecutive audio samples with the same value are unusual, so RLE is not very effective for sound. Image files are better candidates for lossless compression. While an image file is still being edited, it is preferable to keep as much of the original data as possible. Thus, a number of image file formats—PNG and TIFF, for example—offer forms of lossless compression such as LZW. (See Chapter 3 for more information on image file types.) Lossless compression can also be used as one step in a more complex algorithm that does include lossy steps. This is the case with Huffman encoding, one step in the JPEG compression algorithm. We will look at Huffman encoding and LZW compression in more detail in Chapter 3.

## 1.5.3 Entropy Encoding

Claude Shannon's work in information theory sheds light on the limits of lossless compression and methods for achieving better compression rates with entropy encoding. Recall that entropy encoding works by means of variable-length codes, using fewer bits to encode symbols that occur more frequently, while using more bits for symbols that occur infrequently. Shannon's equation, below, gives us a way a judging whether our choice of number of bits for different symbols is close to optimal.

Borrowing the term entropy from physics, Shannon defines the ***entropy of an information source*** S as follows:

---

### 🔑 KEY EQUATION

Let $S$ be a string of symbols and $p_i$ be the frequency of the $i^{th}$ symbol in the string. ($p_i$ can equivalently be defined as the probability that the $i^{th}$ symbol will appear at any given position in the string.) Then

$$H(S) = \eta = \sum_i p_i \log_2\left(\frac{1}{p_i}\right)$$

---

Applying ***Shannon's entropy equation***, you can determine an optimum value for the average number of bits needed to represent each symbol-instance in a string of symbols, based on how frequently each symbol appears. Shannon proves that you can't do better than this optimum. You'll see more clearly what this means in the example below. Let's step through the equation and an example to get a better understanding.

Think about an image file that has exactly 256 pixels in it, each pixel of a different color. Then the frequency of each color is 1/256. Thus, Shannon's equation reduces to

$$\sum_{0}^{255} \frac{1}{256}\left(\log_2\left(\frac{1}{\frac{1}{256}}\right)\right) = \sum_{0}^{255} \frac{1}{256}(\log_2(256)) = \sum_{0}^{255} \frac{1}{256}(8) = 8$$

This means that the average number of bits needed to encode each color is eight, which makes sense in light of the fact that $\log_2 256 = 8$.

What if you had an image file that had many instances of some colors, but only a few instances of others? For example, what if you had an image file of 256 pixels and only eight colors in the image with the following frequencies:

**TABLE 1.10   Color Frequencies**

| Color | Frequency | Optimum Number of Bits to Encode This Color | Relative Frequency of the Color in the File | Product of Columns 3 and 4 |
|-------|-----------|---------------------------------------------|---------------------------------------------|----------------------------|
| black | 100 | 1.356 | 0.391 | 0.530 |
| white | 100 | 1.356 | 0.391 | 0.530 |
| yellow | 20 | 3.678 | 0.078 | 0.287 |
| orange | 5 | 5.678 | 0.020 | 0.111 |
| red | 5 | 5.678 | 0.020 | 0.111 |
| purple | 3 | 6.415 | 0.012 | 0.075 |
| blue | 20 | 3.678 | 0.078 | 0.287 |
| green | 3 | 6.415 | 0.012 | 0.075 |

Then Shannon's equation becomes

$$\frac{100}{256}\log_2\left(\frac{256}{100}\right) + \frac{100}{256}\log_2\left(\frac{256}{100}\right) + \frac{20}{256}\log_2\left(\frac{256}{20}\right) + \frac{5}{256}\log_2\left(\frac{256}{5}\right)$$

$$+ \frac{5}{256}\log_2\left(\frac{256}{5}\right) + \frac{3}{256}\log_2\left(\frac{256}{3}\right) + \frac{20}{256}\log_2\left(\frac{256}{20}\right) + \frac{3}{256}\log_2\left(\frac{256}{3}\right)$$

$$\approx 0.530 + 0.530 + 0.287 + 0.111 + 0.111 + 0.075 + 0.287 + 0.075 \approx 2.006$$

So what's the significance of this? Let's see how Shannon's equation can be applied to compression. Consider each term individually. The first term corresponds to the color black. Relative to the size of the entire file, the symbol for black carries $\log_2\left(\frac{256}{100}\right) = 1.356$ bits of information every time it appears in the file, a measure of how many times black appears relative to the size of the file. The third term corresponds to the color yellow. Yellow conveys $\log_2\left(\frac{256}{20}\right) = 3.678$ bits of information each time it appears.

The implication is that if we were to encode each color with a number of bits equal to its information content, this would be an optimum encoding. That is, we couldn't encode the file in any fewer bits. Overall, the minimum value for the average number of bits required to represent each symbol-instance in this file is 2.006. This implies that in an optimally compressed file, the average number of bits used to encode each symbol-instance cannot be less than 2.006.

Keep in mind that the implication in Shannon's equation is that we don't necessarily need to use the same number of bits to represent each symbol. A better compression ratio is achieved if we use fewer bits to represent symbols that appear more frequently in the file. Algorithm 1.1, the *Shannon-Fano algorithm*, describes one way that Shannon's equation can be applied for compression. It attempts to approach an optimum compression ratio by assigning relatively shorter code words to symbols that are used infrequently, and vice versa.

## ALGORITHM 1.1

```
algorithm Shannon-Fano_compress
/*Input: A file containing symbols. The symbols could represent characters of text,
colors in an image file, etc.
Output: A tree representing codes for the symbols. Interior nodes contain no data.
Each leaf node contains a unique symbol as data.*/
{
    list = a list of the symbols in the input file, sorted by their frequency of appearance
    code_tree = split_evenly(list)
}
algorithm split_evenly(list)
/*Input: A sorted list of symbols, list.
Output: A tree representing the encoding of the symbols in list.*/
{
    if the size of list = =1, then {
        create a node for the one symbol in list, giving it NULL children
        put the symbol as the data of the node
        return the node
    }
    else {
    Divide list into two lists list1 and list2 such that the sum of the frequencies in list1
is close as possible to the sum of the frequencies in list.
        t = a tree with one node
        lchild = split_evenly(list1)
        rchild = split_evenly(list2)
        attach lchild as the left child of t
        attach rchild as the right child of t
        return t
    }
}
```

The algorithm takes a recursive top-down approach, each recursive step dividing the symbols in half such that the symbols in the two halves have approximately the same number of instances in the file being compressed. The algorithm returns a code-tree where the branches are implicitly labeled with 0s and 1s. Gathering the 0s and 1s down each path from root to leaf node gives you the code for the symbol related to the leaf node. In our example, the tree could look like the one shown in Figure 1.23. Colors are abbreviated, and frequencies are shown beside the colors.

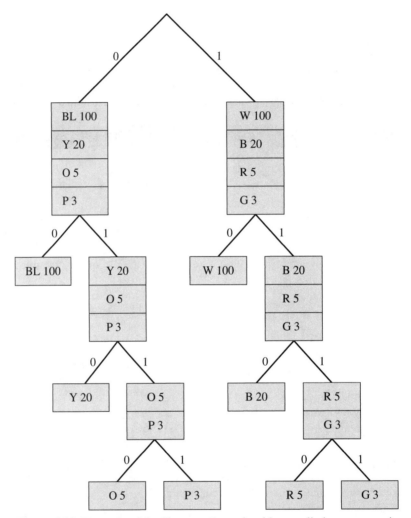

**Figure 1.23** Example of the Shannon-Fano algorithm applied to compression

The Shannon-Fano algorithm for compression works toward achieving the theoretical minimum number of bits per symbol by the method described in Algorithm 1.1.

In this example, the colors would be encoded as shown in Table 1.11. The codes vary in length from two to four bits. How close is the number of bits per symbol used in this encoding to the minimum of 2.006 determined by Shannon's equation? All the symbols for black and white are encoded with two bits, all the symbols for yellow and blue are encoded with three bits, and so forth. This give us

$$(100 * 2) + (100 * 2) + (20 * 3) + (5 * 4) + (5 * 4) + (3 * 4) + (20 * 3) + (3 * 4) = 584$$

| TABLE 1.11 | Codes Resulting from Application of Shannon-Fano Algorithm | |
|---|---|---|
| Color | Frequency | Code |
| black | 100 | 00 |
| white | 100 | 10 |
| yellow | 20 | 010 |
| orange | 5 | 0110 |
| red | 5 | 1110 |
| purple | 3 | 0111 |
| blue | 20 | 110 |
| green | 3 | 1111 |

The colors require 584 bits to encode. For 256 symbols in the file, this is an average of $\frac{584}{256} = 2.28$ bits per symbol-instance—close to the minimum average number of bits per symbol given by Shannon's equation. If we assume that before compression, eight bits were used for each symbol, then the compression rate is $\frac{8}{2.28}$, which is about 3.5:1.

As an aside, you might also want to consider why the word entropy—borrowed from physics—has been adopted in the context of information theory and encoding. The most common definition you will see for the word entropy is disorder. However, a better definition in most situations is multiplicity in the way something can be ordered. Here's a simple example. On a pair of dice, there are six different ways you can roll a value of seven, while there is only one way to roll a value of two. Thus, the value seven has greater entropy than the value two. In the latter definition, entropy is a measure of the number of ways that you can produce a seven. How does this relate to Shannon's equation, and why did Shannon use the term entropy to describe the average minimum number of bits needed to represent each symbol in a string of symbols? You could think of it this way. A file that has a large number of symbols in it relative to the file size will yield a large number from Shannon's equation, compared with a file that has a small number of symbols relative to its size. It has greater entropy because the more symbols you have, the more unique ways those symbols could be arranged. Thus, each encoded symbol carries with it more information, and you need a greater number of distinct codes.

More importantly for our purposes, when you see the term entropy encoding related to digital media, you should understand it to mean encoding that is based on a statistical analysis of the file or type of data being encoded. This analysis could yield the frequency of occurrence of each symbol in an actual file that is to be compressed. Alternatively, the analysis could yield the probability that certain symbols will appear in a *type* of file. For example, in text files, we can expect that some characters will appear more frequently than others. The letter *e* appears frequently in English-language text, while *q* and *x* are more rare. Either type of analysis can be used to create the frequency table upon which entropy encoding is based. Entropy encoding also implies variable-length codes. The benefit in compression arises from using shorter codes for more frequently occurring symbols.

Huffman encoding is another type of entropy encoding that is useful in image compression. We will see in Chapter 3 that it uses the same strategy of statistically based variable-length encoding, while improving upon the Shannon-Fano algorithm in the compression rate.

## 1.5.4 Arithmetic Encoding

One drawback to the Shannon-Fano algorithm is that each symbol must be treated individually; each symbol has its own code, and that code must be represented in an integral number of bits. Huffman encoding has the same disadvantage. By Shannon's equation, we may be able to determine that an optimum encoding is achievable by using a noninteger number of bits for each code. In our example above, if it were possible to use exactly 1.3561 bits to encode black and white, 3.6781 bits to encode yellow and blue, 5.6781 bits to encode orange and red, and 6.415 bits to encode purple and green, then we could achieve an optimum compression rate. (Each of these values is given by $\log_2\left(\dfrac{1}{p_i}\right)$.) The problem is that using the Shannon-Fano algorithm, the optimum encoding isn't possible because we have to use an integer number of bits for each code.

*Arithmetic encoding* overcomes some of the disadvantage of the Shannon-Fano algorithm. Like the Shannon-Fano algorithm, arithmetic encoding is based on a statistical analysis of the frequency of symbols in a file. It differs, however, in that it derives additional advantage from encoding an entire file (or string of symbols) as one entity rather than creating a code symbol by symbol.

The idea is that a string of symbols will be encoded in a single floating point number. In theory, this floating point number can be represented in whatever number of bits is needed for the compression at hand. To implement this with no limit on the number of bits used, we would need infinite precision in the representation of floating point numbers, which is not possible. Let's put this issue aside for now. Later, we will give a sketch of how arithmetic encoding is implemented, but for the moment let's focus on the basic idea.

Arithmetic encoding uses the same strategy as entropy encoding, beginning with a list of the symbols in the input file and their frequency of occurrence. Say that you have a file that contains 100 pixels in five colors: black (K), white (W), yellow (Y), red (R), and blue (B). The frequency of appearance of each color in the file is given in Table 1.12. The frequencies are expressed as numbers between 0 and 1, shown in column two. Each color symbol is assigned a *probability interval* whose size corresponds to its frequency of occurrence, as shown in column three. The entire range between 0 and 1 is called the *probability range*, and the section assigned to one symbol is a probability interval. For example, black's probability interval is 0–0.4. (Assume that these are half open intervals, for example [0, 0.4)). The order of color symbols in the probability range is not important, as long as the symbols are given the same order by the encoder and decoder.

| TABLE 1.12 | Frequencies of Colors Relative to Number of Pixels in File | |
|---|---|---|
| Color | Frequency Out of Total Number of Pixels in File | Probability Interval Assigned to Symbol |
| black (K) | 40/100 = 0.4 | 0–0.4 |
| white (W) | 25/100 = 0.25 | 0.4–0.65 |
| yellow (Y) | 15/100 = 0.15 | 0.65–0.8 |
| red (R) | 10/100 = 0.1 | 0.8–0.9 |
| blue (B) | 10/100 = 0.1 | 0.9–1.0 |

| TABLE 1.13 | Values for encoding the example problem | | |
|---|---|---|---|
| Range | Low Value for Probability interval | High Value for Probability Interval | Symbol |
| $1 - 0 = 1$ | $0 + 1 * 0.4 = 0.4$ | $0 + 1 * 0.65 = 0.65$ | White |
| $0.65 - 0.4 = 0.25$ | $0.4 + 0.25 * 0 = 0.4$ | $0.4 + 0.25 * 0.4 = 0.5$ | Black |
| $0.5 - 0.4 = 0.1$ | $0.4 + 0.1 * 0 = 0.4$ | $0.4 + 0.1 * 0.4 = 0.44$ | Black |
| $0.44 - 0.4 = 0.04$ | $0.4 + 0.04 * 0.65 = 0.426$ | $0.4 + 0.04 * 0.8 = 0.432$ | Yellow |
| $0.432 - 0.426 = 0.006$ | $0.426 + 0.006 * 0.8 = 0.4308$ | $0.426 + 0.006 * 0.9 = 0.4314$ | Red |
| $0.4314 - 0.4308 = 0.0006$ | $0.4308 + 0.0006 * 0.9 = 0.43134$ | $0.4308 + 0.0006 * 1 = 0.4314$ | Blue |

Now let's consider only the first six pixels in the file to make the example manageable. These pixels have the colors white, black, black, yellow, red and blue—represented by the symbols W, K, K, Y, R, and B. The arithmetic encoding algorithm assigns a floating point number to a sequence of symbols by successively narrowing the range between 0 and 1 (Table 1.13). In our example, the first symbol is W. This means that the floating point number encoding the total string will fall somewhere in the probability interval assigned to W, between 0.4 and 0.65, as shown at the step 2 of Figure 1.24.

The second symbol is K. At step 2, the range has a size of 0.25, going from 0.4 to 0.65. K was originally assigned the probability interval 0 to 0.4. Moving to step 3, we want to narrow the probability range so that it begins at 0.4 and ends at $0.4 + 0.25 * 0.4$. Thus, the range at step 3 goes from 0.4 to 0.5. At successive steps, we narrow the range in accordance with the size and position of the symbol just read, as described in Algorithm 1.2. In the final step, the low value of the range can be taken as the encoding of the entire string. We've cut our example short by considering only the first six pixels in the file, but the idea is the same.

## ALGORITHM 1.2

```
algorithm arithmetic_encoding
/*Input: A string of symbols and their assigned probability intervals.
Output: A floating point number that encodes the string*/
    low = 0.0
    high = 1.0
    while input symbols remain {
        s = the next input symbol
        range = high – low
        /*s_high (s) represents the high value of symbol s's assigned probability interval,
and s_low (s) represents the low value of symbols's assigned probability interval. */
        high = low + range * s_high(s)
        low = low + range * s_low(s)
    }
    return (low + high)/2
}
```

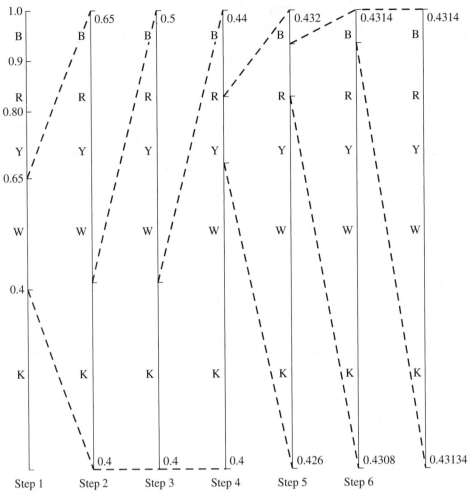

**Figure 1.24** Example of arithmetic encoding

You can probably see for yourself how decoding would proceed. Given a floating point number, you can determine the first symbol of the encoded string by finding, from the initial probability range, the probability interval into which this number fits. Suppose our final encoding from the previous example was 0.43137. The number 0.43137 fits in the interval assigned to W, so W is the first symbol from the encoded string. You now remove the scaling of W's interval by subtracting the low value from W's probability interval and dividing by the size of W's interval, yielding

$$(0.43137 - 0.4)/0.25 = 0.12548$$

The value 0.12548 lies in the probability interval of K. Thus, you subtract K's low range, 0, and divide by the size of K's interval, 0.4, giving

$$0.12548/0.4 = 0.3137$$

This value again lies in K's probability interval.

| TABLE 1.14 | Values for decoding in the example problem | | | |
|---|---|---|---|---|
| Floating Point Number f, Representing Code | Symbol Whose Probability Interval Surrounds f | Low Value for Symbol's Probability Interval | High Value for Symbol's Probability Interval | Size of Symbol's Probability Interval |
| 0.43137 | W | 0.4 | 0.65 | 0.25 |
| (0.43137 − 0.4)/(0.65 − 0.4) = 0.12548 | K | 0 | 0.4 | 0.4 |
| (0.12548 − 0)/(0.4 − 0) = 0.3137 | K | 0 | 0.4 | 0.4 |
| (0.3137 − 0)/(0.4 − 0) = 0.78425 | Y | 0.65 | 0.8 | 0.15 |
| (0.78425 − 0.65)/(0.8 − 0.65) = 0.895 | R | 0.8 | 0.9 | 0.1 |
| (0.895 − 0.8)/(0.9 − 0.8) = 0.95 | B | 0.9 | 1.0 | 0.1 |

The computation proceeds as described in the decoding procedure given in Algorithm 1.3, yielding the values in Table 1.14. Although our example worked out nicely, with a maximum of five digits after the decimal point, you should be able to see that a larger example would require very high precision arithmetic. In fact, this appears to make arithmetic encoding impractical in the implementation, but there are ways around the problem.

## ALGORITHM 1.3

```
algorithm arithmetic_decoding
/*Input:   A floating point number, f, encoding a string of symbols, a list of symbols
encoded by the number, and the probability intervals assigned to these symbol.
Output:   The string of symbols, s, decoded
Assumptions: A terminator symbol has been encoded at the end of the string*/

   symbolDecoded = NULL
   while symbolDecoded ! = TERMINATOR_SYMBOL {
     s = a symbol whose probability interval contains f
     output s
     /*Let s_high(s) represent the high value of symbol s's probability interval, and
s_low(s) represent the low value of s's probability interval*/
     range = s_high(s) − s_low(s)
     f = (f − s_low(s)) / range
   }
}
```

Actual implementations use integer arithmetic and bit shifting operations that effectively accomplish the procedure described here, without requiring infinite precision floating point operations—in fact, without using any floating point operations at all. There are other issues not discussed here that have been fine-tuned in various implementations, including how to terminate the input string and how to speed up what can be a time-consuming compression method. The important facts to note about arithmetic encoding are these:

- Arithmetic encoding is a form of entropy encoding, where the number of bits that a symbol contributes to the compressed string is proportional to the probability of that symbol appearing in the original input string.
- In arithmetic encoding, an entire input string is encoded as one value. In comparison, Huffman encoding—another example of entropy encoding—uses variable-length codes assigned on a symbol-by-symbol basis.
- Because arithmetic encoding theoretically can encode a symbol in a fractional number of bits, it is closer to optimal than Huffman encoding.
- Arithmetic encoding can be applied as one step in JPEG compression of photographic images.
- IBM and other companies hold patents on algorithms for arithmetic encoding.

## 1.5.5 Transform Encoding

The compression algorithms we have looked at so far are all lossless. With these algorithms, a digital image, audio, or video file can be compressed, and the original data can be perfectly reconstructed when it is decompressed (not considering rounding errors that may result from floating point arithmetic).

The disadvantage of lossless methods is that they do not always give enough compression, especially for large audio and video files. Lossy methods are needed. Fortunately, these methods are designed so that the information lost is relatively unimportant to the perceived quality of the sound or images.

Lossy methods are often based upon *transform encoding*. The idea is that changing the representation of data can sometimes make it possible to extract sounds or visual details that won't be missed because they are beyond the acuity of human perception. Thus, this type of compression begins with a *transform* of the data from one way of representing it to another. Two of the most commonly used transforms in digital media are the *discrete cosine transform* (*DCT*) and the *discrete Fourier transform* (*DFT*). You should note that it is not the transform that is lossy. No information is lost in the DCT or DFT. However, when a transform is used as one step in a compression algorithm, it becomes possible to discard redundant or irrelevant information in later steps, thus reducing the digital file size. This is the lossy part of the process.

The discrete cosine transform is applied to digital images to change their representation from the spatial to the frequency domain. We introduced the notion of the frequency of an image earlier in this chapter, and we will go into more detail in Chapter 2. What we want to point out here is that transforming image data to the frequency domain with the DCT can be the first step in compression. Once you have separated out the high frequency components of an image, you can remove them. High frequency components correspond to quick fluctuations of color in a short space—changes that aren't easy for the human eye to see. When this information is removed, later steps in the compression (e.g., Huffman encoding) are even more effective. What we have just described is the basis of JPEG compression.

The discrete Fourier transform is applied to sound, transforming audio data from the temporal to the frequency domain. With the frequency components separated out, it is possible to determine which frequencies mask or block out other ones and then discard the masked frequencies. By this method, transform encoding is followed by perceptual encoding, and the result is a smaller audio file.

## 1.5.6 Compression Standards and Codecs

Thus far in this chapter, we have looked at types of compression methods and the concepts behind them. In practice, compression algorithms are implemented in a wide variety of ways that are fine-tuned and optimized in their details. It is not uncommon for methods to be used in combination with each other, as is the case with JPEG and MPEG compression, which combine the DCT, run-length encoding, and Huffman encoding for compression of photographic images. Some algorithms are standardized by official committees so that the various implementations all produce files in the same format. If a standardized algorithm is patented, then commercial companies must pay a license fee to implement the algorithm and sell it in a commercial product. Two prominent examples of standardized compression algorithms are DV for camcorder-generated digital video and the family of MPEG algorithms. Arithmetic encoding is an example of an image compression algorithm that is covered by patents.

Specific implementations of compression algorithms are called *codecs*—short for compression/decompression. The word codec is usually reserved for audio/video compression (as opposed to still images), since real-time decompression is just as important as initial compression with these time-based media. Some codecs are offered as shareware or freeware. Most codecs are commercial products. Codecs can be embedded in image, audio, or video processing programs, or they can be sold and used separately. Sorenson is an example of a codec that is embedded in other environments (e.g., QuickTime) and also available in a professional-grade version that runs apart from other application programs. The professional-grade Sorenson compressor is actually a suite of codecs that includes implementations of MPEG and DV compression and the standard Sorenson codec.

With most codecs, the compression rate can be adjusted by the user in accordance with the desired quality, up to the maximum compression ability of the codec. The choice may be offered in terms of quality, perhaps as a percentage or on a scale from one to ten. Alternatively, the user may have the option of compressing at different bit rates. The bit rate represents the number of bits that are transferred per second. Bit rate and compression rate are inversely related. Increasing the compression rate reduces the bit rate; if there are fewer bits after the data has been compressed, then fewer bits need to be transferred per second to play the sound or video in real time. A lower bit rate makes it possible to play the media on a device that has a relatively low transfer rate—like a CD-ROM rather than a DVD player. However, the higher the compression rate, the more chance there is that the quality of the sound will degrade as compared to the original uncompressed audio. Fortunately, compression algorithms have evolved to the point where they can compress audio and video at a high rate without unduly sacrificing quality.

Table 1.15 lists examples of standardized or patented algorithms and popular codecs (as of the writing of this chapter). These algorithms and codecs will be examined more closely in the chapters on digital audio and digital video.

| TABLE 1.15 | Examples of Standardized and Patented Compression Algorithms and Codecs | | | |
|---|---|---|---|---|
| **Examples of Standardized or Patented Compression Algorithms** | | | | |
| **Algorithm** | **Source Material** | **Developer** | **Compression Rate and/or Bit Rate\*** | **Comments** |
| LZW and variants | still images | • Lempel, Zev, and Welch | • varies with input<br>• works best on images with large contiguous sections of the same color | • the basic compression algorithm for *.gif* files<br>• optional compression for *.tiff* files<br>• Unisys held the patent on LZW until 2003 |
| arithmetic encoding | still images | • evolved through Shannon, Elias, Jelinek, Pasco, Rissanen, and Langdon | • varies with input<br>• usually better than Huffman encoding | • a number of variants have been created, mostly patented by IBM |
| MP3 (MPEG -1, Audio Layer III) | audio | • invented and patented by an institute of the Fraunhofer Society | • 10:1 or greater compression rate<br>• generally used for bit rates from about 96 to 192 kb/s | • Lame is an open-source MP3 encoder that gives high-quality compression at bit rates of 128 kb/s or higher |
| AAC (Advanced Audio Coding; MPEG-2 version updated to MPEG-4) | audio | • patented by Dolby Labs in cooperation with other developers | • generally achieves same quality as MP3 with a 25–40% increase in compression rate<br>• reports bit rates of 64 kb/s with good quality | • got recognition when used in Apple's iPod<br>• also used in RealAudio for bit rates >128 kb/s |
| MPEG-1, 2, 4 | audio/video | • developed by a working group of the ISO/IEC<br>• see ISO/IEC 11172 (MPEG-1), ISO/IEC 13818 (MPEG-2), and ITU-T H.200 (MPEG-4) | • MPEG-1 ~ 1.5 Mb/s<br>• MPEG-2 ~ 4 Mb/s<br>• MPEG-4 ~ 5 kb/s to 10 Mb/s<br>• MPEG7 and 21 are next in evolution of standard | • standards focused primarily on defining a legal format for the bitstream and specifying methods of synchronization and multiplexing<br>• implemented in a variety of ways in codecs such as DivX and Sorenson |
| DV (Digital Video) | video | • a consortium of 10 companies: Matsushita (Panasonic), Sony, JVC, Philips, Sanyo, Hitachi, Sharp, Thomson Multimedia, Mitsubishi, and Toshiba | • usually 5:1<br>• like JPEG and MPEG, uses discrete cosine transform | • the consumer video format for camcorder, recorded onto a cassette tape<br>• compression is done as video is recorded<br>• transferred by Firewire to computer |

**TABLE 1.15**    *continued*

| Examples of Popular Codecs | | | | |
|---|---|---|---|---|
| **Codec** | **Source Material** | **Developer** | **Compression Rate and/or Bit Rate*** | **Comments** |
| IMAADPCM (Interactive Multimedia Association Adaptive Differential Pulse Code Modulation) | audio | • Apple, migrated to Windows | • 4:1 compression of 16 bit samples<br>• built into QuickTime | • some incompatibility between Mac and Windows versions<br>• comparable to the ITU G.726 and G.727 international standard for ADPCM<br>• somewhat outdated |
| Vorbis | audio | • non-proprietary, unpatented format created by Xiph.org foundation | • bit rate comparable to MP3 and AAC with comparable quality | • a family of compression algorithms, the most successful one being Ogg Vorbis |
| FLAC (Free Lossless Audio Codec) | audio | • non-proprietary, unpatented format created by Xiph.org foundation | • compression rates range from about 1.4:1 to 3.3:1 | • a lossless compression algorithm |
| Sorenson | video | • Sorenson Media | • wide variety of compression rates available, including very high compression with good quality | • a suite of codecs available in a "pro" version<br>• standard Sorenson codec is part of QuickTime<br>• other codecs in the suite offer MPEG-4 and AVC compression |
| Indeo | video | • Intel, later acquired by Ligos | • CD-quality compression (352 × 240 resolution NTSC, 1.44 Mb/s bit rate), comparable to MPEG-1<br>• you can set compression quality | • faster compression than Cinepak<br>• good for images where background is fairly static |
| Cinepak | video | • originally developed by SupermacRadius | • CD-quality compression | • originally good for 2x CD-ROM<br>• takes longer to compress than decompress<br>• can be applied to QuickTime and Video for Windows movies |
| DivX | video | • DivX | • reports 10:1<br>• compresses video so that it can be downloaded over DSL or cable modem | • uses MPEG-4 standard |

# 1.6 STANDARDS AND STANDARDIZATION ORGANIZATIONS FOR DIGITAL MEDIA

In the previous section, we spoke of standards being set for multimedia algorithms and data so that application programs and hardware are able to communicate with each other. In your work in multimedia, you'll encounter references to the organizations and workgroups that set the standards, so you'll want to be familiar with their names and acronyms. The topic of standards is very complicated; whole books are written on the subject. We just want you to be familiar with the main types of standards and the prominent standardization organizations. If you need to know more in your work, you can take it from there.

Standards can be divided into three main types: proprietary, *de facto*, and official. ***Proprietary standards*** are set and patented by commercial companies. Companies lay claim to their way of doing things and naturally hope to make money from their designs and inventions. The competition for better ways of doing things constantly leads to newer and better products, though some would argue that too much insistence on proprietary standards slows development because of lack of coherence and interoperability in the industry. The patents on LZW compression and arithmetic encoding are examples of proprietary standards.

The term ***de facto standard*** is used to describe a method or format that has become the accepted way of doing things in the industry without any official endorsement. For example, TIFF files are considered by many to be the de facto standard for image files. Nearly all image processing programs and operating systems are equipped to handle TIFF files.

***Official standards*** are developed by large industry consortia and/or government agencies. These organizations can exist on either a national or an international level. The main international standardization bodies with which you should be familiar are the ***International Telecommunications Union*** (***ITU***), ***International Organization for Standardization*** (***ISO***, pronounced "eye-so"), and the ***International Electrotechnical Commission*** (***IEC***).

The ITU (formerly called CCITT) is an international organization where governments and the private sector coordinate global telecom networks and services. It has some regulatory power—allocating radio frequency bands, for example. It is divided into three sectors: ITU-T for telecommunications standards, ITU-R for radiocommunications standards, and ITU-D for telecommunications development. The standards most relevant to multimedia are the G and H series. The G series covers speech coding and telephone communication. For example, the G.700 series relates to the coding of analog to digital telephone using methods such as ADPCM. The H series is the realm of real-time digital audio and video communication. For example, H.323 is a standard for voice and video over packet-switched networks (*i.e.*, the internet). H.262 gives the standard for MPEG compression.

Using MATLAB to model digital sound and images

interactive tutorial

ISO, an international body that develops industrial and commercial standards, is composed of representatives from various national standards organizations. The American National Standards Institute (ANSI) is the agency representing the United States. Working closely with ISO is the IEC, which formulates standards for electrical, electronic, and related technologies. ISO and the IEC have formed a joint committee called ISO/IEC JTC1, and through this committee they develop standards in information technology. For example, their ISO/IEC 11172 standard defines MPEG-1, and ISO/IEC 13818 defines MPEG-2.

# 1.7 MATHEMATICAL MODELING TOOLS FOR THE STUDY OF DIGITAL MEDIA

Modeling sound
as a waveform

mathematical
modeling
worksheet

This book focuses on the mathematics, science, and algorithms behind digital media to give you greater understanding of and control over your work environment. As you make your way through the remaining chapters, you may often find it helpful to graph functions, visualize waveforms, and solve problems with real values so that you can see the results for yourself rather than just talking about abstractions. Mathematical modeling tools are helpful in this regard. A widely used tool for this purpose is MATLAB. The online tutorial associated with Chapter 1 shows you how to use MATLAB to model waveforms. Even if you don't have access to MATLAB, you should go through this tutorial because it contains an introduction to waveforms used to model digital sound and images. (Octave is free software that works similarly to MATLAB.)

Modeling images
as waveforms

mathematical
modeling
worksheet

With the names, terminology, and basic concepts covered in Chapter 1, you should be ready now to look more deeply into each medium. Pick your focus, or cover it all, and don't forget to look at the online learning supplements, including worksheets, creative exercises, and interactive demos and tutorials.

## EXERCISES

1. What is the frequency of the sine wave below, in cycles per second? What is its angular frequency?

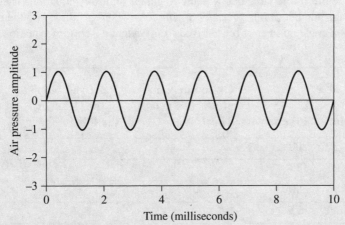

**Figure 1.25** Sine wave

2. What is the equation for a sine wave that has a frequency of 660 Hz?

3. You have a digital image in eight-bit color that has blocky areas of color, lacking the subtle gradations from one color to the next that you would like to see. Is this a matter of aliasing or quantization error? Explain.

4. If you are recording an audio file and you expect that the highest frequency in the file will be 10,000 Hz, what is the minimum sampling rate you can use to ensure that you won't get audio aliasing?

5. How many different colors can be represented with 12 bits?

6. True or false? You can't represent as wide a range of colors with eight bits as you can with 16 bits. Explain your answer.

7. According to the definitions of kilobytes, megabytes, and gigabytes used by computer scientists, 4,276,012,000 bytes is equal to approximately how many kilobytes, how many megabytes, and how many gigabytes?

8. What is the signal-to-noise ratio of a sound file represented with eight bits per sample?

9. Compute the number of bytes needed for one minute of uncompressed video that has $720 \times 576$ pixels per frame, 25 frames per second, three bytes per pixel, and CD-quality stereo audio.

10. What is the data rate of a communication medium with a bandwidth of 3 MHz using 4 different signal levels?

11. Do a run-length encoding of the following sequence of grayscale values. Explain your encoding strategy, and compute the compression rate.

   240 240 240 240 240 240 240 238 238 238 238 238 230 230 230 230 229 228 228 227 227 227 227 227 227 227 227 227 227 227 227 227 227 227 227 227 227 227 227 227

12. Do a Shannon-Fano encoding of an image file on the basis of the frequency table below. Fill in the table below using Shannon's entropy equation. Then compare the average number of bits per color arising from your encoding with the minimum possible average number of bits derived from Shannon's entropy equation.

| Color | Frequency | Optimum Number of Bits to Encode This Color | Relative Frequency of the Color in the File | Product of Columns 3 and 4 |
|-------|-----------|---------------------------------------------|---------------------------------------------|----------------------------|
| black | 200 | | | |
| white | 175 | | | |
| yellow | 90 | | | |
| orange | 75 | | | |
| red | 70 | | | |
| purple | 35 | | | |
| blue | 20 | | | |
| green | 10 | | | |

13. Say that you have an image that has 100 pixels. The first six colors of the image are W K Y B R Y. Do the first six steps of arithmetic encoding based on the frequency table on next page.

| Color | Frequency Out of Total Number of Pixels in File | Probability Interval Assigned to Symbol |
|---|---|---|
| black (K) | $40/100 = 0.4$ | 0–0.4 |
| white (W) | $30/100 = 0.3$ | 0.4–0.7 |
| yellow (Y) | $15/100 = 0.15$ | 0.7–0.85 |
| red (R) | $10/100 = 0.1$ | 0.85–0.95 |
| blue (B) | $5/100 = 0.05$ | 0.95–1.0 |

14. Computer technology changes very quickly. At the time of the writing of this book, Table 1.8 and Table 1.9 list data rates for common communication links and storage devices. Do some research to determine if new technology is now available that gives faster data rates, and update the tables accordingly.

15. The arithmetic encoding algorithm described in this chapter operates as if your computer is capable of infinite precision arithmetic, which of course it is not. Do some research to find out how this algorithm is made practical.

16. Using MATLAB to model digital sound and images, interactive tutorial, online

17. Modeling sound as a waveform, mathematical modeling exercise, online

18. Modeling images as waveforms, mathematical modeling exercise, online

## APPLICATIONS

1. Take inventory of the software available to you for work in digital media, in the following categories:
   - digital image processing
   - vector graphics
   - digital sound processing
   - digital video
   - multimedia programming

   What software was included on your computer when you bought it? What software is available in computer labs to which you have access? What type of multimedia work would you like to do? What software do you need for this work? Compare the features of the products in each category. Do some web research to find out what is available and what each piece of software costs. What can you afford? If there are types of software that are out of your price range, see if you can find scaled-down versions that are less expensive, or freeware or shareware alternatives. If you simply want to experiment with certain application programs, find out if trial versions are available. Often, you can use a trial version for 30 days, although sometimes these versions don't offer all the features of the full program.

2. Look at the specifications of your computer and other hardware to determine its suitability for work in digital media, in the following categories:
   - amount of RAM
   - amount of hard disk space
   - processor speed

Does your computer meet the minimum requirements of the digital media software you'd like to use?

3. As you work through this book, you'll be learning how to create and edit digital images, sound, and video. The last chapter will introduce you to multimedia authoring languages like Director, Flash, and Java, where you can put together your images and sound. One way to tie all of your learning together is to develop a long-term project as you work through the book. Here are some suggestions:

- a game program (e.g. Tic-Tac-Toe, Othello, Mancala, Connect Four, Master Mind, or a Solitaire)
- an interactive tutorial (e.g., "How to Do Long Division," "How to Change a Tire," or whatever you want to teach)
- your own interactive résumé and/or portfolio of your work
- an interactive commercial website

Plan a project that will tie together the media that you study in this book. Decide what media you need for your project. Just for practice, you might want to incorporate as many different types of media as possible—digital photographs, vector graphic animations, digital audio, MIDI, and digital video. As you go through the chapters on each medium, develop the material you'll need for your project. For example, if you're creating a game program for, say, a checkers game, you could create digital images for the splash screen as you work through Chapters 2 and 3, digital audio and MIDI-generated music as you work through Chapters 4 and 5, and digital video as you work through Chapters 6 and 7. Then in Chapter 8, you'll learn how to weave these together with multimedia authoring environments and languages.

*Additional exercises or applications may be found at the book or author's website.*


## REFERENCES

### Print Publications

Chapman, Nigel, and Jenny Chapman. *Digital Multimedia*. 2nd ed. West Sussex, England: John Wiley & Sons, Ltd., 2005.

Comer, Douglas E., and Ralph E. Droms. *Computer Networks and Internets*. 4th ed. Upper Saddle River, NJ: Prentice Hall, 2003.

Couch, II, Leon W. *Digital and Analog Communication Systems*. 7th ed. Upper Saddle River, NJ: Prentice Hall, 2006.

Fano, R. *Transmission of Information*. Cambridge, MA: MIT Press, 1961.

Gibson, Jerry D., et al. *Digital Compression for Multimedia: Principles & Standards*. San Francisco: Morgan Kaufmann Publishers, 2006.

Halsall, Fred. *Multimedia Communications: Applications, Networks, Protocols, and Standards*. Harlow, England: Pearson Education/Addison Wesley, 2000.

Hanselman, Duane, and Bruce Littlefield. *Mastering MATLAB 7*. Upper Saddle River, NJ: Pearson/Prentice Hall, 2005.

Howard, P. G., and J. S. Vitter. *Practical Implementation of Arithmetic Coding*. In *Images and Text Compression*. Boston: Kluwer Academic Publishers, 1992.

Li, Ze-Nian, and Mark S. Drew. *Fundamentals of Multimedia*. Upper Saddle River, NJ: Pearson/Prentice Hall, 2004.

Nyquist, H. Certain Topics in Telegraph Transmission Theory. *Transactions of AIEE*, 47 (April 1928): 617-644. (Reprinted as a class paper in *Proceedings of IEEE*, 90 (2): 280–305, 2003.)

Pasco, R. Source Coding Algorithms for Fast Data Compression. Ph.D. dissertation, Stanford University, 1976.

Rissanen, J. 1976. "Generalized Kraft Inequality and Arithmetic Coding." *IBM Journal of Research and Development* 20: 198–203.

Rissanen, J. July 1984. Universal Coding, Information, Prediction, and Estimation. *IEEE Trans. on Information Theory* IT-30: 629–636.

Rissanen, J., and G. G. Langdon. 1979. "Arithmetic Coding." *IBM Journal of Research and Development*, 23(2): 149–162.

Shannon, C. E. 1948. A Mathematical Theory of Communication. *Bell System Technical. Journal* 27: 379–423, 623–656.

Shannon, C. E. *The Mathematical Theory of Communication*. Champaign, IL: University of Illinois Press, 1949.

Tranter, Jeff. *Linux Multimedia Guide*. Cambridge, MA: Oreilly and Associates, 1996.

Witten, I. H., R. M. Neal, and J. G. Cleary. June 1987. Arithmetic Coding for Data Compression. *Communications of the ACM* 30 (6): 520–540.

## Websites

ISO (International Organization for Standardization).
   http://www.iso.org
ITU (International Telecommunication Union).
   http://www.itu.int/home/
IEC (International Electrotechnical Commission).
   http://www.iec.ch/

# Digital Image Representation

# 2

*Beauty in art has the same base as truth in philosophy. What is the truth? The conformity of our judgements with that of others. What is a beautiful imitation? The conformity of the image with the thing.* —Denis Diderot

## OBJECTIVES FOR CHAPTER 2

- Understand the difference between bitmap and vector graphic representations of image data.
- Understand the difference between representing image data in the spatial versus the frequency domain, and be able to visualize image data as they are represented graphically in each domain.
- Be able to transform image data between the spatial and frequency domains by means of the discrete cosine transform.
- Know how base frequencies of the discrete cosine transform are represented as sinusoidal waves and visualized as changing grayscale or color values.
- Apply the Nyquist theorem to an understanding of aliasing and moiré patterns.
- Understand an example demosaicing algorithm for color aliasing.
- Understand an example anti-aliasing algorithm.
- Understand color models, be able to visualize the important models graphically, and be able to transform from one model to another as needed.
- Understand how parametric curves are created in vector graphics, and be able to apply the equations that define them.
- Understand algorithms for producing fractal images.

## 2.1 INTRODUCTION

Digital images are created by three basic methods: *bitmapping*, *vector graphics*, and *procedural modeling*. *Bitmap images* (also called *pixmaps* or *raster graphics*) are created with a pixel-by-pixel specification of points of color. *Bitmaps* are commonly created by digital cameras, scanners, paint programs like Corel Paint Shop Pro, and image processing programs like Adobe Photoshop. Vector graphic images—created in programs such as Adobe Illustrator and Corel Draw—use object specifications and mathematical equations to describe shapes to which colors are applied. A third way to create digital images is by means of procedural modeling—also called *algorithmic art* because of its aesthetic appeal—where a computer program uses some combination of mathematics, logic, control structures, and recursion to determine the color of pixels and thereby the content of the overall picture. Fractals and Fibonacci spirals are examples of algorithmic art.

Bitmaps are appropriate for photographic images, where colors change subtly and frequently in small gradations. Vector graphic images are appropriate for cleanly delineated shapes and colors, like cartoon or poster pictures. Procedurally modeled images are algorithmically interesting in the way they generate complex patterns, shapes, and colors in nonintuitive ways. All three methods of digital image creation will be discussed in this chapter, with the emphasis on how pixels, colors, and shapes are represented. Techniques for manipulating and compressing digital images are discussed in Chapter 3.

## 2.2 BITMAPS

### 2.2.1 Digitization

A *bitmap* is two-dimensional array of pixels describing a digital image. Each *pixel*, short for *picture element*, is a number representing the color at position $(r, c)$ in the bitmap, where $r$ is the row and $c$ is the column.

> **ASIDE:** A bitmap is a pixel-by-pixel specification of points of color in an image file. The prefix *bit* seems to imply that each pixel is represented in only one bit and thus could have only two possible values, 0 or 1, usually corresponding to black and white (though it could be any two colors). It seems that the word *pixmap*, short for *pixel map*, would be more descriptive, but *bitmap* is the commonly used term even when referring to images that use more than one bit per pixel.

There are three main ways to create a bitmap. One is through software, by means of a paint program. With such a program, you could paint your picture one pixel at a time, choosing a color for a pixel, then clicking on that pixel to apply the color. More likely, you would drag the mouse to paint whole areas with brush strokes, a less tedious process. In this way, you could create your own artwork—whatever picture you hold in your imagination—as a bitmap image.

More commonly, however, bitmap images are reproductions of scenes and objects we perceive in the world around us. One way to create a digital image from real world objects or scenes is to take a snapshot with a traditional analog camera, have the film developed, and then scan the photograph with a digital scanner—creating a bitmap image that can be stored on your computer.

A third and more direct route is to shoot the image with a digital camera and transfer the bitmap to your computer. Digital cameras can have various kinds of memory cards—sometimes called *flash memory*—on which the digital images are stored. You can transfer the image to your computer either by making a physical connection (*e.g.*, USB) between the camera and the computer or by inserting the camera's memory card into a slot on your computer, and then downloading the image file. Our emphasis in this book will be on bitmap images created from digital photography.

Digital cameras use the same digitization process discussed in Chapter 1. This digitization process always reduces to two main steps: sampling and quantization. Sampling rate for digital cameras is a matter of how many points of color are sampled and recorded in each dimension of the image. You generally have some choices in this regard. For example, a digital camera might allow you to choose from $1600 \times 1200$, $1280 \times 960$, $1024 \times 768$, and $640 \times 480$. Some cameras offer no choice.

In digital cameras, quantization is a matter of the color model used and the corresponding bit depth. We will look at color models more closely later in this chapter. Suffice it to say for now that digital cameras generally use RGB color, which saves each pixel in three bytes, one for each of the color channels: red, green, and blue. (A higher bit depth is possible in RGB, but three bytes per pixel is common.) Since three bytes is 24 bits, this makes it possible for $2^{24} = 16,777,216$ colors to be represented.

Both sampling and quantization can introduce error in the sense that the image captured does not represent, with perfect fidelity, the original scene or objects that were photographed. If you don't take enough samples over the area being captured, the image will lack clarity. The larger the area represented by a pixel, the blurrier the picture because subtle transitions from one color to the next cannot be captured.

We illustrate this with the figures below. Imagine that you are looking at a natural scene like the one pictured in Figure 2.1. Suppose that you divide the image into 15 rows and 20 columns. This gives you $15 \times 20$ rectangular sample areas. You (a hypothetical camera)

**Figure 2.1** Digital image

**Figure 2.2** Image, undersampled

**Figure 2.3** Image, reduced bit depth

sample the image once per rectangle, using as your sample value the average color in each square. If you then create the image using the sample values, the image (Figure 2.2) obviously lacks detail. It is blocky and unclear.

A low bit depth, on the other hand, can result in patchiness of color. The bit depth used by digital cameras is excellent for color detail. However, after taking a picture and loading it onto your computer, you can work with it in an image processing program and from there reduce its bit depth. (You might do this to reduce the file size.) Consider this exaggerated example, to make the point. If you reduce the number of colors in the boat picture from a maximum of 16,777,216 to a maximum of 12, you get the image in Figure 2.3. Whole areas of color have become a single color, as you can see in the clouds. This is the effect of quantization error on a digital image.

## 2.2.2 Pixel Dimensions, Resolution, and Image Size

We defined pixel in the context of a bitmap, but it has another meaning in the context of a computer display—where pixel is defined as a physical object a point of light on the screen. Sometimes the terms *logical pixel* and *physical pixel* are used to distinguish between the two usages. When you display a bitmap image on your computer, the logical pixel—that is, the number representing a color and stored for a given position in the image file—is mapped to a physical pixel on the computer screen.

For an image file, *pixel dimensions* is defined as the number of pixels horizontally (*i.e.*, width, $w$) and vertically (*i.e.*, height, $h$) denoted $w \times h$. For example, your digital camera might take digital images with pixel dimensions of 1600 × 1200. Similarly, your computer screen has a fixed maximum pixel dimensions—*e.g.*, 1024 × 768 or 1400 × 1050.

Digital cameras are advertised as offering a certain number of ***megapixels.*** The megapixel value is derived from the maximum pixel dimensions allowable for pictures taken with the camera. For example, suppose the largest picture you can take, in pixel dimensions, for a certain camera is 2048 × 1536. That's a total of 3,145,728 pixels. That makes this camera a 3 megapixel camera (approximately). (Be careful. Camera makers sometimes exaggerate their camera's megapixel values by including such things as "digital zoom," a software method for increasing the number of pixels without really improving the clarity.)

***Resolution*** is defined as the number of pixels in an image file per unit of spatial measure. For example, resolution can be measured in pixels per inch, abbreviated *ppi.* It is assumed that the same number of pixels are used in the horizontal and vertical directions, so a 200 ppi image file will print out using 200 pixels to determine the colors for each inch in both the horizontal and vertical directions.

Resolution of a printer is a matter of how many dots of color it can print over an area. A common measurement is ***dots per inch*** (DPI). For example, an inkjet printer might be able to print a maximum of 1440 DPI. The printer and its software map the pixels in an image file to the dots of color printed. There may be more or fewer pixels per inch than dots printed. You should take a printer's resolution into consideration when you create an image to be printed. There's no point to having more resolution than the printer can accommodate.

***Image size*** is defined as the physical dimensions of an image when it is printed out or displayed on a computer, *e.g.,* in inches (abbreviated ″) or centimeters. By this definition, image size is a function of the pixel dimensions and resolution, as follows:

---

### 🔑 KEY EQUATION

For an image with resolution $r$ and pixel dimensions $w \times h$ where $w$ is the width and $h$ is the height, the printed image size $a \times b$ is given by

$$a = w/r$$

and

$$b = h/r$$

---

For example, if you have an image that is 1600 × 1200 and you choose to print it out at 200 ppi, it will be 8″ × 6″.

You can also speak of the image size as the image appears on a computer display. For an image with pixel dimensions $w \times h$ and resolution $r$, the displayed image size is, as before, $w/r \times h/r$. However, in this case $r$ is the display screen's resolution. For example, if your computer display screen has pixel dimensions of 1400 × 1050 and it is 12″ × 9″, then the display has a resolution of about 117 ppi. Thus, a 640 × 480 image, when shown at 100% magnification, will be about 5½″ × 4″. This is because each logical pixel is displayed by one physical pixel on the screen.

> ### 🔑 KEY EQUATION
>
> For an image with pixel dimensions $w \times h$ where $w$ is the width and $h$ is the height displayed on a computer display with resolution $r$ at 100% magnification, the displayed image size $a \times b$ is given by
>
> $$a = w/r$$
>
> and
>
> $$b = h/r$$
>
> (It is assumed that the display resolution is given in pixels per inch or centimeters per inch.)

Supplement on pixel dimensions, resolution, and image size:

hands-on exercise

The original pixel dimensions of the image file depend on how you created the image. If the image originated as a photograph, its pixel dimensions may have been constrained by the allowable settings in your digital camera or scanner that captured it. The greater the pixel dimensions of the image, the more faithful the image will be to the scene captured. A $300 \times 400$ image will not be as crisp and detailed as a $900 \times 1200$ image of the same subject.

You can see the results of pixel dimensions in two ways. First, with more pixels to work with, you can make a larger print and still have sufficient resolution for the printed copy. Usually, you'll want your image to be printed at a resolution between 100 and 300 ppi, depending on the type of printer you use. (Check the specifications of your printer to see what is recommended.) The printed size is $w/r \times h/r$, so the bigger the $r$, the smaller the print. For example, if you print your $300 \times 400$ image out at 100 ppi, it will be $3'' \times 4''$. If you print it out at 200 ppi, it will be $1\frac{1}{2}'' \times 2''$.

The second way you see the result of pixel dimensions is in the size of the image on your computer display. Since logical pixels are mapped to physical pixels, the more pixels in the image, the larger the image on the display. A $300 \times 400$ image will be 1/3 the size of a $900 \times 1200$ on the display in each dimension. It's true that you can ask the computer to magnify the image for you, but this won't create detail that wasn't captured in the original photograph. If you magnify the $300 \times 400$ image by 300% and compare it to an identical image that was originally taken with pixel dimensions of $900 \times 1200$, the magnified image won't look as clear. It will have jagged edges.

Thus, when you have a choice of the pixel dimensions of your image, you need to consider how you'll be using the image. Are you going to be viewing it from a computer or printing it out? How big do you want it to be, either in print size or on the computer screen? If you're printing it out, what resolution do you want to use for the print? With the answers to these questions in mind, you can choose appropriate pixel based on the choices offered by your camera and the amount of memory you have for storing the image.

There are times when you can't get exactly the pixel dimensions you want. Maybe your camera or scanner has limitations, maybe you didn't take the picture yourself, or maybe you want to crop the picture to cut out just the portion of interest. (*Cropping*, in an image processing program, is simply cutting off part of the picture, discarding the unwanted pixels.) Changing the number of pixels in an image is called ***resampling***. You can increase the pixel dimensions by ***upsampling*** or decrease the dimensions by ***downsampling***, and you may have valid reasons for doing either. But keep in mind that resampling always involves some kind of interpolation, averaging, or estimation, and thus it cannot improve the quality of an image in the sense of making it any more faithful to the picture being represented. The additional pixels created by upsampling are just "estimates" of what the original pixel values would have been if you had originally captured the image at higher pixel dimensions, and pixel values you get from downsampling are just averages of the information you originally captured. In Chapter 3, we'll look more closely at how resampling is done.

The lack of clarity that results from a sampling rate that is too low for the detail of the image is an example of aliasing. You may recall from Chapter 1 that aliasing is a phenomenon where one thing "masquerades" as another. In the case of digital imaging, if the sampling rate is too low, then the image takes on a shape or pattern different what was actually being photographed—blockiness, blurriness, jagged edges, or moiré patterns (which, informally defined, are patterns that are created from two other patterns overlapping each other at an angle). Similarly, a digitized sound might adopt false frequencies heard as false pitches, or digitized video might demonstrate motion not true to the original, like spokes in a bicycle wheel rotating backwards. As explained in Chapter 1, the Nyquist theorem tells us that aliasing results when the sampling rate is not at least twice the frequency of the highest frequency component of the image (or sound or video) being digitized. To understand this theorem, we need to be able to think of digital images in terms of frequencies, which may seem a little counterintuitive. It isn't hard to understand frequency with regard to sound, since we're accustomed to thinking of sound as a wave and relating the frequency of the sound wave to the pitch of the sound. But what is frequency in the realm of digital images?

## 2.3 FREQUENCY IN DIGITAL IMAGES

Chapter 1 gives a general discussion of how data can be represented by functions in a variety of domains, and how the representation can be translated from one domain to another without loss of information. Let's look at this more closely in the context of digital images. Our goal is understand how a digital image can be translated from the spatial domain to the frequency domain, because once we see how this is done, we can understand what the Nyquist theorem means when applied to digital images.

To begin, let's think of an image as a function that can be represented in a graph. It's easier to visualize this with a function in one variable, so let's consider just one line of color across an image as a function $y = f(x)$, where $x$ is the position of one point of color. Function $f$ is *a function over the spatial domain* in that the $x$ values correspond to points in space. $y$ is the color value at position $x$.

Figure 2.4 shows an image of grayscale values that vary from lighter gray (a grayscale value of 168) to darker gray (a grayscale value of 85) and back again. (All examples in this section will be based on grayscale images. The observations are easily generalized to RGB images, where each of the red, green, and blue channels has values between 0 and 255. Each channel can be individually translated from the spatial to the frequency domain.) Grayscale values for one horizontal line across the image are graphed as the function $y = f(x)$ in Figure 2.5, assuming that the pattern repeats. Notice that the graph is sinusoidal—the shape of a sine or cosine wave. Because this is such a simple example, it is easy to see the image in terms of frequency. An important concept to remember is that in the realm of digital imaging, *frequency refers to the rate at which color values change.*

**Figure 2.4** An image in which color varies continuously from light gray to dark gray and back again

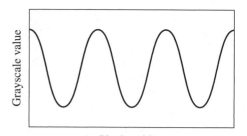

Pixel position

**Figure 2.5** Graph of function $y = f(x)$ for one line of color across the image. $f$ is assumed to be continuous and periodic

This image changes at a perfectly regular and continuous rate, resulting in a sinusoidal shape to the graph.

So far we've been treating the color values in an image as a continuous function, but to work with these values in a digital image we need to discretize them. Figure 2.6 is a discretized version of Figure 2.4 in that it has discrete bands of colors and the change from one color to the next is abrupt. Assume that this is a 8 × 8 pixel image, and imagine extending the image horizontally such that the eight-pixel pattern is repeated four times. Then consider just one row of pixels across the image. Figure 2.7 shows how such an image would be graphed in the spatial domain. We can still consider this a waveform, though it is not smooth like a sine or cosine wave. All bitmap images, even those with irregular patterns of pixel values like the picture of the sparrow shown in Figure 2.8, can be viewed as waveforms. Figure 2.9 shows the graph of one row of pixels taken from the sparrow picture.

**Figure 2.6** Discretized version of gradient

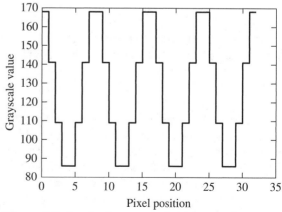

Pixel position

**Figure 2.7** Graph of one row of pixels over the spatial domain (Assume the pattern shown in Figure 2.6 is repeated four times in this graph, making a 32 pixel width.)

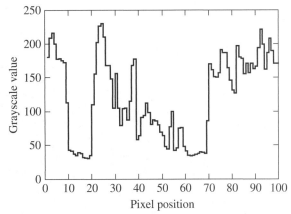

**Figure 2.8** A grayscale bitmap image

**Figure 2.9** Graph of one row of sparrow bitmap over the spatial domain

Extending these observations to two-dimensional images is straightforward. If we assume that the picture in Figure 2.6 is an 8 × 8 pixel bitmap, then the corresponding graph over the spatial domain (Figure 2.10) is a three-dimensional graph where the third dimension is the pixel value at each $(x, y)$ position in the image. The graph for the picture of the sparrow is shown in Figure 2.11. When the two-dimensional bitmap images are graphed, you can imagine that each row (and each column) is a complex waveform.

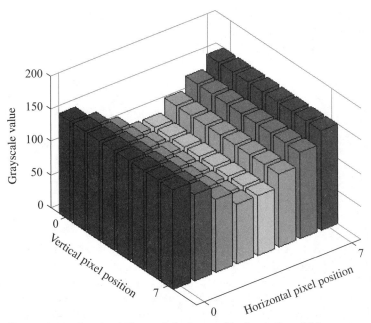

**Figure 2.10** Graph of Figure 2.6, assumed to be an 8 × 8 bitmap image

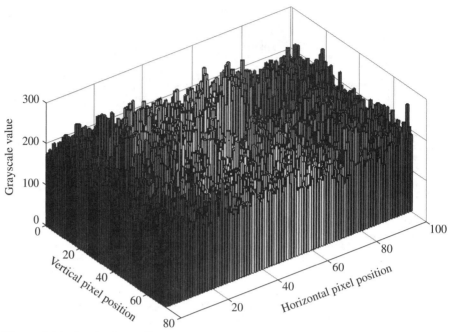

**Figure 2.11**  Graph of two-dimensional bitmap of sparrow

## 2.4 THE DISCRETE COSINE TRANSFORM

**ASIDE:** Fourier theory was developed by mathematician and physical scientist Jean Baptiste Joseph Fourier (1768–1830) and is applicable to a wide range of problems in engineering and digital signal processing.

All of the graphs we've looked at so far have been represented in the spatial domain. To separate out individual frequency components, however, we need to translate the image to the frequency domain. Fourier theory tells us that any complex periodic waveform can be equated to an infinite sum of simple sinusoidal waves of varying frequencies and amplitudes. To understand what this means, think first about just one horizontal line of image data, picturing it as a complex waveform. The fact that this waveform can be expressed as an infinite sum of simple sinusoidals is expressed in the equation below.

$$f(x) = \sum_{n=0}^{\infty} a_n \cos(n\omega x)$$

$f(x)$ is a continuous periodic function over the spatial domain whose graph takes the form of a complex waveform. The equation says that it is equal to an infinite sum of cosine waves that make up its frequency components. Our convention will be to use $\omega$ to represent angular frequency, where $\omega = 2\pi f$ and $f$ is the fundamental frequency of the wave. As $n$ varies, we move through these frequency components, from the fundamental frequency on through multiples of it. $a_n$ is the amplitude for the $n$th cosine frequency component.

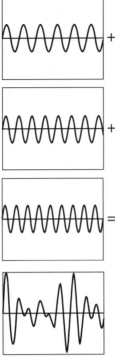

**Figure 2.12** Adding frequency components

We already showed you a simple example of this in Chapter 1. Figure 2.12 shows a sound wave that is the sum of three simple sine waves. (All other frequency components other than those shown have amplitude 0 at all points.)

Let's look at how this translates to the discrete world of digital images. We continue to restrict our discussion to the one-dimensional case—considering a single line of pixels across a digital image, like the one pictured in Figure 2.13. Any row of $M$ pixels can be represented as a sum of the $M$ weighted cosine functions evaluated at discrete points. This is expressed in the following equation:

$$f(r) = \sum_{u=0}^{M-1} \frac{\sqrt{2}C(u)}{\sqrt{M}} F(u)\cos\left(\frac{(2r+1)u\pi}{2M}\right) \text{ for } 0 \le r < M$$

$$\text{where } C(u) = \frac{\sqrt{2}}{2} \text{ if } u = 0 \text{ otherwise } C(u) = 1$$

**Equation 2.1**

You can understand Equation 2.1 in this way. $f(r)$ is a one-dimensional array of $M$ pixel values. For Figure 2.13, these values would be [0, 0, 0, 153, 255, 255, 220, 220]. $F(u)$ is

**Figure 2.13** A one-dimensional image of eight pixels (enlarged). Pixel outlines are not part of image.

one-dimensional array of coefficients. Each function $\cos\left(\dfrac{(2r + 1)u\pi}{2M}\right)$ is called a ***basis function***. You can also think of each function as a ***frequency component***. The coefficients in $F(u)$ tell you how much each frequency component is weighted in the sum that produces the pixel values. You can think of this as "how much" each frequency component contributes to the image.

For $M = 8$, the basis functions are those given in Figures 2.14 through 2.21. They are shown as cosine functions (made continuous) and then as $8 \times 8$ bitmap images whose color values change in accordance with the given basis function. As the values of the cosine function decreases, the pixels get darker because 1 represents white and $-1$ represents black.

$$\cos\left(\frac{(2r + 1)0\pi}{16}\right)$$
$$= \cos(0)$$

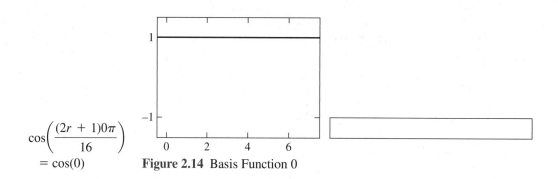

**Figure 2.14** Basis Function 0

$$\cos\left(\frac{(2r + 1)\pi}{16}\right)$$

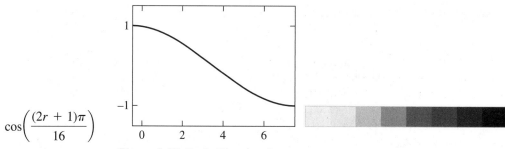

**Figure 2.15** Basis Function 1

$$\cos\left(\frac{(2r + 1)2\pi}{16}\right)$$

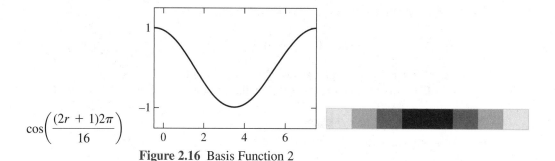

**Figure 2.16** Basis Function 2

$$\cos\left(\frac{(2r + 1)3\pi}{16}\right)$$

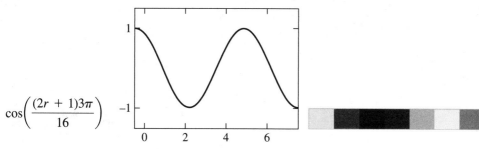

**Figure 2.17** Basis Function 3

$$\cos\left(\frac{(2r + 1)4\pi}{16}\right)$$

**Figure 2.18** Basis Function 4

$$\cos\left(\frac{(2r + 1)5\pi}{16}\right)$$

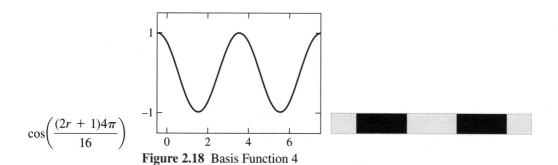

**Figure 2.19** Basis Function 5

$$\cos\left(\frac{(2r + 1)6\pi}{16}\right)$$

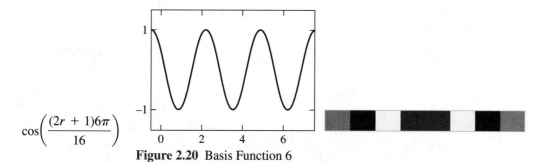

**Figure 2.20** Basis Function 6

$$\cos\left(\frac{(2r + 1)7\pi}{16}\right)$$

**Figure 2.21** Basis Function 7

The pictures of grayscale bars correspond to the sinusoidal graphs as follows: Evaluate the basis function at $r = i$ for $0 \le r \le 7$ from left to right. Each of the resulting values corresponds to a pixel in the line of pixels to the right of the basis function, where the grayscale values are scaled in the range of $-1$ (black) to $1$ (white). Thus, frequency component $\cos\left(\frac{(2r + 1)\pi}{16}\right)$ (basis function 1) corresponds to a sequence of eight pixels that go from white to black.

Equation 2.1 states only that the coefficients $F(u)$ *exist*, but it doesn't tell you how to compute them. This is where the *discrete cosine transform (DCT)* comes in. In the one-dimensional case, the discrete cosine transform is stated as follows:

$$F(u) = \sum_{r=0}^{M-1} \frac{\sqrt{2}C(u)}{\sqrt{M}} f(r) \cos\left(\frac{(2r + 1)u\pi}{2M}\right) \text{ for } 0 \le u < M$$

$$\text{where } C(u) = \frac{\sqrt{2}}{2} \text{ if } u = 0 \text{ otherwise } C(u) = 1$$

**Equation 2.2**

Equation 2.2 tells how to transform an image from the spatial domain, which gives color or grayscale values, to the frequency domain, which gives coefficients by which the frequency components should be multiplied. For example, consider the row of eight pixels shown in Figure 2.13. The corresponding grayscale values are [0, 0, 0, 153, 255, 255, 220, 220]. This array represents the image in the spatial domain. If you compute a value $F(u)$ for $0 \le u \le M - 1$ using Equation 2.2, you get the array of values [389.97, −280.13, −93.54, 83.38, 54.09, −20.51, −19.80, −16.34]. You have applied the DCT, yielding an array that represents the pixels in the frequency domain.

What this tells you is that the line of pixels is a linear combination of frequency components—that is, the basis functions multiplied by the coefficients in **F** and a constant and added together, as follows:

$$f(r) = \frac{389.97}{\sqrt{M}}\cos(0) + \frac{\sqrt{2}}{\sqrt{M}}\left(-280.13\cos\left(\frac{(2r + 1)\pi}{2M}\right) - 93.54\cos\left(\frac{(2r + 1)2\pi}{2M}\right)\right.$$

$$+ 83.38\cos\left(\frac{(2r + 1)3\pi}{2M}\right) + 54.09\cos\left(\frac{(2r + 1)4\pi}{2M}\right) - 20.51\cos\left(\frac{(2r + 1)5\pi}{2M}\right)$$

$$\left. - 19.80\cos\left(\frac{(2r + 1)6\pi}{2M}\right) - 16.34\cos\left(\frac{(2r + 1)7\pi}{2M}\right)\right)$$

You can understand this visually through Figure 2.22.

Supplements on discrete cosine transform:

interactive tutorial

programming exercise

worksheet

mathematical modeling

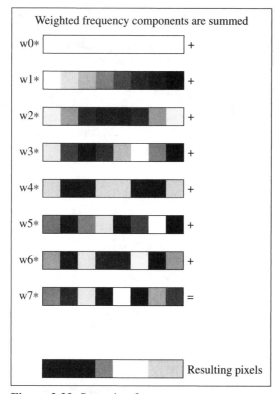

**Figure 2.22**  Summing frequency components

Having a negative coefficient for a frequency components amounts to adding the inverted waveform, as shown in Figure 2.23.

As a matter of terminology, you should note that the first element $F(0)$—is called the **DC component**. For a periodic function represented in the frequency domain, the DC component is a scaled average value of the waveform. You can see this in the one-dimensional case.

$$F(0) = \sqrt{\frac{1}{M}} \left( \begin{array}{l} \cos(0)f(0) + \cos(0)f(1) + \cos(0)f(2) + \cos(0)f(3) + \\ \cos(0)f(4) + \cos(0)f(5) + \cos(0)f(6) + \cos(0)f(7) \end{array} \right)$$

$$= \sqrt{\frac{1}{M}} \left( \begin{array}{l} f(0) + f(1) + f(2) + f(3) + \\ f(4) + f(5) + f(6) + f(7) \end{array} \right)$$

All the other components ($F(1)$ through $F(M - 1)$) are called **AC components**. The names were derived from an analogy with electrical systems, the DC component being

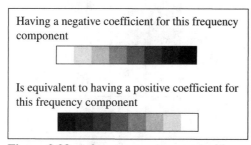

**Figure 2.23**  A frequency component with a negative coefficient

comparable to direct current and the AC component being comparable to alternating current.

We've been looking at the one-dimensional case to keep things simple, but to represent images, we need two dimensions. The two-dimensional DCT is expressed as follows:

## KEY EQUATION

Let $f(r, s)$ be the pixel value at row $r$ and column $s$ of a bitmap. $F(u, v)$ is the coefficient of the frequency component at $(u, v)$, where $0 \leq r, u \leq M - 1$ and $0 \leq s, v \leq N - 1$.

$$F(u, v) = \sum_{r=0}^{M-1} \sum_{s=0}^{N-1} \frac{2C(u)C(v)}{\sqrt{MN}} f(r, s) \cos\left(\frac{(2r + 1)u\pi}{2M}\right) \cos\left(\frac{(2s + 1)v\pi}{2N}\right)$$

where $C(\delta) = \dfrac{\sqrt{2}}{2}$ if $\delta = 0$ otherwise $C(\delta) = 1$

The equations above define the 2D *discrete cosine transform*.

**Equation 2.3**

(Matrices are assumed to be treated in row-major order—row by row rather than column by column.) Equation 2.3 serves as an effective procedure for computing the coefficients of the frequency components from a bitmap image. (Note that since $C(u)$ and $C(v)$ do not depend on the indices for the summations, you can move the factor $\dfrac{2C(u)C(v)}{\sqrt{MN}}$ outside the nested summation. You'll sometimes see the equation written in this alternative form.)

You can think of the DCT in two equivalent ways. The first way is to think of the DCT as taking *a function over the spatial domain*—function $f(r, s)$—and returning *a function over the frequency domain*—function $F(u, v)$ Equivalently, you can think of the DCT as taking a bitmap image in the form of a matrix of color values $-f(r, s)$ – and returning the frequency components of the bitmap in the form of a matrix of coefficients $-F(u, v)$. The coefficients give the amplitudes of the frequency components.

Rather than being applied to a full $M \times N$ image, the DCT is generally applied to $8 \times 8$ pixel subblocks (for example, as a key step in JPEG compression), so our discussion will be limited to images in these dimensions. An enlarged $8 \times 8$ pixel image is shown in Figure 2.24,

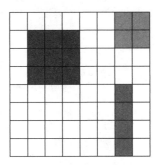

**Figure 2.24** $8 \times 8$ bitmap image. Pixel outlines are not part of image

| TABLE 2.1 | Color Values for Image in Figure 2.24 | | | | | | |
|---|---|---|---|---|---|---|---|
| 255 | 255 | 255 | 255 | 255 | 255 | 159 | 159 |
| 255 | 0 | 0 | 0 | 255 | 255 | 159 | 159 |
| 255 | 0 | 0 | 0 | 255 | 255 | 255 | 255 |
| 255 | 0 | 0 | 0 | 255 | 255 | 255 | 255 |
| 255 | 255 | 255 | 255 | 255 | 255 | 100 | 255 |
| 255 | 255 | 255 | 255 | 255 | 255 | 100 | 255 |
| 255 | 255 | 255 | 255 | 255 | 255 | 100 | 255 |
| 255 | 255 | 255 | 255 | 255 | 255 | 100 | 255 |

| TABLE 2.2 | Amplitudes of Frequency Components for Image in Figure 2.24 | | | | | | |
|---|---|---|---|---|---|---|---|
| 1628 | −61 | 39 | 234 | 173 | −128 | 171 | 22 |
| −205 | −163 | 74 | 222 | 1 | 74 | −30 | 111 |
| 81 | 150 | −95 | −82 | −42 | −11 | −6 | −53 |
| 188 | 231 | −135 | −188 | −53 | −36 | −2 | −103 |
| 96 | 71 | −42 | −78 | −32 | 2 | −17 | −32 |
| 25 | −42 | 25 | 3 | −14 | 27 | −26 | 19 |
| 70 | 15 | −6 | −51 | −17 | 7 | −16 | −13 |
| 94 | 72 | −38 | −87 | −18 | −14 | −4 | −40 |

and its corresponding bitmap values (matrix $f$) and amplitudes of the frequency components computed by the DCT (matrix $F$) are given in Table 2.1 and Table 2.2, respectively.

The discrete cosine transform is invertible. By this we mean that given the amplitudes of the frequency components as $F$, we can get color values for the bitmap image as $f$. This relationship is described in the following equation:

## KEY EQUATION

Let $F(u, v)$ be the coefficient of the frequency component at $(u, v)$. $f(r, s)$ is the pixel value at row $r$ and column $s$ of a bitmap, where $0 \leq r, u \leq M - 1$ and $0 \leq s, v \leq N - 1$.

$$f(r, s) = \sum_{u=0}^{M-1} \sum_{v=0}^{N-1} \frac{2C(u)C(v)}{\sqrt{MN}} F(u, v) \cos\left(\frac{(2r + 1)u\pi}{2M}\right) \cos\left(\frac{(2s + 1)v\pi}{2N}\right)$$

where $C(\delta) = \dfrac{\sqrt{2}}{2}$ if $\delta = 0$ otherwise $C(\delta) = 1$

These equations define the 2D *inverse discrete cosine transform*.

**Equation 2.4**

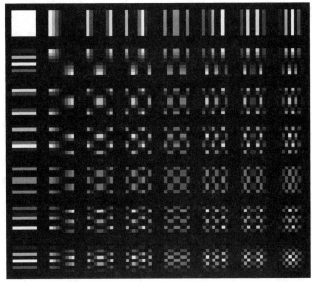

**Figure 2.25** Base frequencies for discrete cosine transform

In essence, the equation states that the bitmap is equal to a sum of $M * N$ weighted frequency components.

The DCT basis functions for an $8 \times 8$ image are pictured in Figure 2.25. Each "block" at position $(u, v)$ of the matrix is in fact a graph of the function $\cos\left(\dfrac{(2r + 1)u\pi}{16}\right)\cos\left(\dfrac{(2s + 1)v\pi}{16}\right)$ at discrete positions $r = [0\ 7]$ and $s = [0\ 7]$. $F(0, 0)$, the DC component, is in the upper left corner. The values yielded by the function are pictured as grayscale values in these positions. The thing to understand is that any $8 \times 8$ pixel block of grayscale values—like the one pictured in Figure 2.24—can be recast as a sum of frequency components pictured in Figure 2.25. You just have to know "how much" of each frequency component to add in. That is, you need to know the coefficient by which to multiply each frequency component, precisely what the DCT gives you in $F(u, v)$ (as in Table 2.2). In the case of color images represented in RGB color mode, the DCT can be done on each of the color components individually. Thus, the process is the same as what we described for grayscale images, except that you have three $8 \times 8$ blocks of data on which to do the DCT—one for red, one for green, and one for blue.

Let's complete this explanation with one more example, this time a two-dimensional image. Consider the top leftmost $8 \times 8$ pixel area of the sparrow picture in Figure 2.8. Figure 2.26 shows a close-up of this area, part of the sidewalk in the background. Figure 2.27 shows the graph of the pixel data over the spatial domain. Figure 2.28 captures the same information about the digital image, but represented in the frequency domain. This graph was generated by the DCT. The DC component is the largest. It may be difficult for you to see at this scale, but there are other nonzero frequency components—for example, at positions (1, 1) and (1, 3) (with array indices starting at 0).

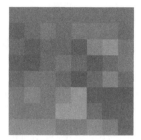

**Figure 2.26**  Close-up of 8 × 8 pixel area (sidewalk) from sparrow picture

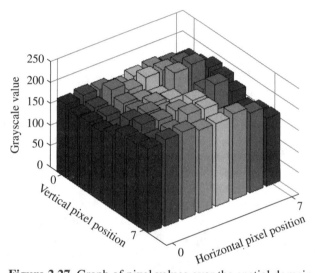

**Figure 2.27**  Graph of pixel values over the spatial domain

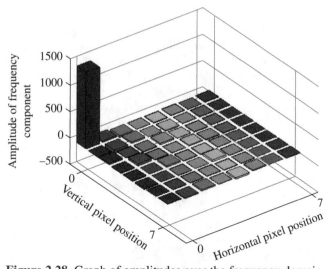

**Figure 2.28**  Graph of amplitudes over the frequency domain

## 2.5 ALIASING

### 2.5.1 Blurriness and Blockiness

Supplements on
aliasing in
sampling:

interactive tutorial

worksheet

The previous section showed that one way to understand frequency in the context of digital images is to think of the color values in the image bitmap as defining a surface. This surface forms a two-dimensional wave. A complex waveform such as the surface shown in Figure 2.11 can be decomposed into regular sinusoidal waves of various frequencies and amplitudes. In reverse, these sinusoidal waves can be summed to yield the complex waveform. This is the context in which the Nyquist theorem can be understood. Once we have represented a bitmap in the frequency domain, we can determine its highest frequency component. If the sampling rate is not at least twice the frequency of the highest frequency component, aliasing will occur.

Let's try to get an intuitive understanding of the phenomenon of aliasing in digital images. Look again at the picture in Figure 2.1 and think of it as a real-world scene that you're going to photograph. Consider just the horizontal dimension of the image. Imagine that this picture has been divided into sampling areas so that only 15 samples are taken across a row—an unrealistically low sampling rate, but it serves to make the point. If the color changes even one time within one of the sample areas, then the two colors in that area cannot both be represented by the sample. This implies that the image reconstructed from the sample will not be a perfect reproduction of the original scene, as you can see in Figure 2.2. Mathematically speaking, the spatial frequencies of the original scene will be aliased to lower frequencies in the digital photograph. Visually, we perceive that when all the colors in a sampling area are averaged to one color, the reconstructed image looks blocky and the edges of objects are jagged. This observation seems to indicate that you'd need a very high sampling rate—that is, large pixel dimensions—to capture a real-world scene with complete fidelity. Hypothetically, that's true for most scenes. Fortunately, however, the human eye isn't going to notice a little loss of detail. The pixel dimensions offered by most digital cameras these days provide more than enough detail for very crisp, clear images.

### 2.5.2 Moiré Patterns

Another interesting example of aliasing, called the ***moiré effect*** or ***moiré pattern***, can occur when there is a pattern in the image being photographed, and the sampling rate for the digital image is not high enough to capture the frequency of the pattern. If the pattern is not sampled at a rate that is at least twice the rate of repetition of the pattern, then a different pattern will result in the reconstructed image. In the image shown in Figure 2.29, the color changes at a perfectly regular rate, with a pattern that repeats five times in the horizontal direction. What would happen if we sampled this image five times, at regularly spaced

**Figure 2.29** A simple image with vertical stripes

intervals? Depending on where the sampling started, the resulting image would be either all black or all white. If we sample more than ten times, however—more than twice per repetition of the pattern—we will be able to reconstruct the image faithfully. This is just a simple application of the Nyquist theorem.

More visually interesting moiré effects can result when the original pattern is more complex and the pattern is tilted at an angle with respect to the sampling. Imagine the image that would result from tilting the original striped picture and then sampling in the horizontal and vertical directions, as shown in Figure 2.30. The red grid shows the sampling blocks. Assume that if more than half a sampling block is filled with black from the original striped image, then that block becomes black. Otherwise, it is white. The pattern in the reconstructed image is distorted in a moiré effect. Once you know what the moiré effect is, you start seeing it all around you. You can see it any time one pattern is overlaid on another—like the shimmering effect of a sheer curtain folded back on itself, or the swirls resulting from looking through a screen at a closely woven wicker chair.

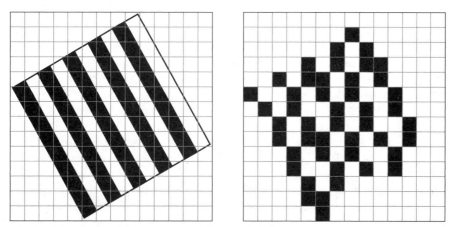

**Figure 2.30**  Sampling that can result in a moiré pattern

Moiré patterns can result both when a digital photograph is taken and when a picture is scanned in to create a digital image, because both these processes involve choosing a sampling rate. Figure 2.31 shows a digital photograph of a computer bag where a moiré pattern is evident, resulting from the sampling rate and original pattern being "out of sync."

**Figure 2.31**  Moiré pattern in digital photograph

**Figure 2.32** Close-up of moiré pattern     **Figure 2.33** True pattern

Figure 2.32 shows a close-up of the moiré pattern. Figure 2.33 shows a close-up of the pattern as it should look. If you get a moiré effect when you take a digital photograph, you can try tilting the camera at a different angle or changing the focus slightly to get rid of it. This will change the sampling orientation or sampling precision with respect to the pattern.

Moiré patterns occur in digital photography because it is based on discrete samples. If the samples are taken "off beat" from a detailed pattern in the subject being photographed, an alias of the original pattern results. But this does not fully explain the source of the problem. Sometimes aliasing in digital images manifests itself as small areas of incorrect colors or artificial auras around objects, which can be referred to as *color aliasing, moiré fringes, false coloration*, or *phantom colors*. To understand what causes this phenomenon, you have to know a little about how color is perceived and recorded in a digital camera.

When a photograph is taken with a traditional analog camera, film that is covered with silver-laden crystals is exposed to light. There are three layers on photographic film, one sensitive to red, one to green, and one to blue light (assuming the use of RGB color). At each point across a continuous plane, all three color components are sensed simultaneously. The degree to which the silver atoms gather together measures the amount of light to which the film is exposed.

We have seen that one of the primary differences between analog and digital photography is that analog photography measures the incident light continuously across the focal plane, while digital photography samples it only at discrete points. Another difference is that it is more difficult for a digital camera to sense all three color components—red, green, and blue—at each sample point. These constraints on sampling color and the use of interpolation to "fill in the blanks" in digital sampling can lead to color aliasing. Let's look at this more closely.

Many current digital cameras use *charge-coupled device (CCD)* technology to sense light and thereby color. (CMOS—complementary metal-oxide semiconductor—is an alternative technology for digital photography, but we won't discuss that here.) A CCD consists of a two-dimensional array of photosites. Each photosite corresponds to one sample (one pixel in the digital image). The number of photosites determines the limits of a camera's resolution. To sense red, green, or blue at a discrete point, the sensor at that photosite is covered with a red, green, or blue color filter. But the question is: Should all three color components be sensed simultaneously at each photosite, should they be sensed at different moments when the picture is taken, or should only one color component per photosite be sensed?

There are a variety of CCD designs in current technology, each with its own advantages and disadvantages. (1) The incident light can be divided into three beams. Three sensors are used at each photosite, each covered with a filter that allows only red, green, or blue to be sensed. This is an expensive solution and creates a bulkier camera. (2) The sensor can be rotated when the picture is taken so that it takes in information about red, green, and blue light in succession. The disadvantage of this method is that the three colors are not sensed at precisely the same moment, so the subject being photographed needs to be still. (3) A more recently developed technology (Foveon X3) uses silicon for the sensors in a method called *vertical stacking*. Because different depths of silicon absorb different wavelengths of light, all three color components can be detected at one photosite. This technology is gaining popularity. (4) A less expensive method of color detection uses an array like the one shown in Figure 2.34 to detect only one color component at each photosite. Interpolation is then used to derive the other two color components based on information from neighboring sites. It is the interpolation that can lead to color aliasing.

| G | R | G | R |
|---|---|---|---|
| B | G | B | G |
| G | R | G | R |
| B | G | B | G |

**Figure 2.34** Bayer color filter array

In the 4 × 4 array shown in the figure, the letter in each block indicates which color is to be detected at each site. The pattern shown here is called a **Bayer color filter array**, or simply a **Bayer filter**. (It's also possible to use a cyan-magenta-yellow combination.) You'll notice that there are twice as many green sensors as blue or red. This is because the human eye is more sensitive to green and can see more fine-grained changes in green light. The array shown in the figure is just a small portion of what would be on a CCD. Each block in the array represents a photosite, and each photosite has a filter on it that determines which color is sensed at that site.

The interpolation algorithm for deriving the two missing color channels at each photosite is called **demosaicing**. A variety of demosaicing algorithms have been devised. A simple **nearest neighbor algorithm** determines a missing color $c$ for a photosite based on the colors of the nearest neighbors that have the color $c$. For the algorithm given below, assuming a CCD array of dimensions $m \times n$, the nearest neighbors of photosite $(i, j)$ are sites $(i - 1, j - 1), (i - 1, j), (i - 1, j + 1), (i, j - 1), (i, j + 1), (i + 1, j - 1), (i + 1, j),$ $(i + 1, j + 1)$ where $0 \leq i \leq m$ and $0 \leq j \leq n$ (disregarding boundary areas where neighbors may not exist). The nearest neighbor algorithm is given as Algorithm 2.1.

---

**ALGORITHM 2.1    NEAREST NEIGHBOR ALGORITHM**

```
algorithm nearest_neighbor
{
    for each photosite (i,j) where the photosite detects color c1 {
        for each c2 ∈ {red,green,blue} such that c2 ≠ c1 {
            S = the set of nearest neighbors of site (i,j) that have color c2
            set the color value for c2 at site (i,j) equal to the average of the color values of
    c2 at the sites in S
        }
}
```

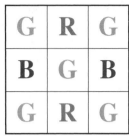

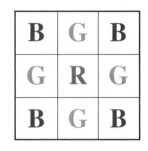

(a) Determining R or B from the center G photosite entails an average of two neighboring sites.

(b) Determining B from the center R photosite entails an average of four neighboring sites diagonal from R.

**Figure 2.35** Photosite interpolation

With this algorithm, there may be either two or four neighbors involved in the averaging, as shown in Figure 2.35a and Figure 2.35b.

This nearest neighbor algorithm can be fine-tuned to take into account the rate at which colors are changing in either the vertical or horizontal direction, giving more weight to small changes in color as the averaging is done. Other standard interpolation methods—linear, cubic, cubic spline, etc.—can also be applied, and the region of nearest neighbors can be larger than 3 × 3 or a shape other than square.

The result of the interpolation algorithm is that even though only one sensor for one color channel is used at each photosite, the other two channels can be derived to yield full RGB color. This method works quite well and is used in many digital cameras with CCD sensors. However, interpolation by its nature cannot give a perfect reproduction of the scene being photographed, and occasionally color aliasing results from the process, detected as moiré patterns, streaks, or spots of color not present in the original scene. A simple example will show how this can happen. Imagine that you photograph a white line, and that line goes precisely across the sensors in the CCD as shown in Figure 2.36. If there is only black on either side of the line, then averaging the neighboring pixels to get the color channels not sensed at the photosites covered by the line always gives an average of 0. That is, no other color information is added to what is sensed at the photosites covered by the

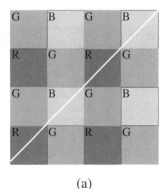

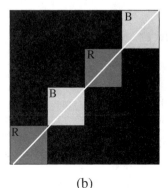

(a)                                        (b)

**Figure 2.36** A situation that can result in color aliasing

line, so each photosite records whatever color is sensed there. The result is the line shown in Figure 2.36b. Generally speaking, when a small area color can be detected by only a few photosites, the neighboring pixels don't provide enough information so that the true color of this area can be determined by interpolation. This situation can produce spots, streaks, or fringes of aliased color.

Some cameras use descreening or anti-aliasing filters over their lenses—effectively blurring an image slightly to reduce the color aliasing or moiré effect. The filters remove high frequency detail in the image that can lead to color aliasing, but this sacrifices a little of the image's clarity. Camera manufacturers make this choice in the design of their cameras—to include the anti-aliasing filter or not—and many high quality cameras do not have the filters because the manufacturers assume that sharp focus is more important to most photographers when weighed against occasional instances of color aliasing or moiré patterns.

### 2.5.3 Jagged Edges

You may have heard the term *aliasing* used to describe the jagged edges along lines or edges that are drawn at an angle across a computer screen. This type of aliasing occurs during rendering rather than sampling and results from the finite resolution of computer displays. A line as an abstract geometric object is made up of points, and since there are infinitely many points on a plane, you can think of a line as being infinitely narrow. A line on a computer screen, on the other hand, is made up of discrete units: pixels. If we assume these pixels are square or rectangular and lined up parallel to the sides of the display screen, then there is no way to align them perfectly when a line is drawn at an angle on the computer screen. This situation is illustrated in Figure 2.37. We assume for purposes of illustration that pixels are nonoverlapping rectangles or squares that cover the display device entirely.

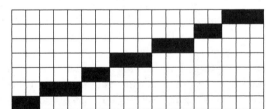

**Figure 2.37** Aliasing of a line that is one pixel wide

Supplements on aliasing in rendering:

interactive tutorial

worksheet

When you draw a line in a draw or a paint program using a line tool, you click on one endpoint and then the other, and the line is drawn between the two points. In order to draw the line on the computer display, the pixels that are colored to form the line must be determined. This requires a line-drawing algorithm such as the one given in Algorithm 2.2. Beginning at one of the line's endpoints, this algorithm moves horizontally across the display device, one pixel at a time. Given column number $x0$, the algorithm finds the integer $y0$ such that $(x0, y0)$ is the point closest to the line. Pixel $(x0, y0)$ is then colored. The results might look like Figure 2.37. The figure and the algorithm demonstrate how a line that is one pixel wide would be drawn. It is not the only algorithm for the purpose, and it does not deal with lines that are two or more pixels wide.

Supplements on
aliasing in line
drawing:

programming
exercise

interactive tutorial

---

**ALGORITHM 2.2** **ALGORITHM FOR DRAWING A LINE**

```
algorithm draw_line
/*Input: x0, y0, x1, and y1, coordinates of the line's endpoints (all integers) c, color
of the line.
Output: Line is drawn on display.*/
{
/*Note: We include data types because they are important to understanding the
algorithm's execution. */
  int dx, dy, num_steps, i
  float x_increment, y_increment, x, y
  dx = x1 − x0
  dy = y1 − y0
  if (absolute_value(dx) > absolute_value(dy) then num_steps = absolute_value(dx)
  else num_steps = absolute_value(dy)
  x_increment = float(dx) / float (num_steps)
  y_increment = float (dy) / float (num_steps)
  x = x0
  y = y0
/*round(x) rounds to the closest integer.*/
  draw(round(x), round(y), c)
  for i = 0 to num_steps−1 {
  x = x + x_increment
  y = y + y_increment
  draw(round(x), round(y), c)
  }}
```

---

To test your understanding, think about how Algorithm 2.2 would be generalized to lines of any width. Figure 2.38 shows a line that is two pixels wide going from point (8, 1) to point (2, 15). The ideal line is drawn between the two endpoints. To render the line in a black and white bitmap image, the line-drawing algorithm must determine which pixels are intersected by the two-pixel-wide area. The result is the line drawn in Figure 2.39. Because it is easy to visualize, we use the assumption that a pixel is colored black if at least half its area is covered by the two-pixel line. Other line-drawing algorithms may operate differently.

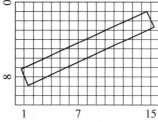

**Figure 2.38** Drawing a line
two pixels wide

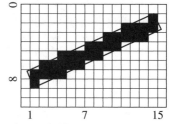

**Figure 2.39** Line two pixels
wide, aliased

*Anti-aliasing* is a technique for reducing the jaggedness of lines or edges caused by aliasing. The idea is to color a pixel with a shade of its designated color in proportion to the amount of the pixel that is covered by the line or edge. In this example, consider the two-pixel-wide line shown in Figure 2.38. If a pixel is completely covered by the line, it is colored black. If it is half covered, it is colored a shade of gray halfway between black and white, and so forth. Using gradations of colors softens the edges. The edges are not sharp, as they would be ideally, but making the lines and edges perfectly straight is impossible due to the finite resolution of the image and the display device. Anti-aliasing helps to compensate for the jagged effect that results from imperfect resolution. The anti-aliased version of our example line is shown in Figure 2.40, enlarged. At normal scale, this line looks smoother than the aliased version.

Bitmaps are just one way to represent digital images. Another way is by means of vector graphics. Rather than storing an image bit-by-bit, a vector graphic file stores a description of the geometric shapes and colors in an image. Thus, a line can be described by means of its endpoints, a square by the length of a side and a registration point, a circle by its radius and center point, etc. Vector graphics suffer less from aliasing problems than do bitmap images in that vector graphics images can be resized without loss of resolution. Let's look at the difference.

When you draw a line with a line tool in a bitmap image, the pixel values are computed for the line and stored in the image pixel by pixel. Say that the image is later enlarged by increasing the number of pixels. This process is called *upsampling*. A simple algorithm for upsampling a bitmap image, making it twice as big, is to make four pixels out of each one, duplicating the color of the original pixel. Obviously, such an algorithm will accentuate any aliasing from the original image. Figure 2.41 shows a one-pixel-wide line from a black and white bitmap image at three different enlargements, the second twice as large and the third three times as large as the first. The jagged edges in the original line look even blockier as the line is enlarged. Other more refined algorithms for upsampling can soften the blocky edges somewhat, but none completely eliminates the aliasing. Algorithms for upsampling are discussed in more detail in Chapter 3.

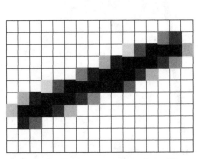

**Figure 2.40**  Line two pixels wide, anti-aliased

**Figure 2.41**  Aliasing of bitmap line resulting from enlargement

Aliasing in rendering can occur in both bitmap and vector graphics. In either type of digital image, the smoothness of lines, edges, and curves is limited by the display device. There is a difference, however, in the two types of digital imaging, and vector graphics has an advantage over bitmap images with respect to aliasing. Aliasing in a bitmap image becomes even worse if the image is resized. Vector graphic images, on the other hand, have only the degree of aliasing caused by the display device on which the image is shown, and this is very small and hardly noticeable.

Changing the size of an image is handled differently in the case of vector graphics. Since vector graphic files are not created from samples and not stored as individual pixel values, upsampling has no meaning in vector graphics. A vector graphic image *can* be resized for display or printing, but the resizing is done by recomputation of geometric shapes on the basis of their mathematical properties. In a vector graphic image, a line is stored by its endpoints along with its color and an indication that it is a line object. When the image is displayed, the line is rendered by a line-drawing algorithm at a size relative to the image dimensions that have been chosen for the image at that moment. Whenever the user requests that the image be resized, the pixels that are colored to create the line are recomputed using the line-drawing algorithm. This means that the jaggedness of the line will never be worse than what results from the resolution of the display device. In fact, to notice the aliasing at all when you work in a vector graphic drawing program, you need to turn off the anti-aliasing option when you view the image. Figure 2.42 shows a vector graphic line at increasing enlargements, with the "view with anti-aliasing" option turned off. The small amount of aliasing is due entirely to the resolution of the display device. The important thing to notice is that as the line gets larger, the aliasing doesn't increase. These observations would hold true for more complex vector graphic shapes as well. (When the lines are printed out on a printer with good resolution, the aliasing generally doesn't show up at all because the printer's resolution is high enough to create a smooth edge.)

**Figure 2.42**  Aliasing does not increase when a vector graphic line is enlarged

In summary, vector graphics and bitmap imaging each has advantages. Vector graphics imaging is suitable for pictures that have solid colors and well-defined edges and shapes. Bitmap imaging is suitable for continuous tone pictures like photographs. The type of images you work with depends on your purpose.

## 2.6 COLOR

### 2.6.1 Color Perception and Representation

Color is both a physical and psychological phenomenon. Physically, color is composed of electromagnetic waves. For humans, the wavelengths of visible colors fall between approximately 370 and 780 nanometers, as shown in Figure 1.19 and 1.20. (A nanometer, abbreviated *nm* in the figure, is $10^{-9}$ meters.) These waves fall upon the color receptors of the eyes, and in a way not completely understood, the human brain translates the interaction between the waves and the eyes as color perception.

Although it is possible to create pure color composed of a single wavelength—for example, by means of a laser—the colors we see around us are almost always produced by a combination of wavelengths. The green of a book cover, for example, may look like a pure green to you, but a spectrograph will show that it is not. A spectrograph breaks up a color into its component wavelengths, producing a spectral density function P($\lambda$). A spectral density function shows the contributions of the wavelengths $\lambda$ to a given perceived color as $\lambda$ varies across the visible spectrum.

Spectral density functions are one mathematical way to represent colors, but not a very convenient way for computers. One problem is that two colors that are perceived to be identical may, on analysis, produce different spectral density curves. Said the other way around, more than one spectral density curve can represent two colors that look the same. If we want to use a spectral density curve to tell a computer to present a particular shade of green, which "green" spectral density curve is the best one to use?

It is possible to represent a color by means of a simpler spectral density graph. (This is basically how color representation is done in the HSV and HLS color models, as will be explained below.) That is, each color in the spectrum can be characterized by a unique graph that has a simple shape, as illustrated in Figure 2.43. The graph for each color gives the color's *dominant wavelength*, equivalent to the *hue*; its *saturation* (*i.e.*, color purity); and its *luminance*. The dominant wavelength is the wavelength at the spike in the graph. The area beneath the curve indicates the luminance L. (This "curve" is a rectangular area with a rectangular spike.) Saturation S is the ratio of the area of the spike to the total area. More precisely with regard to Figure 2.43,

$$L = (d - a)e + (f - e)(c - b)$$

$$S = \frac{(f - e)(c - b)}{L}$$

**ASIDE:** The differences between the power, energy, luminance, and brightness of a light can be confusing. Two colored lights can be of the same wavelength but of different power. A light's power, or energy per unit time, is a physical property *not* defined by human perception. Power is related to brightness in that if two lights have the same wavelength but the first has greater power, then the first will appear brighter than the second. *Brightness* is a matter of subjective perception and has no precise mathematical definition. *Luminance* has a mathematical definition that relates a light's wavelength and power to how bright it is perceived to be. Interestingly, lights of equal power but different wavelengths do not appear equally bright. The brightest wavelengths are about 550 nm. Brightness decreases from there as you move to longer or shorter wavelengths. In general, the more luminant something is, the brighter it appears to be. However, keep in mind that brightness is in the eye of the beholder—a matter of human perception—while luminance has a precise definition that factors in power, wavelength, and the average human observer's sensitivity to that wavelength.

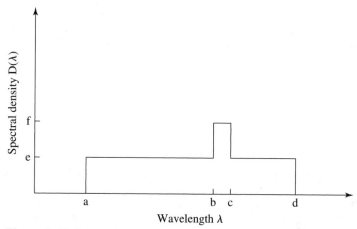

**Figure 2.43** Spectral density graph showing hue, saturation, and lightness

This representation has intuitive appeal, since it is natural to consider first a color's essential hue and then consider varying shades and tones. However, the dimensions of hue, saturation, and brightness do not correspond very well to the way computer monitors are engineered. (We use the terms monitor and display interchangeably to refer to the viewing screen of a computer.) An alternative way to look at a color is as a combination of three primaries. Cathode ray tube (CRT) monitors, for example, display colored light through a combination of red, green and blue phosphors that light up at varying intensities when excited by an electron beam. Similarly, liquid crystal display (LCD) panels display color with neighboring pixels of red, green, and blue that are either lit up or masked by the liquid crystals.

So what is the best way to model color for a computer? There is no simple answer, since different models have advantages in different situations. In the discussion that follows, we will look at *color models* mathematically and find a graphical way to compare their expressiveness.

## 2.6.2 RGB Color Model

One method to create a wide range of colors is by varying combinations of three primary colors. Three colors are primary with respect to one another if no one of them can be created as a combination of the other two. Red, green, and blue are good choices as primary colors because the cones of the eyes—the colors receptors—are especially sensitive to these hues.

$$C = rR + gG + bB$$

where $r$, $g$, and $b$ indicate the relative amounts of red, green, and blue energy respectively. $R$, $G$, and $B$ are constant values based on the wavelengths chosen for the red, green and blue components. The values $r$, $g$, and $b$ are referred to as the values of the RGB *color components* (also called *color channels* in application programs).

The color space for the RGB color model is easy to depict graphically. Let R, G, and G correspond to three axes in three-dimensional space. We will normalize the relative amounts of red, green, and blue in a color so that each value varies between 0 and 1. This color space is shown in Figure 2.44. The origin (0, 0, 0) of the RGB color cube corresponds to black. White is the value (1, 1, 1). The remaining corners of the cube correspond to red, green, blue, and their complementary colors—cyan, magenta, and yellow, respectively. Others colors are created at values between 0 and 1 for each of the components. For

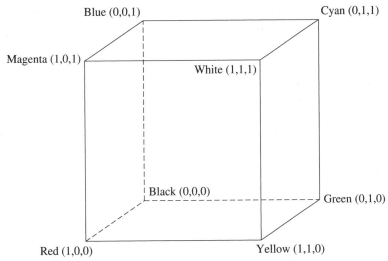

**Figure 2.44** RGB color cube

example, (1, 0.65, 0.15) is light orange, and (0.26, 0.37, 0.96) is a shade of blue. Shades of gray have equal proportions of red, green, and blue and lie along the line between (0, 0, 0) and (1, 1, 1). Notice that if you decrease each of the values for light orange in (1, 0.65, 0.15) but keep them in the same proportion to each other, you are in effect decreasing the brightness of the color, which is like adding in more black. The color moves from a light orange to a muddy brown. You can't increase the brightness of this color and maintain the proportions in Photoshop's HSB color model, because one of the components is already 1, the maximum value. The color is at 100% brightness. On the other hand, the color (0.32, 0.48, 0.39) is a shade of green not at full brightness. You can multiply each component by 2 to get (0.64, 0.96, 0.78), a much lighter shade of green.

You may want to note that in mathematical depictions of the RGB color model, it is convenient to allow the three color components to range between 0 and 1. However, the corresponding RGB color mode in image processing programs is more likely to have values ranging between 0 and 255, since each of the three components is captured in eight bits. What is important is the relative amounts of each component, and the size of these amounts with respect to the maximum possible values. For example, the light orange described as (1, 0.65, 0.15) above would become (255, 166, 38) in an RGB mode with maximum values of 255.

It's interesting to note that grayscale values fall along the RGB cube's diagonal from (0,0,0) to (1,1,1). All grayscale values have equal amounts of R, G, and B. When an image is converted from RGB color to grayscale in an image processing program, the equation can be used for the conversion of each pixel value. This equation reflects the fact that the human eye is most sensitive to green and least sensitive to blue.

### KEY EQUATION

Let an RGB color pixel be given by (R, G, B), where R, G, and B are the red, green, and blue color components, respectively. Then the corresponding grayscale value is given by (L, L, L), where

$$L = 0.30R + 0.59G + 0.11B$$

Since all three color components are equal in a gray pixel, only one of the three values needs to be stored. Thus a 24-bit RGB pixel can be stored as an 8-bit grayscale pixel.

## 2.6.3 CMY Color Model

Like the RGB color model, the ***CMY color model*** divides a color into three primaries, but using a subtractive rather than an additive color creation process. The CMY model can be depicted in a unit cube similar to the RGB model. The difference is that the origin of the cube is white rather than black, and the value for each component indicates how much red, green and blue are subtracted out, effectively combining the color components cyan, magenta, and yellow, their respective complements. Assuming that each of the three RGB (or CMY) components is a value between 0 and 1, the corresponding CMY components can be computed as follows:

---

### KEY EQUATIONS

For a pixel represented in RGB color, the red, green, and blue color components are, respectively, $R$, $G$, and $B$. Then the equivalent $C$, $M$, and $Y$ color components are given by

$$C = 1 - R$$
$$M = 1 - G$$
$$Y = 1 - B$$

Similarly, RGB values can be computed from CMY values with

$$R = 1 - C$$
$$G = 1 - M$$
$$B = 1 - Y$$

---

(The values can be given in the range of [0 255] or normalized to [0 1].)

The CMY model, used in professional four-color printed processes, indicates how much cyan, magenta, and yellow ink is combined to create color. Theoretically, the maximum amount of cyan, magenta, and yellow ink should combine to produce black, but in fact they produce a dark muddy brown. In practice, the four-color printing process used in professional presses adds a fourth component, a pure black ink, for greater clarity and contrast. The amount of $K$, or black, can be taken as the smallest of the $C$, $M$, and $Y$ components in the original CMY model. Thus the CMYK model is defined as follows:

---

### KEY EQUATIONS

For a pixel represented in the CMY color model, the cyan, magenta, and yellow color components are, respectively, $C$, $M$, and $Y$. Let $K$ be the minimum of $C$, $M$, and $Y$. Then the equivalent color components in the CMYK model, $C_{new}$, $M_{new}$, $Y_{new}$, and $K$ are given by

$$K = \min(C, M, Y)$$
$$C_{new} = C - K$$
$$M_{new} = M - K$$
$$Y_{new} = Y - K$$

---

(The definition above theoretically gives the values for CMYK. However, in practice, other values are used due to the way in which colored inks and paper interact.)

## 2.6.4 HSV and HLS Color Models

Instead of representing color by three primary color components, it is possible to speak of a color in terms of its hue (*i.e.*, the essential color), its lightness (or value or luminance), and its saturation (*i.e.*, the purity of the color). Both the ***HSV color model*** (also called HSB) and the ***HLS model*** represent color in this manner. Geometrically, the HSV color space is a distortion of the RGB space into a kind of three-dimensional diamond called a hexacone. Picture turning the RGB cube around and tilting it so that you are looking straight into the origin (white/black) with the remaining corners visible—two on the top, two on the bottom, one on the left, and one on the right, as shown in Figure 2.45. Imagine this as a flat, two-dimensional hexagon where the center white/black point is connected by a line to each vertex, as shown in Figure 2.46. The six primary colors and their complements are at the outside vertices of this shape. Now imagine expanding this into three dimensions again by pulling down on the center point. You have created the HSV color space, as shown in Figure 2.47.

To see how this shape captures the HSV color model, draw an imaginary circle that touches all the vertices of the hexacone's base. The hue is represented by a position on this circle given in degrees, from 0 to 360, with red conventionally set at 0. As the hue values increase, you move counterclockwise through yellow, green, cyan, etc. Saturation is a function of the color's distance from the central axis (*i.e.*, the value axis). The farther a color is from this axis, the more saturated the color. The value axis lies from the black point of the hexacone through the center of the circle, with values ranging from 0 for black to 1 for white, where 0 is at the tip and 1 is on the surface of the hexacone. For example, (58°, 0.88, 0.93) is a bright yellow.

The HLS color model is essentially the same. To create the HLS color space from the HSV space (and hence from RGB), go through the same steps illustrated in Figure 2.45, Figure 2.46, and Figure 2.47. Then take a mirror image of the shape in Figure 2.47 and connect it to the top, as in Figure 2.48. Hue and saturation are given as before, but now lightness varies from 0 at the black tip to 1 at the white tip of the double cones.

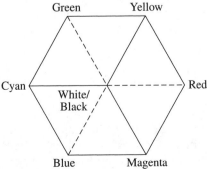

**Figure 2.45** RGB color cube viewed from the top

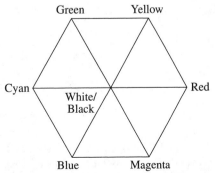

**Figure 2.46** RGB color cube collapsed to 2D

Supplement on transforming color spaces:

interactive tutorial

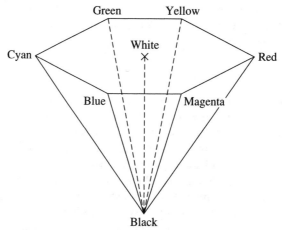

**Figure 2.47** HSV color space, a hexacone

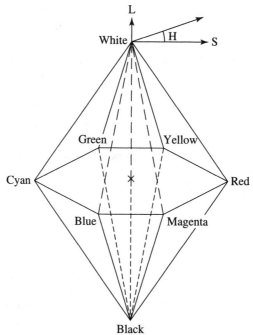

**Figure 2.48** HLS Color Space

The distortion of the RGB color space to either HSV or HLS is a non-linear transformation. In other words, to translate from RGB to HSV, you can't simply multiply each of the R, G, and B components by some coefficient. Algorithm 2.3 shows how to translate RGB to HSV. Algorithm 2.4 translates from RGB to HLS. The inverse algorithms are left as an exercise.

## ALGORITHM 2.3    RGB TO HSV

algorithm RGB_to_HSV
/*  Input: r, g, and b, each real numbers in the range [0 . . . 1].
Output: h, a real number in the range of [0 . . . 360), except if s = 0, in which case h is
undefined. s and v are real numbers in the range of [0 . . . 1].*/
```
{
  max = maximum(r,g,b)
  min = minimum(r,g,b)
  v = max
  if max ≠ 0 then s = (max − min)/max
  else s = 0
  if s == 0 then h = undefined
  else {
    diff = max − min
    if r == max then h = (g − b) / diff
    else if g == max then h = 2 + (b − r) / diff
    else if b == max then h = 4 + (r − g) / diff
    h = h * 60
    if h < 0 then h = h + 360
  }
}
```

## ALGORITHM 2.4    RGB TO HLS

algorithm RGB_to_HLS
/* Input r, g, and b, each real numbers in the range [0 . . . 1] representing the red, green,
and blue color components, respectively
Output: h, a real number in the range of [0 . . . 360] except if s = 0, in which case h is
undefined. L and s are real numbers in the range of [0 . . . 1]. h, L, and s represent hue,
lightness, and saturation, respectively.*/
```
{
  max = maximum(r,g,b)
  min = minimum(r,g,b)
  L = average(max, min)
  if max == min then s = 0
  else {
    sum = max + min
    diff = max − min
    if L ≤ 0.5 then s = diff / sum
    else s = diff / (2 − max + min)
    r_temp = (max − r) / diff
    g_temp = (max − g) / diff
    b_temp = (max − b) / diff
    if r == max then h = b_temp − g_temp
    else if g == max then h = 2 + r_temp − b_temp
    else if b == max then h = 4 + g_temp − r_temp
    h = h * 60
    if h < 0 then h = h + 360
  }
}
```

## 2.6.5 Luminance and Chrominance Color Models

Another way to specify a color is to capture all the luminance information in one value and put the color (*i.e.*, ***chrominance***) information in the other two values. The YIQ model is one example that takes this approach.

The YIQ model is a simple translation of the RGB model, separating out the information in a way that is more efficient for television broadcasting. In the early days of color television, both black and white and color signals had to be transmitted because not all consumers had color television sets. It was convenient to consolidate all of the "black and white" information—which is luminance—in one of the three components and capture all the color information in the other two. That way, the same transmission worked for both kinds of consumers. A linear transformation of the values makes this possible. Specifically,

---

### 🔑 KEY EQUATION

For a pixel represented in RGB color, let the red, green, and blue color components be, respectively, $R$, $G$, and $B$. Then the equivalent $Y$, $I$, and $Q$ color components in the YIQ color model are given by

$$\begin{bmatrix} Y \\ I \\ Q \end{bmatrix} = \begin{bmatrix} 0.299 & 0.587 & 0.114 \\ 0.596 & -0.275 & -0.321 \\ 0.212 & -0.523 & 0.311 \end{bmatrix} \begin{bmatrix} R \\ G \\ B \end{bmatrix}$$

(Note that the values in the transformation matrix depend upon the particular choice of primaries for the RGB model.)

---

$Y$ is the luminance component, and $I$ and $Q$ are chrominance. The inverse of the matrix above is used to convert from YIQ to RGB. The coefficients in the matrix are based on primary colors of red, green, and blue that are appropriate for the standard National Television System Committee (NTSC) RGB phosphor.

YIQ is the model used in U.S. commercial television broadcasting. Isolating luminance in one of the three terms has a further advantage, aside from its advantage in color/black and white broadcasting. Perhaps surprisingly, human vision is more sensitive to differences in luminance than differences in color. Therefore, it makes more sense to give a more finely nuanced representation of the luminance component than of the chrominance. In practical terms, this means that we don't need as many bits—and therefore as much bandwidth—for the transmission of the I and Q components relative to the Y component. It would not be possible to make this savings in bandwidth using the RGB model because in RGB the luminance is not a separate element but instead is implicit in the combination of the three components.

The YUV color model, originally used in the European PAL analog video standard, is also based upon luminance and chrominance. The YCbCr model is closely related to the YUV, with its chrominance values scaled and shifted. YCbCr is used in JPEG and MPEG compression. These compression techniques benefit from the separation of luminance from chrominance since some chrominance information can be sacrificed during compression without visible loss of quality in photographic images. This is called ***chroma subsampling***. Chapters 3 and 6 will explain chroma subsampling in more detail.

## 2.6.6 CIE XYZ and Color Gamuts

The RGB color model has the advantage of relating well to how the human eye perceives color and how a computer monitor can be engineered to display color, in combinations of red, green, and blue light. Its main disadvantage is that there exist visible colors that cannot be represented with positive values for each of the red, green, and blue components.

It may seem that the obvious way to generate all possible colors is to combine all possible intensities of red, green, and, blue light—or at least enough of these values at discrete intervals to give us millions of choices. For example, we could vary the intensity of the red light through 256 evenly-spaced increments, and the same for green and blue. This would give us 256 * 256 * 256 = 16,777,216 colors. That must cover the range of possible colors, right? Wrong. In fact, there exist colors outside the range of those we can create in RGB, colors that we *cannot* capture with any combination of red, green, and blue. But how does anyone know this?

We know this by an experiment called color matching. In this experiment, human subjects are asked to compare pure colors projected onto one side of a screen to composite colors projected beside them. The pure colors are created by single wavelength light. The composite colors are created by a combination of red, green, and blue light, and the amounts of the three components are called the ***tristimulus values***. For each pure color presented to the human observer, these colors ranging through all of the visible spectrum, the observer is asked to adjust the relative intensities of the red, green, and blue components in the composite color until the match is as close as possible. It turns out that there are pure colors in the visible spectrum that cannot be reproduced by positive amounts of red, green, and blue light. In some cases, it is necessary to "subtract out" some of the red, green, or blue in the combined beams to match the pure color. (Effectively, this can be done by adding red, green, or blue to the pure color until the two light samples match.) This is true no matter what three visible primary colors are chosen. No three visible primaries can be linearly combined to produce all colors in the visible spectrum.

> **ASIDE:** There is no fixed shade of red, green, and blue that must be used for RGB. The only requirement is that they be primary colors relative to each other in that no two can be combined in any manner to create the third. The actual wavelengths of *R*, *G*, and *B* chosen for particular monitors depend on the characteristics of the display itself. For example, for a CRT monitor, the persistence of the phosphors in the monitor will determine in part the choice of *R*, *G*, and *B*. ***Persistence*** refers to the length of time the phosphors continue to glow after excitation by an electron beam.

The implication of this experiment is that no computer monitor that bases its color display on combinations of red, green, and blue light can display all visible colors. The range of colors that a given monitor can display is called its ***color gamut***. Since computer monitors may vary in their choice of basic red, green, and blue primaries, two computer monitors based on RGB color can still have different gamuts. By similar reasoning, the gamut of a color system based on the CMYK model will vary from one based on RGB. In practical terms, this means that there will be colors that you can represent on your computer monitor but you cannot print, and vice versa.

It would be useful to have a mathematical model that captures all visible colors. From this model, we could create a color space in which all other color models could be compared. The first step in the direction of a standard color model that represents all visible colors was called CIE XYZ, devised in 1931 by the Commission Internationale de l'Eclairage. You can understand how the ***CIE color model*** was devised by looking graphically at the results of the color matching experiment. Consider the graph in Figure 2.49. (See the worksheet associated with Exercise 10 at the end of this chapter for an explanation of how this graph was created.) The *x*-axis shows the wavelength, $\lambda$, ranging through the colors of the

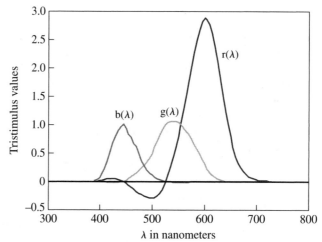

**Figure 2.49** Color matching functions

Supplements on
XYZ color and the
CIE chromaticity
diagram:

mathematical
modeling

programming
exercise

visible spectrum. The $y$-axis shows the relative amounts of red, green, and blue light energy that the "average" observer combines to match the pure light sample. (Units are unimportant. It is the relative values that matter.) Notice that in some cases, red has to be "subtracted" from the composite light (*i.e.*, added to the pure sample) in order to achieve a match.

Mathematically, the amount of red light energy needed to create the perceived pure spectral red at wavelength $\lambda$ is a function of the wavelength, given by $r(\lambda)$, and similarly for green (the function $g(\lambda)$) and blue (the function $b(\lambda)$). Let $C(\lambda)$ be the color the average observer perceives at wavelength $\lambda$. Then $C(\lambda)$ is given by a linear combination of these three components, that is,

$$C(\lambda) = r(\lambda)R + g(\lambda)G + b(\lambda)B$$

Here, $R$ refers to pure spectral red light at a fixed wavelength, and similarly for $G$ and $B$.

The CIE model is based on the observation that, although there are no three visible primary colors that can be combined in *positive* amounts to create all colors in the visible spectrum, it is possible to use three "virtual" primaries to do so. These primaries—called $X$, $Y$, and $Z$—are purely theoretical rather than physical entities. While they do not correspond to wavelengths of visible light, they provide a mathematical way to describe colors that exist in the visible spectrum. Expressing the color matching functions in terms of $X$, $Y$, and $Z$ produces the graphs in Figure 2.50. We can see that $X$, $Y$, and $Z$ are chosen so that all three functions remain positive over the wavelengths of the visible spectrum. We now have the equation

$$C(\lambda) = x(\lambda)X + y(\lambda)Y + z(\lambda)Z$$

to represent all visible colors.

We are still working toward finding a graphical space in which to compare color gamuts, and the CIE color model is taking us there. The dotted line in Figure 2.52 graphs the values of $x$, $y$, and $z$ for all perceived colors $C(\lambda)$ as $\lambda$ varies across the visible spectrum.

**ASIDE:** As is the case with any set of primaries, there is not just one "right" set of values for X, Y, and Z, but X, Y, and Z are in fact fixed by the CIE standard. They must be primaries with respect to each other, and we want them to be combinable in positive amounts to produce all colors in the visible spectrum. It was also found that by a proper choice of Y, function $y(\lambda)$ could be modeled such that its shape is the same as *the luminous efficiency function.* The luminous efficiency function is the eye's measured response to monochromatic light of fixed energy at different wavelengths. With Y chosen in this fashion, $y(\lambda)$ is always equal to the overall luminance of the light in $C(\lambda)$.

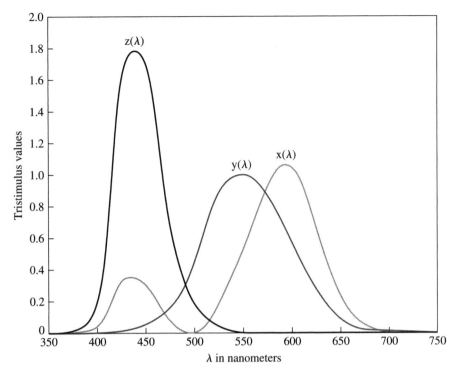

**Figure 2.50** XYZ color matching functions

By the choice of X, Y, and Z, all values $x(\lambda)$, $y(\lambda)$, and $z(\lambda)$ lie in the positive octant. Clearly, not all visible colors are contained within the RGB gamut.

To see the different colors and where the gamuts do or do not overlap, we will picture this in two dimensions. To simplify things further, it is convenient to normalize the values of $x(\lambda)$, $y(\lambda)$, and $z(\lambda)$ so that they sum to 1. That is, the three colors combine to unit energy. Furthermore, the normalized values show each component's fractional contribution to the color's overall energy. Thus we define

$$x'(\lambda) = \frac{x(\lambda)}{x(\lambda) + y(\lambda) + z(\lambda)}, y'(\lambda) = \frac{y(\lambda)}{x(\lambda) + y(\lambda) + z(\lambda)}, z'(\lambda) = \frac{z(\lambda)}{x(\lambda) + y(\lambda) + z(\lambda)}$$

In this way, any two of the color components give us the third one. For example,

$$x'(\lambda) = 1 - y'(\lambda) - z'(\lambda)$$

$x'(\lambda)$, $y'(\lambda)$, and $z'(\lambda)$ are called the ***chromaticity values***. Figure 2.51 shows where the chromaticity values fall within the CIE three-dimensional space. Let $s(\lambda)$ and $s'(\lambda)$ be parametric functions defined as follows:

$$s(\lambda) = (x(\lambda), y(\lambda), z(\lambda))$$
$$s'(\lambda) = (x'(\lambda), y'(\lambda), z'(\lambda))$$

Each point from function $s(\lambda)$ can be plotted in 3D space where $x(\lambda)$ lies on the X-axis, $y(\lambda)$ lies on the Y-axis, and $z(\lambda)$ lies on the Z-axis (and similarly for $s'(\lambda)$). Because we have stipulated that $x'(\lambda) + y'(\lambda) + z'(\lambda) = 1$, $s'(\lambda)$ must lie on the $X + Y + Z = 1$ plane.

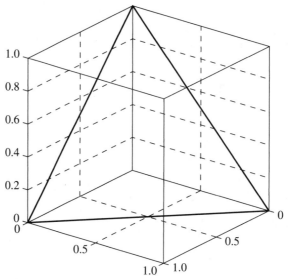

**Figure 2.51** $X + Y + Z = 1$ plane

We also know that $x(\lambda)$, $y(\lambda)$, and $z(\lambda)$ are always positive because we defined primaries X, Y, and Z so that they would be. Thus, we need only look at the area in the positive octant where $X + Y + Z = 1$, represented by the triangle in the figure. The curve traced on this plane shows the values of $s'(\lambda)$ for the pure spectral colors in the visible spectrum. These are fully saturated colors at unit energy. The colors in the interior of this curve on the $X + Y + Z = 1$ plane are still at unit energy, but not fully saturated.

In Figure 2.52, $s(\lambda)$ is the finely-dotted line, the $X + Y + Z = 1$ plane is a triangle drawn with solid lines, and the projection of $s(\lambda)$ onto the $X + Y + Z = 1$ plane is $s'(\lambda)$,

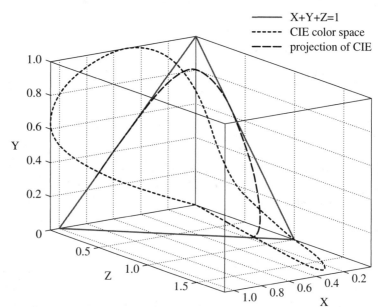

**Figure 2.52** Visible color spectrum projected onto the $X + Y + Z = 1$ plane

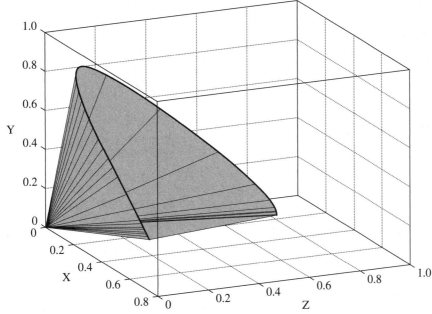

**Figure 2.53** Visible colors in CIE color space

the horseshoe-shaped coarsely dotted line, which forms the perimeter of the cone seen in Figure 2.53. The horseshoe-shaped outline from Figure 2.52 is projected onto the *XY* plane. The 2D projection on the *XY* plane is called the CIE Chromaticity Diagram (Figure 2.54). In this two-dimensional diagram, we have a space in which to compare the gamuts of varying color models. However, we have said that color is inherently a three-dimensional phenomenon in that it requires three values for its specification. We must have dropped some information in this two-dimensional depiction. The information left out here is energy. Recall

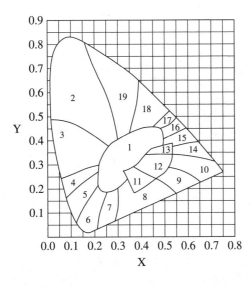

1. Illuminant Area
2. Green
3. Blue Green
4. Green Blue
5. Blue
6. Blue Purple
7. Purple
8. Purple Red
9. Red Purple
10. Red
11. Purple Pink
12. Pink
13. Orange Pink
14. Red Orange
15. Orange
16. Yellow Orange
17. Yellow
18. Yellow Green
19. Green Yellow

**Figure 2.54** CIE chromaticity diagram

that we have normalized the chromaticity functions so that they combine for unit energy. Unit energy is just some fixed level, the only one we consider as we compare gamuts within the CIE diagram, but it's sufficient for the comparison.

Figure 2.53 shows a cone shape that defines the outer surface of the CIE color space. Imagine extending this shape out infinitely into the positive octant. This surface and all the points in its interior represent all the visible colors out to (and beyond) maximum visible luminance. As you move toward (0,0,0), the colors are decreasingly luminant.

> **ASIDE:** Not all visible colors are represented in the CIE chromaticity diagram. Color perceptions that depend in part on the luminance of a color are absent from the diagram—brown, for example, which is an orange-red of low luminance.

Figure 2.55 shows the gamuts for the RGB color vs. the CMYK color space. Note that for each, we must be assuming particular wavelengths for $R$, $G$, and $B$ and pigments for $C$, $M$, $Y$, and $K$. Thus, the RGB gamut could be the gamut for a specific computer monitor, given the wavelengths that it uses for its pure red, green, and blue. For any given choice of $R$, $G$, and $B$, these primary colors can be located in the CIE chromaticity diagram by the $x$ and $y$ coordinates given below. For example, a reasonable choice or $R$, $G$, and $B$ would be located at these positions in the CIE diagram:

|   | $R$ | $G$ | $B$ |
|---|------|------|------|
| $x$ | 0.64 | 0.30 | 0.15 |
| $y$ | 0.33 | 0.60 | 0.06 |

According to these values, the color red lies at 0.64 along the horizontal axis in the CIE diagram and 0.33 along the vertical axis.

The gamut for RGB color is larger than the CMYK gamut. However, neither color space is entirely contained within the other, which means that there are colors that you can

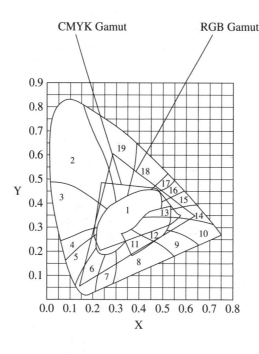

CMYK Gamut        RGB Gamut

1. Illuminant Area
2. Green
3. Blue Green
4. Green Blue
5. Blue
6. Blue Purple
7. Purple
8. Purple Red
9. Red Purple
10. Red
11. Purple Pink
12. Pink
13. Orange Pink
14. Red Orange
15. Orange
16. Yellow Orange
17. Yellow
18. Yellow Green
19. Green Yellow

**Figure 2.55** RGB vs. CMYK gamuts

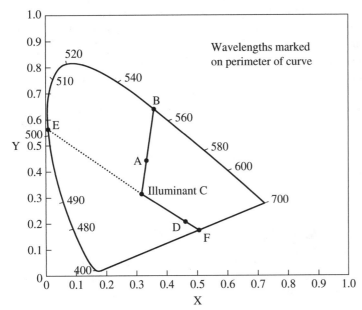

**Figure 2.56** Illuminant C

display on the computer monitor that cannot be printed, and vice versa. In practice this is not a big problem. The range of colors for each color model is great and the variations from one color to the next are sufficiently detailed, and usually media creators do not require an exact reproduction of their chosen colors from one display device to the next. However, where exact fidelity is aesthetically or commercially desirable, users need to be aware of the limits of color gamuts.

CIE diagram is helpful in illustrating color concepts and relationships. In Figure 2.56, point C is called ***illuminant C***, or fully saturated white. Points along the edge of the curved horseshoe shape are fully saturated spectral colors. Colors along the straight line base are purples and magentas, colors that cannot be produced by single-wavelength spectral light nor isolated from daylight spectrographically. The line joining any two colors in the graph corresponds to the colors that can be created by a combination of these colors. To find the dominant wavelength of a color that lies at point A, it is possible to create a line between points C and A and extend it to the nearest point on the perimeter of the horseshoe shape. For example, the dominant wavelength of point A in Figure 2.56 is approximately 550, and the color is a shade of green. If a point is closest to the base of the horseshoe, it is called a ***nonspectral color***. D in Figure 2.56 is an example. Points like D have no spectral dominant wavelength. However, if we draw a line from D through C and find where it crosses the horseshoe shape (at point E), we find the complementary dominant wavelength of a nonspectral point.

Let $\overline{AC}$ denote the length of line segment AC. Then the saturation of the color at point A is defined by the ratio $\dfrac{\overline{AC}}{\overline{BC}}$ (Figure 2.56). The closer to the perimeter, the more saturated a color is. For example, point A is closer to illuminant C than to point B. Thus, it is a pastel or light green. For non-spectral colors such as D, saturation is defined as $\dfrac{\overline{DC}}{\overline{DF}}$.

A third advantage of the CIE Chromaticity Diagram is that it gives us a way to standardize color representation. Say that you have a color and you want to tell someone else exactly what that color is. It is possible, with the right instruments, to measure the $x$, $y$, and $z$ values of your color and communicate these to someone else as a precise specification. In the reverse, other instruments allow you to re-create a color specified in $x$, $y$, and $z$ coordinates.

The conversion from CIE-XYZ to RGB is a simple linear transformation. The coefficients in the conversion matrix are dependent on the wavelengths chosen for the primaries for the RGB model as well as the definition of white. As noted previously, the RGB values can vary from one computer monitor to another. A reasonable transformation matrix is given below.

---

### 🔑 KEY EQUATION

For a pixel represented in XYZ color, let the values for the three color components be $X$, $Y$, and $Z$. Then the equivalent $R$, $G$, and $B$ color components in the RGB color model are given by

$$\begin{bmatrix} R \\ G \\ B \end{bmatrix} = \begin{bmatrix} 3.24 & -1.54 & -0.50 \\ -0.97 & 1.88 & 0.04 \\ 0.06 & -0.20 & 1.06 \end{bmatrix} \begin{bmatrix} X \\ Y \\ Z \end{bmatrix}$$

---

Conversion from RGB to CIE-XYZ uses the inverse of the above matrix.

## 2.6.7 CIE L*a* b*, CIE L*U*V*, and Perceptual Uniformity

The CIE XYZ model has three main advantages: it is device-independent; it provides a way to represent all colors visible to humans; and the representation is based upon spectrophotometric measurements of color. The RGB and CMYK color models, on the other hand, are not device-independent. They begin with an arbitrary choice of complementary primary colors, from which all other colors in their gamuts are derived. Different computer monitors or printers can use different values for R, G, and B, and thus their gamuts are not necessarily identical. The RGB and CMYK models are not comprehensive, either. Regardless of the choice of primary colors in either model, there will exist colors visible to humans that cannot be represented.

The development of the CIE XYZ color model overcame these disadvantages, but there was still room for improvement. A remaining disadvantage of the CIE XYZ model is that it is not perceptually uniform. In a *perceptually uniform color space*, the distance between two points is directly proportional to the perceived difference between the two colors. A color space that is perceptually uniform is easier to work with at an intuitive level, since colors (as they look to the human eye) change at a rate that is proportional to changes in the values representing the colors.

It is possible for a color model to be perceptually uniform in one dimension but not perceptually uniform in its three dimensions taken together. For example, in the HSV color model, hues change at a steady rate as you rotate from 0 to 360 degrees around the plane denoting hue. Similarly, brightness varies steadily up and down the brightness axis. However, equidistant movement through the three combined planes does not result in equal perceived color changes.

The Commission Internationale de l'Eclairage continued to refine its color model and by 1976 produced the CIE L*a*b* and CIE L*U*V* models. CIE L*a*b* is a subtractive color model in which the L* axis gives brightness values varying from 0 to 100, the *a* axis moves from red (positive values) to green (negative values), and the *b* axis moves from yellow (positive values) to blue (negative values). CIE L*U*V is an additive color model that was similarly constructed to achieve perceptual uniformity, but that was less convenient in practical usage.

Because the CIE L*a*b* model can represent all visible colors, it is generally used as the intermediate color model in conversions between other color models, as described in Section 2.4.

## 2.6.8 Color Management Systems

As careful as you might be in choosing colors for a digital image, it is difficult to ensure that the colors you choose will be exactly the colors that others see when your picture is placed on the web or printed in hard copy. There are a number of reasons for this. As we have seen, the gamut of colors representable by an RGB monitor is not identical to the gamut printable in a CMYK color processing system, so you may lose color fidelity in going from the electronic to the hard copy format. Even if you remain in RGB color and display your picture only on computers, you can't be sure that the RGB space of one monitor is the same as the RGB space of another. The color space of your own monitor can even change over time as your computer ages and the screen's ability to glow and show color diminishes. There are perceptual and environmental influences as well. Colors look different depending on the ambient lighting, the incidental surrounding colors like background patterns on your computer screen, and the reflection of your own clothing on the computer monitor.

Most of the time, the shifts in a picture's colors from one environment to the next are subtle and insignificant. However, artists may have aesthetic reasons for seeking color consistency, or an advertising agency may have commercial ones. In cases where color consistency is important, a color management system is needed. Different hardware devices and application programs—for example, scanners, computer monitors, printers, and image processing programs—each have their own color spaces and basic color settings. A *color management system* communicates the assumptions about color spaces, settings for primary colors, and the mapping from color values to physical representations in pixels and ink from one device to another. Using the CIE color space as a universal, device-independent language, a color management system serves as a translator that communicates color settings from one device or software program to another.

Color management involves five steps: calibrating your monitor, characterizing your monitor's color profile, creating an individual image's color profile that includes choices for color model and rendering intent, saving the color profile with the image, and reproducing the image's color on another device or application program on the basis of the source and destination profiles.

*Monitor calibration and characterization* can be done with specialized hardware or software. The operating system of your computer or your image processing program probably have a color management system that allows you to calibrate and profile your monitor, or you can use more precise hardware-based systems. Calibration should be done before the monitor is characterized. For good results, it should be done in typical lighting conditions, on a monitor that has been warmed up, and with a background screen of neutral gray. Generally this step begins with the choice of a basic ICC (International Color Consortium) profile, to which changes can be made. The first adjustment is setting the monitor's *white point* as measured in degrees Kelvin. Daylight is 6500° Kelvin—generally the default hardware setting—while warm white is 5000°. While usually you'll want to keep the white point set to the hardware default, in some cases you may want to adjust it to reflect the conditions in which you expect your images to be viewed. Calibration also involves gamma correction, or adjustment of the midtone brightness. When the adjustments have been made, the new monitor profile is saved. If precise color reproduction is important to your work, it may be necessary to recalibrate your monitor periodically as image specifications or working environments change.

Once your monitor has been properly calibrated, a *color management policy* can be created and saved with each individual image. The image's color management policy is based upon the monitor profile, to which special settings are added for a particular image or group of images that determine how color is translated from one space to another. Typically, your color management system will provide a set of predefined standard color management policies that are sufficient for most images. For example, sRGB is a color management policy devised to be suitable for the typical PC monitor and accepted as a standard in many monitors, scanners, and printers.

In addition to these standard policies, it is also possible to create a profile that customizes the settings for *rendering intent*, dot gain, and the color management engine to be used. The color management engine determines how pixel values in the image file convert to the voltage values applied to—and thus the colors of—the pixels on the computer screen. The rendering intent determines how a color in one color space will be adjusted when it is out of the gamut of the color space to which it is being converted, which could happen, for example, when moving from RGB to CMYK color space. One rendering intent might seek to preserve colors in the manner that they are perceived by the human eye relative to other colors; another might sacrifice color similarities for the saturation, or vividness, of the overall image. *Dot gain* is a matter of the way in which wet ink spreads as it is applied to paper, and how this may affect the appearance of an image. The color management policy created for an image can be saved and shared with other images. It is also embedded in individual image file and is used to communicate color, expressed in terms of the device-independent CIE color space, from one device and application program to another.

Most of us who work with digital image processing don't need to worry very much about color management systems. Your computer monitor has default settings and is initially calibrated such that you may not find it necessary to recalibrate it, and the default color management policy in your image processing program may be sufficient for your purposes. However, it is good to know that these tools exist so that you know where to turn if precise color management becomes important.

# 2.7 VECTOR GRAPHICS

Supplements on the
mathematics of
curve-drawing:

## 2.7.1 Geometric Objects in Vector Graphics

Section 2.2 discussed how data is represented in bitmaps, which are suitable for photographic images with continuously varying colors. We now turn to *vector graphics*, an image file format suitable for pictures with areas of solid, clearly separated colors—cartoon images, logos, and the like. Instead of being painted pixel by pixel, a vector graphic image is drawn object by object in terms of each object's geometric shape.

interactive tutorial

Although there are many file formats for vector graphics—*.fh* (Freehand), *.ai* (Adobe Illustrator), *.wmf* (Windows metafile), *.eps* (encapsulated Postcript), etc.—they are all similar in that they contain the parameters to mathematical formulas defining how shapes are drawn. A line can be specified by its endpoints, a square by the length of a side, a rectangle by the length of two sides, a circle by its radius, and so forth. However, not everything you might want to draw can be pieced together by circles, rectangles, and lines. What if you want to draw a curved flower vase, a winding path disappearing into the woods, a tree branch, or a plate of spaghetti? Curves are the basis of many of the interesting and complex shapes you might want to draw.

worksheet

Consider how a curve is rendered on a computer display. If you were working in a drawing program that offered no curve-drawing tool, what would you do? You'd have to create a curve as a sequence of short line segments connected at their endpoints. If the line segments were short enough, the curve would look fairly smooth. But this would be a very tedious way to draw a curve, and the curve would be difficult to modify. A better way would be to select just a few points and ask a curve-drawing tool to smooth out the curve defined by these points. This is how curve tools work in drawing programs. In the next section, we look behind the scenes at the mathematical basis for curve-drawing tools (called pen tools). These tools make your work easy. You simply choose a few points, and a curve is created for you. But how are these curve-drawing tools themselves implemented?

In the sections that follow, we will present the mathematics underlying the implementation of curves in vector graphics applications. A side note about terminology: If you've encountered the term *spline* in your work in digital media, you may wonder what the difference is between a curve and a spline. The word spline was borrowed from the vocabulary of draftspersons. Before computers were used for CAD design of airplanes, automobiles, and the like, drafters used a flexible metal strip called a spline to trace out smooth curves along designated points on the drafting table. Metal splines provided smooth, continuous curves that now can be modeled mathematically on computers. Some sources make a distinction between curves and splines, reserving the latter term for curves that are interpolated (rather than approximated) through points and that have a high degree of continuity (as in natural cubic splines and B-splines). Other sources use the terms curve and spline interchangeably. We will distinguish between Hermite and Bézier curves on the one hand and natural cubic splines on the other following the terminology used in most sources on vector graphics. We restrict our discussion to Hermite and Bézier curves.

## 2.7.2 Specifying Curves with Polynomials and Parametric Equations

Specifying a curve as a sequence of piecewise linear segments is tedious and inefficient. It's much handier simply to choose a few points and ask the drawing program to fit the

Supplements on
curve-drawing:

interactive tutorial

worksheet

curve to these. But for this to happen, the drawing program needs to use something more powerful than linear equations to define the curve. In the discussion that follows, we show that *parametric cubic polynomial functions* are an excellent formulation for curves. We will step you through the basic mathematics you need in order to understand curve creation, including a review of polynomials, functions, and parametric equations. With this background, you'll be able to understand how the pen tool works in programs such as Illustrator or GIMP.

An *n*th *degree polynomial* is a function that takes the form

$$a_n t^n + a_{n-1}t^{n-1} + a_{n-2}t^{n-2} + \cdots + a_1 t + a_0$$

where $a_n \neq 0$ and $a_0, a_1, \ldots, a_n$ are the coefficients of the polynomial. Cubic polynomials (*i.e.*, 3$^{rd}$ degree polynomials, where the highest power is 3), are a good way to represent curves. They offer sufficient detail for approximating the shape of curves while still being efficient and easy to manipulate.

The polynomial functions used to describe curves can be expressed in one of three ways: as explicit functions, as implicit functions, or as parametric representations. Both explicit functions and implicit functions are non-parametric forms. You will see that parametric representations are most convenient for curves. Before looking at a variety of parametric cubic polynomials that are used to represent curves, let's review the difference between parametric and non-parametric forms.

The *explicit form of a function* with one independent variable is

$$y = f(x)$$

**Equation 2.5**

For example, the explicit form of the equation for a half-circle is

$$y = \sqrt{r^2 - x^2}$$

where $r$ is the radius of the circle—a constant for any given circle. A function such as this represents a one-dimensional function in that it has only one independent variable—in this case, $x$. Note that a one-dimensional function can be graphed as a shape in two-dimensional space. In the discussion that follows, we will use one-dimensional functions. The observations are easily generalized to two-dimensional functions graphable in 3D space.

The *implicit form of the function* equivalent to Equation 2.5 is

$$f(x, y) = 0$$

For example, the implicit form of the equation for a circle is

$$x^2 + y^2 - r^2 = 0$$

Both the explicit and the implicit forms given above are *nonparametric representations*, and neither one is particularly convenient for representing curves. In the case of the explicit form, each value for $x$ gives only one value for $y$, and this makes it impossible to represent ellipses and circles. Furthermore, representing curves with vertical tangents is difficult because the slope of such a tangent would be infinity. In the case of the implicit functional form, it is difficult to specify just part of a circle. To overcome these and other problems, the parametric functional representation is used to define curves.

The *parametric representation of a function* takes the general form

$$P(t) = (x(t), y(t))$$

for $t$ varying within some given range. Generally, the range of $t$ is taken to be between 0 and 1, but other ranges are possible. (The range can always be normalized to between 0 and 1 if needed.) $P$ effectively gives us the points on the Cartesian plane which constitute the curve, with the points' positions given by an equation for each of the variables in the function, as in

$$x = x(t) \quad \text{and} \quad y = y(t)$$

As mentioned above, cubic polynomials are used in the parametric representation for curves. This means that for a curve, the $x$ and $y$ positions of the points in the curve are given by two parametric equations as follows:

$$x(t) = a_x t^3 + b_x t^2 + c_x t + d_x$$

and

$$y(t) = a_y t^3 + b_y t^2 + c_y t + d_y$$

**Equation 2.6**

It is sometimes convenient to represent the parametric equations in matrix form. This gives us:

$$P(t) = [x(t) y(t)] = \begin{bmatrix} t^3 & t^2 & t & 1 \end{bmatrix} \begin{bmatrix} a_x & a_y \\ b_x & b_y \\ c_x & c_y \\ d_x & d_y \end{bmatrix} \quad 0 \le t \le 1$$

or, in short,

$$P = T * C$$

where

$$T = \begin{bmatrix} t^3 & t^2 & t & 1 \end{bmatrix} \quad \text{and} \quad C = \begin{bmatrix} a_x & a_y \\ b_x & b_y \\ c_x & c_y \\ d_x & d_y \end{bmatrix} = \begin{bmatrix} a \\ b \\ c \\ d \end{bmatrix}$$

So let's think about where this is leading us. We define ***control points*** to be points that are chosen to define a curve. We want to be able to define a curve by selecting a number of control points on the computer display. In general, $n + 1$ control points make it possible to model a curve with an $n$-degree polynomial. Cubic polynomials have been shown to be good for modeling curves in vector graphics, so our $n$ will be 3, yielding a 3rd degree polynomial like the one in Equation 2.6. What we need now is an algorithm that can translate the control points into coefficients $a_x$, $b_x$, $c_x$, $d_x$, $a_y$, $b_y$, $c_y$, and $d_y$, which are then encoded in the vector graphics file. That is, we want to get matrix $C$. When the curve is drawn, the coefficients are used in the parametric equation, and $t$ is varied along small discrete intervals to construct the curve.

Given a set of points, what's the right or best way to connect them into a curve? As you may have guessed, there's no single right way. A number of different methods have been devised for translating points into curves, each with its own advantages and disadvantages depending on the application or work environment. Curve-generating algorithms can be divided into two main categories: interpolation algorithms and approximation algorithms. An ***interpolation algorithm*** takes a set of control points and creates a curve that runs directly through all of the points. An ***approximation algorithm*** creates a curve that does not necessarily pass through all the control points. Approximation algorithms are sometimes preferable in that they allow the user to move a single control point and alter just one part of the curve without affecting the rest of it. This is called *local control*. Hermite curves and natural cubic splines are based on interpolation algorithms. Bézier curves are based on an approximation algorithm. We'll focus on Bézier curves here since they are the basis for curve-drawing tools in commonly used vector graphics environments.

The general strategy for deriving the coefficients for the parametric equations from the control points is this: To derive an $n$th degree parametric equation, you must find $n + 1$ coefficients, so you need $n + 1$ equations in $n + 1$ unknowns. In the case of a cubic polynomial, you need four equations in four unknowns. These equations are formulated from constraints on the control points. For Bézier curves, for example, two of the control points are constrained to form tangents to the curve. Let's see how this can be derived.

## 2.7.3 Bézier Curves

Bézier curves are curves that can be approximated with any number of control points. It simplifies the discussion to think of the curve in segments defined by four control points. We divide these control points into two types: two endpoints, $p_0$ and $p_3$; and two interior control points, $p_1$ and $p_2$. Bézier curves are uniform cubic curves in the sense that it is assumed that the control points are evenly distributed along the range of parameter $t$. Thus the control points $p_0, p_1, p_2$, and $p_3$ correspond to the values of $t = 0, 1/3, 2/3$, and 1. The curve is defined by the constraints that $p_0$ and $p_3$ are endpoints, the line from $p_0$ to $p_1$ is a tangent to one part of the curve, and the line from $p_2$ to $p_3$ is a tangent to another part of the curve. We use $P'$ to indicate the first derivative of $P$. Thus, $P'(0)$ is the rate of change of the line segment from $p_0$ to $p_1$, yielding

$$3 * a * 0^2 + 2 * b * 0 + c = (p_1 - p_0)/(1/3 - 0)$$
$$\therefore c = 3(p_1 - p_0)$$

Similarly, $P'(1)$ is the rate of change of the line segment from $p_2$ to $p_3$, yielding

$$3 * a * 1^2 + 2 * b * 1 + c = (p_3 - p_2)/(1 - 2/3)$$
$$\therefore 3a + 2b + c = 3(p_3 - p_2)$$

The constraints that $p_0$ is the first point on the curve and $p_3$ is the last are stated as

$$a * 0^3 + b * 0^2 + c * 0 + d = p_0$$
$$\therefore d = p_0$$
$$a * 1^3 + b * 1^2 + c * 1 + d = p_3$$
$$\therefore a + b + c + d = p_3$$

These four constraint equations in matrix form are

$$
\begin{bmatrix} 0 & 0 & 0 & 1 \\ 1 & 1 & 1 & 1 \\ 0 & 0 & 1 & 0 \\ 3 & 2 & 1 & 0 \end{bmatrix} *
\begin{bmatrix} a \\ b \\ c \\ d \end{bmatrix} =
\begin{bmatrix} p_0 \\ p_3 \\ 3 * (p_1 - p_0) \\ 3 * (p_3 - p_2) \end{bmatrix}
$$

or

$$A * G_B = C$$

Solving for $C$, the coefficient vector, we get the form $C = A^{-1} * G_B$, or

$$C = \begin{bmatrix} a \\ b \\ c \\ d \end{bmatrix} = \begin{bmatrix} 0 & 0 & 0 & 1 \\ 1 & 1 & 1 & 1 \\ 0 & 0 & 1 & 0 \\ 3 & 2 & 1 & 0 \end{bmatrix}^{-1} * \begin{bmatrix} p_0 \\ p_3 \\ 3*(p_1 - p_0) \\ 3*(p_3 - p_2) \end{bmatrix}$$

Thus

$$C = \begin{bmatrix} a \\ b \\ c \\ d \end{bmatrix} = \begin{bmatrix} 2 & -2 & 1 & 1 \\ -3 & 3 & -2 & -1 \\ 0 & 0 & 1 & 0 \\ 1 & 0 & 0 & 0 \end{bmatrix} * \begin{bmatrix} p_0 \\ p_3 \\ 3*(p_1 - p_0) \\ 3*(p_3 - p_2) \end{bmatrix}$$

Simplifying, we get the following key equation:

## KEY EQUATION

Let $P(t) = (x(t), y(t))$ denote the parametric representation of a curve where $(x, y)$ are the pixel positions across the curve, $x(t) = a_x t^3 + b_x t^2 + c_x t + d_x$, and $y(t) = a_y t^3 + b_y t^2 + c_y t + d_y$. Let the coefficients of $x(t)$ and $y(t)$ be given by

$$C = \begin{bmatrix} a \\ b \\ c \\ d \end{bmatrix} = \begin{bmatrix} a_x & a_y \\ b_x & b_y \\ c_x & c_y \\ d_x & d_y \end{bmatrix}.$$ Then a Bézier curve is defined by control points $p_0, p_1, p_2$, and

$p_3$ and the equation

$$C = \begin{bmatrix} -1 & 3 & -3 & 1 \\ 3 & -6 & 3 & 0 \\ -3 & 3 & 0 & 0 \\ 1 & 0 & 0 & 0 \end{bmatrix} * \begin{bmatrix} p_0 \\ p_1 \\ p_2 \\ p_3 \end{bmatrix}$$

**Equation 2.7**

To create an even simpler form of Equation 2.7, let

$$M = \begin{bmatrix} -1 & 3 & -3 & 1 \\ 3 & -6 & 3 & 0 \\ -3 & 3 & 0 & 0 \\ 1 & 0 & 0 & 0 \end{bmatrix}$$

and

$$G = \begin{bmatrix} p_0 \\ p_1 \\ p_2 \\ p_3 \end{bmatrix}$$

This yields

$$C = M * G$$

$M$ is called the **basis matrix**. $G$ is called the **geometry matrix**. The basis matrix and geometry matrix together characterize a type of curve drawn by means of particular control points based on constraints on these points—in this case, in the manner used to define a Bézier curve.

With $M$ and $G$, we can derive another convenient representation for Bezier curves, in terms of the curve's **blending functions**, as they are called. Recall that $T = \begin{bmatrix} t^3 & t^2 & t & 1 \end{bmatrix}$. A Bézier curve is defined by a cubic polynomial equation.

$$P(t) = T * M * G$$

The blending functions are given by $T * M$. That is,

$$P(t) = (T * M) * G = (1 - t)^3 p_0 + 3t(1 - t)^2 p_1 + 3t^2(1 - t)p_2 + t^3 p_3$$

(You should verify this by doing the multiplication and simplifying $T * M$.) The multipliers $(1 - t)^3$, $3t(1 - t)^2$, $3t^2(1 - t)$, and $t^3$ are the **blending functions** for Bézier curves and can be viewed as weights for each of the four control points. They are also referred to as **Bernstein polynomials**.

A more general formulation of Bézier curves allows for polynomials of any degree $n$ and describes the curves in terms of the blending functions. It is as follows:

$$P(t) = \sum_{k=0}^{n} p_k \, blending_{k,n}(t) \quad \text{for} \quad 0 \le t \le 1$$

In the equation, $blending_{k,n}(t)$ refers to the blending functions, where $n$ is the degree of the polynomial used to define the Bézier curve, and $k$ refers to the "weight" for the $k$th term in the polynomial. $blending_{k,n}(t)$ is defined as follows:

$$blending_{k,n}(t) = C(n, k)t^k(1 - t)^{n-k}$$

and $C(n, k)$ is defined in turn as

$$C(n, k) = \frac{n!}{k!(n - k)!}$$

In the case of the cubic polynomials that we have examined above, $n = 3$, and the blending functions are

$$blending_{0,3} = (1 - t)^3$$
$$blending_{1,3} = 3t(1 - t)^2$$
$$blending_{2,3} = 3t^2(1 - t)$$
$$blending_{3,3} = t^3$$

One of the easiest ways to picture a cubic Bézier curve is algorithmically. The **de Casteljau algorithm** shows how a Bézier curve is constructed recursively from the four control points. Consider points $p_0, p_1, p_2$, and $p_3$ shown in Figure 2.57. Let $\overline{p_m, p_n}$ denote a line segment between $p_m$ and $p_n$. First we find the midpoint $p_{01}$ of $\overline{p_0, p_1}$, the midpoint $p_{12}$ of $\overline{p_1, p_2}$, and the midpoint $p_{23}$ of $\overline{p_2, p_3}$. We then find the midpoint $p_{012}$ of $\overline{p_{01}, p_{12}}$ and the midpoint $p_{123}$ of $\overline{p_{12}, p_{23}}$. Finally, we draw $\overline{p_{012}, p_{123}}$ and find its midpoint $p_{0123}$. This point will be on the Bézier curve. The same procedure is repeated, based on initial points

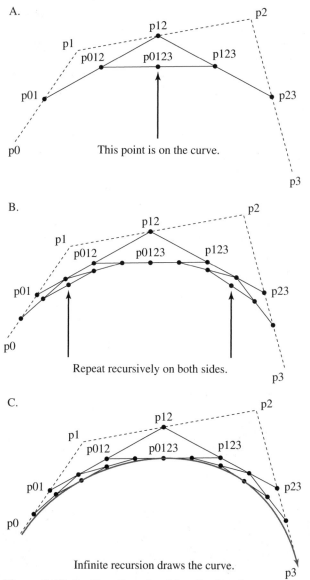

A.

This point is on the curve.

B.

Repeat recursively on both sides.

C.

Infinite recursion draws the curve.

**Figure 2.57** De Casteljau algorithm for drawing a Bézier curve

$p_0, p_{01}, p_{012}$, and $p_{0123}$ on one side and $p_{0123}, p_{123}, p_{23}, p_3$ on the other. This goes on recursively, theoretically down to infinite detail—or, more practically, down to pixel resolution—thereby tracing out the Bézier curve. Analyzing this recursive procedure mathematically is another method for deriving the Bernstein polynomials.

To conclude this section, it may be helpful to return to an intuitive understanding of Bézier curves by considering their properties and looking at some examples as they commonly appear in drawing programs. Bézier curves have the following characteristics:

- Bézier curves can be based on $n$-degree polynomials of degrees higher than three. However, most drawing programs create Bézier curves from cubic polynomials, and thus the curves are defined by four control points. The number of control points is always one more than the degree of the polynomial.

- A Bézier curve with control points $p_0, p_1, p_2$, and $p_3$ passes through the two endpoints $p_0$ and $p_3$ and is approximated through the two interior control points $p_1$ and $p_2$. The lines between $p_0$ and $p_1$ and between $p_2$ and $p_3$ are tangent to the curve.
- Bézier curves are fairly easy to control and understand in a drawing program because the curve will always lie within the convex hull formed by the four points. The convex hull defined by a set $S$ of points is the polygon formed by a subset of the points such that all the points in $S$ are either inside or on an edge of the polygon.
- The mathematics of moving, scaling, or rotating a Bézier curve is easy. If the operation is applied to the control points, then the curve will be appropriately transformed. (Note that transformations such as moving, scaling, and rotating are called ***affine transformations***. An affine transformation is one that preserves colinearity and ratios of distances among points.)

Supplement on pen tool and curve drawing:

hands-on worksheet

Figure 2.58 shows the stepwise creation of a Bézier curve as it is done using the pen tool in programs such as Illustrator or GIMP. We'll have to adjust our definition of control points in order to describe how curves are drawn in these application programs. The control points defined in the Bézier equation above are $p_0, p_1, p_2$, and $p_3$. We need to identify another point that we'll call $p_x$. To make a curve defined by the mathematical control points $p_0, p_1, p_2$, and $p_3$, you click on four physical control points $p_0, p_1, p_2$, and $p_x$. as follows:

- Click at point $p_0$, hold the mouse down, and drag to point $p_1$.
- Release the mouse button.

With pen tool in application programs like Illustrator or GIMP:
Step 1. Click p0, holding down mouse button.
Step 2. Drag to p1. Let go mouse button.
Step 3. Click p3, holding down mouse button.
Step 4. Drag to px and doubleclick to end curve.

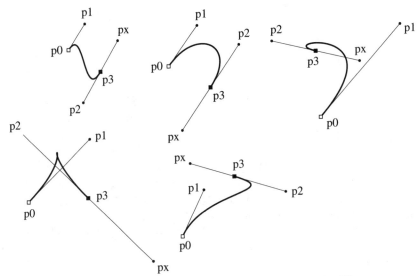

**Figure 2.58** Examples of Bézier curves drawn in, for example, Illustrator or GIMP

- Move the cursor to your desired endpoint $p_3$, click, and pull to create a "handle" that ends at $p_x$.
- Release the mouse button.

As you pull from $p_3$ to $p_x$, a handle extends equidistant from $p_3$ but in the opposite direction from $p_x$, ending in control point $p_2$. Notice that both $p_0$ and $p_3$ will have handles that can be pulled. The handles appear and disappear as you select and deselect endpoints. After you create the initial curve, you can modify the curve's shape by pulling on the handles. The length of the line segments $\overline{p_0, p_1}$ and $\overline{p_2, p_3}$ define how strongly the curve is pulled toward $p_1$ and $p_2$, respectively. Their orientations determine the direction of the curves on each side.

## 2.8 ALGORITHMIC ART AND PROCEDURAL MODELING

Supplement on algorithmic art:

interactive tutorial

So far, we've talked about two types of digital images: bitmap graphics and vector graphics. Bitmaps are created by means of either digital photography or a paint program. Vector graphic images are created by vector drawing programs. Paint and vector drawing programs allow you to work with powerful tools at a high level of abstraction. However, if you're a computer programmer, you can also generate bitmaps and graphical images directly by writing programs at a lower level of abstraction. To "hand-generate" and work with bitmaps, you need to be adept at array manipulation and bit operations. To work at a low level of abstraction with vector graphics, you need to understand the mathematics and algorithms for line drawing, shading, and geometric transformations such as rotation, displacement, and scaling. (These are topics covered in graphics courses.) In this book, we emphasize your work with high-level tools for photographic, sound, and video processing; vector drawing; and multimedia programming. However, we try to give you the knowledge to descend into your image and sound files at a low level of abstraction when you want to have more creative control.

There is a third type of digital image that we will call *algorithmic art*. (It is also referred to as procedural modeling.) In algorithmic art, you create a digital image by writing a computer program based on some mathematical computation or unique type of algorithm, but the focus is different from the type of work we've described so far. In vector graphics (assuming that you're working at a low level of abstraction), you write programs to generate lines, three-dimensional images, colors, and shading. To do this, you first picture and then mathematically model the objects that you are trying to create. In algorithmic art, on the other hand, your focus is the mathematics or algorithm rather than on some preconceived object, and you create an image by associating pixels with the results of the calculation. The image emerges naturally as a manifestation of the mathematical properties of the calculation or algorithm.

One of the best examples of algorithmic art is fractal generation. A *fractal* is a graphical image characterized by a recursively repeating structure. This means that if you look at the image at the macro-level—the entire structure—you'll see a certain geometric pattern, and then when you zoom in on a smaller scale, you'll see that same pattern again. For fractals, this self-embedded structure can be repeated infinitely.

Fractals exist in natural phenomena. A fern has the structure of a fractal in that the shape of one frond of a fern is repeated in each of the small side-leaves of the frond.

**Figure 2.59** Natural fractal structures

Supplement on
Koch snowflake:

programming
exercise

Similarly, a cauliflower's shape is repeated in each subcluster down to several levels of detail (Figure 2.59).

You can create a fractal with a recursive program that draws the same shape down to some base level. This is an example of algorithmic art because the self-replicating structure of the image results from the recursive nature of the algorithm. The **Koch snowflake**, named for Swedish mathematician Helge von Koch, is an example of a fractal structure that can be created by means of a recursive program. Here's an explanation of how you can draw one by hand. First, draw an equilateral triangle. Then draw another triangle of the same size, rotate it 180°, and align the two triangles at their center points. You've created a six-pointed star. Now, consider each point of the star as a separate equilateral triangle, and do the same thing for each of these. That is, create another triangle of the same size as the point of the star, rotate it, and align it with the first. You've just created six more stars, one for each point of the original star. For each of these stars, do the same thing that you did with the first star. You can repeat this to whatever level of detail you like (or until you can't add any more detail because of the resolution of your picture). If you fill in all the triangles with a single color, you have a Koch snowflake (Figure 2.60).

Another recursively defined fractal structure is **Sierpinski's gasket** (Figure 2.61), which is built in the following manner: Begin with an equilateral triangle with sides that are one unit in length. The triangle is colored black (or whatever solid color you like). Create a white triangle inside the first one by connecting the midpoints of the sides of the original triangle. Now you have three small black triangles and one white one, each with sides half the length of the original. Subdivide each of the black triangles similarly. Keep doing this to the level of detail your resolution allows. This can easily be described by a recursive algorithm.

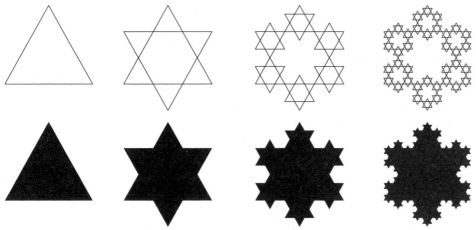

**Figure 2.60** Koch's snowflake, a recursively defined fractal

**Figure 2.61** Sierpinski's gasket

Another very intriguing type of fractal was discovered by Benoit Mandelbrot in the 1970s. Mandelbrot's method is interesting in that the mathematical computation does not explicitly set out to create a fractal of infinitely repeating shapes; instead, a beautiful and complex geometry emerges from the nature of the computation itself.

The Mandelbrot fractal computation is based on a simple iterative equation.

 KEY EQUATION

A Mandelbrot fractal can be computed by the iterative equation

$$f(z) = z^2 + c$$

where $z$ and $c$ are complex numbers. The output of the $i$th computation is the input $z$ to the $i + 1$st computation.

Complex numbers have a real and an imaginary number component. For $c$, we will call these components $c_r$ and $c_i$, and for $z$ the components are $z_r$ and $z_i$.

$$c = c_r + c_i i \text{ and } z = z_r + z_i i \text{ where } i \text{ is } \sqrt{-1}$$

To create a Mandelbrot fractal, you relate values of $c$ on the complex number plane to pixel positions on the image bitmap, and you use these as initial values in computations that determine the color of each pixel. $c_r$ corresponds to the horizontal axis on the plane, and $c_i$ corresponds to the vertical axis. The range of $-2.0$ to $2.0$ in the horizontal direction and $-1.5$ to $1.5$ in the vertical direction works well for the complex number plane. Let's assume that we're going to create a fractal bitmap that has dimensions of $1024 \times 768$ pixels. Given these respective dimensions for the two planes, each pixel position $(x, y)$ is mapped proportionately to a complex number $(c_r, c_i)$ (Figure 2.62).

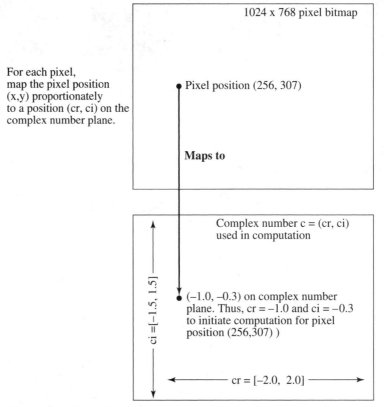

**Figure 2.62** Mapping from pixel plane to complex number plane for Mandelbrot fractal

To compute a pixel's color, you iteratively compute $f(z) = z^2 + c$, where $c$ initially is the complex number corresponding to the pixel's position, and $z$ is initially 0. After the first computation, the output of the $i$th computation is the input $z$ to the $i + 1$st computation. If, after some given maximum number of iterations, the computation has not revealed itself as being unbounded, then the pixel is painted black. Otherwise, the pixel is painted a color related to how many iterations were performed before it was discovered that the computation was unbounded. The result is a Mandelbrot fractal like the ones shown in Figure 2.63.

Algorithm 2.5 describes the Mandelbrot fractal calculation. We have not shown in this pseudo-code how complex numbers are handled, nor have we been specific about the termination condition. For details on this, see the related programming assignment.

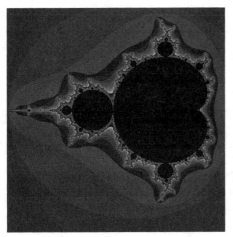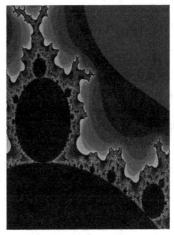

**Figure 2.63** Mandelbrot fractals, the one on right "zoomed in"

---

**ALGORITHM 2.5**

algorithm mandelbrot_fractal
/*Input: Horizontal and vertical ranges of the complex number plane.
Resolution of the bitmap for the fractal.
Color map.
Output: A bitmap for a fractal.*/
{
/*constant MAX is the maximum number of iterations*/
   for each pixel in the bitmap {
     map pixel coordinates (x,y) to complex number plane coordinates (cr, ci)
     num_iterations = 0
     z = 0
     while num_iterations < MAX and not_unbounded* {
       z = z$^2$ + c
       num_iterations = num_iterations + 1
     }
/*map_color(x,y) uses the programmer's chosen color map to determine the color of
each pixel based on how many iterations are done before the computation is found to
be unbounded*/
     if num_iterations == MAX then color(x,y) = BLACK
     else color(x,y) = map_color(num_iterations)
   }
}
/*We have not explained *not_unbounded* here. For an explanation of the termination
condition and computations using complex numbers, see the programming assignment related to this section.*/

A variation of the Mandelbrot fractal, called the **Julia fractal**, can be created by relating $z$ rather than $c$ to the pixel's position and appropriately selecting a value for $c$, which remains constant for all pixels. Values for $c$ that create interesting-looking Julia fractals can be determined experimentally, by trial and error. Each different constant $c$ creates a fractal of a different shape.

  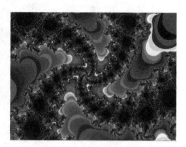

**Figure 2.64**  Three Julia fractals using different starting values for $c$

# EXERCISES

**1.** a. What type of values would you expect for the DCT of the enlarged 8 pixel $\times$ 8 pixel image below (*i.e.*, where do you expect nonzero values)? The grayscale values are given in the matrix. Explain your answer.

**Figure 2.65**

| 0 | 255 | 155 | 155 | 255 | 255 | 200 | 255 |
|---|-----|-----|-----|-----|-----|-----|-----|
| 0 | 255 | 155 | 155 | 255 | 255 | 200 | 255 |
| 0 | 255 | 155 | 155 | 255 | 255 | 200 | 255 |
| 0 | 255 | 155 | 155 | 255 | 255 | 200 | 255 |
| 0 | 255 | 155 | 155 | 255 | 255 | 200 | 255 |
| 0 | 255 | 155 | 155 | 255 | 255 | 200 | 255 |
| 0 | 255 | 155 | 155 | 255 | 255 | 200 | 255 |
| 0 | 255 | 155 | 155 | 255 | 255 | 200 | 255 |

b. Compute the values. You can use computer help (*e.g.*, write a program, use MATLAB, etc.)

**2.** Say that your 1-CCD camera detects the following RGB values in a 3 pixel $\times$ 3 pixel area. What value would it record for the three pixels that are in boldface, assuming the nearest neighbor algorithm is used? (Give the R, G, and B values for these pixels.)

| G = 240 | R = 255 | G = 239 | R = 244 | G = 236 |
|---------|---------|---------|---------|---------|
| B = 238 | **G = 229** | **B = 224** | G = 230 | B = 222 |
| G = 244 | R = 255 | G = 238 | **R = 250** | G = 236 |
| B = 230 | G = 226 | B = 222 | G = 232 | B = 228 |
| G = 244 | R = 255 | G = 238 | R = 250 | G = 236 |

**3.** Answer the following questions based on the diagram below.

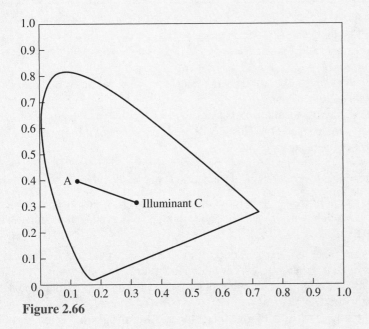

**Figure 2.66**

    a. What color is point A?
    b. How would you find the dominant wavelength of this color?
    c. What does the line segment between A and C represent?
    d. How would you determine the saturation of the color at point A?

**4.** Pixel dimensions, resolution, and image size, hands-on exercise, online

**5.** DCT, interactive tutorial, worksheet, programming exercise, and mathematical modeling exercise, online.

**6.** Aliasing in sampling, interactive tutorial and worksheet, online

**7.** Aliasing in rendering, interactive tutorial and worksheet, online

**8.** Line drawing, interactive tutorial and programming exercise, online

**9.** Color model conversions, programming exercise, online

**10.** XYZ color and the CIE chromaticity diagram, mathematical modeling exercise and programming exercise, online

11. Curve drawing, interactive tutorial, worksheet, and hands-on exercise, online

12. Algorithmic art, interactive tutorial, online

13. Koch snowflakes, programming exercise, online

14. Mandelbrot and Julia fractals, interactive tutorial and programming exercise, online

## APPLICATIONS

1. Examine the specifications on your digital camera (or the one you would like to have), and answer the following questions:
   - Does your camera allow you to choose various pixel dimension settings? What settings are offered?
   - How many megapixels does the camera offer? What does this mean, and how does it relate to pixel dimensions?
   - What type of storage medium does the camera use? How many pictures can you take on your storage medium? This will depend on the size of the storage medium and the size of the pictures. Explain.
   - How can you get your pictures from the camera to your computer?
   - What technology does your camera use for detecting color values?

2. What are the pixel dimensions of your computer display? Can you change them? If so, change the pixel dimensions and describe what you observe about the images on your display. Explain.

3. Examine the specifications of your printer (or the one you would like to have). Is it inkjet? Laser? Some other type? What is its resolution? How does this affect the choices you make for initial pixel dimensions and final resolution of digital images that you want to print?

   **Examine the features of your digital image processing program, vector graphic (*i.e.*, draw), and/or paint programs and try the exercises below with features that are available.**

4. Open the applications program or programs and examine the color models that they offer you. Which of the color models described in this chapter are offered in the application program? Are there other color models available in the application program that are not discussed in this chapter? Examine the interface—sometimes called a "color chooser." Look at the Help of your application program. How is color saved by the application program? If you specify color in HLS rather than RGB, for example, using the color chooser, is the internal representation changing, or just the values you use to specify the color in the interface?

5. Do some experiments with the color chooser of your image processing, paint, or draw program in RGB mode to see if you can understand what is meant by the statement "the RGB color space is not perceptually uniform."

*Additional exercises or applications may be found at the book or author's websites.*

# REFERENCES

## Print Publications

Briggs, John. *Fractals: The Patterns of Chaos*. New York: Simon & Schuster/A Touchstone Book, 1992.

Foley, James D., Steven K. Feiner, John F. Hughes, and Andries Van Dam. *Computer Graphics: Principles and Practice*. 2nd ed. Boston: Addison-Wesley, 1996.

Hargittai, Istvan, and Clifford A. Pickover. *Spiral Symmetry*. Singapore: World Scientific, 1992.

Hearn, Donald, and M. Pauline Baker. *Computer Graphics with OpenGL*. 3rd ed. Upper Saddle River, NJ: Pearson/Prentice-Hall, 2003.

Hill, F. S., Jr. *Computer Graphics Using Open GL*. 2nd ed. Upper Saddle River, NJ: Prentice-Hall, 2001.

Hofstadter, Douglas R. *Gödel, Escher, Bach: An Eternal Golden Braid*. New York: Basic Books, 1979. (Reprinted with a new preface in 1999.)

Livio, Mario. *The Golden Ratio: The Story of Phi, The World's Most Astonishing Number*. New York: Broadway Books, 2002.

Pickover, Clifford. *The Pattern Book: Fractals, Art, and Nature*. Singapore: World Scientific, 1995.

Pickover, Clifford. *Chaos and Fractals: A Computer Graphical Journey*. Elsevier, 1998.

Pokorny, Cornel. *Computer Graphics: An Object-Oriented Approach to the Art and Science*. Franklin Beedle and Associates, 1994.

Rao, K. R., and P. Yip. *Discrete Cosine Transform: Algorithms, Advantages, Applications*. San Diego: Academic Press, 1990.

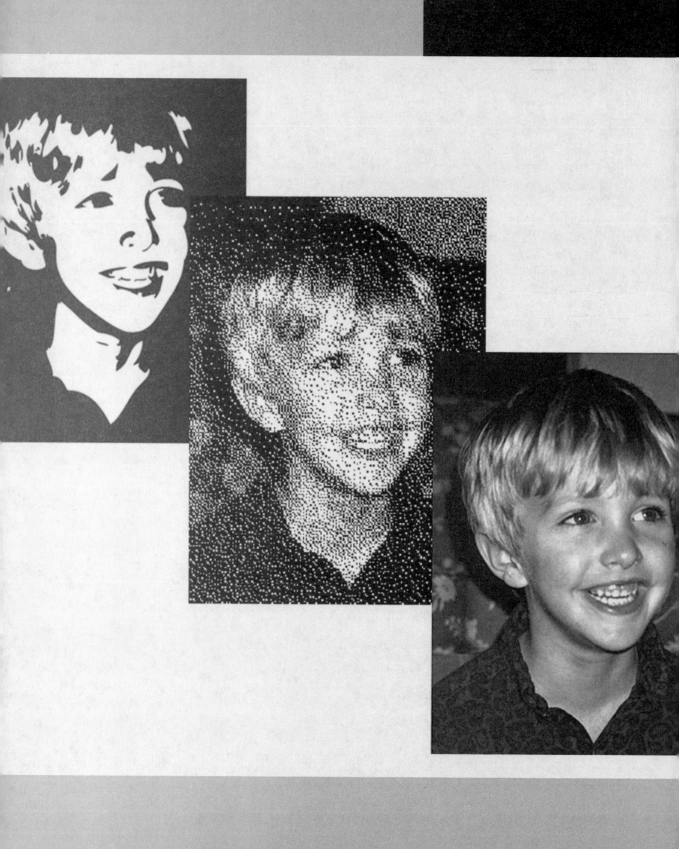

# Digital Image Processing

# 3

*I want to reach that state of condensation of sensations that constitutes a picture.*
—Henri Matisse

### OBJECTIVES FOR CHAPTER 3

- Know the important file types for digital image data by name, basic format, and application.
- Understand the difference between fixed-length and variable-length encoding schemes.
- Understand the implementation and application of LZW compression, Huffman encoding, and JPEG compression.
- Understand the notation, motivation, and application of luminance/chrominance downsampling.
- Understand the motivation, implementation, and application of a variety of indexed color algorithms and the differences among them.
- Understand the implementation and application of a variety of dithering algorithms and the differences among them.
- Understand how pixel point processing is done in digital image processing.
- Understand how convolutions are applied in filtering for enlarging, reducing, or sharpening images.
- Understand the mathematics and application of histograms.
- Understand the mathematics of resampling.

## 3.1 TOOLS FOR DIGITAL IMAGE PROCESSING

In Chapter 2, we examined how image data is captured and represented. We now turn to digital image processing—what you can *do* with images to refine them for creative or practical purposes.

Chapter 3 begins with a brief overview of the tools you need to work with digital images—cameras, scanners, printers, and application programs. The focus of the chapter, however, is on the mathematics and algorithms that make these tools work.

Image processing programs give you great power to alter bitmap images in interesting and creative ways. These tools do a lot of the work for you, and you don't need to know all the underlying mathematics to use them effectively. Then what motivates us to learn the science and mathematics upon which the tools are based? One motivation is that someone needs to create these tools and application programs to begin with, and knowing the science and mathematics of digital media technology makes it possible for you to contribute to its development. A second, more immediate, motivation for looking behind the scenes is that it gives you the ability to work on digital images at a lower level of abstraction. You can create digital image files "from scratch" using programs that you write yourself, or you can take raw image data created with the standard tools and alter it with your own programs.

Let's begin now with your work environment.

To create an original digital image, you can use a digital camera, a scanner, or a paint or image processing program.

Digital cameras come in three basic types—point-and-shoot, prosumer, and professional level. Point-and-shoot digital cameras are what is called "consumer level"—less expensive, easy to use, compact, but with few options. These cameras don't give you much control over pixel dimensions, compression, and file type. There might be only one possible image size, in pixel dimensions, and the images might all be saved in JPEG format. A prosumer camera—which lies between the consumer and professional levels in quality and expense—has more options of pixel dimensions, file type, compression levels, and settings such as white balance, image sharpening, and so forth. Professional level digital cameras are usually *single-lens reflex cameras* (*SLR*). In an SLR camera, when you look through the viewfinder, you're seeing exactly what the lens sees, whereas in a prosumer or point-and-shoot camera your view is offset from the lens's view. SLR cameras have high-quality, detachable lenses, so that you can change lenses, using different focal lengths for different purposes. A disadvantage of SLR cameras is the weight and size compared to point-and-shoot.

A digital image makes its way to your computer as a file by means of a physical or wireless connection or by means of a memory card that can be inserted into a card holder on the computer or printer. Common physical connections are USB or IEEE1394 (Firewire). Memory cards—for example, CompactFlash—can be inserted into adaptors that fit in the PCMCIA port of a computer. The number of images you can fit on a memory card depends on the size of the card, the pixel dimensions, and the file type of the images. If you want to take a lot of pictures with high pixel dimensions and little or no compression, you need a large memory card, a gigabyte or more.

When you have a choice of pixel dimensions in your camera, you should consider how much memory you have in your storage medium, how many pictures you want to take at once, and how you want to use your digital images. High pixel dimensions give you a lot of detail to work with, but the pictures take up a lot of memory. The pixel dimensions offered by your camera might also imply different aspect ratios. The *aspect ratio* of a digital image is the ratio of the width to the height, which can be written $a:b$. Pixel dimensions of $640 \times 480$, for example, give an aspect ratio of $4:3$. If you want to print your image as $8'' \times 10''$, you'll have to adjust the aspect ratio as you edit the image.

You can also capture a digital image using a scanner. A scanner is like a copy machine that turns the copy into a file of digital data. Like a digital camera, a scanner takes samples at evenly spaced points. The number of samples it takes in the horizontal and vertical dimension equates to the pixel dimensions of the image. The object being scanned is a physical object with dimensions that can be measured in inches or centimeters. Thus, we can talk of the resolution of a scanner in pixels per inch or centimeters per inch. (Some people use the term dots per inch—DPI—with regard to scanners, but pixels is a better term, since the scanner is saving the information as pixels in a file.) A scanner has a maximum resolution, limited by the number of sensors it has. You may be allowed to choose a higher resolution than the scanner can physically produce, but in that case the additional pixels are interpolated. High-quality scanners have resolutions of $1200 \times 1200$ pixels per inch and higher.

A third way to create a digital image is through a paint, draw, or image processing program. A *paint program*, sometimes called a *raster graphics editor*, allows you to create bitmap images with software tools that simulate pencils, brushes, paint buckets, type tools, and more. Paint Shop Pro and Microsoft Paint are two examples. A *drawing program* gives you more facilities for vector graphics (*e.g.*, Illustrator and Freehand). Image processing programs (*e.g.*, Photoshop and GIMP) have many of these same tools as paint and draw programs and even more features for editing digital images you may have created through a camera or scanner. The distinction between paint, drawing, and image processing programs is not a sharp one since the tools overlap. These programs can be very sophisticated and powerful—sometime expensive—but freeware and shareware versions also exist (*e.g.*, GIMP).

## 3.2 DIGITAL IMAGE FILE TYPES

If you take a picture with a digital camera or scan a photograph with a digital scanner, you'll have a choice of file types in which to save the image. You'll also have a choice of file types when you save an image in an image processing, paint, or drawing program. Not all color modes can be accommodated by all file types, and some file types require that the image be compressed while some do not. Some of the image file types, identified by the suffix on the file name, are *.tiff* (also *.tif* ), *.jpg* (also *.jpeg*), *.gif*, *.png*, and *.bmp*. Our convention in this book is to refer to these file types using all capital letters, such as GIF, since the suffixes can take multiple forms.

Table 3.1 lists some commonly used file formats, categorized into bitmap images, vector graphics, and a hybrid of the two, sometimes called *metafiles*. Bitmap images are listed first in the table. The four most important things to know about a bitmap filetype are its color model (*e.g.*, RGB, CMYK, or indexed color); its bit depth; its compression type, if any (*e.g.*, LZW, RLE, or JPEG); and the operating systems, browsers, and application software that support it. The possible bit depths for bitmap images include 1, 4, 8, 16, 24, 32, 48, and 64 bits. A 1-bit bitmap image uses only black and white. An 8-bit grayscale image allows 256 shades of gray (including pure black and white). Some file types allow 16-bit grayscale. Bitmap files in RGB and CMYK color mode use 24 bits per pixel—one byte for each of three color channels. Bitmap files in indexed color mode generally use 8 bits (or more) per pixel to store an index into a color table, called a *palette* (although the number of bits can vary).

Because they can be compressed to a small size, GIF files (Graphics Interchange Format) are commonly used for images presented on the web. GIF files allow only 8-bit indexed color. For this reason, they are most suitable for poster-like or cartoon-like images and for photographic images that don't require more than 256 colors. GIF files use lossless LZW compression (discussed below). GIF files support transparency in that you can choose a color from the color palette and designate it to be transparent. This is commonly done for the background of an image. Animated GIF files can be created by sequences of single images.

Like GIF files, JPEG files (Joint Photographic Experts Group) are also widely used on the web. They are good for continuous tone photographic images, where colors change gradually from one point to the next and many colors are needed for detail and clarity. By JPEG files, we mean files that are compressed with the JPEG compression algorithm (explained later in this chapter). The file format is actually called JFIF for JPEG File Interchange Format. You can often select the level of compression you want when you save and compress the file, making a choice between file size and level of detail. GIF files can be saved in an interlaced format that allows progressive download of web images. In *progressive download*, a low-resolution version of an image is downloaded first, and the image gradually comes into focus as the rest of the data is downloaded.

BMP files are a bitmap format that can be uncompressed, or compressed with RLE. BMP files are in 1-bit black and white; 8-bit grayscale; 16-, 24- or 32-bit RGB color; or 4- or 8-bit indexed color. (Indexed color will be discussed below.) BMP files don't support CMYK color. Transparency is supported for individual pixels as in GIF files. Alpha channels are supported in new versions of BMP. An *alpha channel* is a channel like R, G, and B—using

| TABLE 3.1 | Common File Types for Vector Graphics, Bitmapped Images, and Metafiles | | | |
|---|---|---|---|---|

| File Suffix | Our Abbreviation | File Type | Characteristics |
|---|---|---|---|
| **Bitmap Images** | | | |
| *.bmp* | BMP | Windows bitmap | 1 to 24-bit color depth, 32-bit if alpha channel is used. Can use lossless RLE or no compression. RGB or indexed color. |
| *.gif* | GIF | Graphics Interchange Format | Used on the web. Allows 256 RGB colors. Can be used for simple animations. Uses LZW compression. Originally proprietary to CompuServe. |
| *.jpeg* or *.jpg* | JPEG | Joint Photographic Experts Group | For continuous tone pictures. Lossy compression. Level of compression can be specified. |
| *.png* | PNG | Portable Network Graphics | Designed as an alternative to *.gif* files. Compressed with lossless method. 1 to 64-bit color with transparency channel. |
| *.psd* | PSD | Adobe Photoshop | Supports a variety of color models and bit depths. Saves image layers created in photographic editing. |
| *.psp* | PSP | Corel Paint Shop Pro | Similar to *.psd*. |
| *.raw* | | Photoshop | Uncompressed raw file. Could be black and white, grayscale, or RGB color. |
| *.tif* or *.tiff* | TIFF | Tagged Image File Format | Often used for traditional print graphics. Can be compressed with lossy or lossless methods, including RLE, JPEG, and LZW. Comes in many varieties. |
| **Vector Graphics** | | | |
| *.ai* | AI | Adobe Illustrator | Proprietary vector format. |
| *.swf* | SWF | Shockwave Flash | Proprietary vector format; can contain stills, animations, video, and sound. |
| *.cdr* | CDR | Corel Draw | Proprietary vector format. |
| *.dxf* | DXF | AutoCAD ASCII Drawing Interchange Format | ASCII text stores vector data. |
| **Metafiles** | | | |
| *.cgm* | CGM | Computer Graphics Metafile | ANSI, ISO standard. |
| *.emf, .wmf* | EMF, WMF | Enhanced metafile and Windows metafile | Windows platform. |
| *.eps* | EPS | Encapsulated Postscript | Used for output to Postscript device. |
| *.pdf* | PDF | Portable Document Format | An open standard working toward ISO standardization. Windows, MAC, Unix, Linux. |
| *.pict* | PICT | Picture | Macintosh. Can use RLE or JPEG compression. Grayscale, RGB, CMYK, or indexed color. |
| *.wmf* | WMF | Windows metafile | 16-bit format. Can be binary or text. Not portable to other platforms. |

the same number of bits (which accounts for the 32-bit RGB color version). The bits in the alpha channel indicate the level of transparency of each pixel.

PNG files (Portable Network Graphics) are similar to GIF files in that the format and compression method used lend themselves to poster-like images with a limited number of colors. PNG works well for photographic images also, although it doesn't achieve the compression rates of JPEG. PNG files allow many variations, including 1, 2, 4, 8, or 16 bits per pixel grayscale; 1, 2, 4, or 8 bits per pixel indexed color; and 8 or 16 bits per channel RGB color. PNG files allow the use of alpha channels. With the addition of an alpha channel, the largest bit depth of a PNG file is 64 bits per pixel (4 channels * 16 bits/channel). PNG uses a lossless compression algorithm that works by predicting the color of a pixel based on previous pixels and subtracting the predicted color value from the actual color. PNG files have an optional interlaced format that allows progressive download. PNG does not support animation.

TIFF files (Tagged Image File Format) allow for a variety of color models, including black and white, grayscale, RGB, CMYK, YCbCr, and CIELab. Either 8 or 16 bits per channel can be used for multi-channel color models. A variety of compression methods can be applied—including LZW, RLE, or JPEG—or a TIFF file can be uncompressed. Multiple images can be included in one image file. TIFF files have other options, which can sometimes create problems in their portability because not all applications that read TIFF files are implemented to support all the variations.

GIF, JPEG, PNG, and TIFF are usable within a wide variety of operating systems (*e.g.*, Windows, Mac, and Unix/Linux), web browsers, and application programs (*e.g.*, Photoshop and GIMP). A number of proprietary file types are also listed in the table. These are supported by certain application programs—*e.g.*, PSP for Paint Shop Pro and PSD for Photoshop.

Also listed for Photoshop is its *.raw* file format. This format is useful if you want to work with an image file at a low level of abstraction—perhaps writing a program to implement LZW compression, a convolution for unsharp masking, or indexed color—algorithms described later in this chapter. In Photoshop, you can save the image as a *.raw* file such that you have just pixel values (black and white, grayscale, or RGB color, depending on what you want to do). You can then read these values into a program that you've written yourself and experiment with how the algorithms work.

There's a difference between Photoshop's *.raw* file format and RAW files that come from your digital camera. The term RAW image file does not refer to a specific file format. Each digital camera can have its own RAW file format that depends on the camera's engineering. In general, a RAW image file contains unprocessed image data exactly as it is detected by the camera's sensors—without any color interpolation, white balancing, or contrast adjustments. For example, consider a one-CCD camera that uses a demosaicing algorithm like the one described in Chapter 2. For such a camera, if you choose to save an image in the RAW format, you have color information for only one of the three color channels from each of the photosites. The camera doesn't do the demosaicing before saving the data. This generally gives you 12 or 14 bits per photosite. This gives you the rawest data possible, allowing you to do your own adjustments in whatever fine-tuned way you like. However, because the RAW file is proprietary to the camera, you'll need special software to read the file when you port the file to your computer.

We turn now to vector graphic file formats and metafiles. As you recall from Chapter 2, vector graphic files are suitable for images with clear edges and cleanly separated colors—images that can be described in terms of geometric shapes. A vector graphic file for a poster-type image generally is smaller than a bitmap file for the same image. The size of a vector graphic file is proportional to the number of graphical objects in it, while the size of a bitmap file always depends only on the pixel dimensions, bit depth, color mode, and finally compression. Vector graphic files have the additional advantage of being rescalable without aliasing effects. This is because the image is rendered at the time it is displayed on whatever scale is indicated at that moment and at the maximum resolution of the display device.

Vector graphic files store image data in terms of geometric objects. The objects are specified by parameters like line styles, side lengths, radius, color, gradients, etc. This information can be stored in either binary or text form. If a vector graphic file is text-based, you can look at it in a text editor and read the statements that define the objects. It is possible to create or alter a text-based vector graphic file "by hand" with a text editor if you know the grammar and syntax of the object definition, but working this way requires a lot of attention to detail, and you usually don't need to edit by hand since drawing programs give you such powerful high-level facilities for creating and manipulating vector graphic objects. A textbased vector graphic file might have statements like those shown in Figure 3.1.

```
LineType 1;
LineWidth 2.0;
LineColr 1;
Line (200,400) (200,600);
Circle (500,600),430;
```

**Figure 3.1** Excerpt from a vector graphic file

Vector graphic files can also be stored in binary form. Typically, these binary files consist of a header identifying the file type and giving global image parameters, a palette (optional), the image data defined in variable-length records, and an end-of-file symbol. Fortunately, editing binary vector graphics files by hand is rarely necessary.

Some file formats combine vector graphics with bitmap images. These are called *metafiles*. The term metafile evolved from attempts to create a platform-independent specification for vector graphics. The Computer Graphics Metafile (CGM), originally standardized under the International Standards Organization (ISO) in 1987 and evolving through several revisions, is an example of a standardized metafile format designed for cross-platform interchange of vector graphics, with the optional inclusion of bitmaps. CGM files can be encoded in human-readable ASCII text or compiled into a binary representation. The original CGM was not widely supported by web browsers, but in recent years, the World Wide Web Consortium (W3C) has supported the development of WebCGM, which is designed to incorporate the CGM vector format into web pages using XML. An alternative to WebCGM for web vector graphics being developed by W3C is Scalable Vector Graphics (SVG). SVG images can be animated. Generally, WebCGM is considered appropriate for technical graphics and SVG is preferable for graphic arts.

You might want to try opening some vector graphic files in a text editor to see if you can decipher them. Because the CGM standard defines both a text and a binary format, your ability to read a CGM file depends on where and how the file was originally made. If you try opening a CGM file in a text editor, you'll probably discover that it has been encoded in binary, and you won't be able to read it. However, file readers exist for CGM raw files that can give you access to the individual objects.

One of the most widely used types of metafile is PDF (Portable Document Format). PDF files can be used on all major operating systems—Mac, Windows, Unix, and Linux. PDF documents can contain text, bitmap images, vector graphics, and hyperlinks. The text is searchable.

Microsoft Windows Metafile Format (WMF) is a combined vector/bitmap format. Parameter descriptions of graphical objects in WMF files are stored in 16-bit words. The revised version of WMF, called Enhanced Metafile Format (EMF), uses 32-bit words and has more graphics primitives. WMF and EMF files are stored as binary and are therefore not directly readable.

SWF, the proprietary vector graphic format of Flash (formerly produced by Macromedia and bought by Adobe), is currently a very popular file format that is used across a variety of platforms. Its wide use arises from that fact that it allows for inclusion of not only bitmaps but also animated vectors, audio, and video, within a small, compressed file size. Browser plugins that handle SWF files have become standard. SWF files are stored in binary form and thus are not readable as text.

Among those listed in Table 3.1, the easiest vector graphic files to read as text are DXF, EPS, and Adobe Illustrator files. Adobe Illustrator files are similar to EPS files, having been designed as a variation of EPS. Both file types can represent either vector objects or bitmaps.

It is possible to compress vector graphic files, and compression is important to file types that include animations, video, and sound. For example, SWF files, which are stored as binary data, use *zlib* compression, a variant of LZW. We will look at LZW and other compression methods in a later section of this chapter.

## 3.3 INDEXED COLOR

In image processing programs, it is likely that you will often work in RGB mode and 24-bit color. This corresponds to the color system and bit depth of most current computer displays. However, there are times when you may want to reduce the number of colors used in an image file. You could have a number of motivations for reducing the bit depth—and thus the number of representable colors. It may be the case that your picture doesn't use a large number of colors; slight differences in color may not be important; or you may have constraints on the file size of your picture because of the time it would take to download it or the space it would take to store it. The process of reducing the number of colors in an image file is called **color quantization**. In image processing programs, the color mode associated with color quantization is called **indexed color**.

Color quantization begins with an image file stored with a bit depth of $n$ and reduces the bit depth to $b$. The number of colors representable in the original file is $2^n$, and the number of colors representable in the adjusted file will be $2^b$. As an example, let's assume your image is initially in RGB mode with 24-bit color, and you want to reduce it to 8-bit color.

The process of color quantization involves three steps. First, the actual range and number of colors used in your picture must be determined. If your image is stored initially in RGB mode with 24-bit color, then there are $2^{24} = 16,777,216$ possible colors. The question is, which of these colors appear in the picture?

The second step in color quantization entails choosing $2^b$ colors to represent those that actually appear in the picture. For our example, the adjusted picture would be limited to $2^8 = 256$ colors.

The third step in color quantization is to map the colors in the original picture to the colors chosen for the reduced bit-depth picture. The $b$ bits that represent each pixel then become an index into a color table that has $2^b$ entries, where each entry is $n$ bits long. In our example, the table would have 256 entries, where each entry is 24 bits long.

One simple way to achieve a reduction from a bit depth of $n$ to a bit depth of $b$ is called the **popularity algorithm**. In the popularity method, the $2^b$ colors that appear most often in the picture are chosen for the reduced-bit depth picture. A straightforward way to map one of the original colors to the more limited palette is by finding the color that is most similar using the minimum mean squared distance. More precisely, let the $2^b$ colors in the reduced color palette be given by their RGB color components such that the $i$th color has components $r_i$, $g_i$, and $b_i$ for $0 \leq i < 2^b$. In our example, this means that each of the 256 rows in our color look-up table corresponds to one of the original 16,777,216 colors, decomposed into its three RGB color components. For an arbitrary pixel in the original image with color components $r$, $g$, and $b$, we want to find the color at index $i$ that minimizes $(R - r_i)^2 + (G - g_i)^2 + (B - b_i)^2$.

The disadvantage of the popularity algorithm is that it completely throws out colors that appear infrequently. A picture with one dramatic spot of red in a field of white snow, trees, and sky may lose the red spot entirely, completely changing the desired effect.

The quantization process can also be described graphically, in terms of color spaces. The range of colors in a picture can be seen as a subspace of the RGB cube, and thus the first step in quantization involves finding the smallest "box" that contains all the colors appearing in the image. In the second step, the "box" can be partitioned into $2^b$ spaces, or in our example, 256 spaces corresponding to the representable colors. A number of methods for achieving this partitioning have been devised.

The *uniform partitioning algorithm* divides the subspace containing the existing colors into $2^b$ blocks of equal size. This can be done by making slices through the initial box in each of the red, green, and blue dimensions. If the quantization is perfectly uniform, the slices in each dimension are equally spaced, but the size of a slice in one dimension does not have to equal the size of a slice in another dimension. The slices must be made such that they partition the color space into no more than 256 blocks. For example, if we are quantizing to 256 colors, then we could have 16 segments in the red direction, 4 in the green direction, and 4 in the blue direction, yielding $16 \times 4 \times 4 = 256$ blocks; or we could have dimensions of $8 \times 8 \times 4$, or any other combination that gives 256 blocks. We could even have fewer than 256 if we don't mind sacrificing some colors, for example using dimensions of $6 \times 6 \times 6$.

Imagine the color space partitioned uniformly giving eight values of red, eight of green, and four of blue. This is a reduction from 256 values for each red to only eight values. In this partitioning, the red component would map to values between 0 and 7 as follows:

| TABLE 3.2 | Uniform Partitioning for Indexed Color | |
|---|---|---|
| **Range of Reds in the Original Image (decimal values)** | **Range of Red in the Original Image (binary values)** | **Index to Which They Map in the Color Table** |
| 0–31 | 00000000–00011111 | 0 |
| 32–63 | 00100000–00111111 | 1 |
| 64–95 | 01000000–01011111 | 2 |
| 96–127 | 01100000–01111111 | 3 |
| 128–159 | 10000000–10011111 | 4 |
| 160–191 | 10100000–10111111 | 5 |
| 192–223 | 11000000–11011111 | 6 |
| 224–255 | 11100000–11111111 | 7 |

Essentially, all colors from the original file whose first three bits are 0 map to position 0 in the color table, all whose first three bits are 001 map to position 1, and so forth. Green would map similarly, and blue would be mapped in a coarser-grained fashion to just four values.

The disadvantage of uniform partitioning is that it does not account for the fact that the equal-sized partitions of the color space may not be equally populated. There may be many colors in one partition, and only a few in another. All the colors in a heavily populated partition will be converted to a single color, and smooth transitions of color will be lost in the image.

A combination of the popularity and the uniform partition algorithms can be achieved as follows: Again assume that $n$ is the bit depth of the original image, and $b$ will be the bit depth of the converted image. Imagine that you want to get a count of how many times each of the $2^n$ colors appears in a picture. You could allocate an array of $2^n$ integers, read the image file, and increment position $i$ in the array each time the corresponding color is encountered. By this brute force method, if $n = 24$, you could need a $2^{24} = 16,777,216$ element array. That's pretty large. Instead, you could allocate a $2^k$ element array, where $b < k < 24$. For example, $k$ could be 12, giving a $2^{12} = 4,096$ element array. Then, for each pixel in the image file, consider only the first $k/3$ bits in each of the color channels. The positions in the color table are incremented each time a color is encountered, but on the basis of the first $k/3$ bits of each of the color channels only. Then the $2^b$ most frequently appearing color-ranges from among the $2^k$ in the color frequency table are chosen for the final color table. As before, the minimum mean squared distance is used to convert each original color to one of the colors in this color table.

Consider how this would work in the case where $n = 24$, $b = 8$, and $k = 12$.

- For each pixel, consider only the first $k/3 = 4$ bits in each of the R, G, and B color channels, for a total of 12 bits total. This is equivalent to taking groups of 4,096 neighboring colors and making them all one "average" color.
- Run through the original image file and count how many of the pixels fall into each of the 4,096 categories.
- Take the $2^b = 256$ most frequently occurring of these categories and use them in the final indexed color table for your image.
- Finally, to convert your image file based on this color table, take each of the original pixels and map it to the closest of the colors in the color table based on minimum mean squared distance.

Supplement on
indexed color
algorithms:

programming
exercise

The *median-cut algorithm* is superior to uniform partitioning in that it does a better balancing of the number of colors in a partition. The first step, as before, is to reduce the RGB color space to the smallest block containing all the colors in the image. The algorithm proceeds by a stepwise partitioning where at each step some sub-block containing $2^n = c$ colors is divided in half along its longest dimension such that $c/2$ of the existing colors from the image are in one half and $c/2$ are in the other. After this halving, the new sub-blocks are placed on a queue, possibly to be divided again later, until there are finally $2^b$ sub-blocks. When the color space has been partitioned, a color in the center of each sub-block can be chosen as representative of all colors in that sub-block.

The *octree algorithm* is similar to the median-cut algorithm in that it partitions the color space with attention to color population. The algorithm is implemented by means of a tree that has a depth of eight where each node can have up to eight children. This yields a maximum of $8^8$ leaf nodes. (Note that $8^8 = 2^{24}$.) However, only $2^b$ leaf nodes are actually created, each leaf node corresponding to a color in the reduced-bit depth image. We assume for this discussion that $n = 24$ and $b = 8$.

The octree algorithm has two major steps—determining the colors to use in the reduced-bit depth image, and converting the original image to fewer colors on the basis of the chosen color table.

Inserting first pixel into octree where pixel's RGB components are

R: 00100111
G: 11101000
B: 01111111

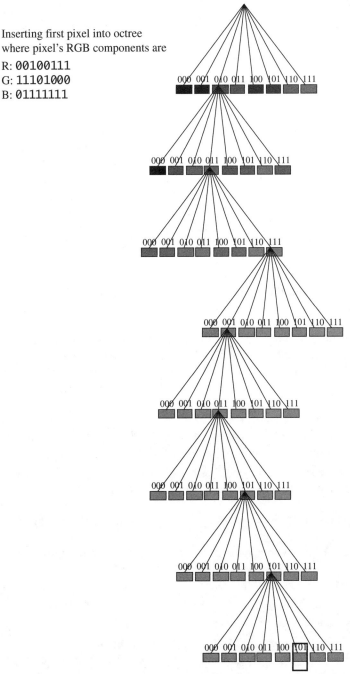

**Figure 3.2**  Building an octree, one pixel inserted

Let's consider creation of the octree first, which essentially gives us a color table. Initially, a root node is created in the octree with the possibility of up to eight children. For each pixel in the image, the R, G, and B components are given in binary as $R = r_1 r_2 r_3 \ldots r_m$, $G = g_1 g_2 g_3 \ldots g_m$, and $B = b_1 b_2 b_3 \ldots b_m$. The algorithm processes each pixel by considering its bits from most significant to least significant, numbering these from 1 to $m$. The numbering of the bits matches the level numbers of the tree, which is numbered from the root beginning at 0. (Note that $m = n/3$.) For each $i$, the bits at position $i$ of the pixel being processed through the tree are concatenated as one value, $r_i g_i b_i$. These three bits together can be taken as a value $j$. Then we create a $j$th child node of the current node.

For example, say that the pixel currently being inserted into the tree is

$R = 11000110$
$G = 01010101$
$B = 11100011$

and $i = 1$. Then $r_1 g_1 b_1 = 101_2$, which has the value 5. Starting at the root node of the tree, we move to the root's 5th child node. If no such child node exists, one is created. It is recorded in this child node that the node has been "visited," *i.e.*, that a pixel has been encountered with this value for the most significant bit of the combined R, G, and B components. The next most significant bits are then considered. They combine to form the decimal value 7, so we move to child 7 of the current node, thus moving down to level 2, and creating the child node if it does not already exist. The child node is marked as having been visited. This continues down the tree to a leaf node, each leaf node corresponding to a 24-bit color. The process repeats for each pixel in the original image file.

We have omitted some details in the description of how a pixel is recorded. Each time a pixel is processed through the tree, there is the possibility that a new leaf node will be created. However, we ultimately want only $2^b$ leaf nodes representing $2^b$ colors to be used in the indexed color image. Thus, if processing a pixel results in the creation of a leaf node $2^b + 1$, some nodes need to be combined. A reducible node—one that has at least two children—must be found at the lowest possible level. If the reducible node has $k$ children, then after it is reduced there will be room for $k - 1$ new leaf nodes in the tree. Reducing a node indicates that, at this point, all the pixels that passed through the reduced node are grouped as a single color. (The tree may grow again later from this node, however.)

As mentioned above, as pixels are processed in each step, the algorithm records at each node in the tree how often the node has been visited, and by what kind of pixel. Say that variables in each node are as follows:

| | |
|---|---|
| *numVisits* | /*the number of times the node has been visited*/ |
| *RTotal* | /*the sum of the R components of all the pixels that passed through this node*/ |
| *GTotal* | /*the sum of the G components of all the pixels that passed through this node*/ |
| *BTotal* | /*the sum of the B components of all the pixels that passed through this node*/ |
| *isLeaf* | /*a Boolean indicating if this is a leaf node*/ |

Then every node in the tree in effect represents a color—the "average" of all the pixels in the image in a certain R, G, and B range, as given by:

$$colorSubstitute = \left( \frac{RTotal}{numVisits} \right), \left( \frac{GTotal}{numVisits} \right), \left( \frac{BTotal}{numVisits} \right)$$

After the octree has been created, the original image file is processed a second time. The octree is traversed in a manner reflecting the way it was originally created. For each pixel in a file, going from the most significant to the least significant bits in the R, G, and B components, $1 \leq i \leq m$, we move down the octree to the child node corresponding to a grouping of the pixel's $i$th most significant bits. The leaf node we arrive at by this means contains the color representative for the pixel being processed. This node could represent the pixel's color in the original image, or it could be an average of pixels that have the same bit values in their R, G, and B components up to the $i$th level of significance.

The octree method has the advantage of using the image's original colors if possible, and averaging similar colors where this is not possible. It is also efficient in its implementation, since the tree never grows beyond a depth of eight.

# 3.4 DITHERING

*Dithering* is a technique for simulating colors that are unavailable in a palette by using available colors that are blended by the eye so that they look like the desired colors. Dithering is helpful when you change an image from RGB mode to indexed color because it makes it possible to reduce the bit depth of the image, and thus the file size, without greatly changing the appearance of the original image.

In an image processing program, if you change an image from RGB mode to indexed mode, you'll probably have a choice of palette sizes and dithering methods. In eight-bit indexed color, if your image is to be placed on the web you may choose to limit the palette to the 216 *web-safe colors*. All web browsers use the same web-safe palette for eight-bit color, and if you choose this palette you know how your picture will look to others, even those whose browsers or monitors are limited to eight bits. For aesthetic reasons or for reasons having to do with file size, you can also limit your image to a smaller bit depth and palette. Whatever your choice of bit depth, you can choose to dither the image or not. If reducing the bit depth of your image creates undesirable sharply delineated areas of solid color, dithering is a good option.

Dithering algorithms are easy to understand if you consider first how dithering would be done to simulate the look of a grayscale image using only pure black and pure white pixels. Let's look at the three dithering methods that are commonly used in image processing programs: noise, pattern, and error diffusion dithering.

First consider what would happen if you have a grayscale image that uses eight bits per pixel and decide to reduce it to a black and white bitmap that uses one bit per pixel. A sensible algorithm to accomplish this would change pixel values less than 128 to black and values greater than or equal to 128 to white. This is called *thresholding*.

As you can see from Figure 3.3, thesholding results in large patches of black and white. *Noise dithering* (also called *random dithering*) eliminates the patchiness and high black/white contrast by adding high frequency noise—speckles of black and white that, when combined by the eye, look like shades of gray. The algorithm for a grayscale image proceeds by choosing a random number between 0 and $2^b - 1$ for each pixel, where $b$ is the bit depth of the indexed image. If the pixel's color value is less than the random number, the pixel is made black; if it's greater, it is white. (Otherwise, choose a new random number.) This algorithm has been applied to the picture in Figure 3.4. It is actually *too* noisy, but the effect can be softened by various means—like not inserting noise with every pixel (using a random number again, to determine when noise will be inserted).

Supplements on dithering:

interactive tutorial

worksheet

programming exercise

**Figure 3.3** Thresholding

**Figure 3.4** Noise (*i.e.*, random) dithering (very noisy)

*Pattern dithering* (also called *ordered dithering* or the *Bayer method*) uses a regular pattern of dots to simulate colors. An $m \times m$ array of values between 1 and $m^2$ is applied to each $m \times m$ block of pixels in the image file. We call this array a *mask*. The numbers in the mask will determine the appearance of the pattern in the dithered image file. Say that they are as shown below:

```
1    7    4
5    8    3
6    2    9
```

For each $m \times m$ block of pixels in the original image, each pixel value $p$ is scaled to a value $p'$ between 0 and $m^2$. In this case, we can divide all the pixels by 25.6 and drop the remainder. Assuming that the values initially are between 0 and 255, this will result in normalized values between 0 and 9. Then the normalized pixel value is compared to the value in the corresponding position in the mask. If $p'$ is less than that value, the pixel is given the value 0, or black; otherwise, it is white. Pattern dithering is easy and fast, but it can result in a

**Figure 3.5** Pattern dithering

crosshatched effect (Figure 3.5). There are many variations of this basic algorithm, applying masks of different sizes and types.

*Error diffusion dithering* (also called the *Floyd–Steinberg algorithm*) is a method that disperses the error, or difference between a pixel's original value and the color (or grayscale) value available. In sketch, here's how it works. For each pixel, the difference between the original color and the color available is calculated. Then this error is divided up and distributed to neighboring pixels that have not yet been visited. After all pixels have been visited, the color used for each pixel is the color in the reduced palette closest to the pixel's new value. Details of the algorithm include a determination of the relative fraction of the error distributed to neighboring pixels, the method for choosing the closest available color, and the order in which pixels are processed. Adjustments can be made to reduce color bleeding (the bleeding of one color into another in the direction in which the error is dispersed).

Consider this example implementation for grayscale images. For each pixel $p$, the error can be distributed in a manner reflected in the mask below.

$$
\begin{array}{ccc}
 & p & 7 \\
3 & 5 & 1
\end{array}
$$

Imagine laying the mask on top of the image, lining it up over the top left $2 \times 3$ pixel area. Each number in the mask pertains to the pixel that it "covers." Call the pixels under the mask $f(r, s)$ where $r$ is the row and $s$ is the column. This gives $p = f(0, 1)$. Let $e$ be the error that would be introduced in changing $p$ if the threshold algorithm were applied, defined as follows: If $p < 128$, then $e = p$ (because thresholding would round $p$ down to 0). If $p \geq 128$, then $e = p - 255$ (because thresholding would round $p$ up to 255, which would become a 1 in a black and white image). Now notice that the numbers in the mask add up to 16. The mask symbolizes that if thresholding would make $p$ greater, then, to compensate, error diffusion should subtract $7/16$ of the error from the pixel to the right of $p$; subtract $5/16$ of the error from the pixel below $p$; subtract $3/5$ from the pixel below and to the left; and subtract $1/16$ from the pixel below and to the right. If thresholding would make $p$ smaller, the corresponding values are added to the neighboring pixels. That is, assignments are made as follows:

$$f(0, 2) = f(0, 2) + (7/16)e$$
$$f(1, 0) = f(1, 0) + (3/16)e$$
$$f(1, 1) = f(1, 1) + (5/16)e$$
$$f(1, 2) = f(1, 2) + (1/16)e$$

The definition of $e$ makes it negative when thresholding would increase $p$. The equations are assignment statements, denoting that the original pixel values are replaced. Thus, when the mask is moved to the right by one pixel, the next step will operate on a pixel that has possibly been changed in a previous step. Pixels can be processed either left to right across each row, or in an alternating motion from left to right and right to left, weaving back and forth. Note that if the error diffusion weaves back and forth, the order of the error multipliers must be flipped accordingly.

After the error has been distributed over the whole image, the pixels are processed a second time. This time for each pixel, if the pixel value is less than 128, it is changed to a 0 in the dithered image. Otherwise it is changed to a 1. The results are shown in Figure 3.6.

**Figure 3.6** Error diffusion dithering

All the dithered images in this section were created "from scratch" using a simple program, one that you could write yourself. (This is why you see pattern edges in the pattern dithering: the edges were handled roughly.) An interesting exercise is to try to write these programs and then compare your results to the dithering done by a professional image processing program that offers the three dithering options we just examined. (See the programming exercise in the learning supplements, which gives more detail to the algorithms.)

## 3.5 CHANNELS, LAYERS, AND MASKS

Digital image processing tools make it easier for you to edit images by allowing you to break them into parts that can be treated separately. Channels are one such breakdown. A channel is a collection of image data, with separate channels for different color components and opacity information. If you're working in RGB mode, there's a channel for each of the red, green, and blue color components. All channels have the same pixel dimensions, those of the overall image. You can edit each channel separately, adjusting its contrast, brightness, saturation, shadows and highlights, and so forth. An additional channel called an *alpha channel* can be added to an image to store the opacity level for each pixel. Figure 3.7 shows the Channels panel from an image editing program, from which you can select a channel for editing. This image includes an alpha channel, at the bottom. The white part of the alpha channel specifies which pixels in the overall image are opaque, and the black part specifies which are transparent.

**Figure 3.7**  R, G, B, and alpha channel (from Photoshop)

A *layer* in image editing is just what the name implies. You can imagine layers to be like sheets of transparent acetate that are laid one on top of another. In areas where there is nothing on a layer, the layer beneath is visible. How can it happen that some areas of a layer have nothing on them? This can happen when you cut something out of one image and paste it into a layer of a second image, as shown in Figure 3.8. The rose was cut out of another image and placed into the image shown. The area around the flower on the layer named *Rose* is transparent, represented by the gray and white checkered pattern. The *Leaves* layer underneath shows through the transparent areas of the *Rose* layer. Notice that each layer has an opacity setting, shown in the Opacity box on the top right of the panel.

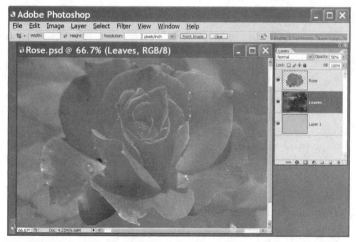

**Figure 3.8**  Layers (from Photoshop)

The *Leaves* layer's opacity is set to 50%, so the solid color background shows through, softening the overall effect and making the rose stand out more.

If you want to specify the opacity level of a layer pixel-by-pixel, you can do this with either an alpha channel or a layer mask, depending on how your image editing software works. An alpha channel is a type of mask in that it can block the visibility of pixels, either fully or partially. The alpha channel has the same pixel dimensions as the overall image. Assuming that the alpha channel is represented by eight bits per pixel, then the closer an alpha channel value is to 255, the more opaque the corresponding pixel in the image. An alpha channel value (alpha value, for short) of 0 corresponds to a fully transparent pixel. (This convention can be reversed in some application programs such that 0 represents fully opaque, so be sure to check.) The alpha values can be normalized to fall between 0 and 1, as shown in Figure 3.9.

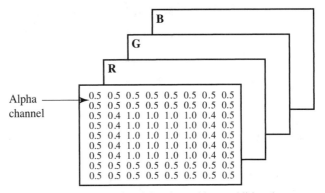

The alpha channel is an additional channel, giving the opacity level of the RGB color.

**Figure 3.9** Alpha channel

*Alpha blending* is a mathematical procedure for putting together multiple images or layers with varying levels of opacity. In the simplest case, you have a foreground pixel with a certain opacity level and an opaque background. In that case, alpha blending works as follows:

## KEY EQUATION

Given is an RGB image with two layers, foreground and background, the background being 100% opaque. Let a foreground pixel be given by $F = (f_r, f_g, f_b)$ a background pixel be given by $B = (b_r, b_g, b_b)$. Let the alpha value for the foreground, representing the opacity level, be $\alpha_f$ where $0 \le \alpha_f \le 1$. Then for each foreground pixel $F$ and corresponding background pixel $B$ at the same location in the image, the resulting composite pixel color $C = (c_r, c_g, c_b)$ created by alpha blending is defined

$$c_r = \alpha_f f_r + (1 - \alpha_f)b_r$$
$$c_g = \alpha_f f_g + (1 - \alpha_f)b_g$$
$$c_b = \alpha_f f_b + (1 - \alpha_f)b_b$$

Henceforth, we'll condense operations such as this to the form $C = \alpha_f F + (1 - \alpha_f)B$, which is meant to imply that the operations are done channel-by-channel.

Let's try an example. If the foreground pixel is (248, 98, 218) with 60% opacity and the background pixel is (130, 152, 74), the result will be (201, 120, 160), as computed below and pictured in Figure 3.10.

$$0.6 * 248 + 0.4 * 130 = 201$$
$$0.6 * 98 + 0.4 * 152 = 120$$
$$0.6 * 218 + 0.4 * 74 = 160$$

In the figure, the area where the blocks overlap is the area of the composite color.

**Figure 3.10** Compositing, pink foreground that is 60% opaque with 100% opaque green background

Alpha blending can get more complicated when there are multiple layers, each with its own opacity level. We'll look at this in more detail in Chapter 7, as it applied to the compositing processes used in digital video.

Image processing programs do the mathematics of alpha blending for you, allowing you to create alpha channels or define opacity levels in a number of different ways. One simple method is to add an alpha channel to an image and paint on it to indicate which parts of the image you want to be transparent. First you choose a grayscale value between 0 and 255 for your paint color. Then you apply that color to the alpha channel by painting with a brush, creating filled geometric shapes, applying gradients, or using any other methods for applying color to pixels. The closer the color on the alpha channel is to black, the more transparent the corresponding pixels will be in the image.

A second way to make an alpha channel is to select the part of an image that you want to be visible in an image and then convert the selection to an alpha channel. This is the way the alpha channel was created in Figure 3.7. The blue background behind the Demon Deacon puppet was selected with a magic wand tool, which selects similar colors within a given tolerance. The selection was then inverted so that the puppet was selected and the background left out. Then the selection was saved as an alpha channel.

The image shown in Figure 3.7 has an alpha channel that effectively makes the background invisible, but there's no layer underneath to show through. In Chapter 7, we'll show you how you can import such an image into a video editing program, lay it over a video track, and allow the images on the video track to show through.

If you want to extract an object from its background and put another background behind it, all within the same image, you can do this with a layer mask. A *layer mask* is an alpha channel applied to a layer in a multiple-layer image (as opposed to an alpha channel applied to the image as a whole). The concept is still the same—*i.e.*, a channel of pixel data indicates the opacity level of each pixel in a layer. We created another picture of the Deacon walking across campus, this time composing the entire image in an image processing program. This was done by putting the Deacon on the top layer, applying a layer mask to that layer, eliminating the background from that layer, and putting a new background on the bottom layer. In Figure 3.11, you can see a layer mask in the Layers panel and a corresponding alpha channel in the Channels panel.

**Figure 3.11** Alpha channel (as a layer mask) on an individual layer

You may want to note that you can have transparent or partially transparent pixels in an image without explicitly having an alpha channel. You've actually seen this already, in the example in Figure 3.8. In this image, part of the rose was selected from its background and the background was erased. Also, the layers themselves have an opacity setting. Thus you see that opacity information can be part of an image file without your having explicit access to the alpha channel. An advantage to explicitly creating an alpha channel is that you don't lose any pixel information by making pixels transparent. The color values are still there, and the alpha channel can easily be edited.

With GIF files, which are in indexed color mode, you can save transparency information without an alpha channel. The transparency information is saved as a pixel color in the color table. You can see this in Figure 3.12. This image, which initially was in RGB mode, was created by first converting the background to a layer, selecting the background, deleting the

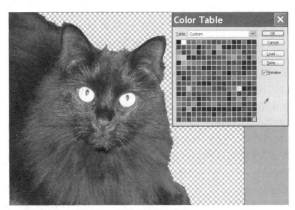

**Figure 3.12** GIF file with one color in color table representing transparency

background, and saving as GIF. You can see in the color table that there is one color reserved to represent transparent pixels (in the lower right corner of the table). Whether or not this transparency information is recognized depends on the application program into which you import the GIF file.

## 3.6 BLENDING MODES

In addition to opacity settings, layers have blending modes associated with them. In the figures shown so far in this section, the blending modes have been set to Normal. (Blending modes can be applied to paint tools as well as to layers, indicating how the painted pixels should combine with already-painted pixels.) The Blending Mode setting for a layer is to the left of the Opacity setting on the Layers panel in Figure 3.11.

Blending modes create a variety of effects in making a composite of a foreground and background image. For example, the darken mode replaces a background pixel with the foreground pixel only if the foreground pixel is darker. The lighten mode does an analogous lightening process. The multiply mode, as the name implies, multiplies the foreground and background pixel values. Since pixel values are normalized to fall between 0 and 1, multiply always darkens an image, unless the background is pure white. The blending operations are

Supplement on
blending modes:

programming
exercise

| TABLE 3.3 | Blending Modes |
|---|---|
| **Blending Mode** | **Equation** |
| normal | $C = F$ |
| multiply | $C = F * B$ |
| divide | $C = \left( \dfrac{B}{F + \dfrac{1}{255}} \right)\left( \dfrac{256}{255} \right)$ |
| screen | $C = 1 - ((1 - F)(1 - B))$ |
| overlay | $C = B(B + 2F(1 - B))$ |
| dodge | $C = \left( \dfrac{B}{\dfrac{256}{255} - F} \right)\left( \dfrac{256}{255} \right)$ |
| burn | $C = 1 - \left( \left( \dfrac{1 - B}{F + \dfrac{1}{255}} \right)\left( \dfrac{256}{255} \right) \right)$ |
| hard light | If $F > 0.5$ then $C = 1 - 2(1 - B)(1 - F)$<br>If $F \leq 0.5$ then $C = 2(F * B)$ |
| soft light | $C = 2(F * B) + B^2 - 2(F * B^2)$ |
| grain extract | $C = B - F + 0.5$ |
| grain merge | $C = B + F - 0.5$ |
| difference | $C = |B - F|$ |
| addition | $C = B + F$ |
| subtraction | $C = B - F$ |
| darken only | $C = \min(B, F)$ |
| lighten only | $C = \max(B, F)$ |

done channel-by-channel. Table 3.3 lists the equations for a number of common blending modes. The pixel values in these equations are assumed to be scaled to a range of 0 to 1.

> Given is an RGB image with two layers, foreground and background, with 100% opacity on each layer. Let a foreground pixel be given by $F = (f_r, f_g, f_b)$ and a background pixel be defined by $B = (b_r, b_g, b_b)$ where $0 \leq f_r, f_g, f_b, b_r, b_g, b_b \leq 1$. Then for each foreground pixel $F$ and corresponding background pixel $B$ at the same location in the image, the resulting composite pixel color $C = (c_r, c_g, c_b)$ is defined for each blending mode in Table 3.3. The equations are applied channel-by-channel, and results are clipped to a range of 0 to 1.

The equations in the table were adapted from a GIMP website. Newer versions of GIMP and other image processing programs may use different equations.

Dissolve, hue, saturation, value are sometimes listed as blending modes as well, although they are not implemented by single channel equations. Dissolve mode operates by randomly dithering the alpha channel of the foreground to black and white. Hue takes the hue of the foreground (where the hue is defined) and the saturation and value of the background. Saturation and value modes operate analogously. Color blending modeworks as a combination of hue and saturation blending modes.

The blending mode equations given in Table 3.3 do not take into account the alpha channels of the foreground and background layers. How blending and alpha channels are combined is implementation-dependent in different application programs. Generally, the foreground's alpha affects only the strength of the blend, while the background's alpha sets the opacity level.

## 3.7 PIXEL POINT PROCESSING

### 3.7.1 Histograms

Supplements on histograms:

interactive tutorial

worksheet

When you work with bitmap images, you generally have something you want to communicate or an effect you want to create. It may be that you simply want your image to be as clear and detailed as possible. If you're working on the image as art, you might want to provoke a certain mood or alter colors and shading that affect the aesthetics of the image. If you're using the image to sell something, you may want to change the focus or emphasis. Whatever your goals, you will find yourself doing operations like adjusting the contrast or brightness, sharpening lines, modifying colors, or smoothing edges. Each of these operations is an example of an image transform—a process of changing the color or grayscale values of image pixels. The following discussion divides image transforms into two types: *pixel point processing* and *spatial filtering*. In pixel point processing, a pixel value is changed based only on its original value, without reference to surrounding pixels. Spatial filtering, on the other hand, changes a pixel's value based on the values of neighboring pixels. (You've already seen an example of spatial filtering: dithering.) This section looks at pixel point processing, and in the next section we'll move on to more examples of spatial filtering.

One of the most useful tools for pixel point processing is the histogram. A *histogram* is a discrete function that describes frequency distribution; that is, it maps a range of discrete values to the number of instances of each value in a group of numbers. More precisely,

---

### KEY EQUATION

Let $v_i$ be the number of instances of value $i$ in the set of numbers. Let *min* be the minimum allowable value of $i$, and let *max* be the maximum. Then the *histogram function* is defined as

$$h(i) = v_i \text{ for } min \leq i \leq max.$$

---

A simple histogram is shown in Figure 3.13 for a group of 32 students identified by class (1 for freshman, 2 for sophomore, 3 for junior, and 4 for senior). You can see that a histogram is graphed as vertical lines (or sometimes vertical bars are used). There are ten freshmen, six sophomores, five juniors, and 11 seniors.

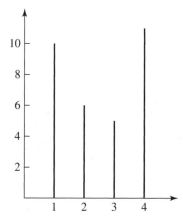

**Figure 3.13** A histogram

An image histogram maps pixel values to the number of instances of each value in the image. A grayscale image and its corresponding histogram are shown in Figure 3.14. Grayscale levels extend from 0 to 255 across the horizontal axis. Each of these values has a vertical line above it indicating the number of pixels in the image that have this value. In practice, image histograms are usually normalized by dividing by the maximum number of instances of a pixel value within the range of values in the image. This is illustrated in the figure below. The value that occurs most frequently in the image is the statistical *mode*. In this example, there are two modes, 141 and 143, occurring with the same frequency. The tallest vertical line is at this point, and it goes to the top of the histogram. Normalizing histograms in this way makes it easier to compare the histograms of two images that don't have the same total number of pixels, since all normalized histograms have a height of one unit.

One of the most important things to observe from a histogram is the extent to which the pixel values cover the possible range. Consider the example in Figure 3.14. The darkest pixel is 58, and the lightest is 210. In other words, the image does not have a wide dynamic

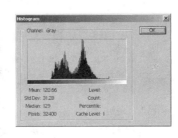

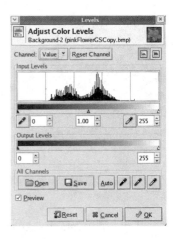

**Figure 3.14** Low contrast grayscale image and its histogram (from Photoshop and GIMP)

range. Consequently, it doesn't have a lot of contrast. All the values are crowded together in the center of the histogram. This generally isn't what you want in an image. Contrast makes the image look sharper and more interesting.

Some histograms, like the one in Figure 3.14, give statistical information about the distribution of pixel values, including the mean, median, and the standard deviation. Assume that you have $n$ samples in a data set. For our purposes, a sample is a pixel value.

---

### 🔑 KEY EQUATION

The *mean*, or average, $\bar{x}$ is defined as:

$$\bar{x} = \frac{1}{n}\sum_{i=1}^{n} x_i$$

---

A *median* is a value $x$ such that at most half of the values in the sample population are less than $x$ and at most half are greater. If the number of sample values is even, the median may not be unique. For example, with [1, 3, 5, 7], any value between 3 and 5 inclusive is a median. Commonly, however, the mean of the two values in the middle is considered the median.

---

### 🔑 KEY EQUATION

The *standard deviation* measures how much the samples vary from the average. It is defined as

$$\sigma = \sqrt{\frac{1}{n}\sum_{i=1}^{n}(x_i - \bar{x})^2}$$

where $x_i$ is the $i$th sample in a population of $n$ samples.

A large standard deviation implies that most of the pixel values are relatively far from the average, so the values are pretty well spread out over the possible range. Generally, this means that a higher standard deviation is indicative of more contrast in the image. However, you have to be careful how you interpret this. If you had only the standard deviation of an image file's histogram and didn't see the image, you might be fooled. The histogram gives you an overview of the pixel values that exist in an image, but it doesn't tell you anything about *where* they are. Think about this: What type of grayscale image would give you the largest standard deviation? One that has an equal number of purely black and white pixels in it, right? The only pixel values in such an image would be at both extremes: 0 and 255. But both of the images in Figure 3.15 fit this description. The one on the left is perceived as having more contrast because the black and white pixels are spatially separated. The image on the left has alternating black and white pixels, so it looks like a shade of gray.

**Figure 3.15** Two figures with the same histogram and standard deviation

Histograms are available in scanner software, digital cameras, and image processing programs. You should check your hardware and software to see what type of histograms they offer and how they are used. In scanner software or digital cameras, a histogram can help you adjust lighting or make settings when you capture an image so that you'll get the maximum amount of appropriate pixel data. With a scanner, you can prescan a digital image and then view the histogram to see what adjustments are necessary before the final scan. With a digital camera, you can take a picture and then view a histogram to decide if you need to take the picture again with different settings or lighting conditions. If most of the pixel values are grouped in the center of the histogram, you may want to adjust your lighting to increase contrast. If most of the values are to the right of center, the image is probably too light. If most are to the left, it's probably too dark.

Sometimes a histogram is displayed along with the image just photographed or prescanned, and the areas that are *clipped* in the image are outlined for you in the image. Clipped values are those that fall outside the sensitivity range of the camera or scanner. If an area is too dark, all the pixels there register as black (0), and if the area is too light they become white (255 in grayscale). Some scanners allow you to increase the *analog gain*— the luminance of the scanner's light source—so that enough light can pass through the source image's darker tones, allowing them to be measured.

Changing the lighting and adjusting analog gain are examples of ways to use a histogram to capture good image data from the outset. Gathering the best data possible from the outset is always the best plan. But even with the best planning, you'll still have many situations where you want to alter the captured image in some way. Histograms are very useful in image processing programs for situations like these.

Before showing you how to adjust contrast or brightness with a histogram, we need to clarify how different color modes are handled. In RGB mode, each pixel has three color channels where the values in each channel range from 0 to 255. (Larger bit depths are possible, but eight bits per channel is common.) A separate histogram can be created for each color channel. The R histogram, for example, shows how many pixels have 0 for their R component, how many have 1 for their R component, and so forth up to 255. A composite RGB histogram can also be constructed, which for $0 \leq j \leq 255$ shows the total number of pixels that have $j$ as their R component plus the pixels that have $j$ as their G component plus the pixels that have $j$ as their B component.

A disadvantage of the composite RGB histogram is that it doesn't correspond directly to the perceived brightness of an image. Among the three color channels, the human eye is most sensitive to green and least sensitive to blue. This fact is reflected in the way that RGB color is transformed to grayscale. Recall from Chapter 2 that a three-byte RGB color can be converted to a one-byte grayscale pixel with value $L$ using

$$L = 0.30R + 0.59G + 0.11B$$

Some scanners or image processing programs give you access to a *luminance histogram* (also called a *luminosity histogram*) corresponding to a color image. A luminance histogram converts the RGB values into luminance, as shown above, and then creates the histogram from these values.

Figure 3.16 shows a histogram that can be manipulated to alter the brightness or contrast of a grayscale image. Notice the triangles on either side of the histogram, marked with the arrows. These triangles can be moved left or right and correspond to values labeled Input Levels. Say that you move the slider on the left to 55 and the one on the right to 186. Assuming that you don't move the middle slider, this maps the input pixel values to output values such that the pixel that was originally 55 becomes 0, the pixel that was previously 186 becomes 255, and everything in between is spread out proportionately. This increases the contrast and allows for more differences between the grayscale values in the image. If you apply this transform and then look at the histogram again, the new histogram looks like Figure 3.17. (Actually, you can open the Histogram window and watch the histogram change there as you move the sliders in the Levels window.) Notice that now the whole range of possible grayscale values is being used.

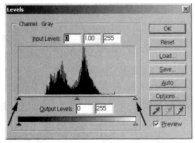

**Figure 3.16** A histogram that can be manipulated to adjust brightness and contrast (from Photoshop)

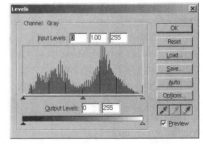

**Figure 3.17** Histogram of image in Figure 3.16 after contrast adjustment (from Photoshop)

The middle value in the Input Levels input fields is called the *gamma level* and relates to the midtones of the image. You can manipulate this value by moving the center triangle-shaped slider on the histogram. If you move the middle slider and leave the left and right sliders where they are, you can manipulate the midtones without affecting the lightest and darkest values—the highlights and shadows—in the image. If you do this, you'll see that the gamma value ranges from 0.10 to 9.99. In the next section, we'll look at the mathematics to see why this range of gamma values makes sense.

## 3.7.2 Transform Functions and "Curves"

Image processing programs sometimes give you another mathematical/graphical view of image data from which you can perform pixel point processing. In programs like Photoshop and GIMP, the Curves feature allows you to think of the changes you make to pixel values as a transform function. Let's look at pixel point processing from this point of view now.

Supplements on curves:

interactive tutorial

worksheet

We define a *transform* as a function that changes pixel values. Expressed as a function in one variable, it is defined as

$$g(x, y) = T(f(x, y))$$

$f(x, y)$ is the pixel value at that position $(x, y)$ in the original image, $T$ is the transformation function, and $g(x, y)$ is the transformed pixel value. Let's abbreviate $f(x, y)$ as $p_1$ and $g(x, y)$ as $p_2$. This gives us

$$p_2 = T(p_1)$$

Transforms can be applied to pixel values in a variety of color modes. If the pixels are grayscale, then $p_1$ and $p_2$ are values between 0 and 255. If the color mode is RGB or some other three-component model, $f(p)$ implies three components, and the transform may be applied either to each of the components separately or to the three as a composite. For simplicity, let's look at transforms as they apply to grayscale images first.

An easy way to understand a transform function is to look at its graph. A graph of transform function $T$ for a grayscale image has $p_1$ on the horizontal axis and $p_2$ on the vertical axis, with the values on both axes going from 0 to 255—that is, from black to white.

Consider the graphs in Figure 3.18. In each case, what would the corresponding transform do to a digital image?

- The transform in Figure 3.18a doesn't change the pixel values. The output equals the input.
- The transform in Figure 3.18b lightens all the pixels in the image by a constant amount.
- The transform in Figure 3.18c darkens all the pixels in the image by a constant amount.
- The transform in Figure 3.18d inverts the image, reversing dark pixels for light ones.
- The transform in Figure 3.18e is a threshold function, which makes all the pixels either black or white. A pixel with a value below 128 becomes black, and all the rest become white.
- The transform in Figure 3.18f increases contrast. Darks become darker and lights become lighter.

Image processing programs have features to automatically adjust the contrast or color levels for you. Many also give you greater control by allowing you to manipulate a graph of the transform function. Figure 3.19 shows the Curves dialog box from Photoshop and GIMP, where you can select points and drag them to adjust contrast or brightness. This makes it

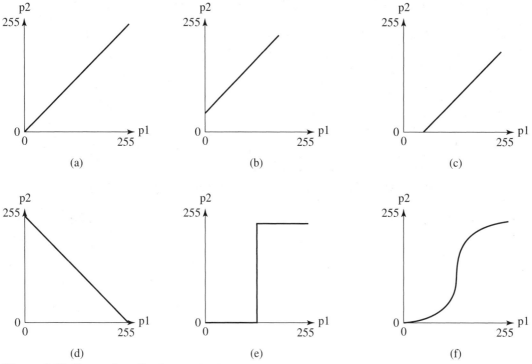

**Figure 3.18** Curves for adjusting contrast

Initially, the "curve" is a straight line. You can select points and drag to reshape the function, as shown on the right.

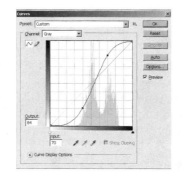

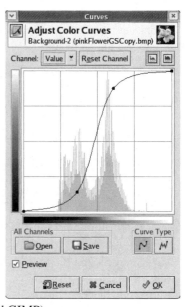

**Figure 3.19** Adjusting the curve of the contrast function (from Photoshop and GIMP)

| (a) Original image | (b) Lighten | (c) Darken |
| --- | --- | --- |
| (d) Invert | (e) Threshold | (f) Increase contrast |

**Figure 3.20** Adjusting contrast and brightness with curves function

possible to create functions like the ones shown in Figure 3.18. In Figure 3.20, we've applied the functions shown in Figure 3.18 so you can see for yourself what effect they have.

The adjustment we made in contrast using the histogram could be done with a graphical view of the transform function as well. Say that you want to adjust the image in Figure 3.16 in a way that would be equivalent to moving the histogram's left slider to 55 and its right slider to 186, as described in Figure 3.17.

Moving the histogram slider on the left from 0 to 55 and on the right from 255 to 186 is equivalent to the transform function pictured in Figure 3.21. If you start with two

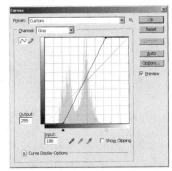

**Figure 3.21** Curve to accomplish the same contrast adjustment as done with the histogram (from Photoshop)

identical images, perform the histogram adjustment on one, perform the curves adjustment on the other, and then look at the new histogram of each, you'll see that you end up with identical histograms and identical images. Both histograms will look like the one in Figure 3.17.

Notice that the transform function we applied to the midtones is linear. When you move the Input Level sliders on the left and right of the histogram but don't move the middle slider, the grayscale values in between are adjusted by a linear function. The histogram's middle slider corresponds to midtones. When the histogram is adjusted, grayscale values are spread out linearly on either side of this value.

A nonlinear function like the S-curve in Figure 3.19 usually does a smoother job of adjusting the contrast. You can create a smooth S-curve like this by clicking on points in the graph and dragging them to new locations. Equivalently, you can change the gamma value in the histogram. We promised earlier to look at the math of the gamma value, and we can do it now with reference to the graph of the transform function.

## 🔑 KEY EQUATION

The *gamma value* $\gamma$ is an exponent that defines a nonlinear relationship between the input level $p_1$ and the output level $p_2$ for a pixel transform function. In particular,

$$p_1 = p_2{}^{\gamma} \text{ where } p_1 \in [0\,1]$$

**Equation 3.1**

Equation 3.1 may seem a little strange because the input level $p_1$ is on the left-hand side of the equation; it seems more natural to think of $p_2$ as a function of $p_1$. We could rewrite the equation to express $p_2$ as the gamma[th] root of $p_1$, but it amounts to the same thing. We give the equation in the form above because it matches the way Photoshop handles the gamma values in its Levels features, as we'll show below.

Think about what the graph of $p_1 = p_2{}^{\gamma}$ would look like for various values of gamma, with $p_1$ defining the horizontal axis and $p_2$ defining the vertical. The graph on the left is for $p_1 = p_2{}^2$ for $0 \le p_1 \le 1$ (which is the same as for $p_2 = \sqrt{p_1}$.) Photoshop's histogram view allows you to use gamma values between 0.1 and 9.99. The graph on the right in Figure 3.22 shows a gamma value of 0.5 as used by Photoshop. (It's the graph for $p_1 = p_2{}^{0.5}$

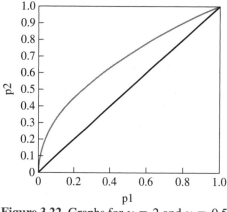
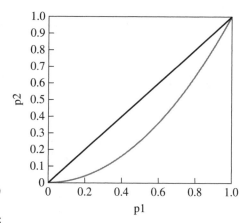

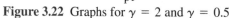

**Figure 3.22** Graphs for $\gamma = 2$ and $\gamma = 0.5$

for $0 \leq p_1 \leq 1$, which is $p_2 = p_1{}^2$.) If you compare the graph to the $p_2 = p_1$ line, you see that this gamma value causes all values to get darker with the exception of 0 and 1. The values in the middle are changed more than those at the end. In general, gamma values less than 1 darken an image while values greater than 1 lighten it.

Changing the gamma value in the histogram view of Figure 3.16 is equivalent to pulling on a point in the graph of the transform function, represented in the Curves view of Figure 3.19. As you pull a chosen point, the graph is stretched as smoothly as possible to accommodate the change, as if you're pulling on an elastic band. The values of lightest and darkest pixels are anchored where they are, but the midtones are lightened or darkened.

Adjustments such as this can be done on color images as well, but the operations are more complicated. If you're working in RGB color, you can adjust the curve function for the full RGB color values, or you can adjust the curve for each color channel separately. One thing that makes it more difficult to work with color than with grayscale, however, is that RGB is not a luminance/chrominance model. For the three color components, equal changes of values do not create equal changes in luminosity or perceived brightness or contrast of the image. The green component contributes the most to luminosity, red the second most, and blue the least. Thus, linear changes to the RGB color levels do not produce linear changes in brightness. Also, the three color components combine in a nonlinear way to create the colors we perceive. In any case, it is possible to work with the color channel curves and visually adjust the colors by moving the graphs. The important thing to understand when you are adjusting a single color channel is that you are changing only that channel's contribution to each pixel in the image.

# 3.8 SPATIAL FILTERING

## 3.8.1 Convolutions

A *filter* is an operation performed on digital image data to sharpen, smooth, or enhance some feature, or in some other way modify the image. A distinction can be made between filtering in the spatial versus the frequency domain. *Filtering in the frequency domain* is performed on image data that is represented in terms of its frequency components. *Filtering in the spatial domain* is performed on image data in the form of the pixel's color values. We'll look at the latter type of filtering in this section.

Spatial filtering is done by a mathematical operation called *convolution*, where each output pixel is computed as a weighted sum of neighboring input pixels. Consider a grayscale image as a matrix of grayscale values. (Generalizing to three color channels is straightforward.) Convolution is based on a matrix of coefficients called a *convolution mask* (Figure 3.23). The mask is also sometimes called a *filter*. (We will use these terms interchangeably.) The mask dimensions are less than or equal to the dimensions of the image. Let's call the convolution mask $c$ and the image $f$. Assume the image is of dimensions $M \times N$ and the mask is $m \times n$. You can picture the mask being placed over a block of pixels in an image, starting in the upper left corner. (You may notice that the filter numbering is "flipped" with regard to the image. This is by convention.) The pixel that is to receive a new grayscale value lies at the center of the mask, which implies that the dimensions of the mask must be odd. Assume that pixel $f(x, y)$ is the one to receive the new value.

Supplements on convolution:

interactive tutorial

worksheet

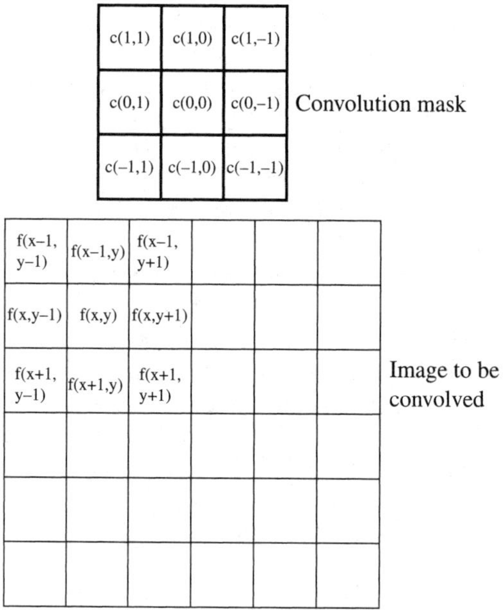

| c(1,1) | c(1,0) | c(1,-1) |
|---|---|---|
| c(0,1) | c(0,0) | c(0,-1) |
| c(-1,1) | c(-1,0) | c(-1,-1) |

Convolution mask

| f(x-1, y-1) | f(x-1,y) | f(x-1, y+1) | | | |
|---|---|---|---|---|---|
| f(x,y-1) | f(x,y) | f(x,y+1) | | | |
| f(x+1, y-1) | f(x+1,y) | f(x+1, y+1) | | | |
| | | | | | |
| | | | | | |
| | | | | | |

Image to be convolved

1. Apply convolution mask to upper left corner of image.
2. Move mask to the right one pixel and apply again.
3. Continue applying mask to all pixels, moving left to right and top to bottom across image.

**Figure 3.23** Convolution

## KEY EQUATION

Let $f(x, y)$ be an $M \times N$ image and $c(v, w)$ be an $m \times n$ mask. Then the equation for a linear convolution is

$$f(x, y) = \sum_{v=-i}^{i} \sum_{w=-j}^{j} c(v, w) f(x - v, y - w)$$

where $i = (m - 1)/2$ and $j = (n - 1)/2$. Assume $m$ and $n$ are odd. This equation is applied to each pixel $f(x, y)$ of an image, for $0 \le x \le M - 1$ and $0 \le y \le N - 1$. (If $x - v < 0$, $x - v \ge M$, $y - w < 0$, or $y - w \ge N$, then $f(x, y)$ is undefined. These are edge cases, discussed below.)

**Equation 3.2**

We have written the convolution equation such that it replaces values in the original image. If you do this, then the new values will be used in the convolution of neighboring pixels. Sometimes this is what you want, and sometimes it isn't, depending on the purpose of the convolution. You should note that sometimes you want to create an entirely new image, and write the new values there so that they aren't used in later computations.

You may wonder what happens at the edges of the image. If we place the mask over the image such that the upper left pixel is the one to receive a new value, then part of the mask

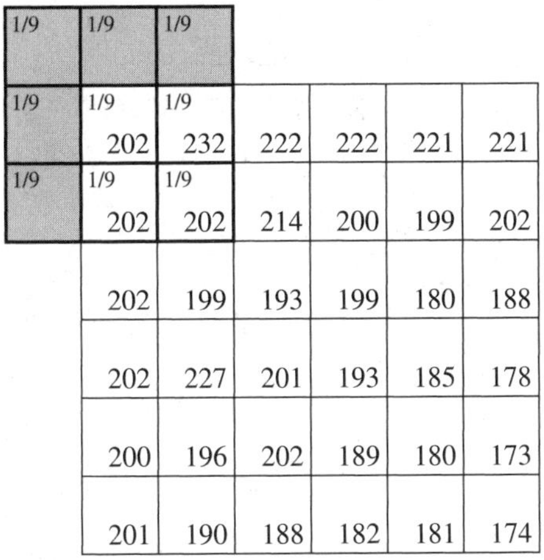

| 1/9 | 1/9 | 1/9 | | | |
|---|---|---|---|---|---|
| 1/9 | 1/9 | 1/9 | | | |
| | 202 | 232 | 222 | 222 | 221 | 221 |
| 1/9 | 1/9 | 1/9 | | | |
| | 202 | 202 | 214 | 200 | 199 | 202 |
| | 202 | 199 | 193 | 199 | 180 | 188 |
| | 202 | 227 | 201 | 193 | 185 | 178 |
| | 200 | 196 | 202 | 189 | 180 | 173 |
| | 201 | 190 | 188 | 182 | 181 | 174 |

Four ways to convolve pixels at the edge of an image:

1. Assume that there are zero-valued pixels around the edges. These would be under the portion of the mask shaded in gray; or

2. Replicate the values from the edges, as shown; ⟶

3. Use only the portion of the mask covering the image and change the weights appropriately for that step; or

4. Don't do convolution on the pixels at the edges.

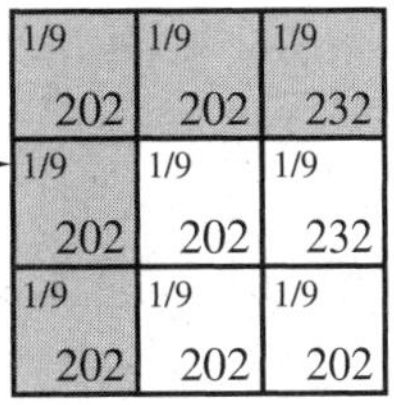

| 1/9 | 1/9 | 1/9 |
|---|---|---|
| 202 | 202 | 232 |
| 1/9 | 1/9 | 1/9 |
| 202 | 202 | 232 |
| 1/9 | 1/9 | 1/9 |
| 202 | 202 | 202 |

**Figure 3.24** Handling edges in convolution

is hanging off the edge of the image. Different ways to handle the edge pixels are summarized in Figure 3.24.

Filters are sometimes used for smoothing or blurring an image. This is done by means of an averaging convolution mask like the one shown in Figure 3.25. There are a number of situations in which blurring is useful. Blurring can be used as a preprocessing step to "pull objects together" so that the main objects in an image can then be detected and extracted. It can be helpful in removing *image noise*, which is manifested as unwanted speckles, which on a grayscale image can look like sprinkles of salt and pepper. It can soften jagged edges or remove moiré patterns in an undersampled image. It can smooth over the blockiness that can be caused by JPEG compression done at a high compression rate. You also might want to smooth an image for aesthetic reasons. Smoothing convolutions are sometimes referred to as *low-pass filters* because their effect is to remove high-frequency components of an image.

The mask shown in Figure 3.25 takes an average of the pixels in a 3 × 3 neighborhood. An alternative for smoothing is to use a *Gaussian blur*, where the coefficients in the convolution mask get smaller as you move away from the center of the mask. It is called a Gaussian blur because the mask values in both the horizontal and vertical directions vary in the shape

| 1/9 | 1/9 | 1/9 |
|-----|-----|-----|
| 1/9 | 1/9 | 1/9 |
| 1/9 | 1/9 | 1/9 |

Convolution mask

| 202 | 232 | 222 | 222 | 221 | 221 |
|-----|-----|-----|-----|-----|-----|
| 202 | 202 | 212 | 200 | 199 | 202 |
| 202 | 222 | 192 | 199 | 180 | 188 |
| 202 | 227 | 201 | 193 | 185 | 178 |
| 200 | 196 | 202 | 189 | 180 | 173 |
| 201 | 190 | 188 | 182 | 181 | 174 |

Image to be convolved

Move the convolution mask over an area of pixels in the original image.

| 1/9  202 | 1/9  232 | 1/9  222 | 222 | 221 | 221 |
|----------|----------|----------|-----|-----|-----|
| 1/9  202 | 1/9  202 | 1/9  214 | 200 | 199 | 202 |
| 1/9  202 | 1/9  199 | 1/9  193 | 199 | 180 | 188 |
| 202 | 227 | 201 | 193 | 185 | 178 |
| 200 | 196 | 202 | 189 | 180 | 173 |
| 201 | 190 | 188 | 182 | 181 | 174 |

This mask will compute an average of the pixels in the neighborhood. The value of the center pixel will become

1/9*202+1/9*232+1/9*222+1/9*202+1/9*202+
1/9*214+1/9*202+1/9*199+1/9*193

**Figure 3.25**　Convolution for averaging pixels in a 3 × 3 neighborhood

of a Gaussian bell curve. These values result in a weighted average of neighboring pixels. In a pure average, all the weights are the same, and they sum to 1. In a weighted average, the coefficients sum to 1, but they are not all the same. For a Gaussian blur, the coefficients closer to the center have more weight than those farther away. A 3 × 3 mask for a Gaussian blur is shown in Figure 3.26. In practice, larger masks are often used for better effect.

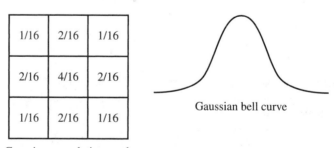

| 1/16 | 2/16 | 1/16 |
|------|------|------|
| 2/16 | 4/16 | 2/16 |
| 1/16 | 2/16 | 1/16 |

Gaussian bell curve

Gaussian convolution mask
**Figure 3.26**　Convolution mask for Gaussian blur

## 3.8.2 Filters in Digital Image Processing Programs

Digital image processing programs like Photoshop and GIMP have an array of filters for you to choose from, for a variety of purposes. Some are corrective filters for sharpening or correcting colors. Some are destructive filters for distorting or morphing images. Some filters create special effects such as simulated brush-strokes, surfaces, and textures. These filters operate by applying convolutions to alter pixel values. (In Chapter 5, we'll show that filtering can equivalently be applied in the frequency domain.) If you understand how different convolution masks will affect your images, you can apply the predefined filters more effectively, even using them in combination with one another. You can also create your own customized masks for creative special effects.

One way to design a convolution mask or predict how a predefined mask will work is to apply it to three simple types of image data: a block of pixels that contains a sharp edge, a block where the center value is different from the rest of the values, and a block where all pixel values are the same. To illustrate these different cases, we'll change our representation of the convolution mask slightly, to make it look more like the way custom filters are presented in Photoshop and GIMP. These application programs allow you to create a custom filter that performs a weighted sum of pixels with a scaling factor and an offset. The pixel values are multiplied by the weights in the mask, the product is divided by the scaling factor, and the offset is added to this total. The custom mask window is shown in Figure 3.27. Assume that blank spaces in the mask are 0s. Since the custom mask varies in its shape and the number of values it contains, and it also involves scaling and offset factors, we need to rewrite Equation 3.2 to describe how each new pixel value is derived from the mask. Let's assume there are $n$ weights in the mask, numbered in row-major order. Let the new pixel value be called $q$ and the weights be given by $w_i$ for $1 \leq i \leq n$. The pixel value corresponding to weight $w_i$ is $p_i$ (that is, the pixel "under" that weight in the mask.) The scale factor is $s$ and the offset is $c$. Then the equation for the new pixel value derived from the mask is

$$q = \left[ \left( \sum_{i=1}^{n} w_i p_i \right) / s \right] + c$$

**Equation 3.3**

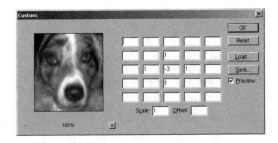
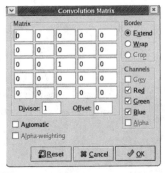

**Figure 3.27**  Custom filter (from Photoshop and GIMP)

In order to preserve the brightness balance of an image, $\sum_{i=1}^{n} w_i / s$ should equal 1. You can easily see this in the case where all the pixels under the mask have the same value. If $\sum_{i=1}^{n} w_i / s > 1$, then the center pixel will be become lighter, and if $\sum_{i=1}^{n} w_i / s < 1$ the center pixel will become darker. You can arrange it so that $\sum_{i=1}^{n} w_i / s = 1$ by making some weights

|||||
|---|---|---|---|
| 255 | 255 | 255 | 255 |
| 255 | 255 | 255 | 255 |
| 255 | 255 | 255 | 255 |
| 0 | 0 | 0 | 0 |
| 0 | 0 | 0 | 0 |
| 0 | 0 | 0 | 0 |

|||||
|---|---|---|---|
| 0 | 0 | 0 | 0 |
| 0 | 0 | 0 | 0 |
| 255 | 255 | 255 | 255 |
| 255 | 255 | 255 | 255 |
| 0 | 0 | 0 | 0 |
| 0 | 0 | 0 | 0 |

| | | |
|---|---|---|
| 1 | 1 | 1 |
| 0 | 0 | 0 |
| –1 | –1 | –1 |

Mask       Block **a**       Block **b**

The mask above applied to block **a** of pixels yields block **b**.

**Figure 3.28** An edge-detection filter

positive and some weights negative, by changing the scaling factor, or by a combination of both methods. Each variation you try has a slightly different effect on how you sharpen (or blur) the entire image or affect primarily the edges in the image.

Let's look at a couple of filters that affect edges. Consider the convolution mask in Figure 3.28 and how it would operate on the block of pixels labeled block **a**. (Assume that for block **a**, the pixel values extend infinitely to the left and right with the same values in each row.) If you do the math, you'll see that along a horizontal edge that goes from light to dark as you move from top to bottom, the filter detects the edge, making that edge white while everything else is black. The effect is illustrated in Figure 3.29. If you swap the row of 1s for the row of –1s, the filter will detect horizontal edges that go from black to white rather than from white to black as you move down the image. This would make a white edge along the girl's bangs rather than along the top of her hair in Figure 3.29. If you arrange the 1s and –1s vertically rather than horizontally, the filter detects vertical edges moving one direction or the other.

**Figure 3.29** Applying an edge-detection filter to a grayscale image

One of the most useful filters in the repertoire is called the ***unsharp mask***. The name is misleading because this filter actually sharpens images. The name is derived from the way the mask is constructed. The idea is that first a blurred ("unsharp") version of the image is produced. Then the pixel values in the original image are doubled, and the blurred version of the image is subtracted from this. The result is a sharpened image, as shown in Figure 3.30. The blur mask shown in Figure 3.30 is different from the one we showed above. Variations of the unsharp mask can be created using different sizes of masks or types of blur masks.

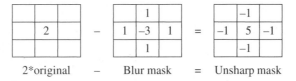

2*original    –    Blur mask    =    Unsharp mask

Original image                    Image with blur filter applied          Image with unsharp mask applied

**Figure 3.30**  Unsharp mask

## 3.9  RESAMPLING AND INTERPOLATION

*Resampling* is a process of changing the total number of pixels in a digital image. There are a number of situations in which resampling might be needed. To understand these, you need to understand the relationship between resolution, the size of an image in pixels, and print size (discussed in Chapter 2).

Here are four scenarios where you might want to change the print size, resolution, or total pixel dimensions of a digital image. See if you can tell which require resampling:

1. You scanned in an $8 \times 10$ inch photograph at a high resolution (300 pixels per inch, abbreviated *ppi*). You realize that you don't need this resolution since your printer can't print in that much detail anyway. You decide to decrease the resolution, but you don't want to change the size of the photograph when it is printed out. If you want your image processing program to change the image size from $8 \times 10$ inches and 300 ppi to $8 \times 10$ inches and 200 ppi, does the image have to be resampled?
2. You scanned in a $4 \times 5$ inch image at a resolution of 72 ppi, and it has been imported into your image processing program with these dimensions. You're going to display it on a computer monitor that has 90 ppi, and you don't want the image to be any smaller than $4 \times 5$ on the display. Does the image have to be resampled?
3. You scanned in an $8 \times 10$ inch photograph at 200 ppi, and it has been imported into your image processing program with these dimensions. You want to print it out at a size of $4 \times 5$ inches. Does the image have to be resampled?
4. You click on an image on your computer display to zoom in closer. Does the image have to be resampled?

So let's see how well you did in predicting when resampling is necessary. The key point to understand is that resampling is required whenever the number of pixels in a digital image is changed. If the resolution—the ppi—is not changed but the print size *is*, resampling is necessary. Resampling is also required if the print size is not changed but the resolution is. Compare your answers to the answers below.

1. The image has to be resampled in this case. If you have 300 ppi and an image that is $8 \times 10$ inches, you have a total of $300 * 8 * 10 = 24,000$ pixels. You want

$200 * 8 * 10 = 16,000$ pixels. Some pixels have to be discarded, which is called *downsampling*.

2. Again, the image has to be resampled. The $4 \times 5$ image scanned at 72 ppi has pixel dimensions of $288 \times 360$. A computer display that can fit 90 pixels in every inch (in both the horizontal and vertical directions) will display this image at a size of $3.2 \times 4$ inches. Retaining a size of at least $4 \times 5$ inches on the computer display requires *upsampling*, a process of inserting additional samples into an image.

3. The image doesn't have to be resampled to decrease its print size, although you can re-sample if you choose to. If you specify that you want to decrease the image print size without resampling, then the total number of samples will not change. The resulting image file will have exactly the same total number of pixels as before. However, without resampling, the number of pixels per inch will be greater because you're decreasing the number of inches. If, on the other hand, you specify that you want to decrease the size and resample, then the resolution will not change, but the total number of pixels *will*. Keeping the same resolution while decreasing the print size implies that you'll have fewer samples in the final image. In that case, the image is downsampled.

4. When you zoom in, the image is being upsampled, but only for display purposes. When you zoom out, the image is being downsampled. The stored image file doesn't change, however.

In practice, here is how resampling works. Figure 3.31 shows the Image Size window in Photoshop and GIMP. The Resample Image is checked. Thus, if you change the width and height in inches, the width and height in pixels will change accordingly so that the resolution does not change. Similarly, if you change the width and height in pixels, the width and height in inches will change.

 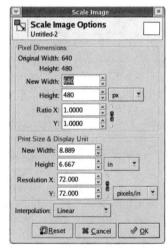

**Figure 3.31** Image Size window, Resample Image checked (from Photoshop and GIMP)

It is interesting to consider what is going on behind the scene when an image processing program resamples an image. The simplest method for upsampling is *replication*, a process of inserting pixels and giving them the color value of a neighboring pre-existing pixel. Replication works only if you are enlarging an image by an integer factor. An example of replication on a small block of pixels is shown in Figure 3.32. For each original pixel, a new pixel with the same color value is inserted to the right, below, and diagonally below and to the right.

| 220 | 230 | 240 |
|-----|-----|-----|
| 235 | 242 | 190 |
| 118 | 127 | 135 |

Original pixels

| 220 | 220 | 230 | 230 | 240 | 240 |
|-----|-----|-----|-----|-----|-----|
| 220 | 220 | 230 | 230 | 240 | 240 |
| 235 | 235 | 242 | 242 | 190 | 190 |
| 235 | 235 | 242 | 242 | 190 | 190 |
| 118 | 118 | 127 | 127 | 135 | 135 |
| 118 | 118 | 127 | 127 | 135 | 135 |

Pixels after replication

**Figure 3.32** Resampling by replication

Correspondingly, the simplest method of downsampling is ***row-column deletion***, the inverse of replication.

Think about how replication and its inverse might affect the quality of an image. Row-column deletion throws away information about the image, so you obviously lose detail. Replication, on the other hand, makes a guess about the colors that might have been sampled between existing samples—if the sampling rate had been higher. The values that are introduced in replication may not be the exact colors that would have been detected if the image had been sampled at a higher resolution to begin with. Thus, even though an upsampled image gains pixels, it doesn't get any sharper. In fact, usually the image loses quality. Since the new pixel values are copied from neighboring pixels, replication causes blockiness in the resampled image. Magnifying a view of an image in an image processing program can be done with simple replication. The image gets bigger, but the blockiness caused by upsampling becomes increasingly evident the more you zoom in. This is illustrated in Figure 3.33. Of course there is no harm done to the file, since the pixel values are upsampled only for display purposes. The values stored in the image file don't change.

**Figure 3.33** Image resampled as you zoom in

You'll notice a similar effect if you upsample a digital image in order to print it out at a larger size. Say that you scan in a 4 × 5 inch image at 200 pixels per inch but decide that you want to print it out at a size of 8 × 10 inches. Increasing the size and keeping the resolution at 200 ppi requires upsampling, since you'll end up with more pixels than you originally captured. But keep in mind that the picture you print out at 8 × 10 inches can't be any clearer or more detailed than the original 4 × 5 inch image.

The point is that the only true information you have about an image is the information you get when the image is originally created—by taking a digital photograph or scanning in a picture. Any information you generate after that—by upsampling—is only an approximation or guess about what the original image looked like. Thus, it's best to scan in digital images with sufficient pixel dimensions from the outset. For example, you could scan the 4 × 5 inch image at 400 ppi so that you could then increase its print size to 8 × 10 inches without resampling. If you deselect "resample image" in your image processing program and then change the image's size to 8 × 10 inches, the number of pixels per inch will change so that the total number of pixels does not change. That is, the resolution will automatically be cut in half as the print size is doubled. Then you'll have your 8 × 10 inches at a resolution of 200 ppi, which may be good enough for the print you want to make, and you won't have had to generate any new pixels that weren't captured in the original scan.

Even with your best planning, there will still be situations that call for resampling. Fortunately, there are interpolation methods for resampling that give better results than simple replication or discarding of pixels. *Interpolation* is a process of estimating the color of a pixel based on the colors of neighboring pixels. In Figure 3.31, notice the drop-down box beside the Resample Image checkbox. This is where you choose the interpolation method: nearest neighbor, bilinear, or bicubic. Nearest neighbor is essentially just replication when the scale factor is an integer greater than 1. However, it can be generalized to non-integer scale factors and described in a manner consistent with the other two methods, as we'll do below. We'll describe these algorithms as they would be applied to grayscale images. For RGB color, you could apply the procedures to each of the color channels.

For this discussion, we describe *scaling* as an affine transformation of digital image data that changes the total number of pixels in the image. An *affine transformation* is one that preserves collinearity. That is, points that are on the same line remain collinear, and lines that are parallel in the original image remain parallel in the transformed image. Clearly, scaling is just another word for resampling, but we introduce this synonymous term so that we can speak of a scale factor. If the *scale factor s* is greater than 1, the scaled image will increase in size on the computer display. If it is less than 1, the image will decrease in size. The scale factor doesn't have to be the same in both directions, but we will assume that it is in this discussion for simplicity.

With the scale factor $s$ we can define a general procedure for resampling using interpolation, given as Algorithm 3.1.

## ALGORITHM 3.1

```
algorithm resample
/*Input: A grayscale image f of dimensions w × h.
Scale factor s.
Output: fs, which is image f enlarged or shrunk by scale factor s.*/
{
   w' = (integer)(w * s)
   h' = (integer)(h * s)
/* create a new scaled image fs with dimensions w' and h'*/
   for i = 0 to h' − 1
     for j = 0 to w' − 1 {
     fs(i, j) = interpolate(i, j, f, method)
     }
}
}
algorithm interpolate(i, j, f, method) {
/*i and j are pixel coordinates in the scaled image fs.*/
   a = i/s /*This is real-number division since s is real.*/
   b = j/s
```

```
/*a and b are coordinates in the original image, f. Note that a and b are not necessar-
ily integers. Interpolation entails finding integer-valued coordinates that are neigh-
bors to a and b.*/
  if method = "nearest neighbor" then
    return f(round(a), round(b))
  else if method = "bilinear" then {
/* Find the coordinates of the top left pixel in the neighborhood of (a, b) */
    x = floor(a)
    y = floor(b)
/*Each pixel's weight is based on how close it is to (a, b)*/
    value = 0
    for m = 0 to 1 {
      for n = 0 to 1 {
        t = a − (x + m)
        u = b − (y + n)
        value = value + (1 − |t|)*(1 − |u|)*f(x + m, y + n)
      }
    }
    return value
  }
  else if method = "bicubic" then {
/*To simplify this algorithm, we assume that f(x, y) always has sixteen neighbors
within the bounds of the image. In practice, the algorithm needs to be adjusted to ac-
count for pixels at edges of the image*/
    x = floor(a)
    y = floor(b)
    value = 0
/*Consider the sixteen neighboring pixels around (a, b)
    for m = −1 to 2
      for n = −1 to 2 {
/*Determine how far position (a, b) is from each of the sixteen neighbors*/
        neighborX = x + m
        neighborY = y + n
        t = |neighborX − a|
        u = |neighborY − b|
        if t < 1
          x_coeff = 1 − 2 * t² + t³
        else
          x_coeff = 4 − 8 * t + 5 * t² − t³
        if u < 1
          y_coeff = 1 − 2 * u² + u³
        else
          y_coeff = 4 − 8 * u + 5 * u² − u³
        value = value + x_coeff * y_coeff * f(neighborX, neighborY)
      }
    return value
  }
}
```

**Step 1. Scale the image.**

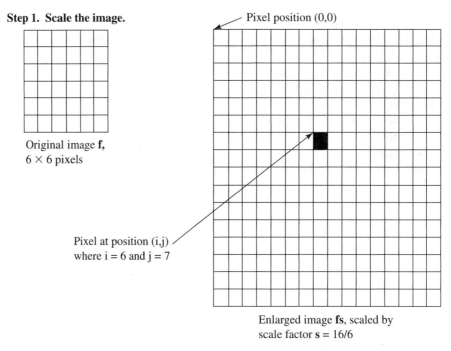

Pixel position (0,0)

Original image **f**,
6 × 6 pixels

Pixel at position (i,j)
where i = 6 and j = 7

Enlarged image **fs**, scaled by
scale factor **s** = 16/6

**Step 2. Map each pixel in the scaled image back to a
position in the original image.**

Position (6,7) in scaled image
maps back to position
(2.25, 2.625) in original image.

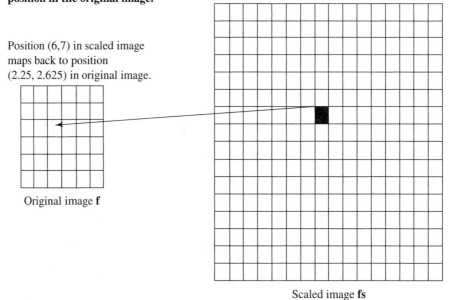

Original image **f**

Scaled image **fs**

**Figure 3.34** The first two steps in resampling

Algorithm 3.1 describes three different interpolation methods—nearest neighbor, bilinear, and bicubic interpolation. All three begin with the same two steps, illustrated in Figure 3.34. First, the dimensions of the scaled image are determined by multiplying the original dimensions by the scale factor. A new bitmap of the scaled dimensions is created. In the example, a 6 × 6 pixel image called $f$ is enlarged to a 16 × 16 image called $fs$, so the scale factor $s$ is

16/6. The values of the pixels in the scaled image are to be determined by interpolation. The second step is to map each pixel position in the scaled image back to coordinates within the original image. A pixel at position $(i, j)$ in *fs* maps back to position $(i/s, j/s)$ in *f*. Clearly, not all pixel positions in *fs* map back to integer positions in *f*. For example, (6, 7) maps back to (2.25, 2.625). The idea in all three interpolation algorithms is to find one or more pixels close to position $(i/s, j/s)$ in *f*, and use their color values to get the color value of *fs*$(i, j)$.

*Nearest neighbor interpolation* simply rounds down to find one close pixel whose value is used for *fs*$(i, j)$ (Figure 3.35). In our example, $f(2, 3)$ is used as the color value of *fs*$(6, 7)$. If you think about this, you'll realize that when $s$ is an integer greater than 1, the nearest neighbor algorithm is effectively equivalent to pixel replication. However, it also works with noninteger scale factors, as shown in our example.

To describe the three interpolation algorithms discussed earlier, it is sufficient to specify the convolution mask for each. Let's do this for nearest neighbor interpolation. We have a $w \times h$ image called $f$ that is being scaled by factor $s$, with the result being written

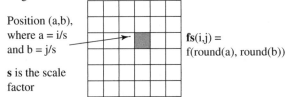

a and b are not necessarily integers, so they don't necessarily correspond to actual pixel coordinates in the original image.

The **nearest neighbor algorithm** assigns to **fs**(i,j) the color value f(round(a), round(b)) from the original image.

Position (a,b), where a = i/s and b = j/s

**fs**(i,j) = f(round(a), round(b))

s is the scale factor

The nearest neighbor is marked in gray.

**Figure 3.35**  Nearest neighbor interpolation

**Nearest neighbor interpolation**

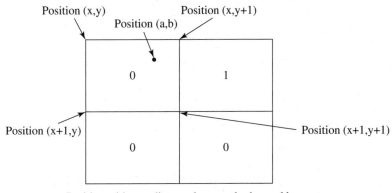

Position (x,y)        Position (x,y+1)

Position (a,b)

| 0 | 1 |

Position (x+1,y)        Position (x+1,y+1)

| 0 | 0 |

Position with coordinates closest to both a and b gets a 1 in the convolution kernel.

**Figure 3.36**  Example of a nearest neighbor convolution mask

to a new image bitmap $fs$ of dimensions $w' = w * s$ and $h' = h * s$. The color value of each pixel $fs(i, j)$ is obtained by mapping $(i, j)$ back to coordinates in $f$ with $a = i/s$ and $b = j/s$.

Let $x = floor(a)$ and $y = floor(b)$. Then the neighborhood of $(a, b)$ in $f$ consists of $f(x, y)$, $f(x + 1, y)$, $f(x, y + 1)$, and $f(x + 1, y + 1)$. For each pixel $fs(i, j)$, define the nearest neighbor convolution mask $\boldsymbol{h}_{nn}(m, n)$ to be a $2 \times 2$ matrix of coefficients as follows:

for $0 \le m \le 1$ and $0 \le n \le 1$,
$\boldsymbol{h}_{nn}(m, n) = 1$ if $-0.5 \le (x + m) - a < 0.5$ and $-0.5 \le (y + n) - b < 0.5$
otherwise $\boldsymbol{h}_{nn}(m, n) = 0$

This effectively puts a 1 in the pixel position closest to $(a, b)$ and a 0 everywhere else, so $fs(i, j)$ takes the value of its single closest neighbor, as shown in the example in Figure 3.36. Note that the position of the 1 in the mask depends on the location of $(a, b)$. The mask is applied with its upper left element corresponding to $f(x, y)$.

You may notice that the numbering of the mask positions is not "flipped" the same way it was in the definition of the linear convolution above. The convolutions for interpolation are different in that they are not applied to every pixel in the original image. The concept is the same, however.

***Bilinear interpolation*** uses four neighbors and makes $fs(i, j)$ a weighted sum of their color values. The contribution of each pixel toward the color of $fs(i, j)$ is a function of how close the pixel's coordinates are to $(a, b)$. The neighborhood is illustrated in Figure 3.37. The method is called bilinear because it uses two linear interpolation functions, one for each dimension. This is illustrated in Figure 3.38. Bilinear interpolation requires more computation time than nearest neighbor, but it results in a smoother image, with fewer jagged edges.

**Bilinear interpolation** uses an average color value of the four pixels surrounding position (a,b) in the original image. Each neighbor's contribution to the color is based on how close it is to (a,b). Let

$x = floor(a)$
$y = floor(b)$

Then the pixels surrounding position (a,b) are

**f**(x, y)
**f**(x+1, y)
**f**(x+1, y+1)
**f**(x, y+1)

Neighborhood is shown in gray.

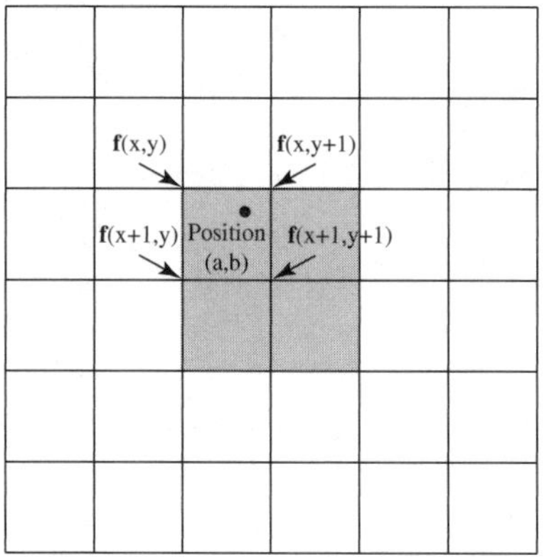

**Figure 3.37** Bilinear interpolation

**Bilinear interpolation**

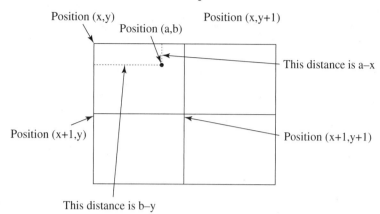

The color of the pixel in image **fs** is a weighted
average of the four neighboring pixels. Weights
come from each pixel's proximity to (a,b).

**Figure 3.38** Weights used in bilinear interpolation

To specify the convolution mask for bilinear interpolation, let $t(m, n) = a - (x + m)$ and $u(m, n) = b - (y + n)$ for $0 \leq m \leq 1$ and $0 \leq n \leq 1$. Then the mask $\boldsymbol{h}_{bl}(m, n)$ is defined as $\boldsymbol{h}_{bl}(m, n) = (1 - |t|)(1 - |u|)$.

*Bicubic interpolation* uses a neighborhood of sixteen pixels to determine the value of $fs(i, j)$. The neighborhood of $(a, b)$ extends from $x - 1$ to $x + 2$ in the vertical direction and from $y - 1$ to $y + 2$ in the horizontal direction, as illustrated in Figure 3.39. The

Supplement on
interpolation for
resampling:

worksheet

**Bicubic interpolation** uses an "average" color value
of the 16 pixels surrounding position (a,b) in the
original image. The weight of each neighbor's
contribution is based on a cubic equation that accounts
for how close each neighbor is.

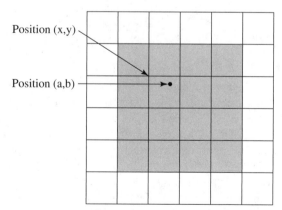

Neighbors are shaded in gray.  The neighborhood of (a,b)
extends from x–1 to x+2 in the vertical direction and
from y–1  to y+2 in the horizontal direction.

**Figure 3.39**  Bicubic interpolation

method is called bicubic because the weighted average of pixels in the $4 \times 4$ pixel neighborhood is based on two cubic interpolation functions, one for each dimension (Figure 3.40). The cubic functions used in our example are sometimes referred to as a "Mexican Hat" convolution mask. Other functions can be used. Bicubic interpolation requires even more computation time and memory than bilinear interpolation, but it creates a smoother image while preserving detail from the original image.

**Bicubic interpolation**

Position (x,y)

| | | | |
|---|---|---|---|
| $\mathbf{g(t(m))g(u(n))}$ | $\mathbf{g(t(m))f(u(n))}$ | $\mathbf{g(t(m))f(u(n))}$ | $\mathbf{g(t(m))g(u(n))}$ |
| $\mathbf{f(t(m))g(u(n))}$ | $\mathbf{f(t(m))f(u(n))}$ | $\mathbf{f(t(m))f(u(n))}$ | $\mathbf{f(t(m))g(u(n))}$ |
| $\mathbf{f(t(m))g(u(n))}$ | $\mathbf{f(t(m))f(u(n))}$ | $\mathbf{f(t(m))f(u(n))}$ | $\mathbf{f(t(m))g(u(n))}$ |
| $\mathbf{g(t(m))g(u(n))}$ | $\mathbf{g(t(m))f(u(n))}$ | $\mathbf{g(t(m))f(u(n))}$ | $\mathbf{g(t(m))g(u(n))}$ |

For $-1<=m<=2$ and $-1<=n<=2$,    Position (a,b)
$\mathbf{t}(m) = a - (x + m)$
$\mathbf{u}(n) = b - (y + n)$

$\mathbf{f(t(m))} = 1 - 2\mathbf{t}(m)^2 + |\mathbf{t}(m)|^3$
$\mathbf{f(u(n))} = 1 - 2\mathbf{u}(n)^2 + |\mathbf{u}(n)|^3$
$\mathbf{g(t(m))} = 4 - 8|\mathbf{t}(m)| + 5\mathbf{t}(m)^2 - |\mathbf{t}(m)|^3$
$\mathbf{g(u(n))} = 4 - 8|\mathbf{u}(n)| + 5\mathbf{u}(n)^2 - |\mathbf{u}(n)|^3$

**Figure 3.40** Convolution mask for bicubic interpolation

# 3.10 DIGITAL IMAGE COMPRESSION

Supplements on
LZW compression:

interactive tutorial

programming
exercise

## 3.10.1 LZW Compression

***LZW compression*** is a method that is applicable to both text and image compression. LZW stands for Lempel-Ziv-Welch, the creators of the algorithm. Lempel and Ziv published the first version of the algorithm in 1977 (called LZ77), and the procedure was revised and improved by Welch in 1984. The algorithm was first widely used in the 1980s in the *compress* Unix utility. It then went through a number of versions and patents with Sperry, Unisys, and CompuServ Corporations. The method is commonly applied to GIF and TIFF image files. The patents are relevant to GIF and TIFF software developers but do not hamper an individual's right to own or transmit files in GIF or TIFF format. In any case, Unisys's main patents for LZW expired in 2003.

The LZW algorithm is based on the observation that sequences of color in an image file (or sequences of characters in a text file) are often repeated. Thus, the algorithm uses a sliding expandable window to identify successively longer repeated sequences. These are put into a code table as the file is processed for compression. An ingenious feature of the algorithm is that the full code table does not have to be stored with the compressed file; only the part of it containing the original colors in the image is needed, and then the rest— the codes for the sequences of colors—can be regenerated dynamically during the decoding process. Let's see how this works.

worksheet

With a first pass over the image file, the code table is initialized to contain all the individual colors that exist in the image file. These colors are encoded in consecutive integers. Now, imagine that the pixels in the image file, going left to right and top to bottom, are strung out in one continuous row. After initialization, the sliding expandable window moves across these pixels. The window begins with a width of one pixel. (The height is always one pixel.) If the pixel sequence is already in the code table, the window is successively expanded by one pixel until finally a color sequence not in the table is under the window. Say that this sequence is $n$ pixels long. Then the code for the sequence that is $n - 1$ pixels long is output into the compressed file, and the $n$-pixel-long sequence is put into the code table. This continues until the entire image is compressed. The procedure is illustrated in Figure 3.41.

The following algorithm that will accomplish the procedure pictured in Figure 3.41.

## ALGORITHM 3.2    LZW COMPRESSION ALGORITHM

```
algorithm LZW
/*Input: A bitmap image.
Output: A table of the individual colors in the image and a compressed version of the
file.
Note that + is concatenation.*/
{
  initialize table to contain the individual colors in bitmap
  pixelString = first pixel value
  while there are still pixels to process {
    pixel = next pixel value
    stringSoFar = pixelString + pixel
    if stringSoFar is in the table then
      pixelString = stringSoFar
    else {
      output the code for pixelString
      add stringSoFar to the table
      pixelString = pixel
    }
  }
  output the code for pixelString
}
```

The decoding process requires only a table initialized with the colors in the image. From this information, the remaining codes are recaptured as the decoding progresses. The decompression algorithm is given as Algorithm 3.3.

**Initial color table:**                     **Space for more codes:**

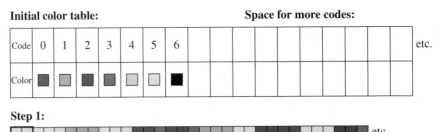

**Step 1:**

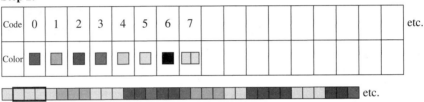

Window is over first sequence of colors not already in table.
Output code for one yellow pixel, and put the new sequence
in the table.

Compressed file so far is **5**.

**Step 2:**

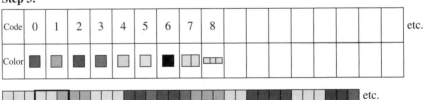

Window slides over to next sequence not yet compressed
and not already in the table. This is three yellow pixels in
a row. Output code for two yellow pixels, and put the new
sequence in the table.

Compressed file so far is **5 7**.

**Step 3:**

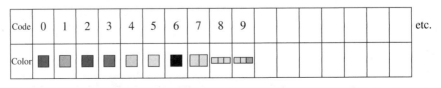

Window slides over to next sequence not yet compressed
and not already in the table. This is two yellow pixels and
one green. Output code for two yellow pixels, and put the
new sequence in the table.

Compressed file so far is **5 7 7**.

**Figure 3.41** A partial trace of LZW compression

## ALGORITHM 3.3    LZW DECOMPRESSION ALGORITHM

```
algorithm LZW_decompress
/*Input: Compressed bitmap image and table of individual colors in image.
Output: Decompressed image.*/
{
  stringSoFar = NULL
  while there are still codes to process in the code string {
    code = next code in the code string
    colors = the colors corresponding to code in the table
    if colors == NULL    /*Case where code is not in the table*/
    /*stringSoFar[0] is the first color in stringSoFar*/
      colors = stringSoFar + stringSoFar[0]
    output colors
    if stringSoFar! = NULL
      put stringSoFar + colors[0] in the table
    stringSoFar = colors
  }
}
```

## 3.10.2 Huffman Encoding

**Huffman encoding** is another lossless compression algorithm that is used on bitmap image files. It differs from LZW in that it is a **variable-length encoding** scheme; that is, not all color codes use the same number of bits. The algorithm is devised such that colors that appear more frequently in the image are encoded with fewer bits. Thus, it is a form of entropy encoding, like the Shannon-Fano algorithm described in Chapter 1. The Huffman encoding algorithm requires two passes: (1) determining the codes for the colors and (2) compressing the image file by replacing each color with its code.

In the first pass through the image file, the number of instances of each color is determined. This information is stored in a frequency table. A tree data structure is built from the frequency table in the following manner: A node is created for each of the colors in the image, with the frequency of that color's appearance stored in the node. These nodes will be the leaves of the code tree. Let's use the variable *freq* to hold the frequency in each node. Now the two nodes with the smallest value for *freq* are joined such that they are the children of a common parent node, and the parent node's *freq* value is set to the sum of the *freq* values in the children nodes. This node-combining process repeats until you arrive at the creation of a root node. The algorithm for this process is given in Algorithm 3.4, and a short trace is given in Figures 3.42 to 3.44.

Consider this simple example. Say that your image file has only 729 pixels in it, with the following colors and the corresponding frequencies:

|       |     |
|-------|-----|
| white | 70  |
| black | 50  |
| red   | 130 |
| green | 234 |
| blue  | 245 |

Supplements on
Huffman encoding:

interactive tutorial

programming
exercise

worksheet

The initial nodes are as pictured in Figure 3.42. The arrangement of the nodes is not important, but moving nodes around as the tree is constructed can make the tree easier to understand.

**Figure 3.42** Leaf nodes of Huffman tree

---

### ALGORITHM 3.4

```
algorithm Huffman_encoding
/*Input: Bitmap image.
Output: Compressed image and code table.*/
{
    /*Let color_freq[] be the frequency table listing each color that appears in the
image and how many times it appears. Without loss of generality, assume that all
colors from 0 to n − 1 appear in the image.*/
    initialize color_freq
/*Assume each node in the Huffman tree contains variable c for color and variable
freq for the number of times color c appears in the image.*/
    for i = 0 to n − 1 {
/*Let nd.c denote the c field of node nd*/
        create a node nd such that nd.c = i and nd.freq = color_freq[i]
    }
    while at least two nodes without a parent node remain {
        node1 = the node that has the smallest freq among nodes remaining that have no
parent node
        node2 = the node that has the second smallest freq among nodes remaining that
have no parent node
/*Assume some protocol for handling cases where two of sums are the same*/
        nd_new = a new node
        nd_new.freq = node1.freq + node2.freq
        make nd_new the parent of node1 and node2
    }
/*Assign codes to each color by labeling branches of the Huffman tree*/
        label each left branch of the tree with a 0 and each right branch with a 1
    for each leaf node {
        travel down the tree from the root to each leaf node, gathering the code for the
color associated with the leaf nodes
        put the color and the code in a code table
    }
    using the code table, compress the image file
}
```

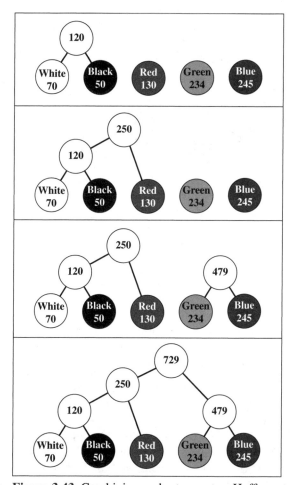

**Figure 3.43** Combining nodes to create a Huffman tree

Combining nodes into a Huffman tree proceeds as pictured in Figure 3.43. Note that at any point in this process, any two nodes that do not already have a parent node can be combined—as long as they are the nodes with the least value. That is, sometimes you might combine two leaf nodes, sometimes two interior nodes, or sometimes a leaf node with an interior node. Also note that if two minimum-value nodes have the same value, the choice of which one to use is arbitrary. This implies that there may be more than one legal Huffman tree—and thus more than one possible code table—derivable from a set of leaf nodes (*i.e.*, for a given image).

Once the tree has been created, the branches are labeled with 0s on the left and 1s on the right. Then for each leaf node, you traverse the tree from the root to the leaf, gathering the code on the way down the tree. This is pictured in Figure 3.44.

After the codes have been created, the image file can be compressed using these codes. Say that the first ten pixels in the image are wwwkkwwbgr (with black abbreviated as k, white as w, red as r, green as g, and blue as b). The compressed version of this string of pixels, in binary, is

00000000000100100000111001

Label branches with 0s on the left and 1s on the right.

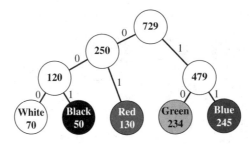

For each leaf node, traverse tree from root to leaf node and gather code for the color associated with the leaf node.

| | |
|---|---|
| White | 000 |
| Black | 001 |
| Red | 01 |
| Green | 10 |
| Blue | 11 |

Note that not all codes are the same number of bits, and no code is a prefix of any other code.

**Figure 3.44** Creating codes from a Huffman tree

If you think about how the Huffman encoding algorithm works, you'll understand why it is designed the way it is. By combining least-valued nodes first and creating the tree from the bottom up, the algorithm ensures that the colors that appear least frequently in the image have the longest codes. Also, because the codes are created from the tree data structure, no code can be a prefix of another code. This is a necessary characteristic of the codes because the codes are not necessarily the same length. Imagine that you had the string 11101011100000001001 to decode, and there was both a 1 (as black, say) and an 11 (the code for white) in the code table. How would you know whether to decode the first two 1s as two black pixels or as a single white pixel? This is the problem you would encounter if one code was a prefix for another.

To understand decoding, picture what you would have in the compressed file. Either a code table, the Huffman tree (in which the codes are implicit), or the frequency table must be saved so that the Huffman tree can be used for the decoding. The easiest way to imagine the decoding process is to assume that the Huffman tree is available to the decoder. Now picture how the decoder would decode the encoded bitmap. Bits are read sequentially from the encoded file, guiding the traversal down the Huffman tree until a leaf node is encountered. A 0 bit means take a left branch. A 1 bit means take a right branch. When the decoder arrives at a leaf node, it finds the color associated with the bit sequence just consumed. Then the code for this sequence is output, and the search continues for the next sequence, with the decoder moving back to the root of the Huffman tree.

To determine the compression rate for a Huffman encoded file, we need to make some assumptions about how the codes are stored in the file. Think about the implications of storing the codes in a code table. The first column of each row would contain one of the original colors from the image file—let's say a 24-bit RGB color. Associated with each color is its code. But since the codes are of variable length, the decoder would have to know how many bits there are in this code. Thus there would first have to be a value indicating the length of this code. An alternative to storing the code table is to store the frequency table and have the decoder regenerate the Huffman tree. Then there would be the encoded image itself in the compressed file. With this in mind, let's compute the compression rate for our example.

Assuming 24-bit color, the original image size is computed as follows:

$$729 \text{ pixels} * 24 \text{ bits/pixel} = 17,496 \text{ bits in the original image}$$

Now for the compressed image. We can get the size of the compressed image by considering that we have 70 white bits encoded with three bits each, 50 black pixels encoded with three bits each, 130 red pixels encoded with two bits each, 234 green pixels encoded with two bits each, and 245 blue pixels encoded with two bits each. That's $(70 + 50) * 3 + (130 + 234 + 245) * 2 = 1,578$ bits in the compressed image. Thus the compression rate is $17,496 : 1,578$, better than $11 : 1$.

You may notice that we didn't really need 24 bits per color if we had only five colors. We could have used just eight bits. Even if we assume only eight bits per color in the original file, we get a compression rate of $3.7 : 1$. This is just a small example (a $27 \times 27$ pixel image), but it gives you the basic concepts.

Huffman encoding is useful as a step in JPEG compression, as we will see in the next section.

### 3.10.3 JPEG Compression

JPEG is an acronym for Joint Photographic Experts Group. In common usage, ***JPEG compression*** refers to a compression algorithm suitable for reducing the size of photographic images or continuous-tone artwork—pictures where the scene transitions move smoothly from one color to another, as opposed to cartoon-like images where there are sharp divisions between colors. If you see a file with the *.jpg* or *.jpeg* suffix, you can assume it has been compressed with the JPEG method, but it is also possible to apply JPEG compression to images saved in TIFF, PICT, and EPS files. Although JPEG is a lossy compression method, it is designed so that the information that is lost is not very important to how the picture looks—that is, the algorithm removes closely spaced changes in color that are not easily perceived by the human eye. This is made possible by transforming the image data from the spatial domain to the frequency domain. When the image is represented in terms of its frequency components, it is possible to "throw away" the high frequency components, which correspond to barely perceptible details in color change.

Another advantage of JPEG compression is that image processing programs allow you to choose the JPEG compression rate, so you can specify how important the image size is versus the image's fidelity to the original subject. JPEG compression on a 24-bit color image yields an excellent compression rate. With a rate of about $10 : 1$ or $20 : 1$, you'll notice hardly any difference from the original to the compressed image. Even compression rates up to $50 : 1$ can give acceptable results for some purposes. The main disadvantage to JPEG compression is that it takes longer for the encoding and decoding than other algorithms require, but usually the compression/decompression time is not noticeable and is well justified when compared with the savings in storage space and download time required for the image file. Without JPEG compression, most people would not want to spend time it would take to download pictures on web pages.

To be precise, the term JPEG does not refer to a standardized file format, but only more generally to a method of compressing image files that was created by the Joint

**Supplements on JPEG compression:**

interactive tutorial

worksheet

Photographic Experts Group in 1990. A standardized JPEG file format with the name *JFIF* (JPEG File Interchange Format) was introduced about a year later by C-Cube Microsystems. An alternative file format designed by C-Cube, called TIFF/JPEG, offers the ability to store more information about the image file, but the simpler JFIF format has become the *de facto* standard.

The algorithm we describe below is the basic method that has been used for JPEG compression since the 1980s, adapted from a scheme proposed by Chen and Pratt. The key step in this algorithm is the transformation of image data from the spatial to the frequency domain by means of the discrete cosine transform (DCT). The main steps are listed in Algorithm 3.5. Let's consider the motivation and then examine some of the details of each of these steps.

---

**ALGORITHM 3.5**

```
algorithm jpeg
/*Input: A bitmap image in RGB mode.
Output: The same image, compressed.*/
{
    Divide image into 8 × 8 pixel blocks
    Convert image to a luminance/chrominance model such as YCbCr (optional)
    Shift pixel values by subtracting 128
    Use discrete cosine transform to transform the pixel data from the spatial domain
    to the frequency domain
    Quantize frequency values
    Store DC value (upper left corner) as the difference between current DC value and
    DC from previous block
    Arrange the block in a zigzag order
    Do run-length encoding
    Do entropy encoding (e.g., Huffman)
}
```

---

**ASIDE:** If you know something about computational complexity, you can understand how dividing the image into 8 × 8 blocks makes execution of the DCT less computationally expensive. Let's assume that an $O(n^3)$ DCT algorithm is used, where $n$ is the dimension of the pixel block horizontally and vertically. If you apply this algorithm on a 16 × 16 block, the algorithm takes on the order of $16^3 = 4096$ steps. Alternatively, you can apply the algorithm on four 8 × 8 blocks. This requires on the order of $4 * 8^3 = 2048$ steps, which is fewer. Applying the DCT on four 8 × 8 blocks covers the same total pixel area as applying it to a 16 × 16 block, but in fewer steps. It's computationally more manageable to use smaller blocks.

**Step 1. Divide the image into 8 × 8 pixel blocks and convert RGB to a luminance/chrominance color model.**

**Motivation:** The image is divided into 8 × 8 pixel blocks to make it computationally more manageable for the next steps. Converting color to a luminance/chrominance model makes it possible to remove some of the chrominance information, to which the human eye is less sensitive, without significant loss of quality in the image.

**Details:** For efficiency reasons, JPEG compression operates on 8 × 8 pixel blocks on the image file. If the file's length and width are not multiples of eight, the bitmap can be padded and the extra pixels removed later.

JPEG compression can be performed on 24-bit color or 8-bit grayscale images. If the original pixel data is in RGB color mode, then there is an 8 × 8 pixel block for each of the color channels.

The blocks for these color channels are processed separately with the steps described below, but the three blocks are grouped so that the image can be reconstructed upon decoding.

Converting the image file from RGB to a model like YCbCr makes it possible to achieve an even greater compression rate by means of chrominance subsampling. As discussed in Chapter 2, the YCbCr color model represents color in terms of one luminance component, Y, and two chrominance components, Cb and Cr. The human eye is more sensitive to changes in light (*i.e.*, luminance) than in color (*i.e.*, chrominance). Thus, we need less detailed information with regard to chrominance, since we won't notice very subtle differences anyway. Transforming directly from RGB to one of the luminance/chrominance models is a straightforward linear operation, as discussed in Chapter 2.

Simply doing this transformation doesn't reduce the number of bits per pixel. However, it does separate the pixel data so that some of it can be discarded. ***Chrominance subsampling*** (also called ***chrominance downsampling***) is a process of throwing away some of the bits used to represent pixels—in particular, some of the color information. For example, with YCbCr color mode, we might choose to save only one Cb value and one Cr value but four Y values for every four pixel values. Three commonly used subsampling rates are pictured in Figure 3.45. The conventional notation for luminance/chrominance subsampling is in the form $a:b:c$. Common subsampling rates are $4:1:1$, $4:2:0$, and $4:2:2$. To understand what these numbers represent, count the number of samples taken for Y and Cb (or Cr, since they are the same) in each pair of four-pixel-wide rows. $a$ is the number of Y samples in both rows. $b$ is the number of Cb samples in the first row (and also the number of Cr samples). $c$ is the number of Cb (and Cr samples) in the second row. Note that we have not specified how the Cb and Cr values are derived. Just one of the values in a sub-block could be used, or the values could be averaged. (In fact, MPEG-1 and MPEG-2 video compression use different methods for determining the single chrominance values corresponding to four luminance values in $4:2:0$ downsampling.)

**4:1:1**

| Y (Cb,Cr) | Y | Y | Y |
|---|---|---|---|
| Y (Cb,Cr) | Y | Y | Y |
| Y (Cb,Cr) | Y | Y | Y |
| Y (Cb,Cr) | Y | Y | Y |

**4:2:0**

| Y (Cb,Cr) | Y | Y (Cb,Cr) | Y |
|---|---|---|---|
| Y | Y | Y | Y |
| Y (Cb,Cr) | Y | Y (Cb,Cr) | Y |
| Y | Y | Y | Y |

**4:2:2**

| Y (Cb,Cr) | Y | Y (Cb,Cr) | Y |
|---|---|---|---|
| Y (Cb,Cr) | Y | Y (Cb,Cr) | Y |
| Y (Cb,Cr) | Y | Y (Cb,Cr) | Y |
| Y (Cb,Cr) | Y | Y (Cb,Cr) | Y |

**Figure 3.45** Chrominance subsampling

With RGB color mode, we can imagine that for each $8 \times 8$ pixel section of the image, there are actually three $8 \times 8$ blocks to be processed, one for each of the R, G, and B color channels. With YCbCr color mode, we have to picture this a little differently. We begin by dividing the image into $16 \times 16$ pixel macroblocks. Then, with $4:2:0$ chroma downsampling, we get four $8 \times 8$ blocks of Y data for every one $8 \times 8$ block of Cb and one $8 \times 8$ block of Cr data. This is pictured in Figure 3.46. Each of the blocks undergoes the

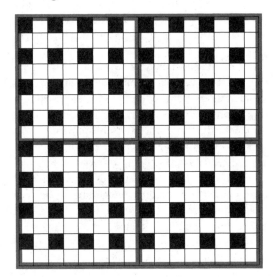

With 4:2:0 YCbCr chrominance subsampling,
a 16 × 16 macroblock yields:
–four 8 × 8 blocks of Y values
–one 8 × 8 block of Cb values
–one 8 × 8 block of Cr values
Each black location represents one Cb
and one Cr sample taken for a block
of four pixels. Y samples are taken
at all locations.

**Figure 3.46**  Chrominance subsampling

remaining steps of the algorithm, and the resulting compressed data is reconstructed upon decoding.

You can see that using a luminance/chrominance color model and then chrominance sub-sampling reduces the image file size even before the rest of the compression steps are performed. Consider the reduction in file size if 4:2:0 downsampling is used by counting the number of bytes in an area of pixels with a width of four pixels and a height of two pixels— eight pixels total. Assuming that each component requires one byte, an unsubsampled image requires 8 * 3 = 24 bytes. Subsampling at a rate of 4:2:0 requires 8 + (2 * 2) = 12 bytes (eight for the Y component but only two for each of the Cb and Cr). This is a 2:1 savings.

Chrominance subsampling is not a required step in JPEG compression, and some JPEG compressors allow you to turn this option off if you think that subsampling will compromise the desired sharpness of your image. Usually, however, this isn't necessary.

We will trace through an example of JPEG compression performed on an 8 × 8 block of a grayscale image. In grayscale images, the RGB color channels all have the same value, so it's necessary to store only one byte value per pixel. Thus, our example will need to show the processing of only one 8 × 8 block for an 8 × 8 pixel area. But keep in mind that if 4 : 2 : 0 chroma subsampled YCbCr color is used, for every 16 × 16 pixel area, there are four 8 × 8 blocks of Y data and one each of Cb and Cr data. If RGB color is used, there are three 8 × 8 blocks—one each for R, G, and B—for every 8 × 8 pixel area.

**Step 2. Shift values by −128 and transform from the spatial to the frequency domain.**

**Motivation:** On an intuitive level, shifting the values by −128 is like looking at the image function as a waveform that cycles through positive and negative values. This step is a preparation for representing the function in terms of its frequency components. Transforming from the spatial to the frequency domain makes it possible to remove high frequency components. High frequency components are present if color values go up and down quickly in a small space. These small changes are barely perceptible in most people's vision, so removing them does not compromise image quality significantly.

**Details:** Let's review briefly what was covered in Chapter 2 concerning the spatial versus the frequency domain: When an $M \times N$ digital image is represented in the spatial domain, it can be stored in a two-dimensional array where each element in the array is the color value—or amplitude—of the image at that point. Thus, a two-dimensional digital image bitmap defines a surface, each pixel value telling how high the surface is at a given point. In this sense, we can view the image data as a two-dimensional waveform. Figure 3.47 shows an $8 \times 8$ grayscale pixel area, and Figure 3.48 gives the corresponding surface in the spatial domain. Viewing the image data as a waveform leads us to an alternative representation of the data that is equivalent to the spatial domain. When digital image data is transformed from the spatial to the frequency domain, each value in the $M \times N$ array indicates "how much" of each frequency component exists in the waveform. That is, the elements in the array are coefficients by which we multiply the cosine basis functions such that these functions can be summed to yield the surface of the image.

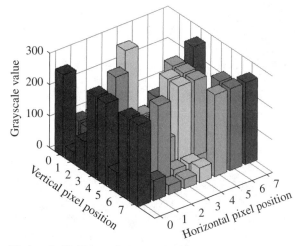

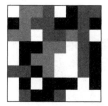

**Figure 3.47** $8 \times 8$ pixel area, enlarged

**Figure 3.48** Figure 3.47 graphed in the spatial domain

If the spatial and frequency domains give equivalent representations of a digital image, why do we need to transform from one to the other? The answer is that sometimes it is convenient to rearrange data so that we can access certain parts more easily. In this case, it is useful to separate out the high frequency components of the image, because these are the parts to which the human eye is least sensitive. High-frequency components in an image correspond to places where colors change in a small space. This kind of detail can be almost imperceptible, so eliminating it has little effect on the perceived difference between the original and the compressed image.

The DCT is a mathematical procedure that transforms image data from the spatial to the frequency domain. Chapter 2 describes this procedure in detail. It is a lossless procedure, aside from the small unavoidable error introduced through floating point arithmetic. The DCT performs the transform in one direction, and the inverse DCT can restore the original data without loss of information.

We will trace through an example to see the effects of JPEG compression. The example is based on an $8 \times 8$ pixel area taken from the picture shown in Figure 3.49.

The pixel values are given in Table 3.4, and the values shifted by $-128$ are given in Table 3.5.

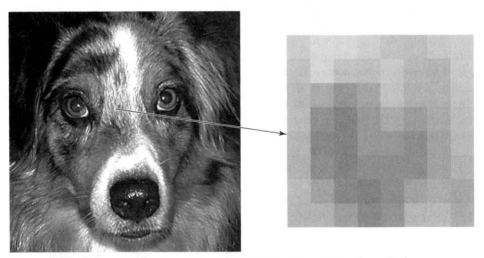

**Figure 3.49** Grayscale image and enlarged $8 \times 8$ pixel area taken from the image

| TABLE 3.4 | Grayscale Values for $8 \times 8$ Pixel Area Shown in Figure 3.49 | | | | | | |
|---|---|---|---|---|---|---|---|
| 222 | 231 | 229 | 224 | 216 | 213 | 220 | 224 |
| 216 | 229 | 217 | 215 | 221 | 210 | 209 | 223 |
| 211 | 202 | 283 | 198 | 218 | 207 | 209 | 221 |
| 214 | 180 | 164 | 188 | 203 | 193 | 205 | 217 |
| 209 | 171 | 166 | 190 | 190 | 178 | 199 | 215 |
| 206 | 177 | 166 | 179 | 180 | 178 | 199 | 210 |
| 212 | 197 | 173 | 166 | 179 | 198 | 206 | 203 |
| 208 | 208 | 195 | 174 | 184 | 210 | 214 | 206 |

| TABLE 3.5 | Pixel Values for Image in Figure 3.49 Shifted by −128 | | | | | | |
|---|---|---|---|---|---|---|---|
| 94 | 103 | 101 | 96 | 88 | 85 | 92 | 96 |
| 88 | 101 | 89 | 87 | 93 | 82 | 81 | 95 |
| 83 | 74 | 55 | 70 | 90 | 79 | 81 | 93 |
| 86 | 52 | 36 | 60 | 75 | 65 | 77 | 89 |
| 81 | 43 | 38 | 62 | 62 | 50 | 71 | 87 |
| 78 | 49 | 38 | 51 | 52 | 50 | 71 | 82 |
| 84 | 69 | 45 | 38 | 51 | 70 | 78 | 75 |
| 80 | 80 | 67 | 46 | 56 | 82 | 86 | 78 |

| TABLE 3.6 | DCT of an 8 × 8 Pixel Area | | | | | | |
|---|---|---|---|---|---|---|---|
| 585.7500 | −24.5397 | 59.5959 | 21.0853 | 25.7500 | −2.2393 | −8.9907 | 1.8239 |
| 78.1982 | 12.4534 | −32.6034 | −19.4953 | 10.7193 | −10.5910 | −5.1086 | −0.5523 |
| 57.1373 | 24.829 | −7.5355 | −13.3367 | −45.0612 | −10.0027 | 4.9142 | −2.4993 |
| −11.8655 | 6.9798 | 3.8993 | −14.4061 | 8.5967 | 12.9151 | −0.3122 | −0.1844 |
| 5.2500 | −1.7212 | −1.0824 | −3.2106 | 1.2500 | 9.3595 | 2.6131 | 1.1199 |
| −5.9658 | −4.0865 | 7.6451 | 13.0616 | −1.1927 | 1.1782 | −1.0733 | −0.5631 |
| −1.2074 | −5.7729 | −2.0858 | −1.9347 | 1.6173 | 2.6671 | −0.4645 | 0.6144 |
| 0.6362 | −1.4059 | −0.7191 | 1.6339 | −0.1438 | 0.2755 | −0.0268 | −0.2255 |

Table 3.6 gives the DCT values corresponding to the pixel values from Table 3.5.

Notice that some of the values are negative. We have said that it is possible to express a digital image as a sum of discretized sinusoidal functions, but sometimes a term in the sum must be negative. You can picture adding a negative amount of a frequency component as adding the inverted waveform.

**Step 3. Quantize the frequency values.**

**Motivation:** Quantization involves dividing each frequency coefficient by an integer and rounding off. The coefficients for high-frequency components are typically small, so they often round down to 0—which means, in effect, that they are thrown away.

**Details:** Not every value in the matrix needs to be divided by the same integer. The amount of error introduced by the rounding is proportional to the size of the integer by which a frequency coefficient is divided. It is preferable to divide the high-frequency coefficients by larger integers, since the human eye is less sensitive to high-frequency components in the image. Because there is not a constant integer by which all frequency coefficients are divided, a quantization table must be stored with the compressed image. We use the divisors given in Table 3.7 and the results in Table 3.8.

| TABLE 3.7 | Quantization Table | | | | | | |
|---|---|---|---|---|---|---|---|
| 8 | 6 | 6 | 7 | 6 | 5 | 8 | 7 |
| 7 | 7 | 9 | 9 | 8 | 10 | 12 | 20 |
| 13 | 12 | 11 | 11 | 12 | 25 | 18 | 19 |
| 15 | 20 | 29 | 26 | 31 | 30 | 29 | 26 |
| 28 | 28 | 32 | 36 | 46 | 39 | 32 | 34 |
| 44 | 35 | 28 | 28 | 40 | 55 | 41 | 44 |
| 48 | 49 | 52 | 52 | 52 | 31 | 39 | 57 |
| 61 | 56 | 50 | 60 | 46 | 51 | 52 | 50 |

| TABLE 3.8 | Quantized DCT Values | | | | | | |
|---|---|---|---|---|---|---|---|
| 73 | −4 | 10 | 3 | 4 | 0 | −1 | 0 |
| 11 | 2 | −4 | −2 | 1 | −1 | 0 | 0 |
| 4 | 2 | −1 | −1 | −4 | 0 | 0 | 0 |
| −1 | 0 | 0 | −1 | 0 | 0 | 0 | 0 |
| 0 | 0 | 0 | 0 | 0 | 0 | 0 | 0 |
| 0 | 0 | 0 | 0 | 0 | 0 | 0 | 0 |
| 0 | 0 | 0 | 0 | 0 | 0 | 0 | 0 |
| 0 | 0 | 0 | 0 | 0 | 0 | 0 | 0 |

Typically in JPEG compression, there will be a lot of zeros at the end of the matrix.

Rounding off after dividing by an integer has effectively thrown away many high-frequency components. Then the strings of zeros make a good compression rate possible when run-length encoding is applied. Rounding during quantization makes JPEG a lossy compression method, but, depending on the compression rate chosen, the information that is lost usually does not unduly compromise the quality of the image.

**Step 4. Apply DPCM to the block.**

**Motivation:** *DPCM* is the abbreviation for *differential pulse code modulation*. In this context, DCPM is simply storing the difference between the first value in the previous 8 × 8 block and the first value in the current block. Since the difference is generally smaller than the actual value, this step adds to the compression.

**Details:** DPCM is a compression technique that works by recording the difference between consecutive data values rather than the actual values. DPCM is effective in cases where consecutive values don't change very much because fewer bits are needed to record the change than the value itself. DPCM can be applied in more complex ways in other compression algorithms for digital sound and image (*e.g.*, see Chapter 5), but in JPEG compression the application is simple: The upper leftmost value in an 8 × 8 block—called the DC component—is stored as the difference from the DC component in the previous block. The abbreviation DC is borrowed from electrical engineering, where it refers to direct current. The DC component is proportional to the average amplitude for all values in an $8 \times 8$ block.

We are considering only one block in our example, so we'll omit the DPCM step.

**Step 5. Arrange the values in a zigzag order and do run-length encoding.**

**Motivation:** The zigzag reordering sorts the values from low-frequency to high-frequency components. The high-frequency coefficients are grouped together at the end. If many of them round to zero after quantization, run-length encoding is even more effective.

**Details:** In Figure 2.25, we show the basis functions corresponding to each position in the $8 \times 8$ block. If you examine this picture, you'll notice that the frequencies increase from left to right in the horizontal direction and from top to bottom in the vertical direction. Thus, if we want to order the coefficients in order of increasing frequency, a good way to do this is the zigzag order pictured in Figure 3.50. The order of quantized values is now 73, $-4$, 11, 4, 2, 10, 3, $-4$, 2, $-1$, 0, 0, $-1$, $-2$, 4, 0, 1, $-1$, 0, 0, 0, 0, 0, 0, $-1$, $-4$, $-1$, $-1$, and 36 zeros. Reordering the coefficients in this way will increase the likelihood that you'll have strings of zeros, and this will increase the compression rate for the digital image.

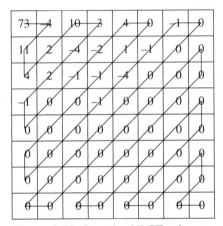

**Figure 3.50** Quantized DCT values rearranged from low- to high-frequency components

Chapter 1 showed a simple way to do run-length encoding. An alternative method can be done using pairs of the form (skip, value) where *skip* is the number of zeros in a row and *value* is the first nonzero value after the string of zeros. A (0, 0) indicates that there are no more nonzero values in the block. The run-length encoding of our example would be as follows:

(0, 73), (0, $-4$), (0, 11), (0, 4), (0, 2), (0, 10), (0, 3), (0, $-4$), (0, 2), (0, $-1$), (2, $-1$), (0, $-2$), (0, 4), (1, 1), (0, $-1$), (6, $-1$), (0, $-4$), (0, $-1$), (0, $-1$), (0, 0)

**Step 6. Do entropy encoding.**

**Motivation:** Additional compression can be achieved with some kind of entropy encoding.

**Details:** *Entropy encoding* is a compression strategy whereby the length of the code for a symbol is proportional to the probability that the symbol will appear in the file. Both Huffman encoding and arithmetic encoding take this approach. See Chapter 1 and the section on Huffman encoding in this chapter for a detailed description.

After these steps have been performed, the compressed file is put into a standardized format that can be recognized by the decompressor. A header contains global information such as the type of file, the width and height, one or more quantization tables, Huffman code tables, and an indication of any pixel-padding necessary to create properly sized coding units. The compressed image is divided into minimum coding units (MCUs). When YCbCr color model is used, an MCU consists of a $16 \times 16$ macroblock of pixels that is divided into four $8 \times 8$ blocks of Y fields and one $8 \times 8$ for each of the Cb and Cr fields.

An alternative JPEG compression method is called *JPEG2000*, noted for its high compression rate and good quality, without some of the blocky artifacts of standard JPEG. This method represents digital image data as wavelets as an alternative to the DCT. Some digital imaging application programs accommodate JPEG2000, at least as a plugin, but it cannot become the new standard until web browsers and digital cameras support it more widely.

## EXERCISES AND PROGRAMS

1. Indexed color algorithms, programming exercise, online

2. Octree algorithm for indexed color interactive tutorial, worksheet, and programming exercise, online

3. Dithering interactive tutorial, worksheet, and programming exercise, online

4. Blending modes, programming exercise

5. Histogram interactive tutorial and worksheet, online

6. Curves interactive tutorial and worksheet, online

7. Convolutions interactive tutorial and worksheet, online

8. Interpolation for resampling worksheet, online

9. LZW compression interactive tutorial, worksheet, and programming exercise, online

10. Huffman encoding interactive tutorial, worksheet, and programming exercise, online

11. JPEG compression interactive tutorial and worksheet, online

## APPLICATIONS

1. Examine the specifications of your digital camera (or the one you would like to have). Is it an SLR camera? In what file format does it save images? Does it have a RAW format? Does the camera allow you to do white balancing? Does it have a software image sharpening feature? If so, is there any indication of the algorithm it uses? Does have a histogram feature?

2. Examine the specifications of your scanner (or the one you would like to have). How many physical sensors does it have? What is its advertised maximum resolution? Are any of the pixels generated through interpolation?

3. Take a photograph with a digital camera. Transport the image to your computer and open it with an image processing program. Let's say that the image is saved by your camera as a JPEG file. Use your image processing program to save the image in different file types. First, save it as a TIFF file. Are you given the option of compressing the file? Describe this. Now save it as a BMP. Are you given the option of compressing the file? Describe this. Now save it as a GIF file. What options are you given when you save the file as GIF? How about PNG?

4. Find a poem or short story that you would like to illustrate with a digital image (or find some other motivation for taking an interesting digital photograph). Plan to create a web-based and a printable version of this photograph. Plan your project before you begin, thinking about the aspect ratio you want for the photograph, the pixel dimensions for the original photograph, the file type you want to work with, the point at which you should crop each image, the final pixel dimensions and resolution, and so forth. Experiment with the features of your image processing program to make refinements on the image and produce special effects. Keep notes on your work, and when you're done, describe your process and the reasons for your decisions. Include a list of questions about features that you would like to use but couldn't figure out.

   **Examine the features of your digital image processing program, vector graphic (*i.e.*, draw), and/or paint programs and try the exercises below with features that are available.**

5. What image file types are supported by your image processing software? What file types are supported by your vector graphics program?

6. Take a photograph with a digital camera. Transport the image to your computer and open it with an image processing program. What file type is it, as created by the camera? Let's say it's JPEG (common for many digital cameras). Change the image to indexed color. Then see if your image processing program will show you the color palette. (There may be a menu selection for color palette or color table.) Reduce the color palette to just eight colors if you can. Do this without dithering. Then select the dithering option. Describe the difference in the original, the reduced-color without dithering, and the reduced-color with dithering versions. Are different dithering algorithms offered? If so, what are they?

7. Look at the filters that are offered in your image processing program, relating the numbers in the convolution mask to the effect they create. If there is a "custom filter" feature, try designing your own custom filter. Explain the numbers you put in the convolution mask, and describe what effect they create.

**8.** a. If you have access to Adobe Illustrator, create a very simple drawing—for example, a single line. Save the image as an AI file. Then try to open the file with a text editor to see if you can read the file as text. Try to decipher what you see.

   b. Create a simple EPS file with whatever software you have available that supports this file type. See if you can read if as a text file. Try to find an example of a CGM file that can be read as text.

**9.** With an image processing or paint program, create an image that is just a blue circle on a white background. Make sure the edge of the circle is anti-aliased. Then make the background transparent. Save the image as a GIF file. Then insert the GIF file into another image that has a different-colored background. What is the undesirable effect that results from the anti-aliasing? What can you learn from this?

*Additional exercises or applications may be found at the book or author's websites.*

## REFERENCES

### Print Publications

*Adobe Photoshop CS2 Classroom in a Book*. Berkeley, CA: Adobe Press, 2005.

Bayer, B. E., "An Optimum Method for Two-Level Rendition of Continuous-Tone Pictures," *IEEE Conference Record of the International Conference on Communications* (1973), pp. 26-11–26-15.

Chen, W.-H., and W. K. Pratt. "Scene Adaptive Coder." *IEEE Transactions on Communications*, COM-32: 255–232, March 1984.

Floyd, R. and Steinberg, L. "An Adaptive Algorithm for Spatial Gray Scale." *Society for Information Display 1975 Symposium Digest of Technical Papers* (1975), p. 36.

Gallagher, R. G. "Variations on a Theme by Huffman." *IEEE Transactions on Information Theory*, 24(6): 668–674, Nov. 1978.

Gervautz, M. and W. Purgathofer. "A Simple Method for Color Quantization: Octree Quantization." *Graphics Gems*, Academic Press, 1990.

Gibson, J. D., et al. *Digital Compression for Multimedia: Principles and Standards*. San Francisco: Morgan Kaufmann Publishers, 1998.

Gonzalez, Rafael C., and Richard E. Woods. *Digital Image Processing*. 2nd ed. Upper Saddle River, NJ: Prentice Hall, 2002.

Heckbert, P. "Color Image Quantization for Frame Buffer Display." *SIGGRAPH 82*, pp. 297–307.

Huffman, D. A. "A Method for the Construction of Minimum-Redundancy Codes." *Proceedings of the Institute for Radio Engineers* [now IEEE], 40(9): 1098–1101, 1952.

Ifeachor, Emmanuel C., and Barrie W. Jervis. *Digital Signal Processing.* 2nd ed. Addison-Wesley Publishing, 2001.

McClelland, Deke. *Photoshop CS Bible: Professional Edition*. Indianapolis, IN: Wiley Publishing, 2004.

Pennebaker, W. B., and J. L. Mitchell. *JPEG Still Image Data Compression Standard*. New York: Van Nostrand Reinhold, 1993.

Sayood, Khalid. *Introduction to Data Compression*, 2nd ed. San Francisco: Morgan Kaufmann Publishers, 2000.

Welch, T. A. "A Technique for High Performance Data Compression." *IEEE Computer*, 17(6): 8–19, June 1984.

Ziv, J., and A. Lempel. "A Universal Algorithm for Sequential Data Compression." *IEEE Transactions on Information Theory*, 23(3): 337–343, 1977.

Ziv, J. and A. Lempel. "Compression of Individual Sequences Via Variable-Rate Coding." *IEEE Transactions of Information Theory*, 24(5): 530–536, September 1978.

## Websites

The JPEG Committee.

  http://www.jpeg.org/

JPEG 2000.

  http://www.jpeg.org/jpeg2000/

The JPEG Standard.

  http://www.w3.org/Graphics/JPEG/itu-t81.pdf
**See Chapter 2 for additional references on digital imaging.**

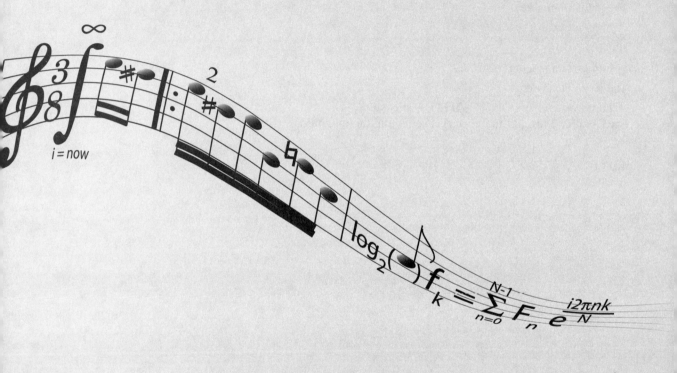

# Digital Audio Representation

*Take care of the sense, and the sounds will take care of themselves.* —Lewis Carroll, Alice's Adventures in Wonderland

## OBJECTIVES FOR CHAPTER 4

- Understand how waveforms represent changing air pressure caused by sound.
- Be able to apply the Nyquist theorem to an understanding of digital audio aliasing.
- Given a sampling rate, be able to compute the Nyquist frequency.
- Given the frequency of an actual sound wave, be able to compute the Nyquist rate.
- Given a sampling rate and the frequency of an actual sound wave, be able to compute the frequency of the resulting aliased wave if aliasing occurs.
- Understand the relationship between quantization level (*i.e.*, sample size or bit depth) to dynamic range of an audio file.
- Given air pressure amplitude for a sound, be able to compute decibels, and vice versa.
- Given a bit depth for digital audio, be able to compute the signal-to-quantization noise ratio assuming linear quantization.
- Understand how dithering is done and be able to choose an appropriate audio dithering function.
- Understand how noise shaping is done.
- Understand the algorithm and mathematics for $\mu$-law encoding.
- Understand the application and implementation of the Fourier transform for digital audio processing.
- Be able to read and interpret a histogram of a waveform.
- Be able to compute the RMS (root-mean-square) power of a digital audio wave.
- Understand the information provided in a frequency or spectral analysis of an audio wave.
- Understand the difference between the formats of MIDI and digital audio sound files.
- Become familiar with basic terminology of MIDI and related areas in musical acoustics and musical notation.
- Be able to interpret a MIDI byte-stream, identifying status and data bytes.

## 4.1 INTRODUCTION

As we introduce each new medium in this book, we place the concepts in context. Why would you want or need to know the mathematical and scientific concepts covered in the next two chapters on digital audio? What work might you be doing that is based on these concepts?

You may find yourself working with digital audio in a variety of situations. You may want to be able to digitally record and edit music, combining instruments and voices. You may want to edit the sound track for a digital video. You may be doing game programming and want to create sound effects, voice, and musical accompaniment for the game. You may work in the theater designing the sound to be used in the performance of a play or dance.

Working with digital audio in these applications entails recording sound, choosing the appropriate sampling rate and sample size for a recording, knowing the microphones to use for your conditions, choosing a sound card and editing software for recording and editing, taking out the imperfections in recorded audio, processing with special effects, compressing, and selecting the right file type for storage.

In this chapter, we'll begin with the basic concepts underlying digital audio representation. In Chapter 5 we'll talk about how to apply these concepts in digital audio processing.

## 4.2 AUDIO WAVEFORMS

The notion of a sound wave is something you've probably become comfortable with because you encounter it in so many everyday contexts. But unless you've had to study it in a high school or college physics course, you might assume that you understand the sense in which sound is a "wave," when really you may never have thought about it very closely. So let's check your understanding, just to be sure.

A good way to understand sound waves is to picture how they act on microphones. There are many kinds of microphones, divided for our purposes into two main categories of electrodynamic and electrostatic types. *Electrodynamic microphones* (also called simply *dynamic microphones*) operate by means of a moving coil or band (Figure 4.1). *Electrostatic microphones* (also called *condenser* or *capacitor microphones*) are based on capacitors that require an external power supply. Both function according to the same principle, which is that changing air pressure produced by sound waves causes the parts inside the microphone to react, and this reaction can be recorded as a "wave." For illustration of the nature of a sound wave, let's use an electrodynamic microphone, since it's easy to picture how it works.

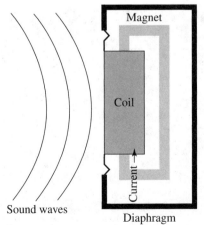

**Figure 4.1** The diaphragm of an electrodynamic microphone

Imagine that a single note is played on a piano, and a microphone is placed close to the piano to pick up the sound. A hammer inside the piano's mechanism strikes a string, vibrating the string. The string's vibrations "push" on the air molecules next to it, causing them alternately to move closer together and then farther apart in a regularly repeating pattern. When air molecules are squeezed together, air pressure rises. When they move apart, air pressure falls. These changes in air pressure are propagated through space. It's just like what happens when you splash in the water at the edge of a pool. The wave ripples through the pool as the water molecules move back and forth.

So how does this sound wave affect the microphone? The basic component of an electrodynamic microphone is a coil of wire wound in the microphone's diaphragm in the presence of a magnetic field. (The diaphragm is the place in a microphone that detects the air vibrations and responds.) If a wire moves in the environment of a magnetic field, a current is induced in the wire. This is what happens when the changes in air pressure reach the wire—the wire moves, and an electrical current proportional to the movement of the wire is created. The electrical current oscillates along with the vibrations of the piano string. The changes in current can be recorded as continuously changing voltages. If you draw a graph of how the voltages change, what you're drawing is the sound wave produced by the striking of the piano key. In essence, the changing voltages model how air pressure changes over time in response to some vibration, changes that are perceived by the human ear as sound.

Physically, the changing air pressure caused by sound is translated into changing voltages. Mathematically, the fluctuating pressure can be modeled as continuously changing numbers—a function where time is the input variable and amplitude (of air pressure or voltage) is the output. Graphing this function with time on the horizontal axis and amplitude on the vertical axis, we have the one-dimensional waveform commonly associated with sound. If the sound is a single-pitch tone with no overtones, the graph will be a single-frequency sinusoidal wave. The wave corresponding to the note A on the piano (440 Hz) is shown in Figure 4.2. Few sounds come to us as single-pitch tones. Even the single spoken word "boo" is a complex waveform, as shown in Figure 1.16.

You saw in Chapter 2 that an image can mathematically be formulated as the sum of its frequency components in two dimensions, horizontally and vertically over space. A complex

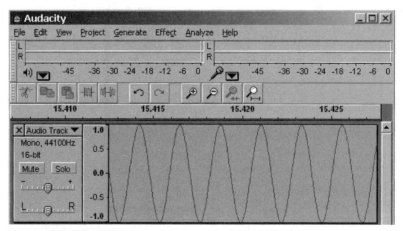

**Figure 4.2** Waveform view of the note A, 440 Hz (from Audacity)

sound wave can be formulated as a sum of its frequency components in one dimension, over time. Later in this chapter, you'll see how the transformation from the time domain to the frequency domain is done with the Fourier transform. For now, let's look at different views of a waveform that give you information about the sound in either the time or the frequency domain.

Figure 4.2 is a waveform view from an audio processing program. A waveform view shows the sound wave with time on the horizontal axis and amplitude on the vertical axis, as shown in the figure above. You may be able change the units on the axes. The vertical axis might be shown in decibels (specifically, dBFS, explained below), sample values, percentages, or normalized values. The horizontal axis might be shown as mm:ss:ddd (*i.e.*, minutes, seconds, and fractions of seconds to the thousandths), sample numbers, or different SMPTE (Society of Motion Picture and Television Engineers) formats.

# 4.3 PULSE CODE MODULATION AND AUDIO DIGITIZATION

Algorithms for sound digitization date back farther than you might imagine. *Pulse code modulation* (*PCM*) is a term that you'll encounter frequently as you read about digital audio. The term has been around for a long time—since it was first invented in 1937 by Alec Reeves, who at that time worked for International Telephone and Telegraph. PCM is based on the methods of sampling and quantization applied to sound. However, when Reeves devised this method in 1937, his focus was on the *transmission* of audio signals—the emphasis being on the word *modulation*. (See Chapters 1 and 6 for more on modulation techniques.) Reeves proposed an alternative to analog-based frequency and amplitude modulation: that signals be sampled at discrete points in time, each sample be quantized and encoded in binary, and the bits be transmitted as pulses representing 0s and 1s. It sounds familiar, doesn't it? When you realize that 1937 predates the advent of digital audio as we know it today, you realize how far ahead of his time Reeves was. The term PCM is still used in digital audio to refer to the sampling and quantization process. In fact, PCM files are files that are digitized but not compressed. When you want to save your files in "raw" version, you can save them as PCM files.

When you create a new audio file in a digital audio processing program, you are asked to choose the sampling rate and bit depth. Audio sampling rates are measured in cycles per second, designated in units of Hertz. In the past, the most common choices were 8000 Hz mono for telephone quality voice, or 44.1 kHz two-channel stereo with 16 bits per channel for CD-quality sound. Digital audio tape (DAT) format uses a sampling rate of 48 kHz. Now higher sampling rates and bit depths have become more common (*e.g.*, sampling rates of 96 or 192 kHz for two-channel stereo DVD with 24 bits per channel). In general, your

> **ASIDE:** A number of bit-saving alternatives to PCM have been devised, especially in the field of telephony, where compressing the signal is important for preserving bandwidth. Statistically based methods rely on the characteristic nature of voice signals. Because the amplitudes of sounds in human speech do not change dramatically from one moment to the next, it's possible to reduce the bit depth by recording only the difference between one sample and the succeeding one. This is called *differential pulse code modulation* (*DPCM*). The algorithm can be fine-tuned so that the quantization level varies in accordance with the dynamically changing characteristics of the speech pattern, yielding better compression rates. This is called *adaptive differential pulse-code modulation* (*ADPCM*).

> **ASIDE:** In the context of digital audio, the bit depth is sometimes referred to as *resolution*, which is a little confusing because in digital imaging *resolution* relates to sampling rate.

sampling rate and bit depth should match that of other audio clips with which you might be mixing the current one. They should also be appropriate for the type of sound you're recording, the storage capacity of the medium on which the audio will be stored, and the sensitivity of the equipment on which it will be played. You may sometimes want to use a higher sampling rate than you will ultimately need so that less error is introduced if you add special effects. Sometimes 32-bit samples are used initially for greater accuracy during sound processing, after which the audio can be downsampled to 16 bits before compression. Most good audio processing programs do this automatically, behind the scenes. This is why it is recommended that you use dither on your output even if you're working with a 16-bit file and saving it as 16 bits. Even though you, the user, may not be doing any bit depth conversions, the software might be behind the scenes.

The concepts of sampling rate and bit depth that you find in digital imaging carry over to digital audio processing as well. Just as was true with digital imaging, the sampling rate for digital audio must obey the Nyquist theorem, meaning that it must be at least twice the frequency of the highest frequency component in the audio being captured. The bit depth puts a limit on the precision with which you can represent each sample, determining the signal-to-quantization-noise ratio and dynamic range. In the next sections, we'll examine these issues closely as they apply to digital audio representation.

## 4.4 SAMPLING RATE AND ALIASING

There are two related, but not synonymous, terms used with regard to the Nyquist theorem: Nyquist frequency and Nyquist rate. Given a sampling rate, the *Nyquist frequency* is the highest actual frequency component that can be sampled at the given rate without aliasing. Based on the Nyquist theorem, the Nyquist frequency is half the given sampling rate. For example, if you choose to take samples at a rate of 8000 Hz (*i.e.*, 8000 samples/s), then the Nyquist frequency is 4000 Hz. This means that if the sound you're digitizing has a frequency component greater than 4000 Hz, then that component will be aliased—that is, it will sound lower in pitch than it should.

Given an actual frequency to be sampled, the *Nyquist rate* is the lowest sampling rate that will permit accurate reconstruction of an analog digital signal. The Nyquist theorem tells us that the Nyquist rate is twice the frequency of the highest frequency component in the signal being sampled. For example, if the highest frequency component is 10,000 Hz, then the Nyquist rate is 20,000 Hz. The two terms are summarized in the key equations below. (Unfortunately, some sources incorrectly use Nyquist frequency and Nyquist rate interchangeably.)

### KEY EQUATION

Given $f_{max}$, the frequency of the highest-frequency component in an audio signal to be sampled, then the *Nyquist rate*, $f_{nr}$, is defined as

$$f_{nr} = 2f_{max}$$

## KEY EQUATION

Given a sampling frequency $f_{samp}$ to be used to sample an audio signal, then the *Nyquist frequency*, $f_{nf}$, is defined as

$$f_{nf} = \frac{1}{2}f_{samp}$$

The main point is that when you're digitizing an analog audio wave and your sampling rate is below the Nyquist rate, **audio aliasing** will occur. That is, when the digitized sound is played, the frequency from the original sound will be translated to a different frequency, so the digitized sound doesn't sound exactly like the original. Let's look at how this happens, beginning with single-frequency waves, from which we can generalize to waves with more than one frequency component.

In essence, the reason a too-low sampling rate results in aliasing is that there aren't enough sample points from which to accurately interpolate the sinusoidal form of the original wave. If we take *more* than two samples per cycle on an analog wave, the wave can be precisely reconstructed from the samples, as shown in Figure 4.3. In this example, the wave being sampled has a frequency of 637 Hz, which is 637 cycles/s. This means that we need to sample it at a Nyquist rate of at least 1274 samples/s (*i.e.*, 1274 Hz). The black dots on the figure show where the samples are taken, at a rate of 1490 Hz, greater than the Nyquist rate. No aliasing occurs when the wave is reconstructed from the samples because there is sufficient information to reconstruct the wave's sinusoidal form.

**ASIDE:** The example where samples are taken exactly twice per cycle illustrates why there is some confusion in the literature over the definition of the Nyquist rate. The *Nyquist rate* is sometimes defined as "at least twice the actual frequency of the highest frequency component" and sometimes as "greater than twice the actual frequency of the highest frequency component." Sampling at exactly twice the frequency of the highest-frequency component can work but isn't guaranteed to work, as shown in the example.

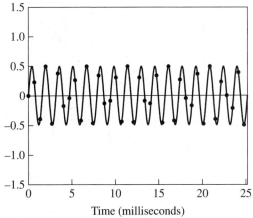

**Figure 4.3** Samples taken more than twice per cycle will provide sufficient information to reproduced the wave with no aliasing

If we have *exactly* two samples per cycle and the samples are taken at precisely the maximum and minimum values of the sine wave, once again the digitized wave can be reconstructed, as shown in Figure 4.4. However, if the samples are taken at locations other than peaks and troughs, the frequency may be correct but the amplitude incorrect. In fact, the amplitude can be 0 if samples are always taken at 0 points.

A wave sampled fewer than two times per cycle cannot be accurately reproduced. In Figure 4.5, we see the result of sampling a 637 Hz wave at 1000 Hz, resulting in an aliased wave of 363 Hz. The inadequate sampling rate skips over some of the cycles, making it appear that the frequency of the actual wave is lower than it really is. (The actual frequency is the sine wave drawn with the dashed line in the background.)

Figure 4.6 shows a 637 Hz wave sampled at 500 Hz. Again, the sampling rate is below the Nyquist rate. In this case, the aliased wave has a frequency of 137 Hz.

Figure 4.7 shows a 637 Hz wave sampled at 400 Hz, yielding an aliased wave at 163 Hz.

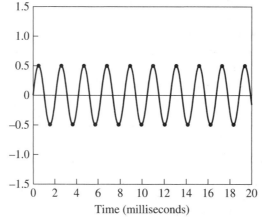

**Figure 4.4** Samples taken exactly twice per cycle *can* be sufficient for digitizing the original with no aliasing

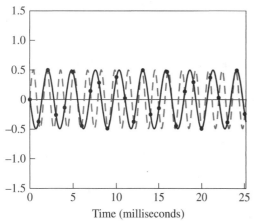

**Figure 4.5** A 637 Hz wave sampled at 1000 Hz aliases to 363 Hz

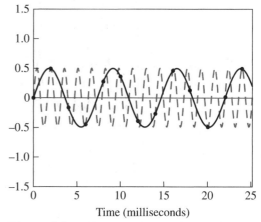

**Figure 4.6** A 637 Hz wave sampled at 500 Hz aliases to 137 Hz

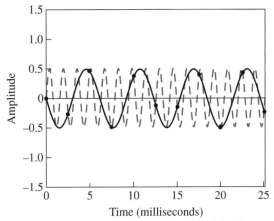

**Figure 4.7** A 637 Hz wave sampled at 400 Hz
aliases to 163 Hz

Algorithm 4.1 shows how to compute the frequency of the aliased wave where aliasing occurs. Let's do an example of cases 2, 3, and 4.

---

**ALGORITHM 4.1**

```
algorithm get_frequency
/*Input:   Frequency of the analog audio wave (a single tone)
           to be sampled, f_act
           Sampling frequency, f_samp
Output:   Frequency of the digitized audio wave, f_obs*/
{
  f_nf = 1/2 f_samp
                /*f_nf is the Nyquist frequency*/
/*CASE 1*/
    if (f_act ≤ f_nf) then
      f_obs = f_act
/*CASE 2*/
    else if (f_nf < f_act ≤ f_samp) then
      f_obs = f_samp − f_act
    else {
      INT = f_act/f_nf /* integer division */
      REM = f_act mod f_nf
/*CASE 3*/
      if (INT is even) then
          f_obs = REM
/*CASE 4*/
      else if (INT is odd) then
          f_obs = f_nf − REM
  }
}
```

**Case 2:**

$f\_act = 637$ Hz; $f\_samp = 1000$ Hz; thus $f\_nf = 500$ Hz

$f\_nf < f\_act \leq f\_samp$

Therefore, $f\_obs = f\_samp - f\_act = 363$ Hz

(See Figure 4.5.)

**Case 3:**

$f\_act = 637$ Hz; $f\_samp = 500$ Hz; thus $f\_nf = 250$ Hz

$f\_act > f\_samp$

$INT = f\_act/f\_nf = 637/250 = 2$

(Note: / is integer division, which means throw away the remainder)

INT is even

$REM = f\_act \bmod f\_nf = 137$

(Note: *mod* saves only the remainder from the division)

Therefore, $f\_obs = REM = 137$ Hz

(See Figure 4.6.)

**Case 4:**

$f\_act = 637$ Hz; $f\_samp = 400$ Hz; thus $f\_nf = 200$ Hz

$f\_act > f\_samp$

$INT = f\_act/f\_nf = 637/200 = 3$

INT is odd

$REM = f\_act \bmod f\_nf = 37$

Therefore, $f\_obs = f\_nf - REM = 200 - 37 = 163$ Hz

(See Figure 4.7.)

It may be helpful to get a sense of how the algorithm works by looking at it as a function with one independent variable and graphing it. Assume that $f\_samp$ is given as a constant, $f\_act$ is the input to the function, and $f\_obs$ is the output. The function is graphed in Figure 4.8. A graph such as this can be drawn for any given sampling rate. Along the horizontal axis you have $f\_act$, and along the vertical axis you have $f\_obs$. The four cases of the algorithm always lie along the same parts of the graph: Case 1 is along the upward slope of the first triangle, case 2 on the downward slope of the first triangle, case 3 on the upward slope of any succeeding triangle, and case 4 on the downward slope of any succeeding triangle. All the triangles peak at $f\_obs = f\_nf$. The sampling rate is fixed for a particular graph, and it determines the Nyquist frequency. That is, $f\_nf = \frac{1}{2} f\_samp$ tells you the highest frequency that can be sampled at the given sampling rate without aliasing. Once you have fixed the sampling rate and corresponding Nyquist frequency and drawn the graph, you can consider any actual frequency $f\_act$ and predict what its corresponding observed frequency $f\_obs$ will be given the sampling rate $f\_samp$.

A different graph can be drawn by fixing the actual frequency of a sound wave and graphing the observed frequency as a function of the sampling rate. As long as the sampling rate is below the Nyquist rate, the observed frequency will always be less than the actual frequency. This is shown in Figure 4.9.

Audio editing programs allow you to resample audio files. You sometimes may want to do this to lower the sampling rate and reduce the file size. As you have seen, using a lower

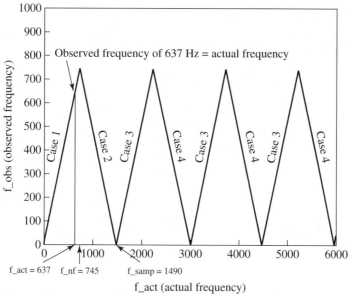

**Figure 4.8** The relationships among sampling rate, actual frequency, and observed frequency when $f_{samp} = 1490$

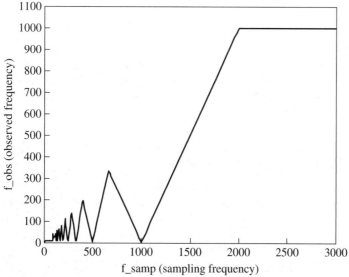

**Figure 4.9** Graph of aliasing function with fixed actual frequency of 1000 Hz

sampling rate may introduce aliased frequencies. However, audio editing programs have filters that will eliminate the high frequency components before resampling in order to avoid aliasing. You should look for these options when you work with your sound files. Filtering is also done in hardware analog-to-digital converters to avoid aliasing when a digital recording is made.

## 4.5 QUANTIZATION AND QUANTIZATION ERROR

### 4.5.1 Decibels and Dynamic Range

As you have seen in the previous section, sampling rate relates directly to the frequency of a wave. Quantization, on the other hand, relates more closely to the amplitude of a sound wave. *Amplitude* measures the intensity of the sound and is related to its perceived loudness. It can be measured with a variety of units, including voltages, newtons/m$^2$, or the unitless measure called decibels. To understand decibels it helps to consider first how amplitude can be measured in terms of air pressure.

In Chapter 1, we described how a vibrating object pushes molecules closer together, creating changes in air pressure. Since this movement is the basis of sound, it makes sense to measure the loudness of a sound in terms of air pressure changes. Atmospheric pressure is customarily measured in pascals (newtons/meter$^2$) (abbreviated Pa or N/m$^2$). The average atmospheric pressure at sea level is approximately $10^5$ Pa. For sound waves, *air pressure amplitude* is defined as the average deviation from normal background atmospheric air pressure. For example, the *threshold of human hearing* (for a 1000 Hz sound wave) varies from the normal background atmospheric air pressure by $2 * 10^{-5}$ Pa, so this is its pressure amplitude.

Measuring sound in terms of pressure amplitude is intuitively easy to understand, but in practice decibels are a more common, and in many ways a more convenient, way to measure sound amplitude. Decibels can be used to measure many things in physics, optics, electronics, and signal processing. A decibel is not an absolute unit of measurement. A decibel is always based upon some agreed-upon reference point, and the reference point varies according to the phenomenon being measured. In networks, for example, decibels can be used to measure the attenuation of a signal across the transmission medium. The reference point is the strength of the original signal, and decibels describe how much of the signal is lost relative to its original strength. For sound, the reference point is the air pressure amplitude for the threshold of hearing. A decibel in the context of sound pressure level is called *decibels-sound-pressure-level* (*dB_SPL*).

> ### 🔑 KEY EQUATION
>
> Let $E$ be the pressure amplitude of the sound being measured and $E_0$ be the sound pressure level of the threshold of hearing. Then *decibels-sound-pressure-level*, (*dB_SPL*) is defined as
>
> $$dB\_SPL = 20 \log_{10}\left(\frac{E}{E_0}\right)$$

Often, this is abbreviated simply as *dB*, but since decibels are always relative, it is helpful to indicate the reference point if the context is not clear. With this use of decibels, $E_0$, the threshold of hearing, is the point of comparison for the sound being measured.

Given a value for the air pressure amplitude, you can compute the amplitude of sound in decibels with the equation above. For example, what would be the amplitude of the audio threshold of pain, given as 30 Pa?

$$dB\_SPL = 20 \log_{10}\left(\frac{30 \text{ Pa}}{0.00002 \text{ Pa}}\right) = 20 \log_{10}(1500000) = 20 * 6.17 \approx 123$$

Thus, 30 N/m$^2$, the threshold of pain, is approximately equal to 123 decibels. (The threshold of pain varies with frequency and with individual perception.) You can also compute the pressure amplitude given the decibels. For example, what would be the pressure amplitude of normal conversation, given as 60 dB?

$$60 = 20 \log_{10}\left(\frac{x}{0.00002 \text{ Pa}}\right)$$

$$60 = 20 \log_{10}\left(\frac{50000x}{\text{Pa}}\right)$$

$$3 = \log_{10}\left(\frac{50000x}{\text{Pa}}\right)$$

$$10^3 = \frac{50000x}{\text{Pa}}$$

$$\frac{1000}{50000}\text{Pa} = x$$

$$x = 0.02 \text{ Pa}$$

Thus, 60 dB is approximately equal to 0.02 Pa.

Decibels can also be used to describe sound intensity (as opposed to sound pressure amplitude). *Decibels-sound-intensity-level (dB_SIL)* is defined as $dB\_SPL = 10 \log_{10}\left(\frac{I}{I_0}\right)$. $I_0$ is the intensity of sound at the threshold of hearing, given as $10^{-12}$ W/m$^2$. (W is watts.) It is sometimes more convenient to work with intensity decibels rather than pressure amplitude decibels, but essentially the two give the same information. The relationship between the two lies in the relationship between pressure (*potential* in volts) and intensity (*power* in watts). In this respect, $I$ is proportional to the square of $E$ (discussed in Chapter 1).

Decibels-sound-pressure-level are an appropriate unit for measuring sound because the values increase logarithmically rather than linearly. This is a better match for the way humans perceive sound. For example, a voice at normal conversation level could be 100 times the air pressure amplitude of a soft whisper, but to human perception it seems only about 16 times louder. Decibels are scaled to account for the nonlinear nature of human sound perception. Table 4.1 gives the decibels of some common sounds. The values in Table 4.1 vary with the frequency of the sound and with individual hearing ability.

**TABLE 4.1    Approximate Decibel Levels of Common Sounds**

| Sound | Decibels (dB_SPL) |
|---|---|
| Threshold of hearing | 0 |
| Rustling leaves | 20 |
| Conversation | 60–70 |
| Jackhammer | 100 (or more) |
| Threshold of pain | 130 |
| Damage to eardrum | 160 |

Experimentally, it has been determined that if you increase the amplitude of an audio recording by 10 dB, it will sound about twice as loud. (Of course, these perceived differences are subjective.) For most humans, a 3 dB change in amplitude is the smallest perceptible change.

While an insufficient sampling rate can lead to aliasing, an insufficient bit depth can create *distortion*, also referred to as *quantization noise*. In Chapter 1, we showed that signal-to-quantization-noise-ratio, SQNR, is defined as $SQNR = 20 \log_{10}(2^n)$ where $n$ is the bit depth of a digital file. This can be applied to digital sound and related to the concept of dynamic range. Dynamic range is the ratio between the smallest nonzero value, which is 1, and the largest, which is $2^n$. For an $n$-bit file, the ratio, expressed in decibels, is then $20 \log_{10}\left(\dfrac{2^n}{1}\right) = 20n \log_{10}(2)$. Thus, the definition is identical to the definition of SQNR, and this is why you see the terms SQNR and dynamic range sometimes used interchangeably.

We can simplify $20n \log_{10}(2)$ even further by taking $\log_{10}(2)$, which is about 0.30103, and multiplying by 20.

---

### KEY EQUATION

Let $n$ be the bit depth of a digital audio file. Then the *dynamic range of the audio file*, $d$, in decibels, is defined as

$$d = 20n \log_{10}(2) \approx 6n$$

---

As a rule of thumb you can estimate that an $n$-bit digital audio file has a dynamic range (or, equivalently, a signal-to-noise-ratio) of $6n$ dB. For example, a 16-bit digital audio file has a dynamic range of about 96 dB, while an 8-bit digital audio file has a range of about 48 dB.

Be careful not to interpret this to mean that a 16-bit file allows louder amplitudes than an 8-bit file. Rather, dynamic range gives you a measure of the range of amplitudes that can be captured relative to the loss of fidelity compared to the original sound. Dynamic range is a relative measurement—the relative difference between the loudest and softest parts representable in a digital audio file, as a function of the bit depth.

There is a second way in which the term dynamic range is used. We've defined it as it applies to any file of a given bit depth. The term can also be applied to a particular audio piece, not related to bit depth. (In this usage, you don't even have to be talking about digital audio.) A particular piece of music can be said to have a wide dynamic range if there's a big difference between the loudest and softest parts of the piece. Symphonic classical music typically has a wide dynamic range. "Elevator music" is produced so that it doesn't have a wide dynamic range, and can lie in the background unobtrusively.

Let's return to the term decibels now. You'll find another variation of decibels when you use audio processing programs, where you may have the option of choosing the units for sample values. Units are shown on the vertical axes in the waveforms of Figure 4.10. On the left, we've chosen the *sample units* view. On the right, we've chosen the *decibels* view. However, the decibels being displayed are *decibels-full-scale (dBFS)* rather than the decibels-sound-pressure-level defined above.

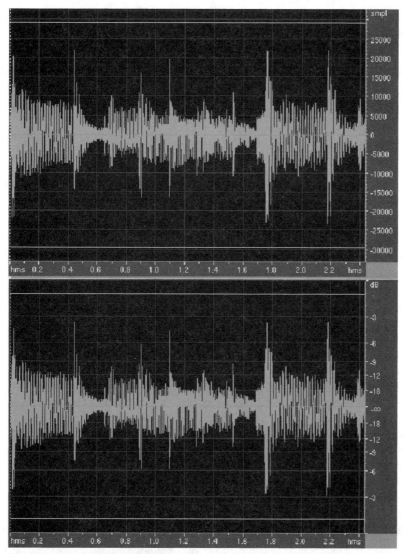

**Figure 4.10** Measuring amplitude in samples or decibels (from Audition)
Units are samples in top window, decibels in bottom window

The idea behind dBFS is that it makes sense to use the maximum possible amplitude as a fixed reference point and move down from there. There exists some maximum audio amplitude that can be generated by the system on which the audio processing program is being run. Because this maximum is a function of the system and not of a particular audio file, it is the same for all files and does not vary with bit depth. This maximum is given the value 0. When you look at a waveform with amplitude given in dBFS, the horizontal center of the waveform is $-\infty$ dBFS, and above and below this axis the values progress to the maximum of 0 dBFS. This is shown in the window on the right in Figure 4.10. The bit depth of each audio file determines how much lower you can go below the maximum amplitude before the sample value is reduced to 0.

This is the basis for the definition of dBFS, which measures amplitude values relative to the maximum possible value. For *n*-bit samples, dBFS is defined as follows:

> ### 🔑 KEY EQUATION
>
> Let $x$ be an $n$-bit audio sample in the range of $-2^{n-1} \le x \le 2^{n-1} - 1$. Then $x$'s value expressed as ***decibels-full-scale*, dBFS,** is
>
> $$dBFS = 20 \log_{10}\left(\frac{|x|}{2^{n-1}}\right)$$

Try the definition of dBFS on a number of values, using $n = 16$. You'll find that a sample value of $-32768$ maps to 0, the maximum amplitude possible for the system; 10,000 maps to $-10.3$; 1 maps to $-90.3$; and 0.5 maps to $-96.3296$. These values are consistent with what you learned about dynamic range. A 16-bit audio file has a dynamic range of about 96 decibels. Any samples that map to decibel values that are more than 96 decibels below the maximum possible amplitude effectively are lost as silence.

## 4.5.2 Audio Dithering

Supplements on audio dithering:

interactive tutorial

mathematical modeling worksheet

***Audio dithering*** is a way to compensate for quantization error. Surprisingly, the way to do this is to add small random values to samples in order to mask quantization error. The rounding inherent in quantization causes a problem in that at low amplitudes, many values may be rounded down to 0. Since 0 is simply silence, this can cause noticeable breaks in the sound. If small random values between 0 and the least significant bit (on the scale of the new bit depth) are added to the signal before it is quantized, some of the samples that would have been lost will no longer fall to 0. Adding a little bit of noise to the signal is preferable to having discontinuities of silence.

Dithering is customarily performed by analog-to-digital converters before the quantization step. You'll also encounter the dithering option if you decide to reduce the bit depth of an audio file. If you know how audio dithering works, you'll know what effect it will have and you'll be able to make a more informed choice of a dithering function.

A good way to understand the effect that quantization error has on sound is to look at it graphically. Figure 4.11 shows a continuous waveform, the wave quantized to 16 quantization levels, and the quantization error wave. Note that the original wave plus the error wave equals the quantized wave. The error wave constitutes another sound component that can be heard as a distortion of the signal.

Although in the previous section we used the term *noise* with regard to quantization error, *distortion* is really more accurate. Notice that the error waveform is periodic; that is, it repeats in a regular pattern, and its period is related to the period of the original wave. This is the distinction that some sources make between distortion and noise. Noise is random, while distortion sounds meaningful even though it is not. For this reason, distortion can be more distracting in an audio signal than noise. The distortion wave moves in a pattern along with the original wave and thus, to human hearing, it seems to be a meaningful part of the sound. It is

> **ASIDE:** The term signal-to-noise ratio is widely used with regard to quantization error, but this type of noise might more correctly be called distortion. However, not all sources make a distinction between distortion and noise.

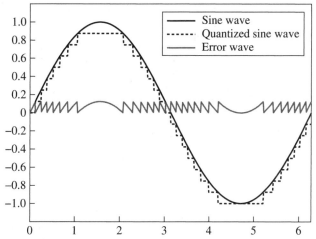

**Figure 4.11** Original wave (the sine wave), quantized sine wave, and quantization error wave

easier for the human brain to tune out noise because it seems to have no logical relationship to the dominant patterns of the sound.

It may be counterintuitive to understand that artificially introducing noise (the random kind) can actually have a helpful effect on sound that is quantized in an insufficient number of bits, but it's possible to add noise to a quantized audio wave in a way that reduces the effects of distortion. Imagine that we add between −1 and 1 unit, on the scale of the reduced bit depth, to each sample. The exact amount, $x$, to be added to the sample could be determined at random by a ***triangular probability density function*** (**TPDF**). The function, shown in Figure 4.12, indicates that there is the greatest probability that 0 will be added to a sample. As $x$ goes from 0 to 1 (and symmetrically as $x$ goes from 0 to −1), the probability that $x$ is the value to be added to a sample decreases. (A simple way to generate values for a triangular probability density function is to take the sum of two random numbers between −0.5 and 0.5.)

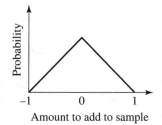

**Figure 4.12** Triangular probability function

Adding this random noise to the original wave eliminates the sharp stairstep effect in the quantized signal. Instead, the quantized wave jumps back and forth between two neighboring quantization levels. Another advantage is that with the addition of the small random value, there aren't as many neighboring low-amplitude values that are rounded to 0 when they are quantized. Neighboring low-amplitude values that become 0 in quantization create disturbing breaks in the audio. (You would be able to picture this better in an actual music audio clip than in the simple waveform pictured in Figure 4.11.)

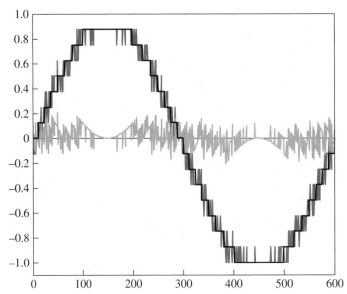

**Figure 4.13** Quantized sine wave, dithered quantized wave, and (along horizontal axis) error wave including dithering

Figure 4.13 shows dithering with the triangular dithering function, which produces random values between −1 and 1. (It's assumed in this figure that the signal is originally at a bit depth of 16 and is being reduced to a bit depth of four. A bit depth of four is unrealistically low but serves to illustrate the effect.) The dithered wave in the figure represents the original quantized wave to which the dither function has been added. The resulting dithered wave generally has fewer disturbing audio artifacts than the undithered wave does. By "artifacts," we mean areas where the sound breaks up or goes to silence.

Other dithering functions include the ***rectangular probability density function*** (**RPDF**), the ***Gaussian PDF***, and ***colored dithering***. The RPDF generates random numbers such that all numbers in the selected range have the same probability of being generated. While the TPDF randomly generates numbers within a range of two units (*e.g.*, −1 to +1), the RPDF works better if numbers are chosen in a range of 1 unit (*e.g.*, 0 to 1). The Gaussian PDF is like the TPDF except that it weights the probabilities according to a Gaussian rather than a triangular shape. Gaussian dither creates noise that resembles common environmental noises, like tape hiss. Colored dithering produces noise that is primarily in higher frequencies rather than in the frequencies of human hearing. It's best to apply colored dithering only if no more audio processing will be done, since the noise it generates can be amplified by other effects applied afterwards. The TPDF is best to use when the audio file will be undergoing more processing.

Supplement on
noise shaping:

mathematical
modeling
worksheet

### 4.5.3 Noise Shaping

*Noise shaping* is another way to compensate for the quantization error. It is an important component in the design of analog-to-digital and digital-to-analog converters. You can also opt to use noise shaping in conjunction with dithering if you reduce the bit depth of an audio file. Noise shaping is *not* dithering, but it is often used along with dithering. The idea behind noise shaping is to redistribute the quantization error so that the noise is concentrated in the higher frequencies, where human hearing is less sensitive. Noise shaping algorithms, first developed by Cutler in the 1950s, work by computing the error that results from quantizing the *i*th sample and adding this error to the next sample, before that next sample is itself quantized. Say that you have an array *F* of audio samples. Consider the following definition of a first-order feedback loop for noise shaping:

## KEY EQUATIONS

Let *F_in* be an array of $N$ digital audio samples that are to be quantized, dithered, and noise shaped, yielding *F_out*. For $0 \leq i \leq N - 1$, define the following:

$F\_in_i$ is the *i*th sample value, not yet quantized.

$D_i$ is a random dithering value added to the *i*th sample.

The assignment statement $F\_in_i = F\_in_i + D_i + cE_{i-1}$ dithers and noise shapes the sample. Subsequently, $F\_out_i = \lfloor F\_in_i \rfloor$ quantizes the sample.

$E_i$ is the error resulting from quantizing the *i*th sample after dithering and noise shaping. For $i = -1, E_i = 0$. Otherwise, $E_i = F\_in_i - F\_out_i$.

**Equation 4.1**

Let's try an example.

Assume that audio is being recorded in 8 bit samples. On the scale of 8 bits, sound amplitudes can take any value between $-128$ and $128$. (These values do not become integers between $-128$ and $127$ until after quantization.)

Say that $F\_in_0 = 68.2, F\_in_1 = 70.4, D_0 = 0.9, D_1 = -0.6$, and $c = 1$. Then

$F\_in_0 = F\_in_0 + D_0 + cE_{-1} = 68.2 + 0.9 + 0 = 69.1$

$F\_out_0 = \lfloor F\_in_0 \rfloor = 69$

$E_0 = F\_in_0 - F\_out_0 = 69.1 - 69 = 0.1$

$F\_in_1 = F\_in_1 + D_1 + cE_0 = 70.4 - 0.6 + 0.1 = 69.9$

$F\_out = \lfloor F\_in_0 \rfloor = 69$

$E_1 = F\_in_1 - F\_out_1 = 69.9 - 69 = 0.9$

To understand the benefit of noise shaping, think about the frequency spectrum of quantization noise—that is, the range of the frequency components—when noise shaping is *not* used. Quantization noise is part of the original audio signal in the sense that it shares the original signal's sampling rate, and thus its frequency components are spread out over the same range. By the Nyquist theorem, the highest valid frequency component is half the frequency of the sampling rate, and without noise shaping, this is where the frequency components of the quantization noise lie. If we filter out frequencies above the Nyquist frequency, we're not losing anything we care about in the sound. The more of the noise's frequency components we can move above the Nyquist frequency, the better. This is what noise shaping does. The idea is that if the error from dithering and quantizing $F_i$ is larger than the previous one, then the error for $F_{i+1}$ ought to be smaller for $F_i$. Making the error wave go up and down rapidly has the effect of moving the error wave to a higher frequency. The feedback loop inherent in noise shaping has the effect of spreading out the noise's frequency components over a broader band so that more of them are at high levels and can be filtered out.

The term *shaping* is used because you can manipulate the "shape" of the noise by manipulating the noise shaping equations, adding more error terms and using different multipliers for the error terms. The general statement for an *n*th order noise shaper noise shaping equation becomes $F\_out_i = F\_in_i + D_i + c_{i-1}E_{i-1} + c_{i-2}E_{i-2} + \cdots + c_{i-n}E_{i-n}$. The coefficients of the error terms can be used to control the frequencies generated. Ninth-order noise shapers are not uncommon. The POW-r noise shaping algorithm, for example, uses a 9th order formula to requantize audio from 24 to 16 bits.

When you reduce the bit depth of an audio file in an audio processing program, you're given the options of using noise shaping along with dithering. Both operations reduce the negative effects of noise, but they do it in different ways. Recall from the previous section that some sources make a distinction between *distortion* and *noise*. Distortion is a certain kind of noise—noise that is correlated with the original signal, in that its frequency pattern follows the frequency pattern of the signal. Noise shaping doesn't do anything to dissociate the noise's frequency pattern from the signal, so it's important to use dithering in conjunction with noise shaping, not alone.

Figure 4.14 shows the effect of requantizing an audio file from 16 down to 4 bits. This is not something you are likely to do, since there's no reason to use so few bits, but it serves to illustrate the effect. Three versions of the quantization error are shown, in both waveform and spectral views. (To generate the error wave, you just subtract the requantized wave from the original one.) The first shows the error that is generated from requantization with no dithering. The second shows the error that results from requantization with dithering. The third shows the error that results from requantization with dithering and noise shaping. Dithering spreads out the error pretty evenly around the frequencies. Noise shaping moves the error to higher frequencies. A small clip of each wave is given on the right, and in this view as well you can see that the frequencies increase.

Dithering and noise shaping algorithms are provided for you in audio processing programs. You are given a choice of noise shaping algorithms to use along with dithering. These choices are associated with the sampling rate of your audio file. If your sampling rate is less than 32 kHz, noise shaping doesn't work very well. This is because the Nyquist frequency for this sampling rate is relatively low, so even when you spread the noise across a wider frequency band, some of it will probably still be in the range of human hearing.

## 4.5.4 Non-Linear Quantization

*Nonlinear encoding*, or *companding*, is an encoding method that arose from the need for compression of telephone signals across low bandwidth lines. The word companding is derived from the fact that this encoding scheme requires compression and then expansion. In sketch, it works as follows:

- Take a digital signal with bit depth *n* and requantize it in *m* bits, $m < n$, using a nonlinear quantization method.

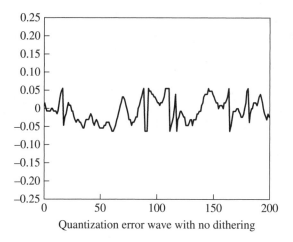

Quantization error wave with no dithering

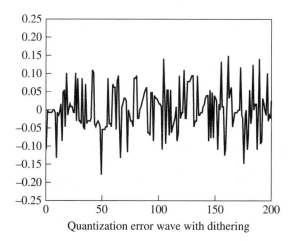

Quantization error wave with dithering

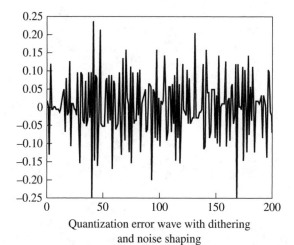

Quantization error wave with dithering
and noise shaping

**Figure 4.14**  Quantization error

- Transmit the signal.
- Expand the signal to $n$ bits at the receiving end. Some information will be lost, since quantization is lossy. However, nonlinear quantization lessens the error for low amplitude signals as compared to linear quantization.

The nonlinear encoding method is motivated by the observation that the human auditory system is perceptually nonuniform. Humans can perceive small differences between quiet sounds, but as sounds get louder our ability to perceive a difference in their amplitude diminishes. Also, quantization error generally has more impact on low amplitudes than on high ones. Think about why this is so. Say that your bit depth is eight. Then the quantization levels range for sound between $-128$ and 127. The sound amplitudes are scaled to this range. So that only integer values are used, values must be rounded to integers. If you consider the percent error for individual samples, you can easily see the relatively greater effect that a low bit depth has on low vs. high amplitude signals. A value of 0.499 rounds down to 0, for 100% error, while a value of 126.499 rounds down to 126, for about 0.4% error. In light of these observations, it makes sense to use *more* quantization levels for low amplitude signals and *fewer* quantization levels for high amplitudes. This is the idea behind nonlinear companding, the method used in $\mu$-law and A-law encoding for telephone transmissions.

Nonlinear companding schemes are widely used and have been standardized under the CCITT (Comité Consulatif Internationale de Télégraphique et Téléphonique) recommendations for telecommunications. In the United States and Japan, **$\mu$-law** (also called **mu-law**) **encoding** is the standard for compressing telephone transmissions, using a sampling rate of 8000 Hz and a bit depth of only eight bits, but achieving about 12 bits of dynamic range through the design of the compression algorithm. The equivalent standard for the rest of the world is called **A-law encoding**. Let's look more closely at $\mu$-law to understand nonlinear companding in general. The encoding method is defined by the following function:

### KEY EQUATION

Let $x$ be a sample value normalized so that $-1 \le x < 1$. Let $sign(x) = -1$ if $x$ is negative and $sign(x) = 1$ otherwise. Then the **$\mu$-law function** (also called **mu-law**) is defined by

$$m(x) = sign(x)\left(\frac{\ln(1 + \mu|x|)}{\ln(1 + \mu)}\right)$$

$$= sign(x)\left(\frac{\ln(1 + 255|x|)}{5.5452}\right) \quad for \quad \mu = 255$$

The $\mu$-law function is graphed in Figure 4.15. You can see that it has a logarithmic shape. Its effect is to provide finer-grained quantization levels at low amplitudes compared to high.

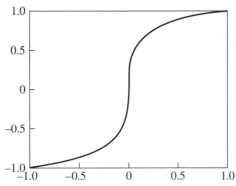

**Figure 4.15** Logarithmic function for nonlinear audio encoding

It may be easier to visualize what this function is doing if you think in terms of sample values rather than normalized values. Say that you begin with 16-bit audio samples with values ranging from −32,768 to 32,767. You're going to transmit the signal at a bit depth of 8, and expand it back to 16 bits at the receiving end.

To apply the $\mu$-law function, first normalize the input values by dividing by 32,768. Then apply the function to get $m(x)$. Then, compute $\lfloor 128m(x) \rfloor$ to scale the value to a bit depth of eight. Try this with an initial 16-bit sample of 16.

Apply the $\mu$-law function:    $m\left(\dfrac{16}{32,768}\right) \approx 0.02$

Scale to 8-bit samples:    $\lfloor 128 * 0.02 \rfloor = 2$

Now let's try an initial value of 30,037.

Apply the $\mu$-law function:    $m\left(\dfrac{30,037}{32,768}\right) = 0.9844$

Scale to 8-bit samples:    $\lfloor 128 * 0.9844 \rfloor = 125$

The nonlinear companding values in Table 4.2 were computed by the method just shown. (Only positive values are shown in the table, but negatives work the same way.) You can see the benefit of nonlinear companding versus linear requantization in this table. Linear quantization using eight bits would create equal-sized quantization intervals— each of them containing $65,536/256 = 256$ sample values ranging from −128 to 127. In nonlinear companding, the quantization intervals are smaller at lower amplitudes, resulting in fewer small-magnitude samples being mapped to the same value. The result is greater accuracy in the requantization at low amplitudes compared to the error you get with linear quantization.

After compression using the $\mu$-law function, samples can be transmitted in eight bits. At the user end, they are decompressed to 16 bits with the inverse function.

Supplements on $\mu$-law encoding:

interactive tutorial

mathematical modeling worksheet

programming exercise

**TABLE 4.2**  **Comparison of Quantization Interval Size with Linear Requantization and Nonlinear Companding**

| Linear Requantization | | Nonlinear Companding | | |
|---|---|---|---|---|
| Original 16-bit Sample Values | 8-bit Sample Values After Linear Requantization (divide by 256 and round down to nearest integer) | Original 16-bit Sample Values | 8-bit Sample Values After Non-linear Companding | Number of Values that are Mapped to the Same Value |
| 0–255 | 0 | 0–5 | 0 | 6 |
| 256–511 | 1 | 6–11 | 1 | 6 |
| 512–767 | 2 | 12–17 | 2 | 6 |
| . . . | . . . | . . . | . . . | . . . |
| 32,000–32,255 | 125 | 28,759–30,037 | 125 | 1,279 |
| 32,256–32,511 | 126 | 30,038–31,373 | 126 | 1,336 |
| 32,512–32,767 | 127 | 31,374–32,767 | 127 | 1,394 |

## KEY EQUATION

Let $x$ be a $\mu$-law encoded sample normalized so that $-1 \leq x < 1$. Let $sign(x) = -1$ if $x$ is negative and $sign(x) = 1$ otherwise. Then the *inverse $\mu$-law function* is defined by

$$d(x) = sign(x)\left(\frac{(\mu + 1)^{|x|} - 1}{\mu}\right)$$

$$= sign(x)\left(\frac{256^{|x|} - 1}{255}\right) \quad for \quad \mu = 255$$

Continuing our example, let's see what happens with the sample that originally was 16. The $\mu$-law function, scaled to an 8-bit scale, yielded a value of 2. Reversing the process, we do the following:

Apply the inverse $\mu$-law function:   $d\left(\dfrac{2}{128}\right) = 0.00035$

Scale to 16-bit samples:   $\lceil 32,768 * 0.00035 \rceil = 11$

We can do the same computation for the sample that originally was 30,037 and yielded a value of 125 from the $\mu$-law function.

Apply the inverse $\mu$-law function:   $d\left(\dfrac{125}{128}\right) = 0.8776$

Scale to 16-bit samples:   $\lceil 32,768 * 0.8776 \rceil = 28,758$

An original sample of value 16 became 11 at the receiving end using $\mu$-law encoding, which is an error of about 31%. An original sample of 30,037 became 28,758 at the receiving end,

| TABLE 4.3 | Comparison of Error with Linear Requantization Vs. Nonlinear Companding (representative values only) | | | | | |
|---|---|---|---|---|---|---|
| | Linear Requantization | | | Nonlinear Companding | | |
| Original 16-bit Sample | 8-bit Sample After Compression | 16-bit Sample After Decompression | Percent Error | 8-bit Sample After Compression | 16-bit Sample After Decompression | Percent Error |
| 1–5 | 0 | 0 | avg. 100% | 0 | 0 | avg. 100% |
| 6–11 | 0 | 0 | avg. 100% | 1 | 6 | avg. 26% |
| 12–17 | 0 | 0 | avg. 100% | 2 | 12 | avg. 16% |
| 18–24 | 0 | 0 | avg. 100% | 3 | 18 | avg. 13% |
| 25–31 | 0 | 0 | avg. 100% | 4 | 25 | avg. 10% |
| 127 | 0 | 0 | 100% | 15 | 118 | 7% |
| 128 | 1 | 256 | 100% | 25 | 118 | 7.8% |
| 383 | 1 | 256 | 33% | 31 | 364 | 4.9% |
| 30,038 | 117 | 29,952 | 0.29% | 126 | 30,038 | 0% |
| 31,373 | 122 | 31,232 | 0.45% | 126 | 30,038 | 4.2% |

for an error of about 4%. There's still more error at low amplitudes than at high, but the situation is improved over the error you would get with linear quantization.

Think about how you might reduce the bit depth for transmission if you simply divided by 256 and rounded the values, as shown below. Say that we use $r(x) = round(x/256)$ for lowering the bit depth (compression) and $s(x) = 256x$ for expanding the bit depth back again (decompression).

Assuming that this is how you would do linear requantization, Table 4.3 shows the amount of error resulting from linear vs. nonlinear quantization at different amplitude levels. In general, nonlinear companding reduces the impact of error on low-amplitude samples, making it less than it would be with linear quantization.

With linear requantization, all 16-bit samples between 0 and 127 compress to 0 and decompress to 0. This is 100% error for the sample values between 1 and 127. In comparison, with nonlinear companding, 16-bit samples between, say, 12 and 17 compress to 2 and decompress to 12, for an average error of 16%.

Percent error for the two methods is graphed in Figure 4.16 and Figure 4.17. Note that the enlargement in Figure 4.16 covers samples only from 0 to 100, while the enlargement in Figure 4.17 shows samples from 0 to 2000.

Percent error has an inverse relation to signal-to-quantization noise ratio. A large SQNR is good; a large percent error is obviously not good. Nonlinear companding increases the SQNR—the dynamic range—compared to what it ordinarily would be for 8-bit samples. You recall that a digital audio file linearly quantized in $n$ bits has a dynamic range of approximately $6n$ decibels. Thus, a bit depth of eight ordinarily would give a dynamic range of 48 dB. $\mu$-law encoding, however, reduces the average error per sample, effectively yielding the equivalent of a 12-bit dynamic range, which is about 72 dB.

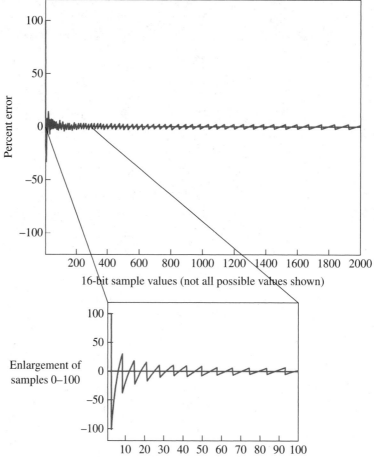

Figure 4.16 Percent error with nonlinear companding

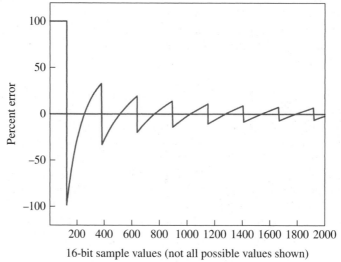

Figure 4.17 Percent error with linear quantization

# 4.6 FREQUENCY ANALYSIS

## 4.6.1 Time and Frequency Domains

In Chapter 1, we introduced the idea that both sound and image data can be represented as waveforms—one-dimensional waveforms for sound and two-dimensional for images. We explained that any complex waveform is actually the sum of simple sinusoidal waves. This makes it possible to store sound and image data in two ways. Sound can be represented either over the time domain or the frequency domain. Similarly, images can be represented either over the spatial domain or the frequency domain. A transform is an operation that converts between one domain and the other. The transform that is used most frequently in digital audio processing is the Fourier transform. It's time to look more closely at the mathematics of this transform.

If you represent digital audio over the *time domain*, you store the wave as a one-dimensional array of amplitudes—the discrete samples taken over time. This is probably the easiest way for you to think of audio data. If you think of it as a function, the input is time and the output is a sample value. But consider the alternative. A complex waveform is in fact equal to an infinite sum of simple sinusoidal waves, beginning with a *fundamental frequency* and going through frequencies that are integer multiples of the fundamental frequency. These integer multiples are called *harmonic frequencies*. To capture the complex waveform, it is sufficient to know the amplitude and phase of each of the component frequencies. The amplitude is, in a sense, how much each frequency component contributes to the total complex wave. This is how the data is stored in the *frequency domain*—as the amplitudes of frequency components. Sometimes we refer to these values as *coefficients*, because they represent the multiplier for each frequency in the summation. If you think of this as a function, the input is frequency and the output is the magnitude of the frequency component. It's useful to be able to separate the frequency components in order to analyze the nature of a sound wave and remove unwanted frequencies. Be sure you understand that the time domain and frequency domain are equivalent. They both fully capture the waveform. They just store the information about the waveform differently.

Audio processing programs provide information about the frequency components of an audio file. Two useful views of an audio file are the frequency analysis view and the spectral view.

In the *frequency analysis view* (also called the *spectrum analysis*), frequency components are on the horizontal axis, and the amplitudes of the frequency components are on the vertical axis. The frequency analysis view is useful for seeing, in a glance, how much of each frequency you have in a segment of your audio file. (The magnitude of the frequency component will be defined formally below.) Notice that you can't take a frequency analysis at some instantaneous point in your audio file. Frequency implies a change in the amplitude of the wave over time, so some time must pass for there to be a frequency. You can select a portion of your audio file and ask for a frequency analysis on this portion. It's also possible to have the frequency analysis shown while an audio file is playing. In this case, the analysis is done over a window of time surrounding the playhead, and you can watch the frequency analysis graph bounce up and down as frequency components change over time. The frequency analysis of the word " boo" is shown in Figure 4.18. The file is in mono. For a stereo file, there would be two frequency graphs, one superimposed over the other.

The *spectral view* (also called the *spectrum*) is another alternative for showing frequency components. In a spectral view, time is on the horizontal axis and the frequency components

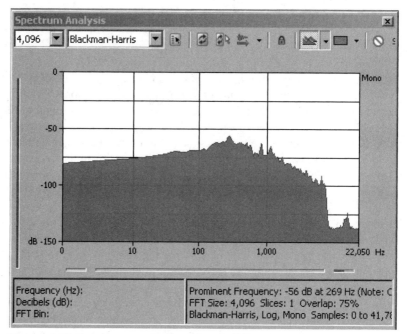

Figure 4.18 Frequency analysis of the word "boo" (from Sound Forge)

are on the vertical axis, with the amplitude of the frequency components represented by color. Generally speaking, the brighter the color, the larger the amplitude for the frequency component. For example, blue could indicate the lowest amplitude for a frequency component. Increasingly high amplitudes could be represented by colors that move from blue to red to orange to yellow or white.

The spectral view computes an "instantaneous spectrum" of frequencies for time $t$ by applying the Fourier transform to a window on the audio data that surrounds $t$. The window is then moved forward in time, and the transform is applied again. Showing the frequency components in one view as they change over time can give you an easily understood profile of your audio data. Figure 4.19 is a spectral view where the lowest amplitude is represented by blue, the medium by red, and the highest by yellow or white.

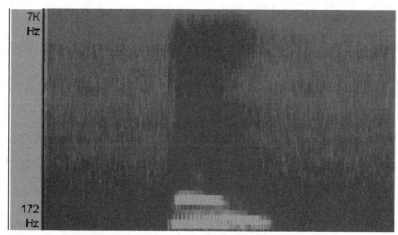

Figure 4.19 Spectral view (from Audacity)

The term *energy* is sometimes applied to frequency and spectral analysis views. Informally defined in the context of a frequency analysis view, the energy is the area under the frequency curve. In Figure 4.18, the energy is concentrated in the low frequencies, which is the usual range of the human voice. In a spectral analysis view, the energy is concentrated in the brightest colors.

In the next section, we'll examine the mathematical operations that make frequency analysis possible.

## 4.6.2 The Fourier Series

If you continue to work in digital media, you're certain to encounter the Fourier transform. The goal of the discussion below is to make you comfortable with the mathematical concepts, relating them to the physical phenomenon of sound so that you can understand what the transforms mean and how they are applied. At the end of the mathematical discussion, we'll summarize the main points as they relate to your work in digital audio processing.

The observation that any complex sinusoidal waveform is in fact a sum of simple sinusoidals can be written in the form of a Fourier series. A *Fourier series* is a representation of a periodic function as an infinite sum of sinusoidals:

$$f(t) = \sum_{n=-\infty}^{\infty} [a_n \cos(n\omega t) + b_n \sin(n\omega t)]$$

**Equation 4.2**

In the context of digital audio, $f(t)$ represents a complex sound wave. Let $f$ be the fundamental frequency we described at the beginning of Section 4.6.1. (Note that $f$ and $f(t)$ are two different things, the former being the fundamental frequency of the sound wave and the latter being the function for the complex waveform.) $\omega$ is the *fundamental angular frequency,* where $\omega = 2\pi f$. As $n$ goes from $-\infty$ to $\infty$, $\omega n$ takes you through the harmonic frequencies related to $f$. For each of these, the coefficients $a_n$ and $b_n$ tell how much each of these component frequencies contributes to $f(t)$.

**ASIDE:** To be more precise, a periodic function satisfying Dirichlet's conditions can be expressed as a Fourier series. Dirichlet's conditions are that the function be piecewise continuous, piecewise monotonic, and absolutely differentiable.

You should note that Equation 4.2 is true only for periodic functions. Also, $f(t)$ is assumed to be continuous. There are different equations for Fourier analysis that vary according to whether the function is periodic or nonperiodic and discrete or continuous. We haven't yet shown you a form of the Fourier transform that is applicable to *digital* audio processing.

You sometimes see Equation 4.2 written in a different form, with the first term of the summation pulled out, as follows:

$$f(t) = a_0 + \sum_{n=-\infty}^{-1} [a_n \cos(n\omega t) + b_n \sin(n\omega t)] + \sum_{n=1}^{\infty} [a_n \cos(n\omega t) + b_n \sin(n\omega t)]$$

**Equation 4.3**

This separation of terms in Equation 4.3 is possible because $\sin(0) = 0$ and $\cos(0) = 1$. In this form, $a_0$ is the *DC component,* which gives the average amplitude value over one period. Given that $T = \dfrac{1}{f}$ is the period of the fundamental frequency, the DC component is given by

$$a_0 = \frac{1}{T} \int_{-T/2}^{T/2} f(t)\,dt$$

In an analogy with electrical currents (AC for alternating and DC for direct), you can picture the DC component graphically as a straight horizontal line at amplitude $a_0$ (*i.e.*, it is the zero-frequency component). The integral in the equation is taking all the values between $-T/2$ and $T/2$, summing them, and dividing by $T$. In other words, it is the average amplitude of the complex waveform. Since the wave is assumed to be periodic, the average amplitude over one period $T$ is the same as the average over the entire wave. Each **AC component** is a pure sinusoidal wave, beginning with the one that has fundamental frequency $f$. The summation in Equation 4.3 creates harmonic components with frequencies that are integer multiples of $f$. The coefficients of each of these frequency components are given by the following equations:

$$a_n = \frac{1}{T} \int_{-T/2}^{T/2} f(t) \cos\left(n\omega t\right) dt$$

$$b_n = \frac{1}{T} \int_{-T/2}^{T/2} f(t) \sin\left(n\omega t\right) dt$$

$$for\ -\infty \le n \le \infty$$

Note that since $\cos(-x) = \cos(x)$, $a_{-n} = a_n$, and since $\sin(-x) = -\sin(x)$, $b_{-n} = -b_n$ and $b_0 = 0$. Rearranging Equation 4.3 and making these substitutions gives yet another form:

$$f(t) = a_0 + \sum_{n=1}^{\infty} \left[ a_{-n} \cos(-n\omega t) + b_{-n} \sin(-n\omega t) + a_n \cos(n\omega t) + b_n \sin(n\omega t) \right]$$

$$= a_0 + \sum_{n=1}^{\infty} \left[ a_n \cos(-n\omega t) - b_n \sin(-n\omega t) + a_n \cos(n\omega t) + b_n \sin(n\omega t) \right]$$

$$= a_0 + \sum_{n=1}^{\infty} \left[ a_n \cos(n\omega t) + b_n \sin(n\omega t) + a_n \cos(n\omega t) + b_n \sin(n\omega t) \right]$$

$$= a_0 + \sum_{n=1}^{\infty} \left[ 2a_n \cos(n\omega t) + 2b_n \sin(n\omega t) \right]$$

$$= a_0 + 2 \sum_{n=1}^{\infty} \left[ a_n \cos(n\omega t) + b_n \sin(n\omega t) \right]$$

**Equation 4.4**

On an intuitive level, it's fairly easy to understand how Equation 4.2, which is expressed in terms of sines and cosines, relates to a complex sound wave. However, this isn't the most common form for the Fourier series. There's another, equivalent way of expressing the Fourier series. It is as follows:

$$f(t) = \sum_{n=-\infty}^{\infty} F_n e^{in\omega t}$$

**Equation 4.5**

where $e$ is the **base of the natural logarithm** (~2.71828); $i$ is $\sqrt{-1}$; $\omega$ is defined as before; and $F_n$ is a complex number. Recall that a complex number $c$ is defined as

$$c = a + bi$$

where $a$ is the real component and $b$ is the imaginary component.

Where does Equation 4.5 come from, and how can it be shown that it is equal to Equation 4.2? The equivalence is derivable from Euler's formula, which states that

$$e^{inx} = \cos(nx) + i\sin(nx)$$

Based on this identity

$$e^{in\omega t} = \cos(n\omega t) + i\sin(n\omega t)$$

> **ASIDE:** One of the greatest mathematicians of all time, Swiss mathematician Leonhard Euler (1707–1783) made contributions to number theory, differential equations, complex numbers, Fermat's theorems, prime numbers, harmonics, optics, and mechanics, to name just some of the areas in which he excelled.

Equation 4.2 and Equation 4.5 really say the same thing. Let's see how they relate to each other. Recall that $F_n$ is a complex number. The real and imaginary components of the complex number correspond to the coefficients of the cosine and sine terms, respectively, in Equation 4.2, as shown below.

$$F_n = a_n - ib_n$$

**Equation 4.6**

We can do substitutions using Euler's identity and the identity given in Equation 4.6, and show that Equation 4.5 is equivalent to Equation 4.2 and Equation 4.4.

$$f(t) = \sum_{n=-\infty}^{\infty} F_n e^{in\omega t}$$

$$= \sum_{n=-\infty}^{\infty} \left[ F_n(\cos(n\omega t) + i\sin(n\omega t)) \right] \qquad \textit{Step 1}$$

$$= \sum_{n=-\infty}^{-1} \left[ (a_n - ib_n)(\cos(n\omega t) + i\sin(n\omega t)) \right] \qquad \textit{Step 2}$$

$$= \sum_{n=-\infty}^{\infty} \left[ a_n\cos(n\omega t) + ia_n\sin(n\omega t) - ib_n\cos(n\omega t) - i^2 b_n\sin(n\omega t) \right] \qquad \textit{Step 3}$$

$$= \sum_{n=-\infty}^{\infty} \left[ a_n\cos(n\omega t) + ia_n\sin(n\omega t) - ib_n\cos(n\omega t) + b_n\sin(n\omega t) \right] \qquad \textit{Step 4}$$

$$= \sum_{n=-\infty}^{-1} \left[ a_n\cos(n\omega t) + ia_n\sin(n\omega t) - ib_n\cos(n\omega t) + b_n\sin(n\omega t) \right] + a_0 - ib_0$$

$$+ \sum_{n=1}^{\infty} \left[ a_n\cos(n\omega t) + ia_n\sin(n\omega t) - ib_n\cos(n\omega t) + b_n\sin(n\omega t) \right] \qquad \textit{Step 5}$$

$$= \sum_{n=-\infty}^{-1} \left[ a_n \cos(n\omega t) + ia_n \sin(n\omega t) - ib_n \cos(n\omega t) + b_n \sin(n\omega t) \right] + a_0$$
$$+ \sum_{n=1}^{\infty} \left[ a_n \cos(n\omega t) + ia_n \sin(n\omega t) - ib_n \cos(n\omega t) + b_n \sin(n\omega t) \right] \qquad Step\ 6$$

$$= \sum_{n=1}^{\infty} \left[ a_{-n} \cos(-n\omega t) + ia_{-n} \sin(-n\omega t) - ib_{-n} \cos(-n\omega t) + b_{-n} \sin(-n\omega t) \right] + a_0$$
$$+ \sum_{n=1}^{\infty} \left[ a_n \cos(n\omega t) + ia_n \sin(n\omega t) - ib_n \cos(n\omega t) + b_n \sin(n\omega t) \right] \qquad Step\ 7$$

$$= a_0 + \sum_{n=1}^{\infty} \left[ \begin{array}{l} a_{-n} \cos(-n\omega t) + ia_{-n} \sin(-n\omega t) - ib_{-n} \cos(-n\omega t) - b_{-n} \sin(-n\omega t) \\ + a_n \cos(n\omega t) + ia_n \sin(n\omega t) - ib_n \cos(n\omega t) + b_n \sin(n\omega t) \end{array} \right]$$
$$\qquad Step\ 8$$

$$= a_0 + \sum_{n=1}^{\infty} \left[ \begin{array}{l} a_n \cos(n\omega t) - ia_n \sin(n\omega t) + ib_n \cos(n\omega t) + b_n \sin(n\omega t) + \\ a_n \cos(n\omega t) + ia_n \sin(n\omega t) - ib_n \cos(n\omega t) + b_n \sin(n\omega t) \end{array} \right] \qquad Step\ 9$$

$$= a_0 + \sum_{n=1}^{\infty} 2 \left[ a_n \cos(n\omega t) + b_n \sin(n\omega t) \right] \qquad Step\ 10$$

$$= a_0 + 2 \sum_{n=1}^{\infty} \left[ a_n \cos(n\omega t) + b_n \sin(n\omega t) \right] \qquad Step\ 11$$

The derivation is justified as follows:

**Step 1:** Substitution based on Euler's identity.

**Step 2:** Substitution of Equation 4.6.

**Step 3:** Distribution of terms.

**Step 4:** $-i^2 = -(\sqrt{-1})^2 = 1$.

**Step 5:** Separation of summation into three parts.

**Step 6:** $b_0 = 0$.

**Step 7:** Change first summation to $\sum_{n=1}^{\infty}$ rather than $\sum_{n=-\infty}^{-1}$ and reverse the sign of $n$ on all terms in the summation.

**Step 8:** Since both summations are now over the same range, combine them.

**Step 9:** $a_n = a_{-n}, b_n = b_{-n}, \cos(-n) = \cos(n),$ and $\sin(-n) = -\sin(n)$.

**Step 10:** Combine terms, and we now have Equation 4.4.

The point is that Equation 4.2 and Equation 4.4 and Equation 4.5 give the same information. They all tell you that a continuous complex waveform is equal to an infinite sum of simple cosine and sine functions. $a_n$ and $b_n$ tell "how much" of each frequency component contributes to the total waveform. $a_n$ and $b_n$ are explicit in Equation 4.2. They are implicit in Equation 4.5, derivable from Equation 4.6.

## 4.6.3 The Discrete Fourier Transform

Recall that $f(t)$ is assumed to be a continuous function that can be graphed as a continuous waveform. Now we need to move to the domain of digital audio, where an audio file is an array of discrete samples. The discrete equivalent of Equation 4.2 is the defined as follows:

### KEY EQUATION

Let $f_k$ be a discrete integer function representing a digitized audio signal in the time domain. Let $F_n$ be a discrete, complex number function representing a digital audio signal in the frequency domain. $i = \sqrt{-1}$ and $\omega = 2\pi f$. Then the **inverse discrete Fourier transform** is defined by

$$f_k = \sum_{n=0}^{N-1} \left[ a_n \cos\left(\frac{2\pi nk}{N}\right) + b_n \sin\left(\frac{2\pi nk}{N}\right) \right]$$

$$= \sum_{n=0}^{N-1} F_n e^{\frac{i2\pi nk}{N}}$$

**Equation 4.7**

(Notice that that we've changed to subscript notation, $f_k$, to emphasize that this is an array of discrete sample values rather than a continuous function.) Since $\omega = 2\pi f$, then the **fundamental frequency** $f$ is $\frac{1}{N}$. As it applies to sound, Equation 4.7 states that a digital audio waveform consisting of $N$ samples is equal to a sum of $N$ cosine and sine frequency components. If you know the amplitude for each component ($a_n$ and $b_n$ for $0 \le n \le N - 1$), you can reconstruct the

**ASIDE:** The fundamental frequency is defined here in terms of cycles per number of samples. You might expect that it would be defined as cycles per unit time. You can assume that time units are implicit in the number of samples.

wave. The DC component, $a_0$, is defined by $a_0 = \frac{1}{N} \sum_{k=0}^{N-1} f_k$, giving an average amplitude.

The AC components $a_n$ and $b_n$, for $1 \le n \le N$, are $a_n = \frac{1}{N} \sum_{k=0}^{N-1} f_k \cos\left(\frac{2\pi nk}{N}\right)$ and $b_n = \frac{1}{N} \sum_{k=0}^{N-1} f_k \cos\left(\frac{2\pi nk}{N}\right)$.

If we view the inverse discrete Fourier transform as an effective procedure, then it begins with a digital audio file in the frequency domain and transforms it to the time domain. But what if you have an array of audio samples over the time domain and want to derive the frequency components? For this you need the discrete Fourier transform.

The **discrete Fourier transform** (**DFT**) operates on an array of $N$ audio samples, returning cosine and sine coefficients that represent the audio data in the frequency domain.

### KEY EQUATION

Let $F_n$ be a discrete, complex number function representing a digital audio signal in the frequency domain. Let $f_k$ be a discrete integer function representing a digitized audio signal in the time domain. $i = \sqrt{-1}$ and $\omega = 2\pi f$. Then the **discrete Fourier transform** is defined by

$$F_n = \frac{1}{N} \sum_{k=0}^{N-1} f_k \cos\left(\frac{2\pi nk}{N}\right) - i f_k \sin\left(\frac{2\pi nk}{N}\right) = \frac{1}{N} \sum_{k=0}^{N-1} f_k e^{\frac{-i2\pi nk}{N}}$$

for $0 \le n \le N - 1$

**Equation 4.8**

Supplements on
Fourier transform:

interactive tutorial

worksheet

programming
exercise

Each $F_n$ is a complex number with real and imaginary parts that correspond to the cosine and sine frequency components. That is, $F_n = a_n - ib_n$. $f_k$ is the $k$th sample in the array of discrete audio samples.

The two forms of Equation 4.8 are equivalent. The first may be a more intuitive way of thinking about complex waveforms—as a sum of simple sinusoidals—but the second is more concise and turns out to be more convenient for computing the Fourier transform, and thus it's the form you see most often in the literature.

Another thing that might confuse you is the seemingly-interchangeable use of either positive or negative exponents along with the imaginary number $i$. For example, Equation 4.8 might have $i2\pi nk$ rather than $-i2\pi nk$ as the power of $e$. The choice of a positive or negative exponent is arbitrary, with one caveat: If the exponent is negative in the forward transform, the sign must be positive in the inverse, and vice versa. And there's one last thing to add to the confusion. Engineers use $j$ instead of $i$ to represent $\sqrt{-1}$.

The purpose of applying the discrete Fourier transform to digital audio data is to separate the frequency components, analyze the nature of an audio clip, and edit it by possibly filtering out or altering some frequencies. The Fourier transform is widely used in both audio and (in the 2-D case) image processing, and it is implemented in a wide variety of mathematical programs and multimedia editing tools.

### 4.6.4 A Comparison of the DFT and DCT

At this point, you may be wondering what the difference is between the discrete Fourier transform and the discrete cosine transform described in Chapter 2. We'll first look at the mathematical differences and then consider how these relate to applications.

Mathematically, the one-dimensional DCT is in fact the DFT applied to $N$ audio samples to which (implicitly) another $N$ samples—a symmetric copy—are appended. By "symmetric copy" we mean that in addition to sample values $[f_0, f_1, \ldots, f_{N-1}]$, the DCT algorithm operates as if there were another $N$ sample values, $[-f_{N-1}, -f_{N-2}, \ldots, -f_0]$. Now think about the sine term in the discrete cosine transform given in Equation 4.8. The sine function is an odd function, which means that $\sin(-x) = -\sin(x)$. The cosine function is an even function, which means that $\cos(-x) = \cos(x)$. Since the DCT algorithm assumes that the data includes the negative of all the given sample values, it is in effect canceling the sine term, since for every term there is also the negative of the term. This leaves only the cosine terms—which give us the one-dimensional discrete cosine transform. (The two-dimensional DCT that we showed in Chapter 2 is an extension of this for image processing.)

When you implement the DCT, you don't really append the extra samples to the data. The algorithm just "pretends" that they are there. This is how the algorithm assumes that the data it is given represents a *periodic* discrete function—one that repeats in a pattern. Mathematically, the statements we make in Equation 4.3 and Equation 4.7—which describe the nature of our function defining the audio data, and the fact that it is decomposable into frequency components—are true only if the function is periodic. We have to assume in what sense the audio function is periodic. In fact, it is probably something quite complex with no single repeated pattern. For the Fourier transform, we assume it is periodic by assuming that the entire set of data points keeps repeating—the whole audio file constitutes one period; that is, sample values $[f_0, f_1, \ldots, f_{N-1}]$ keep repeating. For the cosine transform, we assume that the data points have appended to them a "mirror image" of themselves, and then this total pattern repeats.

What are the practical consequences of these simplifying assumptions? In the case of the DFT, one important consequence is that for an audio file of $N$ samples, the DFT yields no more than $N/2$ valid frequency components. The emphasis is on the word *valid*. You saw in Chapter 2 that the DCT yields $N$ frequency components for $N$ samples. The reason the DFT yields only $N/2$ frequency components is based on the Nyquist theorem. Let's do the math. Our variables are defined as follows:

Supplements on DCT and DFT:

interactive tutorial

$N$ = number of samples
$T$ = total sampling time
$s = N/T$ = sampling rate

worksheet

By the Nyquist theorem, if we sample at a frequency of $s$, then we can validly sample only frequencies up to $s/2$. This implies that when we perform the DFT, there's no point in detecting frequency components above $s/2$, since they couldn't have been sampled by this sampling rate to begin with. The DFT actually yields $N$ output values, but we don't want to use all $N$ of them; some of the higher ones must be discarded.

Let's look more closely at how the DFT chooses the component frequencies to measure. It does so by dividing the total time of the audio data being transformed, $T$, into $N$ equal parts. The frequency components correspond to $k/T$ for $0 \leq k \leq N - 1$. $1/T$ is the fundamental frequency (using units of time rather than samples). This makes sense, because $T$ is assumed to be the period of the wave. $2/T$ is the second harmonic frequency, and so forth. For what value of $k$, with $0 \leq k \leq N - 1$, do we find $k/T = s/2$? This would correspond to the highest valid frequency component. We can easily solve this as follows:

$$\frac{k}{T} = \frac{s}{2}$$

$$k = \frac{Ts}{2} = \frac{T(N/T)}{2} = \frac{N}{2}$$

When we reach $N/2$, we have reached the limits of the usable frequency components from the output.

Here's an example: Say that you have an audio clip that is a pure tone at 440 Hz. The sampling rate is 1000 Hz. You are going to perform a Fourier transform on 1024 samples. Thus $T = 1024/1000 = 1.024$ sec . The frequency components that are measured by the transform are separated by $1/T = 0.9765625$ Hz. There are $N/2 = 512$ valid frequency components, the last one being $0.9765625 * 512 = 500$ Hz. This is as it should be, since the sampling rate is $2 * 500$ Hz $= 1000$ Hz, so we are not violating the Nyquist limit.

The DCT works differently. Because it takes $N$ sample points and assumes it has $N$ more, it implicitly has $2N$ samples per period, so $N$ frequency components are given as output.

You may think now that the DCT is inherently superior to the DFT because it doesn't trouble you with complex numbers, and it yields twice the number of frequency components. But it isn't as simple as that. Because of their mathematical properties, the DCT works better for some applications, the DFT for others.

Discarding the DCT's sine component may make you a little suspicious anyway. If it occurs to you that the DFT must contain more information, you're right. Thinking about the relationship between the **trigonometric form** of the DFT (the one containing sines and cosines) with the **exponential form** (the one containing $e$ to a power) will help you to understand the additional information contained in the DFT but not in the DCT.

$\boldsymbol{F_n}$ in the exponential form of the Fourier transform is a complex number, having a real and an imaginary part. The cosine term in the trigonometric form relates to the real-number part of $F_n$, and the sine term relates to the imaginary part. Specifically, $F_n = a_n - ib_n$. (The DCT, in comparison, has only a real-number part.) Earlier in this chapter, we said that in the spectral view of a waveform, color represents the amplitudes of the frequency components. We can now be more precise about this. $a_n$ and $b_n$ can be recombined to yield the magnitude and phase of the $n$th frequency component.

---

### 🔑 KEY EQUATION

Let the equation for the inverse discrete Fourier transform be as given in Equation 4.7. Then the *magnitude of the $n$th frequency component*, $A_n$, is given by

$$A_n = \sqrt{a_n^2 + b_n^2} \quad \text{for} \quad 0 \leq n \leq N - 1$$

---

### 🔑 KEY EQUATION

Let the equation for the inverse discrete Fourier transform be as given in Equation 4.7. Then the *phase of the $n$th frequency component*, $\phi_n$, is given by

$$\phi_n = -\tan^{-1}\left(\frac{b_n}{a_n}\right) \quad 0 \leq n \leq N - 1$$

---

This gives us yet one more way to describe a complex waveform—the magnitude/phase form of the inverse DFT, as a sum of cosine waves offset by their phase.

---

### 🔑 KEY EQUATION

Let the equation for the inverse discrete Fourier transform be as given in Equation 4.7. Then the *magnitude/phase form of the inverse DFT* is given by

$$f_k = \sum_{n=0}^{N-1} A_n \cos(2\pi nk + \phi_n)$$

---

(Some sources use a sine function rather than a cosine in this magnitude/phase form, but that's fine since a sine function is just a phase-offset cosine.)

Now you can see that with the sine term that is part of the DFT, we have information about the phase of the signal. Is phase important? In the realm of sound, can we hear phase differences? Some sources will tell you that the human ear doesn't really detect phase differences, so it's information that in many situations can be discarded. Ohm's phase law, formulated in the 1800s, states that the phase of a waveform has no effect on how humans perceive the sound waveform. Let's be precise about what this means. That is,

**ASIDE:** German physicist George Simon Ohm (1789–1854) is best known for his research in electrical current and his precise formulation of the relationship between potential and current in electrical conduction. The unit of electrical resistance was named in his honor.

a pure-tone sound wave could be sent to you at one moment. Then later, the same tone could be sent, but with the phase shifted. You would hear no difference in these two sounds. However, if both of these tones were sent to you at the same time—with the phase of one shifted—you would be able to hear the destructive interference that results from summing the two out-of-phase tones. In environments where sounds are reverberating a great deal anyway, phase differences can be masked. But in more controlled environments, phase distortion is audible to discriminating ears. Stereo speakers that are out-of-phase can be quite annoying to audiophiles, for example.

And what about phase in images? Perhaps surprisingly, it is easier experimentally to show the importance of phase in images than in sound. Experiments show that if you take two images—call them A and B—that are decomposed into their magnitude and phase components, and you replace B's phase component with A's while leaving the magnitude component unchanged, image B will then look more like A than what it originally looked like. That is, the phase component dominates in our perception. This is one of the things that makes the two-dimensional Fourier transform very useful in image editing and restoration.

The Fourier transform also can be applied to fast implementations of convolutions. In Chapter 3, we described a convolution as a kind of two-dimensional spatial filter, altering pixels that are represented in the spatial domain. Convolutions can also be done in one dimension on audio data that are represented in the time domain. An alternative to performing the convolution in the time/space domain is to transform the data to the frequency domain by means of the Fourier transform. Then the operations can be done more efficiently by simple multiplications. In short, the Fourier transform can be the basis for a very efficient implementation of convolution.

For digital audio, the Fourier transform is primarily used to analyze an audio signal. Figure 4.2 showed how it is used to create a frequency spectrum of an audio file based on the magnitudes of the frequency components. From the frequency spectrum, you can identify which frequencies are present and which are not, and you can detect areas in the file that may need to be corrected.

On the other hand, the main application of the DCT is image compression. The DCT is one of the main steps in JPEG compression. It is a good choice in this context because the DCT concentrates energy into the coefficients corresponding to the low-frequency components. This is where we want to store the most detailed information as compression is performed. As you saw in Chapter 3, it's possible to discard more of the high-frequency information because the human eye can't detect it very well anyway.

The bottom line is that both the DCT and the DFT are useful. Fourier analysis in general, under which both the DCT and the DFT are subsumed, has wide applications that extend beyond digital imaging and digital audio into cryptography, optics, number theory, statistics, oceanography, signal processing, and other areas.

## 4.6.5 The Fast Fourier Transform

The usefulness of the discrete Fourier transform was extended greatly when a fast version was invented by Cooley and Tukey in 1965. This implementation, called the *fast Fourier transform* (**FFT**), reduces the computational complexity from $O(N^2)$ to $O(N \log_2(N))$. For those of you who haven't yet studied computational complexity, this means that you can transform much larger audio or image sample files through the FFT than through the DFT and still finish the computation in a reasonable amount of time. The time it takes to do the computation of the DFT grows at the same rate that $N^2$ grows, while the time for the FFT grows at the same rate that $N \log_2(N)$ grows, where $N$ is the number of samples. This is a big savings in computational time in light of the fact that CD quality stereo, for example, has 44,100 samples in every second, giving you a very large $N$ in just a few minutes. Let's look at the time savings more closely.

The ratio of the time it takes to compute the DFT versus the time it takes to compute the FFT is given by $\dfrac{N^2}{N \log_2(N)} = \dfrac{N}{\log_2(N)}$. You can see how fast this ratio grows by trying increasingly large values of $N$.

For $N = 256$, you get $\dfrac{256}{\log_2(256)} = \dfrac{256}{8} = 32$.

For $N = 1024$, you get $\dfrac{1024}{\log_2(1024)} = \dfrac{1024}{10} \approx 102$.

For $N = 65{,}536$, you get $\dfrac{65{,}536}{\log_2(65{,}536)} = \dfrac{65{,}536}{16} = 4096$.

It takes the DFT more than 100 times longer to compute a Fourier transform on a block of 1024 samples than it takes the FFT. The larger the $N$, the more important it is that you use the FFT. Otherwise, it simply takes too long to do the computation. The FFT is more efficient than the DFT because redundant or unnecessary computations are eliminated. For example, there's no need to perform a multiplication with a term that contains $\sin(0)$ or $\cos(0)$. We know that $\sin(0) = 0$, so a term containing $\sin(0)$ can be discarded, and $\cos(0) = 1$, so a term containing $\cos(0)$ can just be added or subtracted without a multiplication. Many repetitive computations can also be identified so that they are done only one time.

The FFT has some details in its implementation that you need to know about because they are considerations when you apply the Fourier transform in digital audio processing programs. The first thing to point out is that you can't perform any kind of Fourier transform—either the DFT or the FFT—on a single sample. You need a block of samples. Imagine looking at the waveform of an audio file you're working on in a digital audio processing program, picking one point in the waveform, and wondering what the frequency components are at precisely that point. The problem is that frequency arises from the changing values in the waveform, but you don't have any changing values if you're only looking at one point.

Another way of thinking about this is in terms of the frequencies (*i.e.*, pitches) that you can hear. Say that you were asked to listen to a pure tone that lasted less than a sixteenth of a second. Do you think you'd be able to identify what pitch it was? Probably not. At best it would sound like a click.

The point is that for the FFT or DFT to divide sound into frequency components, it needs a block of samples—not a just one sample—to work with. So why not just take the whole audio file—the entire waveform—and perform the transform on the whole thing? You can't do this with the FFT. Because of the way it weeds out redundant and unnecessary calculations, the FFT algorithm has to operate on blocks of samples where the number of samples is a power of 2. The DFT can work with a sample set of any block size. Because it is so fast, the FFT is the form of the Fourier transform used in digital audio programs. When you use it, you can specify the window size, which is the number of samples per block processed by the FFT. The number might vary from, say, 64 to 65,536. When you choose a point in the audio file and ask for a frequency analysis, the FFT determines the frequency components in an area of the specified window size, around the point you selected. The frequency analysis view you'll get will look something like Figure 4.18.

Some audio processing tools require that you choose an FFT window size for their required frequency analysis. For example, noise reduction generally begins with a frequency analysis of a portion of audio that ought to be silent but that contains background noise. The size of the FFT window is significant here because adjusting its size is a tradeoff between frequency and time resolution. You have seen that for an FFT window of size $N$, $N/2$ frequency components are produced. Thus, the larger the FFT size, the greater the frequency resolution. However, the larger the FFT size, the smaller the time resolution. Think about why this is so. A larger FFT window covers a longer span of time. A noise profiler divides the selected portion of audio—the portion that ought to be silent—and repeatedly does an FFT analysis of blocks of size $N$ within this window. The average of the frequency components yielded from each block becomes the frequency profile for the selected portion of audio. A larger FFT size looks at larger blocks of time, losing some of the audio detail that occurs over time (*i.e.*, sudden changes in amplitude. If the FFT size is too large, the result is time slurring, a situation where the FFT of the audio selection doesn't capture sufficient detail over time).

The frequency analysis in Figure 4.20 was done on a simple waveform representing a pure tone at 440 Hz. Since there is only one frequency in the wave, it doesn't matter what point you select for the transform. You'll always get the same frequency analysis because the frequency doesn't change over time. But you would expect that there would be just one frequency component, a single spike in the graph at 440 Hz. Why is this not the case?

The problem has to do with the assumption that the FFT makes about the periodicity of the signal. When the FFT operates on a window of $N$ samples, it assumes that this constitutes one period of a periodic signal. Even the simplest case—a pure sinusoidal wave—reveals the problem with this assumption. Assume that the FFT is operating on 1024 samples of a 440 Hz wave sampled at 8000 samples per second. The window size of 1024 samples would cover about 56.32 cycles of the wave—a non-integer multiple. This means that the end of the window would break the wave in the middle of a cycle. For the operation of the FFT, the file is assumed to consist of repeated periods of this

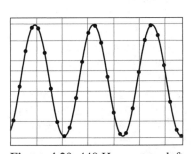
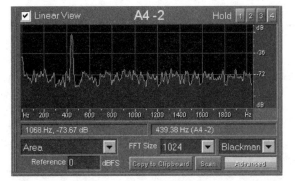

**Figure 4.20**  440 Hz wave on left and its frequency analysis on the right (from Audition)

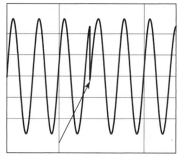

**Figure 4.21** Discontinuity caused by an FFT window that does not cover an integral number of cycles

interactive tutorial

worksheet

mathematical modeling worksheet

shape. Figure 4.21 shows what it looks like when you put two of these periods end-to-end. They are out-of-phase, ending about a third of the way through a cycle at the end of the first period, and jumping to the beginning of the cycle at the beginning of the second period. Thus, the wave the FFT assumes it is analyzing doesn't correctly represent the true frequency of the audio clip. The FFT interprets the discontinuity as additional frequency components. This phenomenon is called *spectral leakage*. As the FFT moves across the entire waveform, each time performing its operations on a window of size 1024, it repeatedly detects the spurious frequencies, which is why you see them in the frequency analysis view of Figure 4.20.

If you could juggle your numbers so that your window covered an integral number of cycles, or if you were lucky enough that the numbers came out evenly on their own, you wouldn't get spectral leakage. For example, if your sampling rate is 1024 Hz, the frequency of the wave is 512 Hz, and you sample for one second, you'll have a block of 1024 samples that cover exactly two cycles, so there would be no spectral leakage. Of course, things don't work this way in the real world. Your sound file has a length and frequencies dictated by the nature of the sound. So the problem of spectral leakage has to be dealt with in some other way.

Spectral leakage is handled in audio processing programs by the application of a windowing function. The purpose of a windowing function is to reduce the effect of the phase discontinuities that result from the assumption that the block on which the FFT is applied is one period in a periodic wave. When you apply the FFT for frequency analysis in an audio processing program, you're asked to specify which windowing function to apply. Common choices are *triangular*, *Hanning*, *Hamming*, and *Blackman windowing functions*. In Figure 4.20, you can see that the Blackman function is being used, with an FFT window size of 1024.

The purpose of a windowing function is to reduce the amplitude of the sound wave at the beginning and end of the FFT window. The phase discontinuities occur at the ends of the window, and these phase discontinuities introduce spurious frequencies into the frequency analysis. If the amplitude of the wave is smaller at the beginning and end of the window, then the spurious frequencies will be smaller in magnitude as well.

Shaping a wave in this way is done by multiplying the wave by another periodic function. When you multiply one sinusoidal wave by another, it's as if you putting the first one in an envelope that is the shape of the second. Thus, each different windowing function is a different sinusoidal multiplier that shapes the original wave in a slightly different way. Four windowing functions are given in Table 4.4 and are graphed in Figure 4.22. Other functions exist, including Blackman-Harris, Welch, and Flat-Top.

| TABLE 4.4 | Windowing Function for FFT |
|---|---|
| $u(t) = \begin{cases} \dfrac{2t}{T} & for \quad 0 \leq t < \dfrac{T}{2} \\[2ex] 2 - \dfrac{2t}{T} & for \quad \dfrac{T}{2} \leq t \leq T \end{cases}$ <br><br> Triangular windowing function | $u(t) = \dfrac{1}{2}\left[1 - \cos\left(\dfrac{2\pi t}{T}\right)\right] \quad for \quad 0 \leq t \leq T$ <br><br> Hanning windowing function |
| $u(t) = 0.54 - 0.46\cos\left(\dfrac{2\pi t}{T}\right) \quad for \quad 0 \leq t \leq T$ <br><br> Hamming windowing function | $u(t) = 0.42 - 0.5\cos\left(\dfrac{2\pi t}{T}\right) + 0.08\cos\left(\dfrac{4\pi t}{T}\right)$ <br> $for \quad 0 \leq t \leq T$ <br><br> Blackman windowing function |

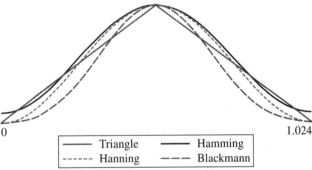

Figure 4.22  Graphs of windowing functions for FFT

Figure 4.23 shows how application of the Hanning windowing function changes the shape of a single-frequency sound wave. The frequency of the wave is 440 Hz. The sampling frequency is 1000 Hz. We want 1024 samples. Thus, the period is $T = 1024/1000 = 1.024$ seconds. Notice that applying the windowing function does not alter the frequency of the sound wave—only the amplitude at the ends.

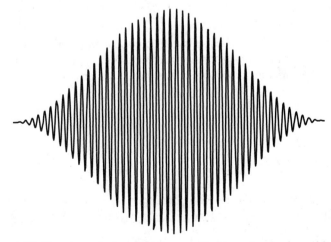

Figure 4.23  Hanning window function applied to a simple sinusoidal wave

From the previous discussion, you should now understand that when you do frequency analysis in an audio processing program, there are two settings that affect your results: the window size and the windowing function applied. The size of the window involves a trade-off between frequency and time resolution. Remember that you're not measuring an instantaneous frequency; instead, you're measuring the frequency over a period of time $T$. Unless you have a perfectly constant sound wave, the frequency changes over that period of time. Applying the FFT to the window gives you the average frequency components over period $T$. A bigger window averages over a bigger span of time, and thus provides a less detailed picture of the changes that occur over period $T$ than would be captured in a smaller window. In short, increasing the window size increases frequency resolution in that it measures more frequency components, but it decreases time resolution in that the frequency components are derived from averages that span a longer period of time.

Loss of time resolution can be partially compensated for by the way in which FFT is implemented. Rather than apply the first FFT to samples 0 through $N - 1$ and then slide over to sample $N$ to $2N - 1$ for the next application of the transform, it's possible to slide the window over by smaller amounts; that is, overlapping windows can be analyzed.

So how do you know what window size to use? Consider first using the default value in your audio processing program. From there, you can experiment with different window sizes to see what information each one gives you. Larger window sizes take more processing time, so this is another factor in your choice. It's possible to play a sound file and watch the frequency analysis view, which changes dynamically to show you how the frequency components change over time. To be able to do this in real time, however, you have to set your window size relatively low—say, 1024 samples or less.

Windowing functions differ in the types of signals for which they are best suited; the accuracy of their amplitude measurements, even for low-level components; their frequency resolution—that is, their ability to differentiate between neighboring frequency components; and their ability to reduce spectral leakage. Hanning and Blackman give good results for most applications. If detailed frequency analysis is important to your work, you should investigate the literature on each windowing function and experiment with them to see what results they yield.

## 4.6.6 Key Points Regarding the Fourier Transform

So that you don't lose the forest in the trees, we end this section with a summary of the key points related to the Fourier transform.

- The Fourier transform is applicable in both audio and image processing. It is performed in one dimension for audio processing and two dimensions for image processing.
- The discrete Fourier transform (DFT) has two equivalent forms,

$$F_n = \frac{1}{N} \sum_{k=0}^{N-1} f_k \cos\left(\frac{2\pi nk}{N}\right) - i f_k \sin\left(\frac{2\pi nk}{N}\right)$$

and

$$F_n = \frac{1}{N} \sum_{k=0}^{N-1} f_k e^{\frac{-i2\pi nk}{N}} \quad \text{where} \quad 0 \le n \le N - 1$$

Either form yields a complex number $F_n = a_n - i b_n$, where $a_n$ and $b_n$ are the coefficients for the cosine and sine frequency components of the waveform being analyzed.

- The Fourier transform can be thought of in pairs: the forward and inverse transforms. The forward transform goes from the time to the frequency domain. The inverse transform goes from the frequency domain to the time domain. The transform is invertible without loss of information (down to rounding errors). The two forms of the inverse discrete Fourier transform corresponding to the forward transform shown above are

$$f_k = \sum_{n=0}^{N-1}\left[a_n\cos\left(\frac{2\pi nk}{N}\right) + b_n\sin\left(\frac{2\pi nk}{N}\right)\right]$$

and

$$f_k = \sum_{n=0}^{N-1}F_n e^{\frac{i2\pi nk}{N}}$$

- One difference between the discrete Fourier and the discrete cosine transform is that the DFT contains phase information while the DCT does not. You can express an audio wave in terms of the magnitude $A_n$ of its frequency components offset by a phase $\phi_n$. This is captured in the magnitude/phase form of the inverse discrete Fourier transform:

$$f_k = \sum_{n=0}^{N-1}A_n\cos(2\pi nk + \phi_n)$$

- The fast Fourier transform (FFT) is a fast implementation of the discrete Fourier transform. Both versions operate on a window of $N$ samples. The FFT requires that $N$ be a power of 2, while the DCT does not. (However, there do exist variants of the FFT that don't have this requirement.) The FFT is the version of the Fourier transform that is generally used in audio processing programs, because it is fast.
- For both the DFT and the FFT, $N/2$ frequency components are given as output, with frequencies $k/T$ for $1 \le k \le N/2$. This is another difference between the DCT and the DFT or FFT. The DCT yields $N$ frequency components for $N$ samples, while the DFT and FFT yield $N/2$ frequency components for $N$ samples.
- Increasing the window size for the FFT increases the frequency resolution but decreases the time resolution.
- Both the DCT and the FFT yield frequency components that aren't actually part of the audio signal. This is because they have to make assumptions about the periodicity of the sample blocks they analyze. The DCT assumes that the block and its mirror image constitute one period of the entire sound wave. The FFT assume that the block alone constitutes one period. Windowing functions are used to help eliminate the spurious frequencies that are output from the transforms.
- Examples of windowing functions are Hanning, Hamming, Blackman, and Blackman–Harris.

Supplement on RMS:

## 4.7 STATISTICAL ANALYSIS OF AN AUDIO FILE

In addition to frequency and spectral views, which analyze sound data in the frequency domain, audio processing programs sometimes offer a statistical analysis of your audio files, which analyze sample values in the time domain. The statistical analysis may include the minimum and maximum possible sample values; the peak amplitude in the file; the number of clipped samples; the DC offset; the total, minimum, maximum, and average root-mean-square (RMS) amplitude; and a histogram.

mathematical modeling worksheet

Let's consider what is meant by the DC offset. You have seen that no matter how complex a sound wave is, you can decompose it into frequency components. Each frequency component is a pure sinusoidal wave that is centered on the horizontal axis. However, analog to digital conversion is not a perfect process, and it can happen that the frequency components of the sampled waveform are not perfectly centered at 0. The amount of deviation is called the **DC offset**. You generally won't hear if your audio file has a DC offset, but it may affect certain audio processing steps, particularly those based on finding places where the waveform crosses 0, called **zero-crossings**. Your audio processing program probably will have a feature for adjusting the DC offset.

The **root-mean-square amplitude** (also referred to as **RMS power** or **RMS level**, depending on your audio processing program) is a measure of the average amplitude in the sound wave over a given period—either over the entire sound wave or over a portion of it that you've selected. It is computed as follows:

---

### 🔑 KEY EQUATION

Let $N$ be the number of samples in an audio signal. $x_i$ is the amplitude of the $i$th sample. Then the **root-mean-square amplitude**, $r$, is defined as

$$r = \sqrt{\frac{1}{N}\sum_{i=1}^{N} x_i{}^2}$$

**Equation 4.9**

---

**ASIDE:** You may also see the RMS equation in the form $r = \dfrac{max}{\sqrt{2}}$ where $max$ is the maximum sample value. This derives from $\sqrt{\dfrac{1}{T_2 - T_1}\int_{T_1}^{T_2}(f(x))^2 dx}$, which is the continuous version of Equation 4.9. When applied to a sine for $k$ full cycles, you get $\sqrt{\dfrac{1}{2k\pi}\int_0^{2k\pi}(max * \sin(x))^2} = \dfrac{max}{\sqrt{2}}$.

**Minimum** or **maximum RMS power** makes sense only if you have defined a window size, which you should be able to do in the statistics view. If the window size is 50 milliseconds, for example, then the minimum RMS power is the minimum RMS amplitude for any 50-millisecond period in the selected waveform. The **average RMS amplitude** (sometimes referred to as **average RMS power**) is the average RMS amplitude for all windows of the specified size.

An **audio histogram** shows how many samples there are at each amplitude level in the audio selection. An example of an audio histogram is given in Figure 4.24.

Supplement audio processing programs:

hands-on worksheet

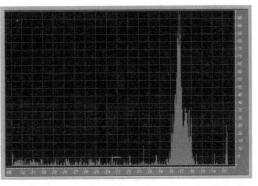

**Figure 4.24** Audio histogram (from Audition)

# 4.8 MIDI

## 4.8.1 MIDI Vs. Sampled Digital Audio

Thus far, we've been considering digital audio that is created from sampling analog sound waves and quantizing the sample values. There's another way to store sound in digital form, however. It's called *MIDI*, which stands for *Musical Instrument Digital Interface*. It may be more precise to say that MIDI stores "sound events" or "human performances of sound" rather than sound itself. Written in a scripting language, a MIDI file contains messages that indicate the notes, instruments, and duration of notes to be played. In MIDI terminology, each message describes an *event* (*i.e.*, the change of note, key, tempo, etc.) as a musical piece is played.

With sampled digital audio, an audio file contains a vector of samples—perhaps millions of them—that capture the waveform of the sound. These are reconstructed into an analog waveform when the audio is played. In comparison, MIDI messages tell what note and instrument to play, and they are translated into sound by a *synthesizer*. If a message says the equivalent of "Play the note middle C for ½ second, and make it sound like a piano," then the computer or MIDI output device either retrieves "piano middle C" from a memory bank of stored sounds, or it creates the sound from mathematical calculations, a process called *FM synthesis*. We'll look at these synthesis methods more closely in a moment.

The difference between sampled digital audio and MIDI is analogous to the difference between bitmapped graphics and vector graphics. Bitmaps store color values at discrete points in space, while vector graphics store symbolic descriptions of shapes—for example, an encoding of "draw a red square." Analogously, sampled digital audio files store sound wave amplitudes at discrete points in time, while MIDI files store symbolic descriptions of musical notes and how they are to be played. Just as vector graphic files are generally much smaller than bitmaps, MIDI files are generally much smaller than sampled digital audio. It's much more concise to encode the instruction "Play a piano note middle C for ½ second" than to store half a second of sound recording the piano's middle C. At 44.1 kHz in stereo, with two bytes per sample per channel, just half a second requires 176,400 bytes when the audio is stored as samples. The MIDI message, in comparison, would require just a few bytes.

Because MIDI stores information in terms of notes and instruments played, it's easier to deal with this information in discrete units and edit it. For example, it's possible to change individual notes, or even to change a whole piece so that it's played with a different instrument. This would be very difficult with sampled digital audio. Think about it. With sampled audio, how would you determine exactly where one musical note ends and another begins? How would you identify what instrument is being played, just on the basis of an audio waveform? How would you change a waveform representing a tuba to a waveform representing a piccolo playing the same piece of music? No easy task.

A disadvantage of MIDI is that it can sound more artificial or mechanical than sampled digital audio. Imagine recording someone playing the flute. Sampled digital audio will capture the sound just as it is played, with all the subtle changes in pitch, tone, resonance, and timing that may be characteristic of the musician's style. The digitally recorded audio retains that human touch. MIDI audio, on the other hand, uses synthesized sounds to recreate each note played on the flute. Without any added audio "color," the same MIDI note played from a flute will always

Supplements on MIDI vs. audio in Chuck:

hands-on worksheet

Supplements of MIDI vs. audio in MAX/MSP:

hands-on worksheet

**ASIDE:** Actually, *"wav* to MIDI converters" *do* exist. They do a fairly good job of converting an audio file into MIDI messages if the audio contains only one instrument. However, it is nearly impossible to separate the frequencies of multiple instruments played simultaneously.

sound exactly the same. However, this disadvantage to MIDI is not as bad as you might imagine. Additional information can be sent in MIDI messages to describe how a note should be bent (as in pitch bend) or modulated. Most MIDI input devices can detect how hard a note is played, so the dynamics of a piece can be better reproduced. And MIDI input devices also allow you to play a piece and capture the exact timing of the performance (or near-exact, down to the maximum timing quantization level of the input and storage devices). So while it is true that it is more difficult to capture the personality of an individual's performance with synthesized sound than with sampled sound, MIDI music still has great expressive capabilities.

A main advantage to MIDI audio is the ease with which you can create and edit a piece of music. With a MIDI keyboard connected to your computer, you can play a piece, record it on your computer in MIDI format, and then edit it with a MIDI-editing program. With such a program, you can change the musical instrument used to play the piece with a click of the mouse. You can edit individual notes, change the key in which the piece is played, and fix errors note by note. And because the MIDI format is an industry standard, you can also easily transport your music from one MIDI device or computer to another.

## 4.8.2 The MIDI Standard

MIDI is a standard or protocol agreed upon by the makers of musical instruments, computers, and computer software. The protocol defines how MIDI messages are constructed, how they are transmitted, how they are stored, and what they mean. The hardware part of the protocol specifies how connections are made between two MIDI devices, including how MIDI ports convert data to electrical voltages, and how MIDI cables transmit the voltages. The software part of the protocol specifies the format and meaning of MIDI messages, and how they should be stored.

The first formal definition of the MIDI protocol was released in 1983 as the MIDI 1.0 Detailed Specification. This protocol evolved from a collaboration of industry representatives from Roland Corporation, Sequential Circuits, Oberheim Electronics, Yamaha, Korg, Kawai, and other companies associated with music. The *MIDI Manufacturers Association* (*MMA*) was subsequently created to oversee changes and enhancements to the MIDI standard. An important part of the MIDI Detailed Specification is the *General MIDI* standard, **GM-1**, adopted by the MMA in 1991. GM standardizes how musical instruments are assigned to *patch numbers*, as they are called. Before the adoption of GM-1, you could create a musical piece on a certain keyboard or MIDI input device, defining the instruments as you wanted them. For example, your keyboard might have stored flute as patch number 74. But you had no assurance that patch number 74 would be interpreted as a flute on some other MIDI device. With GM-1, 128 standard patch numbers were adopted, as listed in Table 4.5. The patches are organized into 16 family types with eight instruments in each family. (FX stands for "special effects.") General MIDI was updated in GM-2 in 1999 and revised again in 2003. *GM-2* increases the number of sounds defined in the standard and also includes character information (*e.g.*, karaoke lyrics). GM-2 is backward compatible with GM-1.

## 4.8.3 How MIDI Files Are Created, Edited, and Played

The first thing you probably want to know is how to create a MIDI file, so let's begin by looking at the features of MIDI hardware and software that make this possible.

Hardware devices that generate MIDI messages are called *MIDI controllers*. MIDI controllers take a variety of forms. A musical instrument like an electronic piano keyboard, a

## TABLE 4.5    General MIDI Mapping of Instruments to Patch Numbers

| Patch/Instrument | Patch/Instrument | Patch/Instrument | Patch/Instrument |
|---|---|---|---|
| **Piano** | **Bass** | **Reed** | **Synth. FX** |
| 1. Acoust. Grand Piano | 33. Acoustic Bass | 65. Soprano Sax | 97. FX 1 (rain) |
| 2. Bright Acoust. Piano | 34. Electric Bass (finger) | 66. Alto Sax | 98. FX 2 (soundtrack) |
| 3. Electric Grand Piano | 35. Electric Bass (pick) | 67. Tenor Sax | 99. FX 3 (crystal) |
| 4. Honky Tonk Piano | 36. Fretless Bass | 68. Baritone Sax | 100. FX 4 (atmosphere) |
| 5. Electric Piano 1 | 37. Slap Bass 1 | 69. Oboe | 101. FX 5 (brightness) |
| 6. Electric Piano 2 | 38. Slap Bass 2 | 70. English Horn | 102. FX 6 (goblins) |
| 7. Harpsichord | 39. Synth. Bass 1 | 71. Bassoon | 103. FX 7 (echoes) |
| 8. Clavichord | 40. Synth. Bass 2 | 72. Clarinet | 104. FX 8 (sci-fi) |
| **Chromatic Percussion** | **Strings** | **Pipe** | **Ethnic** |
| 9. Celesta | 41. Violin | 73. Piccolo | 105. Sitar |
| 10. Glockenspiel | 42. Viola | 74. Flute | 106. Banjo |
| 11. Music Box | 43. Cello | 75. Recorder | 107. Samisen |
| 12. Vibraphone | 44. Contrabass | 76. Pan Flute | 108. Koto |
| 13. Marimba | 45. Tremolo Strings | 77. Blown Bottle | 109. Kalimba |
| 14. Xylophone | 46. Pizzicato Strings | 78. Shakuhachi | 110. Bagpipe |
| 15. Tubular Bells | 47. Orchestral Harp | 79. Whistle | 111. Fiddle |
| 16. Dulcimer | 48. Timpani | 80. Ocarina | 112. Shanai |
| **Organ** | **Ensemble** | **Synth. Lead** | **Percussive** |
| 17. Drawbar Organ | 49. String Ensemble 1 | 81. Lead 1 (square) | 113. Tinkle Bell |
| 18. Percussive Organ | 50. String Ensemble 2 | 82. Lead 2 (sawtooth) | 114. Agogo |
| 19. Rock Organ | 51. Synth. Strings 1 | 83. Lead 3 (calliope) | 115. Steel Drums |
| 20. Church Organ | 52. Synth. Strings 2 | 84. Lead 4 (chiff) | 116. Woodblock |
| 21. Reed Organ | 53. Choir Aahs | 85. Lead 5 (charang) | 117. Tailo Drum |
| 22. Accordian | 54. Voice Oohs | 86. Lead 6 (voice) | 118. Melodic Tom |
| 23. Harmonica | 55. Synth. Voice | 87. Lead 7 (fifths) | 119. Synth. Drum |
| 24. Tango Accordian | 56. Orchestra Hit | 88. Lead 8 (bass + lead) | 120. Reverse Cymbal |
| **GUITAR** | **BRASS** | **SYNTH. PAD** | **SOUND FX** |
| 25. Acoustic Guitar (nylon) | 57. Trumpet | 89. Pad 1 (new age) | 121. Guitar Fret Noise |
| 26. Acoustic Guitar (steel) | 58. Trombone | 90. Pad 2 (warm) | 122. Breath Noise |
| 27. Electric Guitar (jazz) | 59. Tuba | 91. Pad 3 (polysynth) | 123. Seashore |
| 28. Electric Guitar (clean) | 60. Muted Trumpet | 92. Pad 4 (choir) | 124. Bird Tweet |
| 29. Electric Guitar (muted) | 61. French Horn | 93. Pad 5 (bowed) | 125. Telephone Ring |
| 30. Overdriven Guitar | 62. Brass Section | 94. Pad 6 (metallic) | 126. Helicopter |
| 31. Distortion Guitar | 63. Synth, Brass 1 | 95. Pad 7 (halo) | 127. Applause |
| 32. Guitar Harmonics | 64. Synth. Brass 2 | 96. Pad 8 (sweep) | 128. Gunshot |

saxophone, a guitar, or a trumpet can serve as a MIDI controller if it is designed for MIDI. Devices that read MIDI messages and turn them into audio signals that can be played through an output device are called ***MIDI synthesizers***. Some MIDI keyboards can serve as both controllers and synthesizers, which means that they can both generate MIDI messages and also serve as the sound output device (through which you hear the sound played). Other MIDI keyboards are silent; that is, they are used only to generate MIDI messages without creating any audible sound. Many computer sound cards are equipped to synthesize MIDI audio, and if your sound card doesn't have this capability, the operating system can provide a MIDI software synthesizer. You can also buy an external sound card (also called a sound interface) if you want to upgrade. A sound studio can have a wide range of MIDI components and setups that link samplers, effects processors, instruments, mixing consoles, and more. However, we'll restrict our discussion in this chapter to a common setup for the average user: an electronic keyboard connected to a personal computer.

A MIDI keyboard looks like a piano keyboard with extra controls. The number of keys, controls, and sensitivity features varies with the keyboard. You can find keyboards with (for example) 25, 32, 49, 61, 76, or 88 keys. (A standard piano has 88 keys.) Some keyboards can detect the velocity with which you strike a key and add this information to the MIDI message. Some can detect how hard you hold down a key after it is pressed. These features make the instrument more sensitive to musical dynamics.

The type of MIDI cable you need depends on the connection type your computer uses. Older computers sometimes use a 15-pin MIDI/joystick connection at the computer side. More commonly, a MIDI cable that connects to the USB port of the computer, connecting at the MIDI keyboard with two 5-pin circular connectors, one for the *in* and one for the *out* port. A through-port is also available on some MIDI devices, (to pass data directly through to another MIDI device). A standard MIDI connection passes data serially at a rate of 31.25 kb/s. High-speed serial ports make it possible to use multiport MIDI interfaces so that a computer can address multiple MIDI devices at the same time.

A ***MIDI sequencer*** is a hardware device or software application program that allows you to receive, store, and edit MIDI data. Stand-alone hardware sequencers exist for storing and editing MIDI files. By "stand-alone," we mean that these devices work independently from a personal computer. However, we're assuming that you're more likely to be working with a computer, and in this case your MIDI sequencer will be an application program running on your computer (for example, Cakewalk Music Creator or Cubase). A sequencer captures the MIDI messages generated by your controller and stores them in General MIDI file format. Many sequencers allow you to view your MIDI file in a variety of formats—a staff view showing musical notation, a piano roll view, or an event list, for example, as shown in Figure 4.25–Figure 4.27.

Closely related to MIDI sequencers are musical notation programs. In musical notation programs, the emphasis is on creating music files in musical notation, but MIDI capability is nearly always included. With both sequencers and musical notation programs, it is also possible to create a MIDI file by inputting musical notes one note at a time. You can do this using a mouse to click on a picture of a keyboard on your computer screen, or you may be able to edit MIDI messages directly with an event editor. This isn't as convenient as playing an actual musical instrument and recording what you play as MIDI, but it works for small pieces.

A third way to capture a MIDI file is simply to read one in from another source. MIDI files with no copyright restrictions are widely available on the web or can be purchased as collections.

**Figure 4.25** Staff view (from Cakewalk Music Creator)

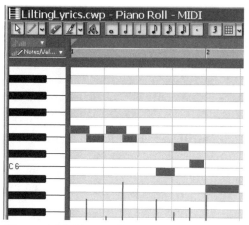

**Figure 4.26** Piano roll view (from Cakewalk Music Creator)

| Trk | HMSF | MBT | Ch | Kind | Data | | |
|---|---|---|---|---|---|---|---|
| 2 | 00:00:00:00 | 1:01:000 | 1 | Note | E 6 | 62 | 546 |
| 2 | 00:00:00:08 | 1:01:488 | 1 | Note | Eb6 | 67 | 505 |
| 2 | 00:00:00:16 | 1:02:073 | 1 | Note | E 6 | 59 | 546 |
| 2 | 00:00:00:23 | 1:02:536 | 1 | Note | Eb6 | 75 | 396 |
| 2 | 00:00:01:01 | 1:03:056 | 1 | Note | E 6 | 52 | 328 |
| 2 | 00:00:01:08 | 1:03:528 | 1 | Note | B 5 | 67 | 515 |
| 2 | 00:00:01:16 | 1:04:066 | 1 | Note | D 6 | 61 | 411 |
| 2 | 00:00:01:23 | 1:04:513 | 1 | Note | C 6 | 63 | 415 |
| 2 | 00:00:02:00 | 2:01:025 | 1 | Note | A 5 | 69 | 911 |
| 2 | 00:00:02:26 | 2:02:683 | 1 | Patch | Normal | ··· Violin | |
| 2 | 00:00:02:26 | 2:02:683 | 1 | Note | E 5 | 58 | 574 |
| 2 | 00:00:03:02 | 2:03:147 | 1 | Note | G#5 | 64 | 727 |
| 2 | 00:00:03:10 | 2:03:632 | 1 | Note | A 5 | 44 | 531 |
| 2 | 00:00:03:18 | 2:04:161 | 1 | Note | B 5 | 65 | 1:115 |

**Figure 4.27** Event view (from Cakewalk Music Creator)

It's important to understand the difference between MIDI sequencers and standard digital audio processing programs—those which work with sampled digital audio. (*e.g.*, Audition, Logic, Audacity, or Sound Forge). Digital audio processing programs may have only limited MIDI capability. For example, they may allow you to import a MIDI file, but then the intention is that you convert the MIDI file into sampled digital audio. Doing the conversion in this direction—from MIDI to, say, WAV or PCM, isn't too hard. The MIDI file can be synthesized to digital audio, played by the sound card, recorded back through the sound card, and saved to a new file. On the other hand, taking a sampled digital audio file and converting it to MIDI would be very difficult. As described above, this would entail identifying where a note begins and ends and what instrument is playing the note, simply on the basis of the sound samples. That's nontrivial.

The beauty of MIDI is that it's so easy to create and edit MIDI files, especially for musicians. Once you've created a MIDI file, you can use your sequencing software to edit it note by note, measure by measure. This is usually done at a high level of abstraction. Musicians are accustomed to looking at musical notation in the form of sheet music, and this is the level of abstraction at which they can work in sequencing software. Easy mouse clicks or menu selections allow you to change the tempo, transpose the key, switch instruments, add or delete individual notes or measures, and correct errors. Complex and interesting musical effects can be created in this way.

### 4.8.4 MIDI for Nonmusicians

MIDI is not only for musicians. MIDI is a protocol for message passing, and applications of MIDI are not restricted to music. A system can be designed to read and interpret MIDI messages in whatever way is desired. For example, MIDI messages can be used to control complex lights, special effects, and multimedia in a theater. Since its inception, new applications have continually been added to the MIDI standard. For example, MIDI Show Control is a command and control language originally designed for theaters and later used in theme parks rides. MIDI Machine Control is used in recording studios to synchronize and remotely control recording equipment. The MIDI format has also been applied to polyphonic ring tones for mobile phones.

Once you understand how MIDI messages are constructed and communicated, you may want to experiment with catching a MIDI message and using it to control an activity. Although MIDI messages are usually intended to describe musical notes, they don't really have to be interpreted that way. If you intercept a MIDI message, you can interpret it to mean whatever you want. So if you're a computer programmer, you can find interesting and creative ways to use a MIDI device as a controller for something that might have nothing to do with music.

If you would like to experiment with MIDI's music, drum, and sound effects capability, there's still a lot you can do even without musical training. You can pick out a tune by ear on a MIDI keyboard and try out the keyboard's auto-accompaniment feature if one is available. You can look at your file in the event or piano roll view and try your hand at editing it by changing notes, changing instruments, adding more notes, changing the timing, and so forth. You can be quite creative without ever reading a note of music. As you work with MIDI, you'll learn something about music terminology and theory. In fact, one of the most common applications of MIDI is in music education. With MIDI, you can train your ear to recognize notes, keys, and intervals between notes, or you can play a piece of music and get feedback on your accuracy. If you're interested in the musical features of MIDI but don't have much background in that area, the next section will help you get started.

### 4.8.5 Musical Acoustics and Notation

If you're a musician and can read music, then you'll already be familiar with most of the terminology in this section, but you may find it helpful to place your knowledge in the context of digital media. If you're not a musician, don't be intimidated. You don't have to know how to read or compose music in order to work with MIDI, but it's good to be familiar with basic concepts and terminology.

In Western music notation, musical sounds—called *tones*—are characterized by their pitch, timbre, and loudness. With the addition of onset and duration, a musical sound is called a *note*. The pitch of a note is how high or low it sounds to the human ear. For musical notes that are simple sinusoidal waves, the higher the frequency of the wave, the higher the pitch. The range of human hearing is from about 20 Hz to about 20,000 Hz. Actually, if you test the frequency limits of your own hearing, you'll probably not be able to hear frequencies as high as 20,000 Hz. As you get older, you lose your ability to hear very high frequency sounds.

Different cultures have developed different terminology with regard to music—that is, different ways of arranging and labeling frequencies within the range of human hearing. Nearly all cultures, however, base their musical terminology on the following observation: If the frequency of one note is $2^n$ times of the frequency of another, where $n$ is an integer, the two notes sound "the same" to the human ear, except that the first is higher-pitched than the second. For example, a 400 Hz note sounds like a 200 Hz note, only higher. This leads to the following definition:

> ## 🔑 KEY EQUATION
>
> Let $g$ be the frequency of a musical note. Let $h$ be the frequency of a musical tone $n$ **octaves** higher than $g$. Then
>
> $$h = 2^n g$$

The note-by-note scale at which the frequencies between two one-octave-apart notes are divided varies from culture to culture. In Western culture, 440 Hz is taken as a starting reference point and is called the note A. The octave between one A and the next higher A is then divided into twelve notes. (The word octave comes from the fact that there are eight whole notes in it: A, B, C, D, E, F, G, and again A.) The twelve notes are called A, A sharp, B, C, C sharp, D, D sharp, E, F, F sharp, G, and G sharp. A sharp can also be called B flat; C sharp can be called D flat; B sharp can be called E flat; F sharp can be called G flat; and G sharp can be called A flat. Sharps are symbolized with #, and flats are symbolized with ♭. Only the letters A through G are used to label notes. After G, the next note is A again.

The way these notes look on a piano keyboard is shown in Figure 4.28. There are black keys and white keys on the keyboard. The sharps are black keys. To show an octave, we could have started with any note, as long as we end on the same note at the end of the octave ("the same" in the sense that it is twice the frequency of the first). This is how notes and their corresponding frequencies are divided in Western music. Other cultures may have more or fewer notes per octave.

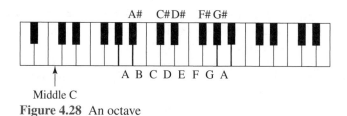

**Figure 4.28** An octave

Given that every twelve notes you double the frequency, if you know the frequency $f1$ of a certain note, you can compute the frequency $f2$ of the succeeding note. Based on the definition of an octave, start with $f1$ and multiply each succeeding frequency by some $x$, doing this 12 times to get to $2f1$. This $x$ will be the multiplier we use to get each successive frequency. Thus, we can derive $x$ from

$$2f1 = (((((((((((f1x)x)x)x)x)x)x)x)x)x)x) = f1x^{12}$$

$$2 = x^{12}$$

$$x = \sqrt[12]{2} \approx 1.05946309436$$

That is, the frequency relationship between any two successive notes $f1$ and $f2$, where $f2$ immediately follows $f1$ on the keyboard is

$$f2 = 1.05946309436 f1$$

If A has frequency 440 Hz, then A# has frequency 440 Hz * 1.05946309436 ≈ 466.16 Hz; B has frequency 466.16 Hz * 1.05946309436 ≈ 493.88 Hz; and so forth.

Musical notation is written on a *musical staff*—a set of lines and spaces, as pictured in Figure 4.25. The staff has a *key signature* at the beginning of the piece, telling which notes are supposed to be played as sharps and flats. (This is another meaning for the term *key*, as opposed to a physical key on the keyboard.) It's good to know this use of the term key as you work with MIDI. With a MIDI sequencer, it is easy to transpose a piece of music to a higher or lower key. If you transpose a piece to a higher key, each note is higher, but all the notes retain their frequency relationship to each other, so the piece sounds exactly the same, only at a higher pitch. The notes will be moved up on the staff if you look at the music in staff view after transposing it.

The *timbre* of a musical sound is its "tone color." Think about two different instruments playing sounds of exactly the same basic pitch—say, a violin and a flute. Even though you can recognize that they're playing the same note, you can also hear a difference. The sounds, when produced by two different instruments, have a different timbre. The timbre of a musical sound is a function of its *overtones*. A sound produced by a musical instrument is not a single-frequency wave. The shape and dynamics of the instrument produce vibrations at other, related frequencies. The lowest frequency of a given sound produced by a particular instrument is its fundamental frequency. It is the fundamental frequency that tells us the basic note that is being played. Then there are other frequencies combined in the sound. Usually, these are integer multiples of the fundamental frequency, referred to as *harmonics*. The fundamental frequency is also called the *first harmonic*. A frequency that is two times the fundamental frequency is called the *second harmonic*, a frequency that is three times the fundamental frequency is the *third harmonic*, and so forth. The harmonics above the fundamental frequency are the sound's overtones. Theoretically, all harmonics up to infinity can be produced, but in fact only some of the harmonics for a note are present at any moment in time, and they change over time, adding even more complexity to the waveform. The intensity of the different-level harmonics is determined by how the instrument is played—how a guitar string is plucked, a horn is blown, or a piano key is struck, for example. Each instrument produces its own characteristic overtones, and thus its own recognizable timbre.

There are instruments that create inharmonic overtones as well—drums, for example. These inharmonic overtones make the fundamental frequency unrecognizable, and the sound is thus more like noise than like a musical note.

*Resonance* affects the perceived sound of an instrument, as well. When an object at rest is put in the presence of a second, vibrating object, the first object can be set into sympathetic vibration at the same frequency. This is resonance. The shape of a musical instrument—like the tubular shape of a horn or the body of a guitar—can cause the frequencies produced by the instrument to resonate, and in this way some of the harmonics are strengthened while others may be lessened. Resonance thus has an effect on an instrument's timbre.

The perceived loudness of a musical sound is a function of the air pressure amplitude. The period covered by a single musical note is called the sound's **amplitude envelope**. The **attack** covers the moment when the sound is first played and reaches its maximum amplitude—for example, when a piano key is struck, a guitar is plucked, or a trumpet is blown. The relatively quick drop in amplitude after the initial attack is called the **decay**. Following this decay, the **sustain** period is the span of time during which the sound continues vibrating at a fairly even level. If the sound is stopped before it fades away naturally, the moment when it is stopped is called its **release**. Each instrument has its own typical sound envelope, and each individual sound produced by an instrument has a particular envelope. For example, a drum beat typically has a sharply peaking attack. A piano note has a fairly sharp attack as well, sharper if it is struck hard and quickly. A flute generally has a less sharply peaked attack because it must be blown to create a sound, and the blowing of a flute is a slower, smoother action than the striking of a key. A piano has a slow, steadily fading sustain, as compared to an organ, where the sound amplitude fades less during the sustain period. The general form of an amplitude envelope is shown in Figure 4.29.

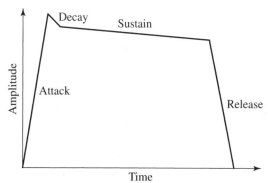

**Figure 4.29** Amplitude envelope

## 4.8.6 Features of MIDI Sequencers and Keyboards

MIDI controllers and sequencers have certain standard features and a variety of additional options, depending on the sophistication of the equipment. One of the most basic features is the ability to set patches. A **patch** number specifies the instrument to be played. In descriptions of MIDI messages, the patch number is referred to as the **program number**. When an instrument is selected on a MIDI keyboard, it is sometimes referred to as a **voice**. A **bank** is a database of patches, each database composed of its own samples.

A MIDI file can be played into any output device that has the ability to synthesize sound from MIDI data. If your computer has a MIDI-equipped sound card (most do), it can become the output device for playing MIDI. If you have a MIDI keyboard connected to your computer, you can play a MIDI file through the keyboard's synthesizer (if it has one) and hear the sound through the speakers of the keyboard. When you're working with a MIDI sequencer, you select which MIDI inputs and outputs you want to use.

The controls, features, and number of keys on a MIDI keyboard vary from one model to the next. A *polyphonic* keyboard is able to play more than one note at a time. For example, a MIDI keyboard may have 32-note maximum polyphony, which means that it can play 32 notes at the same time. A *multitimbral* MIDI output device can play different instruments at the same time. An output device must be polyphonic in order to be multitimbral, but the maximum number of notes and instruments it can play simultaneously doesn't have to be the same. You may be able to set a *split-point* for your keyboard—a division between two keys on the keyboard such that options can be set differently above and below that point. For example, you could designate that the keys above the split-point to sound like one instrument, and the keys below the split-point to sound like a different instrument. With a split-point set, you could play one part with your right hand and it could sound like a piano, while the part you play with your left hand sounds like a bass guitar.

A *touch-sensitive* keyboard can detect the velocity with which you strike a key, encode this in a MIDI message, and control the loudness of notes accordingly. In addition to sensing velocity, some keyboards can also sense how hard a key is held down after it is pressed, called *aftertouch*. A key that is held down relatively hard after it is pressed can be a signal that a note should swell in volume as it is sustained—a realistic effect for horns and brass. *Monophonic aftertouch* assigns the same aftertouch value to all notes that are played at the same time. *Polyphonic aftertouch* can make one note in a chord grow louder while other notes played at the same time don't change in volume.

**ASIDE:** To be more precise, a velocity message can be interpreted however you like in a MIDI track. For example, when you play the MIDI file via a MIDI sampler, you can set the sampler control to interpret a velocity message as a change in timbre.

Two important MIDI terms that are sometimes confused are channel and track. A MIDI *channel* is a path of data communication between two MIDI devices. A *track* is an area in memory where MIDI data is stored, with a corresponding area on the sequencer's timeline where the MIDI notes can be viewed. In a MIDI sequencer's user interface, the track view shows you each track separately. You always have to record to a specific track. You can also record on more than one track simultaneously; you can designate tracks as either MIDI or audio; and you can mute tracks and listen to them separately on playback. Tracks are shown in Figure 4.30.

There is a close relationship between channels and tracks, but they are not the same. The following recording scenarios should help you to understand the difference between a track and a channel. (Your ability to re-enact these scenarios depends on the features of your equipment.)

When you play something on your MIDI keyboard, you record it to a certain track. Then you may want to record something else—something that will be played at the same time as the first clip. You can rewind to the beginning and record the second clip on the same track with the first, selecting the option to blend the two recordings rather than have the second overwrite the first. As an alternative, you can record the second clip onto a different track. What's the advantage of recording on a different track? The advantage is that the two clips are stored in separate areas in memory, so you can edit them separately. You can mute one track and play the other alone. You can change the patch on the two tracks separately, so that they play different instruments. You can delete either one without affecting the other.

So how does a channel relate to this? We said above that you can change the patch on the two tracks separately so that they play different instruments. But you can do this only if the two tracks are able to play on two different channels. The channel is the path along which the MIDI messages are passed from the place where they are stored, on your computer, to

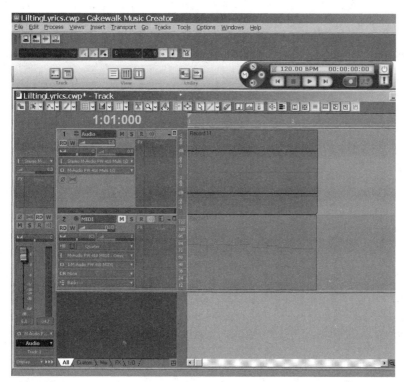

**Figure 4.30**  Two tracks (from Cakewalk Music Creator)

the place where they are played, on your keyboard or some other synthesizer. The GM standard calls for 16 channels on a MIDI device. In your MIDI sequencing software, you can designate that track 1 plays on channel 1 and track 2 plays on channel 2, and then if tracks 1 and 2 are set to play different instruments, you'll actually hear two different instruments played. But if both tracks are set to channel 1, then you'll hear only one of the two instruments playing both tracks. Figure 4.30 shows two tracks, the first set to channel 1 to play as a grand piano, and the second set to channel 2 to play as an alto sax. Since they are playing on separate channels, they can play different instruments.

In the MIDI standard, channel 10 is designated to carry drum and percussion sounds. If you set a track to record from channel 10, then each key you play at the keyboard will be recorded as some drum or percussion instrument as defined by the Percussion Key Map shown in Table 4.6. For example, if you record middle C, C#, and D on channel 10, you'll hear the hi bongo, low bongo, and mute hi conga in succession when you play it back. (Middle C is note 60.)

A *sustain pedal* can be connected to some keyboards so that you can delay the release of a note. This pedal works just like the sustain pedal on a piano. Other types of pedals (*e.g.*, sostenato pedal or soft pedal) can also be added.

A keyboard may also have a ***pitch bend wheel***. The pitch bend wheel can be slid up or down to move the pitch of a note up or down as it is being played. The wheel slides back to its original position when you let it go. If you do this when your instrument is set to

**ASIDE:** The sustain pedal causes a *sustain* MIDI message to be sent and recorded, but that message could be interpreted later in whatever way you want. For example, you could specify by means of your sampler that a *sustain* message should trigger reverb.

| TABLE 4.6 | Percussion Key Map | |
|---|---|---|
| **Key #/Percussion Sound** | **Key #/Percussion Sound** | **Key #/Percussion Sound** |
| 35. Acoustic bass drum | 51. Ride cymbal 1 | 67. High agogo |
| 36. Bass drum 1 | 52. Chinese cymbal | 68. Low agogo |
| 37. Side stick | 53. Ride bell | 69. Cabasa |
| 38. Acoustic snare | 54. Tambourine | 70. Maracas |
| 39. Hand clap | 55. Splash cymbal | 71. Short whistle |
| 40. Electric snare | 56. Cowbell | 72. Long whistle |
| 41. Low floor tom | 57. Crash cymbal 2 | 73. Short guiro |
| 42. Closed hi-hat | 58. Vibraslap | 74. Long guiro |
| 43. High floor tom | 59. Ride cymbal 2 | 75. Claves |
| 44. Pedal hi-hat | 60. Hi bongo | 76. Hi wood block |
| 45. Low tom | 61. Low bongo | 77. Low wood block |
| 46. Open hi-hat | 62. Mute hi conga | 78. Mute cuica |
| 47. Low-mid tom | 63. Open hi conga | 79. Open cuica |
| 48. Hi-mid tom | 64. Low conga | 80. Mute triangle |
| 49. Crash cymbal 1 | 65. High timbal | 81. Open triangle |
| 50. High tom | 66. Low timbal | |

Supplement on
MIDI:

hands-on
worksheet

some kind of guitar, it sounds like you're manipulating the guitar string while you're playing the note. The wheel has an analogous effect with other instruments.

A *metronome* is an audible timing device that ticks out the beats as you play. You can usually turn the metronome on from both the sequencer and the controller. By keeping pace with the metronome, you can maintain a consistent beat as you play. The sound of the metronome does not have to be recorded with the music.

A wide variety of changes and effects can be achieved with MIDI sequencing software. Some of the important features are *transposition* (changing the key signature), *timing quantization* (moving notes to more evenly spaced timing intervals), tempo change, and digital signal processing (DSP) effects like flange, reverb, delay, and echo. With many sequencers, it is also possible to have digital audio—for example, vocals or sound effects—on one track and MIDI on another. The tracks can be mixed down to a digital audio file if this is your final intent.

## 4.8.7 MIDI Behind the Scenes

### 4.8.7.1 Types and Formats of MIDI Messages

A MIDI message is a packet of data that encodes an event. MIDI events describe how music is to be played. There are two main types of MIDI messages: channel messages and system messages. *Channel messages*, as the name implies, always contain information relevant to channels. *Channel voice messages* are the most common, indicating when a note begins (Note On), when a note ends (Note Off), what the note is, how hard it is pressed (Velocity), how hard it is held down (Aftertouch), what instrument is played (Program Change), what channels are activated, and so forth. *Channel mode messages* tell the MIDI

Types of MIDI messages

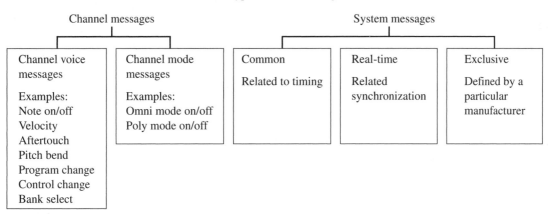

**Figure 4.31** Types of MIDI messages

receiving device—the device that plays the sound—what channels to listen to and how to interpret what it hears. For example, the Omni On message allows the receiver to listen to messages on any channel. The Mono On message indicates that the receiver is to play only one note at a time. *System messages* contain information that is not specific to any particular channel—for example, messages about timing, synchronization, and setup information. The general classification of MIDI messages is shown in Figure 4.31.

MIDI messages are transmitted in 10-bit bytes. Each byte begins with a start bit of 0 and ends with a stop bit of 1. The start and stop bits mark the beginnings and endings of bytes at the serial port. It's important to know that they're there when you compute the data rate for MIDI messages, but you don't need to take the start and stop bits into account if you capture and read MIDI messages through the port. The information part of the data is contained in a standard eight-bit byte, and you read only eight bits at a time for a byte. (For example, if you write a C program to capture MIDI messages, you can read the bytes into variables of type *unsigned char*, which are eight bits long.)

For each message, one *status byte* and zero or more *data bytes* are sent. The status byte tells what type of message is being communicated. Status bytes can be distinguished from data bytes by their most significant bit (MSB). The MSB of a status byte is 1, while the MSB of a data byte is 0. This implies that the value of a status byte always lies between 128 and 255, while the value of a data byte always lies between 0 and 127.

We'll look closely only at channel voice messages, since these are the most common. The complete specification of MIDI messages can be found at the MMA website. Channel voice messages tell what note is played and how it is played, requiring both a status byte and data bytes. The four least significant bits of each channel voice message tell the channel on which the note is to be transmitted. (Four bits can encode values 0 through 15, but at the user level the channels are referred to as 1 through 16, so the mapping is offset by one.) The four most significant bits of a channel voice message tell what action is to be taken— for example, begin playing a note, release the note, make the note swell; modulate, pan, turn up the volume, or create or some other effect; change the instrument; or bend the pitch. Seven channel voice messages are described in Table 4.7. The x before numbers in the second column indicate that they are given in hexadecimal. The equivalent binary numbers are in the third column. From this table, consider what the three-byte message x91 x3C x64

| TABLE 4.7 | Channel Voice Messages | | |
|---|---|---|---|
| **Message** | **Status Byte in Hex (n is channel)** | **Status Byte in Binary** | **Information in Data Bytes** |
| Note On | x9n | 1001 ---- | Note being played and velocity with which the key is struck (two bytes) |
| Note Off | x8n | 1000 ---- | Note being released and velocity with which key is released (two bytes) |
| Aftertouch for one key | xAn | 1010 ---- | Note, pressure (two bytes) |
| Aftertouch for entire channel | xDn | 1101 ---- | Pressure (one byte) |
| Program change | xCn | 1100 ---- | Patch number (one byte) |
| Control change | xBn | 1011 ---- | Type of control (*e.g.,* modulation, pan, etc.) and control change (two bytes) |
| Pitch bend | xEn | 1110 ---- | The range of frequencies through which the pitch is bent (two bytes) |

would mean. (This would be 10010001 00111100 01100100 in binary.) Hexadecimal is base 16, so x3C = 3 * 16 + 12 = 60 and x64 = 6 * 16 + 4 = 100. The first byte, x91, indicates "Note on, channel 1" The second byte indicates that the note to be played is note 60, which is middle C. The third byte indicates that the note should be played with a velocity of 100.

In addition to the messages shown in Table 4.7, it is also possible to signal the selection of a new bank of patches using a sequence of control change messages followed by appropriate data bytes.

### 4.8.7.2 Transmission of MIDI Messages

Supplement on MIDI:

programming exercise

MIDI messages are transmitted serially in 10-bit bytes at a rate of 31.25 kb/s. Each message is a data packet that begins with 0 for the start bit and ends with 1 for the stop bit. In between, the data is transmitted from the least to the most significant bit. Each message has a status byte and zero or more data bytes. Usually, there are two or three data bytes, but there can be even more. Think about what this implies. A Note On message requires three 10-bit bytes. That's 30 bits. What if you have a piece of piano music that has a single note being played by the right hand and a three-note chord being played by the left hand—all simultaneously? Now you have four notes at 30 bits each, or 120 bits. At a rate of 31.25 kb/s, it takes approximately 0.004 seconds to transmit the notes—about 0.001 seconds per note (and we haven't even accounted for the Note Off messages). If the time between notes isn't too long, it won't be detected by the human ear, so the notes sound like they're being played at the same time. But we haven't considered other messages that might be pertinent to these notes, like pitch bend or control change. Rolling the pitch bend wheel on the keyboard generates tens, or sometimes even hundreds of messages. With the relatively slow serial bit rate, the number of messages can start to clog the transmissions. When this happens, there is a audible lag between notes.

*Running status* is a technique for reducing the amount of MIDI data that needs to be sent by eliminating redundancy. The idea is simple. Once a status byte is communicated, then it doesn't have to be repeated as long as it still applies to the data bytes that follow. For example, if you have a three-note chord requiring that three Note On messages be sent in a

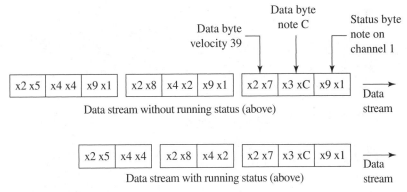

Notes: Start and stop bits not shown.
x indicates hexadecimal representation

**Figure 4.32** Running status

row, all to be transmitted on the same channel, then the status byte for Note On is given only once, followed by the notes and velocities for the three notes to be played. A comparison of the bit streams is given in Figure 4.32.

### 4.8.7.3 Synthesized Sound

The device that reads and plays a MIDI file—a sound card or a MIDI keyboard, for example—must be able to synthesize the sounds that are described in the messages. Two methods for synthesizing sound are *frequency modulation synthesis* (FM synthesis) and *wavetable synthesis*.

FM synthesis is done by performing mathematical operations on sounds that begin as simple sinusoidal frequencies. The operations begin with a carrier frequency which is altered with a modulating frequency. Assume that the original frequency can be modeled by a sinusoidal function. This frequency can be altered in complex and interesting ways by making another sinusoidal function an argument to the first—*e.g.*, taking a sine of a sine. The outer function then can be multiplied by an amplitude envelope function that models the kind of amplitude envelope shown in Figure 4.29. Additional functions can be applied to change how the sound is modulated over time, thereby creating overtones. FM synthesis can capture the timbre of real instruments fairly well, and it can also be used to create interesting new sounds not modeled after any particular musical instrument. Sound cards can use FM synthesis as a relatively inexpensive way to produce MIDI.

Wavetable synthesis is based on stored sound samples of real instruments. The software or hardware device in which the sounds are stored is called a *sampler*. (See Figure 4.33.) Wavetable synthesis is more expensive than FM synthesis in the amount of storage it requires, but it also reproduces the timbre of instruments more faithfully. Because of its greater fidelity, wavetable synthesis is generally preferred over FM synthesis, and it is made affordable by methods for decreasing the number and size of samples that must be stored.

Let's consider the number of samples that would have to be stored for an instrument, and how this number could be reduced. Is one sample enough to represent an instrument? Do you need a sample for each note played by an instrument? The answer actually lies somewhere in between. Although it's possible to take a single sample and shift its pitch with mathematical operations, if the pitch is shifted too far the sample begins to lose the characteristic timbre of the instrument. An instrument's timbre results in part from the

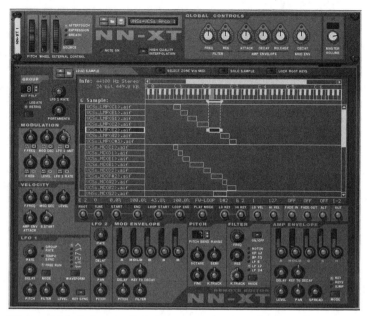

**Figure 4.33** Software digital sampler (from Reason)

overtones of notes, appearing at frequencies higher than the fundamental. Shifting the pitch can cause these overtones to be aliased, inserting false frequencies into the sample. Thus, numerous samples of each instrument are stored—but it isn't necessary to store a sample for each note. Instead, the range of notes is divided into regions, called *key splits*. One sample is taken per key split, and then all other notes within the split are created by pitch-shifting this sample.

Other ways have been devised to reduce the storage requirements for sampled sound. The size of the samples themselves can be reduced. Specifically, only a small representative sample of a note's sustain section has to be recorded. When the sample is played, a loop (possibly with some fading) is created over this section to make it the appropriate length. Digital filtering techniques can be applied to improve the accuracy of pitch shifting such that key splits can be larger. Finally, samples can also be compressed in ways that preserve their dynamic range. With these combined techniques, wavetable synthesis has become affordable enough to be widely adopted.

## EXERCISES AND PROGRAMS

1. Convert 160 dB_SPL (damage-to-eardrum level) to air pressure amplitude in Pa. Show your work.

2. Convert 20 Pa (approximately the air pressure level of very loud music) to dB_SPL. Show your work.

3. What is the dBFS equivalent of a 16-bit sample value of 5000?

4. If the frequency of a note B is about 494 Hz, what is the frequency of the next note E up the scale from this B?

5. If the frequency of a note A is about 440 Hz, what's the frequency of an A two octaves below the 440 Hz A?

6. What does this MIDI message xC2 x39 say?

7. What is the savings in bytes for a sequence of MIDI messages that has six notes played simultaneously, using running status instead of a Note On message for each note?

8. The fast Fourier transform assumes that a wave is periodic. What does it assume to be the length of the period when the FFT uses a window of 4096 samples on a file with a sampling rate of 44.1 kHz? What's the fundamental frequency? What's the third harmonic frequency?

9. Audio aliasing interactive tutorial, worksheet, and mathematical modeling exercise, online

10. Audio dithering interactive tutorial, worksheet, and mathematical modeling exercise, online

11. Noise shaping mathematical modeling exercise, online

12. $\mu$-law encoding interactive tutorial, programming exercise, and mathematical modeling exercise, online

13. Fourier transform interactive tutorial, worksheet, and programming exercise

14. Comparison of Fourier and discrete cosine transforms interactive tutorial and worksheet

15. Windowing functions interactive tutorial, worksheet, and mathematical modeling exercise

16. Root-mean-square amplitude mathematical modeling worksheet

## APPLICATIONS

1. By generating single-frequency tones in an audio processing program, identify the highest and lowest frequencies you're able to hear.

2. Generate a simple frequency tone of $x$ Hz. Generate another at $2x$ Hz. Mix them into one file. Play them. What do you expect to hear? What do you hear? Make another wave that is $3x$ the frequency of the first. What do you expect to hear when you play it together with the first wave? Play the mixed waves to confirm your prediction. Make another wave that is *not* an integer multiple of the first. What do you expect to hear when you play it together with the first wave? Play the mixed waves to confirm your prediction.

**Examine the features of your audio processing program and try the exercises below with features that are available. You should be able to find sample WAV files on the web to experiment with.**

3. Can you generate a single-frequency tone in your audio processing program at an arbitrary sampling rate? If so, create a file with a sampling rate of 1000 Hz and try to generate a tone that is 600 Hz. What happens? Why?

4. Can you get a frequency analysis and/or a spectral view of sound waves? If so, look at some sound waves and analyze the information given to you in these views. Select different portions of the file and look at the frequency analysis. Play the file and watch the frequency analysis change over time. Can you change the window size and/or windowing function for the frequency analysis? If so, try different sound files, window sizes, and windowing functions and observe the results.

5. Change an audio file to a raw format. Examine the values in the file.

6. Can you reduce the bit depth of an audio file in your audio processing program? If so, experiment with bit depth reduction. Reduce the bit depth of a file, and then listen to it. At what bit depth do you get noticeable quantization distortion? Find places where values are reduced to 0 and listen to how these sections sound.

7. Try reducing an audio file from 16 to 8 bits per sample, with no dithering. Then for comparison, take the original audio file and save it in an 8-bit $\mu$-law encoded format. Compare the two versions by listening to them. Can you hear the difference in quality? (Try a piece of music that has a wide dynamic range, and listen with good earphones.)

8. Does your audio processing program give you statistics regarding an audio file? If so, look at the RMS amplitude and histograms of an audio file. Interpret them as they relate to the audio file.

9. Working with audio, hands-on worksheet, online

10. Working with audio and MIDI in Chuck, worksheet, online

11. Working with audio and MIDI in MAX/MSP, worksheet, online

12. Working with MIDI, hands-on worksheet, online

13. Capturing and interpreting MIDI signals, programming exercise, online

*Additional exercises or applications may be found at the book or author's websites.*

# REFERENCES

## Print Publications

Adobe Creative Team. *Adobe Audition 2.0 Classroom in a Book*. Berkeley, CA: Adobe Press, 2006.

Cutler, C. C. 1960. Transmission Systems Employing Quantization. U.S. Patent No. 2,927,962.

Huntington, John. *Control Systems for Live Entertainment*, 2nd ed. Oxford: Focal Press, 2000.

Ifeachor, Emmanuel C., and Barrie W. Jervis. *Digital Signal Processing: A Practical Approach*. Addison-Wesley Publishing, 1993.

Kientzle, Tim. *A Programmer's Guide to Sound*. Reading, MA; Addison-Wesley Developers Press, 1998.

Kirk, Ross, and Andy Hunt. *Digital Sound Processing for Music and Multimedia*. Oxford: Focal Press, 1999.

Lehrman, Paul D., and Tim Tully. *MIDI for the Professional*, New York: Amsco Publications, 1993.

Loy, Gareth. *Musimathics: The Mathematical Foundations of Music. Vols. I and II*. Cambridge, MA: The MIT Press, 2006.

Messick, Paul. *Maximum MIDI: Music Applications in C++*. Greenwich: Manning Publications, 1998.

Penfold, R. A. *Electronic Music and MIDI Projects*. Kent, UK: PC Publishing, 1994.

Petelin, Roman, and Hury Petelin. *Cool Edit Pro 2 In Use*. Wayne, PA: A-List Publishing, 2003.

Petelin, Roman, and Hury Petelin. *Adobe Audition: Soundtracks for Digital Video*. Wayne, PA: A-List Publishing, 2004.

Pohlmann, Ken C. *Principles of Digital Audio*, 4th ed. New York: McGraw-Hill, 2000.

Phillips, Dave. *Linux Music and Sound*. San Francisco, CA: No Starch Press, 2000.

Roads, Curtis. *The Computer Music Tutorial*. Cambridge, MA: The MIT Press, 1996.

Roberts, Lawrence G. February 1962. "Picture Coding Using Pseudo-Random Noise." *IEEE Transactions on Information Theory* 8, 2: 145–154.

Rothstein, Joseph. *MIDI: A Comprehensive Introduction*, 2nd ed. Madison, WI: A-R Editions, 1995.

Schuchman, L. December 1964. "Dither Signals and Their Effect on Quantization Noise." *IEEE Transactions on Communications* 12, 4: 162–165.

Smith, Julius O., III. *Mathematics of the Discrete Fourier Transform (DFT) with Audio Applications*. 2nd ed. Seattle: Book Surge Publishing, 2007.

Smith, Steven W. *Digital Signal Processing: A Practical Guide for Engineers and Scientists*. Burlington, MA: Elsevier Science, 2003.

Tranter, Jeff. *Linux Multimedia Guide*. Cambridge, MA: O'Reilly, 1996.

Winkler, Todd. *Composing Interactive Music: Techniques and Ideas Using MAX*. Cambridge, MA: The MIT Press, 1998.

## Websites

MIDI Manufacturers Association, MMA.
  http://www.midi.org/

ChucK: Strongly-timed, Concurrent, and On-the-fly Audio Programming Language.
  http://chuck.cs.princeton.edu/

**See references in previous chapters for additional sources on multimedia and digital signal processing applicable to this chapter.**

# Digital Audio Processing

## OBJECTIVES FOR CHAPTER 5

- Know the basic hardware and software components of a digital audio processing environment.
- Know the common file types for digital audio and be able to choose an appropriate file type and compression for audio files.
- Understand the difference between destructive and nondestructive audio editing.
- Understand how normalization, compression, expansion, equalization, and reverb are applied and what they do to digital audio.
- Understand methods for audio restoration.
- Understand how filters are applied and how they work mathematically.
- Understand the concept and examples of time-based encoding for digital audio.
- Understand the concept and examples of perceptual encoding for digital audio.
- Understand the concept, implementation, and application of MPEG audio compression.

# 5.1 TOOLS FOR DIGITAL AUDIO PROCESSING

## 5.1.1 Digital Audio Work Environments

In Chapter 4, we introduced basic concepts of digital audio representation. Now it's time to consider how you actually record and edit digital audio. Throughout this book, the goal is to uncover the mathematics and algorithms that underlie work in digital media and to give you knowledge that lasts longer than the short shelf-life of most editions of digital media application programs. But because being able to *do something* with your knowledge is one of the biggest motivators you can have, we chose the book's topics based on real hands-on work. So this chapter begins with an overview of the hardware and software tools for working with digital audio.

There are two main environments in which you might work with audio: during live performance or in a sound recording studio. Let's look at the equipment for live performances first—the kind of equipment you would use as a sound engineer for a theater play, musical, or concert—comparing an analog to a digital hardware setup.

Figure 5.1 is a diagram of the type of analog equipment you could use to manage sound during a live performance or in studio recording. Central in this configuration is the *mixer*, also called a *mixing console* or *soundboard*. A mixer is used to gather inputs from microphones and instruments and dynamically adjust their amplitudes, equalize the frequency components, compress the dynamic range, apply special effects, and route the processed sound to outputs such as speakers. Each input to the mixer is designated as a *channel*, with 24 or more channels in larger mixers. Multiple channels can be gathered into a *bus* (a subsignal that is the sum of the inputs to it), and the effects can be applied to the bus. The signal

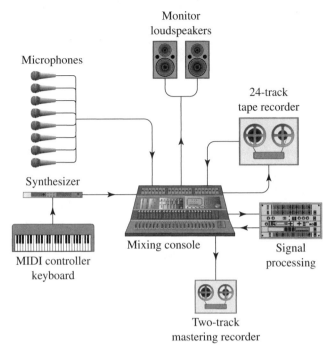

**Figure 5.1**  Analog sound equipment

can be split to multiple outputs so that speakers can be set up appropriately around an auditorium to create the desired sound environment.

Figure 5.2 shows what your live performance audio set-up would look like if you used a digital mixer. Notice how much hardware is absorbed into the software of the digital mixer. Inside the digital mixer is an analog-to-digital converter (ADC). As the signal enters the mixer, it is immediately converted to digital form so that further processing can be done on it in software. Before it is sent to the outputs, it is converted back to analog form with a digital-to-analog converter (DAC).

Sound processing can also take place in settings other than live performances—for example, in sound recording studios. Much of the equipment is the same, with the difference that the sound is recorded, refined, processed with special effects, and finally compressed and packaged for distribution. Much of this work can be done by means of a personal computer equipped with the right sound card, microphones, and audio processing software.

In this book, we're going to assume that you're working in a mostly digital environment, using your personal computer as the central component of your *digital audio workstation* (*DAW*). The most basic element of your DAW is a sound card or external sound interface. A *sound card* is a piece of hardware that performs the following basic functions:

- provides input jacks for microphones and external audio sources
- converts sound from analog to digital form as it is being recorded, using an ADC
- provides output jacks for headphones and external speakers
- converts sound from digital to analog form as it is being played, using a DAC
- synthesizes MIDI sound samples using either FM or wavetable synthesis, more often the latter. (Most sound cards have this capability.)

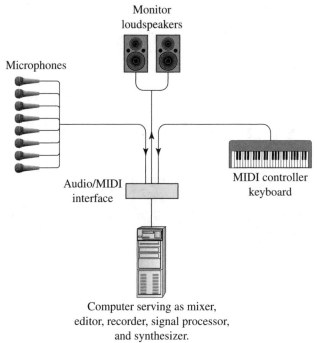

**Figure 5.2** Digital sound equipment

If the sound card that comes with your computer doesn't do a very good job with ADC, DAC, or MIDI-handling, or if it doesn't offer you the input/output interface you want, you may want to buy a better internal sound card or even an external sound interface. An external sound interface can offer extra input and output channels and connections, including MIDI, and a choice of XLR, ¼ inch TRS, or other audio jacks to connect the microphones (Figure 5.5). To complete your DAW, you can add digital audio processing software, headphones, and good quality monitors. If you want to work with MIDI, you can also add hardware or software MIDI samplers, synthesizers, and/or a controller.

Many computers have built-in microphones, but their quality isn't always very good. The two types of external microphones that you're most likely to use are dynamic and capacitor mics. A *dynamic mic* (Figure 5.3) operates by means of an induction coil attached to a diaphragm and placed in a magnetic field such that the coil moves in response to sound pressure oscillations. Dynamic mics are versatile, sturdy, and fairly inexpensive, and they're good enough for most home or classroom recording studio situations.

A *capacitor mic* (also called a *condenser mic*) has a diaphragm and a backplate that together form the two plates of a capacitor (Figure 5.4). As the distance between the plates is changed by vibration, the capacitance changes, and in turn, so does the voltage representing the sound wave. The material from which the plates are made is lighter and thus more sensitive than the coil of a dynamic mic.

The main differences between dynamic and capacitor mics are these:

- A dynamic mic is less expensive than a capacitor mic.
- A capacitor mic requires an external power supply to charge the diaphragm and to drive the preamp. A dynamic mic is sometimes more convenient because it doesn't require an external power supply.

**Figure 5.3** Dynamic mic

**Figure 5.4** Condenser mic

- A dynamic mic has an upper frequency limit of about 16 kHz, while the capacitor's frequency limit goes to 20 kHz and beyond. This difference is probably most noticeable with regard to the upper harmonics of musical instruments.
- A dynamic mic is fine for loud instruments or reasonably close vocals. A capacitor mic is more sensitive to soft or distant sounds.
- A capacitor mic is susceptible to damage from moisture condensation.

You can't really say that one type of microphone is better than another. It depends on what you're recording, and it depends on the make and model of the microphone. Greater sensitivity isn't always a good thing, since you may be recording vocals at close range and don't want to pick up background noise; in this case a dynamic mic is preferable.

Microphones can also be classified according to the direction from which they receive sound. The *cardioid mic* is most commonly used for voice recording, since its area of sensitivity resembles a heart-shape around the front of the mic. An *omnidirectional mic* senses sound fairly equally in a circle around the mic. It can be used for general environmental sounds. A *bidirectional mic* senses sound generally in a figure-eight area. The direction from which sounds are sensed depends in part on the frequency of the sound. In the case of high frequencies, the directional response of a microphone depends in part on the angle from which the sound arrives. Some high quality microphones have switches that allow you to change their patterns of optimum reception. You can see the icon's for different reception patterns on the microphone in Figure 5.4.

Another property of microphones is their frequency response—the range of frequencies that it picks up. The Shure SM50 microphone has a frequency response between 50 and 15000 Hz. A good condenser mic like the one pictured in Figure 5.4 could have a frequency response of 20 to 20000 Hz.

You may want to buy monitors for the audio work you do on your computer. A *monitor* is just another name for a speaker—but one that treats all frequency components equally. Speakers can be engineered to favor some frequencies over others, but for your audio work you want to hear the sound exactly as you create it, with no special coloring. For this reason, you should pay particular attention to the frequency characteristics of the speakers or monitors you use. It's nice to have a good set of earphones as well, so that you can listen to your audio without environmental background noise.

You'll need a variety of cables and connectors to complete your digital audio workstation. Figure 5.5 shows commonly used audio connectors. To connect your computer to an external audio or hard disk drive, you'll probably use *Firewire* or *USB*. Firewire provides a high speed data connection, and thus it is very popular for audio, video, and hard disk drive connections. USB and USB2 are used for the same purpose. USB connections can be convenient in that an external device may be able to draw its power from the USB connection and therefore doesn't require a power cord. Firewire is advertised as having a data rate of 400 Mb/s and USB2 a data rate of 480 Mb/s. However, USB2 goes through the CPU to determine the direction of data flow, and Firewire does not. Thus, Firewire actually turns out to be faster, not stealing any CPU time that could be used for audio processing. Firewire connections come in two types—six pin or four pin. You need to be sure to have the right type for your equipment. You might need a Firewire cable that is six pin on both ends, six pin on one end and four on the other end, and so forth.

If you're connecting a digital audio recorder to your computer or external sound interface, you use an S/PDIF connection, which stands for Sony Phillips Digital Interface. S/PDIF is made to transmit audio data that is already digitized, so it doesn't have to go through an analog-to-digital converter in the sound interface.

The remaining connectors discussed in this section are analog, which link a microphone—which is an analog device—to an analog-to-digital converter that resides in your computer's sound card or in an external sound interface. The connector type that this entails depends on the type of microphone.

Inexpensive consumer microphones generally have an ⅛″ stereo miniplug on the end that go directly to your computer's internal sound card. This type of microphone doesn't provide professional quality recording.

TRS and TR ¼ inch connectors are used with a wide variety of consumer and professional equipment such as microphones amplifiers, guitars, headphones, and speakers. The ¼ connectors can be balanced or unbalanced (explained below).

To use a good quality microphone, you'll need an XLR cable. External sound interfaces generally have XLR inputs. The sound interface provides a female three pin connection port and the microphone has a male three pin connection. The XLR cable that connects the

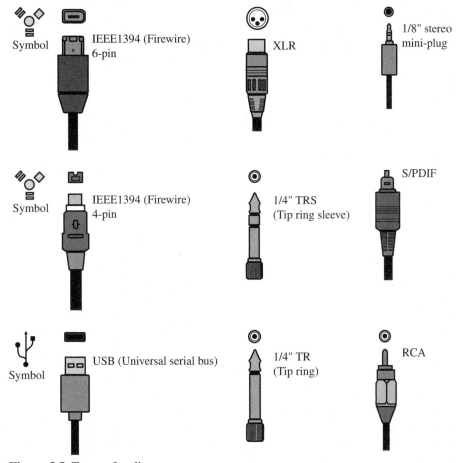

**Figure 5.5** Types of audio connectors

two is female on the microphone end and male on the sound interface end. XLR connectors provide a high quality, balanced, low impedance signal.

If your sound card has ¼ inch inputs and you want to connect a microphone that uses XLR connections, you can get an XLR to ¼ inch adaptor. However, the transformation of the signal that is done via the adaptor sacrifices some audio quality in your recording.

RCA connectors have been around for a long time as part of consumer audio and video equipment. They often are used with devices like external tape decks or video cameras. You have probably seen them in color coded three-jack connections for where the yellow plug is for composite video, white is for the left or mono audio connection, and red is for the right audio connection. (See Figure 6.11.) RCA connectors transmit an unbalanced signal.

As you consider the types of connections you need, you'll encounter the terms impedance and balance. *Impedance* (abbreviated Z) is the measure of the total opposition to current flow in an alternating current circuit. Measured in ohms, impedance is the sum of two components, resistance (R) and reactance (X). Ohms is abbreviated $\Omega$, 1,000 ohms is abbreviated k$\Omega$, and 1,000,000 ohms is abbreviated M$\Omega$.

The source of an audio signal—like a microphone or electric guitar—is called the *source* or *output*. The place where you plug this source into a sound card, external sound interface, or mixer is called the *load* or *input*. The significance of impedance is that it affects what types of outputs should be plugged into what kinds of inputs.

A microphone up to about 600 Ω is low impedance, between 600 and 10,000 Ω is medium impedance, and 10,000 Ω or more is high impedance. A high impedance mic or instrument generally outputs a higher amplitude signal, measured in voltage, than a lower impedance one. This does not imply that high impedance is better than low impedance. Most good mics are low impedance, particularly those with XLR connectors.

It's not good to connect a higher impedance output to a lower impedance input because the frequencies that are recorded may be distorted. An electric guitar generally is a high impedance source. It often has a ¼ inch TRS output connection like the one shown in Figure 5.5. You shouldn't connect a high impedance electric guitar to a low impedance input jack. Some external audio interfaces provide ¼ inch inputs that are designed to receive an electric guitar for direct recording of its output. You can check the specifications of your sound interface to see if an input is provided with correct impedance for an electric guitar. (USB outputs also exist for electric guitars.)

Another thing you should know about high impedance output that it isn't good when you have to connect the output to the input by means of a long cable. With a long cable, there's more chance that high frequencies will be lost in the audio signal. This is because high frequencies are affected more by reactance. Also, a longer cable provides more chance for the high impedance output to attract electrical interference on its way to the input. This can add noise to the recording in the form of a hum. A low-impedance mic can be used with hundreds of feet of cable without picking up hum or losing high frequencies. A medium-impedance mic cable is limited to about 40 feet, and a high-impedance mic is limited to about ten feet. The extent to which high frequencies are lost depends also on the capacitance of the cable.

The other consideration is whether a connection transmits a balanced or unbalanced signal. *Balanced signals* have two signal conductors and one shield. The two signal conductors are identical except that they are 180 degrees out of phase with each other. (Note that adding two sine waves that are 180 degrees out of phase yields 0 amplitude at all points.) If noise is added to the line, it is identical in both of the signals. Thus, adding the two signals cancels the original signal and yields two times the noise. This identifies the frequency components of the noise in the signal, which can then be eliminated. The significance of this is that a balanced connection generally has less noise than an unbalanced one. *Unbalanced signals* use only two signal conductors—a center conductor and a grounded shield. The shield is intended to protect the center signal from electrical interference, but it doesn't block all the interference. When interference does get through, it results in a hum or buzz added to an audio recording. This is more likely to happen when the cable between the output and input is long.

The bottom line is that balanced low impedance microphones (e.g., those with XLR connections) provide a superior audio signal in recording.

## 5.1.2 Digital Audio Processing Software

Digital audio processing software and MIDI controllers give you an interface to your sound card, allowing you to record, edit, compress, and save audio and MIDI files. As of the writing of this chapter, Digidesign Pro Tools (Mac or Windows), Adobe Audition (Windows), Apple Logic (Mac), Sony Sound Forge (Windows), and Nuendo (Mac or Windows) are among the most popular commercial audio application programs. Cakewalk Music Creator and Cakewalk Sonar are combined audio/MIDI processing packages. Propellerhead Reason (Mac or Windows) is a sophisticated audio/MIDI software package that provides a sequencer, drum machines, and a wide variety of software synthesizers that are visually and functionally modeled after analogous hardware. Reason can be used as a stand-alone or as a plug-in to other audio processing software. Acid Pro is a loop-based music creation tool. Max/MSP (Mac and Windows), developed by Cycling '74, is an interesting development environment for interactive music and audio processing. Many freeware, shareware, and commercial digital audio tools are available for Linux and Unix, also, including (at the time of this writing) DAP, MixViews, ReZound, Slab, JoKosher, KWave, Brahms, Jazz++, TiMidity++, Playmidi, BladeEnc, and aRts. Audacity is an open source program that runs under Mac, Windows, and Linux operating systems.

Features that you generally find in digital audio processing software include the following:

- the ability to import and save audio files in a variety of formats
- an interface (called *transport controls*) for recording and playing sound
- a waveform view that allows you to edit the wave, often down to the sample level
- multitrack editors
- audio restoration tools to remove hisses, clicks, pops, and background noise
- the ability to take input from or direct output to multiple channels
- special effects such as reverb, panning, or flange
- controls for equalizing and adjusting volume and dynamic range
- frequency filters
- the ability to handle the MIDI format along with digital audio and to integrate the two types of data into one audio file
- the ability to record samples and add to the bank of MIDI patches
- compression codecs

Not all audio application programs include all the features listed above. In some cases, you have to install plug-ins to get all the functionality you want. Three common plug-in formats are VST (Virtual Studio Technology), TDM (time division multiplexing), DirectX, and Audio Units by Core Audio. Plug-ins provide fine-tuned effects such as dynamic compression, equalization, reverb, and delay (explained later in this chapter).

In digital audio processing programs, you often have a choice between working in a *waveform view* or a *multitrack view*. The waveform view gives you a graphical picture of sound waves like we have described in Chapter 4. You can view and edit a sound wave down to the level of individual sample values, and for this reason the waveform view is sometimes called the *sample editor*. The waveform view is where you apply effects and processes that cannot be done in real-time, primarily because these processes require that the whole audio file be examined before new values can be computed. When such processes are executed, they permanently alter the sample values. In contrast, effects that can be applied in real-time do not alter sample values.

The waveform view of an audio file displays time across the horizontal axis and amplitude up the vertical axis. The standard representation of time for digital audio and video is *SMPTE*, which stands for *Society of Motion Picture and Television Engineers*. SMPTE divides the timeline into units of hours, minutes, seconds, and frames. The unit of a frame is derived from digital audio's association with video. A video file is divided into a sequence of individual still images called *frames*. One standard frame rate is 30 frames per second, but this varies according to the type of video. A position within an audio file can be denoted as $h:m:s:f$. For example, $0:10:42:14$ would be 10 minutes, 42 seconds, and 14 frames from the beginning of the audio file. Audio editing programs allow you to slide a "Current

Position Cursor" to any moment in the audio file, or alternatively you can type in the position as $h:m:s:f$. Other time formats are also possible. For example, some audio editors allow you to look at time in terms of samples, bars and beats, or decimal seconds.

The multitrack view allows you to record different sounds, musical instruments, or voices on separate tracks so that you can work with these units independently, modifying frequency or dynamic range, applying reverb or phase shifts, whatever you want for your artistic purposes. A *track* is a sequence of audio samples that can be played and edited as a separate unit. Often, different tracks are associated with different instruments or voices. You can record one instrument on one track and then you can record a second instrument or voice on another. If you play the first track while recording the second, you can easily synchronize the two. With the right digital processing software and a good computer with plenty of RAM and external storage, you can have your own sound studio. If you're also a musician, you can do all of the musical parts yourself, recording one track after another. In the end, you'll probably want to *mix down* the tracks, collapsing them all into one unit. This is very much like flattening the layers of a digital image. Once you have done this, you can't apply effects to the separate parts (but if you're smart, you'll have kept a copy of the multitrack version just in case). The mixed-down file might then go through the mastering process. *Mastering* puts the final touches on the audio and prepares it for distribution. For example, if the audio file is one musical piece to be put on a CD with others, mastering involves sequencing the pieces, normalizing their volumes with respect to one another so one doesn't sound much louder than another, altering their dynamic ranges for artistic reasons, and so forth.

A channel is different from a track. A *channel* corresponds to a stream of audio data, both input and output. Recording on only one channel is called monophonic or simply *mono*. Two channels are *stereo*. When you record in stereo, the recording picks up sound from slightly different directions. When the sound is played back, the intention is to send different channels out through different speakers so that the listener can hear a separation of the sound. This gives the sound more dimension, as if it comes from different places in the room. Stereo recording used to be the norm in music, but with the proliferation of DVD audio formats and the advent of home theaters that imitate the sound environments of movie theatres, the popularity of multichannel audio is growing. A 5.1 multichannel setup has five main channels: front center, front right, front left, rear right, rear left, and a *low frequency extension channel* (*LFE*). LFE, often called a *subwoofer*, has frequencies from 10 to 120 Hz. A 6.1 multichannel setup has a back center channel as well.

## 5.1.3 Destructive Vs. Nondestructive Editing

Changes made to digital audio files by means of audio processing software are generally handled in one of two ways: by means of *destructive editing* or *nondestructive editing*.

Think about what happens when you work on an audio file that you previously recorded and saved in permanent storage—say, on your hard disk. Audio files can be very large, so the whole file will not be held in RAM and operated on there as you edit it. The audio processing program will have to record your changes as you work by writing to a file on the disk drive. The question is, will it change your original audio file even before you do a "Save" operation? In immediately destructive editing, this is exactly what would happen. If you added reverb to your sound, a destructive editor would immediately apply the reverb operation to the original file on disk, so you couldn't get the original file back.

Fortunately, audio processing programs generally don't handle editing in this manner. Instead, they create a temporary (temp) file on the hard disk and write any changes you make to this temporary copy of the audio file. If you never save the edited version, the temp file goes away. If you do save the edited audio, the previous version is overwritten with the temp file.

If most edits are not *immediately* destructive, then what's the distinction between destructive and non-destructive edits? In most audio processing programs, destructive edits are handled in the manner described in the previous paragraph. If your editing environment allows "undos"—and most of them do—then your operations will be saved in a series of temp files, and you can revert back to previous states by undoing instructions. The editing operations don't become permanent until you save the audio file.

Nondestructive edits are handled by means of additional instructions that are added to the audio file. For example, you could indicate that you want a volume change in a portion of the audio. Instead of altering the amplitudes of the samples, the editing program would save an instruction indicating the level, beginning point, and ending point of the volume change. The assumption here is that you would be saving the audio file in a file format that accommodates these extra instructions—for example, the proprietary file format of the audio processing program. If you eventually decide to mix your audio down to another standard file format like WAV, at that point the changes become destructive in that the sample values are changed.

Sometimes a distinction is made between the waveform view and the multitrack view, the former being an environment for destructive edits and the latter for nondestructive. You should consult your application program's Help so you know how editing is handled in your working environment. You'll also want to set your maximum number of "undos." It's nice to be able to undo a lot of operations, but you'll need sufficient disk space for all the temp files.

Real-time processing is always nondestructive. It's amazing to discover just how much real-time processing can go on while an audio file is playing or being mixed in live performance. It's possible to equalize frequencies, compress dynamic range, add reverb, or even combine these processing algorithms. The processing can happen so quickly that the delay isn't noticed. However, all systems have their limit for real-time processing, and you should be aware of these limits. In mixing of live performances, there are also times when you have to pay attention to the delay inevitably introduced in any kind of digital audio processing. ADC and DAC themselves introduce some delay right off the top, to which you have to add the delay of special effects.

## 5.1.4 Digital Audio File Types

If you have worked at all with digital audio, you've seen that audio files are saved in a variety of formats, as indicated by the many file extensions: *.wav, .au, .mp3, .aac,* and so forth. How do you know which is right for your application? What distinguishes one file type from another?

File formats differ in how they answer the following questions:

- How are the samples encoded?
  - Using linear quantization?
  - Using logarithmic quantization?
  - Are sample values signed or unsigned?
- What is the format of the data?
  - Is there a header?
  - Are bytes stored in little-endian or big-endian order?
  - Are channels interleaved?

- What type of information is stored in the file?
  - Are there constraints on the sampling rate and/or bit depth?
  - Are there constraints on the number of channels?
  - Is extra information allowed, like timestamps or loop points?
- Is the file compressed?
  - Using a lossy procedure?
  - Using a lossless procedure?
- Is the format "open" or proprietary?
  - Is the code open source?
  - Does the format follow a widely accepted standard such as IMA or IFF?

Let's consider uncompressed files first. An audio file format that is described as ***linear PCM*** stores a sequence of audio samples encoded in linearly spaced quantization intervals, which means that each interval is the same size. (See Chapter 1.) An alternative is to use logarithmic quantization, where low amplitude samples are represented with more precision than are high amplitude samples. In other words, quantization intervals get progressively larger as the amplitude of the audio samples get larger. The advantage to this method is that you can make finer distinctions between amplitude levels at lower amplitudes, where the human ear is more sensitive to differences. A-law and $\mu$-law encoding are examples of logarithmic quantization methods. The file extensions *.u*, *.al*, *.l8*, and *.l16* can be recognized, respectively, as 8-bit $\mu$-law, 8-bit A-law, 8-bit linear PCM, and 16-bit linear PCM, all assumed to be at a sampling rate of 8000 Hz.

Raw files have nothing but sample values in them. There's no header to indicate the sampling rate, sample size, or type of encoding. If you try to open a *.raw* file in an audio processing program, you'll be asked to provide the necessary information.

Sometimes the file extension of an audio file uniquely identifies the file type, but this isn't always the case. Often it's necessary for the audio file player or decoder to read the header of the file to identify the file type. For example, the *.wav* extension is used for files in a variety of formats: uncompressed, A-law encoded, $\mu$-law encoded, ADPCM encoded, or compressed with any codec. The header of the file specifies exactly which format is being used. WAV files are the standard audio format of Microsoft and IBM.

To facilitate file exchange, a standard format called IFF—the Interchange Format File—has been devised. IFF files are divided into chunks, each with its own header and data. Files with the *.wav* or *.aif* (Apple) extension are versions of the IFF format. They differ in that Microsoft/IBM use little-endian byte order while Macintosh uses big-endian. In little-endian byte ordering, the least significant byte comes first, and in big-endian the most significant byte comes first.

It is sometimes difficult to separate audio file formats from codecs. Codecs are compression/decompression algorithms that can be applied within a variety of file formats. For example, the fact that a file has the *.wav* file extension says nothing about whether or not the file is compressed. The file could be compressed with any one of a number of codecs, as specified in the file's header. However, if a file has the file extension *.mp3* or *.aac*, then you know that it has been compressed with the MP3 or AAC codec, respectively. Some codecs are proprietary (*e.g.*, WMA) and some are open source (*e.g.*, FLAC and Ogg Vorbis). Some provide lossy compression, some lossless.

Representative audio file formats and codecs are listed in Table 5.1. Your choice of audio file format depends on a number of factors. On what platforms do you expect to deliver the audio? What sampling rate and bit depth are appropriate to the type of audio you're

| TABLE 5.1 | Representative Audio File Formats | |
|---|---|---|
| **File Extension** | **File Type or Codec** | **Characteristics** |
| .aac | Advanced Audio Coding | Lossy compression method designed as an improvement of .mp3 files; used by iPods, cell phones, and portable PlayStations. |
| .aif | Audio Interchange File Format, Apple's standard wave format | Uncompressed PCM format supporting mono or stereo, 16-bit or 8-bit, and a wide range of sample rates; big-endian byte order. |
| .au | NeXT/Sun (Java) | Can be uncompressed or can use variants of CCITT $\mu$-law, A-law, or G.721; supports mono or stereo, 16-bit or 8-bit, and a range of sampling rates when uncompressed; often used for distribution on the Internet and for inclusion in Java applications and applets. |
| .flac | Free Lossless Audio Codec, Xiph.Org Foundation | A free codec providing lossless compression at a ratio of about 1.5 : 1 or 2 : 1; popular for lossless compression of web-based audio; competitive with .tta. |
| .mp3 | MPEG-1 Layer 3 audio | High compression rate with good quality; dominant web-based format for many years. |
| .ogg | Ogg Vorbis, Xiph.Org Foundation | Open, free codec; high compression rate with high fidelity; competitive with .mp3. |
| .raw | Raw files | Raw sample values with no header; when a raw file is opened, you're asked for the sampling rate, resolution, and number of channels. |
| .rm | RealMedia | Supports streamed audio, which allows you to begin listening to the audio without having to download the entire file first. |
| .tta | True Audio | A free codec providing lossless compression at a ratio of about 1.5 : 1 or 2 : 1; popular for lossless compression of web-based audio; competitive with .flac. |
| A-law or $\mu$-law .wav | CCITT standard G.711 standard formats | 8-bit per sample files created from 16-bit per sample using A-law or $\mu$-law encoding, achieving the equivalent of about 13-bit dynamic range (about 78 dB). |
| DVI/IMA .wav | International Multimedia Association version of ADPCM .wav format with ADPCM compression | Uses a different (faster) method than Microsoft ADPCM; a good alternative to MPEG with fast decoding and good quality of compressed audio. |
| Microsoft ADPCM .wav | Microsoft | Uses ADPCM; yields 4-bit per channel compressed data for 4 : 1 compression ratio. |
| Windows PCM .wav | Microsoft | Standard Windows .wav format for uncompressed PCM audio; supports both mono and stereo at a variety of bit depths and sample rates; follows RIFF (Resource Information File Format) specification, allowing for extra user information to be saved with the file. |
| .wma or .asf | Microsoft Windows Media (audio) | Microsoft proprietary codec; allows you to choose quality settings, including constant bit rate (CBR) vs. variable bit rate (VBR) and lossy vs. lossless compression; competitive with .aac; uses .asf file extension if encapsulated in Advanced Systems Format; supports streaming audio. |

recording? Not all file types offer all the choices you might want in sampling rate and bit depth. Remember to keep the file in an uncompressed form while you're working on it in order to maintain the greatest fidelity possible. But if file size is ultimately an issue, you need to consider what codec to use for the audio's final deliverable form. Will your user have the needed codec for decompression? Is lossy compression sufficient for the desired quality, or do you want lossless compression? All these decisions should become clearer as you work more with audio files and read more about audio file compression later in this chapter.

## 5.2 DYNAMICS PROCESSING

*Dynamics processing* is the process of adjusting the dynamic range of an audio selection, either to reduce or to increase the difference between the loudest and softest passages. An increase in amplitude is called *gain* or *boost*. A decrease in amplitude is called *attenuation* or, informally, a *cut*. Dynamics processing can be done at different stages while audio is being prepared, and by a variety of methods. The maximum amplitude can be limited with a hardware device during initial recording, gain can be adjusted manually in real-time with analog dials, and hardware compressors and expanders can be applied after recording. In music production, vocals and instruments can be recorded at different times, each on its own track, and each track can be adjusted dynamically in real-time or after recording. When the tracks are mixed down to a single track, the dynamics of the mix can be adjusted again. Finally, in the mastering process, dynamic range can be adjusted for the purpose of including multiple tracks on a CD and giving the tracks a consistent sound. In summary, audio can be manipulated through hardware or software; the hardware can be analog or digital; the audio can be processed in segments or holistically; and processing can happen in real-time or after recording.

The information in this section is based on digital dynamics processing tools: hard limiting, normalization, compression, and expansion. These tools alter the amplitude of an audio signal and therefore change its dynamics   the difference between the softest and the loudest part of the signal. Limiting sets a maximum amplitude. Normalization finds the maximum amplitude sample in the signal, boosts it to the maximum possible amplitude (or an amplitude chosen by the user), and boosts all other amplitudes proportionately. Dynamic compression decreases the dynamic range of a selection. (This type of compression has nothing to do with file size.) Dynamic expansion increases it.

The purpose of adjusting dynamic range is to improve the texture or balance of sound. The texture of music arises in part from its differing amplitude levels. Instruments and voices have their characteristic amplitude or dynamic range. The difference between peak level amplitude and average amplitude of the human voice, for example, is about 10 dB. In a musical composition, instruments and voices can vary in amplitude over time—a flute is played softly in the background, vocals emerge at medium amplitude, and a drum is suddenly struck at high amplitude. Classical music typically has a wide dynamic range. Sections of low amplitude are contrasted with impressive high amplitude sections full

**ASIDE:** You should be careful to distinguish among the following: *possible dynamic range* as a function of bit depth in digital audio; *actual dynamic range* of a particular piece of audio; and *perceived loudness* of a piece. The possible dynamic range for a piece of digital audio is determined by the bit depth in which that piece is encoded. In Chapters 1 and 4, we derived a formula that tells us that the possible dynamic range is equal to approximately $6 * n$ dB where $n$ is the number of bits per sample. For CD quality audio, which uses 16-bit samples, this would be 96 dB. However, a given piece of music doesn't necessarily use that full possible dynamic range. The dynamic range of a piece is the difference between its highest amplitude and lowest amplitude sample. The overall perceived loudness of a piece, which is a subjective measurement, is related to the average RMS of the piece. The higher the average RMS, the louder a piece seems to the human ear. (RMS—root-mean-square—is explained in Chapter 4.)

of instruments and percussion. You probably are familiar with Beethoven's Fifth Symphony. Think of the contrast between the first eight notes and what follows:

*BUM BUM BUM BAH!*
*BUM BUM BUM BAH!*
*Then softer . . .*

In contrast, "elevator music" or "Muzak" is intentionally produced with a small dynamic range. Its purpose is to lie in the background, pleasantly but almost imperceptibly.

Musicians and music editors have words to describe the character of different pieces that arise from their variance in dynamic range. A piece can sound "punchy," "wimpy," "smooth," "bouncy," "hot," or "crunchy," for example. Audio engineers train their ears to hear subtle nuances in sound and to use their dynamics processing tools to create the effects they want.

Deciding when and how much to compress or expand dynamic range is as much art as science. Compressing the dynamic range is desirable for some types of sound and listening environments and not for others. It's generally a good thing to compress the dynamic range of music intended for radio. You can understand why if you think about the way radio sounds in a car, which is where radio music is often heard. With the background noise of your tires humming on the highway, you don't want music that has big differences between the loudest and softest parts. Otherwise, the soft parts will be drowned out by the background noise. For this reason, radio music is dynamically compressed, and then the amplitude is raised overall. The result is that the sound has a higher average RMS, and overall it is perceived to be louder.

There's a price to be paid for dynamic compression. Some sounds—like percussion instruments or the beginning notes of vocal music—have a fast **attack time**. The attack time of a sound is the time it takes for the sound to change amplitude. With a fast attack time, the sound reaches high amplitude in a sudden burst, and then it may drop off quickly. Fast-attack percussion sounds like drums or cymbals are called **transients**. Increasing the perceived loudness of a piece by compressing the dynamic range and then increasing the overall amplitude can leave little **headroom**—room for transients to stand out with higher amplitude. The entire piece of music may sound louder, but it can lose much of its texture and musicality. Transients give brightness or punchiness to sound, and suppressing them too much can make music sound dull and flat. Allowing the transients to be sufficiently loud without compromising the overall perceived loudness and dynamic range of a piece is one of the challenges of dynamics processing.

While dynamic compression is more common than expansion, expansion has its uses also. Expansion allows more of the potential dynamic range—the range made possible by the bit depth of the audio file—to be used. This can brighten a music selection.

Using downward expansion, it's possible to lower the amplitude of signals below the point where they can be heard. The point below which a digital audio signal is no longer audible is called the **noise floor**. Say that your audio processing software represents amplitude in dBFS—decibels full scale—where the maximum amplitude of a sample is 0 and the minimum possible amplitude—a function of bit depth—is somewhere between 0 and $-\infty$. For 16-bit audio, the minimum possible amplitude is approximately $-96$ dBFS. Ideally, this is the noise floor, but in most recording situations there is a certain amount of low amplitude background noise that masks low amplitude sounds. The maximum amplitude of the background noise is the actual noise floor. If you apply downward expansion to an audio selection and you lower some of your audio below the noise floor, you've effectively

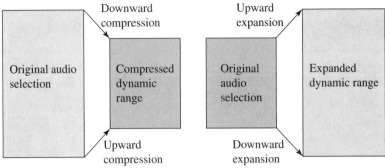

**Figure 5.6** Types of dynamic range compression and expansion

lost it. (On the other hand, you could get rid of the noise within the music piece itself by downward expansion, moving the background below the $-96$ dB noise floor).

To understand how dynamic processing works, let's look more closely at the tools and the mathematics underlying dynamics processing, including hard limiting, normalization, compression, and expansion.

We've talked mostly about dynamic range compression in the examples above, but there are four ways to change dynamic range: downward compression, upward compression, downward expansion, and upward expansion, as illustrated in Figure 5.6. The two most commonly applied processes are downward compression and downward expansion. You have to look at your hardware or software tool to see what types of dynamics processing it can do. Some tools allow you to use these four types of compression and expansion in various combinations with each other.

- *Downward compression* lowers the amplitude of signals that are above a designated level, without changing the amplitude of signals below the designated level. It reduces the dynamic range.
- *Upward compression* raises the amplitude of signals that are below a designated level without altering the amplitude of signals above the designated level. It reduces the dynamic range.
- *Upward expansion* raises the amplitude of signals that are above a designated level, without changing the amplitude of signals below that level. It increases the dynamic range.
- *Downward expansion* lowers the amplitude of signals that are below a designated level without changing the amplitude of signals above this level. It increases the dynamic range.

Audio *limiting*, as the name implies, limits the amplitude of an audio signal to a designated level. Imagine how this might be done in real-time during recording. If *hard limiting* is applied, the recording system does not allow sound to be recorded above a given amplitude. Samples above the limit are clipped. *Clipping* cuts amplitudes of samples to a given maximum and/or minimum level. If *soft limiting* is applied, then audio signals above the designated amplitude are recorded at lower amplitude. Both hard and soft limiting cause some distortion of the waveform.

*Normalization* is a process which raises the amplitude of audio signal values and thus the perceived loudness of an audio selection. Because normalization operates on an entire audio signal, it has to be applied after the audio has been recorded.

The normalization algorithm proceeds as follows:

- find the highest amplitude sample in the audio selection
- determine the gain needed in the amplitude to raise the highest amplitude to maximum amplitude (0 dBFS by default, or some limit set by the user)
- raise all samples in the selection by this amount

A variation of this algorithm is to normalize the RMS amplitude to a decibel level specified by the user. RMS can give a better measure of the perceived loudness of the audio. In digital audio processing software, predefined settings are sometimes offered with descriptions that are intuitively understandable—for example, "Normalize RMS to −10 dB (speech)."

Often, normalization is used to increase the perceived loudness of a piece after the dynamic range of the piece has been compressed, as described above in the processing or radio music. Normalization can also be applied to a group of audio selections. For example, the different tracks on a CD can be normalized so that they are at basically the same amplitude level. This is part of the mastering process.

Compression and expansion can be represented mathematically by means of a transfer function and graphically by means of the corresponding transfer curve. Digital audio processing programs sometimes give you this graphical view with which you can specify the type of compression or expansion you wish to apply. Alternatively, you may be able to type in values that indicate the compression or expansion ratio. The transfer function maps an input amplitude level to the amplitude level that results from compression or expansion. If you apply no compression or expansion to an audio file, the transfer function graphs as a straight line at a 45° angle, as shown in Figure 5.7. If you choose to raise the amplitude of the entire audio piece by a constant amount, this can also be represented by a straight line of slope 1, but the line crosses the vertical axis at the decibel amount by which all samples are raised. For example, the two transfer functions in Figure 5.7 show a 5 dB increase and a 5 dB decrease in the amplitude of the entire audio piece.

Supplements on dynamics processing:

interactive tutorial

worksheet

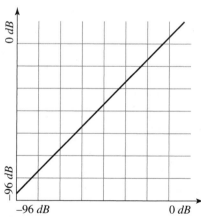
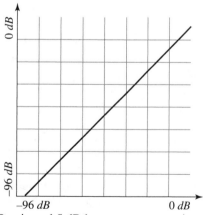

**Figure 5.7** Linear transfer functions for 5 dB gain and 5 dB loss—no compression or expansion

To apply downward compression, you designate a ***threshold***—that is, an amplitude above which you want the amplitude of the audio signal to be lowered. (For upward compression, amplitudes below the threshold would be raised.) Figure 5.8 shows the transfer

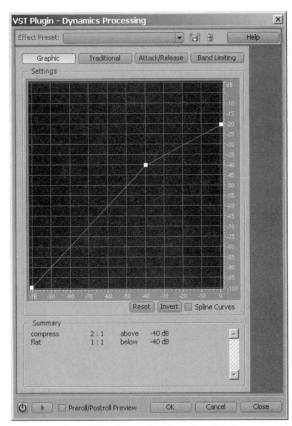

**Figure 5.8** Graph of transfer function for downward compression (from Audition)

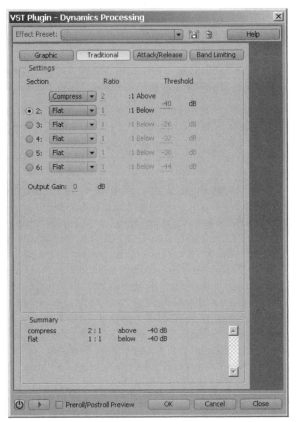

**Figure 5.9** Downward compression, traditional view (from Audition)

function graph corresponding to downward compression where the rate of change of sample values higher than −40 dB is lowered by a 2 : 1 ratio. Figure 5.9 shows the traditional view. Compression above the threshold is typically represented as a ratio $a : b$. If you indicate that you want a compression ratio of $a : b$, then you're saying that, above the threshold, for each $a$ decibels that the signal increases in amplitude, you want it to increase only by $b$ decibels. For example, if you specify a dynamic range compression ratio of 2 : 1 above the threshold, then if the amplitude raises by 1 dB from one sample to the next, it will actually go up (after compression) by only 0.5 dB. Notice that, beginning at an input of −40 dB and continuing to the end, the slope of the line is $b/a = 1/2$.

Often, a gain makeup is applied after downward compression. You can see in Figure 5.9 that there is a place to set Output Gain. The Output Gain is set to 0 in the figure. If you set the output gain to a value $g$ dB greater than 0, this means that after the audio selection is compressed, the amplitudes of all samples are increased by $g$ dB. Gain makeup can also be done by means of normalization, as described above. The result is to increase the perceived loudness of the entire piece. However, if the dynamic range has been decreased, the perceived difference between the loud and soft parts is reduced.

Upward compression is accomplished by indicating that you want compression of sample values that are *below* a certain threshold, or decibel limit. For example, Figure 5.10 shows how you indicate that you want samples that are below −30 dB to be compressed by

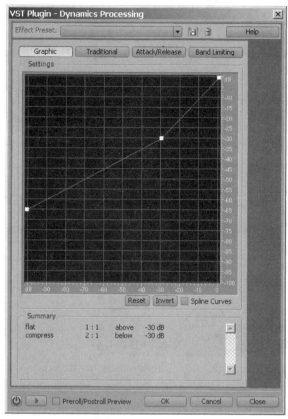

**Figure 5.10** Upward compression by 2 : 1 below −30 dB (from Audition)

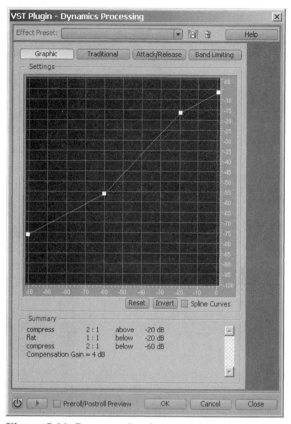

**Figure 5.11** Downward and upward compression (from Audition)

a ratio of 2 : 1. If you look at the graph, you can see that this means that sample values will *get larger*. For example, a sample value of −80 dB becomes −54 dB after compression. This may seem counterintuitive at first, since you may think of compressing something as making it smaller. But remember that it is the dynamic range, not the sample values themselves, that you are compressing. If you want to compress the dynamic range by changing values that are below a certain threshold, then you have to make them larger, moving them toward the higher amplitude values at the top. This is what is meant by upward compression.

With some tools, it's possible to achieve both downward and upward compression with one operation. Figure 5.11 shows the graph for downward compression above −20 dB, no compression between −20 and −60 dB, and upward compression below −60 dB. To this, an output gain of 4 dB is added. An audio file before and after such dynamics processing is shown in Figure 5.12. The dynamic range has been reduced by both downward and upward compression.

Sometimes, normalization is used after dynamic range compression. If we downward and upward compress the same audio file and follow this with normalization, we get the audio file pictured in Figure 5.13.

It is also possible to compress the dynamic range at both ends, by making high amplitudes lower and low amplitudes higher. Following is an example of expanding the dynamic range by "squashing" at both the low and high amplitudes. The compression is performed

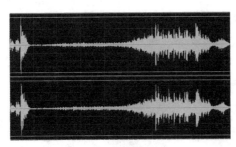
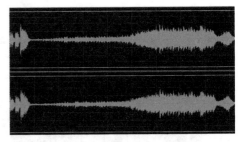

(a) Uncompressed audio            (b) Compressed audio

**Figure 5.12** Audio file before and after dynamics processing

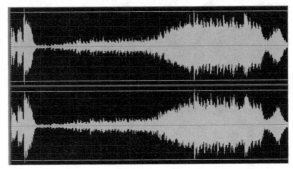

**Figure 5.13** Downward and upward compression followed by normalization

on an audio file that has three single-frequency tones at 440 Hz. The amplitude of the first is −5 dB, the second is −3 dB, and the third is −12 dB. Values above −4 dB are made smaller (downward compression). Values below −10 dB are made larger (upward compression). The settings are given in Figure 5.15. The audio file before and after compression is shown in Figure 5.14a and Figure 5.14b. (The three sine waves appear as solid blocks because the view is too far out to show detail. You can see only the amplitudes of the three waves.)

There's one more part of the compression and expansion process to consider. The **_attack_** of a dynamics processor is defined as the time between the appearance of the first sample value beyond the threshold and the full change in amplitude of samples beyond the threshold. Thus, attack relates to how quickly the dynamics processor _initiates_ the compression or

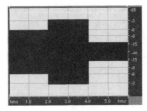
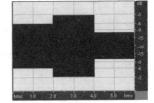

(a) Before compression         (b) After compression

**Figure 5.14** Audio file (three consecutive sine waves of different amplitudes) before and after dynamic compression

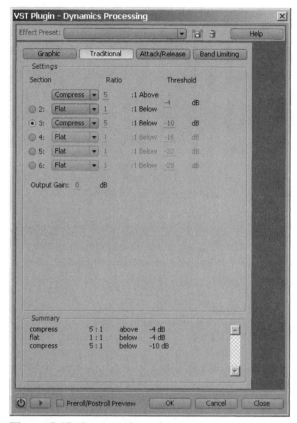

**Figure 5.15** Compression of dynamic range at both high and low amplitudes (from Audition)

expansion. When you downward compress the dynamic range, a slower attack time can sometimes be more gradual and natural, preserving transients by not immediately lowering amplitude when the amplitude suddenly, but perhaps only momentarily, goes above the threshold. The *release* is the time between the appearance of the first sample that is *not* beyond the threshold (before processing) and the cessation of compression or expansion.

## 5.3 AUDIO RESTORATION

Background noise arises from a variety of sources during audio recording: the whir of a spinning disk drive, noises in the environment like air conditioners or wind, inadvertent taps on the microphone, tape hiss (if the audio is being copied from an analog tape), or a puff of air when a "p" is spoken too close to the mic, for example. Three basic types of audio restoration are used to alleviate these problems: noise gating, noise reduction, and click and pop removal.

The operation of a *noise gate* is very simple. (See Figure 5.16.) A noise gate serves as a block to signals below a given amplitude threshold. When samples fall below the threshold, the gate closes and the samples are not passed through. When the samples rise above

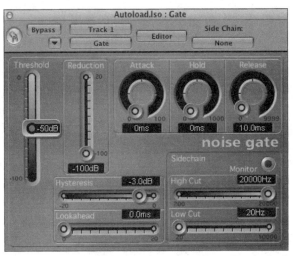

**Figure 5.16** Interface to a noise gate (from Logic Pro)

the threshold, the gate opens. Some noise gates allow you to indicate the *reduction level*, which tells the amplitude to which you want the below-threshold samples to be reduced. Often, reduction is set at the maximum value, completely eliminating the signals below the threshold. The *attack* time indicates how quickly you want the gate to open when the signal goes above the threshold. If you want to preserve transients like sudden drum beats, then you would want the attack to be short so that the gate opens quickly for these. A lookahead feature allows the noise gater to look ahead to anticipate a sudden rise in amplitude and open the gate shortly before the rise occurs. Some instruments like strings fade in slowly, and a short attack time doesn't work well in this case. If the attack time is too short, then at the moment the strings go above the threshold, the signal amplitude will rise suddenly. The *release* time indicates how quickly you want the gate to close when the signal goes below the threshold. If a musical piece fades gradually, then you want a long release time to model the release of the instruments. Otherwise, the amplitude of the signal will drop suddenly, ruining the decrescendo. Some noise gaters also have a *hold* control, indicating the minimum amount of time that the gate must stay open. A *hysteresis* control may be available to handle cases where the audio signal hovers around the threshold. If the signal keeps moving back and forth around the threshold, the gate will open and close continuously, creating a kind of *chatter*, as it is called by audio engineers. The hysteresis control indicates the difference between the value that caused the gate to open (call it $n$) and the value that will cause it to close again (call it $m$). If $n - m$ is large enough to contain the fluctuating signal, the noise gate won't cause chatter.

Noise reduction tools can eliminate noise in a digital audio file after the file has been recorded. The first step is to get a profile of the background noise. This can be done by selecting an area that should be silent, but that contains a hum or buzz. The noise reduction tool does a spectral analysis of the selected area in order to determine the frequencies in the noise and their corresponding amplitude levels. Then the entire signal is processed in sections. The frequencies in each section are analyzed and compared to the profile, and if these sections contain frequency components similar to the noise, these

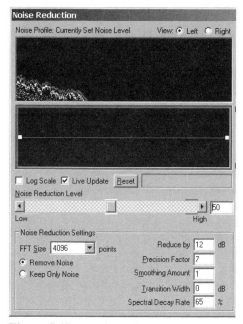

**Figure 5.17** Interface of a noise reduction tool (from Audition)

**Figure 5.18** Interface of a noise reduction tool (from Logic Pro)

can be eliminated below certain amplitudes. Noise reduction is always done at the risk of changing the character of the sound in unwanted ways. Music is particularly sensitive to changes in its frequency components. A good noise reduction tool can analyze the harmonic complexity of a sound to distinguish between music and noise. A sound segment with more complex harmonic structure is probably music and therefore should not be altered. In any case, it is often necessary to tweak the parameters experimentally to get the best results.

Some noise reduction interfaces, such as the one in Figure 5.17, give a graphical view of the frequency analysis. The graph in the top window is the noise profile. The horizontal axis moves from lower to higher frequencies, while the vertical axis shows amplitude. The original signal is in one color (the data points at the top of the graph), the amount of noise reduction is in a second color (the data points at the next level down in amplitude), and the noise is in a third color (the data points at the bottom of the graph). The main setting is the amount of noise reduction. Some tools allow you to specify how much to "reduce by" (Figure 5.17) and some say exactly the level to "reduce to" (Figure 5.18).

You can see from the interface in Figure 5.17 that the noise profile is done by Fourier analysis. In this interface, the size of the FFT of the noise profiler can be set explicitly. Think about what the profiler is doing—determining the frequencies at which the noise appears, and the corresponding amplitudes of these frequencies. Once the noise profile has been made, the frequency spectrum of the entire audio file can be compared to the noise profile, and sections that match the profile can be eliminated. With a larger FFT size, the noise profile's frequency spectrum is divided into a greater number of frequency components—that is, there is greater frequency resolution. This is a good thing, up to a point, because noise is treated differently for each frequency component. For example, your audio sample may have a −70 dB background hum at 100 Hz. If the frequency resolution isn't fine enough, the noise reducer may have to treat frequencies between 80 and 120 Hz all the same way, perhaps doing more harm than good. On the other hand, it's also possible to set the FFT size too high because there is a tradeoff between frequency resolution and time resolution. The higher the frequency resolution, the lower the time resolution. If the FFT size is set too high, time slurring can occur, manifested in the form of reverberant or echo-like effects.

Noise reducers often allow you to set parameters for smoothing. Time smoothing adjusts the attack and release times for the noise reduction. Frequency smoothing adjusts the extent to which noise that is identified in one frequency band affects amplitude changes in neighboring frequency bands. Transition smoothing sets a range between amplitudes that are considered noise and those that are not considered noise.

Noise reducers can also be set to look for certain types of noise. **White noise** is noise that occurs with equal amplitude (or relatively equal) at all frequencies (Figure 5.19). Another way to say this is that white noise has equal energy in frequency bands of the same size. (Intuitively, you can think of the energy as the area under the curve—the "colored" area—for a frequency band.) **Pink noise** has equal energy in octave bands. Recall from Chapter 4 that as you move from one octave to the same note in the next higher octave, you double the frequency. Middle C on the piano has a frequency of about 261.6 Hz, and the next higher C has a frequency of 2 * 261.6, which is about 523 Hz. In pink noise, there is an equal amount of noise in the band from 100 to 200 Hz as in the band from 1000 to 2000 Hz because each band is one octave wide. Human perception is logarithmic in that our sensitivity to the loudness of a signal drops off logarithmically as frequency increases. Thus, pink noise is perceived by humans to have equal loudness at all frequencies. If you know the character of the noise in your audio file, you may be able to set the noise reducer to eliminate this particular type of noise.

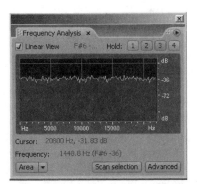

**Figure 5.19** White noise with energy equally distributed across frequency spectrum (from Audition)

A click or pop eliminator can look at a selected portion of an audio file, detect a sudden amplitude change, and eliminate this change by interpolating the sound wave between the start and end point of the click or pop. Figure 5.20 shows how a waveform can be altered by click removal.

An unwanted click in
an audio file

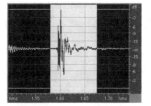

Zooming in and selecting
the click

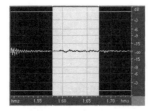

The click removed
**Figure 5.20**  Click removal (from Audition)

## 5.4 DIGITAL AUDIO FILTERS AND RELATED PROCESSING

### 5.4.1 Types of Digital Audio Filters

A digital audio filter is a linear system that changes the amplitude or phase of one or more frequency components of an audio signal. Picture a filter as a black box. The sound goes in one end with certain frequency and phase characteristics, and it comes out the other end altered. While an analog filter uses hardware components to operate on the physical properties of a wave, a digital filter—whether it is implemented in hardware or software—uses mathematical algorithms to alter sample values. A digital audio filter can be applied to either analog or digital audio signals. If it is applied to an analog signal, then there is an analog-to-digital converter at the input end and a digital-to-analog converter at the output end.

**Figure 5.21**  Audio filter

Digital audio filters are applied for a variety of reasons. They can be used to separate and analyze frequency components in order to identify the source of sounds. For example, undersea sounds could be detected and analyzed to determine the marine life in the area. Filters can also be used for restoration of a poorly recorded or poorly preserved audio recording, like an old, scratched vinyl record disk that is being digitized. Digital filters are the basis for common digital audio processing tools for equalization, reverb, and special effects.

Digital audio filters can be divided into two categories based on the way they're implemented: *FIR* (*finite-impulse response*) and *IIR* (*infinite-impulse response*) *filters*. Mathematically, FIR and IIR filters can be represented as a convolution operation. Let's look at the FIR filter first. The FIR filter is defined as follows:

---

### KEY EQUATION

Let $x(n)$ be a digital audio signal of $L$ samples for $0 \le n \le L - 1$. Let $y(n)$ be the audio signal after it has undergone an FIR filtering operation. Let $h(n)$ be a convolution mask operating as an FIR filter where $N$ is the length of the mask. Then an *FIR filter function* is defined by

$$y(n) = h(n) \otimes x(n) = \sum_{k=0}^{N-1} h(k)\, x(n - k)$$

where $x(n - k) = 0$ if $n - k < 0$

**Equation 5.1**

---

**ASIDE:** $h(n)$ goes by different names, depending on your source. It can be called the *convolution mask*, the *impulse response*, the *filter*, or the *convolution kernel*.

Note that in this section, we will use notation that is standard in the literature. Instead of using subscripts for discrete functions to emphasize that they are arrays, as in $x_n$, we use $x(n)$ and $y(n)$. These functions are in the time domain. (To emphasize this, we could call it $x(Tn)$ where $T$ is the interval between time samples, but $x(n)$ captures the same information with T implicit.) $\otimes$ is the convolution operator.

Consider what values convolution produces and, procedurally, how it operates.

$$y(0) = h(0)x(0)$$
$$y(1) = h(0)x(1) + h(1)x(0)$$
$$y(2) = h(0)x(2) + h(1)x(1) + h(2)x(0)$$

In general, for $n \ge N, y(n) = h(0)x(n) + h(1)x(n - 1) + \cdots + h(N - 1)\ x(n - N + 1)$

We already covered convolution in Chapter 3 as applied to two-dimensional digital images. Convolution works in basically the same way here, as pictured in Figure 5.22. $h(n)$ can be thought of as a convolution mask that is moved across the sample values. The values in the mask serve as multipliers for the corresponding sample values. To compute succeeding values of $y(n)$, the samples are shifted left and the computations are done again. With digital images, we applied a two-dimensional mask. For digital sound, convolution is applied in only one dimension, the time domain. You may notice that the mask is "flipped"

Filter on top, samples on bottom

| $h(4)$ | $h(3)$ | $h(2)$ | $h(1)$ | $h(0)$ |
|---|---|---|---|---|
| $x(0)$ | $x(1)$ | $x(2)$ | $x(3)$ | $x(4)$ |

$x(5)\ x(6)\ x(7)\ x(8)\ x(9)\ ...$

At time $n = 4$, $y(4)$ is computed.
Filter size is $N = 5$

**Figure 5.22** Visualizing the order of coefficients in a filter relative to the samples

relative to the sample values. That is, $x(0)$ is multiplied by $h(N - 1)$, and $x(N - 1)$ is multiplied by $h(0)$.

Equation 5.1 describes an FIR filter. The essence of the filtering operation is $h(n)$, which is just a vector of multipliers to be applied successively to sample values. The multipliers are usually referred to as coefficients, and the number of coefficients is the **order of a filter**. Engineers also call the coefficients **taps** or **tap weights**. The central question is this: How do you determine what the coefficients $h(n)$ should be, so that $h(n)$ changes a digital signal in the way that you want? This is the area of digital filter design, an elegant mathematical approach that allows you to create filters to alter the frequency spectrum of a digital signal with a great amount of control. We'll return to this later in the chapter.

Now let's consider IIR filters. To describe an IIR, we need a mask of infinite length, given by the following equation:

## KEY EQUATION

Let $x(n)$ be a digital audio signal of $L$ samples for $0 \leq n \leq L - 1$. Let $y(n)$ be the audio signal after it has undergone an IIR filtering operation. Let $h(n)$ be a convolution mask operating as an IIR filter where $N$ is the length of the forward filter and $M$ is the length of the feedback filter. Then **the infinite form of the IIR filter function** is defined by

$$y(n) = h(n) \otimes x(n) = \sum_{k=0}^{\infty} h(k)x(n - k)$$

where $x(n - k) = 0$ if $n - k < 0$ and $k$ is theoretically infinite.
An equivalent form, called **the recursive form**, is

$$y(n) = h(n) \otimes x(n) = \sum_{k=0}^{N-1} a_k x(n - k) - \sum_{k=1}^{M} b_k y(n - k)$$

**Equation 5.2**

Again, we use notation that is standard in the literature.

Notice that $y(n)$ depends on present and past input samples as well as on past outputs. The dependence on past outputs is a kind of feedback. Intuitively, you can understand the sense in which the recursive equation is equivalent to an infinite summation when you consider that once you have the first output, you'll continue infinitely to have more outputs. This is because $y(i)$ is used to create a value $y(j)$ where $j > i$.

The recursive form of Equation 5.2 expands to a convolution of the form

$$y(n) = a_0x(n) + a_1x(n-1) + a_2x(n-2) + \cdots + b_1y(n-1)$$
$$+ b_2y(n-2) + b_3y(n-3) + \cdots$$

If you have coefficients $h(n)$ for an FIR filter or coefficients $a_k$ and $b_k$ for an IIR filter, you can perform a filter as a convolution. The task, then, is to understand how to derive these coefficients based on specifications for the desired filter. We'll see how to do this in later in the chapter.

The main advantage of IIR filters is that they allow you to create a sharp cutoff between frequencies that are filtered out and those that are not. More precisely, FIR filters require larger masks and thus more arithmetic operations to achieve an equivalently sharp cutoff as compared to what could be achieved with an IIR filter. Thus, FIR filters generally require more memory and processing time. A second advantage of IIR filters is that they can be designed from equivalent analog filters. FIR filters do not have analog counterparts. On the other hand, FIR filters have an important advantage in that they can be constrained to have a ***linear phase response***. In a filter with linear phase response, phase shifts for frequency components are proportional to the frequency. Thus, harmonic frequencies are shifted by the same proportions so that harmonic relationships are not distorted. Clearly, linear phase response is important for music. Finally, FIR filters are not as sensitive to noise resulting from low bit depth and round-off error.

## 5.4.2 Impulse and Frequency Response

The convolution mask $h(n)$ for an FIR or IIR filter is sometimes referred to as the ***impulse response***. Let's examine the origin of the term.

FIR and IIR filters are examples of linear systems. In the digital audio realm, a system operates on and changes the values of an audio signal, which is just a vector of sample values. A system is a ***linear system*** if it has the properties of homogeneity and additivity. With the property of homogeneity, a change in the input signal's amplitude results in a corresponding change in the output signal's amplitude. With the property of additivity, if the system takes $x(i)$ as input to yield output $y(i)$ and takes $x(j)$ as input to yield output $y(j)$, then $x(i) + x(j)$ yields output $y(i) + y(j)$.

A ***unit impulse***, also called a ***delta function***, is a vector of values where the 0th value in the vector is 1 and all the rest are 0. The FIR and IIR filtering functions as defined in Equation 5.1 and Equation 5.2 are linear systems. The output to either system is $h(n)$ when the delta function is the input. This is why $h(n)$ is called the impulse response; it is the response you get from the FIR or IIR function when an impulse is sent through it. That is, if you do a convolution on a vector of samples that has the shape of a delta function— a 1 followed by 0s—and you use $h(n)$ as the convolution mask, you'll get the mask $h(n)$ as the output.

A counterpart to the impulse response is the ***frequency response***. By convention, if the impulse response is denoted $h(n)$, then the frequency response is denoted $H(z)$. We'll explain why this is so later in the chapter, but for now let's just consider the concept of a frequency response and its corresponding graph. A ***frequency response graph*** describes how a filter acts on an audio signal. In the ideal, it looks like the graphs in Figure 5.23. Each of the four graphs depicts a different filter in the abstract. The low-pass filter retains low-frequency components and eliminates higher frequencies. The high-pass filter does the opposite. The

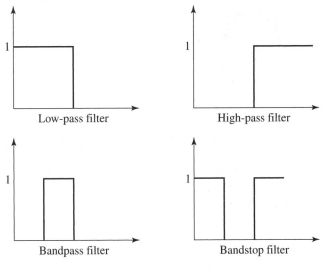

Horizontal axis:   Frequency component
Vertical axis:      Fraction of frequency component
                    retained in filtered signal

**Figure 5.23**  Frequency response graphs

bandpass filter retains frequency components across a particular band. The bandstop filter eliminates frequencies in a particular band. All of these graphs are idealized. In reality, it isn't possible to filter out frequency components with perfect accuracy. However, idealized graphs like this can describe the general behavior of a filter.

## 5.4.3 Filters and Related Tools in Digital Audio Processing Software

The filters and filter-related tools that you'll find in audio processing hardware and software generally go by these names:

- *band filters*
  - *low-pass filter*—retains only frequencies below a given level.
  - *high-pass filter*—retains only frequencies above a given level.
  - *bandpass filter*—retains only frequencies within a given band.
  - *bandstop filter*—eliminates all frequencies within a given band.
- *IIR filters* (also called *scientific filters*)—Bessel, Butterworth, Chebyshev1, and Chebyshev2 filters, all four of which are infinite-impulse response filters that can give fine-tuned control over the frequency bands that are permitted to pass through and the way in which phase is affected.
- *comb filters*—add delayed versions of a wave to itself, resulting in phase cancellations that can be perceived as echo. Phase cancellations eliminate frequency components when two sine waves that are out-of-phase with each other are summed. Thus, the frequency response has the shape of a comb (Figure 5.24).
- *convolution filters*—FIR filters that can be used to add an acoustical environment to a sound file—for example, mimicking the reverberations of a concert hall.

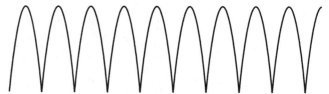

**Figure 5.24** Frequency response of a comb filter

- *graphic equalizer*—gives a graphical view that allows you to adjust the gain of frequencies within an array of bands.
- *parametric equalizer*—similar to a graphic equalizer but with control over the width of frequency bands relative to their location.
- *crossover*—splits an input signal into several output signals, each within a certain frequency range, so that each output signal can be directed to a speaker that handles that range of frequencies best.

We'll look at some of these tools more closely in the context of digital processing software, and then return to the mathematics that makes them work.

## 5.4.4 Equalization

*Equalization* (*EQ*) is the process of selectively boosting or cutting certain frequency components in an audio signal. In digital audio processing, EQ can be used during recording to balance instruments, voices, and sound effects; it can be used in post-processing to restore a poorly recorded signal, apply special effects, or achieve a balance of frequencies that suits the purpose of the audio; or it can be applied when audio is played, allowing frequencies to be adjusted to the ear of the listener.

EQ is a powerful and useful audio processing tool, but it must be applied carefully. When you change the relative amplitudes of frequency components of an audio piece, you run the risk of making it sound artificial. The environment in which music is recorded puts an acoustic signature on the music, adding resonant frequencies to the mix. The frequency spectra of instruments and voices are also complex. Each instrument and voice has its own timbre, characterized by its frequency range and overtones. Separating the frequency components of different instruments and voices is next to impossible. You may think that by lowering the high-frequency components you're only affecting the flutes, but really you may also be affecting the overtones of the oboes. The point is that generally, it's better to get the best quality, truest sound when you record it rather than relying on EQ to "fix it in post-processing." Nevertheless, there are times when a good equalizer is an invaluable tool, one that is frequently used by audio engineers.

You've probably already used EQ yourself. The bass/treble controls on a car radio are a simple kind of equalizer. These *tone controls*, as they are sometimes called, allow you to adjust the amplitude in two broad bands of frequencies. The bass band is approximately 20 to 200 Hz while the treble is approximately 4 to 20 kHz. Figure 5.25 shows four *shelving filters*. Frequency is on the horizontal axis and gain is on the vertical axis. The gain level marked with a 1 indicates the level at which the filter makes no change to the input signal. The other lines indicate five levels to which you can boost or cut frequencies, like five discrete levels you might have for both bass and treble on your car's tone controls. A negative gain cuts the amplitude of a frequency. A shelving filter for cutting or boosting low frequencies is called a *low-shelf filter*. A *high-shelf filter* boosts or cuts high frequencies. Shelving filters are similar to low- and high-pass filters except that they boost or cut frequencies up to a certain *cutoff*

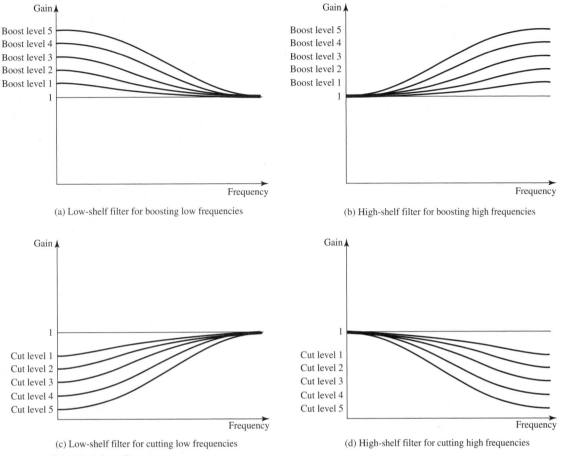

(a) Low-shelf filter for boosting low frequencies

(b) High-shelf filter for boosting high frequencies

(c) Low-shelf filter for cutting low frequencies

(d) High-shelf filter for cutting high frequencies

**Figure 5.25** Shelving filters

*frequency* (or starting at a cutoff frequency) after which (or before which) they allow the frequencies to pass through unchanged. Low- and high-pass filters, in contrast, completely block frequencies lower or higher than a given limit, as we'll see later in this chapter.

Consider the low-shelf filter for boosting low frequencies in Figure 5.25a. For any of the five boost levels, as frequencies increase, the amount of gain decreases such that higher frequencies, above the cutoff level, are not increased at all.

You may also be familiar with more fine-tuned control of EQ in the form of a ***graphic equalizer*** on your home stereo. A graphic equalizer divides the frequency spectrum into bands and allows you to control the amplitude for these bands individually, usually with sliders. Digital audio processing tools have their equivalent of graphic equalizers, and with an interface that looks very much like the interface to the analog graphic equalizer on your home stereo (Figure 5.26). With graphic equalizers, you can select the number of frequency bands. Typically, there are ten frequency bands that are proportionately divided by octaves rather than by frequency levels in Hz. Recall that if two notes (*i.e.*, frequencies) are an octave apart, then the higher note has twice the frequency of the lower one. Thus, the starting point of each band of the graphic equalizer in Figure 5.26 is twice that of the previous band. If you ask for 20 bands, then the bands are separated by half an octave and thus are spaced by a factor of $2^{\frac{1}{2}} = \sqrt{2}$. If the first band starts at 31.5, then the next starts at $31.5 * \sqrt{2} \approx 44$ Hz, the next starts at $44 * \sqrt{2} \approx 63$ Hz, and so forth. If you divide the

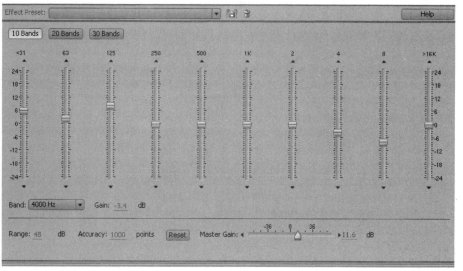

**Figure 5.26** Graphic equalizer (from Audition)

spectrum into 30 bands, the bands are separated by a third of an octave and thus are spaced by a factor of $2^{\frac{1}{3}} = \sqrt[3]{2} \approx 1.26$.

Figure 5.26 shows the interface to a graphic equalizer in an audio processing program. The Accuracy setting relates to the length of the filter used to achieve EQ. If you're equalizing only high frequencies, you can use a smaller Accuracy number. To adjust low frequencies, you need a larger Accuracy number. A larger filter has more terms in the filtering equation and thus yields better frequency resolution. This is analogous to the significance of window size in the discrete Fourier transform, as discussed in Chapter 4. The bigger the window size, the more frequency components are computed by the DFT. Greater frequency resolution is necessary when you're working with the low frequency bands because these bands are narrower than the high frequency ones. The cost of a larger filter, however, is increased processing time.

A *parametric EQ* is more flexible for equalization in that it allows you to focus on individual bands of frequencies. Rather than having a number of fixed bandwidths, as in the graphic equalizer, with the parametric equalizer you can set the center point of a band and its bandwidth and adjust the frequencies in this band as you desire. An example of a simple digital parametric equalizer interface is shown in Figure 5.27. This EQ operates on only one band at a time.

Parametric EQs are based on bandpass and bandstop filters. A bandpass filter allows frequencies in a certain band to pass through and filters out frequencies below and above the band.

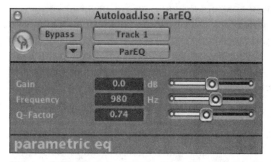

**Figure 5.27** Parametric equalizer (from Logic Pro)

Ideally, the unwanted frequencies would be filtered out entirely, but in reality this isn't possible. Thus, the frequency response graph for a bandpass filter looks more like the bell curve in Figure 5.28. This type of filter is sometimes called a *peaking filter*. If you set the gain to a positive number, the peak is pointed upward and you create a bandpass filter around your central frequency. If you set the gain to a negative number, the peak is pointed downward and you create a bandstop filter. A very narrow bandstop filter is also called a *notch filter*. The *Q-factor* (also called *quality factor* or simply *Q*) determines how steep and wide the peaking curve is. The higher the Q-factor, the higher the peak in relation to the width of the frequency band.

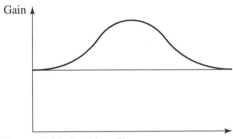

**Figure 5.28** Peaking filter

Q-factor is a term adopted from physics and electronics. In physical and electrical systems, Q-factor measures the rate at which a vibrating system dissipates its energy, a process called *damping*. More precisely, it is the number of cycles required for the energy to fall off by a factor of 535. (The rate 535 is actually $e^{2\pi}$, a number chosen because it simplified related computations.) The Q-factor of an inductor is the ratio of its inductance to its resistance at a given frequency, which is a measure of its efficiency. Q-factors are also used in acoustics to describe how much a surface resonates. A surface with a high Q-factor resonates more than one with a low Q-factor. Instruments and sound speakers have Q-factors. A bell is an example of a high-Q system, since it resonates for a long time after it is struck. Although a high Q-factor seems to imply better quality, the right Q-factor depends on the situation. If your speakers' Q-factor is too high, they may prolong the normal decay of the instruments, or "ring" if a signal suddenly stops, making the music sound artificial or distorted.

A graph can be drawn to depict how a system resonates, with frequency on the horizontal axis and energy on the vertical axis. The same type of graph is used to depict a peaking filter. It is essentially a frequency response graph, depicting which bands of frequencies are filtered out or left in, except that it plots energy (rather than amplitude) against frequency. This is shown in Figure 5.29. The peaking filter graph is parameterized by its Q-factor, a high Q-factor corresponding to a steep peak. Formally, Q-factor can be defined as follows:

## 🔑 KEY EQUATION

Given the graph of a peaking filter, let $f_{width}$ be the width of the peak measured at a point that is $\frac{1}{2}$ times the peak's height, and let $f_{center}$ be the frequency at the geometric center of the peak, both in Hz. Then the Q-factor, $Q$, is defined as

$$Q = \frac{f_{center}}{f_{width}}$$

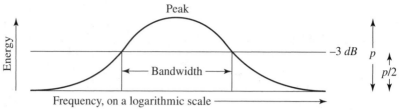

**Figure 5.29** Resonance graph of energy plotted against frequency

In Figure 5.29, frequency is shown in a logarithmic scale. On this graph, the center frequency $f_{center}$ is in the geometric center of the peak, and the bandwidth $f_{width}$ is measured at a point that is half the peak height, called the **−3 dB point**. Note that the geometric center is $(min*max)^{\frac{1}{2}}$ rather than $\left(\dfrac{min + max}{2}\right)$. On a frequency response graph of the filter that plots amplitude (rather than energy) against frequency, the bandwidth would be measured at a point that is $\dfrac{1}{\sqrt{2}}$ times the peak height.

When defined in terms of octaves, the definition of $Q$ becomes the following:

> ### KEY EQUATION
>
> Let $n$ be the bandwidth of a peaking filter in octaves. Then the filter's Q-factor, $Q$, is defined as
>
> $$Q = \frac{\sqrt{2^n}}{2^n - 1}$$

Given the Q-factor, you can compute the bandwidth of the filter.

> ### KEY EQUATION
>
> Let $Q$ be the Q-factor of a peaking filter. Then the bandwidth of the filter, $n$, is given by
>
> $$n = 2\log_2\left(\frac{1}{2Q} + \sqrt{\left(\frac{1}{2Q}\right)^2 + 1}\right)$$

When you use a parametric EQ, you may not need the equations above to compute a precise bandwidth. The main point to realize is that the higher the Q, the steeper the peak of the band. The parametric EQ pictured in Figure 5.27 allows Q to be set in the range of 0.10 to 10, the former being a fairly flat peak and the latter a steep one. Some EQ interfaces actually show you the graph and allow you to "pull" on the top of the curve to adjust Q, or you can type in numbers or control them with a slider.

Different types of filters—low-pass, high-pass, shelving, and bandpass—can be grouped into one EQ tool, sometimes called a **paragraphic equalizer**. Figure 5.31, Figure 5.32,

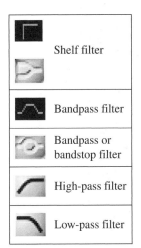

**Figure 5.30** Icons for filters

**Figure 5.31** A paragraphic equalizer (from Waves Native Power Pack)

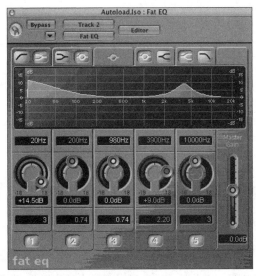

**Figure 5.32** An EQ that combines high-pass, bandpass/stop, shelving, and low-pass filters (from Logic Pro)

Figure 5.33, and Figure 5.34 show four paragraphic EQs. Note that frequency is on a logarithmic scales in these figures. Common icons for filters that are used in audio processing software are shown in Figure 5.30.

When different filters are applied to different frequency bands, as is the case with a paragraphic EQ, the filters are applied in parallel rather than serially. The audio signal is input

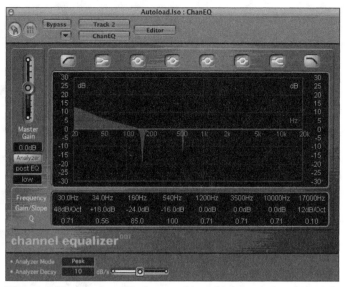

**Figure 5.33**  Another EQ that combines high-pass, bandpass/stop, shelving, and low-pass filters (from Logic Pro)

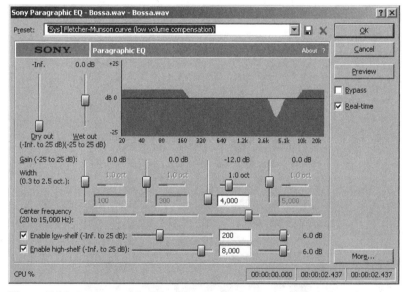

**Figure 5.34**  A paragraphic EQ with wet and dry control (from Sound Forge)

separately into each of the filters, and the outputs of the filters are combined after processing. A parallel rather than serial configuration is preferable because any phase distortions introduced by a single filter will be compounded by a subsequent phase distortion when filters are applied serially. If phase linearity is important, a linear phase EQ can be applied. Linear phase filters will not distort the harmonic structure of music because if there is a phase shift at a certain frequency, the harmonic frequencies will be shifted by the same amount. A linear phase filter is pictured in Figure 5.35.

**Figure 5.35** A linear phase EQ (from Waves Native Power Pack)

Some EQs allow you to set the master gain, which boosts or cuts the total audio signal output after the EQ processing. You may also be able to control the amount of wet and dry signal added to the final output. A *wet signal* is an audio signal that has undergone processing. A *dry signal* is unchanged. A copy of the dry signal can be retained, and after the signal has been processed and made wet, varying amounts of wet and dry can be combined for the final audio output. A paragraphic EQ with wet and dry controls is shown in Figure 5.34.

## 5.4.5 Comb Filters, Delay, Reverb, and Convolution Filters

A type of filter of particular interest is the *comb filter*. A comb filter is created when an earlier audio sample is added to a later one, causing certain resonant frequencies to be eliminated, as if they are "combed out" at regular frequency intervals. Comb filters can be either nonrecursive FIR filters or recursive IIR filters. A simple nonrecursive comb filter is described by $y(n) = x(n) + gx(n - m)$ where $m$ is the amount of the delay in numbers of samples and $|g| \leq 1$. A simple recursive comb filter is described by $y(n) = x(n) + gy(n - m)$ where $m$ is the amount of the delay in numbers of samples and $|g| < 1$. This filter is recursive in that you feed back the output $gy(n - m)$ into a later output.

You should be able to get an intuitive understanding of what these filters do. In a nonrecursive filter, a fraction of an earlier sample is added to a later one, but there's no feedback. The result would be simple repetition of part of the sound. The distance from the original sound is controlled by $m$. But what if the result of a previous computation is fed back into a later one, as is the case with a recursive comb filter? A single earlier sound would continue to affect later sounds, but with decreasing intensity (because each time its effect is scaled down again by the coefficient $g$, which we assume is less than 1). That would sound more like an echo.

Filters are often represented by flow diagrams. The flow diagram for the nonrecursive and recursive filters are shown in Figure 5.36. $z^{-m}$ symbolizes a delay of $m$ samples in the term $gx(n - m)$ or $gy(n - m)$. (You'll understand this notation even better after you read the section on z-transforms.)

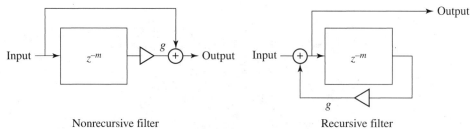

Nonrecursive filter                          Recursive filter

**Figure 5.36** Flow diagrams of simple nonrecursive and recursive filters

The comb filters given above can be used to create simple delay effects. Changing the co-efficients, changing the delay $m$, and cascading filters can create different effects similar to real-world echoes and reverberation. The phase characteristics of these filters, however, are not very natural, and thus a single filter like those above isn't the best for creating realistic echo and reverberation. What is unnatural is that the phases of all the frequencies aren't changed suffi-ciently relative to each other. This isn't how real audio echoes and reverberations happen.

Imagine that you stand in the middle of a room and play a note on a musical instrument. You hear the initial sound, and you also hear reflections of the sound as the sound waves move through space, bounce off the walls and objects in the room, and repeatedly come back to your ears until the reflections finally lose all their energy and die away. The way in which the sound waves reflect depends on many factors—the size of the room, the materi-als with which it's built, the number of objects, the heat and humidity, and so forth. Further-more, different frequencies are reflected or absorbed differently, low frequencies being absorbed less easily than high. (Have you ever sat beside another car at a traffic light and heard only the booming bass of the other person's stereo?)

Another type of filter, the ***all-pass filter***, is often used as a building block of reverbera-tion effects. Adding the all-pass filter to a chain or bank of comb filters helps to make the reflections sound like they're arriving at different times. The all-pass filter doesn't change the frequencies of the wave on which it acts. It only changes the phase, and it does so in a way that "smears" the harmonic relationships more realistically. A simple all-pass filter is defined by $y(n) = -gx(n) + x(n - m) + gy(n - m)$ where $m$ is the number of samples in the delay and $|g| < 1$. The flow diagram is shown in Figure 5.37.

Different echo and reverberation effects can be created by combining the above filters in various ways—in series, in parallel, or nested. One of the first designs that combined filters in this way was made by Manfred Schroeder. Filter designs for reverberation have gone be-yond this simple configuration, but the diagram in Figure 5.38 serves to illustrate how the simple filters can be put together for more realistic sound than is possible with a single filter.

Digital audio processing programs offer tools for delay, multi-tap delay, chorus, flange, and reverberation. More sophisticated algorithms can be found in audio effects plug-ins

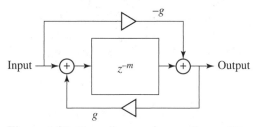

**Figure 5.37** Flow diagram for an all-pass filter

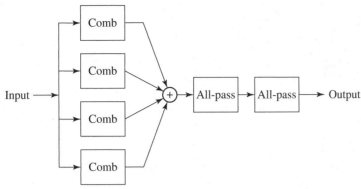

**Figure 5.38** Schroeder's Filter

that you can add to your basic software. ***Reverb*** (short for ***reverberation***) is one of the most useful effects for giving vibrance and color to sound. It can simulate not only how music and voice sound in different listening spaces, but also how it is produced by particular instruments, microphones, loudspeakers, and so forth. Reverb can also enhance the timbre of instruments and voices, making a recording that is otherwise flat and dull sound interesting and immediate. Let's look at how these effects are presented to you in audio processing software. The distinction between the different delay-based effects is not a strict one, and the methods of implementation are mostly transparent to the user, but the following discussion will give you an idea of what to expect.

Some audio processing programs make no distinction between delay and echo, while others have separate tools for them. If the features are separated, then the ***delay effect*** is less realistic, possibly implemented with nonrecursive delay units that create simple repetition of the sound rather than trailing echoes. From the interface in an audio processing program, you're able to set the delay time and the amount of wet and dry signal to be added together. The ***multi-tap delay effect*** compounds the effects of multiple delays, a ***tap*** being a single delay. When an echo effect is considered separate from delay, ***echo effect*** is more realistic in that the spectrum of the signal is changed. That is, a special filter may be used so that the

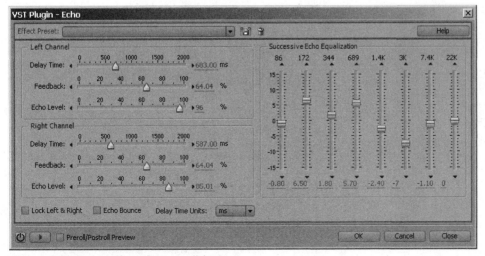

**Figure 5.39** Echo effect (from Audition)

phases of echoed sounds are changed to simulate the way different frequencies are reflected at different rates. The echo effect uses feedback, and thus interfaces to echo tools generally allow you to control this parameter.

The **chorus effect** takes a single audio signal—presumably a voice—and makes it sound like multiple voices singing or speaking in unison. You can choose how many voices you want, and the chorus effect delays the different copies of the signal one from the other. This isn't enough, however, for a realistic effect. When people sing together, they sing neither in perfect unison nor at precisely the same pitch. Thus, the frequencies of the different voices are also modulated according to your settings. Too much modulation makes the chorus sound off-pitch as a group, but the right amount makes it sound like a real chorus.

The **flange effect** uses a comb filter with a variable delay time that changes while the music is played, varying between about 0 and 20 milliseconds. You can picture the teeth of the comb filter moving closer together and then farther apart as the delay time changes. Rather than creating an echo, the flange effect continuously boosts some frequencies, cuts some frequencies, and filters others out completely, but which frequencies are affected which way changes continuously over time, which is the distinguishing characteristic of the flange effect. The resulting sound is described variously as "swooshy," "warbly," "wah wah" and so forth, depending on the audio clip to which the effect is applied and the parameters that are set. Parameters that a flange tool will probably allow you to set include the initial and final delay time and the amount of feedback.

Reverb can alter an audio signal so that it sounds like it comes from a particular acoustical space. Let's consider how reverb can be used to simulate the way sound travels in a room, as depicted in Figure 5.40. Imagine that a sound is emitted in a room—an instantaneous impulse. The line marked *direct sound* indicates the moment when the sound of the impulse first reaches the listener's ears, having traveled directly and with no reflections. In the meantime, the sound wave also propagates toward the walls, ceilings, and objects in the room and is reflected back. The moments when these first reflections reach the listener's ears are labeled *first-order reflections*. When the sound reflects off surfaces, it doesn't reflect perfectly. It's not like a billiard ball striking the side of a billiard table, where the angle of incidence equals the angle of reflection. Some of the sound is diffused, meaning that a wave reflects back at multiple angles. The first-order reflections then strike surfaces again, and these are the **secondary reflections**. Because of the diffusion of the sound, there are even more reflections at a higher

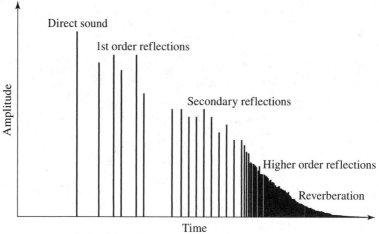

**Figure 5.40** Sound reflections in an acoustical space

order than there were at a lower order. However, each time the waves reflect, they lose some of their energy to heat, as shown by the decreasing amplitude of higher-order reflections. Eventually, there can be so many reflected waves that there is barely any time between their moments of arrival to the listener's ear. This blur of reflections is perceived as reverb.

Two basic strategies are used to implement reverb effects. The first is to try to model the physical space or the acoustical properties of an instrument or recording device. For rooms, this involves analyzing the size of the room, the angles and spacing of walls and ceilings, the objects in the room, the building and decorating materials, the usual temperature and humidity, the number of people likely to be in the room, and so forth. One standard measure of an acoustical space is its reverberation time—the time it takes for a sound to decay by 60 dB from its original level. Based on the analysis of the space, the space's effect on sound is simulated by arranging multiple recursive and all-pass filters in serial, in parallel, or in nested configurations. The many possible arrangements of the filters along with the possible parameter settings of delay time and coefficients allow for a wide array of designs.

A second method, called the ***impulse response method***, is something you could try experimentally yourself. This method is applied to modeling the way things sound in a particular listening space. The idea is to test the acoustics of a space by recording how a single quick impulse of sound reverberates, and then using that recording to make your own sound file reverberate in the same manner. Ideally, you would go into the listening room and generate a pure, instantaneous impulse of sound that contains all audible frequencies, recording this sound. In practice, you can't create an ideal impulse, but you can do something like clap your hands, pop a balloon, or fire a starter pistol. This recording is your impulse response—a filter—that can be convolved with the audio file to which you're applying the effect. This technique is sometimes called ***convolution reverb***. There are some hitches in this if you try it experimentally. The impulse you generate may be noisy. One way to get around this is to use a longer sound to generate the impulse—a sine wave that sweeps through all audible frequencies over several seconds. Then this recorded sound is deconvolved so that, hypothetically, only the reverberations from the room remain, which can be used as the impulse response. (Deconvolution begins with the output that would result from applying this filter and determines the input signal.)

Trying to generate your own impulse response file is interesting and illustrative, but for more polished results you have recourse to hundreds of libraries of impulse files (sometimes called ***IRs***) available commercially or free on the web. These IRs simulate the reverberance of concert halls, echo chambers, electric guitars, violins, specialized mics—just about any sound environment, instrument, voice, or audio equipment you can think of. In fact, if you have reverberation software that takes IRs as input, you can use any file at all, as long as it's of the expected format (*e.g.*, WAV or AIFF). You can get creative and add the resonance of your own voice, for example, to a piece of music.

# 5.5 THE RELATIONSHIP BETWEEN CONVOLUTION AND THE FOURIER TRANSFORM

It can be shown that the Fourier transform is just another side of the coin of convolution. Let's think about how filtering might be done with the Fourier transform and see how this relates to filtering as convolution. What you're trying to do is the following: Let $x(n)$ be a digital audio signal. Let $X(z)$ be the discrete Fourier transform of $x(n)$. (The notation used in this section is standard in digital signal processing.) You want to filter $X(z)$, creating output $Y(z)$, such that $Y(z)$ has the frequency components at the desired levels. Thus, you want to find some $H(z)$ such that $Y(z) = H(z)X(z)$. Note that $Y(z)$ is the audio signal represented in the frequency domain. Thus, the inverse discrete Fourier transform of $Y(z)$ will give you $y(n)$, the filtered signal in the time domain. In summary, the steps are these:

- take the discrete Fourier transform of digital audio signal $x(n)$, which gives $X(z)$
- describe the specifications of your filter
- from these specifications, find $H(z)$ such that $Y(z) = H(z) X(z)$ and $Y(z)$ has the desired frequency components
- perform the multiplication $H(z)X(z)$ to get $Y(z)$
- take the inverse discrete Fourier transform of $Y(z)$, which gives $y(n)$, your filtered signal represented in the time domain

The difficult part of the process above is finding $H(z)$, just as the difficult part of designing a convolution filter is finding $h(n)$. Actually, the two processes amount to the same thing. Performing $Y(z) = H(z)X(z)$ and then taking the inverse discrete Fourier transform of $Y(z)$ to get $y(n)$ is equivalent to doing a convolution operation described as $y(n) = h(n) \otimes x(n) = \sum_{k=0}^{N} h(k)x(n - k)$. The point here is that convolving in the time domain is equivalent to multiplying in the frequency domain. This is expressed in the *convolution theorem*:

> Let $H(z)$ be the discrete Fourier transform of a convolution filter $h(n)$, and let $X(z)$ be the discrete Fourier transform of a digital audio signal $x(n)$. Then $y(n) = h(n) \otimes x(n)$ is equivalent to the inverse discrete Fourier transform of $Y(z)$, where $Y(z) = H(z)X(z)$.

In fact, doing multiplication in the frequency domain and then inverting to the time domain is more computationally efficient than doing convolution in the time domain (if the Fast Fourier transform is used for the implementation).

The bottom line is that to design a particular filter yourself, you still have to determine either $h(n)$ or $H(z)$.

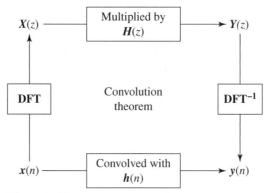

**Figure 5.41** Equivalent operations in time and frequency domains

# 5.6 DESIGNING AND IMPLEMENTING YOUR OWN FILTERS

## 5.6.1 FIR Filter Design

Let's turn now to the design of FIR filters. At the end of this section, we give an algorithm for creating an FIR filter. You could apply this algorithm without understanding how it works. If you do want to understand how it works, you should read on through this section to look at the underlying mathematics, or you can skip ahead to the algorithm and try to learn by application.

The convolution mask $h(n)$ is also called the **impulse response**, representing a filter in the time domain. Its counterpart in the frequency domain, the **frequency response $H(z)$**, is also sometimes referred to as the **transfer function**. The relationship between the impulse response and the frequency response of a digital audio filter is precisely the relationship between $h(n)$ and $H(z)$ described in the previous section.

A frequency response graph can be used to show the *desired* frequency response of a filter you are designing. For example, the frequency response of an ideal low-pass filter is shown in Figure 5.42. In the graph, angular frequency is on the horizontal axis. The vertical axis represents the fraction of each frequency component to be permitted in the filtered signal. This figure indicates that frequency components between $-\omega_c$ and $\omega_c$ are to be left unchanged, while all other frequency components are to be removed entirely. $\omega_c$ is the angular cutoff frequency. It can be assumed that the angular frequency in this graph is normalized. This is done by mapping the Nyquist angular frequency—which is half the sampling frequency—to $\pi$. That is, if $f_{samp}$ is the sampling frequency in Hz and $f_c$ is the cutoff frequency in Hz, then $f_c$, normalized, is $\dfrac{f_c}{f_{samp}}$. In angular units, this gives us the normalized $\omega_c = 2\pi\dfrac{f_c}{f_{samp}}$. It makes sense to normalize in this way because the only frequencies that can be validly digitized at a sampling frequency of $f_s$ are frequencies between 0 and $\dfrac{f_s}{2}$. Note also that normalization implies that the cutoff frequency $\omega_c$ must be less than $\pi$.

This frequency response is ideal in that it displays a completely sharp cutoff between the frequencies that are removed and those that are not changed. In reality, it isn't possible to design such a filter, but the ideal frequency response graph serves as a place to begin. The first

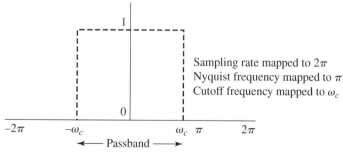

Sampling rate mapped to $2\pi$
Nyquist frequency mapped to $\pi$
Cutoff frequency mapped to $\omega_c$

**Figure 5.42** Frequency response of an ideal low-pass filter

**ASIDE:** A sinc function is the product of a
sine function and a monotonically decreasing
function. Its basic form is

$$\text{sinc}(x) = \begin{cases} \dfrac{\sin(x)}{x} & \text{for } x \neq 0 \\ 1 & \text{for } x = 0 \end{cases}$$

The sinc function is the Fourier transform of the
rectangle function, and vice versa.

step in FIR filter design is to determine what ideal impulse response
corresponds to the ideal frequency response.

The frequency response graph shown in Figure 5.42 is an example of a **rectangle function**, which has a value of 1 in a certain finite
range and 0s everywhere else. This graph represents an idealized
version of how we'd like our filter to behave. You can think of it as
an idealized form of $H(z)$. Then what would be the corresponding
ideal impulse response, an idealized $h(n)$?

It can be shown that the inverse Fourier transform of a rectangle
function in the frequency domain is a **sinc function** in the time
domain, shown in Figure 5.43. The rectangle and sinc functions
arise frequently in digital signal processing and are convenient because of the relationship
they have with each other through the Fourier transform.

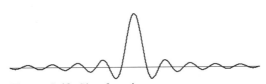

**Figure 5.43** Sinc function

**ASIDE:** If you compare this ideal impulse response equation with Equation 4.5, you should
note the following relationships:

| function | $h_{ideal}(n)$ | $f(t)$ |
| --- | --- | --- |
| time | $n$ | $t$ |
| frequency | $\omega$ | $n\omega$ |
| freq. range | $-\pi \ldots \pi^*$ | $-\infty \ldots \infty$ |
| base frequency | infinitesimal | $\omega$ |
| freq. domain function | $H_{ideal}(\omega)$ | $F_n$ |
| periodic? | no | yes |
| continuous? | yes | yes |

*Actually, it is $-\infty \ldots \infty$, but we normalize fre-
quencies so that $H_{ideal}(\omega) = 0$ when $|\omega| \geq$, so
the integral is 0 outside the range $-\pi \ldots \pi$.

Let's see how this works mathematically. Recall the relationship
between the frequency response and the impulse response. The former is the Fourier transform of the latter. In other words, the inverse
Fourier transform of the ideal frequency response $H_{ideal}(\omega)$ gives us
the ideal impulse response $h_{ideal}(n)$. (An integral rather than a summation is used because the function is not assumed to be periodic.)

$$h_{ideal}(n) = \frac{1}{2\pi} \int_{-\pi}^{\pi} H_{ideal}(\omega) e^{i\omega n} d\omega$$

This equation can be simplified as follows:

**Step 1:**
$$h_{ideal}(n) = \frac{1}{2\pi} \int_{-\pi}^{\pi} H_{ideal}(\omega) e^{i\omega n} d\omega$$

$$= \frac{1}{2\pi} \int_{-\omega_c}^{\omega_c} e^{i\omega n} d\omega$$

**Step 2:**
$$= \frac{1}{2\pi} \int_{-\omega_c}^{\omega_c} \cos(\omega n) + i\sin(\omega n) d\omega$$

**Step 3:**
$$= \frac{\sin(\omega_c n)}{\pi n}$$

**Step 4:**
$$= \frac{\sin(2\pi f_c n)}{\pi n} \quad \text{for } -\infty \leq n \leq \infty, n \neq 0$$
$$\text{and } 2f_c \text{ for } n = 0$$

In short, we get

$$h_{ideal}(n) = \frac{\sin(2\pi f_c n)}{\pi n} \quad \text{for } -\infty \leq n \leq \infty, n \neq 0$$
$$\text{and } 2f_c \text{ for } n = 0$$

**Equation 5.3**

In step 1, the integral is limited to the range of $-\omega_c$ to $\omega_c$ because $H_{ideal}(\omega)$ is equal to 1 between $-\omega_c$ and $\omega_c$, and 0 everywhere else under the assumption that $\omega_c < \pi$. Step 2 does a substitution using Euler's identity. (See Chapter 4.) Step 3 does the integration. Notice that the sine term falls out because its integral is −cosine, which is an even function, and the negatives cancel the positives. In step 4, we use the substitution $\omega_c = 2\pi f_c$, from the relationship between angular frequency and frequency in Hz. The case where $n = 0$ results from taking the limit as $n$ goes to 0, by l'Hôpital's rule. We have derived a form of the sinc function, as expected. The importance of this derivation is that Equation 5.3 gives you the ideal impulse response based on your desired cutoff frequency $f_c$. By a similar process, it is possible to derive the equations for ideal high-pass and bandpass filters, which are given in Table 5.2.

| TABLE 5.2 | Equations for Ideal Impulse Responses for Standard Filters, Based on Cutoff Frequency $f_c$ and Band Edge Frequencies $f_1$ and $f_2$ | |
|---|---|---|
| **Type of filter** | $h_{ideal}(n), n \neq 0$ | $h_{ideal}(0)$ |
| Low-pass | $\dfrac{\sin(2\pi f_c n)}{\pi n}$ | $2f_c$ |
| High-pass | $-\dfrac{\sin(2\pi f_c n)}{\pi n}$ | $1 - 2f_c$ |
| Bandpass | $f_2 \dfrac{\sin(2\pi f_2 n)}{\pi n} - f_1 \dfrac{\sin(2\pi f_1 n)}{\pi n}$ | $2(f_2 - f_1)$ |
| Bandstop | $f_1 \dfrac{\sin(2\pi f_1 n)}{\pi n} - f_2 \dfrac{\sin(2\pi f_2 n)}{\pi n}$ | $1 - 2(f_2 - f_1)$ |

But we're still in the realm of the ideal. We don't yet have a workable FIR filter. The problem is that a sinc function goes on infinitely in the positive and negative directions, as shown in Figure 5.43. The amplitude continues to diminish in each direction but never goes to 0. We can't use this ideal, infinite sinc function as an impulse response (*i.e.*, a convolution mask) for an FIR filter. Think about the problem of trying to apply a convolution mask like this in real-time. To compute a new value for a given audio sample, we'd need to know all past sample values on to infinity, and we'd need to predict what future sample values are on to infinity.

The next step in FIR filter design is to take this ideal, infinite sinc function and modify it to something that is realizable as a convolution mask of finite length. However, a consequence of the modification is that you can't achieve an *ideal* frequency response. Modifying the ideal impulse response by making it finite creates ripples in the corresponding frequency response.

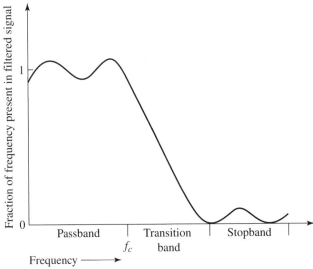

**Figure 5.44** Frequency response of a realistic low-pass filter

Now let's consider a realistic frequency response graph. Figure 5.44 shows the kind of frequency response graph you'll encounter in the literature and documentation on digital audio filters. Such a graph could represent the specifications of a filter design, or it could represent the behavior of an existing filter. As with the graph of the ideal frequency response, the horizontal axis corresponds to frequency and the vertical axis gives the fraction of the frequency that will remain in the audio file after it is filtered, corresponding to attenuation. In Figure 5.44, frequency is given in Hz rather than radians, and only the positive portion need be shown since the graph is implicitly symmetrical around 0, but otherwise the graph is the same in nature as the ideal frequency response graph in Figure 5.42. As before, we consider the frequency components only up to one-half the sampling rate, which is the Nyquist frequency, since no other frequencies can be validly sampled. In frequency response graphs, units on the vertical axis are sometimes shown in decibels. Measured in decibels, attenuation is equal to $20 \log_{10}\left(\dfrac{a_{out}}{a_{in}}\right) dB$, where $a_{in}$ is the amplitude of frequency component $f$ before the filter is applied, and $a_{out}$ is the amplitude after the filter is applied. In the graph shown, the units are normalized to range from 0 to 1, indicating the fraction by which each frequency component is attenuated. In the case of normalization, attenuation is measured as $\dfrac{a_{out}}{a_{in}}$.

Compare the realistic frequency response graph to an ideal one. In a realistic graph, the **passband** is the area from 0 up to the cutoff frequency $f_c$ and corresponds to the frequencies the filter tries to retain. Ideally, you want frequencies up to $f_c$ to pass through the filter unchanged, but in fact they may be slightly attenuated in either the positive or negative direction, shown as a **ripple**, fluctuations in the frequency magnitude. The **stopband** corresponds to the frequencies the filter attenuates or filters out. In the realistic graph, the stopband has ripples like the passband, indicating that the unwanted frequencies are not filtered out perfectly. The **transition band** lies in between. Unlike the transition in an ideal filter, in a real filter the *transition region rolloff*—the slope of the curve leading to the transition band—is not infinitely steep.

When you design an FIR filter, you specify certain parameters that define an acceptable, though not ideal, frequency response. For example, you could specify:

- for a low-pass filter, the cutoff frequency marking the end of the passband ($f_c$ above)
- for a low-pass filter, transition width, the maximum acceptable bandwidth from the end of the passband to the beginning of the stopband
- for a stopband or bandpass filter, $f_1$ and $f_2$, the beginning and end frequencies for the stopband or passband
- passband deviation, the maximum acceptable range of attenuation in the passband due to rippling
- stopband deviation, the maximum acceptable range of attenuation in the stopband due to rippling

So how do you realize a workable FIR filter based on your design specifications? This takes us back to the ideal impulse response functions we derived in Table 5.2. One way to design an FIR filter is to take an ideal impulse response and multiply it by a windowing function $w(n)$. The purpose of the windowing function is to make the impulse response finite. However, making the impulse response finite results in a frequency response that is less than ideal. It has ripples in the passband or stopband, like those shown in Figure 5.44. Thus, you need to select a windowing function that minimizes the ripples in the passband or stopband and/or creates your desired cutoff slope.

The simplest windowing function is rectangular. It has the value 1 in some finite range across the infinite impulse response and 0s everywhere else. Multiplying by this window simply truncates the infinite impulse response on both sides. The disadvantage of a rectangular windowing function is that it has the effect of providing only limited attenuation in the stopband. Four other commonly used windowing functions are the triangular, Hanning, Hamming, and Blackman windows. The triangular, Hamming, Hanning, and Blackman windows are tapered smoothly to 0 at each end. The effect is that when you multiply a sinc function by one of these windowing functions, the resulting frequency response has less of a ripple in the stopband than would be achieved if you multiply by a rectangular window. The disadvantage is that the transition band will generally be wider.

**ASIDE:** These are essentially the same Hanning, Hamming, and Blackman function as discussed in Chapter 4, through they look a little different in form. The functions in Chapter 4 were expressed as continuous functions going from 0 to T. In Table 5.3 they are expressed as discrete functions going from $-\frac{1}{2}N$ to $\frac{1}{2}N$. This shift of values symmetric around 0 results in terms being added rather than subtracted in the function.

| TABLE 5.3 | Windowing Functions |
|---|---|
| 1<br><br>Rectangular windowing function | $w(n) = 0.5 + 0.5\cos\left(\dfrac{2\pi n}{N}\right)$<br><br>Hanning windowing function |
| $w(n) = 0.54 + 0.46\cos\left(\dfrac{2\pi n}{N}\right)$<br><br>Hamming windowing function | $w(n) = 0.42 + 0.5\cos\left(\dfrac{2\pi n}{N-1}\right) + 0.08\cos\left(\dfrac{4\pi n}{N-1}\right)$<br><br>Blackman windowing function |

The process discussed in this section is called the ***windowing method of FIR filter design***. In summary, the steps are given in Algorithm 5.1. The algorithm is for a low-pass filter, but a similar one could be created for a high-pass, bandpass, or bandstop filter simply by replacing the function with the appropriate one from Table 5.2 and including the needed parameters. One parameter needed for all types of filters is the order of the filter, $N$ (*i.e.*, the number of coefficients). The order of the filter will have an effect on the width of the transition band. Call the width of the transition band $b$. Assume that the Nyquist frequency in Hz is normalized to 0.5 and that $b$ is on this scale. Then the relationship between $b$ and $N$ is given by $b = 4/N$. Thus, if you know the width you'd like for your transition bandwidth, you can determine an appropriate order for the filter. A higher-order filter gives a sharper cutoff between filtered and unfiltered frequencies, but at the expense of more computation.

## ALGORITHM 5.1

```
algorithm FIR_low_pass filter
/*Input: f_c, the cutoff frequency for the lowpass filter, in Hz
          f_samp, the sampling frequency of the audio signal to be filtered, in Hz
          N, the order of the filter; assume N is odd
   Output: a low-pass FIR filter in the form of an N-element array */
{
  /*Normalize f_c and ω_c so that π is equal to the Nyquist angular frequency*/
  f_c = f_c/f_samp
  ω_c = 2*π*f_c
  middle = N/2     /*Integer division, dropping remainder*/
  /*Create the filter using the low-pass filter function from Table 5.2*/
  /*Put a dummy value in for n = 0 to avoid a divide by 0 error)*/
  for n = −N/2 to N/2
     if (n = 0) ftr(middle) = 1
     else fltr(n+middle) = sin(2*π*f_c*n)/(π *n)
  fltr(middle) = 2*f_c
  /*Multiply the elements of fltr by a windowing function chosen from Table 5.3.
  We use the Hanning window function/
  for n = 0 to N-1
     fltr(n) = fltr(n) * (0.5 + 0.5*cos((2*π*n)/N))
}
```

Supplement on windowing method for FIR filter design:

mathematical modeling worksheet

We've described the windowing method of FIR filter design because it gives an intuitive sense of the filters and related terminology and is based on the mathematical relationship between the impulse and frequency responses. However, it isn't necessarily the best method. Two other methods are the optimal method and the frequency sampling method. The optimal method is easy to apply and has the advantage of distributing the ripples more evenly over the passband and stopband, called ***equiripple***. The advantage of the frequency sampling method is that it allows FIR filters to be implemented both nonrecursively and recursively and thereby leads to computational efficiency. Another important implementation issue is the effect of quantization error on filter performance. We refer you to the references for details on these filter design approaches and issues.

In this section, we've given you the basic mathematical knowledge with which you could design and implement your own software FIR filters. Of course you don't always have to design filters from scratch. Signal processing tools such as MATLAB allow you to design filters at a higher level of abstraction, but to do so, you still need to understand the terminology and processes described here. Even when you use the predesigned filters that are available in audio processing hardware or software, it helps to understand how the filters operate in order to choose and apply them appropriately.

## 5.6.2 The Z-Transform

For a complete understanding of IIR and FIR filters, you need to be familiar with the *z-transform*. Terminology related to z-transforms can be used in filter design and in descriptions of predesigned filters. The manner in which frequencies are altered by a filter can be represented conveniently by means of z-transforms. Another application of z-transforms is to analyze the effects of quantization error on digital filter performance.

Consider a sequence of discrete values $x(n)$ for $n = 0, 1, \ldots$. The z-transform of this sequence is defined as $X(z) = \sum_{n=0}^{\infty} x(n)z^{-n}$ where $z$ is a complex variable. This defines a *one-sided z-transform*, with values of $n$ going from 0 to $\infty$. A full z-transform sums from $-\infty$ to $\infty$, but the one-sided transform works for our purposes.

Notice the naming convention that $x(n)$ is transformed to $X(z)$, $y(n)$ is transformed to $Y(z)$, $h(n)$ is transformed to $H(z)$, and so forth.

First, think of the z-transform in the abstract. It doesn't really matter what $x(n)$ corresponds to in the real world. Try applying the definition to $x(n) = [5, -2, 3, 6, 6]$, assuming that $x(n) = 0$ for $n > 4$. (Henceforth, we'll assume $x(n) = 0$ if no value is specified for $x(n)$. Array positions are numbered from 0.)

$$X(z) = 5 - 2z^{-1} + 3z^{-2} + 6z^{-3} + 6z^{-4}$$

You can see that $X(z)$ is a function of the complex variable $z$.

It's no coincidence that the functions are called $H(z)$, $X(z)$, and $Y(z)$ as they were in the previous sections. This is because you can turn the z-transform into something more familiar if you understand that it is a generalization of the discrete Fourier transform. Let's see how this works.

In general, $X(z)$ is a function that runs over all complex numbers $z$. However, consider what you get if you specifically set $z = e^{i\theta}$ and apply the z-transform to a vector of length $N$. This gives you

$$\text{for } 0 \le k < N, X(z_k) = \sum_{n=0}^{N-1} x(n)e^{-i\theta n} = \sum_{n=0}^{N-1} x(n)e^{\frac{-i2\pi kn}{N}} \quad \text{for } z = e^{i\theta} \quad \text{and} \quad \theta = \frac{2\pi k}{N}$$

**Equation 5.4**

Equation 5.4 is the discrete Fourier transform of $x(n)$. The subscript $k$ indicates that the summation is performed to determine each $k$th frequency component. We will omit the $k$ when it is not important to the discussion, but you should keep in mind that the summation is performed for every frequency component that is computed. In the context of this equation, we are considering discretely spaced frequency components. The $N$ frequency components are spaced by $\frac{2\pi}{N}$, and the $k$th frequency component is frequency $\theta = \frac{2\pi k}{N}$. Thus, although

$X(z)$ is defined over the whole complex plane, when we perform the discrete Fourier transform of $x(n)$, we are only evaluating $X(z)$ at $N$ specific points on the complex plane. These points represent different frequency components, and they all lie evenly spaced around the unit circle.

We already observed that convolution in the time domain is equivalent to multiplication in the frequency domain in the sense that performing $y(n) = h(n) \otimes x(n)$ is equivalent to performing $Y(z) = H(z)X(z)$ and then taking the inverse Fourier transform of $Y(z)$. So why do you need z-transforms, since you can focus on a special case of the z-transform, which is the Fourier transform? The reason is that expressing things using the notation of a z-transform is more convenient mathematically because it helps to lay bare how a given filter will behave. An IIR filter is defined as a convolution by $y(n) = h(n) \otimes x(n)$. The equivalent relation in terms of the z-transform is $Y(z) = H(z)X(z)$, from which it follows that

$$H(z) = \frac{Y(z)}{X(z)}$$

This form of $H(z)$, expressed as $\dfrac{Y(z)}{X(z)}$, is referred to as a ***transfer function***. Note that this form is closely related to the recursive form of an IIR filter.

---

## KEY EQUATION

Let $y(n) = h(n) \otimes x(n) = \displaystyle\sum_{k=0}^{N-1} a_k x(n-k) - \sum_{k=1}^{M} b_k y(n-k)$ be an IIR filter,

as defined in Equation 5.2. Let $H(z) = \dfrac{Y(z)}{X(z)}$ be the transfer function for this filter. Then

$$H(z) = \frac{a_0 + a_1 z^{-1} + a_2 z^{-2} + \cdots}{1 + b_1 z^{-1} + b_2 z^{-2} + \cdots} = \frac{a_0 z^N + a_1 z^{N-1} + \cdots}{z^N + b_1 z^{N-1} + \cdots}$$

---

We'll see in the next section that the transform function gives us a convenient way of predicting how a filter will behave, or designing an IIR filter so that it behaves the way we want it to.

## 5.6.3 Zero-Pole Diagrams and IIR Filter Design

Previously, we looked at graphs of the frequency response, calling the function $H(z)$—for example, Figure 5.23. More precisely, this is a graph of the frequency magnitude response. Recall that the discrete Fourier transform yields frequency components as complex numbers. The magnitude of a complex number $a + bi$ is equal to $\sqrt{a^2 + b^2}$. The frequency response of a filter can also be visualized by plotting $H(z)$ on the complex number plane. For a complex number $a + bi$, the horizontal axis of the complex number plane represents the real-number component, $a$, while the vertical axis represents the coefficient of the imaginary component, $b$. This is pictured in Figure 5.45. $\overrightarrow{a}$ , $\overrightarrow{b}$, and $\overrightarrow{r}$ are vectors, while $a$, $b$, and $r$ denote the magnitudes of these vectors. Consider a circle of radius $r = 1$ around

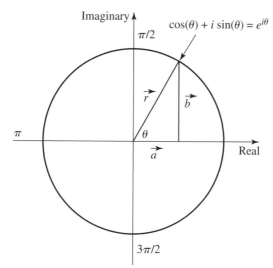

**Figure 5.45** A circle with radius 1 on the complex-number plane

the origin. If $r = 1$, then the points that lie on this circle correspond to the complex numbers $e^{i\theta}$. We can see this from simple geometry and vector addition.

$$a = r|\cos\theta| = |\cos\theta|$$
$$b = r|\sin\theta| = |\sin\theta|$$
$$\vec{a} = (\cos\theta, 0)$$
$$\vec{b} = (0, \sin\theta)$$
$$\vec{r} = (\cos\theta, \sin\theta)$$

The point $(\cos\theta, \sin\theta)$ corresponds to $\cos\theta + i\sin\theta$ in the complex number plane. By Euler's identity, this is $e^{i\theta}$.

Why do we want to trace a circle on the complex number plane using the point $e^{i\theta}$? Because this circle is exactly the circle on which we evaluate the z-transform for each frequency component. By Equation 5.4, the $k$th frequency component, $H(z_k)$, is obtained by evaluating the discrete Fourier transform at $z = e^{i\theta} = e^{i\frac{2\pi k}{N}}$. Since $H(z)$ yields the frequency response, evaluating $H(z_k)$ tells us how much the $k$th frequency component is attenuated by the filter.

We know that $H(z) = \dfrac{Y(z)}{X(z)}$. Notice that as $Y(z)$ gets closer to 0, $H(z)$ gets smaller. As $X(z)$ gets closer to 0, $H(z)$ gets larger. The places where $Y(z) = 0$ are called the **zeros** of $H(z)$. The places where $X(z) = 0$ are called the **poles** of $H(z)$.

The zeros and poles for a given filtering function can be placed on this same graph. Placing the zeros and poles on the graph makes it possible to get a general picture of how a filter affects the digital signal it operates on, without having to evaluate $H(z_k)$ for every $k$. To see how the filter defined by $H(z)$ will affect a digital signal, you determine its zeros and poles from $H(z) = \dfrac{Y(z)}{X(z)}$ and plot them on the zero-pole graph. Once you know where the zeros and poles are, you can see how frequency components are affected by the filter. For example, you may be able to see that high frequencies, beyond a certain point, are attenuated while frequencies less than this cutoff are unchanged.

This may seem confusing at first. You need $\dfrac{Y(z)}{X(z)}$ to get a filter's zeros and poles. But $Y(z)$ is the z-transform of $y(n)$, and $y(n)$ is the output of the filter. How can you determine $Y(z)$ without actually running the filter? Actually, you do it algebraically. Let's try a simple example of an FIR filter to see how you might get values for the zeros and poles, and from these you can predict the overall effect of the filter.

Let $h(n) = [1, -0.5]$. Then its z-transform, $H(z)$, is $1 - 0.5z^{-1}$. We can divide this into a numerator and denominator by multiplying by $\dfrac{z}{z}$. This gives us $H(z) = \dfrac{z - 0.5}{z}$. Thus, $H(z)$ has a zero at $z = 0.5$ and a pole at $z = 0$.

Another way to get a zero and a pole associated with $h(n) = [1, -0.5]$ is as follows. The difference equation form of this convolution is

$$y(n) = \sum_{k=0}^{1} h(k)x(n - k) = x(n) - 0.5x(n - 1)$$

The z-transform has a property called the **delay property** whereby the z-transform of $x(n - 1)$ equals $z^{-1}X(z)$. The z-transform also has the **linearity property,** which states that if two functions are equal, then their z-transforms are equal, and the z-transform of a sum of terms is equal to the sum of the z-transforms of the terms. Thus, if we take the z-transform of both sides of the equation $y(n) = x(n) - 0.5x(n - 1)$, we get

$$Y(z) = X(z) - 0.5z^{-1}X(z)$$

Dividing both sides by $X(z)$ yields

$$\frac{Y(z)}{X(z)} = H(z) = 1 - 0.5z^{-1} = \frac{z - 0.5}{z}$$

Thus, we have a zero at $z = 0.5$ (where the numerator equals 0) and a pole at $z = 0$ (where the denominator equals 0).

Once you know the zeros and poles, you can plot them on the complex plane in a graph called a **zero-pole diagram**. From this you can derive information about the frequency response of the filter. At point $z = 0.5$, there is no imaginary component, so this point lies on the horizontal axis. The pole is at the origin. This is shown in Figure 5.46.

To predict the filter's effect on frequencies, we look at each $k$th point—called it $P_k$— around the unit circle, where $P_0$ falls on the $x$-axis. The angle formed between $P_k$, the origin, and $P_0$ is $\theta$ (which is equal to $\dfrac{2\pi k}{N}$). Each such angle corresponds to a frequency component of a signal being altered by the filter. Since the Nyquist frequency has been normalized to $\pi$, we consider only the frequencies between 0 and $\pi$, in the top semicircle. Let $d_{zero}$ be the distance between $P_k$ and the zero of the filter, and let $d_{pole}$ be the distance between $P_k$ and the pole. The frequency response $H(z)$ will be larger or smaller in proportion to $\dfrac{d_{zero}}{d_{pole}}$. In this case, because the pole of the filter is at the origin, $d_{pole}$ is the distance

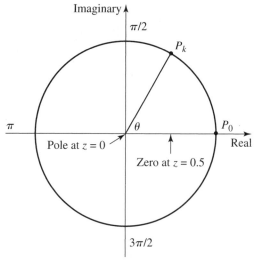

**Figure 5.46** A zero-pole diagram

from the origin to the unit circle, which is always 1, so the size of $\dfrac{d_{zero}}{d_{pole}}$ depends entirely on $d_{zero}$. As $d_{zero}$ gets larger, the frequency response gets larger, and $d_{zero}$ gets increasingly large as you move from $\theta = 0$ to $\theta = \pi$, which means the frequency response gets increasingly large. Thus, the zero-pole diagram represents a high-pass filter in that it attenuates low frequencies more than high frequencies.

Now let's try deriving and analyzing the zero-pole diagram of an IIR filter. Say that your filter is defined by the difference equation

$$y(n) = x(n) - x(n - 2) - 0.64y(n - 2)$$

This can be written as

$$y(n) + 0.64y(n - 2) = x(n) - x(n - 2)$$

The delay and linearity properties of the z-transform yields

$$Y(z) + 0.64z^{-2}Y(z) = X(z) - z^{-2}X(z)$$

The rest of the derivation goes as follows:

$$Y(z)(1 + 0.64z^{-2}) = X(z)(1 - z^{-2}) \Rightarrow$$

$$\frac{Y(z)}{X(z)} = \frac{1 - z^{-2}}{1 + 0.64z^{-2}} = \frac{z^2 - 1}{z^2 + 0.64} = \frac{(z + 1)(z - 1)}{(z + 0.8i)(z - 0.8i)} = H(z)$$

The zeros are at $z = 1$ and $z = -1$, and the poles are at $z = 0.8i$ and $z = -0.8i$. (Note that if the imaginary part of $z$ is nonzero, roots appear as conjugate pairs $a \pm ib$.) The zero-pole diagram is in Figure 5.47. This diagram is harder to analyze by inspection because we have more than one zero and more than one pole. To determine when the frequency response gets larger, we have to determine when $H(z) = \dfrac{(z + 1)(z - 1)}{(z + 0.8i)(z - 0.8i)}$ grows, which is the

Supplement on z-transforms, zero-pole diagrams, and IIR filters:

interactive tutorial

worksheet

Supplement on creating FIR and IIR filters in MATLAB:

mathematical modeling worksheet

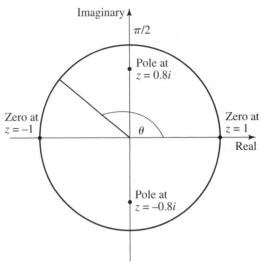

**Figure 5.47** A zero-pole diagram for an IIR filter

Supplement on
creating a filter via
a transfer function:

mathematical
modeling
worksheet

same thing as determining how $(z + 1)(z - 1)$ gets large relative to $(z + 0.8i)(z - 0.8i)$. In fact, this diagram represents a bandpass filter, with frequencies near $\pi/2$ being the least attenuated.

We've looked at how you analyze an existing filter by means of its zero-pole diagram. It is also possible to design a filter using a zero-pole diagram—by placing the zeros and poles in relative positions such that they create the desired frequency response. This is feasible, however, only for simple filters.

The most commonly used design method for IIR filters is to convert analog filters into equivalent digital ones. This method relies on the z-transform as well as the equivalent transform in the continuous domain, the Laplace transform. We won't go into the details of this method of filter design. However, you should be aware of four commonly used types of IIR filters, the Bessel, Butterworth, Chebyshev, and elliptic filters.

Recall that FIR filters are generally phase linear, which means that phase shifts affect frequency components in a linear fashion. The result is that harmonic frequencies are shifted in the same proportions and thus don't sound distorted after filtering, which is important in music. In IIR filters, on the other hand, care must be taken to enforce phase linearity.

***Bessel filters*** are the best IIR filters for ensuring a linear phase response. ***Butterworth filters*** sacrifice phase linearity so that they can provide a frequency response that is as flat as possible in the passband and stopband (*i.e.*, they minimize ripples). A disadvantage of Butterworth filters is that they have a wide transition region. ***Chebyshev filters*** have a steeper roll-off than Butterworth filters, the disadvantage being that they have more nonlinear phase response and more ripple. However, the amount of ripple can be constrained, with tradeoffs between ripple and roll-off or between ripple in the passband (Chebyshev 1 filters) and ripple in the stopband (Chebyshev 2 filters). ***Elliptic filters***, also called Cauer filters, have the worst phase linearity of the common IIR filters, but they have the sharpest roll-off relative to the number of coefficients and are equiripple in the passband and stopband. The choice of filter depends on the nature of your audio signal and how you want it to sound after filtering.

# 5.7 DIGITAL AUDIO COMPRESSION

## 5.7.1 Time-Based Compression Methods

Chapter 4 covered some methods that effectively reduce the size of audio files. Nonlinear quantization (*e.g.*, $\mu$- or A-law encoding) reduces the amount of data in voice signals by quantizing high-amplitude signals more coarsely than low-amplitude ones. This works well because the human ear distinguishes more finely among relatively low amplitudes (1000 to 5000 Hz) than among high (10,000 to 20,000 Hz). Also, when the technique is applied to a voice signal such as a telephone transmission, the reduction in quality resulting from effectively reducing the bit depth isn't objectionable.

Differential pulse code encoding is another way of making an audio file smaller than it would be otherwise—by recording the difference between one sample and the next rather than recording the actual sample value. Variations of DPCM include ADPCM and delta modulation.

A-law encoding, $\mu$-law encoding, delta modulation, and other variations of PCM are time-based methods. That is, there is no need to transform the data into the frequency domain in order to decide where and how to eliminate information. In a sense, these methods aren't really compression at all. Rather, they are ways of reducing the amount of data at the moment an audio signal is digitized, and they are often considered conversion techniques rather than compression methods.

The most effective audio compression methods require some information about the frequency spectrum of the audio signal. These compression methods are based on psychoacoustical modeling and perceptual encoding.

## 5.7.2 Perceptual Encoding

Perceptual encoding is based upon an analysis of how the ear and brain perceive sound, called ***psychoacoustical modeling***. Just as digital image compression takes advantage of visual elements to which the human eye is not very sensitive, perceptual encoding exploits audio elements that the human ear cannot hear very well. In the case of digital images, human eyes are not very good at perceiving high frequency changes in color, so some of this information can be filtered out. The same method would not work with digital audio, however, since filtering out high frequency sound waves would effectively filter out high-pitched sounds that are a meaningful component of an audio signal. Then what *can* be filtered out of digital audio? What kinds of sounds do humans not hear very well, and in what conditions?

Psychoacoustical tests have shown that there is a great deal of nonlinearity in human sound perception. The pitch of frequencies is perceived in a nonlinear fashion, for example. Octaves are separated by frequencies that are multiples of each other, such that the width in Hz of a lower octave is much smaller than the width in Hz of a higher octave. The octave from middle C (called C4) to C5 ranges from 261.63 Hz to 523.25 Hz, while C5 to C6 ranges from 523.25 to 1046.50 Hz. But the distance from C4 to C5 subjectively sounds the same as the distance from C5 to C6.

Humans hear best in the 1000 to 5000 Hz range, the frequency range of human speech. If you have two tones—the first at, say, 100 Hz and the second at 1000 Hz, you have to play the 100 Hz tone louder than the 1000 Hz tone to make them equally loud. The same difference holds true between 1000 Hz and 10,000 Hz tones. Again, you have to play the higher frequency tone louder to make it sound as loud as the 1000 Hz tone, because the 1000 Hz tone is in the range where humans hear the best.

Human ability to distinguish between frequencies decreases nonlinearly from lower to higher frequencies. At low frequencies, we can distinguish between sound waves that are only a few Hz apart. At high frequencies, the frequencies must be a hundred or more Hz apart for us to hear the difference. The reason for this is that the ear is divided into frequency bands called *critical bands*. When a sound wave arrives at the ear, it is perceived by a section—that is, a band—of the inner ear that responds to that wave's particular frequency. Within a small window of time, sound waves with neighboring frequencies—which must be sensed by the ear's same critical band—have an effect on each other in that the loudest frequency sound can overpower the others in the band. This phenomenon is called *masking*. Critical bands are narrower for low- than for high-frequency sounds. Between 1 and 500 Hz, bands are about 100 Hz in width. The critical band at the highest audible frequency is over 4000 Hz wide. Think about the implications of relatively narrow bands at low frequencies: Narrow bands imply that that interference among frequencies occurs over a narrower range, which explains why we have greater frequency resolution at low frequencies.

The phenomenon of critical bands is one of the most important in perceptual encoding, since it gives us a basis for eliminating sound information that is not perceived anyway. The masking phenomenon is pictured in Figure 5.48. Recall from Chapter 1 that the limit below which you can't hear is called the threshold of hearing. Masking causes the threshold of hearing to change in the presence of a dominant frequency component in a band. For example, a 500 Hz frequency component is easy to hear, but when a 400 Hz tone occurs at about the same time and at sufficient amplitude, it can mask the 500 Hz component. Another way to say this is that the threshold of hearing for 500 Hz is higher in the presence of the 400 Hz signal. A frequency that raises the threshold of hearing of another frequency is called a *masking frequency* or *masking tone*. As shown in Figure 5.48, the threshold of hearing for all the frequencies within the critical band of the masking frequency are raised, indicated by the *masking threshold* in the figure. All frequencies that appear at amplitudes beneath the masking threshold will be inaudible. This graph represents the effect of just one masking tone within one critical band at one window in time. These effects happen continuously over time, over all the critical bands. The important point to note is that frequencies that are

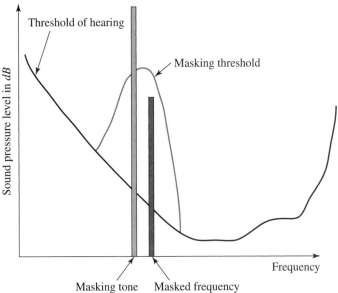

**Figure 5.48** Threshold of hearing and a masking tone

masked out in an audio signal cannot be heard, so they do not need to be stored. Eliminating masked information results in compression.

Here's a sketch of how the masking phenomenon can be applied in compression: A small window of time called a *frame* is moved across a sound file, and the samples in that frame are compressed as one unit. Spectral analysis by means of a *filter bank* divides each frame into bands of frequencies; 32 is often the number of bands used. A masking curve for each band is calculated based upon the relative amplitudes of the frequencies in that band. Analysis of the masking curve reveals the information that can be discarded or compressed. This is done by determining the lowest possible bit depth that can be used for the band such that the resulting quantization noise is under the masking curve. Further refinements can be made to this scheme. For example, temporal masking can be applied, based on the phenomenon of one signal blocking out another that occurs just before or just after it. Following the perceptual filtering step, the remaining information is encoded at the bit depth determined for each band.

In the sections that follow, we will use MPEG compression to illustrate how perceptual encoding is implemented. MPEG coding has been one of the dominant audio compression methods since the 1990s. Other important audio coding schemes exist that we won't examine here. For example, AC3-Dolby audio is a widely used audio codec that is used in DVD video, digital TV, and video playstations. Based on perceptual encoding, AC3-Dolby uses many of the techniques used in MPEG compression.

## 5.7.3 MPEG Audio Compression

### 5.7.3.1 Overview of MPEG

*MPEG*, an acronym for the *Motion Picture Experts Group*, represents a family of compression algorithms for both digital audio and video. In Chapter 7, we'll cover MPEG video compression algorithms. In this section we focus only on the audio portion of MPEG.

Standardized by ISO/IEC, MPEG has been developed in a number of phases since the 1990s: MPEG-1 (1991), MPEG-2 (1994), MPEG-4 (1998), and MPEG-7 (2003). Each is targeted at a different aspect of multimedia communication. *MPEG-1* covers CD quality and audio suitable for video games. *MPEG-2* covers multichannel surround sound. *MPEG-4* covers a wide range of audio including simple voice, MIDI, high-end audiophile sound, and interactive systems. *MPEG-7*, also called Multimedia Content Description, supports searching and filtering of multimedia data. The phases of the MPEG audio standard are also divided into three layers, *Audio Layers I, II, and III*. The compression algorithms increase in sophistication from Layer I to Layer III, requiring more computation for encoding and decoding, but generally with better playback quality in proportion to the bit depth. The naming convention is a little confusing, but just remember that the Arabic numerals indicate phases and the Roman numerals indicate layers within a phase. (Unfortunately, not all sources adhere to this distinction.) Sometimes abbreviations are used. The well-known *MP3* audio file format is actually *MPEG-1 Audio Layer III*.

*AAC compression*, which stands for *Advanced Audio Coding*, is not standardized as a layer, but it is available in both MPEG-2 and MPEG-4. AAC has been implemented in proprietary form as AT&T's a2b music and as Liquid Audio. It supports a wide range of sampling rates and number of channels with excellent quality at relatively low bit rates.

You may find yourself confused by the various bit rates that you'll see cited for different implementations of MPEG audio. The bit rate tells you how much data there is per second of

> **ASIDE:** The term *version* is sometimes used to distinguish MPEG-1, 2, 4, and 7, but this isn't the most appropriate term. Versions are generally implementations that are developed over time, each with improvements and additions over the previous. MPEG phases have different purposes, targeted at different systems and types of multimedia.

compressed audio. Think about what might cause this number to be relatively larger. If you start with a higher sampling rate and bit depth, you're going to get a higher bit rate. For example, a sampling rate of 48 kHz results in a higher bit rate than a sampling rate of 44.1 kHz. Also, more stereo channels yield a higher bit rate. Finally, a compression algorithm that is less lossy gives a higher bit rate. A range of bit rates is associated with each MPEG audio layer because the layer's compression method can be applied to audio files of different sampling rates, either mono or stereo. In Table 5.4, for example, the lowest bit rate cited for MPEG-1 results from compressing 32 kHz mono signals. The highest bit rate in MPEG-1 Layer I (448 kb/s) corresponds to compressing a 48 kHz stereo file. The fact that the maximum bit rate in a layer gets smaller from Layer I to Layer III is a result of the greater complexity of the Layer III compression algorithm compared to the Layer I algorithm—that is, the Layer III can compress more without loss of quality, but it takes more time to do so.

**TABLE 5.4  Phases and Layers of MPEG Audio Compression**

| Version | Data Rates | Applications | Channels | Sampling Rates Supported |
|---|---|---|---|---|
| **MPEG-1** | | CD, DAT, ISDN, video games, digital audio broadcasting, music shared on the web, portable music players | mono or stereo | 32, 44.1, and 48 kHz |
| Layer I | 32–448 kb/s | | | |
| Layer II | 32–384 kb/s | | | |
| Layer III | 32–320 kb/s | | | |
| **MPEG-2 LSF (Low Sampling Frequency)** | | audio files with low sampling frequency | mono or stereo | 16, 22.05, and 24 kHz |
| Layer I | 32–256 kb/s | | | |
| Layer II | 8–160 kb/s | | | |
| Layer III | 8–160 kb/s | | | |
| **MPEG-2 Multichannel** | | multichannels, multilingual extensions | 5.1 surround | 32, 44.1, and 48 kHz |
| Layer I | max 448 kb/s | | | |
| Layer II | max 384 kb/s | | | |
| Layer III | max 32 kb/s | | | |
| **AAC in MPEG-2 and MPEG-4** (Advanced Audio Coding) | 8–384 kb/s | multichannels, music shared on the web, portable music players, cell phones | up to 48 channels | 32, 44.1, and 48 kHz and other rates between 8 and 96 kHz |

The amount of time needed for encoding and decoding has the greatest impact on real-time audio, such as for two-way voice conversations. In general, a delay of more than 10 milliseconds can be disturbing in a voice conversation. MPEG audio encoding delays are on the order of between 15 milliseconds for Layer I and 60 milliseconds for Layer III, dependent on the hardware and the software implementation.

The compression rates that you may see cited for different layers of MPEG give you the general picture that higher layers yield better compression. For example, MPEG-1 Layer 1 is cited as having a compression rate of about 4 : 1, Layer 2 as about 7 : 1, and Layer III as about 11 : 1. However, as with bit rates, compression rates don't mean much unless you consider what type of audio is being compressed. To get a sense of the compression rate, consider that uncompressed CD-quality stereo requires 32 bits per sample * 44,100 samples/s = 1.4112 Mb/s. Compressing CD-quality stereo to 128 kb/s using MP3 encoding yields a

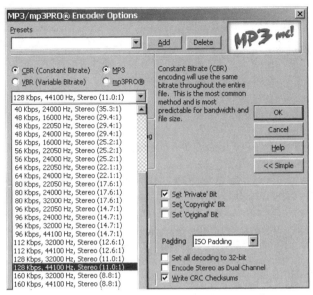

**Figure 5.49** MP3 compression bit rate options

compression rate of $11:1$. But MP3 can also be compressed at 192 kb/s, which is a rate of about $7:1$. You can see that to generate specific compression rates, you need to compare the initial bit rate with the final bit rate. To some extent, the final bit rate is your own choice. When you compress an audio file with an MPEG compressor, you get a list of bit rate options, as shown in Figure 5.49. The lower the bit rate, the more compression you get, but at the sacrifice of some sound fidelity. Notice that you can also choose between *constant bit rate* (***CBR***) and *variable bit rate* (***VBR***). CBR uses the same number of bits per second regardless of how complex the signal is. VBR uses fewer bits for passages with a smaller dynamic range, resulting overall in a smaller file.

The MPEG audio layer and bit rate that is best for a given application depends on the nature of the audio files being compressed and how high a bit rate the user can tolerate. For example, MPEG-1 Layer 2 (sometimes referred to as MP2) gives better quality sound than MP3 if you don't mind relatively higher bit rates, and it requires lower encoding delays. For these reasons, it is widely used for digital radio. MP3 compresses well and has been extremely popular for music files that are shared through the web. The usual MP3 bit rate of 128 or 192 kb/s creates reasonable-size files that don't take too much time to download and that have good quality for playback.

MPEG layers are backward compatible so that, for example, a Layer III decoder can decode a Layer I stream. MPEG-2 decoders are backward compatible with MPEG-1. Proprietary implementations of MPEG such as AT&T's a2b and Liquid Audio are not mutually compatible.

### 5.7.3.2 MPEG-1 Audio Compression

We focus on MPEG-1 compression because it illustrates perceptual encoding concepts well, and it can be explained understandably in a fairly short space. MPEG-2 and AAC use many of the same techniques as those described in this section, but with additional refinements to further improve the audio quality and handle other special applications.

None of the MPEG phases prescribe an encoding algorithm. Instead, they offer psychoacoustical models of audio compression. The MPEG-1, for example, proposes two psychoacoustical models, one more complex and offering higher compression than the other. What

## ALGORITHM 5.2

```
algorithm MPEG-1_audio
/*Input: An audio file in the time domain
  Output: The same audio file, compressed*/
{
   Divide the audio file into frames
   For each frame {
      By applying a bank of filters, separate the signal into frequency bands.
      For each frequency band {
         Perform a Fourier transform to analyze the band's frequency spectrum
         Analyze the influence of tonal and nontonal elements (i.e., transients)
         Analyze how much the frequency band is influenced by neighboring bands
         Find the masking threshold and signal-to-mask ratio (SMR) for the band,
         and determine the bit depth in the band accordingly
         Quantize the samples from the band using the determined bit depth
         Apply Huffman encoding (optional)
      }
      Create a frame with a header and encoded samples from all bands
   }
}
```

*is* dictated by the standard is how the bit stream must look to the decoder. Implementers can create whatever ingenious algorithms they can imagine, as long as the compressed bit stream is in the format the decoder expects. The advantage to this is that algorithms can be refined and improved, and existing decoders will still work on the new implementations.

Algorithm 5.2 and Figure 5.50 show the basic steps common to most implementations of MPEG-1 compression, which is sufficient to give the flavor of MPEG compression in general. First, try to get an overview of the method, and then you can focus on some of the motivations and details of each step.

**1. Divide the audio file into frames and analyze the psychoacoustical properties of each frame individually.**

**Motivation:** Each frame covers a sequence of samples in a small window of time. To analyze how one frequency component might mask neighboring ones, it's necessary to look at samples that are close to each other in time. The masking phenomenon happens only when different frequencies are played at close to the same time.

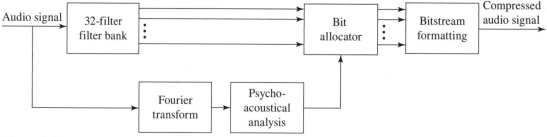

**Figure 5.50** MPEG audio compression

**Details:** Frames can contain 384, 576, or 1152 samples, depending on the MPEG phase and layer. It may seem odd that these numbers are not powers of two. However, when frequency analysis is done on these samples, a larger window is placed around the sample, and the window *is* a power of two.

For the remainder of these steps, it is assumed that we're operating on an individual frame.

### 2. By applying a bank of filters, separate the signal into frequency bands.

**Motivation:** The samples are divided into frequency bands because the psychoacoustical properties of each band will be analyzed separately. Each filter removes all frequencies except for those in its designated band. Once the psychoacoustical properties of a band are analyzed, the appropriate number of bits to represent samples in that band can be determined.

**Details:** The use of filter banks is called *subband coding*. Say that there are $n$ filters in the filter bank. $n$ copies of the signal are generated, and a copy is sent through each of the filters. (In MPEG-1, for example, $n = 32$.) Time-domain bandpass filters are applied such that each filter lets only a range of frequencies pass through. Note that the $n$ frequency bands are still represented in the time domain—that is, they contain samples of audio consecutive points in time. Also, the amount of data does *not* increase as a result of dividing the frame into bands. If, for example, 384 samples entered the 32 filters, each filter produces 12 samples. There is no increase in data.

The previous section on FIR and IIR filters shows that bandpass filters are never ideal in that you cannot perfectly isolate the band of filters you want. The frequency response graph is never a perfect rectangle like the one pictured in Figure 5.42, with a sharply vertical cutoff between the desired frequencies and the filtered-out frequencies. Instead, the cutoff between the frequencies is a sloped line, called an *attenuation slope*. For this reason, the frequency bands overlap a little. If this overlap is not accounted for, then there will be aliasing when the signal is reconstructed. *Quadrature mirror filtering* (*QMF*) is a technique that eliminates the aliasing. It does so by making the attenuation slope of one band a mirror image of the attenuation slope of the previous band so that the aliased frequencies cancel out when the signal is reconstructed. This is pictured in Figure 5.51.

In MPEG-1 Layers I and II, the frequency bands created by the filter banks are uniform in size. This means that their width doesn't match the width of the critical bands in

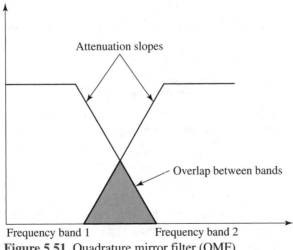

Figure 5.51  Quadrature mirror filter (QMF)

human hearing, which are wider at high frequencies. However, the way in which the frequency components of a band are analyzed can compensate somewhat for this disparity. In MP3 encoding, the ***modified discrete cosine transform*** (***MDCT***) is used to improve frequency resolution, particularly at low-frequency bands, thus modeling the human ear's critical bands more closely. Also, MP3 uses nonlinear quantization, where (like in $\mu$-law encoding) the quantization intervals are larger for high amplitude samples.

**3. Perform a Fourier transform on the samples in each band in order to analyze the band's frequency spectrum.**

**Motivation:** The filters have already limited each band to a certain range of frequencies, but it's important to know exactly how much of each frequency component occurs in each band. This is the purpose of applying a Fourier transform. From the frequency spectrum, a masking curve can be produced for each band. Then the number of bits with which to encode each band can be chosen in a way that pays attention to the elevated noise floor produced from masking.

**Details:** Another copy of each frame, called a ***sidechain***, is created so that the Fourier transform can be applied. A 512 or 1024-sample window is used. You may notice that this is not the same size as the number of samples in a frame. In fact, the Fourier transform is done on a window that surrounds the frame samples. For example, if a frame has 384 samples, 1024 samples that encompass this window are used for the Fourier transform. If the frame has 1152 samples, two 1024-sample Fourier transforms are done, covering two halves of the frame.

**4. Analyze the influence of tonal and nontonal elements in each band. (Tonal elements are simple sinusoidal components, such as frequencies related to melodic and harmonic music. Nontonal elements are transients like the strike of a drum or the clapping of hands.)**

**Motivation:** It would not be good to allow masking to eliminate nontonal elements that punctuate an audio signal in meaningful ways. Also, if nontonal elements are not compressed properly, ringing or pre-echo effects can result.

**Details:** The longer the time window is in frequency analysis, the better the frequency resolution, but the worse the time resolution. The effect of poor time resolution is that sound elements that occur very close to one another in time might not be distinguished sufficiently, one from the other. This in turn can mean that transient signals are not properly identified. Layers II and III have a longer time window than Layer I, so they have better time resolution.

**5. Determine how much each band's influence is likely to spread to neighboring frequency bands.**

**Motivation:** It isn't sufficient to deal with bands entirely in isolation from each other, since there can be a masking effect between bands.

**Details:** Empirically determined spreading functions can be applied.

**6. Find the masking threshold and *signal-to-mask ratio* (*SMR*) for each band, and determine the bit depth of each band accordingly.**

**Motivation:** Within each band, a high amplitude frequency component can mask other frequency components. The precision with which samples need to be represented depends on the ratio of the loudest sample among them to the amplitude below which they can't be heard, even if they are present. This is in fact the definition of SMR: the ratio between the peak sound pressure level and the masking threshold is the SMR (Figure 5.52). This ratio determines how many bits are needed to represent samples within a band.

**Details:** The main idea you should get from this is that the masking phenomenon causes the noise floor within a band to be raised. The number of bits per sample varies from band

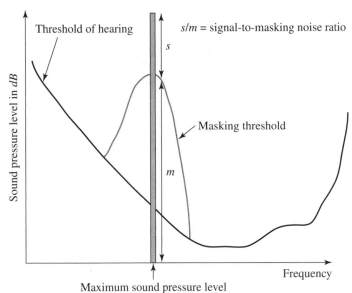

**Figure 5.52** Signal-to-masking noise ratio

to band depending on how high the noise floor is. When the noise floor is high relative to the maximum sound pressure level within a band, then fewer bits are needed. Fewer bits create more quantization noise, but it doesn't matter if that quantization noise is below the masking threshold. The noise won't be heard anyway.

MP3 has interesting variation in its design, allowing for a *bit reservoir*. In a constant bit rate (CBR) encoding, all frames have the same number of bits at their disposal, but not all frames need all the bits allocated to them. A bit reservoir scheme makes it possible to take unneeded bits from a frame with a low SMR and use them in a frame with a high SMR. This doesn't increase the compression rate (since we're assuming CBR), but it does improve the quality of the compressed audio.

**7. Quantize the samples for the band with the appropriate number of bits, possibly following this with Huffman encoding.**

**Motivation:** Some bit patterns occur more frequently than others. Huffman encoding allows the frequently occurring bit patterns to be encoded with fewer bits than patterns that occur infrequently.

**Details:** MPEG-1 Layers 1 and 2 use linear quantization, while MP3 uses nonlinear.

After quantization, the values can be scaled so that the full dynamic range offered by the bit depth is used. The scale factor then has to be stored in the frame.

In MP3 encoding, the frame data is reordered after quantization and divided into regions so that Huffman tables can be applied. These empirically generated tables reflect the probabilities of certain bit patterns in each region.

A refinement in the above algorithm is related to the compression of stereo information. There are a number of different ways to compress stereo. The *joint stereo* compression method allows one stereo channel to carry the information that is identical in both channels, while the other channel carries the differences. This is a lossless method that gives fairly good compression. The *intensity stereo* compression method replaces a left and right signal with one signal plus a vector representing directional information. This yields the highest stereo compression rate, but obviously it is a lossy method. *Mid/side stereo coding*

| Header<br><br>(Sync word, phase and layer #s, bit rate, sampling frequency, etc.) | CRC (Layers i and ii) | Bit allocation by band | Scale factor by band | Sample values | Extra info<br><br>(Artist, album, year, etc.) |
|---|---|---|---|---|---|
| | | | | | |

**Figure 5.53** MPEG bit stream

calculates a middle channel as (left + right)/2 and side channel as (left − right)/2, which then is encoded with fewer bits than straightforward stereo representation. Mid/side stereo coding has a less detrimental effect on phase information than intensity stereo does.

The MPEG standard defines how a compressed bit stream must look. The compressed signal is divided into frames. A sketch of an MPEG frame is shown in Figure 5.53. Each frame begins with a sync word to signal that this is the beginning of a new frame. The header then tells the bit rate, sampling frequency, mono or stereo mode, and so forth. CRC stands for *cyclic redundancy check*, which is an error-checking algorithm to ensure that no errors have been inserted in transmission. Following the CRC, the number of bits used in each band is listed. Then the scale factor for each band is given. The largest part of the frame is devoted to the samples. Extra information may be added to a frame in the form of ID3 tags. ID3 is an informal standard for giving information about music files being compressed, including copyright, artist, title, album name, lyrics, year, and web links.

### 5.7.3.3 MPEG-2, AAC, and MPEG-4

The MPEG-2 audio standard is complicated by the fact that it is divided into three formats: *MPEG-2 Multichannel*, *MPEG-2 LSF* (*low sampling frequency*), and *MPEG-2 AAC* (Advanced Audio Coding). The first two of these are further subdivided into Layers, as shown in Table 5.4.

MPEG-2 Multichannel, as the name indicates, has features to accommodate more than one channel—up to *5.1 stereo surround sound*. This type of surround sound allows music to be played through three front speakers, two back speakers, and one subwoofer for bass tones. MPEG-2 Multichannel is backward compatible with MPEG-1 so that an audio file compressed with an MPEG-1 encoder can be played by an MPEG-2 decoder.

MPEG-2 LSF allows sampling rates of 16, 22.05, and 24 kHz. It is sometimes called MPEG-2.5. This format offers better frequency resolution, and hence better quality in the compressed file, if lower sampling rates can be used.

A third format—MPEG-2 AAC—was designed to take advantage of newly developed psychoacoustical models and corresponding compression techniques. Applying these techniques, however, meant that the AAC could not be backward compatible with MPEG-1. Thus, AAC was originally referred to as MPEG-2 NBC (not backward compatible), while MPEG-2 Multichannel was called MPEG-2 BC.

AAC handles multiple channels up to 5.1 surround sound, compressing down to a bit rate of 64 kb/s per channel, which yields 384 kb/s total. AAC achieves this bit rate with even better quality than MPEG-2 Multichannel. Listening tests show, for example, that a music file compressed as MPEG-2 AAC at, say 96 kb/s sounds better than the same one compressed as MP3 at 128 kb/s. Because of its good quality, AAC has gained popularity for use in portable music players and cell phones, two of the biggest markets for compressed audio files.

The AAC psychoacoustical model is too complicated to describe in detail in a short space. The main features include the following:

- The modified discrete cosine transform improves frequency resolution as the signal is divided into frequency bands.
- Temporal noise shaping (TNS) helps in handling transients, moving the distortion associated with their compression to a point in time that doesn't cause a pre-echo.
- Predictive coding improves compression by storing the difference between a predicted next value and the actual value. (Since the decoder uses the same prediction algorithm, it is able to recapture the actual value from the difference value stored.)
- Not all scale factors need to be stored since consecutive ones are often the same. AAC uses a more condensed method for storing scale factors.
- A combination of intensity coding and mid/side stereo coding is used to compress information from multiple channels.
- A model for low-delay encoding provides good perceptual encoding properties with the small coding delay necessary for two-way voice communication.

The AAC compression model is a central feature of both MPEG-2 and MPEG-4 audio. MPEG-4, however, is a broad standard that also encompasses DVD video, streaming media, MIDI, multimedia objects, text-to-speech conversion, score-driven sound synthesis, and interactivity.

We refer you to the sources at the end of this chapter and Chapter 4 if you're interested in more implementation details of AAC, MPEG-4, and the other compression models.

## EXERCISES AND PROGRAMS

1. Say that the first 30 values of a digital audio file, $x(n)$, are those given below, and you apply the nine-tap FIR filter, $h(n)$, below. What is the value of the 10th digital sample after filtering?

   $x(n) = [138, 232, 253, 194, 73, -70, -191, -252, -233, -141, -4, 135, 230, 253, 196, 77, -66, -189, -251, -235, -144, -7, 131, 229, 253, 198, 80, -63, -186, -251]$

   $h(n) = [0.0788, 0.1017, 0.1201, 0.1319, 0.1361, 0.1319, 0.1201, 0.1017, 0.0788]$

2. Say that you have an IIR filter $y(n) = \sum_{k=0}^{N-1} a_k x(n-k) - \sum_{k=1}^{M} b_k y(n-k)$ where $a = [0.389, -1.558, 2.338, -1.558, 0.389]$ and $b = [2.161, -2.033, 0.878, -0.161]$. Note that vector $a$ is numbered starting at index 0 and vector $b$ is numbered starting at index 1.

   To find $h(n)$ for this filter so that you can define it with

   $$y(n) = h(n) \otimes x(n) = \sum_{k=0}^{\infty} h(k)x(n-k),$$

   you can evaluate a unit impulse run through the function $y(n) = \sum_{k=0}^{N-1} a_k x(n-k) - \sum_{k=1}^{M} b_k y(n-k)$. Do this to get $h(n)$. You'll have to give it a finite length. Try 32 taps. You might want to write a program to do the computation for you. Graph the impulse response that you get.

3. Say that you have a graphic equalizer that allows you to divide the frequency spectrum into 30 bands, each separated by a third of an octave. If the first band is at 31 Hz, where are the remaining 29 bands, in Hz?

4. For a peaking filter, assume that you want the center frequency of the curve defining the peak to be at 8000 Hz, and you want the bandwidth of the peak to be 1000 Hz.
   a. What is the Q-factor?
   b. What is the corresponding bandwidth of this filter, in octaves?
   c. What is the Q-factor of a peaking filter with a central frequency of 2000 Hz and a bandwidth of 1000 Hz?
   d. What is the corresponding bandwidth of the filter, in octaves?
   e. What is Q if you want the peaking filter to span one octave?

5. The step response of a continuous filter is the integral of the filter—the area under the curve that graphs the filter. Thus, the step response of a discrete filter would be the sum of the discrete points that define the filter. Create the impulse response of a low-pass filter, or find some values in another source. (See the online worksheets for how to create an FIR filter.) Then determine the corresponding step response and graph it. Describe what the step response tells you about the filter, with regard to the steepness of the step.

6. Dynamics processing, interactive tutorial and worksheet, online

7. Windowing method for FIR filter design, mathematical modeling worksheet, online

8. Z-transforms, zero-pole diagrams, and filters, interactive and worksheet online

9. Creating FIR and IIR filters with MATLAB.

10. Creating a filter via a transfer function, mathematical modeling worksheet, online

## APPLICATIONS

1. Examine the specifications of your sound card (or the one you would like to have). What kind of input and output ports does it have? What is its signal-to-noise ratio? Does it handle MIDI? If so, how?

2. Examine the specifications of your microphone (or the one you would like to have). Is a dynamic mic, a condenser mic, or some other kind? Does your microphone require power? What frequencies does it handle best? Do you need different mics for different purposes?

3. If you have access to more than two microphones with significantly different characteristics, try making similar recordings with both of them. Listen to the recordings to see if you can hear the difference. Then look at the frequency spectrum of the recordings and analyze them. Are the results what you expect, based on the specifications of the mics?

4. Create a one-minute radio commercial for a hypothetical product, mixing voices, music, and sound effects. Record the commercial at your digital audio workstation using multitrack editing software. Record and edit the different instruments, voices, and so forth on different tracks. Experiment with filters, dynamics processing, and special effects. When you've finished, mix down the tracks, and save and compress the audio in an appropriate file type. Document and justify your steps and choices of sampling rate, bit depth, editing tools, compression, and final file type.

5. If you don't know already, find out what loops are. Find a source of free online loops. Create background music for a hypothetical computer game by combining and editing loops. (At the time of this writing, Acid Loops is an excellent commercial program for working with loops. Royalty Free Music is a source for free loops.) If you create a computer game when you get to Chapter 8, you can use your music in that game.

6. See if you can replicate the impulse response method of creating a convolution filter for reverb that makes an audio file sound like it was recorded in a certain acoustical space. (If you do a web search, you should be able to find descriptions of the details of this method. Look under "convolution reverb." For example, at the writing of this chapter, a paper entitled "Implementation of Impulse Response Measurement Techniques" by J. Shaeffer and E. Elyashiv could be found at www.acoustics.net/objects/pdf/IR-paper.pdf.) **Examine the features of your digital audio processing program or programs and try the exercises below with features that are available.**

7. What file types are supported by your audio editing software? What compressions methods?

8. Make a simple audio file and intentionally put a click or pop in it. See if you can remove the click or pop with your audio editing program.

9. Examine the tools for dynamics processing offered in your audio editing program. Try compressing the dynamic range of an audio file. Then try expansion. Experiment with different attack and release times and listen to the differences.

10. Examine the types of filters offered in your audio editing program. See if your software has a graphic equalizer, parametric EQ, paragraphic EQ, notch filters, and/or convolution. Can you tell if they are implemented with FIR or IIR filters? What parameters do you have to set to use these filters?

11. Examine the types of reverb, echo, and delay effects available in your audio editing program and experiment with the effects.

*Additional exercises or applications may be found at the book or author's websites.*

## REFERENCES

### Print Publications

Coulter, Doug. *Digital Audio Processing*. Lawrence, KS: R & D Books, 2000.

Embree, Paul M., and Damon Danieli. *C++ Algorithms for Digital Signal Procssing.* 2nd ed. Upper Saddle River, NJ: Prentice Hall, 1999.

Noll, Peter. Sept. 1997. "MPEG Digital Audio Coding." *IEEE Signal Processing Magazine*, 14 (5): 59–81.

Pan, Davis. 1995. "A Tutorial on MPEG/Audio Compression." *IEEE Multimedia* 2 (2): 60–74.

Phillips, Dave. *The Book of Linux Music & Sound.* San Francisco: No Starch Press/Linux Journal Press, 2000.

Smith, Steven W. *The Scientist and Engineer's Guide to Digital Signal Processing.* San Diego: California Technical Publishing, 1997.

Weeks, Michael. *Digital Signal Processing Using MATLAB and Wavelets.* Hingham, MA: Infinity Science Press LLC, 2007.

*See Chapter 4 for additional references on digital audio.*

### Websites

aRts-project.
   http://www.arts-projects.org.

Audacity.
   http://jackit.sourceforge.net.

# Digital Video Data Representation and Communication

CHAPTER

**6**

# CHAPTER

# 6

*Wisdom and Spirit of the universe! Thou soul, that art the eternity of thought, And giv'st to forms and images a breath And everlasting motion.* —William Wordsworth, "Influence of Natural Objects," 1799

## OBJECTIVES FOR CHAPTER 6
- Be familiar with the standard formats for analog and digital video.
- Understand the difference between the ways that analog and digital video are represented and communicated.
- Understand the main properties of analog and digital video such as frame rate, image aspect ratio, pixel aspect ratio, color model, sampling method, color signal transmission, resolution, and bandwidth.
- Understand how the bandwidth of an input signal is related to frame rate and resolution, in both analog and digital video.
- Understand the fundamental concepts of carrier signal modulation and how this relates to the bandwidth of frequency channels.
- Understand how streaming video data are represented and transmitted.
- Know the differences among standard television, digital television, and high definition television.

# 6.1 FILM, TELEVISION, MOVIES, AND VIDEO: WHAT'S IN A NAME?

## 6.1.1 The Context

Video is fascinating, and it is complicated. It's fascinating because it can capture reality on the one hand, and create complex fantasies on the other. It's fascinating because it's easy, even for the novice, to "do video," yet it's hard to do it well. It's fascinating because it includes images and sound, interweaving the science of both media. It's fascinating because it arises out of film and television, media that permeate our popular culture.

Video is complicated for the same reasons. To understand the science of digital video, you need to understand sampling and resolution, mathematical filters and transforms, color models, and compression—topics covered in the first five chapters of this book. You have to keep straight the differences between analog and digital, film and video, and standard definition and high definition television. To some extent, you have to make your way through a tangle of standards that have evolved through analog television and film, on through digital video, and then to HDTV.

This chapter includes information about analog video, television technology, and film—areas that are not strictly digital video, but that are such close relatives that it would be an oversight not to talk about them. Analog video is included because when you understand how data is communicated in an analog manner, it gives you a point of comparison in understanding digital data communication. Also, the standards for digital video—for example, the number of lines in a frame and the rate at which frames are displayed—evolved from the standards for analog video, so having some background in analog video helps you make sense of the numbers. The concept of *bandwidth* is crucial in video technology. Video implies "lots of information." How do you know just how much is needed? It's interesting to see how this is worked out in both the analog and digital domain. It's also economically compelling because there's only so much bandwidth—in the airwaves or within computer networks—and those in the telecommunications industries care very much about who gets what, and how their individual bandwidth allotments are divided up into different programming. Television and film are included in this chapter because they are so much a part of our popular culture and daily lives. Digital technology is all around you, and it should be satisfying for you to know something about the specifications for television screen sizes, resolution, and the like. Just what is a 1080i DLP television, anyway? Finally, you will probably be interested in learning just how much digital video is used in today's television and film production. Is film really film anymore, or is it shot digitally? Are television programs shot on film or on videotape? Is there any way to tell the difference, just by looking at the final product? We'll try to answer some of these questions in this chapter.

> **ASIDE:** Although we prefer the term *pixel dimension* when referring to the width and height of a video frame, the term *resolution* is more common, so we adopt this term when speaking of video.

This chapter will give you an idea of what you might be able to do with knowledge of digital video. If digital video is your passion, you have a growing array of areas to apply your skills and creativity, including advertising, websites, video games, music videos, theme park rides, television, documentaries, and commercial feature-length movies. All of these areas now use *digital* video, which has become the most time- and money-efficient medium for moving pictures. In any of these areas, you could work in a collaborative environment of hundreds of coworkers using millions of dollars worth of technical equipment, or you could work just with your own video camera and computer workstation.

The historical overview in Table 6.1 will show you how we have gotten to this exciting point.

| TABLE 6.1 | History of Film, Television and Digital Video | | | | | |
|---|---|---|---|---|---|---|
| **1830–1890** | **1884** | **1890s** | **1895** | **Late 1800s** | **Early 1900s** | **1927** |
| Mechanical precursors to film projectors and cameras are invented, including the Fantascope, zoetrope, and chronophotographic camera | Eastman invents photographic film | Edison develops and patents the motion picture camera | Lumière brothers invent a combination movie camera and projector | Mechanical models for television are developed, based on Nipkow's rotating disks | CRT is developed for television display | The first feature-length talkie including dialog—*The Jazz Singer*—makes its debut |
| **1920s** | **1932** | **1939** | **1941** | **1940s** | **1952** | **1953** |
| Baird builds first mechanical television; Farnsworth develops a complete electronic television system | With backing of RCA executive Zarnoff, Zworykin invents a television system with 343 lines, 60 cycles per second, and 30 interlaced fields | New York World's Fair is televised with system invented by Zworykin | FCC issues the NTSC standards for black and white television | Coaxial cable is developed for transmission of TV signals; cable TV is introduced for those in areas receiving poor airwave signals | 70 cable systems serve 14,000 subscribers in U.S. | NTSC adopts RCA's color system for TV broadcast |

(continued)

| TABLE 6.1 | *Continued* | | | | | |
|---|---|---|---|---|---|---|
| **1950s** | **1962** | **1972** | **1975** | **1970s** | **1981** | **1970s and 80s** |
| First color television programs are broadcast; Ampex develops a videotape system to replace kinescope | First transatlantic television signal is sent via TELSTAR | Philips introduces video cassette recorders (VCRs) for the home | RCA launches first satellite that is exclusively for use of major TV networks | Cable TV takes advantage of satellite transmission, launching HBO and CNN | NHK (Japanese broadcasting company) introduces HDTV with 1125 lines of resolution | Betamax and VHS format vie for market dominance in VCRs, VHS eventually winning |
| **1980s** | **1987** | **1980s and 90s** | **1990s** | **1990s** | **1993** | **1994** |
| Nearly 53 million households subscribe to cable | Hornbeck invents DLP projection at Texas Instruments | Satellite broadcasts become available for home TV; 18-inch digital satellite dishes are introduced | Cable providers upgrade their networks to broadband, using fiber optics; cable now offers high-speed internet access, digital cable, and HDTV | MPEG-2 becomes the compression standard for digital video broadcasts; high compression allows cable to transmit more channels and facilitates interactive TV | Grand Alliance is formed to develop HDTV equipment and standards | RCA's DirectTV becomes North America's first high-power direct broadcast satellite (DBS) for consumer TV |
| **1996** | **1997** | **2000** | **Early 2000s** | **Early 2000s** | **2006** | **2008** |
| FCC approves ATSC standards for HDTV and makes plan for transition within television industry | Mini-DV digital video cameras are introduced and become popular for home use; FCC mandates that by 2006, all TV broadcasts must be fully digital (later moved to 2009) | DVDs introduced as storage medium for digital video | Cable providers offer a growing array of pay-per-view and continue to develop interactive TV | Flat screen TVs become popular, including plasma and LCD televisions for the home; DLP projection is popularized | 25 or 50 GB Blu-Ray disks become popular; competition continues between Blu-Ray and HD-DVD, Blu-Ray eventually taking the lead | Toshiba announces discontinuance of HD-DVD, thus ending the HD war |
| **2000s** | **2000s** | **2000s** | **2000s** | **2000s** | **2000s** | |
| convergence of media in telecommunications industry; MIDs (mobile internet devices) and SmartPhones include email, web browsing, digital cameras, and music and video players | internet video popularized by youtube.com | time/place shifting devices DVR, Slingbox, and Tivo are popularized | VoD (video on demand) gains ground when iTunes enters the movie rental market | Stereo/3D technology advances | Satellite and possibly cable start to move to MPEG4 rather than MPEG2 | |

## 6.1.2 Video, Film, and Television Compared

So what should we call this moving picture phenomenon? *Movie* is a good generic term: a story told with moving images and sound. The word *motion picture* has more grandiose connotations than the plain-clothes term movie, but essentially they're the same thing. The word *film*, on the other hand, might seem more high-brow, maybe more arty. It also seems to imply a movie that is shot and/or stored on cellulose film. But is there any digital video processing involved in films? In fact, there generally is. Movie-making is now a hybrid process that can involve a combination of film and digital video. A feature film is often shot on film, transferred to digital video for ease-of-editing, and then transferred back to film for distribution. Many TV series are shot on film because it creates the rich and sometimes grainy appearance that viewers like, even if they aren't conscious of what attracts them to the look. (The *24* series is an example.) The worlds of film, television, and digital video have converged, introducing new creative fields referred to variously as electronic cinema, digital filmmaking, and digital cinema. We'll take a closer look at these fields at the end of the chapter.

Let's begin by comparing film and video. Film and video both rest on the same phenomenon of human perception, called *persistence of vision*—the tendency of human vision to continue to "see" something for a short time after it is gone. A related physiological phenomenon is *flicker fusion*—the human visual system's ability to fuse successive images into one fluid moving image. Because of these phenomena, if your eyes are presented with a quick succession of still images—assuming these images represent incrementally moving objects—you'll perceive these images as a moving picture. You can observe this phenomenon yourself by drawing a simple sequence of stick figures, where in each successive picture the arms or legs of the stick figure are moved just a little. When you put your pictures in order and flip through them with your thumb, you have a moving picture. This is precisely how film and television create moving pictures—by a fast sequence of images, called frames.

The speed at which images are shown is the *frame rate*. Subjective experiments have shown that a frame rate of about 40 frames per second is needed in order for successive images to be perceived as smooth motion with no flicker. The frame rate adopted for film is 24 frames per second, which seems like it would be insufficient. However, film projectors have a shutter that opens and closes, causing each frame to be displayed twice. Oddly enough, this actually prevents the viewer from perceiving a flicker, since 48 images are displayed in one second.

The word film comes from the physical medium on which frames are recorded—celluloid or cellulose tape. Film stock is characterized by its width, usually measured in millimeters. The space on the film is shared by the frame, the sprocket holes, and possibly a soundtrack. Sprocket holes—also called *perforations*—are holes on the sides of the film used to pull the film through the projector. Depending on the type of film being used, there may be a soundtrack and timecodes for synchronizing the soundtrack printed along the edge of the tape.

A section of 35 millimeter (abbreviated mm) film is pictured in Figure 6.1. It's called *4-perf* because it has four perforations per frame. The perforations, frame, and sound codes can be arranged in different ways on the film stock, balancing the frame size and the space needed for multiple soundtracks, timecodes, and keycode. Sound isn't printed on the original film negative. It is recorded separately and added to a later print.

When the film is projected, each frame is projected all at once. Light shines through the frame and a lens enlarges the frame as it is projected onto a big screen. Film inherently has such high resolution that it can be blown up quite a lot and still look very clear and focused. Film doesn't have a specific resolution in the same sense that digital video does. A film

**Figure 6.1** 4-perf 35 mm film

frame is a continuous image. The picture is right there in the frame, represented by microscopic grains of dye or silver. It isn't encoded digitally, in discrete units called pixels. The resolution of a certain kind of film stock, like 35 mm, is measured by how much detail the viewer can discern—for example, how many neighboring lines of alternating color. This is a complex combination of the physical nature of the film stock and the graininess it gives to the picture, the nature of the lens projecting the film, the viewing conditions, and so forth. Resolution takes on new importance when film is transferred to digital video. Film-to-video scanners are used to encode film frames digitally. These scanners have resolution settings. The question is, how many pixels should be gathered in the horizontal and vertical directions for each film frame? There must be a point of diminishing returns, a maximum resolution, beyond which you don't get a clearer image as it is viewed by human eyes. Film scanners record thousands of pixels per inch, often with 12-bit color (*i.e.*, 12 bits for each of the color channels rather than eight). You can imagine that this creates a huge amount of data, but compression of the digital data makes the process manageable. It is common practice now to digitize film. This can be done as a way of preserving old films. Film stock, as a physical medium, deteriorates over time. Digital media—in electronic form—is more robust. Digitizing film to create an intermediate, more easily edited form, has also become common in the film industry. We'll talk more about this process later in the chapter.

Silent movies and early sound movies were shot mostly on 16 mm film, introduced by Eastman Kodak in 1923. Silent movies were shot on 16 mm film with an aspect ratio of 1.33 : 1. **Aspect ratio** is the ratio of the width to the height of a frame, expressed as *width : height*. The 1.33 : 1 aspect ratio is called the **Academy aspect ratio** or **Academy aperture**, named for the Academy of Motion Picture Arts and Science (Figure 6.2). Sound movies of the 1930s to early 1950s were shot on 35 mm film with an aspect ratio of 1.37 : 1, called **Academy full screen**. The comparable standard in Europe was 1.66 : 1.

Academy aspect ratio 1.33:1            Widescreen, 1.85:1                    Anamorphic widescreen, 2.39:1

**Figure 6.2** Standard film aspect ratios

When television came along and starting competing for audience attention, the film industry moved toward the **widescreen** aspect ratios of 1.85 : 1 as a way of heightening the totally immersive experience of watching a movie in the theater. A number of methods can be used to achieve the wider aspect ratio. The simplest method is simply to crop some of the top and bottom off a frame, but this compromises the image composition. As an alternative, Paramount pictures created VistaVision in the 1950s, which achieved the wider aspect ratio by rotating the frame by 90 degrees on the film stock, in effect running the frames horizontally through the projector. That way, the width of the frame wasn't constrained by the width of the film stock. *White Christmas* and *The Ten Commandments* are examples of movies that were shot in VistaVision. The disadvantage of VistaVision was that it required more film footage. Another way to achieve widescreen is through **anamorphic lenses**, which squeeze images into the standard 35 mm frame as the film is being shot and stretch

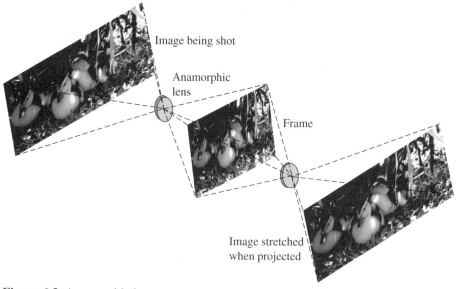

Image being shot

Anamorphic
lens

Frame

Image stretched
when projected

**Figure 6.3** Anamorphic lens

the images when the movie is projected (Figure 6.3). This is the method that was used by Cinemascope in the 1950s in movies such as *How To Marry a Millionaire*, *The Robe*, and *Twenty Thousand Leagues Under the Sea*. Early anamorphic lenses achieved an aspect ratio of 2.35 : 1, and those after 1970 increased the aspect ratio to 2.39 : 1 (sometimes rounded to 2.4).

An even wider aspect ratio and higher resolution can be had at the cost of 70 mm film. This film gauge is sometimes referred to as 65 mm, since this is the size of the film in the camera. The processed film has 5 more mm, which includes the sound track encoded on the side. The aspect ratio varies according to usage. Standard 70 mm aspect ratio is 2.2 : 1, as illustrated by *Lawrence of Arabia*. IMAX movies are shot on 70 mm film with aspect ratio of 1.43 : 1. Frames are laid horizontally on IMAX film as they were with VistaVision. This gives room for a larger frame, but not just for the purpose of widening the aspect ratio. IMAX movies are on very large screens, so the frames have to be enlarged more than they are in standard movie projection. To retain high resolution, frames have to be larger on the film stock. IMAX productions were originally special made-for-IMAX releases, but now many film companies are remastering some of their more popular films for IMAX—for example, *The Matrix Reloaded* and *Star Wars Episode II*. Also, IMAX versions of newly released movies are often created along with regular theater versions.

This information about frame rates, film size, and aspect ratio in feature films sets the stage for a discussion of similar topics in the realm of video. It will also be relevant to the later explanation of how film is translated into digital form.

We've established that the key characteristic of a movie-as-film is the physical medium on which the movie is shot, but filmmaking overlaps widely with digital video processing. Now we need to ask, what's the difference between video and television? At what point does television become digital rather than analog? What's the difference between standard-definition and high-definition television? Is cable television always digital? Is satellite television always digital? Is HDTV always digital? Is digital television always HDTV? The answers to these questions might not always be what you expect.

In the beginning, television was transmitted as an analog signal. In comparison to the newer HDTV, we now sometimes refer to this as *SDTV* (*standard-definition television*). SDTV was broadcast through radio waves by land-based broadcast stations (terrestrial broadcast). Home television sets in North America were on the order of 20 inches or so wide with an aspect ratio of $4:3$.

In the 1970s, satellite broadcasts became possible on network television. The first satellite broadcasts were still analog in nature, but digital satellite broadcasts followed in the 1980s and 90s. Direct Broadcast Satellite (DBS) is received directly in the home, which must be equipped with a satellite dish. DirectTV emerged in 1994 as the first large, successful commercial DBS company in North America. Its competitor, EchoStar's Disk Network, was launched in the same year. Commercial satellite television providers such as these use an encoding and encryption scheme that requires special receivers in the consumers' homes.

In 1981, NHK, the Japanese broadcasting network, began broadcasting what came to be known as *high-definition television, HDTV*. The Japanese version of HDTV was transmitted in analog form and had 1125 lines/frame, an aspect ratio of $16:9$, and a frame rate of 30 frames/s. Thus, HDTV is not necessarily digital—at least, not historically.

The current definition of HDTV is television that has an aspect ratio of $16:9$, surround sound, and one of three resolutions: $1920 \times 1080$ using interlaced scanning, $1920 \times 1080$ using progressive scanning, or $1280 \times 720$ using progressive scanning. (The terms *interlaced* and *progressive* are explained in the next section.) The width (*i.e.*, horizontal resolution) is the first number, and the height (*i.e.*, vertical resolution) is the second. These three standard resolutions are referred to in abbreviated form as *1080i, 1080p*, and *720p*. Sometimes the frame rate is given as well, as in *1080i60*, indicating a frame rate of 60 frames/s (actually, 59.94). Digital encoding is not part of this definition, and, historically, HDTV was not always digital. In reality, however, HDTV and digital encoding are natural partners, and you can now assume that all HDTV is digital.

What about looking from the other direction? Is digital television (DTV) always HDTV? No, not necessarily. It's possible to transmit video digitally without its being at the aspect ratio and high resolution of HDTV. The only requirement of DTV is that the video be digitized—encoded as 0s and 1s.

Is cable television necessarily HDTV? Is cable always digital? No, of course not. Homes have received cable television as an analog signal for decades. But cable companies now offer both digital cable and HDTV. HDTV requires a great deal of bandwidth, and cable companies and consumers see a trade-off between the higher resolution and better sound quality of HDTV versus the number of programming choices you have if the bandwidth is spread out among lower-resolution broadcasts. Some of the bandwidth might even be reserved for interactive television—enabling activities like pay-per-view, voting, game playing, and so forth by means of your television. This is an area getting increasing attention by the television and cable industries.

So, to put it simply, cable and satellite can be used to transmit analog TV, DTV, and HDTV, but they can also transmit digital, and, in fact, standardizing agencies have mandated that the television industry convert to "all digital." The age of digital television and HDTV has arrived, requiring providers and consumers to purchase new equipment accommodating digital television. Consumers are replacing their old analog television sets with digital-enabled widescreen TVs, and pretty soon all terrestrial, cable, and satellite television transmissions will be digital.

The bottom line: Television, along with film, is "going digital."

# 6.2 VIDEO STANDARDS

You're going to see a lot of abbreviations and acronyms if you work in digital video. This section introduces you to the standardizing agencies and how they have evolved from analog to digital video.

Three main standards emerged in the early days of analog television: *NTSC* (developed by the *National Television Systems Committee*), *PAL* (*Phase Alternating Line*), and *SECAM* (*Système Electronique Couleur Avec Mémoire*). These began as analog standards that have evolved to cover digital video as well.

NTSC governs standards in North America, Japan, Taiwan, and parts of the Caribbean and South America. NTSC was instrumental in helping the television industry move from monochrome transmission (what we ordinarily call black and white) to color in a way that was backward compatible. The first commercial television program was broadcast in monochrome in the United States in 1941, with standards developed by NTSC. NTSC's standards for color television were published in 1954, and they now cover video cassette recorders (VCRs), digital cable, high-definition television, and digital video.

Because European monochrome television was based on a technology different from that used in the United States, a different standard for color television was needed. A number of competing technologies were studied in the decade following the adoption of the NTSC standard, and in 1967 PAL was adopted for color television broadcasts in the United Kingdom and Germany. PAL has a number of variants that are now used in Europe (*e.g.*, Italy, Belgium, Austria, Germany), the United Kingdom, Australia, and countries in Asia, Africa, and South America.

SECAM was developed in France and accepted for color broadcasting in 1967. It was later adopted by other countries in Eastern Europe. In Africa, Asia, and Latin America, countries have generally adopted PAL, SECAM, or NTSC based on their colonial histories.

With the advent of digital video, new standards were needed to define how a digital video signal should be transmitted and how digital video data should be stored. These standards needed to be backward-compatible with the analog standards. Development of digital video standards was handled by consortia of industry representatives in cooperation with international government agencies.

The *ITU* (*International Telecommunication Union*) is an organization within the United Nations System that brings together representatives of government and the private sector to develop standards for global telecommunications. Its three main departments are ITU-R (radio communication), ITU-T (telecom standardization), and ITU-D (telecom development). An ITU standard that you'll probably encounter frequently in your work in digital media is ITU-R BT.601, which gives specifications for storage and communication. This standard originated as CCIR601, developed by the Consultative Committee for International Radio, and it is often still referred to by this older name. BT.709 is another often-cited standard, developed for HDTV.

You've probably seen the *SMPTE* (*Society for Motion Picture and Television Engineers*) acronym most often as it relates to timecodes, but SMPTE has also been instrumental in the development of international digital video standards. In the 1990s, SMPTE worked in consultation with ITU to help ensure that digital video files from NTSC, PAL, and SECAM sources could be exchanged. Many digital video standards bear the SMPTE prefix.

In the 1990s, the development of international standards for the transmission of *digital television* (*DTV*) became a hot topic. There are three main standards organizations for DTV: ATSC in North America, DVB in Europe, and ISDB in Japan. All three standards use

| TABLE 6.2 | Standards for Digital Terrestrial Television | | |
|---|---|---|---|
| | **ATSC** | **DVB** | **ISDB** |
| Origin | United States | Europe | Japan |
| video compression | MPEG-2 main profile | | |
| audio compression | Dolby AC-3 | MPEG-2 or Dolby AC-3 | MPEG-2 AAC |
| transmission type | 8-vestigial sideband | COFDM (coded orthogonal frequency division multiplexing) | bandwidth segmented transmission of COFDM |
| bit rate | 19.4 Mb/s | 3.7–31.7 Mb/s | 4–21.5 Mb/s |

MPEG-2 video compression and Dolby audio compression. The major difference lies in the radio frequency modulation schemes for airwave transmission. (See Table 6.2.)

*ATSC* (*Advanced Television Systems Committee*) is an international nonprofit organization that develops voluntary standards for digital television. It includes member organizations from the computer, cable, satellite, broadcast, motion picture, and consumer electronics industries. ATSC developed DTV standards for the United States and Canada. These standards were adopted by the FCC in 1996. This was the beginning of the transition to digital and high-definition television mandated by the FCC, requiring that new televisions have digital tuners and TV broadcasting stations provide digital signals by the year 2009.

In Europe, standards for digital television were developed by *DVB* (*Digital Video Broadcasting Project*). DVB is an international consortium of broadcasters, manufacturers, network operators, software developers, and regulatory bodies aimed at designing global standards for digital television. DVB standards are promulgated by *ETSI* (*European Telecommunications Standards Institute*). DVB standards are divided into terrestrial (DVB-T), satellite (DVB-S), and handheld (DVB-H).

Standards for digital video in Japan go by the name of *ISDB* (*Integrated Services Digital Broadcasting*). The ISDB system was developed by *ARIB* (*Association of Radio Industries and Businesses*). Like ATSC and DVB, ISDB uses MPEG-2 video compression and Dolby audio compression. Both ISDB and DVB also have standards for MPEG audio compression.

Historically, digital television and HDTV are not the same thing. The first HDTV system actually predates DTV. In the late 1960s, the Japanese government undertook the challenge of innovating their television broadcast system to use a larger width-to-height ratio and better sound. Rather than interfere with terrestrial broadcast channels, the Japanese chose to transmit HDTV by satellite, governed by their NHK public broadcast system. Geographically, it was feasible to do this and reach all the Japanese islands with one or two satellites. At its inception Japanese HDTV was analog, not digital. Japanese HDTV went through a number of versions. The 1990 version, still essentially analog but with compression methods borrowed from digital technology, was known in the United States as MUSE, for Multiple sub-Nyquist Sampling Encoding. This version had 1125 lines/frame, 30 frames/s, an aspect ratio of 16:9, and a bandwidth of 24 MHz.

By the 1980s, the United States and Europe realized that it was time for them to respond with their own proposals for HDTV standards. The stakes were high in defining the standards. Because of its higher resolution and enhanced audio, HDTV required a wide bandwidth. Compression methods had not yet advanced to the point where it was possible to squeeze HDTV bandwidth into the 6 MHz channels allocated for standard analog television. If HDTV was to be broadcast by terrestrial broadcast channels, it appeared that the channels might have to be reallocated. Broadcast channels are a finite and precious commodity, and the prospect of dividing them up differently got special interest groups motivated. The alternative prospect of moving broadcasts to satellite also worried terrestrial broadcasters because they feared that their services might then be less valuable. Definition of standards also affected the competing computer and television industries. Should interlaced scanning be used for the new HDTV monitors, a legacy of analog television displays? Or should the standard move to progressive scanning and be more compatible with computer displays? (Progressive and interlaced scanning are explained below.)

Simultaneous with the evolution of HDTV, standards were being developed for digital television in the United States, Europe, and Japan. In the United States, the new technology was called *advanced television systems*, covering digital SDTV and HDTV. In 1987, the FCC established an Advisory Committee to help them set technical and public policy regarding advanced television. Initially, 23 different systems were proposed to the Advisory Committee, ranging from systems that offered relatively small improvements to the quality of the existing analog television broadcasts to systems with wide HDTV aspect ratios and improved sound. In 1990, General Instruments Corporation introduced the first completely digital HDTV system, and shortly thereafter three other digital HDTV systems appeared. A challenge went out to industry leaders to create an HDTV format that would combine the best of these four systems, motivating the formation of the Grand Alliance, a consortium of industry leaders including General Instruments, AT&T, Massachusetts Institute of Technology, David Sarnoff Research Center, Philips, Zenith, and Thomson Electronics. The Grand Alliance put together a prototype HDTV system, and the FCC Advisory Committee oversaw its testing from 1993 to 1995. The ATSC was tasked with writing detailed specifications for the advanced television standard based on the Grand Alliance system. It became clear that the specification needed to cover the entire spectrum of DTV, so the ATSC added digital SDTV to the proposed standard. In 1996, the FCC accepted the ATSC's DTV proposal, which became the ATSC A/53 standard.

Essentially, acceptance of the ATSC standard amounted to a mandate that digital terrestrial television broadcasts be phased in and eventually replace analog terrestrial broadcasts entirely. HDTV first was to be broadcast alongside analog, and eventually all analog broadcasts would end and digital HDTV would take over the terrestrial airwaves. The timetable for the transition had to be adjusted to more realistically match the pace at which the television industry and consumers were able and willing to make the change. Electronics companies had to manufacture the new HDTV recording equipment and home television sets, television networks had to begin offering HDTV broadcasts, and consumers had to be willing to upgrade the new technology in their homes. Eventually, a deadline of 2009 was set for the transition to digital HDTV (superseding the original 2006 deadline).

In the meantime, Europe and Japan were developing their own standards for DTV and HDTV. The DVB project was organized in 1993 with the mission of creating a completely digital broadcasting system for the European market. The DVB-T standard was approved in 1995. Like the ATSC system, DVB uses MPEG-2 compression for video. The main differences between the DVB and ATSC systems lie in how the audio is encoded and how the signal is modulated onto a carrier frequency. DVB uses MPEG audio encoding in addition to the Dolby digital audio compression (AC-3) used by ATSC. For signal modulation, DVB uses Coded Orthogonal Frequency Division Multiplexing (COFDM), while ATSC uses 8 Vestigial Sideband Modulation (8-VSB).

Japan's development of digital television standards began in 1994, culminating in 1999 in a digital terrestrial broadcast system approved by the ITU-R. The Japanese system is known as Integrated Services Digital Broadcasting for Terrestrial (ISDB-T), applicable to both television and radio. Like the United States' system, it uses MPEG-2 compression for video. It uses a form of MPEG for compression for audio as well.

The ATSC, DVB, and ISDB standards have been adopted in countries outside of their countries of origin. Canada, Taiwan, South Korea, Argentina, and Mexico use the ATSC standard. The United Kingdom, Spain, and Sweden have adopted the DVB standard. Only Japan uses ISDB. The three standards for digital terrestrial television are summarized in Table 6.2.

## 6.3 VIDEO AND FILM DISPLAYS

It's hard to separate analog from digital when you talk about televisions and video displays. Often, a television can accept either an analog or a digital signal—it just needs to know how to translate that signal into its internal display technology. A more meaningful comparison is between video display and film display.

Like film, video is created by a sequence of discrete images, called frames, shown in quick succession. Film is displayed at 24 frames/s. The standard frame rate for NTSC video is about 30 frames/s. The frame rate for PAL and SECAM video is 25 frames/s. This is true whether the video frames are conveyed in an analog or a digital manner.

Think again about the difference between how film and video frames are displayed. A film frame is a continuous image, enlarged and projected as a whole onto the movie screen. Video frames, in contrast, are divided into lines. Television has to be transmitted as a signal, line-by-line. The amount of time taken for the transmission of one line is fixed by a standard. The number of lines per frame is also standardized. This way, the receiving device knows exactly when one line ends and another begins. The number of lines per frame in NTSC, PAL, and SECAM analog video is 525, 625, and 625, respectively. (You'll see later that the number of lines for digital video is set so that the timing matches the timing for analog video.) Picturing how these lines are captured and displayed will help you to understand the nature of video signal transmission.

Video is displayed (and recorded) by a process called *raster scanning*. The raster refers to a single frame. The scanning process is a movement from left to right and top to bottom. When the scanner has finished with one line, it moves back to the left to start another in a motion called *horizontal retrace*. *Vertical retrace* takes the scanner from the bottom of the monitor to the top again. In the case of a video camera (assuming it uses scanning technology), the purpose of the scanning is to record the data that will be saved and/or transmitted as the video signal—in particular, the color of the framed picture being recorded at points in space. In the case of a video display device, the purpose of the scanning is to activate physical pixels so that they emit the appropriate colors.

For many years, the dominant video display technology was the *cathode ray tube* (*CRT*). Most home television sets were built from CRTs, as were the first computer monitors. A scanning method is used to display video on a CRT. Inside the CRT, an electron gun is focused through vacuum tubes onto a phosphor-coated screen. A phosphor is any material that emits light when it is exposed to radiation such as a beam of electrons. The intensity of the electron beam emitted by the scan gun varies in proportion to the value stored in the scan line, and this in turn controls how brightly the phosphor glows. In a monochrome television, there is one phosphor cell per pixel location. In a color television, there are three phosphors—one for each of the red, green, and blue channels—and three corresponding electron beams. In both monochrome and color CRTs, the electron gun scans one line at a time. (See Figure 6.4.)

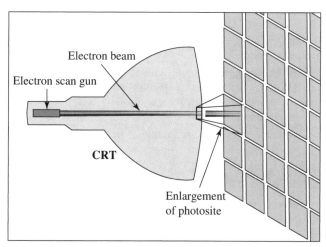

**Figure 6.4**  Raster scanning in a CRT

Scanning can be done by one of two methods: either interlaced or progressive scanning (Figure 6.5). In *interlaced scanning*, which is the method used by analog television displays, the lines of a frame are divided into two *fields*: The odd-numbered lines, called the *upper field* (also called the *top* or *odd field*); and the even-numbered lines, called the *lower field* (also called the *bottom* or *even field*). In many systems the lower field is scanned first, and then the upper one, but this varies by system.

Video standards are sometimes described in terms of *field rate* rather than frame rate. For example, PAL and SECAM analog video use interlaced scanning with a field rate of 50 fields/s, which is equivalent to a frame rate of 25 frames/s since a field is half a frame. You'll often see the NTSC frame rate quoted as 30 frames/s , but it is actually slightly less than this. Analog NTSC video uses interlaced scanning and has a field rate of 59.94 for a frame rate of 29.97 frames/s.

Interleaved scanning became the dominant method in television displays early in the industry because it helped to solve the problem of flicker. The human eye needs about 40 frames per second to see a continuous image, this number varying with distance from the image, size of the image, and lighting conditions. In the early days of television, the technology had not yet advanced to the point where it was possible to send the data fast enough. Interlaced scanning is a compromise that satisfies the eye. Half the image is refreshed every 1/60th second, and this is enough to achieve the illusion of smooth motion.

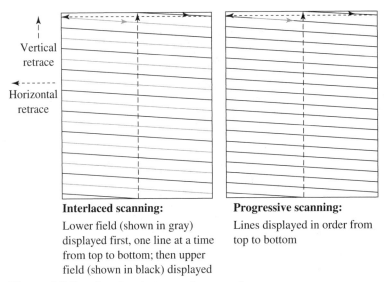

Vertical
retrace

Horizontal
retrace

**Interlaced scanning:**
Lower field (shown in gray)
displayed first, one line at a time
from top to bottom; then upper
field (shown in black) displayed

**Progressive scanning:**
Lines displayed in order from
top to bottom

**Figure 6.5** Interlaced and progressive scanning

In *progressive scanning*, each frame is scanned line-by-line from top to bottom. For progressive scanning, the frame rate and field rate are the same because a frame has only one field. Computer monitors and many digital televisions use progressive scanning. You will sometimes see *i* or *p* appended to video specifications, usually in lower case but sometimes capitalized. This refers to the use of interlaced or progressive scanning, respectively. For example, 24p would indicate a frame rate of 24 frames/s with progressive scanning.

The aspect ratio of standard CRT-based television sets, in keeping with the aspect ratio of NTSC, PAL, and SECAM analog video, is 4 : 3. This is the same as 1.33 : 1, and you see the aspect ratio described either way.

Early television sets used CRT technology, but as HDTV became available in the 2000s, new types of displays were developed to take advantage of higher resolution and wider aspect ratio in the video signal. *LCD displays* are based on liquid crystals to which electrical currents are applied. The electrical currents cause the crystals to untwist, changing the angle at which light passes through them. This action can be engineered so that different colors are emitted according to the voltages applied. LCD displays can be flat and lightweight, not requiring the depth of rear-projection systems. They also provide a very bright clear picture and a wide viewing angle. There were size limitations on the first models of LCD displays, but size limits began to disappear as the technology improved, and by 2008 LCDs became the most popular display technology. LCDs are used for both television and computer displays.

*Plasma displays* use inert gases such as xenon and neon, to which electric voltages are applied. Thousands of tiny gas-filled elements are pressed between two glass plates. An electrical current causes the release of photons, which in turn excite phosphors that emit visible light. Like LCDs, plasma displays can be flat and provide a bright clear picture. In their initial releases, plasma displays could offer higher resolution per dollar than LCDs and thus they quickly gained popularity.

An alternative technology to LCDs and plasma monitors is rear-projection televisions. They are less expensive than plasmas and LCDs but have the disadvantage of a less brilliant and clear image. Many rear-projection sets are based on DLP displays.

*DLP* (*digital light processing*) *displays* use either DMD (digital micromirror device) or LCoS (liquid crystal on silicon) technology. DMD has millions of microscopic mirrors arranged in a rectangular array. The mirrors are tilted at varying angles to project light and thus color onto the display screen. LCoS uses liquid crystals instead of individual mirrors. DLPs gained popularity because they could be made in larger sizes than plasmas and LCDs, at affordable prices, offering good clarity and high resolution. The disadvantage is that rear-projection DLPs aren't as flat as LCDs and plasmas and thus can't be wall-mounted.

LCDs, plasmas, and DLPs became popular display types for televisions in the early 2000s, available in sizes from about 30″ to 100″. They have aspect ratios suitable for HDTV, which is $16:9$ (also cited as $1.78:1$). They come in three versions:

1080i: $1920 \times 1080$ with interlaced scanning
1080p: $1920 \times 1080$ with progressive scanning
 720p: $1280 \times 720$ with progressive scanning

These dimensions should not be interpreted as the exact number of physical pixels on the display. A 720p television doesn't necessarily have $1280 \times 720$ pixels. What this means is that it accepts a signal with $1280 \times 720$ pixels per frame and displays them with progressive scanning. It may in fact have a different *native resolution*. For each frame, the *logical pixels*—pieces of information saved and transmitted in a video signal—have to be mapped to the *physical pixels*—points of light on the video display. There isn't always a one-to-one mapping between the number of logical pixels received and the physical pixels on the display.

When a 1080p television receives a 1080i signal, the signal must be deinterlaced. This will be discussed in a later section, since it also relates to television-to-film transformations.

You can also watch video on your computer—a digital video, that is. For example, you can play a DVD movie either on a television or on a computer. How is that possible? And what's the resolution of the movie? What's the resolution of the computer?

Standard computer display resolutions range from 17 to 30 inches for desktops and 8 to 20 for laptops with resolutions of $1024 \times 728$ (XGA/XVGA), $1280 \times 1024$ (SXGA), $1400 \times 1050$ (SXGA+), $1600 \times 1200$ (UXGA), and upwards. Various forms of Wide XGA give aspect ratios that are approximately $16:9$ or $16:10$, including WSXGA ($1440 \times 900$) and WUXGA ($1920 \times 1200$). Here we're talking physical pixels on the computer display.

Now let's say you have a video on a DVD in standard definition format. It's in digital form and has a resolution of $720 \times 480$, because that's what's prescribed by the standard. You'll read that the format for DVD standard-definition videos is $720 \times 480$ with an aspect ratio of $4:3$. That doesn't sound right, does it? $720 \times 480$ is $3:2$, not $4:3$. The discrepancy lies in the difference between logical and physical pixels. The resolution of $720 \times 480$ is logical pixels. When you play the video on your computer, it maps to $640 \times 480$ physical pixels, which *is* $4:3$. (Or you can blow it up to full screen. It will then be bigger, but less clear.) You can also put the DVD in a DVD player connected to a standard definition television set. The DVD player knows how to translate the digital signal into something your television can understand. The DVD video will fit nicely into the $4:3$ aspect ratio of SDTV.

16:9 Aspect ratio

16:9 Aspect ratio displayed
on a 4:3 screen (letter box)

4:3 Aspect ratio

4:3 Aspect ratio displayed
on a 16:9 screen (pillar box)

**Figure 6.6** Comparison of 4 : 3 and 16 : 9 image aspect ratio

The 4 : 3 and 16 : 9 aspect ratios are compared in Figure 6.6. When a 4 : 3 video is shown on a 16 : 9 screen, one option is to show it in pillar box view, with black bars filling the sides. Similarly, a 16 : 9 movie shown on a 4 : 3 screen can be shown in letter box view. An alternative is pan-and-scan, a conversion of a narrower-format movie to wider format that is done by editors. In this method, the editors choose which part of the wide frame to include, frame by frame.

Another issue to consider with regard to video display is ***pixel aspect ratio***, the ratio of the width to the height of a physical pixel. Pixels on televisions and computers are not the same shape. Standard television pixels are rectangular, with a pixel aspect ratio of 0.9 : 1. Computer pixels are square. You sometimes need to be aware of this difference in pixel aspect ratio when you work in digital video processing. For example, if you create a single image in a photographic processing program on your computer and incorporate it into a video, you have to be sure that the pixel aspect ratio of your image matches the pixel aspect ratio of the video. The pixel aspect ratios of televisions and computers are shown in Figure 6.7 The pixels are shown as a combination of red, green, and blue channels, an abstraction of the technology used to create color at the pixel level. The pixels are small and the color channels are combined by the eye to create a single color.

Television
pixel is rectangular

Computer
pixel is square

**Figure 6.7** Pixel aspect ratios

# 6.4 VIDEO CAMERAS AND CONNECTIONS

## 6.4.1 Video Connections

As you work with video, you'll need to be familiar with the cables and interfaces that connect one device to another. Some transmit an analog signal, some digital, and some either. Table 6.3 shows three types of *analog video transmission formats*: component, S-video, and composite. Recall from Chapter 2 that color models divide color into three components. For digital still images, you often work with RGB mode, where a color is separated into its red, green, and blue components. In analog video, luminance/chrominance models like YUV and YIQ work better. Like RGB, luminance/chrominance color models require three pieces of information—one luminance and two chrominance—to represent a color. In the realm of analog video, the three pieces of information can be sent in one of three ways—in component, S-video, or composite form. When we say "sent," we could mean through a physical connection or through the airwaves. In this section, we're talking about physical connections, like the type of cables you would use to connect digital video to television. In the section on analog bandwidth, we'll be talking about sending the information through the airwaves.

| TABLE 6.3 | Standards for Analog Video Recording Equipment | | | | |
|---|---|---|---|---|---|
| Video Format | Year Introduced | Color Transmission Format | Horizontal Resolution | Tape Width | Quality |
| VHS | 1976 | composite | ~240 | ½" (12.5 mm) | consumer |
| Betamax | 1976 | composite | ~240 | ½" (12.5 mm) | consumer |
| 8mm (Video 8) | 1984 | composite | ~240–300 | 8 mm | consumer |
| S-VHS | 1987 | S-video | ~400–425 | ½" (12.5 mm) | high-end consumer |
| Hi-8 | 1998 | S-video | ~400–425 | 8 mm | high-end consumer |
| U-Matic | 1971 | composite | ~250–340 | ¾" (18.75 mm) | professional |
| M-II | 1986 | component | ~400–440 | ½" (12.5 mm) | professional |
| Betacam | 1982 | component | ~300–320 | ½" (12.5 mm) | consumer |
| Betacam SP | 1986 | component | ~340–360 | ½" (12.5 mm) | professional |

NOTE:
Vertical resolution depends on whether the camera is NTSC-, PAL-, or SECAM-compliant.

In *component video* (Figure 6.8, left), a separate signal is sent for each part of the three luminance/chrominance components. Component video has three separate paths for the information and three connectors at the end. This is the most accurate and expensive format for representing and transmitting video, eliminating crosstalk between the different components. A few high-end analog camcorders like Betacam use component video connections.

The next step down in video quality is *S-video*, which uses two data paths: one for the luminance component, and one for the two chrominance components. An S-video jack thus has one connection at the display end, with two channels of information carried through the connection. Figure 6.9 shows a standard S-video jack. In the pin assignments of the jack,

**Figure 6.8** RGB component video connection (left) and composite video with two audio jacks (right)

4 'C' color (chrominance) ——— 3 'Y' intensity (luminance)

2 'C' ground ——— 1 'Y' ground

**Figure 6.9** Standard S-video connection and pin assignments

there is one pin for the color components and one for the luminance component. Hi-8 video and S-VHS use the S-video standard.

*Composite video* is a video signal that is sent on just one channel. Compositing the signal makes it possible to use just one broadcast channel through the airways or one physical connection from device to device. For example, video cassette recorders (VCRs) that take VHS tape are designed for composite signals. Thus if you want to hook a video camera up to a VHS-type VCR, there is just one physical connection going into the tape deck, like the one pictured in Figure 6.8. The disadvantage to this technology is that crosstalk can occur between the color and luminance components, making composite video the lowest quality of all the alternatives.

There are two main types of digital video transmission format: *DVI (digital video interface),* and *HDMI (high definition multimedia interface). DVI* is a digital video interface that connects an uncompressed digital video source (e.g., from a video card) to a digital display device like a computer or television. DVI superceded the VGA connection for computer video, and before the advent of HDMI, it was commonly used to connect a computer video signal to HDTV LCD and plasma displays. There are three basic DVI formats: DVI-D, for a true digital-to-digital connection; DVI-A, which connects and converts a digital signal to an analog display; and DVI-I, which can transmit both digital-to-digital and analog-to-analog. A DVI connection is pictured in Figure 6.10.

*HDMI* is an audio/video connection for transmitting uncompressed digital data. It is backward compatible with DVI in that no signal conversion needs to take place between

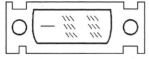

**Figure 6.10** DVI-D interface

**Figure 6.11** HDMI interface

the two. However, HDMI also accommodates audio data on the signal. HDMI is used to connect audio/video sources such as set-top boxes, DVD players, digital cameras, computers, and video game consoles to digital audio players, digital monitors, and digital televisions. HDMI connections can apply ***HDCP (high bandwidth digital content protection)*** to the signal if this is required by the video source. HDCP is a digital copy protection protocol that prevents unauthorized copying or viewing of protected material. An HDMI connection is picutred in Figure 6.11.

## 6.4.2 Videotape

In the early days of television, everything was live. The actors acted out their dramas or told their jokes, and these images were broadcast directly into the consumers' homes. Videotape had not yet been invented. Without videotape, it was difficult to broadcast television programs across long distances. Antennas could broadcast at only a limited distance, and cable didn't reach all homes. Another problem was scheduling. For example, programs shown at 8:00 pm prime time on the east coast of the United States would have to be viewed at 5:00 pm on the west coast. The first solution to this problem was ***kinescope***, a method for filming television by aiming a camera at a television monitor and recording onto 16 mm or 35 mm film. Flat television screens were used—as flat as was possible in those days—and the filming mechanism was timed to correspond to the video refresh rate to avoid flicker. Still, you can imagine that this process didn't yield very good quality. The film was developed and then projected and captured again with a video camera when it was rebroadcast. These films are the only record we have of some of the early television programs, like Jackie Gleason's *The Honeymooners*. Programs that didn't undergo kinescope, like Ernie Kovacs' comedies, are lost to us. A later, more technically sophisticated method was to film the program on stage, even using multiple cameras to switch shots, and then transfer the film to video. This was the innovation introduced by the Desilu Company for *I Love Lucy*. Videotape technology wasn't invented until around 1956 and gradually replaced the kinescope process.

Videotape is different from film. Instead of recording a whole frame in a rectangle, a video camera records an image line-by-line, on a magnetized piece of plastic. The audio track lies in a straight line along the edge, and the video information—which takes much more space—is written diagonally on the tape. (Some videotape formats store the audio in a diagonal pattern along a strip on the edge. There may also be control information on a strip on the edge of the tape.) This is pictured in Figure 6.12. Although the information is arranged diagonally, it is essentially linear. This is a basic difference between film and videotape. In an analog video camera, light comes through the lens and hits an imaging chip, which reacts to the light with continuously varying voltages. The stronger the light, the stronger the voltages is. These voltages, after magnification and signal processing, magnetize the tape particles in a continuously varying pattern that mirrors the signal.

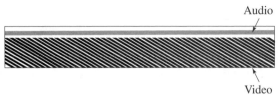

**Figure 6.12** Videotape

The most popular type of video camera (and the corresponding VCR) in the United States during the 1980s was VHS. VHS was an inexpensive and attractive format in its day, but it has been replaced by much higher resolution, higher color-quality formats. S-VHS and Hi-8 improved the color quality with an S-video color signal, also offering better resolution. 8mm and Hi-8 video uses a smaller tape, and thus the corresponding video cameras are generally smaller than for VHS.

Betacams were a breakthrough for television news since they used small tape sizes, and thus smaller cameras than news people previously had to use, with extremely high quality.

The number of horizontal lines in a frame is called the *vertical resolution* of an image because lines are stacked up vertically as you move down a frame. As you look at Table 6.6, you might wonder why the vertical resolution, but no horizontal resolution, is specified. The resolution of any given video camera depends on whether it is NTSC-, PAL-, or SECAM-compliant. The number of lines for each of these standards is 525, 625, and 625, respectively. The horizontal resolution is just an estimate. Unlike digital video, horizontal resolution is not fixed but lies within a range. This is because analog video sends picture information as a continuous waveform rather than as discrete pixels.

Analog video has quickly become outmoded now that digital video has arrived on the scene and is affordable for personal use. VHS doesn't have the quality of DV video, a consumer format that we'll look at in the next section. But all is not lost. If you have an analog video camera or old VHS tapes, you still can capture these analog videos on your computer. For example, you can connect an analog video camera to your computer and—assuming that you have the appropriate software and video capture card—you can capture video footage in digital directly on your computer. Or you can play an VHS tape and, with the right interface, capture the video on your computer. Video capturing is the processing of digitally encoding and saving video on a computer.

## 6.4.3 Digital Video Cameras

Like analog video cameras, digital video cameras move across an image line-by-line, detecting light coming in through the lens. However, instead of recording the light as continuously changing voltages, they digitally encode the light intensity. The encoded pixel values can be stored on a videotape, just as they are for an analog camera, but information is represented differently.

Throughout the 1980s to the 2000s, the digital format evolved through a series numbered D1 through D12. (Note that they skipped D4 and D8.) Along the way, the DV standard emerged for consumer-grade, compressed digital video.

D1, the first major professional digital videotape format, specified uncompressed digital video stored on ¾" (19 mm) tape and transmitted via a component signal using YUV 4:2:2 subsampling. The standard retained the BT.601 raster format. With no compression and with component transmission, the D1 format required a wide bandwidth. The D2 format reduced the bandwidth by allowing the data to be transmitted in a composite signal. Both D1 and D2 were formats used by Sony. Panasonic implemented the D3 format on ½" tape, which was their equivalent of D2. Panasonic later introduced D5, another uncompressed digital format on ½" tape. D1 through D5 are all uncompressed formats.

Compressed formats for digital video began appearing in 1996. The *DV* standard, including a description of the DV compression method, was originally released in 1999 in a document known as the *Blue Book*, which is now called IEC 61834. (IEC refers to the International Electrotechnical Commission, a standards organization related to ITU.) DV is the term you will probably hear most often with regard to consumer-grade digital video equipment. It comes in a number of variations, including DVCPRO (*i.e.*, D7), Digital-S (*i.e.*, D9), DVCAM, DVCPRO-50, and Digital-8.

All the DV variants share the DV compression algorithm, which is based on intraframe compression. The basic DV compression rate is $5:1$ to achieve a fixed bit rate of 25 Mb/s. DVCPRO-50 uses chrominance subsampling and more compression for a bit rate of 50 Mb/s. Consumer-grade DV camcorders often use Firewire for data transfer. They also generally have composite video outputs to interface with analog equipment. High-end DV camcorders may have outputs such as SDI (serial digital interface) and HD-SDI. The basic DV standard allows for two 16-bit audio channels at a 48 kHz sampling rate, or four 12-bit audio channels at a 32 kHz sampling rate. We will look more closely at DV compression in Chapter 7.

New digital video standards have continued to emerge, especially with the advent of HDTV. Tables 6.4 and 6.5 provide an historical trace of the evolution of digital video. By the time you read this chapter, there will be more standards that ought to be added to the list. One thing to glean from the table is an understanding of the parameters that vary from one standard to another. As you choose to buy or use a digital camcorder, you should note what type of storage media it uses, the cost of storage, the compression method, the data rate, and whether it has a component or composite signal. Chrominance subsampling of $4:2:2$ retains more color information than $4:1:1$ but leads to a larger video file. The lower the compression rate, the higher the bit rate, requiring fast connections and lots of storage space. The wider the videotape, the more robust the signal, though the technology has improved so that very narrow tapes now yield excellent quality. Some formats are interoperable. For example, DV, DVCAM, and DVCPRO are compatible. An advantage of Digital-8 is that it uses conventional analog Video Hi-8 tapes. Some Digital-8 camcorders allow you to turn your old analog tapes into DV format. Other parameters of interest not listed on the table are the number of minutes per videotape and, with regard to the camcorder you purchase, the connection type and the camcorder's weight.

The DV videotape formats have been extended to include HDTV. The first of the HDTV videotape standards was D6, an uncompressed format that uses $4:2:2$ chrominance subsampling to achieve a bit rate of about 1.2 Gb/s. D5, originally an SDTV format, was adapted by Panasonic to use a motion-JPEG codec that compresses high-definition footage at a ratio of $5:1$. This came to be known as D5 HD (or, alternatively, HD D5). In 1997–1998, Sony introduced HDCAM, an HDTV videotape format with a resolution of $1440 \times 1080$, either interlaced or progressive scanning, a choice of frame rates, $3:1:1$ chrominance subsampling, and M-JPEG-type compression similar to DV that achieves a data rate of 135 Mb/s. ($3:1:1$ chrominance subsampling takes one chrominance sample for every three luminance samples, reducing from nine bytes to five for every three pixels.) HDCAM was standardized by SMPTE as D11. Panasonic launched DVCPRO100 in 2000, soon to be known

| TABLE 6.4 | | Standards for Digital Videotape and Camcorders | | | | | | | |
|---|---|---|---|---|---|---|---|---|---|
| Type | Year | Standard | Maker | Compression | Approximate Bit Rate, Mb/s | Color Sampling | Signal Type | Tape Size | User |
| D1 | 1987 | SMPTE 224M to 228M | Sony | none | 172 video, 225 all | 4:2:2 | component | ¾" | pro |
| D2 | 1990 | SMPTE 224M to 248M | Sony/ Ampex | none | 94 video, 127 all | 4f$_{sc}$ | composite | ¾" | pro |
| D3 | 1993 | SMPTE 264M and 265M | Panasonic | none | 94 video, 127 all | 4f$_{sc}$ | composite | ½" | pro |
| Digital Betacam | 1993 | not SMPTE standard | Sony, Thompson | 2.7:1 | 90 video, 128 all | 4:2:2 | component | ½" | pro |
| D5 | 1994 | SMPTE 279M | Panasonic | none | 220 video, 330 all | 4:2:2 | component | ½" | pro |
| DVCAM | 1996 | IEC 61834 | Sony | DV compression, 5:1 | 25 video, 42 all | 4:1:1 (NTSC) 4:2:0 (PAL) | component | ¼" | prosumer |
| DV and Mini-DV | 1996 | IEC 61834 | Sony, Panasonic, JVC, Canon, Sharp, etc. | DV compression, 5:1 | 25 video, 42 all | 4:1:1 | component | ¼" | consumer |
| Betacam SX | 1996 | not SMPTE standard | Sony | MPEG-2, 10:1 | 18.7 video, 44 all | 4:2:2 | component | ½" | pro |
| D7 (DVC-PRO) | 1998 | SMPTE 306M, 307M, 314M | Panasonic, Ikegami, Philips, Hitachi | DV compression, 5:1 | 25 video, 42 all | 4:1:1 (NTSC and PAL) | component | ¼" | pro |
| Digital-8 | 1998 | IEC 61834 | Sony | DV compression, 5:1 | 25 video, 42 all | 4:1:1 (NTSC) 4:2:0 (PAL) | component | 8 mm | consumer |
| DVC-PRO 50 | 1998 | SMPTE 314M | Panasonic | DV compression, 3.3:1 | 50 video, 80 all | 4:2:2 | component | ¼" | pro |
| D9 (Digital-S) | 1999 | SMPTE 316M, 317M | JVC | DV compression, 3.3:1 | 50 video, 80 all | 4:2:2 | component | ½" | pro |
| D10 IMX | 2001 | SMPTE 386M | Sony | MPEG-2 I-frame only | 50 video 105 all | 4:2:2 | component | ½" | pro |

*4f$_{sc}$ means four times the frequency of the subcarrier signal of the video signal. For NTSC, this is 14.3 MHz. For PAL it is 17.7 MHz.
**NOTES:**
No D4 standard was created, reputedly because four is an unlucky number in Asian culture.
D6, D11, and D12 are omitted from the table because they are for HDTV. No D8 standard was created to avoid confusion with Digital-8, Video8, and 8mm.

| TABLE 6.5 | Standards for HDTV Digital Videotape and Camcorders | | | | | |
|---|---|---|---|---|---|---|
| Type | Year | Maker | Compression | Approximate Video Bit Rate in Mb/s | Chrominance Subsampling | Tape Size |
| D5 HD | 1994 | Panasonic | motion-JPEG, 5:1 | 270 | 4:2:2 | ½" |
| D6 | 1995 | | none | 1188 | 4:2:2 | ¾" |
| D9 (Digital S) | 1996 | JVC | MPEG-2 | 50 | 4:2:2 | ½" |
| D11 HDCAM | 1997 | Sony | M-JPEG-type | 140 | 3:1:1 | ½" |
| D12 DVCPRO HD | 2000 | Panasonic | combination of codecs | 100 | 4:2:2 | ½" |
| HDCAM SR | 2003 | Sony | MPEG-4 studio profile | 440 or 880 | 4:4:4 | ½" |
| HDV | 2003 | JVC, Sony, Canon, Sharp | MPEG-2 | 17 or 25 | 4:2:0 | ¼" |
| XDCAM | 2003 | Sony | MPEG-2, DV25, and MPEG4 | 18, 35, or 50 | 4:2:0 | optical disk |
| AVCHD | 2006 | Sony, Panasonic, Canon | MPEG-4 H.264 | 12–24 | 4:2:0 | DVD disk, hard disk, memory stick, or internal flash |
| XDCAM EX | 2007 | Sony | MPEG-2 long GOP | 25 or 35 | 4:2:2 | SxS memory card |
| Red 3K Scarlet, 4K, One, 5K Epic | 2006– 2008 | Red | uncompressed or compressed as Redcode raw | 28–36 MB/s | 4:2:2 | hard disk or flash memory |

by the name DVCPRO HD and later standardized by SMPTE as D12. DVCPRO HD uses 1080i or 720p resolution, 4:2:2 subsampling, and a combination of four codecs to achieve a bit rate of 100 Mb/s. (Not all DVCPRO HD have full 1920 width resolution.)

HDV is a high-definition format that is affordable at the consumer level. JVC and Sony launched this format, and now Canon, Sharp, and Panasonic make HDV cameras as well. Data rates for HDV are 19.7 Mb/s for 720p and 25 Mb/s for 1080i. HDV advertised as 1080i does not have the full 1920 vertical resolution; it's actually 1440 × 1080. There is currently no 1080p in the HDV format. You may notice that 25 Mb/s is the same data rate as cited for regular DV cameras. HDV achieves the higher data rate by using MPEG-2 compression. HDV uses the same type of tapes as are used for the popular mini-DV cameras, which makes them even handier. AVCHD became popular with Sony and Panasonic around 2006. First and second generation AVCHD cameras were 1440 × 1080; the third generation were 1920 × 1080. A summary of HDTV videotape formats is in Table 6.5.

# 6.5 ANALOG VIDEO RESOLUTION AND BANDWIDTH

What is the difference between the ways that analog and digital video are represented and communicated, and what are the implications for picture clarity? The engineering details of analog and digital data communication fill up large textbooks. But let's think about them abstractly for the moment so that we can see the essential difference.

Video originated as television—"pictures coming from a distance," and in this context the information transmission is the key point. Instead of a strip of film moving through a projector displaying whole frames at a time, we have electronic signals moving through the air or through cables, line-by-line. Consider a single line from a video frame. A line from a video frame is just like a single line in a still image. As you saw in Chapter 2, a line from an image can be represented by a waveform where the amplitude of the wave changes in relation to how the colors of the image change across the line. For television, the wave is recorded live or saved on a videotape and can be transmitted by continuously varying voltages or by a radio frequency airwave signal. It's easy to picture this for a grayscale image, where the wave goes up and down in accordance with the luminance level, as shown in Figure 6.13. The data that is stored by the video camera indicates how the receiving device lights up physical pixels on a video screen, line-by-line from top to bottom, frame-by-frame.

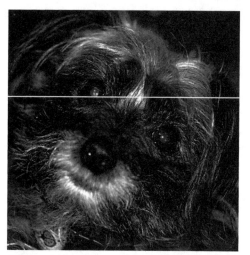 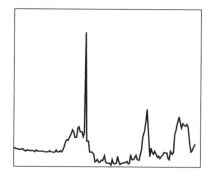

**Figure 6.13** Line of a grayscale image as an analog waveform

In comparison, digital video is encoded as a sequence of 0s and 1s. (This is not to say that there are only two levels, but that whatever amplitude a sample value has can be encoded in 0s and 1s.) Discrete pixel positions across one line of the image are sampled and encoded in binary. You can picture this binary data being sent as two voltage levels—a high level for 1s and a low level for 0s. The 1s and 0s are gathered into meaningful units at the receiving end. If 24-bit RGB color is being used, each 8 bits constitute a color channel for one pixel. The receiver figures out the color of each successive pixel and lights the pixels up accordingly.

Of course it's not that simple. Modulation schemes are used in digital data transmission, just as they are in analog; luminance/chrominance subsampling is used; and the signal is compressed. But the previous descriptions capture the essential difference between analog and digital data communication.

You should note a couple of things before we go on. Video is a time-dependent medium. The lines of video that are being transmitted in the video signal have to arrive fast enough for the lines and frames to stream by in the sight of the viewer, giving the illusion of continuous motion. Secondly, the receiving device needs to know where one line ends and the next begins so that it can make its horizontal retrace. Thus, the vertical resolution of video has to be set at a specific value, both in number of lines per frame and in the time it takes for one line to be transmitted. This is true for both analog and digital video; they both have a fixed vertical resolution (though this resolution may vary according to NTSC, PAL, or SECAM).

Horizontal resolution is a different matter. That is, you can talk about a specific horizontal resolution for digital video, but not for analog. Think about the digital case first, since that's easier to picture. "Things digital" are discrete in nature. A specific number of samples are taken in both the horizontal and vertical directions for a digital video frame. These samples are saved and transmitted as logical pixels. The receiver (*i.e.*, the video display) may not necessarily have the same exact number of physical pixels per line as are sent in the video signal. The logical pixels have to be mapped to physical pixels at the receiving end, but that's another matter. The point here is that the digital video signal itself has a specific resolution in logical pixels in the horizontal and vertical directions.

Analog video, in contrast, has no precise horizontal resolution, but there *are* limits that depend on the video equipment and signal bandwidth. You can understand how horizontal resolution for analog video relates to frequency if you think about the nature of the analog signal. Consider the three video lines in Figure 6.14. Each is represented by a waveform on the right. The one that changes from black to white most frequently (*i.e.*, the highest frequency line) has the most detail, and in that sense it has the highest resolution. To put it simply, a high frequency wave has "bumps" that are close together. These bumps represent color changes that happen in close proximity to each other—detail in the image. A wave corresponding to a video signal is more complex than the ones in Figure 6.14, but it is mathematically a sum of simple component frequencies. The horizontal resolution is a function of the highest frequency component of the wave.

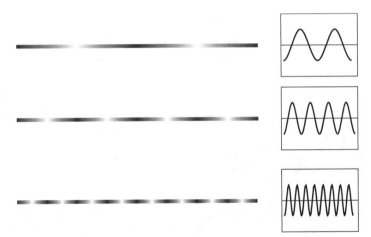

**Figure 6.14** Frequency of color change

What determines how high this frequency is, and thus the horizontal resolution? A video camera has technological limits on how much detail it can record—that is, how fast it can detect changing colors and record that signal. The rate at which the camera can do this limits its horizontal resolution. The specifications for analog video cameras show horizontal resolution either as a range or as a maximum that one can expect from the camera, as shown in Table 6.3. The faster the camera's sensing device can alternate between neighboring colors, the higher its horizontal resolution. VHS has less resolution than Video-8, and Video-8 has less than S-VHS.

Horizontal resolution of analog video is directly related to bandwidth. Bandwidth is defined as the number of times a signal can change per unit time. Thus, it is measured in cycles per second, which is also a frequency measure. There are limits on the bandwidth of an analog video signal as set by the NTSC, PAL, and SECAM standards, and these bandwidths put limits on horizontal resolution. According to the NTSC standard, an analog video signal is allocated a bandwidth of 6.0 MHz, 4.2 MHz for luminance and 1.5 for chrominance, and the remainder for audio (Table 6.6). This bandwidth puts a limit on the highest frequency component that can be sent in the signal. We'll look at this mathematically in the next section.

| TABLE 6.6 | NTSC, PAL, and SECAM Standards for Analog Television Composite Signals | | |
|---|---|---|---|
| Property | NTSC | PAL (version G) | SECAM (version D) |
| frame rate | 29.97 | 25 | 25 |
| type of scanning | interlaced | interlaced | interlaced |
| number of lines | 525 | 625 | 625 |
| number of active lines | ~480 | ~575 | ~575 |
| time to display one line (including horizontal retrace) | 63.56 μsec | 64 μsec | 64 μsec |
| horizontal retrace | 10.9 μsec | 12 μsec | 12 μsec |
| aspect ratio | 4:3 | 4:3 | 4:3 |
| color model | YIQ | YUV | YDbDr |
| luminance bandwidth | 4.2 MHz | 5.0 MHz | 6.0 MHz |
| chrominance bandwidth | 1.5 MHz (I), 0.5 MHz (Q) | 1.3 MHz (U), 1.3 MHz (V) | 1.0 MHz (Db), 1.0 MHz ( Dr) |
| method of color modulation | QAM | QAM | FM |
| frequency of color subcarrier | 3.58 MHz | 4.43 MHz | 4.25 MHz (Db), 4.41 MHz (Dr) |
| frequency of audio subcarrier | 4.5 MHz | 5.5 MHz | 6.5 MHz |
| composite signal bandwidth | 6.0 MHz | 8.0 MHz | 8.0 MHz |

Notice that neither the video camera nor the signal bandwidth dictates that there *will* be a certain horizontal resolution, only that the resolution will have to be within the bandwidth limits of the camera and the signal. If the signal for each line is an analog signal, there is no specific number of pixels being transmitted and thus no specific horizontal resolution, as there is in the case of digital video.

Standards for NTSC, PAL, and SECAM analog composite video signals are compared in Table 6.6. Let's see if we can make sense of these numbers and what they tell us about bandwidth.

In the previous section, we considered a line of a grayscale images as a wave (Figure 6.13). This abstraction of an analog video signal doesn't take into account the many engineering details related to how the signal is repackaged for transmission. There are actually

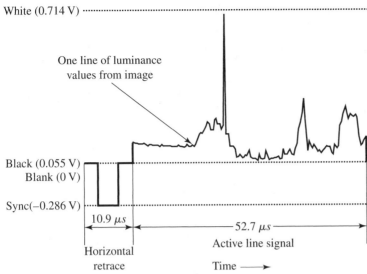

White (0.714 V)

One line of luminance
values from image

Black (0.055 V)
Blank (0 V)

Sync(−0.286 V)

10.9 μs

Horizontal
retrace

52.7 μs

Active line signal

Time ⟶

**Figure 6.15** One active line scanned, NTSC analog video

three color components, represented in a luminance/chrominance color model, with implicit compression by means of subsampling. Audio data is sent along with the video signal. The total signal is modulated onto a carrier signal by means of amplitude, frequency, or phase modulation. This means that mathematical operations between the carrier wave and the video/audio wave encode the video/audio wave onto the carrier, to be decoded at the receiving end.

Figure 6.15 shows the timing of one line of NTSC analog video. It indicates how changing voltages can be used to communicate one line of a video signal. The drop in voltage at the beginning of the line indicates that the scanner should go back to the beginning of a line on the display device—the horizontal retrace. Transmission/display of one line is allotted about 63.56 μsec, with 10.9 μsec of this time taken up by the horizontal retrace. When the scanner reaches the end of a frame, it must return to the top left corner. This is called the ***vertical retrace*** (or in some sources, the ***vertical blanking interval***, ***VBI***). The timing for the vertical retrace is not shown in this figure because it is done for every frame, not for every line.

As can be seen from Table 6.6, in analog video a distinction is made between total lines and ***active lines***. The total number of lines for NTSC is 525, but only 480 of these are active lines. Let's see if the arithmetic works out, multiplying the time allotted for one line by the total number of lines to get a frame rate.

$$0.00006356 \, s/line * 525 \, lines/frame = 0.33369 \, s/frame \approx 29.97 \, frame/s$$

You can see that if we take the number of lines in a video frame to be 525, we get the desired frame rate of 29.97 frames/s. So what is meant by "active lines"? You can think of the 525 lines as 525 lines of data coming in to the video receiver. However, not all these lines of data contain information relating to pixel colors. Some of the lines of data are reserved for the vertical retrace and other auxiliary information. There are only about 480 active lines—lines that contain information.

It's necessary to stipulate a vertical resolution and the time allotted to one line of video so that the recording device knows how many lines to record and the receiving device knows when one line ends and another begins. On the other hand, we've already noted the following about the horizontal resolution:

- A video camera has a maximum horizontal resolution.
- Table 6.3 shows the horizontal resolution of a number of analog video recording formats.
- Maximum horizontal resolution of a video signal is implicit in the maximum bandwidth of the video transmission. (For example, for the luminance component of NTSC video it is 4.2 MHz).

To understand how bandwidth and frequency relate, look at the simplest case—a wave of maximum frequency $f$, and a single cycle of that wave. This wave represents changing luminance (grayscale values). The maximum value of the wave communicates "white" and the minimum communicates "black." The limiting case on the television screen is that you could have two picture elements side-by-side, one white and the other black (or vice versa). This information cannot be communicated faster than in one cycle. Thus, the maximum frequency component of the wave sets a limit on how fast you can communicate information about the change in grayscale value from white to black. In a single cycle, the wave can say "one picture element is white, and the neighboring one is black"—two pieces of information. This is a basic concept—one cycle of a wave with maximum frequency component $f$ can communicate two pieces of information—samples, if you will—yielding a sample rate of $2f$. If the maximum frequency of the wave is 10,000 cycles per second, then you can communicate at most 20,000 samples per second. The sample rate is twice the frequency. In this sense, the bandwidth allocated to a signal determines its maximum frequency which in turn puts a limit on the maximum amount of horizontal detail that can be communicated. (This explanation is an oversimplification, but it gives an intuitive sense of the relationship between bandwidth and frequency.)

Television stations are allocated a certain bandwidth in the form of frequency channels. An NTSC analog video signal is allotted 6 MHz in bandwidth, with 4.2 MHz for luminance information. This means that the color signal can change at a frequency of 4.2 million cycles per second, which puts an upper limit on the resolution of the color signal. As you can picture from Figure 6.14, the faster you can change the color signal, the more detail you'll have in the picture—that is, the higher the resolution. The luminance bandwidth given in the NTSC standard puts a limit on this resolution.

Implicitly, Table 6.6 also gives us information about how analog television channels must be set up—how wide the frequency bands need to be for analog television transmission. In Chapter 1, we introduced the concept of bandwidth and channels. Table 1.7 lists the frequency bands, or channels, allocated to radio and television stations, and stated that AM radio, FM radio, television, and HDTV require bandwidths of 10 kHz, 200 kHz, 6 MHz, and 20 MHz, respectively. Where do these numbers come from? Why is 6 MHz the right bandwidth for NTSC analog video? How do you know that a sufficient amount of information can be sent in that bandwidth, for picture and sound clarity of analog television?

Let's take the luminance bandwidth, given as 4.2 MHz, and work backwards to see if this number makes sense. Does it yield a horizontal resolution that fits the given vertical resolution of 480 active lines per frame? From our previous argument, you know that a bandwidth of 4.2 MHz can yield 8.4 million samples per second.

$$4,200,000 \, cycles/s * 2 \, samples/cycle = 8,400,000 \, samples/s$$

The samples for one line have 52.7 μsec allotted for their display. This gives us

$$8,400,000 \, samples/s * 0.0000527 s/line = 443 \, samples/line$$

Our arithmetic yields a horizontal resolution of 443, for a total resolution of 443 × 480, which is a ratio of about 0.923 to 1. We have an aspect ratio of 0.923 : 1, not the 1.33 : 1 aspect ratio that we expect for analog video.

One way to explain the numbers is by arguing that while 480 lines are transmitted for each frame, you can't actually capture 480 distinct lines with a video camera, so the effective vertical resolution is less than 480. This was the argument made by an RCA engineer in the 1930s as he studied the vertical resolution achievable by the video technology of his day. Imagine that you are using a video camera to record exactly 480 alternating black and white lines on a frame. Although your camera may have the ability to record 480 lines of data, the sensing devices of your camera might not line up precisely with the lines you're trying to record. By subjective experiments, it was determined that the best you could do would be to get about 70% of the lines. Thus, the **Kell factor**, as it was called, was determined to be about 0.7. (You'll see different numbers in different contexts. We'll use 0.6875 for four significant digits.) The Kell factor is a factor by which you multiply the ideal vertical resolution to get the actual, achievable vertical resolution.

The Kell factor is somewhat controversial. Engineers still debate what the right number is, what types of systems it applies to, and whether modern engineering has made it irrelevant. But it helps you to understand why 4.2 MHz is the prescribed bandwidth of NTSC analog video. Instead of a vertical resolution of 480 corresponding to the 480 active lines of information, we get 480 * 0.6875, or 330 lines in the vertical direction, yielding a resolution of 440 × 330. These numbers are a little more satisfying to look at. They match what you'll read in the literature about the resolution of standard television, they match the reported aspect ratio of 4 : 3 of analog video, and they match the 4.2 MHz specified for analog video.

We've worked backwards to make sense of the given bandwidth of 4.2 MHz to convince ourselves that the standard makes sense, yielding a horizontal resolution that is proportional to the vertical. It is also possible to work in the other direction. You'll sometimes see a formula like Equation 6.1 in the literature.

## KEY EQUATION

For a video signal transmission, let $a$ be the aspect ratio, $v$ be the number of active lines, $t$ be the time to transmit one line, and $k$ be the Kell factor. Then the bandwidth of the transmission, $b$, is defined by

$$b = \frac{akv}{2t}$$

**Equation 6.1  Formula for computing bandwidth**

For our example, bandwidth $b$ of the luminance component can be approximated by Equation 6.1, assuming $k = 0.6875$; $a = 4/3$; $v = 480$; and $t = 52.7$ μsec/line.

This equation follows the same reasoning that was used above. Multiply the Kell factor by the number of active lines to get the effective number of active lines.

$$0.6875 * 480 = 330$$

Multiply the resulting value by the aspect ratio to get a horizontal resolution that is in the correct ratio to the vertical resolution.

$$330 * 4/3 \approx 440$$

The result so far indicates that for a vertical resolution of 480, you want a horizontal resolution of about 440 samples. What frequency signal does this require? A video line is transmitted in $t$ seconds. Thus, calculate the number of lines transmitted per second as follows:

$$1/t = 1 \; line/0.0000527 \; s = 18{,}975 \; lines/s$$

Frequency is then computed.

$$440 * 18{,}975 = 8{,}349{,}146 \; samples/s$$

A cycle of the signal can communicate two samples. Thus, bandwidth is computed.

$$8{,}349{,}146/2 \approx 4.17 \, \text{MHz}$$

A bandwidth of 4.17 MHz should be sufficient. This number is close enough to the 4.2 MHz you expect from the bandwidth listed for NTSC, given that some of the numbers (*e.g.* the Kell factor) are approximate.

The total bandwidth allotted for an NTSC analog video signal is 6.0 MHz. This includes luminance, chrominance, audio data, and auxiliary information. Figure 6.16 shows how the bandwidth is divided up into subbands for the different components. Keep in mind that this is a composite signal, the total signal modulated onto a carrier signal.

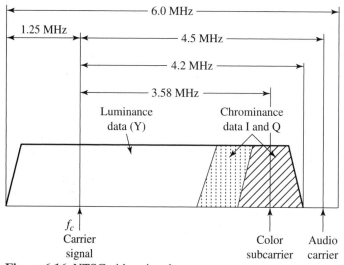

**Figure 6.16** NTSC video signal spectrum

The previous discussion shows that a frequency of 6 MHz is high enough to communicate the horizontal resolution we want in an analog video signal proportional to the vertical resolution. But from the explanation just given, it may sound like every television station is sending a luminance signal with frequency components that lie between 0 and 6 MHz. If that were the case, how would receivers be able to distinguish one station's frequencies from another, if they're all in the same frequency range? In fact, each station gets a band of frequencies—called a *channel*—with a bandwidth of 6 MHz (Figure 6.17).

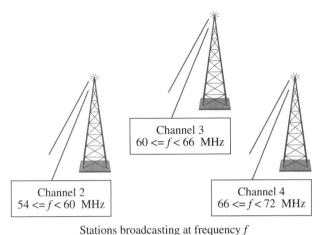

Channel 3
$60 <= f < 66$ MHz

Channel 2
$54 <= f < 60$ MHz

Channel 4
$66 <= f < 72$ MHz

Stations broadcasting at frequency $f$

**Figure 6.17** Bandwidth of analog television channels

The analog waveform shown in Figure 6.13—where the amplitude of the wave varies with the grayscale level across a line of the image—is a simplification. In fact, an analog video signal is written on a carrier wave by some form of amplitude, frequency, or phase modulation, as discussed in Chapter 1. To complete the discussion of bandwidth, we need to show how a *carrier signal* can be modulated by a *data signal* of some maximum bandwidth so that the resulting signal never falls outside the frequency band allotted to the television station. This will clarify the notion of bandwidth as a frequency channel.

Amplitude modulation is easy to understand and gives you the flavor of how modulation works in general, so let's use it as an example. With amplitude modulation, the amplitude of a carrier wave is varied over time as a way of encoding the video information, which can be done by a simple multiplication of the sinusoidal functions.

## KEY EQUATION

Let $\omega_c$ be the angular frequency of a carrier signal. Let $\omega_d$ be the angular frequency of a data signal to be amplitude-modulated onto the carrier signal. Then the function defining the amplitude-modulated wave is

$$\cos(\omega_c t)(1.0 + \cos(\omega_d t))$$
$$= \cos(\omega_c t) + (\cos(\omega_c t)\cos(\omega_d t))$$
$$= \cos(\omega_c t) + \frac{1}{2}\cos(2\pi(f_c + f_d)t) + \frac{1}{2}\cos(2\pi(f_c - f_d)t)$$

**Equation 6.2  Amplitude modulation**

The third step in deriving Equation 6.2 comes from applying the cosine product rule: $\cos(f_1)\cos(f_2) = \frac{1}{2}(\cos(f_1 + f_2)) + \frac{1}{2}(\cos(f_1 - f_2))$. Notice that there are three terms in Equation 6.2, corresponding to three different cosine waves. This is to say that there are three frequency components to the amplitude-modulated wave. The first term, $\cos(\omega_c t)$,

Supplement
on amplitude
modulation:

mathematical
modeling
worksheet

is the carrier frequency. The second term, $\frac{1}{2}\cos(2\pi(f_c + f_d)t)$, is a second frequency component called the ***upper sideband***. The third term, $\frac{1}{2}\cos(2\pi(f_c - f_d)t)$, is a third frequency component called the ***lower sideband***. Figure 6.18 shows a graph of these frequency components. Notice that the bandwidth of the signal is $b = (f_c + f_d) - (f_c - f_d) = 2f_d$. With this method of modulation, if the channel has a bandwidth of $2f_d$, that will be sufficient to carry the signal with frequency $f_d$. Actually, because the lower sideband is just a mirror image of the upper, only half this bandwidth, $f_d$, is needed for the modulated signal.

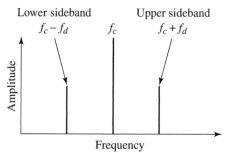

**Figure 6.18** Frequency bands from amplitude modulation

A hypothetical example will illustrate how this works. Assume that the largest frequency component that will ever be transmitted on a channel is 250 Hz. Let's say that initially, to accommodate the two sidebands created by amplitude modulation, the channel must be at least 2*250 Hz = 500 Hz in bandwidth. Suppose the carrier frequency is 4000 Hz and, at some moment in time, a frequency to be transmitted is 200 Hz. Then by the explanation above, aside from the carrier frequency we'll have a frequency component at $4000 - 200$ Hz and one at $4000 + 200$ Hz—that is, sidebands at 3800 Hz and 4200 Hz. Say that the receiver applies a bandpass filter to receive only the frequencies between 3750 and 4250 Hz. The filtered signal is then sampled at a sampling rate equal to the width of the channel, 500 Hz. This results in aliasing because frequencies between 3750 and 4250 are above the Nyquist frequency of 250 Hz. We can compute the aliased frequencies for the 3800 and 4200 Hz sidebands using Algorithm 4.1. Both come out to be 200 Hz, which is the frequency originally transmitted. From this we can see that only one of the sidebands need be transmitted in order to reconstruct the signal at the receiving end. Thus, the channel needs to be only $f_{d\,max}$ in bandwidth rather than $2f_{d\,max}$. In reality, other modulation schemes are used, but this example gives the basic concepts of modulated data transmission.

This argument can be extended to more complex signals. You saw in Chapter 1 that a complex wave is a sum of single-frequency sinusoidal components. Imagine that the data signal is such a complex waveform. When the carrier signal $f_c$ is amplitude-modulated using the data signal, each frequency component of the data signal creates a pair of sidebands around $f_c$. Say that $f_{d\,max}$ is the highest frequency component in the data signal. Then a channel with a bandwidth of at least $f_{d\,max}$ will be sufficient to hold the signal. If the channel is not this wide, some of the frequency components of the data signal will spill over into the neighboring channel.

You can see from Table 6.6 and Figure 6.16 that analog video uses a luminance/chrominance color model, which separates luminance from color information. The analog standards for NTSC, PAL, and SECAM call for YIQ, YUV, and YDbDr color, respectively. Luminance/chrominance models for analog color television were adopted for two reasons. First, they made the transition from monochrome to color television easier. With the signal divided into two chrominance (color) components and one luminance (brightness) component, black-and-white television sets could receive color signals and just ignore the color information. Secondly, luminance/chrominance models lend themselves better to compression. The human eye is more sensitive to brightness than to color. Thus, less data needs to be stored with regard to color. This makes *subsampling* possible. Subsampling is achieved in the analog domain by allocating less bandwidth to the chrominance components than to luminance. (Chapter 2 shows how subsampling is done in the digital domain—by taking fewer samples for the two chrominance components than for the luminance component. See the figures in Chapter 2 illustrating $4:1:1$, $4:2:2$, and $4:2:0$ subsampling.)

So let's finish the picture of the 6 MHz bandwidth for analog NTSC video. First, our estimate for bandwidth was based on a monochrome signal. A color signal has three pieces of color information to transmit: two chrominance and one luminance. To accomplish subsampling, more bandwidth is allocated for luminance than for chrominance. NTSC analog video is transmitted in composite format, where the luminance and chrominance components are modulated onto one signal. Analog video uses two efficient forms of modulation—quadrature amplitude modulation (QAM) and vestigial sideband modulation (VSM). QAM is used for compositing the Y, I, and Q components. Then vestigial sideband modulation is applied to the entire signal. In contrast with amplitude modulation, VSB creates a lower sideband that is only 1.25 MHz lower than the carrier signal. The 6 MHz reported as the bandwidth of NTSC analog video is the sum of 1.25 MHz lower sideband, the 4.2 MHz upper sideband, and 0.55 MHz for audio data. The NTSC signal spectrum is shown in Figure 6.16. This introduction gives you a taste of the engineering issues that go into analog video and that have evolved into standards for digital video, both standard and high definition.

## 6.6 DIGITAL VIDEO RESOLUTION AND BANDWIDTH

An important step in converting the video industry from analog to video was creating a standard for the conversion. Given that a frame of NTSC analog video has 525 lines, 480 of which are active lines, how many lines should a corresponding digital frame have? Should PAL and SECAM digital video have the same number of lines? We've seen that analog video has no specific horizontal resolution. What should the horizontal resolution of digital video be? BT.601 was a groundbreaking standard that answered these questions, specifying the sampling rate and resolution to be used converting from analog to digital video.

One of the goals in the standard was to make it easier to exchange NTSC, PAL, and SECAM video files. Converting from one standard to another was made easier by setting a horizontal resolution standard for digitized video that was the same for NTSC, PAL, and SECAM, while allowing just the number of active lines to be different. In this way, the clock rate for sampling could be consistent, and only the timing of the blanking interval had to vary from one standard to another.

Figure 6.19 shows one digital frame as it is encoded in the BT.601 standard. The BT.601 standard adopted the number of lines that were standard for NTSC and PAL analog video and divided the lines into samples. In NTSC analog video, there are 525 lines, 480 of which

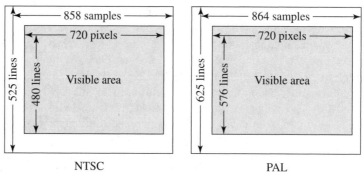

NTSC                         PAL

**Figure 6.19** Spatial resolution according to ITU-RBT.601 standard, converting analog to digital video

relate to the actual image. BT.601 stipulates that there be 858 samples in each line, 720 of these corresponding to visible pixels.

Imagine the analog signal being sent to an analog-to-digital converter. The converter has to read 858 samples in each of the 525 lines in each of the 29.97 frames. From this we get the sampling rate.

sampling rate = horizontal resolution * vertical resolution * frames/s

NTSC: (858 * 525) samples/frame * 29.97 frames/s ≈ 13,500,000 samples/s = 13.5 MHz

PAL: (864 * 625) samples/frame * 25 frames/s = 13,500,000 samples/s = 13.5 MHz

Thus, NTSC and PAL digital video both are described as having a horizontal resolution of 720 pixels and a sampling rate of 13.5 MHz. An NTSC frame is 720 × 480, and a PAL frame is 720 × 576.

With this information, it is possible to determine both the bandwidth and the data rate for different types of digital video. Assume that you have 720 × 480 pixels in a frame, 29.97 frame/s, and 4:2:2 subsampling. (These are the specifications of D1 video, as shown in Table 6.4.) Recall from Chapter 2 that 4:2:2 subsampling uses 16 bits/pixel (Figure 6.20). Bit rate can be computed as follows:

$$720 * 480 \, pixels/frame = 345,600 \, pixels/frame$$

$$345,600 \, pixels/frame * 29.97 \, frames/s = 10,357,632 \, pixels/s$$

$$10,357,632 \, pixels/s * 16 \, bits/pixel = 165,722,112 \, bits/s \approx 166 \, Mb/s$$

(The difference between this value of 166 Mb/s and the value of 172 Mb/s shown in Table 6.4 can be accounted for by overhead—*e.g.*, error checking, etc.)

Bit rate tells you two things: how much data would have to be processed per second if you wanted to display the video in real time, as it's being transmitted, and how much data is generated for each second of video, which has implications for memory requirements if the video is being stored. You can see that uncompressed digital video is prohibitively expensive. A data rate of 172 Mb/s is 21.5 MB/s, which is 77.4 GB per hour of uncompressed video (defining Mb and MB here in powers of 10 rather than 2, which is most common for data rates). Fortunately, video compression methods are very effective at reducing file size while retaining quality. Generally, video is compressed even while it is being shot. For example, DV video, a popular consumer format, is compressed at a rate of almost 5:1.

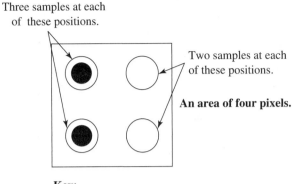

Three samples at each of these positions.

Two samples at each of these positions.

**An area of four pixels.**

**Key:**

⬤ Both chrominance components are sampled at this position

◯ One luminance component is sampled at this position

Assuming one byte per sample and eight bits per byte, 4:2:2 chrominance subsampling yields 8 bytes/4 pixels = 16 bits/pixel.

**Figure 6.20** Bits/pixels required for $4:2:2$ subsampling

## 6.7 DIGITAL VIDEO DISTRIBUTION MEDIA

Now let's get an overview of types of CDs and DVDs and how they differ (Table 6.7). This overview will introduce you to types of permanent portable storage, and the background knowledge should help you understand the technology as it continues to evolve.

A *CD* (*compact disk*, also spelled *disc*) is an optical disk for the storage of data. CDs were originally developed in the late 1970s for 16-bit, 44.1 kHz digital audio data, holding about 74 minutes per disk. In the mid-1980s, the first data CDs and computer CD-ROMs appeared. For data storage, a standard CD holds about 700 MB of data.

| TABLE 6.7 | Digital Video Distribution Media | | | | |
|---|---|---|---|---|---|
| **Format** | **VCD** | **SVCD** | **DVD** | **HD-DVD** | **Blu-ray** |
| NTSC Resolution | 352 × 240 | 480 × 480 | 720 × 480 | 1920 × 1080 | 1920 × 1080 |
| Video Compression | MPEG-1 | MPEG-2 | MPEG-2 | MPEG-2, MPEG-4 AVC, SMPTE-VC1 | MPEG-2, MPEG-4 AVC, SMPTE-VC1 |
| Audio Compression | MP1 | MP1 | PCM, DD, DTS Surround | PCM, DD, DD⁺, DD, TrueHD, DTS, DTS-HD | PCM, DD, DD⁺, DD, TrueHD, DTS, DTS-HD |
| Video Bit Rate | ~1.2 Mb/s | ~2 Mb/s | ~10 Mb/s | ~28 Mb/s | ~40 Mb/s |
| Length (in time) | 74 min. on CD | 35–60 min. on CD | 1–4 hours or more of SD | 2 hours or more of HD, depending on the number of layers | 2 hours or more of HD, depending on the number of layers |

Before the popularization of DVDs, consumers who wanted to produce their own digital videos had to try to squeeze the data onto a CD. A commonly used digital video file format for CD-video was *SIF* (which stands for *standard input format, source intermediate format*, or *source input format*, depending on who you ask). SIF digital video, standardized by ISO-MPEG, has a file resolution of 352 $\times$ 240 for NTSC and 352 $\times$ 288 for PAL and frame rates of 30p or 25p frames/s, respectively. (The size of the video viewed on the screen is 320 $\times$ 240.) Other frame rates may be permitted also, depending on the development platform. MPEG-1 and 4:2:0 chrominance subsampling are used to compress the 30 Mb/s raw data rate down to about 1.2 Mb/s. SIF digital video has quality that is about the same as the quality of analog VHS video, which isn't quite as good as broadcast analog television.

A later standard format for storing digital video on a CD is *VCD* (*video CD*). Derived from the SIF standard, VCD has the same resolution and compression type as described in the previous paragraph. Since the bit rate of VCD is approximately the same as the bit rate for standard CD audio, the number of minutes of VCD video per CD is the same as the number of minutes of audio—74.

*SVCD* (*super video CD*) is an improved version of VCD that uses MPEG-2 rather than MPEG-1 video compression, allowing a data rate up to 2.6 Mb/s with a resolution of 480 $\times$ 480 (NTSC) or 480 $\times$ 576 (PAL). The result is a picture quality almost as good as for DVD video. Eight audio channels are permitted using compressed MPEG multichannel surround sound. About 35 to 60 minutes of SVCD video can fit on a standard CD.

VCDs and SVCDs can be played on dedicated CD players, computers, and some DVD players. Some DVD players will not play VCDs that have been created by means of personal computer CD burners. (They require VCDs created by a professional pressing process.)

A *DVD* is also an optical storage disk, but with a greater storage capacity than a CD. DVD originally was an abbreviation for digital video disk, but when DVDs became adapted to multiple uses it was suggested that this be changed to digital versatile disk. With no clear consensus, the official decision of the DVD Forum was that DVD is just the name and stands for nothing in particular. The DVD Forum is the official standard-setting body for DVDs.

DVDs have evolved through a number of different types, and the technology continues to advance. A DVD-ROM (read-only memory) is permanently stamped with data that can only be read by the consumer. A DVD-R/RW disk allows you to record and re-record. A DVD-RAM disk allows you to record and then go back at a later time and add more to the same recording (as opposed to completely overwriting). A DVD+ type of DVD was created by the DVD+RW Alliance, a consortium that decided to create their own standards outside the DVD Forum's umbrella. DVD+R/RWs work the same as DVD-R/RWs, and most DVD players can play either type.

DVDs can have one or two sides of data, and one or two layers of data per side. The data transfer rates of DVDs are multiples of 10.8 Mb/s, the rate for a 1X DVD. Thus, a 2x is 2*10.8 Mb/s, etc.

DVDs have the capacity to hold audio, video, or regular data. DVD-Audio offers higher fidelity than CD-quality, with sampling rates of 44.1, 48, 88.2, 96, 176.4, and 192 kHz and a variety of sample sizes. Audio compression options include MPEG and AC3. DVD-Video normally uses a resolution of 720 $\times$ 480 (NTSC) or 720 $\times$ 576 (PAL) and is compressed with MPEG-2 compression to a rate of about 3 to 5 Mb/s. About two hours of this type of digital video can be stored on a standard DVD.

In 2003, the DVD Forum approved a new format to succeed DVD, called ***HD-DVD*** (***High Density DVD***), a format intended for high-definition video. HD-DVD was pioneered by Toshiba, NEC, Microsoft, and Intel. HD-DVD disks have three to four times the capacity of DVDs. Like DVDs and CDs, HD-DVDs come in read-only (ROM), writable (R) and rewritable (RW) versions. An HD-DVD can hold 15 GB of data per side. Dual-layer versions hold 30 GB.

The Blu-Ray disk was introduced at the same time as HD-DVD, leading to an HD war for market dominance. Promoted by Sony, this format holds 25 GB per layer. A dual-layer Blu-Ray disk can store about 9 hours of high-definition video and 23 hours of regular video. With the possibility of more than two layers, Blu-Ray disks are projected to have a capacity up to 200 GB. HD-DVD and Blu-Ray are intended for HDTV at 1080p. HD-DVD and Blu-Ray file formats offer the same choice of compression codecs, including the standard MPEG-2 as well as H.264, MPEG-4, Video Codec 1 (VC1, based on the Windows Media 9 format). MPEG-2 yields a bit rate of about 25 Mb/s for high-definition video. MPEG-4 and Video Codec 1 compress to about 15 Mb/s. In 2008, Toshiba announced discontinuing HD-DVD, and Blu-Ray became the accepted standard.

Aside from the standards already mentioned, a variety of proprietary and open source codecs are available for digital video: Sorenson, RealMedia, Cinepak, Intel Indeo, Windows Media Video, XviD, and DivX, to name a few. The concepts and methods underlying these compression algorithms will be covered in detail in Chapter 7.

## 6.8 DIGITAL VIDEO, FILMMAKING, AND TELEVISION PRODUCTION

### 6.8.1 Advantages of Digital Video

We have now entered the digital age, where both film and television are being produced and transmitted in digital format. The advantages of digital video have made it worthwhile for the television, film, and home video industries to make the transition to new technology.

If you compare analog to digital video, digital video comes out the clear winner. Here are some of the reasons why:

- With the bit depth and compression rates that are now possible, **digital video is generally superior in quality to analog, especially at the consumer level**. It has better resolution. You can see this if you compare the picture quality of VHS and DV digital video.
- **Analog video is more susceptible to noise.** If you're old enough, you may remember the noisy—sometimes called "snowy"—pictures in the early days of television. Analog television had to be tuned in, a tricky process of turning knobs and moving antennae to get the clearest possible picture. The 0s and 1s of digital video can be transmitted, received, and interpreted more precisely, with less error, than analog video. The picture comes in with the clarity that its high resolution allows, without any tuning on your part.
- **It's easier to copy video in digital form than in analog form**. When you make a copy of an analog videotape, it is copied mechanically onto another tape and you introduce noise. Each successive copy introduces more noise. This is called *generational loss*. There's no generational loss with digital video. Each copy is a perfect duplicate of the original.

- **Digital video can be edited nonlinearly**, one its biggest advantages. Think about how you would edit analog video that's on tape. What if you wanted to add something into the middle of it? You'd have to make a copy of the original tape up to the point where you wanted to insert the new material, then record the new material, and then copy the remainder of the original onto the new tape. This is a time-consuming linear editing process. It's called *linear editing* because you have to move in a linear manner through the tape; you can't just jump into the middle, nor can you edit one portion while you're working on another. The recopying also introduces generational loss. Digital video can be handled with a *nonlinear editor* (*NLE*). In a nonlinear editing process, you don't have to start at the beginning of a film and edit it in a straight line to the end. You can jump around. Different parts of the film can be edited at the same time, resulting in an efficient specialization of labor. One group can be capturing on-location shots while another is creating computer-generated objects and creatures and another is editing sound.

- **Nonlinear digital editing makes it easier to separate the work on visuals and sound**. In the days when movies were edited entirely on film, sound editing was the last step and couldn't begin until all the film had been sequenced. At that point, the sound track was created and printed along the edge of the film. This slowed down final production. When a movie is edited digitally, sound editing can be done in parallel with the editing of visuals. Also, the director and production crew can actually hear the sound when watching the dailies, since there is no complicated matter of syncing up the sound with the film. (*Dailies* are movie footage shot during one day and reviewed by director, crew, and sometimes cast after the day's work.) Furthermore, digital editing tools have revolutionized sound editing itself.

- **The editing process for digital video is much easier than for film**. Film editing (without the aid of digital translation) requires actually cutting pieces of film and splicing them together again. If a film is edited entirely in film form, thousands of feet of film are shot and this footage has to be reviewed and kept sorted in physical film clips. Choosing segments to use entails searching through all the clips, cutting the film, and splicing it together. In computer-based editing environments (*e.g.*, Avid, Premiere Pro, Final Cut, etc.) sorting clips, shortening them to the desired length, and splicing them together is a matter of simple mouse and keyboard clicks. Furthermore, it is nondestructive. You don't lose part of a clip when you cut it in a computer-based editing environment. The original file is still saved on your hard drive.

- **Special effects such as fade ins/outs, slow motion, background mattes, green screening, and color adjustments are easier to apply digitally than on film**. In the past, these effects had to be created by special lenses, color filters, and optical compositing. Without the aid of digital encoding, special effects must be done by means of an optical printer, which takes multiple film segments, aligns them, applies filters as desired, and rephotographs them onto a new piece of film. Putting multiple shots together in this way is called *optical compositing*. This is tedious and time-consuming, and it's difficult to control the results. Also, each re-recording of the film can introduce generational loss since there's another chance that the film could become dirty and scratched. Compositing and optical effects revolutionized the advent of computer-based video editing systems.

- **Video allows the directors and artists to see results more quickly**. Film has to be sent to the lab for processing. Video can be viewed immediately, so the staging and composition of a scene can be evaluated even on-location and changes made immediately.

Filmmakers began using analog video dailies in the 1960s and 1970s, and now digital video dailies have replaced the analog.

- **Movie scenes can be simulated digitally to see if they are workable**. Actually shooting the scene may require an expensive cast and crew, challenging or dangerous locations, stunt work, and so forth. Simulating the scene first can help the director determine if the scene is worth shooting. If it is, he or she can work out the bugs and prepare the scene so that it can be shot in less time.
- **Videotape physically degenerates over time, while bits in a digitized video file do not**. Film, as a physical medium, is fairly delicate. Nitrate-based film stock, which was the stock used before 1951, decays and even becomes flammable over time. Digital video is more robust. It can be saved on computer hard drives with multiple identical backups at various locations for additional safety.
- **Asset management is easier with digital video than film**. The different components of a movie's production can be organized and stored on a computer with files shared among all the specialist working groups. These components can be broken down to a fine level of detail. Each working group may have its own breakdown of labor and the components they produce. For example, the special effects group has 3-D modelers, lighting experts, shaders, and so forth, each group producing parts of figures at different levels of completion. Storing these in shared files in an organized way streamlines the collaborative process. Exchanging files can be instantaneous, even among collaborators who are on opposite sides of the globe. Moreover, creative assets can be saved and used in multiple productions, even crossing over to spin-off moneymakers like home videos, video games, theme parks, etc.
- **Video editing is much less expensive than film editing**, for all the reasons above.

## 6.8.2 The Allure of Film

Computers are now used in nearly all aspects of movie production. Digital video is an intermediate form used in most movies, which are shot in film, edited in video, and transferred back to film. Some feature-length commercial movies are now produced entirely in video. Still, digital video has not completely usurped film's place as an artistic medium. Many movie makers and television producers still prefer film over video for its look. Just what *is* that look? What creates it? Do you know it when you see it?

Film stock comes in a wide variety of types that vary in their graininess and ability to absorb light. This gives cinematographers a wide range of artistic choices. Working with film offers a certain artistic satisfaction because the film can be manipulated physically. Its graininess is thought to add a desirable texture preferable to the look of digital video. Ironically, the brightness and clarity of digital video are considered drawbacks by many traditionalists, who see video as slick, plastic, or artificial looking. Film, created from analog frames of visual information, inherently has very high resolution, and it is said to offer more subtle color variations and a wider contrast from light to dark. Also, film can have a more gradual transition from sharp to out-of-focus areas, which can give it a softer look. Viewers perceive these differences, whether consciously or unconsciously. A television program that is produced entirely on videotape looks different from one that is shot originally on film. There's something more "immediate" about the videotape—as if you're on the set with the actors—but something more "authentic" about film—a desirable artistic distance between the story and the audience.

Because of film's interesting visual properties, the associations that viewers have made with it over time, and the traditionalists' attachment to it, film is not going to disappear from movie making any time soon, if ever. Nevertheless, digital video has the many advantages listed above. Not the least of these advantages is that video is generally much cheaper than film, and thus a large part of the movie making process is now handled by means of digital video.

### 6.8.3 The Advent of Electronic Cinema and Digital Filmmaking

Two of the early proponents of using computers in filmmaking were George Lucas, director of *American Graffiti* and the *Star Wars* series; and Francis Ford Coppola, director of *Apocalypse Now* and the *Godfather* series. Coppola even coined a term for the revolution in filmmaking: *electronic cinema*. Together, Lucas and Coppola founded American Zoetrope film studio, which made groundbreaking advances in the use of computers for storyboarding, pre-visualization of scenes, automated synchronization of images and sound, and automated sequencing of dailies stored on analog videotape. This was in the 1970s and 1980s, before digital video had entered the scene, so the innovations of electronic cinema were aimed at using computers in planning, scheduling, and automatically synchronizing the activities of the technical equipment. Lucas later went on to found Industrial Light & Magic (ILM), a special effects company that pioneered the use of computer-generated imagery (CGI). CGI employs advanced methods of computer modeling, graphics, and 3D animation, seamlessly integrating computer-animated figures and special effects into scenes shot with traditional filming techniques. ILM is now considered by many to be the best CGI company in the world, with movies like *The Abyss, Jurassic Park*, and *Pirates of the Caribbean: Dead Man's Chest* to its credit, among many others.

Even before the days of digital video, filmmakers recognized the handiness of viewing their work on videotape. Videotape was cheaper, it didn't require lab development, and—after timecode stamping was invented—it was an easier format for synchronizing sound and visuals. It became common practice to generate a video tap alongside film as it was being shot. A video tap used an attachment to a film camera to catch frames in a video signal. This made it possible for more than one person to view the scene without having to look through the film camera's viewfinder. The technology soon became available to make copies of the video to be viewed as dailies.

### 6.8.4 Telecine and Pulldown

The word *telecine* refers to both the process that transfers film to video and the machine that performs the process. Telecine (along with its derivative, high-resolution film scanning) is used in both the television and film industry. In either context, it can be used to transfer film to an intermediate digital format for editing. Because of film's high resolution, its visual qualities, and the experience that artists and professionals have with it, movies are generally shot first on film, and television programs often are shot on film. More and more, digital video is being used in movie and television production. The different workflows that are possible are outlined later in this chapter (Figure 6.23). In all these workflows, transferring film to video is essential.

You can easily picture what a telecine has to do. Light must pass through a film frame and be received by a sensor, which translates the wavelengths of the light into an electronic video signal, which may be analog or digital in nature. This is done for each frame of the film. Flying spot scanners are based on CRT technology. A tiny beam of light is shot through the film frame from left to right and onto a phosphor-coated receiver, which separates the light into its R, G, and B wavelengths and converts these into an electrical video signal. An alternative technology is based on CCD. In this design, light is passed through the whole frame, separated by a prism, received by the photosites on the CCD, and translated into an electrical video signal. In both of these technologies, the process must be done frame-by-frame.

The major difficulty in either of these designs is that film and television have different frame rates. The frame rate for NTSC video is 29.97 frames/s. For PAL and SECAM it is 25 frames/s. The frame rate for film is 24 frames/s. How can you make these match?

One simple method is to translate 24 frames/s of film directly into 24 frames/s of video. Since video is displayed at a faster rate than 24 frames/s, the action is "sped up" when it is viewed. For PAL and SECAM, this isn't so bad, since PAL and SECAM video are displayed at a rate of 25 frames/s. This is a speedup of 1 frame for every 24, or about 4%. The speedup results in a raising of sound pitch, but this can be corrected by a pitch shifter. This simple method of dealing with the frame discrepancy has been used for PAL and SECAM video for many years.

A better way, one that creates smoother video and truer audio, is called ***pulldown***. ***Pulldown*** is a method for using interlaced fields more than once, across frames, to make up for a discrepancy in frame rates as film is translated to video.

Let's look at NTSC video first, which uses ***3:2 pulldown***. The first step in 3:2 pulldown is to slow down the film by 0.1% so that we can get to an integer-based ratio of frame rates. If you multiply 24 * 0.999, you get 23.976. This gives you a ratio of 23.976/29.97, which is 4/5. Now these numbers are something we can deal with. For each four frames of film, we need to create five frames of video.

Figure 6.21 illustrates 3:2 pulldown. The name reflects the pattern of how many fields are used from a frame. The pattern shown in the picture is actually 2:3:3:2, indicating how often the fields of frames A, B, C, and D are used, respectively. This pattern would repeat for each four frames of film.

| | | |
|---|---|---|
| Film frame A | Field A even | Video frame 1 |
| | Field A odd | |
| Film frame B | Field B even | Video frame 2 |
| | Field B odd | |
| | Field B odd | Video frame 3 |
| Film frame C | Field C even | |
| | Field C even | Video frame 4 |
| | Field C odd | |
| Film frame D | Field D even | Video frame 5 |
| | Field D odd | |

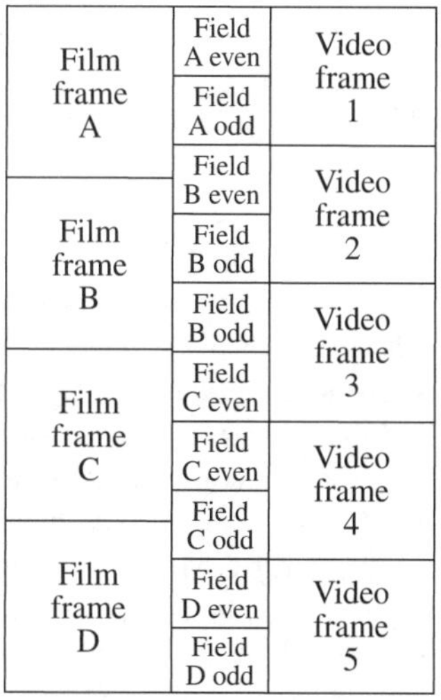

**Figure 6.21**  3:2 pulldown

Analog video frames, and some digital, use interlaced scanning, so the film frames need to be scanned line-by-line and divided into even fields and odd fields. Consider just the first four frames of a film clip that you want to convert to video, and call these frames A, B, C, and D. (The process we're about to describe repeats for every four frames.) The video frames to be created are numbered 1 through 5. The even and odd fields of film frame A are used to create video frame 1. The even and odd fields of film frame B are used to create video frame 2. Then the odd field of film frame B is used again, along with the even frame of film frame C to create video frame 3. This reuse of fields is what gets you five video frames out of four film frames, and it creates fairly smooth video despite the repetition. Sometimes there's a little jerkiness to the movement, called *telecine judder*, but generally the results are good.

A similar method can be used for PAL and SECAM conversions. Here, you need only one additional frame of video for each 24 frames of film. If a field is reused every 12 film frames, an extra video frame is created for every 24 frames. (Two fields make a frame.) Thus the pattern is $2:2:2:2:2:2:2:2:2:2:2:3$.

Since analog and digital video have the same frame rate (as long as you stay within one standard—NTSC, PAL, or SECAM), this pulldown method works whether telecine is producing analog or digital video. It is also adaptable to high-definition formats.

The telecine and pulldown processes can be reversed. Increasingly, film production involves creating the original footage on film, transferring to video for editing, and then transferring back to film for final distribution. When the video is inverse-telecined, the fields have to be properly deinterlaced to ensure smooth motion, as described in the next section.

The original telecines have evolved into high resolution scanners like the Kodak Cineon, Philips Spirit DataCine, and the Cintel Klone. The newer scanners, sometimes called high-end telecines, can achieve resolutions on the order of 4000 ppi in the horizontal direction, and even higher, from a 35 mm film frame. The resolutions for high-end scanners are customarily abbreviated as 2K (*e.g.*, $2048 \times 1536$), 4K (*e.g.*, $4096 \times 3072$), and so forth. Just how much resolution is enough is a subjective judgment. Since film is inherently analog— each frame is a continuous image with gradually changing colors—a film frame has no precise horizontal or vertical resolution. By most estimates, 4K resolution is enough. At some point, no more information is acquired by a higher resolution scanner. Since scanning so much information takes time, a practical limit has to be placed on the resolution.

New file formats have been designed specifically to accommodate digital video that is created from scanned film. One of the first to be widely used was called *Cineon*, created by Kodak. The word Cineon was first used for an entire workstation, including the scanner, tape drives, film recorder, and notably, the software for editing the intermediate digital form. The Cineon software is no longer sold, and now the word refers to a file format for digital video scanned from film, including information about gamma values and printing density. Pixels in digital video files scanned from film are typically stored with a bit depth of 10 bits. Cineon files have evolved into the *DPX format*, standardized by ANSI/SMPTE.

The transfer from video to film is done by *digital film recorders*. These can be CRT-based (*e.g.*, those made by Celco) or laser-based (*e.g.*, the Arrilaser). *Tron* was the first movie to be recorded from digital to film using a Celco recorder. Later film credits for Celco include *Hotel Rwanda* and *Apocaplyto*. The IMAX *Sharks 3D* was recorded using the Celco Fury. The laser-based film-scanning technology invented by Arrilaser received a Scientific and Technical Award in 2001 from the Academy of Motion Picture Arts and Sciences. Arrilaser was used to record *Lord of the Rings*, *Harry Potter and the Sorcerer's Stone*, and *102 Dalmations*, among others. Both types of digital film recorders are still in use. In addition to their use in the film-making process, digital film recorders are important in film restoration and preservation.

## 6.8.5 Deinterlacing

*Deinterlacing* is the process of putting fields together in a way that creates a coherent frame that can be shown by a progressive-scanning display. It is required in two situations: When material has been transferred from film to video and is being transferred back to film; and when video material in interlaced format is being shown on a display device that uses progressive scanning. (Film is like a progressive scanning display in that it shows the whole frame at one time.) This second situation arises when HDTV is transmitted in 1080i format and received by a television that is 1080p.

Let's first consider how deinterlacing works in the case of the film-to-video-to-film translation, since this is fairly simple. If film has been transferred to video by a telecine or film-scanning process, then the pattern of field usage is known, as described above for 3:2 pulldown. If nothing changed the frames after they were scanned to video, this pattern could simply be reversed. The difficulty is that the video is edited before being returned to film, and the pattern is disrupted. Image analysis techniques have to be employed, to find segments where the pulldown patterns may still be intact. Where pulldown patterns are not intact, interpolation methods have to be applied.

The second application of deinterlacing is for translating interlaced video into progressive video. Think about how this situation differs from the previous one. With video that was created from film, during the film-scanning process, if two fields are created from one frame, you know that they belong to a picture that was captured at a single moment in time because that's the nature of a film frame. If the inverse telecine process can find the correct two fields, they will go together perfectly, with no combed edges.

Video frames that were created *as video* from the start are different. With video frames, the even and odd fields from one frame are captured at different moments in time. Thus, if there is motion in the scene, objects aren't in the same place in the second field as they were in the first. This is alright when the video is displayed in an interlaced manner, since the two fields are not displayed at exactly the same time. However, if you put the two fields into one progressively scanned frame and show that frame all at once, you get a combed-edge effect. You can see this in Figure 6.22, where two fields representing a moving object are captured as one still image. Progressive scanning doesn't really display the two deinterlaced fields all at once—it scans them in. But is does so at a rate of 29.97 frames per second, with the deinterlaced fields shown side by side about every 1/30th of a second. This makes the combining effect apparent. Deinterlacing must put two neighboring fields together in a way that eliminates the combing.

An easy way to accomplish interlacing is called **doubling**: choosing either the even or the odd field and using the chosen field twice to create a frame. An alternative is to average

Combed effect from combining even          Deinterlacing by interpolation
and odd interlaced fields

**Figure 6.22** Combed effect from interlaced scanning

the even and odd fields and use the average for both. Both doubling and averaging reduce the resolution of the frame. Motion compensation can be added to these techniques to predict the direction in which objects are moving so that the pixels in the fields can be modified accordingly.

Deinterlacing can be done automatically by a television if it is engineered that way. That is, televisions that are designed for progressive scanning can receive interlaced video transmission and deinterlace it for display. Deinterlacing filters are also offered in image processing programs. For example, you can export a single frame from a video processing program, import it into a still image processing program and deinterlace it. You won't be able to get perfect resolution, but the picture will be smoother, as shown in Figure 6.22.

### 6.8.6 Integrating Film and Digital Video in Commercial Movie-Making

It's hard to say where film ends and video begins in the world of movie and television production. For one thing, it's a moving target. As of the writing of this book, HDTV is coming into its own, with everything changing to higher resolution, wider aspect ratios, and immersive sound. Film and video are closely intertwined in production methods. Television and movie directors still like film, and it's probably a fair generalization to say that most movies and dramatic television series are shot initially on film and return to film after intermediate digital processing. But producers and directors don't reveal all their tricks, and the situation continues to change. A movie may start as film, go to video for editing, and return to film. Or some parts of it may go through one process, and some parts another. Depending on the scenes and theme that a director is to trying to convey, a movie could be made with a combination of 35 mm and 16 mm film, professional videotape formats, and even consumer-level videotape. And now, some movies are even being made entirely on video—not just the animated ones like *Toy Story* and *Finding Nemo*, but human dramas.

To sort this out, it may be helpful to look back at the traditional filmmaking process, and compare it to new workflows. The four main stages of filmmaking are preproduction, production, postproduction, and distribution. Preproduction is the planning period. The script is developed, a budget made, a crew is assembled, and locations are scouted. In production, the movie is shot. In postproduction, the movie is edited, which includes choosing the segments to use, sequencing them, applying special effects, adjusting color and lighting, and making final prints. Then the film is distributed to movie theaters and promoted with advertising and special appearances of its cast.

Computers are used in all aspects of this process. Computer software is used for storyboarding, budgets, set design, artists' models of scenes and animated creatures, effects editing, the control of camera movement, advertising—just about any part of the process you can think of. It's the postproduction stage, however, that involves digital video.

Four possible workflows for moviemaking are shown in Figure 6.23. (Note that these workflows and the following discussion do not include animated movies or movies that contain no camera work.) The first workflow is traditional filmmaking, involving no digital elements. Around the 1970s and 1980s, starting with the work of George Lucas, this traditional way of making films began to change. Science fiction and movies like *Star Wars*, the *Indiana Jones* series, and the *Jurassic Park* series became very popular, requiring advanced methods of computer modeling and animation to be woven in with filmed real-world scenes. Also, nonlinear digital video editing tools became available, facilitating the editing process. Thus, the second workflow emerged, where digital video was used as an intermediate form. Not all sources agree on who was first, but some sources credit *Breaking the Waves*, a 1996

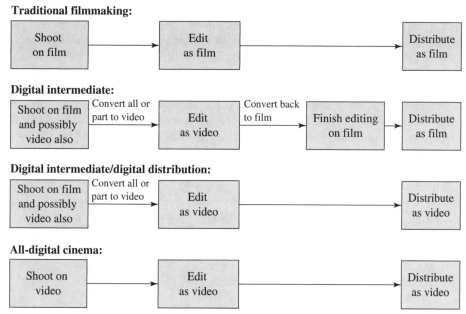

**Figure 6.23** Movie-making workflows

Swedish production, as being the first commercial movie to be transferred entirely to an intermediate digital form and then transferred back to film. *Pleasantville* (1998) is another good example of the digital intermediate workflow (although only part of the move was digitized). In this movie, which transports two teenagers into their television sets and the black and white world of early TV, characters slowly begin to see color as they throw off their stereotypes. This effect was easily created in the digital format. *O Brother, Where Art Thou?* (2000) also was among the first movies to go through an entirely digital intermediate stage. Its DVD release included a behind the scenes segment entitled "Painting with Pixels" that described the digital postprocessing coloring of the movie.

The third and fourth workflows in the figure are becoming increasingly popular, both of them using digital distribution and projection, which is called *digital cinema*. Digital projection requires an initial investment to equip theaters with new digital projection equipment and computer-automated management systems for uploading and displaying digital movies. This cost is being shared between theater owners and film distributors. A consortium of movie studios and vendors called the Digital Cinema Initiatives (DCI), together with the SMPTE committee, has developed a common format for projectors and sound systems in digital cinema theaters. These specifications include either $2048 \times 1080$ or $4096 \times 2160$ resolution; 36 bits per pixel in the XYZ color model; JPEG 2000 compression; a maximum bit rate of 250 Mb/s; and 24 bits/sample audio at a sampling rate or 48 or 96 kHz, uncompressed.

Digital distribution has clear advantages. It's much cheaper to send movies as digital data files rather than as physical reels of film. Making film prints to be released around the world costs millions of dollars because of the cost of film stock and the duplication process. In contrast, digital data is very easy to duplicate. At a rate of 250 Mb/s, a feature-length movie could fit into a few hundred gigabytes, and sometimes less. Digital movies can be distributed on recyclable hard drives or sent through high-speed networks. Another advantage is the ability to encrypt the movie so that it can be played only by the right kind of projector, which makes it more difficult to copy, protecting against copyright infringements.

Released by satellite broadcast in the United States in 1998, *The Last Broadcast* is credited as being the first movie to be released digitally. In 1999, *Bicentennial Man* was shown digitally in some venues with DLP projection. *Star Wars Episode I: The Phantom Menace* is a good example of the film-to-digital-projection workflow. Most of this movie was shot on film, with a few scenes shot on video. The movie was transferred to video and computer-generated images that were seamlessly integrated. Then, in a 1999 limited release, a digital version of the movie was shown. (In most theaters, the movie was shown on film.)

*Star Wars Episode II: Attack of the Clones* is an example of the last workflow in Figure 6.23. It is cited as the first movie to be shot entirely with digital cameras (to which CGI was added) and released in an encrypted digital format. New high-resolution video cameras have made entirely digital movies possible. New high-resolution digital video cameras (*e.g.*, the Dalsa Origin) go beyond the 1920 ppi horizontal resolution of HDTV, offering 4K resolution that rivals the detail of film. These new cameras are also adaptable to the 24 frames/s rate of film. With the new technology, it's possible to make high-definition video look very much like film, so finishing on video is becoming more and more common. Film and video are merging and to some extent converging, and the technology is changing every day. If you want to be in the middle of it all, digital video is the place to be.

## EXERCISES

1. This chapter shows how to arrive at the reported 4.2 MHz luminance bandwidth for NTSC video. Do the same type of computation for PAL to see if you arrive at a luminance bandwidth of about 5.0 MHz. Show your work.

2. How many bits/pixel are required for 4:1:1 subsampling?

3. What is the speed of a 12X DVD burner?

4. Amplitude modulation, mathematical modeling exercise, online

## APPLICATIONS

1. Examine the specifications of the display on your computer and/or television. Is it CRT, LCD, plasma, or DLP? What is its resolution? Does it use progressive or interlaced scanning? Describe other important specifications.

2. Examine the features of your image processing software. Does it have a feature for adjusting pixel aspect ratio so that you can create an image to be incorporated into video? When and why does the aspect ratio have to be adjusted? What will happen if you create an image intended to be displayed on a computer monitor and it is shown on a video monitor with rectangular pixels?

3. Check the connection types on your video camera, VCR, and/or DVD player. What type of connections are possible? Composite video? S-video? What type do you use, and why? Does the device allow for component video?

4. Examine the specifications of your digital video camera (or the one you would like to have). What is the storage medium? Do you have choices of storage media? What is the type of video (*e.g.*, D1, DV, etc.)? Is video compressed as it is shot? Are different compression methods possible?

# REFERENCES

## Print Publications

Ascher, Steven, and Edward Pincus. *The Filmmaker's Handbook: A Comprehensive Guide for the Digital Age*. New York: Plume, 1999.

Couch, II, Leon W. *Digital and Analog Communication Systems*. 6th ed. Upper Saddle River, NJ: Prentice Hall, 2001.

Hsu, Stephen C. Feb. 1986. "The Kell Factor: Past and Present." *SMPTE Journal* 95(2): 206–214.

Jack, Keith. *Video Demystified: A Handbook for the Digital Engineer*. 3rd ed. Eagle Rock, VA: LLH Technology Publishing, 2001.

Kell, R. D., A. V. Bedford, and G. L. Fredendall,. July 1940. "A Determination of the Optimum Number of Lines in a Television System," *RCA Review* 5: 8–30.

Long, Ben, and Sonja Schenk. *The Digital Filmmaking Handbook*. 3rd ed. Hingham, MA: Charles River Media, Inc., 2006.

Malkiewicz, Dris, and M. David Mullen. *Cinematography: The Classic Guide to Filmmaking, Revised and Updated for the 21st Century*. 3rd ed. New York: Simon & Schuster/Fireside, 2005.

Ohanian, Thomas A., and Michael E. Phillips. *Digital Filmmaking: The Changing Art and Craft of Making Motion Pictures*. Boston: Focal Press, 2000.

Poynton, Charles. *Digital Video and HDTV Algorithms and Interfaces*. San Francisco: Morgan Kaufmann, 2003.

Read, Paul. April 2001. "The Digital Intermedia Post-Production Process in Europe." *Journal of Film Preservation*, pp. 57–70.

Wang, Yao, Jorn Ostermann, and Ya-Qin Zhang. *Video Processing and Communications*. Upper Saddle River, NJ: Prentice Hall, 2002.

## Websites

ARIB (Association of Radio Industries and Businesses).
    http://www.arib.or.jp.
ATSC (Advanced Television Systems Committee).
    http://www.atsc.org.
Blu-ray.com
    http://www.blu-ray.com
DVB (Digital Video Broadcasting).
    http://www.dvb.org.
ITU (International Telecommunication Union).
    http://www.itu.int/home.
SMPTE (Society for Motion Picture and Television Engineers).
    http://www.smpte.org.

# Digital Video Processing

CHAPTER

7

*Whatever you think you can do or believe you can do, begin it. Action has magic, grace, and power in it.* —Johann Wolfgang Von Goethe

## OBJECTIVES FOR CHAPTER 7
- Know the basic components of a digital video editing workstation.
- Know the main steps in digital video editing.
- Know how alpha channels are created and used and understand the mathematics of alpha blending.
- Know how mattes are created and used and understand the mathematics of chroma keying.
- Know how keyframes are used.
- Understand the difference between drop-frame and nondrop-frame timecode.
- Know the difference between constant and variable speed change in digital video.
- Be familiar with how color correction tools are applied in digital video.
- Be familiar with common digital video file types and codecs.
- Understand the basic concept of vector quantization.
- Be familiar with various types of MPEG compression.
- Understand the basic MPEG compression algorithm.
- Be familiar with the algorithm for motion estimation.

## 7.1 WHY, WHAT, AND HOW

Digital video has arrived. Television producers use digital video. Cinematographers use it. In 2006, YouTube exploded on the web, inviting anyone and everyone to share videos of just about any type you can think of. In 2006, *Time* magazine named YOU the person of the year, reflecting this new power to make yourself seen and heard. Video isn't just for big shots. YOU can do it, too. You can you shoot your son's birth, your daughter's wedding, your family's Christmas, and your treks through Tibet—collecting miles of unedited videotape, editing the tapes, and saving them on disks. You can even learn to do this *well*. You can create videos for practical reasons, as part of your work. You can create them as a form of creative expression. And the web gives you an immediate audience, if you want one. You can share your videos with the world, if you like. If you have access to a digital video camera, a video cell phone, a computer, the right software—digital video is within your grasp.

In Chapter 6, we explained how digital video is represented, comparing it to its analog ancestor. We put it in the context of film and television production, and gave you an idea of the professional arenas in which you could use your knowledge of digital video. In this chapter, we'll introduce you to the process of digital video production. The hardware and software described will be mostly consumer-level, since this is where you're most likely to start—working with DV video in environments like Adobe Premiere Pro, Apple Final Cut Pro, Avid Media Composer, Cinelerra, or Kino.

Video is a moving target. Feature-length films are moving to digital production, as are many television series. Home video and television equipment is making the transition from standard to high definition. Television and computer technology is beginning to converge, along with the rest of the telecommunications industry. Models for video cameras change every few months, as does video editing software.

This chapter includes some screen captures of digital video processing programs. The interfaces to your own video processing software may be a little different, but the features will be basically the same. When we describe a feature and tell you that you "can" do this or that, we mean of course "depending on the video processing program you're using." You'll need to become familiar with your own work environment to see what features are available. Reading through our examples should prepare you for the activities involved in video processing, and seeing a variety of interfaces should make you aware that you have to be flexible in moving from one environment to another.

We assume that you've read about the science of imaging and sound in the previous chapters. This chapter is presented at a higher level of abstraction than earlier chapters, giving you an overview of digital video processing and showing you the steps you typically go through in shooting, capturing, and editing digital video. The second part of this chapter returns to algorithms, explaining how digital video compression is done.

## 7.2 DIGITAL VIDEO WORKSTATIONS

In Chapter 6, we listed the recent formats for digital video cameras. In the early 2000s, DV became the most popular format at the consumer level. DV has many varieties, including professional (DVCAM and DVCPRO 50) and high-definition formats (HDV and DVCPRO HD). The version used most by consumers is called mini-DV, so named because the cassettes are small. Standard DV cameras, also called *camcorders*, come in the single CCD, 3-CCD or CMOS varieties and shoot in the standard 4:3 aspect ratio. HD cameras shoot in 16:9 aspect ratio. Many of them store on tape, with a compression ratio of about 5:1. This format is good if you want to transfer video to your computer for editing. Although DV video is compressed, the compression occurs only within frames, not between frames. Thus, each frame remains a separate entity, making it possible to edit DV video frame by frame. HDV, AVDHD, and other high definition formats use both intra- and interframe compression. If you need the very highest quality video, you'll have to use a professional-grade camera and an uncompressed format.

Video cameras can also have on-board hard or DVD drives, or memory cards that allow you to compress and save directly in MPEG-1 or MPEG-2 format, which have higher compression ratios than DV. These cameras are good if you don't plan to edit your video footage since they compress the video in a distributable format right away. Also, it's easier to transfer the footage to your computer, since it's a simple file copy rather than a real-time capture. The disadvantage is that MPEG-1 and MPEG-2 are lossy compression methods. If you compress your footage from the outset but want to edit it before creating a final version, you've already lost some resolution. To edit the footage, you may have to decompress it and export it again to an editable format, like DV. So the bottom line is that if you don't ever plan to edit your video footage, cameras that immediately compress to MPEG are very convenient. But if you *are* going to edit and want to have better resolution in the end, this is not the right camera for you.

Around 2006, high-definition DV cameras (HDV) began to drop in price and increase in popularity as consumers wanted to match their camera formats with the new widescreen televisions that they were buying. The cameras come in the 720p and 1080i formats designed for televisions.

When choosing a camera, you need to decide whether you want standard definition or high definition. You need to weigh the convenience of cameras that immediately compress to

MPEG versus those that compress minimally, allowing you to edit and compress to final form later. You should consider the convenience of the on-board storage medium, whether it is tape, DVD, hard disk, or a memory card. You should also be aware of the output type of your camera and the corresponding bit rate, because this bit rate determines how much storage space you'll need for your video footage. (Bit rates are given in the table in Chapter 6.)

As of the writing of this book, you can buy a consumer-level digital video camera for as little as $200, with prices ranging up to about $3000. Professional digital video cameras cost in the thousands or tens of thousands of dollars. Digital cinema cameras are so specialized and expensive that often they are rented rather than bought by film producers.

In addition to a camera, you need a computer powerful enough for digital processing. You should check your video processing software to see what its system requirements are, but you can expect that you'll need at least a 1 GHz processor and 2 GB of RAM, a display with resolution of at least $1440 \times 900$, and *lots* of hard disk space. You should consider what type of video you'll be using, look up its data rate, and get an estimate of how much data you'll be generating per hour of video. For example, DV format has a data rate of about 25 Mb/s for video alone. At that data rate, you'll generate over 11 GB of data in an hour—twice that for HD. A terabyte of disk space isn't too much. An essential investment is a removable hard drive for backing up and transporting your work.

If you want to be able to convert an analog video signal to digital on your computer, you'll need a ***video capture card***. ***Capturing*** is the process of transferring video to your computer. The video footage could originate in a digital video camera. In this case, it is already digitized, and the capturing step is a matter of transferring the file to your computer via a software interface. Alternatively, the video footage could originate from an analog source, like an analog video camera or a television broadcast signal. In this case, a video capture card is needed to do the analog-to-digital conversion. Video capture cards are PCI-e or USB cards that fit into expansion slots. There isn't a lot of room directly on this interface for all the connection types you might want, like XLR for sound and S-video for analog. If you want to have a variety of connections available to the card, you have to get an external interface called **a *breakout box***.

Capturing is a real-time process. That is, if you have 60 minutes on a videotape, it takes 60 minutes to capture it. Capturing video requires a hard drive and data connection that can keep up with the data rate of digital video. Compressed digital video has a data rate that ranges from about 25 to 100 Mb/s, depending on the resolution and how much it is compressed. If this much data is going to travel from a digital video camera to the computer's hard disk, then the data transport cable, the computer's internal bus, and the hard disk drive have to be able to keep up. Otherwise, frames will be dropped. A type of cable connection that is often used with consumer-grade digital camcorders is ***IEEE 1394***—known as ***Firewire*** or ***iLink***. ***USB (Universal Serial Bus)*** and ***USB 2.0***, ***component***, ***HD-SDI***, and ***HDMI*** connections are also common. ***SDI*** (***serial data interface***), ***SDDI*** (***Sony digital data interface***), or ***SDTI*** (***serial digital transport interface***) are used with some high-end camcorders. The transfer cable goes from the digital camcorder to the computer for digital video capture or direct recording. (See Tables 1.4 and Table 1.5 in Chapter 1 for data transfer rates of common communication links and storage devices.)

With the power of today's digital video editing suites, it's possible for the non-professional to create polished video from his or her home computer. Video editing software has become reasonably affordable, and the steps in video editing are kept at a high level of abstraction so that the layperson can figure out how to use the software.

The basic components of a digital video editing suite are an environment for capturing and sequencing clips in a timeline, one for applying special effects, and a compression/DVD burning program. You may not need all of these depending on the type of movie you're making and how you want to distribute it, and two or three of these functions may be wrapped in one software package. Basic clip-sequencing software gives you the ability to place transitions between clips, add sound, and apply simple special effects like mattes, resizing, blurs, blue- or greenscreening, and so forth. For more computationally difficult special effects like smoke, fire, or frame distortions and colorations, you may need a dedicated special effects package. To compress and package your movie for distribution, you may be able to use the same software environment in which you edited the movie, or you may want to export the movie and import it into another environment that offers specialized compression algorithms or allows you to author a DVD with a tailored user interface.

Recall from Chapter 6 that a digital video editing environment can be referred to as an NLE (nonlinear editor). We'll use NLE for brevity in this chapter.

# 7.3 VIDEO PROCESSING

## 7.3.1 The Main Steps

The main steps in digital video processing are these:

- shooting video footage
- gathering your media in a video processing environment
  - ○ capturing video clips from your camera to the NLE's native video format or transferring the files directly in a tapeless workflow
  - ○ importing clips previously captured on or copied to the computer
  - ○ importing sounds, still images, vector graphics, motion graphics, etc. as needed
- editing and sequencing clips
  - ○ marking in and out points of individual video or sound clips
  - ○ placing video clips, sound clips, and/or still frames in the timeline
  - ○ applying transitions between clips
  - ○ adjusting timing
- applying special effects
  - ○ compositing by applying transparency, mattes, chroma or luma keys, etc.
  - ○ changing colors, shape, motion, etc. for special purposes
- editing sound
- applying final color adjustments and balances
- rendering
- exporting the movie to an appropriate file format with compression
- burning the video to a DVD, placing it on a website, or otherwise distributing it

In a ***tapeless workflow***, the footage is captured to a medium like a hard drive or memory card in the camera. Then the footage can be transferred directly to the computer as a file transfer, without the real-time capturing step. This has become a popular workflow.

## 7.3.2 Shooting and Capturing Video

Shooting video is the process of pointing a video camera at something and recording what the camera sees. How to shoot *good* video is a big topic itself—the art of cinematography. It's not the subject of this book, but we refer you to the references at the end of this chapter if it's a subject you're interested in.

Supplement on
video processing:

hands-on project

Let's say you have a video camera of some type. Now how do you get the video footage onto your computer where you can edit it? Here are five common ways:

**Shoot video on a digital video camera, storing it on the camera's internal hard drive, DVD, or memory card. Then transfer the video file to your computer.** Some digital video cameras have internal hard disk drives, DVD writers, or memory cards. These cameras digitize the video and compress it at the same time, generally in MPEG-1 or MPEG-2 format. The video file then can be transferred directly to your computer. The camera is connected to the computer with the type of cable described above, and the transfer can be as simple as a file drag-and-drop. This type of camera avoids the real-time capture step, but it automatically compresses the video, making it harder to edit.

**Shoot video on a digital video camera, storing it on videotape. Then capture the video on your computer.** This is a two-step process. First, you *shoot* the video. The camera digitizes the image and saves it on videotape. Then you *capture* the video on your computer. *Capturing video* is the process of transferring digital video from an external source—in this case, digital videotape—to a computer file.

**Connect a digital video camera to the computer and record the video directly onto the hard drive of the computer.** This method avoids the capture step, since recording and capturing are condensed into one step. The disadvantage is that it isn't always convenient to connect a video camera directly to a computer and record from there. To do this, you have to stay physically connected to the computer, which obviously limits your video shooting situations.

**Connect an analog video device to the computer and record the video directly onto the hard drive of the computer.** Analog isn't completely outmoded. You can still record in real time with an analog video camera, capturing on the computer as you record. You'll need a video capture card on your computer to do this. The video capture card digitizes the analog video and sends it to permanent storage on the computer. If you have some old VHS tapes and want to digitize them, you can also play them through a cassette deck attached to the computer and capture them as digital video.

**Copy digital video files from an external source.** If you have video footage that you created previously or uncopyrighted footage that someone else created, you can simply transfer the files as you would any other computer files.

### 7.3.3 Gathering Media

Representative NLEs are shown in Figure 7.1, Figure 7.2 and Figure 7.3. Generally, they include the following components:

- a capture window
- a window for gathering and organizing your media
- a window for editing clips before placing them in the timeline—for example, choosing *In* and *Out* points, which is how you trim a clip to the desired length. (This window is called the *Source* view in Premiere Pro, the *Viewer* in Final Cut Pro.)
- a window for viewing clips that are in the timeline and applying special effects to them (called the *Program* view in Premiere Pro, the *Canvas* in Final Cut Pro)
- a timeline for sequencing clips, stills, and sound files

Capturing can be a simple matter of connecting your digital video camera to the computer, opening the capture window on the computer, and clicking the play button. Once you've captured video, you have a file in the editing program's native file format—AVI, MPG, M2T, or MXP for Premiere Pro or MOV for Final Cut Pro, for example. The video footage is now a *clip* that you can work with.

**Figure 7.1** Capture window (Ulead VideoStudio)

**Figure 7.2** Video editing environment (from Premiere Pro) (Markings of Source and Program were added.)

You begin creating a movie by gathering your ***media***, also called ***assets***—all the video footage, still images, and sound that will be put together in the movie. In addition to capturing new clips, you can import clips that you captured in a previous work session or maybe others that you've gotten from an outside source. You also can import still images and audio files—for example. BMP, GIF, JPEG, PNG, WAV or MP3 files. You can import a still image with an alpha channel and preserve the alpha channel in the video environment. Then part of the image will be transparent, and if you put this image on top of a video clip, the clip will show through the transparent part of the overlying image.

Note that a video editing project *links* to the media that you import into it. In essence, it creates a pointer to the external media rather than embedding it directly into the project file. This means that if you delete from your computer any clips that were part of a project, the project will mark these clips as being unavailable and ask you to relink, skip, or delete them.

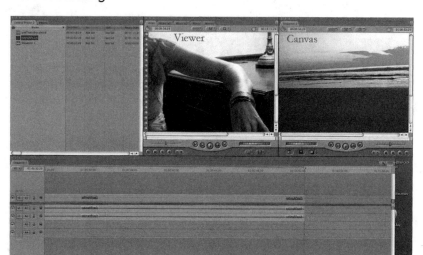

**Figure 7.3** Another video editing environment (from Final Cut Pro) (Markings of Viewer and Canvas were added.)

The advantage to this is the ease with which you can upgrade your media. Consider what happens if you overwrite an image file saved on your computer with a new copy. The video editing project knows the file by its name, so it will be automatically linked to the new copy.

## 7.3.4 Sequencing

Now you've gathered your clips, and you're ready to select the ones you want to use, placing them one after another on the timeline with transitions in between. You've probably shot much more footage than you'll use in the edited movie. But it's easy to be selective with digital editing. You don't have to use entire clips; you can trim individual clips to just the portions you want. Fortunately, this is a nondestructive process in that it doesn't alter the original video clip stored on your computer. Some programs allow you to mark the In and Out points on a clip before you place it in the timeline, and only the parts between the In and Out points will be included in that part of the movie. If you recorded audio with the clip, it will go along with the video frames in the timeline. You can also import audio files separately. Transitions can be applied between clips in the timeline. A wide range of transitions are available, including fade in, fade out, cross fade, wipe, peel, and so on (Figure 7.4).

Some video editing environments allow you to organize your clips into *sequences* of clips, which are like scenes in a movie or chapters in a book. Sequences can be nested within other sequences, and they can be exported and reused in movies. You may even be able to save an entire project and import it as a sequence into another project.

**Figure 7.4** Transitions (from Ulead VideoStudio)

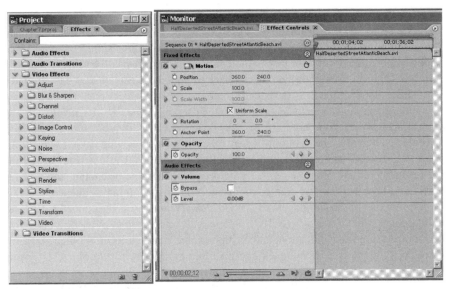

**Figure 7.5**  Effects (from Premiere Pro)

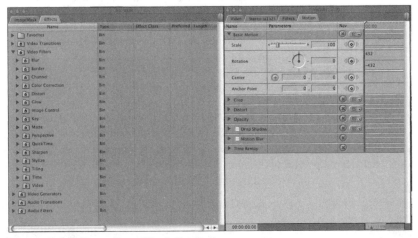

**Figure 7.6**  Effects (from Final Cut Pro)

You can apply effects to clips in the timeline. Basic effects (sometimes called *fixed effects* or *motion effects*) include changing the size, shape, position, or opacity of a clip. These are shown on the right hand side of Figure 7.5 and Figure 7.6. Special effects such as distortions of shape or chroma keying are grouped by type. These are shown on the left-hand side of the corresponding figure. You apply a special effect by dragging and dropping it onto a clip in the timeline. Then you adjust the parameters as you like.

## 7.3.5 Digital Compositing

### 7.3.5.1 Alpha Channels and Alpha Blending

If all you could do was to string clips one after the other on a timeline, you wouldn't have much room for creativity. But that's not all there is to it. Through the process of *compositing*, you can combine multiple clips and still images. The timeline in an NLE has tracks so that you can put different clips and images on different tracks, possibly covering the same span of time. Tracks in video are just like layers in still images. The clip or still image that is on the top track will lie on top of one on a lower track. If the one on top is shrunk so that it doesn't cover the whole frame, or if it is made partially transparent, then you'll be able to see the one underneath. You can even erase an object's background and place another background behind it. This is done all the time in special effects for movies—from making spaceships fly in *Star Wars* to making sea monsters rise from the deep in *Pirates of the Caribbean*.

In the early days of film, compositing was done optically: Two or more pieces of film were projected together and shot onto a new piece of film. Now with digital video, digital compositing methods are used to mathematically combine pixel values from two or more images to create a new final image. A frame of video is simply an image, and when you process these images frame-by-frame, you have a composited digital sequence.

A basic digital compositing operation called *alpha blending* was introduced in Chapter 3. Recall that if you have a two-layer RGB image with a foreground pixel $F$, a background pixel $B$ at the same image location, and an alpha value $\alpha$ at that location, then—assuming that the background is fully opaque—the resulting composite pixel color $C$ is given by $C = \alpha F + (1 - \alpha)B$. These operations are done channel-by-channel.

Let's take this a step further. What if you want to make a composite of two layers, both of which have less than 100% opacity. You need a method that allows you to do this from the bottom up, saving at each step a "remainder alpha value," $\alpha'$. The equations are as follows:

## KEY EQUATION

Given an RGB image with two layers, foreground and background, let a foreground pixel be given by $F = (f_r, f_g, f_b)$ and a background pixel be given by $B = (b_r, b_g, b_b)$. Let the alpha value for the foreground be $\alpha_f$ and the alpha value for the background be $\alpha_b$ where $0 \leq \alpha_f, \alpha_b \leq 1$. Then for each foreground pixel $F$ and corresponding background pixel $B$ at the same location in the image, the resulting composite pixel color $C = (c_r, c_g, c_b)$ created by alpha blending is defined by

$$C = (\alpha_f F + (1 - \alpha_f)\alpha_b B)/\alpha'$$

where

$$\alpha' = \alpha_f + \alpha_b(1 - \alpha_f)$$

and operations are done channel-by-channel.

**Equation 7.1**

You should be able to see intuitively how these equations work, applying a fraction of the color to each pixel in proportion to the alpha channel for each layer. Let's try an example to see if it gives reasonable results.

Say that you have the situation pictured in Figure 7.7 Considering the layers from the bottom up, we have black, blue, green, and pink blocks of color overlapping in various ways. The blue block has RGB color (40, 100, 255), the green block is RGB (130, 152, 74), and the pink block is RGB (248, 98, 218). Assume that the green block has a 40% opacity, and the blue block has a 80% opacity. The black background is fully opaque. To determine the pixel colors, you can work from the bottom up or from the top down, as shown in Table 7.1.

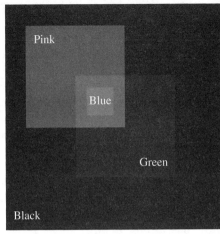

Layers, from top down:

Pink block, 60% opaque
Green block, 40% opaque
Blue block, 80% opaque
Black background, 100% opaque

**Figure 7.7** Alpha blending of multiple layers

| TABLE 7.1 | Alpha Blending |
|---|---|
| **Bottom Up** | **Top Down** |
| blue over black<br>0.8 * 40 = 32<br>0.8 * 100 = 80<br>0.8 * 255 = 204 | pink over green<br>$\alpha' = 0.6 + 0.4 * (1 - 0.6) = 0.76$<br>(0.6 * 248 + 0.4 * (1 − 0.6) * 130)/0.76 = 223<br>(0.6 * 98 + 0.4 * (1 − 0.6) * 152)/0.76 = 109<br>(0.6 * 218 + 0.4 * (1 − 0.6) * 74)/0.76 = 188 |
| green over black<br>0.4 * 130 = 52<br>0.4 * 152 = 61<br>0.4 * 74 = 30 | green over black<br>0.4 * 130 = 52<br>0.4 * 152 = 61<br>0.4 * 74 = 30 |
| pink over black<br>0.6 * 248 = 149<br>0.6 * 98 = 59<br>0.6 * 218 = 131 | pink over black<br>0.6 * 248 = 149<br>0.6 * 98 = 59<br>0.6 * 218 = 131 |
| green over (blue over black)<br>$\alpha' = 1$<br>(0.4 * 130 + 0.6 * 32)/1 = 71<br>(0.4 * 152 + 0.6 * 80)/1 = 109<br>(0.4 * 74 + 0.6 * 204)/1 = 152 | (pink over green) over blue<br>$\alpha' = 0.76 + 0.8 * (1 - 0.76) = 0.952$<br>(0.76 * 223 + 0.8 * (1 − 0.76) * 40)/0.952 = 186<br>(0.76 * 109 + 0.8 * (1 − 0.76) * 100)/0.952 = 107<br>(0.76 * 188 + 0.8 * (1 − 0.76) * 255)/0.952 = 202 |
| pink over (green over (blue over black))<br>$\alpha' = 1$<br>(0.6 * 248 + 0.4 * 73)/1 = 177<br>(0.6 * 98 + 0.4 * 108)/1 = 102<br>(0.6 * 218 + 0.4 * 139)/1 = 192 | ((pink over green) over blue) over black<br>$\alpha' = 0.952 + 1 * (1 - 0.952) = 1$<br>(0.952 * 186 + (1 − 0.952) * 1 * 0)/1 = 177<br>(0.952 * 107 + (1 − 0.952) * 1 * 0)/1 = 102<br>(0.952 * 202 + (1 − 0.952) * 1 * 0)/1 = 192 |
| pink over (green over black)<br>$\alpha' = 1$<br>(0.6 * 248 + 0.4 * 52)/1 = 170<br>(0.6 * 98 + 0.4 * 61)/1 = 83<br>(0.6 * 218 + 0.4 * 30)/1 = 143 | (pink over green) over black<br>$\alpha' = 0.76 + 1 * (1 - 0.76) = 1$<br>(0.76 * 223 + (1 − 0.76) * 1 * 0)/1 = 170<br>(0.76 * 109 + (1 − 0.76) * 1 * 0)/1 = 83<br>(0.76 * 188 + (1 − 0.76) * 1 * 0)/1 = 143 |

The equation $C = \alpha F + (1 - \alpha)B$ is applied to composite two colors, and Equation 7.1 is applied when more than two colors are composited. If you work from the bottom up, $\alpha'$ always carries over as 1 from the previous layer. This is because the background is opaque black. You can lay something that is partially transparent over an opaque background, but the result will always be opaque. (If you started with a background that is not totally opaque, $\alpha'$ would not always be 1.) When working from the top down, if you have two layers, neither of which is entirely opaque, the resulting layer will not be entirely opaque, so the $\alpha'$ that you carry to the next layer down will not be 1.

One way that alpha blending is applied in digital video editing is by means of the opacity setting on each track, which defines an alpha value for that track. The alpha blending equations can be applied frame by frame in the same way that they are applied to still images.

Alpha channels can play a part in digital compositing in another way. You can import a still image into an NLE and cause that image to be displayed for any number of frames. In Chapter 3, we created an image of a Demon Deacon puppet extracted from its background. This image has only one layer and thus no layer to show through the transparent area. However, you could save this image in a format that supports alpha channels (*e.g.*, PSD, BMP, or PNG) and import it into an application program that supports the transparency information of the file type—for example, a video editing environment like Premiere Pro, Final Cut Pro, Cinelerra, or a multimedia programming language like Director. Say that we import it into a video editing program and place it on the track above a video clip. The alpha channel defines which pixels in the still image are visible and which are not. In areas where the still image is invisible, the clip below shows through. It looks like the object is superimposed over the video clip of the campus scene, which becomes its new background (Figure 7.8).

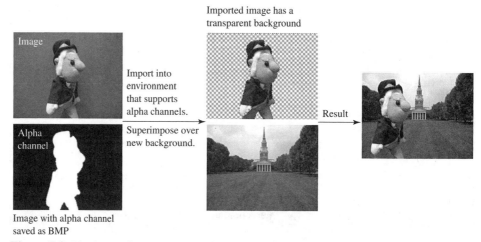

**Figure 7.8** Placing an image with an alpha channel on a track of an NLE timeline with another clip or image on a lower track

You could also do the reverse of this. That is, you could cut out an oval or rectangle of transparent pixels from a colored background, and save the opacity information as an alpha channel. Then when you put this image with the alpha channel on a track above a video clip, the clip will show through the hole, being framed by the visible part of the image.

### 7.3.5.2 Mattes

Another way to make a composite digital video sequence is by means of a matte. Mattes come from the world of analog photography and filmmaking, where in the *optical compositing* process they are used to block out the chemical processing of portions of an image as it is being combined with another. You can picture a matte as a piece of cardboard with something cut out from it. You lay the matte over a lens or piece of film, and the only part of the film that gets exposed is the part where light passes through the cut-out. A matte is like an overlay with holes cut in it to define which parts of a picture you do and don't want to see.

The basic idea is the same in digital video. In digital video, a matte is a file containing values related to pixels, usually having the same dimensions as the video frames to which it is applied. An *image matte* (also called an *image mask*) is an image whose pixel values determine the opacity levels of the pixels in the video frames to which the matte is applied. To put an image matte on a video clip in an NLE, you go through the following basic steps:

- Create the matte, perhaps in an image editing environment.
- Choose an image matte or image mask effect from the Effects list and drop it onto a track in the NLE. The special effects list is called Filters in some programs.
- In the place where parameters are set for the effect, specify the type of matte you want—either a luma or an alpha matte. Also, specify the file that is to serve as the matte.

A *luma matte* is an image matte that uses luminosity values to specify opacity levels. An *alpha matte* is an image file with an alpha channel; alpha values in the image matte define the opacity levels of pixels in the frames to which the matte is applied.

The difference between applying an image matte to a video clip, as just described, and inserting an image with an alpha channel on a track, as illustrated in Figure 7.8, is that the image matte is not placed on a track in the video timeline. Instead, an effect or filter is placed on the clip—specifically, an image mask filter (as it is called in Final Cut Pro) or an image matte effect (as it is called in Premiere Pro). Then the image to be used as the matte is specified as a parameter to the filter or effect.

Figure 7.9 shows the effect of applying an image matte operating as a luma matte. The matte is a grayscale image, with pixels between 0 and 255, normalized to range from 0 to 1, indicating their luminosity. In general, the darker a pixel in the matte, the more transparent the pixel in the frame to which the matte is applied, allowing the background underneath to show through.

A matte can also be defined by points within a frame. Since these points can be moved over time, this type of matte is called a *track matte* or a *traveling matte*. Say that a track matte

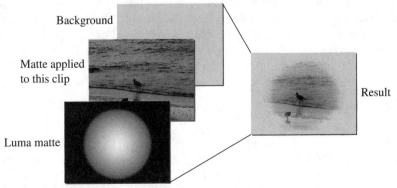

**Figure 7.9** A luma matte (aka a grayscale image matte)

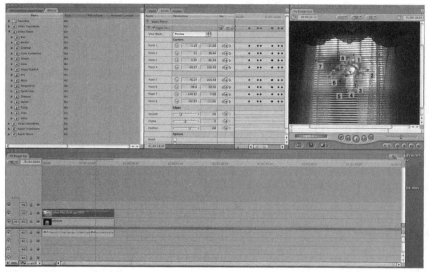

**Figure 7.10** A traveling matte (from Final Cut Pro)

is applied to clip A, which is on a track higher than clip B. Then the area of clip A that is inside the points specified for the matte will be visible, and the rest of clip A will be invisible, allowing clip B to show through. Figure 7.10 shows this type of matte, which follows an enlarged fly as it "walks around" in a window. The matte is defined by eight points. We can see only the portion of the fly clip that is inside the polygon defined by the eight points. The rest is masked out. The positions of the points change over time in a way that follows the movement of the fly. A traveling matte such as this one is sometimes called a ***garbage matte***. Everything outside of the area delineated by the chosen points is garbage—thrown out of the scene.

### 7.3.5.3 Chroma Keying

Chroma keying—the process of eliminating pixels that are of a certain color, within some tolerance—operates according to the same principle as matting. When you identify a color to be eliminated in a frame, you are essentially requesting that a matte be created that specifies the opacity level of each pixel in that frame. ***Chroma keying*** makes pixels transparent based on how close they are to some specified color.

If you want to be strict about the definition of chroma keying—with the emphasis on the word chroma—you would define it as a matting process that derives alpha values only from chroma values in the matte, which implies that its implementation depends on using a color model that separates out the color information. In the context of an HLS color model, for example, chroma keying could be a simple process of identifying the unwanted hue $h_{key}$ and setting $\alpha = 0$ for all pixels of hue $h_{key}$ within a certain tolerance $t$.

---

**KEY EQUATION**

Let the color of a pixel be $C = (h, l, s)$ where $0 \le h, l, s \le 1$. Then given a hue $h_{key}$ that is to be eliminated from an image and a tolerance $t$, the alpha value for the pixel can be computed by

$$\alpha = 0 \quad \text{if} \quad (h_{key} - t) < h < (h_{key} + t) \quad \text{and} \quad \alpha = 1 \text{ otherwise}$$

This method has shortcomings, the main one being that two pixels that have the same hue but different saturation and lightness can look very different.

Better control can be asserted over the keying process if alpha values are created for all three components and these are then weighted to create an alpha value for each pixel.

---

### KEY EQUATION

Let the color of a pixel be $C = (h, l, s)$ where $0 \leq h, l, s \leq 1$. Let weights be given as $w_h$, $w_l$, and $w_s$, where $w_h + w_l + w_s = 1$. Then given a color $K = (h_{key}, l_{key}, s_{key})$ that is to be eliminated from an image and tolerances $t_h$, $t_l$, and $t_s$, the alpha value, $\alpha$, for the pixel can be computed by

$$\alpha = w_h \alpha_h + w_l \alpha_l + w_s \alpha_s$$

where

$\alpha_h = 0$   if   $(h_{key} - t_h) < h < (h_{key} + t_h)$,   and   $\alpha_h = 1$ otherwise
$\alpha_l = 0$   if   $(l_{key} - t_l) < l < (l_{key} + t_l)$,   and   $\alpha_l = 1$ otherwise
$\alpha_s = 0$   if   $(s_{key} - t_s) < s < (s_{key} + t_s)$,   and   $\alpha_s = 1$ otherwise

---

Chroma key methods that work in YCbCr space also exist. These methods have the advantage of working in the same color space as MPEG compression. However, they are not very effective on DV video, which downsamples the two chrominance components at a rate of $4:1:1$ (for NTSC). Chroma mattes for DV video tend to have jagged edges. You can compensate for this by adding a chroma blur prior to the keying. Better chroma keying results can be obtained with uncompressed digital formats like D1 or D5 or lightly compressed formats like Digital Beta or DVCPro 50, which use $4:2:2$ subsampling.

You'll find that the term *chroma keying* is used in any situation where color is removed, regardless of the color model in which the color removal is implemented. The most common application of chroma keying is to remove an object from its background and place it in another background. For example, you might videotape someone in front of a solid blue (or green) background so that you can later remove the background and replace it with, say, a beach scene. This is a specific kind of chroma keying called *bluescreening* (or *greenscreening*), an effect you've probably heard of in the context of television production and movie making. Bluescreening was first developed for film by Arthur Widmer in 1950. In those days it was a complicated process of optical compositing. Now digital bluescreening (or more often, greenscreening) is used every day in the production of television weather forecasts. The weather reporter is shot in front of a green background, which is replaced by moving weather maps. The reporter can tell where he or she should be pointing by watching the monitors.

In what follows, we will use the term bluescreening, but the observations apply equally to chroma keying using other colors. Blue and green were originally chosen for this process because human skin contains few blue or green tones.

To achieve a good bluescreen effect, you need to set up your conditions carefully, with the following guidelines:

- The background is a consistent blue color.
- The background is smooth.
- Lighting is as uniform as possible on the background to avoid reflections and shadows.
- The foreground object doesn't contain the shade of blue used in the background.

- The foreground object is several feet away from the background screen.
- You're using the best digital video format you have available.

Even with your best effort, it's impossible to set up ideal conditions. You can't make the background perfectly uniform, so instead of trying to key out a single blue color, you have to eliminate a range of blues. Then it's likely that some of these blues may be in your foreground as shadows or texture. Also, there will probably be some color spill onto your foreground subject—some color reflected from the background onto the foreground. If you eliminate these pixels, you'll lose some of the fine detail around the foreground, like wisps of hair or edges of garments. The challenge is to find the right balance between erasing the background and losing some of the foreground.

In the early 1960s, Vlahos developed a bluescreening method based on his optical compositing work in filmmaking. From experience and observation, Vlahos determined that better results are obtained by identifying pixels where the blue component dominates the red and green components and deriving the alpha value accordingly.

---

### 🔑 KEY EQUATION

Let the color of a pixel be $C = (c_r, c_g, c_b)$, where $0 \leq c_r, c_g, c_b \leq 1$. Then the alpha value for the pixel is computed by **the color difference keying method for bluescreening**

$$\alpha = 1 - (c_b - \max(c_r, c_g))$$

with the result clipped to the range [0  1].

**Equation 7.2**

---

Supplement on chroma keying:

programming exercise

Equation 7.2 gives $\alpha = 0$ for pixels that are pure blue, $\alpha$ close to 0 for those that are predominantly blue, and $\alpha = 1$ for pixels that have no blue in them at all. This approach has been refined through many versions by the Ultimatte Corporation. (Vlahos received a Lifetime Achievement Award for this work from the Academy of Motion Picture Arts and Sciences in 1994.)

An alternative bluescreening method was devised by Mishima in 1992 and came to be known as the Primatte Keyer. This method can be described in RGB color space. Within the RGB color cube, the foreground and background colors are separated into two areas (S3 and S1, respectively), with a transition area between them (S2). The system works interactively with the user, who identifies pixels that are part of the background. As more pixels are identified, the smallest possible convex hull is drawn around these colors in RGB color space. For simplicity, this convex hull is pictured as the dark gray sphere, S1, in Figure 7.11. (In fact, 128-face triangular mesh surfaces are used.) Working from the opposite direction, the user also identifies pixels that are in the foreground image, and the largest possible convex hull is drawn such that *none* of the foreground pixels are contained in the hull. This is the light gray sphere, S2, in the figure. Any pixels whose colors are in S1 have $\alpha = 0$. Any pixels whose colors are not in S1 or S2 are in S3 and have $\alpha = 1$. Let **P** be a point in S2, and let C be the color corresponding to that point. Draw a line from **P** to the outer edge of S2, yielding line segment $\overline{YP}$. Draw a line from **P** to the outer edge of S1, yielding line segment $\overline{XP}$. (See the figure.) Then any pixel whose color is C will have $\alpha = \dfrac{|\overline{XP}|}{|\overline{XY}|}$. ($|\overline{XP}|$ denotes the size of $\overline{XP}$). A pixel's alpha value will be smaller in proportion to its closeness to the S1 region.

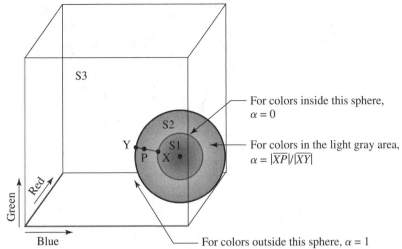

For colors inside this sphere, $\alpha = 0$

For colors in the light gray area, $\alpha = |\overline{XP}|/|\overline{XY}|$

For colors outside this sphere, $\alpha = 1$

**Figure 7.11** Primatte method of bluescreening

In practice, you have access to the chroma keying effects either as part of a standard NLE, as a plugin to an NLE, or as a separate application devoted entirely to matting or chroma keying. You'll need to experiment with your tools to see what works best for your applications.

## 7.3.6 Keyframes

With many of the video effects you apply, you will want the effect to change over time. Keyframes and tweening are essential to this process.

A *keyframe* is a frame that is marked as a reference point. *Tweening* is the process of making a parameter change gradually from one keyframe to another. By *parameter*, we mean a property like size, position, or color related to some object. In video editing, you set keyframes and parameters for a given effect by selecting a clip on the timeline, going to the window where controls for that clip are accessible, and finding the place where parameters for the effect can be set. Then you can move through a timeline associated with the selected clip and choose moments in time that you want to be keyframes. Finally, for each of those moments in time you set the parameters for the effect you're applying.

You can use keyframes to move a clip, blur it, change the saturation of its colors, move a mask across it, twirl it at a certain speed and angle—anything that can happen as an effect that changes over time. Figure 7.10 shows how keyframing is used to change the position of a mask on one clip that is superimposed on a second clip. The top-layer clip shows a fly that is only partially visible, the rest made transparent. Underneath this clip is a still frame covering several seconds and showing a curtained window. The mask follows the fly as it walks around on top of the window.

Figure 7.12 shows the tweening of a twirl. The parameters related to the twirl effect are angle, radius, and center. The effects control gives you access to a mini-timeline—that is, a timeline just for the clip on which you've applied the effect. If you click the clock icon (indicated with an arrow), you can then set keyframes at points on this timeline. You do this for any parameter you want to change over time. Only the angle and radius are changed in this example, using three keyframes. The keyframes are marked by diamonds in the keyframe timeline. One keyframe is indicated with an arrow in the first figure.

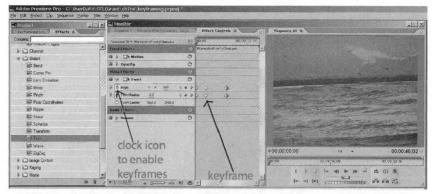

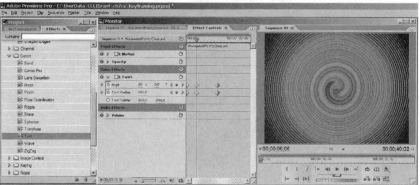

**Figure 7.12** Using keyframes for a twirl (from Premiere Pro)

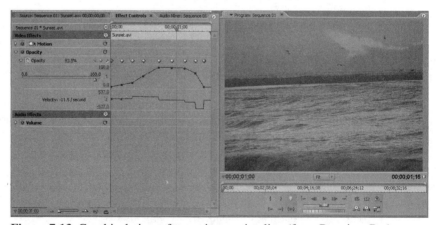

**Figure 7.13** Graphical view of tweening on timeline (from Premiere Pro)

Some video editing and motion graphics programs give you the option of looking at a graph of keyframed parameter changes. Figure 7.13 is an example of this.

## 7.3.7 Timecodes

The standard way of denoting time in video editing is with SMPTE video timecode, given in terms of *hours:minutes:seconds:frames*. In a video editing environment, time is shown for the duration of a clip, for In and Out points, and for the position of the playhead in the

**Figure 7.14** Timecode for In and Out points (from Premiere Pro)

timeline. For example, in Figure 7.14, the In point of the clip is at 03 : 31 : 18 and the Out point is 26 seconds and 9 frames later.

If you think about the timing of NTSC standard video, which has 29.97 frames/s, you might wonder how the noninteger number of frames per second is handled. Actually, there are two options, and you can choose which you prefer in your timecode display. One option, called ***nondrop-frame timecode***, rounds 29.97 up to 30. The *frames* field of *hours:minutes:seconds:frames* ticks from 0 to 29 and then rolls over to 0 again as the *seconds* field is incremented. The problem with this is that it creates a discrepancy between the timecode reading and the actual length of a clip or movie. Every 29.97 seconds, you're adding an additional 0.03 seconds to the length, so the timecode display for a clip makes the clip appear to be longer than it really is.

The other option is called ***drop-frame timecode***. This method doesn't actually drop any frames—it just changes the numbering of frames so that the time shown accurately reflects the length of a clip. Specifically, frames are renumbered so that the numbers of the first two frames of every minute are skipped, except for minutes ending in 0 (*i.e.*, minute 0, minute 10, and so forth). For example, the frame after 0;0;59;29 is labeled 0;1;00;02, the frame after 0;1;59;29 is labeled 0;2;00;02, and so forth. But the frame after 0;9;59;29 is labeled 0;10;00;00 (no skipping).

Think about how this adjusts the overall time. For a frame rate of 29.97 frames/s, how many frames should there be in 10 minutes?

$$29.97 \text{ frames/s} * 60 \text{ sec/min} * 10 \text{ min } = 17{,}982 \text{ frames}$$

How many frames will you get by the method described above? If you used 30 frames/s, then in each minute you'd have 1800 frames, but you're going to drop two of these for each of the first 9 minutes, so that gives you 1798 frames/min for the first 9 minutes. Then you add 1800 for the 10th minute.

$$(1798 * 9) + 1800 = 17{,}982$$

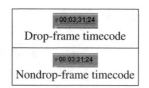

**Figure 7.15** SMPTE timecode

It works. If 17,982 frames are passed every 10 minutes, then the timecode shown correctly reflects the frame rate and the actual length of the movie or clip.

You can generally select which way you want the timecode displayed. Semicolons are used between fields to indicate that drop-frame timecode is being used. Colons are used for non-drop-frame (Figure 7.15).

Be sure that you understand that no frames are actually dropped. Drop-frame timecode just changes the numbers of frames so that the timecode displayed accurately matches the real-time of the movie.

## 7.3.8 Adjusting Speed

Timecode is just a way of indicating where you are in a clip or how long the clip is. Changing the timecode display doesn't change the clip's timing or speed in any way.

You *can* change the speed of a clip, making it play in slow or fast motion. If you indicate that you want the speed change to be constant throughout a clip, then changing the speed of the clip also changes its duration. This is called a ***constant speed change***. For example, if you want to play a clip in slow motion—say at 50% speed—it's going to take twice as long for the clip to play. The speed-change setting has to do something to make the clip take twice as long to play. One way is to make a duplicate of each frame. However, this can create a jerky, "strobed" effect. Some NLEs allow you to specify that you want new frames to be a blend of neighboring frames. Motion blur also can be applied to smooth things over.

It is also possible to vary the speed of a clip *without* changing its duration. This is called a ***variable speed change***, and it's done by indicating what frame in the clip you want to be on-screen at what point in time. Say that you have a clip that covers the first 60 seconds of your movie. You want the 90th frame of this clip to appear at exactly the 5th second. You can mark this accordingly. This will cause the first 90 frames to be slowed down so that the 90th frame arrives after 5 seconds rather than after about 3, as it ordinarily would. Then the rest of the frames will have to be sped up afterwards so that the length of the clip overall doesn't change.

## 7.3.9 Color Correction

Although NLEs have excellent tools for color correction, as is true in all aspects of video production your aim should be to gather the best material from the outset rather than to fix problems in post-production. Of course you want to use the best video camera you have available. A three-CCD or CMOS camera will give you better color fidelity than a one-CCD. Lighting should be carefully evaluated for each shot, and if you're shooting a scene from multiple angles, the lighting should be consistent from one shot to another. One helpful habit is to begin each clip by shooting something that you consider true white in your scene's lighting. You can then use this white as a reference when you color balance the scene in post-production. Chip charts like the one shown in Figure 7.16 are also used for black/white calibration of digital video cameras (i.e., white balance). If you're shooting a scene with more

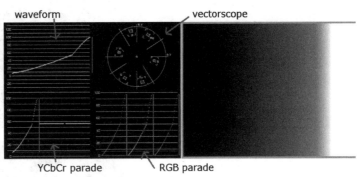

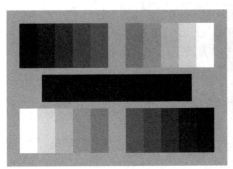

**Figure 7.16** Chip chart

**Figure 7.17** Color correction view (from Premiere Pro)

than one camera, getting an initial shot of the chip chart with each camera can help you to match the color and lighting balance of the two shots in post-production.

Even with careful attention to how you capture your scenes, you may need to adjust color in various ways after sequencing clips into a movie. You could have a number of different reasons for adjusting color, including these:

- to call attention to important elements in a scene
- to create a mood or look
- to remove unwanted color casts caused by lighting
- to balance the colors among clips, which may have been shot under different lighting or with different cameras
- to ensure that luminosity and chroma are within broadcast standards (if you're preparing video for television broadcast)

NLEs provide you with a number of tools for checking color. The views shown in Figure 7.17 are commonly available, including a vectorscope, a waveform view, and "parade" views that graph color components. The views in this figure correspond to the frame to the right of the graphs, a gradient of grayscale values.

A *vectorscope* shows you the hue and saturation of a video frame plotted on a circular graph. (Vectorscopes are available within the cameras, also.) The hue of each pixel plotted on this graph is given by the angle the pixel makes with the center point. The positions of the primary colors and their complements are shown in Figure 7.18. Points closer to the perimeter of the circle correspond to more saturated colors. Black and white are at the center of the circle. Since the image being graphed in the vectorscope is grayscale, only one point shows in the vectorscope, right in the middle. The line running between red and yellow marks approximately where human flesh tones lie, marked automatically by the system for reference.

The *waveform view* shows how the brightness of the selected frame varies from left to right. In Figure 7.17, the frame is a simple grayscale gradient. We use this example because it is easy to interpret the waveform view's information. You can see in the waveform view that the frame increases in brightness as you move from left to right—getting brighter faster on the right-hand side. The *RGB parade* shows that the frame has equal amounts of red, green, and blue, which is as it should be since it is grayscale. The *YCbCr parade* shows that the luminance increases but the chrominance components stay steady across the frame. Both the RGB and YCbCr parades represent the frame as it changes from left to right, repeated three times—once for each of the three components. You can also select to see a histogram, as shown in Figure 7.19.

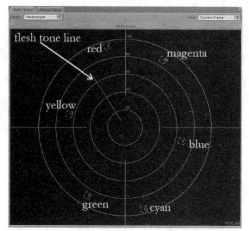

**Figure 7.18** Vectorscope (from Final Cut Pro)

This clip exceeds broadcast standards for luminance.

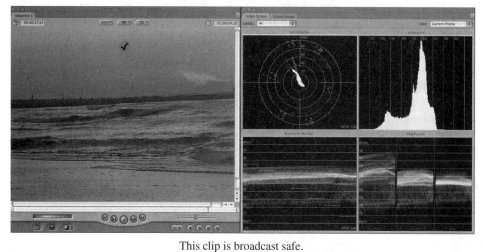

This clip is broadcast safe.

**Figure 7.19** Comparing color on two clips (from Final Cut Pro)

The color correction graphs are informational only; you can't adjust color through these graphs. However, they do help you to see things that might be difficult to detect through the naked eye, like subtle color casts. The graphs also can help you compare two clips so that you can make their color balances more similar. For example, what if you wanted to use, in sequence, the two clips in Figure 7.19, which are sunrises taken on two different days. Are the colors and lighting similar enough? If not, how do they differ? The histogram shows that the top image has more contrast than the bottom. The vectorscopes reveal that although the two images are in approximately the same color areas, the top image is more saturated than the bottom. You can see this in the way the white "blob" in the center of the top vectorscope is pulled more toward the perimeter of the circle. (The "blob" is a plot of the pixels in the image.)

If your video is to be broadcast on television, you need to be sure that the colors are broadcast safe. Each network has its own standards for the maximum luminance and chrominance permitted. If you exceed the limits, your colors may bleed, or they may be adjusted so that they become washed out. Color correcting views can show you if your video is within legal bounds. In Figure 7.19, the *range check* option has been turned on, causing red stripes to indicate any places where luminance or chrominance levels have been exceeded. Portions of the sky in the top clip are marked, and an exclamation point calls attention to the fact that broadcast safe range has been exceeded. The bottom clip is marked with a check, indicating that its luminance and chrominance values are within the safe range.

### 7.3.10 Rendering

To some extent, you can preview what your final movie is going to look like as you edit it. As you work, the NLE does its best to approximate how filters and special effects will be applied so that you have a working copy of your video to assess as you go, although this may be at a reduced frame rate. However, sometimes the effects you apply are computationally intensive and can't be applied on the fly. Compositing, adjusting color with multiple filters, scaling, rotating, and so forth can put too many demands on the processor for real-time computation. This means that some preliminary computation needs to be performed before you can see what the total effect will be. The computation that gives you your final video with all effects applied is called *rendering*.

It's important to be aware that special effects will be rendered in a particular order, and changing the order can change what results you get. Some of the basic effects may have a predefined order. For example, in Premiere Pro, position, scale, rotation, and opacity are rendered in the order just given. If you want to change this order, you have to apply the effect as a special effect. (These effects are listed again in the special effects listing.) Special effects are rendered in the order in which you apply them.

In many NLEs, any section in the timeline that needs to be rendered is marked with a colored bar above it. If you don't render such a section before previewing, you can get only a sketchy view of what the final effect will be. Before you compress the final movie for distribution, it will need to be rendered completely.

## 7.4 PREPARING DIGITAL VIDEO FOR DISTRIBUTION

### 7.4.1 Digital Video Files

The last step in video production is to prepare your video for distribution by choosing a file type and codec. These decisions are based on your target audience, the operating system and codec they are most likely to have, the medium on which you're distributing the video (*e.g.*, CD, DVD, or web), the bandwidth available for downloading, and memory requirements if the file is to be saved.

As is true with audio files, the suffix used on a video file doesn't give you complete information about the file's contents. For example, if you find a file with the *.avi* or *.mov* suffix, you don't know from the file name if it is compressed, and if it *is* compressed, you don't know with what codec. AVI, MOV, and WMV are actually ***container file*** formats—a type of metafile format—that can hold media of different types. They all allow a wide variety of codecs to be used.

AVI (Audio Video Interleave) files, introduced by Microsoft in 1992, are in RIFF format (Resource Interchange File Format), which groups data in tagged chunks. MOV files are QuickTime movies, created by Apple in 1991. WMV files were originally a Microsoft proprietary Advanced Systems format, but they have now been standardized by SMPTE. MPEG files contain one of the many MPEG standardized codecs. RealMedia is a proprietary container format developed by RealNetworks. OGG is an open-source format that accommodates many different codecs, and also has its own MPEG-4 implementation, a codec called Theora. Table 7.2 summarizes these commonly used multimedia container file formats.

| TABLE 7.2 | Common Digital Video File Types | |
|---|---|---|
| **File Extension** | **Container File Type** | **Characteristics** |
| *.avi* | Audio/Video Interleaved | A type of RIFF file designed for Windows Media. Created for the PC platform, now used on Mac and Linux also. Can be uncompressed, or compressed with a variety of codecs, including DivX, Cinepak, Indeo, MJPEG, or DV. |
| *.mov* (sometimes *.qt*) | QuickTime Movie | A multimedia container file framework created by Apple; it stores different media—including video, sound, and text—in different tracks. Cross-platform, for Mac, PC, and Linux. Accommodates a variety of audio and video codecs, including Sorensen, MPEG, Cinepak, and DivX. |
| *.mpg* (also *.mpeg*, *.m1v*, *.m2v*, *.m2t*, *.mp4*, *.mpv2*) | MPEG | A file that has been compressed with some version of the MPEG codec. MPEG-1 is greatly compressed with small resolution, for use on CD or web. MPEG-2 is the standard for video on DVD. MPEG-4 has highest compression rate and serves as a container file, modeled after QuickTime. |
| *.flv*, *.f4v*, *.f4p*, *.f4a*, *.f4b* | Flash video | Encoded audio and video streams playable by the Flash player, which can exchange audio, video, and data over RTMP (real-time messaging protocol) connections with Adobe Flash Media Server. Now used widely on the web. |
| *.ogg* | Ogg (by Xiph Foundation) | An open-source format, good for internet streaming. |
| *.rm* and *.rmvb* | Real Media | A proprietary file format with accompanying codecs, developed by RealNetworks; it works on multiple platforms, including Windows, Mac, Linux, and Unix. |
| *.wmv* (sometimes *.asf*) | Microsoft Windows Media | Originally Microsoft proprietary codec for Windows Media Player, standardized by SMPTE; uses Advanced Systems format (a container format) sometimes with *.asf* suffix. Uses its own codec. |

The currently dominant video file format on the web is FLV, Flash video. One reason for its popularity is the fact that FLV files are playable by means of the Flash player, which is a standard plugin in web browsers. Initially, FLV files were encoded under Sorenson Spark, a variant of the H.263 standard. With Flash Player 8, the On2 TrueMotion VP6 standard for video bitstreams was also supported in the encoding. This provided better visual quality than Sorenson Spark at lower bitrates. Flash Player 9 Update 3 moved to support the H.264 video standard, for an even better quality/bitrate ratio. Early FLV versions accommodated uncompressed, MP3, and ADPCM audio. In 2007, Adobe announced that it would support MPEG4 and H.264 video along with AAC audio and MP4, M4V, M4A, 3GP, and MOV container formats. The Flash video standard also supports *3GPP timed text specification*, which allows for standardized subtitles.

To encode FLV files, you can use Adobe Flash, On2 Flix, Sorenson Squeeze, and other third party tools. There are three options for delivering Flash video:

- Embedding the video within an SWF file and playing it with a Flash Player from a web page.
- Using progressive download, via HTTP, which allows for random-access at any point in the video file
- Streaming video by means of RTMP (real-time multimedia protocol) from your own Flash Media Server or a hosted server using Flash Video Streaming Services.

The process of creating and distributing Flash video entails acquiring the video, deciding on a delivery mechanism, encoding the video as FLV, adding the video to a web page, and publishing the web page. The ubiquity of the Flash Player makes the video viewable to a wide audience. This ease of encoding and distributing Flash video has made it extremely popular.

When you save and compress a video production, you choose—whether implicitly or explicitly—both the container file type and the codec to be used for compression. The interfaces to the Export functions vary from one NLE to another. In NLEs that shelter you from the details, you just say that you want to export for CD or DVD or whatever medium you choose, and the NLE will make the appropriate settings. In the case of CD export, for example, it may give you a resolution of 320 × 240 at 15 frames/s. Other NLEs give you more control, and you may find yourself faced with all kinds of options, including not only codecs but also bit rate, pixel aspect ratio, and image aspect ratio. For example, in Adobe Premiere Pro, if you choose to export a file as QuickTime, you'll then have numerous options for compressors, as shown in Figure 7.20. You may also be able to choose from among some standard settings, as is the case with the Adobe Media Encoder.

## 7.4.2 Codecs

### 7.4.2.1 Properties of Codecs

Digital video files are very large. With no compression or subsampling, NTSC standard video would have a data rate of over 240 Mb/s; HD would have a data rate of about 1 Gb/s. As you compile your footage into a polished production of, say, an hour's length, you accumulate quite a lot of data. To fit this on a DVD or post it on the web requires considerable compression.

In Chapter 3, you saw how compression is achieved on individual still images. These methods can be applied in the realm of digital video, where each frame is nothing more than a still image. Finding ways to remove redundancies and extraneous information within one

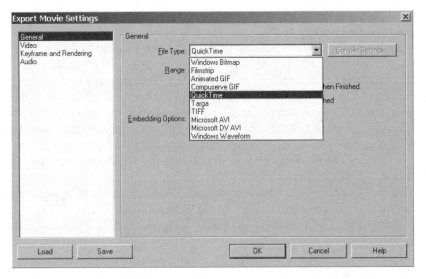

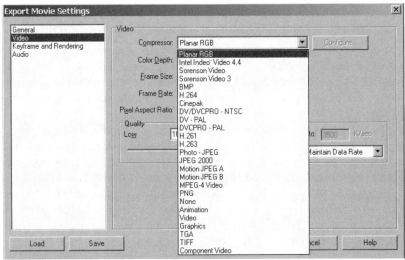

**Figure 7.20** Export Movie settings (from Premiere Pro)

frame is called *intraframe compression*. It also can be referred to as *spatial compression*. There are two commonly used methods for accomplishing spatial compression: transform encoding and vector quantization. If you read Chapter 3, you're already familiar with transform encoding—changing the representation of each frame from the spatial to the frequency domain by means of the discrete cosine transform and then quantizing in a manner that sacrifices some high-frequency information. This is the method used in JPEG compression, and it can be applied to the frames of video. Vector quantization is an entirely different approach—encoding a sequence of pixels by finding its closest match in a color key in a table. We'll look at vector quantization more closely in a moment.

Digital video has another dimension that provides opportunities for compression, and that is time. *Temporal compression* is a matter of eliminating redundant or unnecessary information by considering how images change over time. Because it relies on comparing neighboring frames, it is also called *interframe compression*. The basic method for compressing between frames is to detect how objects move from one frame to another, represent this as a vector, and then use differential encoding along with the motion vector. Determining the motion vector is done by a method called *motion estimation*, another compression technique that we'll examine more closely in a later section.

Some codecs allow you to select either *constant* or *variable bit rate encoding* (*CBR* and *VBR*, respectively). Variable bit rate varies the bit rate according to how much motion is in a scene. If there isn't a lot of motion, the scene can be compressed more, yielding a lower bit rate for that section. Scenes with more motion don't lend themselves as well to compression, so in order to maintain the quality level, you have to raise the bit rate for these scenes. The variances in the bit rate must come out to some predictable average so that the buffer holding the incoming video data does not overflow.

Codecs are mostly *asymmetrical*. This means that the time needed for compression is not the same as the time needed for decompression. (It's usually much greater.) Some codecs are more asymmetrical than others. For example, the early Cinepak had the disadvantage of requiring a long time for compression, but decompression could be done comparatively quickly. The time needed for compression could be one factor in your choice of codecs when you export your video for distribution. In any case, you should allow for a good block of time to render and compress your video. It can take hours, depending on the codec, the length of your video, and the speed of your processor.

## 7.4.2.2 Vector Quantization

The first popular codecs were designed to fit video within the limitations of the low-bandwidth systems that were available at the time—for example, 1X CD-ROM players. MPEG compression had not been "invented" yet. The early codecs used, instead, a method called *vector quantization*. This method, while complicated in the details, is based on concepts that should be familiar to you at this point—the rounding off process of quantization coupled with a code table. The basic method involves the following steps:

- Create a palette for a frame. The palette represents the frame's dominant colors and color patterns and serves as a code table.
- Divide the frame into areas—say, 4 pixels $\times$ 4 pixels. Search in the code table for the best color match to this area.
- Encode the area by an index into the code table.

This may sound similar to the method for converting to indexed color, explained in Chapter 3. The difference is that an area of pixels, rather than a single pixel, is encoded by one index into the code table.

The essence of this method is easy to understand, but the details are complicated. You might immediately wonder how a code table is created for a frame. This is a computationally complex procedure, as is the matching of an area of pixels to some color in the code table. For this reason, codecs that use vector quantization take a long time to compress. Decompression is much faster, as it entails primarily just a code table lookup.

The three best-known codecs based on vector quantization are Cinepak, Indeo, and Sorenson.

*Cinepak* is one of the older codecs, originally bundled with QuickTime for Macintosh computers but then ported to the Windows environment. Intended for video to be distributed on CD or the web, it encodes at a resolution of 320 $\times$ 240 and 12 frames/s. It achieves high compression rates, but can result in blockiness at edges. Cinepak Pro is a recent upgrade.

*Indeo*, like Cinepak, is one of the earlier codecs intended for CD-playback, thus compressing at high rates. It was originally developed as a vector quantization-based method by Intel, was later sold to Ligos, and evolved into different implementations that have remained largely proprietary.

*Sorenson* is another codec that initially came to prominence through its association with QuickTime. It was first released as part of QuickTime 3 in 1998 and remained with QuickTime through versions 4 and 5. Sorenson is more powerful than Cinepak and Indeo. Its reputation spread as it was used for movie trailers on the web, like *Star Wars: The Phantom Menace*. In 2002, QuickTime adopted MPEG-4, and Sorenson moved to a licensing agreement with Macromedia Flash (afterwards bought by Adobe). Sorenson Spark is a Video Codec used by YouTube, Yahoo, and Google. Sorenson Squeeze is a compression suite for Windows Media, Adobe Flash, and MPEG-4, allowing for variable bit rates and HD video. Its compression method is proprietary.

### 7.4.2.3 Motion JPEG Compression

If you apply what you know already about compressing individual images, you could come up with a fairly effective video compression method. Since each frame is just a still image, you could apply JPEG compression frame-by-frame, right? This method is called *Motion JPEG* (*MJPEG*). Initially, MJPEG was an informal name rather than a formal standard, but now that QuickTime includes MJPEG-A and MJPEG-B in their package, Motion JPEG has achieved some level of standardization. Both MJPEG-A and MJPEG-B apply spatial compression separately to each of two interlaced fields. The difference between A and B is that A allows markers in the bitstream while B does not. Like JPEG compression on which it is based, MJPEG allows you to specify the quality of video—applying more compression if small file size is more important than fine resolution. Quality settings in the context of video are done by specifying a data rate. MJPEG has been used in some digital still cameras, allowing them to have a "movie" mode without much modification to the hardware. Now, better algorithms are available that combine intra- and interframe compression, and MJPEG is not used a great deal.

### 7.4.2.4 DV Compression

DV is another format that relies solely on intraframe compression. Standard *DV compression* produces resolutions of $720 \times 480$ for NTSC and $720 \times 576$ for PAL. DV cameras take an RGB color signal, convert it to YCbCr, downsample to $4:1:1$ (NTSC) or $4:2:0$ (PAL), and then apply the discrete cosine transform, adaptive quantization, and variable length encoding. Transform encoding of interlaced video can be done one of two ways. If there isn't much motion between the companion fields, they are combined and the DCT is applied to the whole frame. Otherwise, the DCT can be applied to each of the fields separately. The result is a video data stream at 25 Mb/s. When the audio and error checking are added, the bit rate is about 36 Mb/s. Professional versions of DV—DVCAM and DVCPRO—use the same compression method as standard DV. DVCPRO50 and DVCPRO HD use $4:2:2$ chroma subsampling and produce video data rates of 50 Mb/s and 100 Mb/s, respectively.

DV is an appropriate intermediate format for video. The compression applied makes the file sizes manageable. Because DV uses only intraframe compression, you can still edit frames individually. When you are working with consumer-level video equipment, you typically capture DV video into an NLE and edit it frame-by-frame.

### 7.4.2.5 MPEG Compression

When you've finished editing your video and are ready to distribute it, you'll want to apply even greater compression. This requires a codec that combines intraframe and interframe compression. One of the most versatile codecs at present is MPEG. MPEG compression was developed in two lines. The first was the work of ITU-T and their subcommittee, the Video Coding Experts Group. We know this line of codecs as the H.26* series. (The * is replaced by a single-digit integer.) The second line emerged from the Motion Picture Experts Group, from which we get the name MPEG. Notably, neither the H.26* nor the MPEG codec prescribes the form of the compressed bitstream. Particular implementations are left to the ingenuity of commercial and open source software developers, to encourage innovation and the benefits of competition. Nevertheless, beginning with H.261, certain fundamental algorithms have emerged from the work of the standardizing agencies, and these algorithms remain the basis of DCT-based codecs as they have been made more powerful and flexible.

*H.261* was developed in 1990 by the ITU-T as a compression standard for video conferencing or digital video to be transmitted over ISDN telephone lines. It supports video resolutions of 352 × 288 (*Common Interchange Format* or *CIF*) and 176 × 144 (¼ of CIF, called *QCIF*) at a data rate of between 64 kb/s and 2 Mb/s. The compression methods developed for H.261—the use of macroblocks, JPEG for intraframe compression and motion prediction for interframe compression—are essential elements of later MPEG and H.26* versions. H.261 calls for $4:2:0$ subsampling, progressive scanning only, and an NTSC frame rate of 29.97 frames/s.

The line of MPEG codecs is complex. It covers both audio and video compression and a wide variety of applications. First, MPEG versions are numbered—MPEG-1, MPEG-2, and MPEG-4. Within each of these versions, there are *parts*. Each parts relates to a specific component (*e.g.*, system, audio, video) or issue (*e.g.*, conformance testing, RTI extensions), defined by a particular standards document. MPEG-1 has 6 parts, MPEG-2 has 9, and MPEG-4 has 23 (and more could be added). MPEG standards are designed to cover very wide-ranging applications, and it would be difficult to implement everything defined within MPEG-1, 2, or 4. Thus, each part is divided into *profiles*, identifying a subset of features that are to be included in an implementation. These features include things like subsampling type, quantization methods, losslessness of certain parts of encoding, and so forth. Dividing the standard into profiles helps developers focus on the part of the implementation of greatest interest to them, and they can make clear which part they have implemented by naming it as a profile. In addition to this, profiles are divided into *levels*, which relate to how much computation has to be done in encoding in order to accommodate the prescribed bit rate and resolution. Finally, audio is divided into *layers*, related to the audio bit rate.

*MPEG-1* emerged as an ISO standard in 1991, using the basic algorithm of H.261 and improving on its motion prediction and quantization methods. MPEG-1 is applied mostly to video to be distributed on CDs or the web, with a resolution of 352 × 240, a frame rate of 29.97 frames/s, a data rate of 1.5 Mb/s, $4:2:0$ subsampling, and progressive scanning. For PAL, the resolution is 352 × 288 and frame rate is 25 frames/s. (Other resolutions and frame rates are possible within the standard, but most people associate MPEG-1 with video on CD or web.) At the data rate of 1.5 Mb/s, MPEG-1 produces VHS-quality images and CD-quality audio. MPEG-1 has three audio layers, MP1, MP2, and the best-known, MP3—which ushered in the era of web audio-download for music lovers. (See Chapter 5.)

*MPEG-2* was approved in 1994, aimed primarily at providing standards for digital television. If you have some experience with digital video, you're probably familiar with

| TABLE 7.3 | MPEG-2 Levels | | |
|---|---|---|---|
| **Level** | **Maximum Resolution** | **Maximum Frame Rate** | **Maximum Data Rate** |
| Low | 352 × 288 | 30 | 4 Mb/s |
| Main | 720 × 576 | 30 | 15 Mb/s |
| High 1440 | 1440 × 1152 | 60 | 60–80 Mb/s |
| High | 1920 × 1152 | 60 | 80–100 Mb/s |

MPEG-2 as the codec used when you put video on a DVD. This has been its primary application, but it reflects only one of four possible *levels* within the MPEG-2 standard. The four MPEG-2 levels are listed in Table 7.3. Abbreviations such as MP@ML (Main Profile at Main Level) are used to describe particular implementations of MPEG-2. (MP@ML is an implementation aimed at DVD video or television broadcast.) ITU-T worked with the Motion Picture Experts Group on the MPEG-2 standard, and *H.262* is identical to the video part of MPEG-2.

MPEG-3 was intended to be the HD version of MPEG-2, but because MPEG-2 could be applied at higher bit rates for HD, MPEG-3 was never developed.

*H.263*, standardized in 1995, adapted the compression methods of H.261 to produce low bit rate video that could be transmitted over regular telephone lines. To achieve the higher bit rate, the codec uses improved motion compensation and quantization methods and adds arithmetic encoding. The bit rate can be as low as 64 kb/s and as high as 1024 kb/s. Resolution ranges from 128 × 96 to 1408 × 1152, but the usual application of H.263 is 352 × 288.

The revolutionary advance in MPEG-4 compression is the use of object-based coding, where media objects (*e.g.*, audio and visual objects) are first-class entities that can be directly manipulated. Object-based coding facilitates indexing, searching, and general user interactivity, one of the chief aims of MPEG-4 encoding. The first versions of MPEG-4 appeared around 1998. The most notable of the MPEG-4 standards are MPEG-4 Part 2 and MPEG-4 Part 10. *MPEG-4 Part 2* was designed to be versatile, with applications ranging from low-data-rate web distribution to DVDs to high-data-rate HDTV broadcast. Its initial design was based on the QuickTime container format. *MPEG-4 Part 10*, sometimes called *MPEG-4 AVC* (Advanced Video Coding) and equivalent to *H.264*, is an improved MPEG-4 version introduced in 2003 that quickly achieved wide adoption for CD, DVD, HD DVD, and Blu-ray disc distribution; web streaming media; videoconferencing; videophone; and broadcast television. MPEG-4 supports data rates ranging from 5 kb/s to 10 Mb/s.

The main steps of MPEG compression are given in Algorithm 7.1. The algorithm we describe gives you an overview of MPEG compression, primarily as it is defined for MPEG-1 and MPEG-2. We suppress or simplify some details for clarity. As we did in Chapter 3 with JPEG compression, we'll look at each of the steps in turn, explaining its motivation and execution. If you understand the basic concepts in this section, you should be able to read the official documents describing any of the specific standards and understand the algorithms and terminology.

**Step 1. Divide the sequence of frames into GOPs, identifying I, P, and B frames.**

**Motivation:** A *GOP* is a *group of pictures*, that is, a group of *n* sequential video frames. The *I frames*, or *intraframes*, are compressed independently, as if they were isolated still images, using JPEG compression. This is spatial compression, as discussed earlier.

**ALGORITHM 7.1**

```
algorithm mpeg
/*Input: A sequence of frames of digital video
  Output: The same sequence, compressed*/
{
      Divide the sequence of frames into groups of pictures (GOPs), identifying I, P,
      and B frames.
      Divide each frame into macroblocks.
      Identify I frames (intraframes, to be compressed spatially with JPEG), P frames
      (forward prediction frames, to be compressed temporally relative to a preceding
      I or P frame), and B frames (bidirectional frames, to be compressed temporally
      relative to preceding and following I and/or P frames).
      For each P and B frame, compare the frame to the related I or P frame to deter-
      mine a motion vector (or more than one motion vector).
      Record differential values for P and B frames (the difference between the ex-
      pected pixel value, adjusted by motion compensation, and the actual value).
      For all frames, compress with JPEG compression
           transform data to the frequency domain with DCT
           arrange in zigzag order
           quantize
           apply entropy encoding (e.g., Huffman encoding)
}
```

I frames serve as reference points for the P frames (**interframes**, also called **forward prediction frames**) and B frames (**bidirectional frames**), which are compressed both spatially and
temporally. Recall that temporal compression involves measuring how the image in a frame
changes over time, which requires a comparison of neighboring frames.

**Details.** Each P frame is compared to its closest previous I or P frame in order to determine how much the image has changed in between. Specifically, a motion estimation algorithm is applied to determine the direction of motion between the two images, if there is
any, and represent this as a motion vector. This motion estimation is done at the macroblock level, a $16 \times 16$ pixel area. Similarly, each B frame is compared to its closest I or
P frame, in both the forward and backward direction. The GOP size and the distance between I and the next P are defined by the encoder. For example, in an MPEG-1 compressor, the GOP could be size 15 and M could be size 3. This would yield two I frames per second. I frames can serve as points of direct access when video is fast-forwarded, since their
decompression does not rely on neighboring frames.

**Step 2. Divide each frame into macroblocks.**

**Motivation:** A **macroblock** is a $16 \times 16$ pixel area. This is a manageable computational
unit. It is also small enough to allow the compressor to focus on motion in one area at a time.
Motion may be different in different parts of a frame. A child might be riding a bicycle in
one part of a frame while a second child is swinging a baseball bat in another. Motion
estimation has to be restricted to small enough areas to account for these differences.

**Details:** A $16 \times 16$ macroblock can be divided into $8 \times 8$ blocks. The way that macroblocks are divided depends on the particular compression standard, differing for H.261,

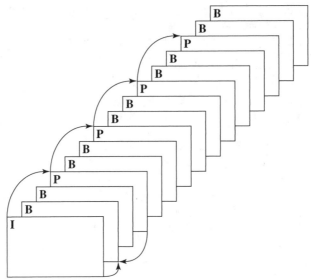

**Figure 7.21** GOP (group of pictures) in MPEG compression

MPEG-1, MPEG-2, MPEG-4 and the various profiles and levels within these, which can apply different types of chrominance subsampling. Let's look at a couple of ways that we can divide the macroblock into $8 \times 8$ blocks.

Consider $4:2:0$ YCbCr subsampling, which is used in H.261 compression. Subsampling at a ratio of $4:2:0$ produces a Y sample at each of the 256 pixels in a $16 \times 16$ area, but it takes only one Cb sample and one Cr sample for every $2 \times 2$ block of pixels. This is the equivalent of sampling every other row and every other column. You can see this in Figure 7.22. Out of $16 \times 16$ pixels, you get one $8 \times 8$ block of Cb samples, and similarly for Cr. Notice also that the $16 \times 16$ Y samples can be divided into four $8 \times 8$ blocks. In sum, you have four $8 \times 8$ blocks of information for Y, one $8 \times 8$ block for Cb, and one $8 \times 8$ block for Cr. In contrast $4:2:2$, subsampling is the equivalent of sampling every other pixel in every row for Cb and Cr, as shown in Figure 7.23. Thus, $4:2:2$ subsampling produces four $8 \times 8$ blocks of information for Y, two $8 \times 8$ blocks for Cb, and two $8 \times 8$ blocks for Cr.

Dividing a frame into macroblocks is more complicated for MPEG-2 compression than for MPEG-1 and H.261 because MPEG-2 supports interlaced video. An interlaced video frame has two fields, top and bottom. One way to handle this is to combine the two fields into one frame, divide the frame into macroblocks, and compare P and B frames with reference frames as described above. However, other options are available within the MPEG-2 standard. For example, it is possible to treat top and bottom fields separately. Then a number of possibilities open up: match a macroblock from the top field of a P frame with the top or bottom field of the preceding I or P frame; match a macroblock from the bottom field with the top field of the same frame; match a macroblock from the bottom field with the bottom field of the preceding I or P frame; and so forth. The fine-tuned motion estimation algorithms for MPEG-2 can produce multiple motion vectors and are very effective at increasing the compression rate while still yielding good quality.

Whatever the subsampling method and the resulting method for dividing the macroblock into $8 \times 8$ blocks, in the end it is the $8 \times 8$ blocks that undergo the DCT and quantization, as described in Step 5 below.

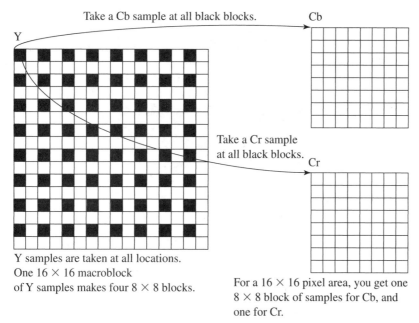

**Figure 7.22** Macroblock for 4 : 2 : 0 subsampling

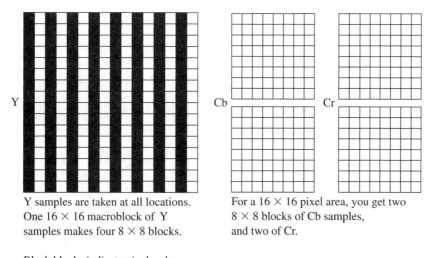

**Figure 7.23** Macroblock for 4 : 2 : 2 subsampling

**Steps 3 and 4. For each P and B frame, compare the frame to the related I frame to determine a motion vector (or more than one motion vector). Record differential values for P and B frames (the difference between the expected pixel value, adjusted by motion compensation, and the actual value).**

**Motivation:** This step is called *motion estimation*. It is motivated by a recognition that sometimes there isn't very much motion between one frame and the next. It's wasteful to repeatedly send the same information for nearly identical frames. It's more economical, in

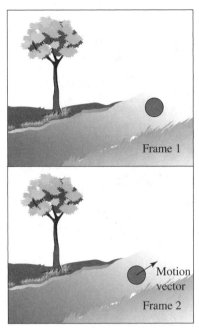

**Figure 7.24** Determining a motion vector

terms of bit rate, to convey the difference between one frame and the next, a method called ***differential encoding***. The value needed to encode the difference between a pixel in one frame and what that pixel was in the previous frame is often a smaller value than the value of the pixel itself. If there's no difference, differential encoding can yield strings of 0s, which lend themselves well to compression.

Motion of objects also has to be accounted for in a differential encoding scheme. Consider this simple scenario. You have video of a big blue ball rolling down a path (Figure 7.24). There is no wind, and nothing changes or moves except the ball. In frame 1, the ball is at one position. In frame 2, it's displaced a little to the left. Motion estimation determines how much a section of a frame has "moved" since the previous frame (or previous reference frame). Say that the ball has moved $x$ pixels to the left and $y$ pixels down between frames 1 and 2. If you can find a way to determine this motion—which in this case could be represented as a horizontal vector pointing right $x$ pixels and up $y$ pixels (pointing back to the original position)—you could use the appropriate area of frame 1 as your reference for encoding the corresponding area of frame 2. That is, you could encode the area of frame 1 as the difference between what it was (accounting for the displacement) and what it is now. The difference would not be great. Some shading differences could result from the way light is falling on the ball, but still, you're comparing part of a blue ball to part of a blue ball, as opposed to dirt or grass or tree bark or leaves. The difference between the macroblock in frame 2 and the matching macroblock in frame 1 is called the ***prediction error***.

**Details:** The P or B frame being compressed is called the ***target frame***. The reference frame to which a P frame is compared is called its ***forward prediction frame***. (The reference frame is previous to the P frame, and forward prediction works from the reference frame toward the P frame.) The reference frame to which a B frame is compared is called its ***backward prediction frame***. With both forward and backward prediction frames, an attempt is made to match a block from the P or B frame with its prediction frame. It's possible that a good match cannot be found from either of the prediction frames, in which case the frame reverts to intraframe compression only. If just one good match is found, one motion vector is used. If a good match is found from both prediction frames, two motion vectors are produced, and the matching blocks from the two prediction frames are averaged before the prediction error is computed. With MPEG-2, when interlaced video is encoded, more than two motion vectors can be generated, depending on how the fields are divided into macroblocks and compared to each other.

As you can easily imagine, motion estimation is a computationally expensive operation. Here's a sketch of how it proceeds, assuming that a full search for a matching block is done.

Assume we have a macroblock in the target frame T. We will search for a matching macroblock in reference frame R. The origin of the target block is its upper left corner, and this origin is at position $x, y$ relative to the entire frame, denoted as point $T(x, y)$. ($T(x, y)$ denotes the pixel value at that point.) The corresponding point in the reference frame would then be $R(x, y)$. We will let the origin identify a macroblock, so the macroblock in frame $R$ with origin $R(x, y)$ will be called $R_{x,y}$. We want to look in the vicinity of $R_{x,y}$ for the macroblock that most closely matches $T_{x,y}$. The vicinity we choose to examine is within a distance $d$ from $R(x, y)$. That is, we are going to compare each macroblock $R_{x+i,y+j}$ to $T_{x,y}$ for $-d \leq i \leq d$ and $-d \leq j \leq d$. We'll choose from all of these macroblocks the one that is the best match. "Best match" could be defined a number of ways. A reasonable definition is to use the average of each pixel's color difference from its corresponding pixel in the reference block. This is called the ***mean absolute difference (MAD)***, defined as follows:

$$MAD(i, j) = \frac{1}{N^2} \sum_{a=0}^{N-1} \sum_{b=0}^{N-1} |T(x + a, y + b) - R(x + i + a, y + j + b)|$$

where $N$ is the size of the macroblock and the origins of $R$ and $T$ are $R(x, y)$ and $T(x, y)$ respectively.

We want to find the vector $(p, q)$ for which $MAD(p, q)$ is the minimum. The vector given by $(p, q)$ is the displacement of the matching macroblock from the $(x, y)$ position.

The full search summarized in Algorithm 7.2 is very expensive computationally. Notice in Figure 7.25 that to do a full search, you have to examine every macroblock whose center is on or within the dotted line. This is $(2d + 1)^2$ macroblocks. Each macroblock contains $N^2$ pixels. Thus, a full search requires on the order of $(2d + 1)^2 N^2$ operations for every macroblock. In a 720 × 480 MPEG-2 frame, there would be $\frac{720 * 480}{N^2}$ macroblocks, at a rate of nearly 30 frames per second. Clearly, doing a full search is not realistic.

An alternative is to do a 2D logarithmic search. In a logarithmic search, you begin by examining only 9 macroblocks, evenly spaced within a distance $d$ around the original macroblock's position: $R_{x-\lceil d/2 \rceil, y-\lceil d/2 \rceil}$, $R_{x,y-\lceil d/2 \rceil}$, $R_{x+\lceil d/2 \rceil, y-\lceil d/2 \rceil}$, $R_{x-\lceil d/2 \rceil, y}$, $R_{x,y}$, $R_{x+\lceil d/2 \rceil, y}$, $R_{x-\lceil d/2 \rceil, y+\lceil d/2 \rceil}$, $R_{x,y+\lceil d/2 \rceil}$, and $R_{x+\lceil d/2 \rceil, y+\lceil d/2 \rceil}$. You then find the best match among these. Say that the best match is $R_{x',y'}$. Then at the next iteration, you focus on a smaller area around this macroblock, examining $R_{x'-\lceil d/4 \rceil, y'-\lceil d/4 \rceil}$, $R_{x',y'-\lceil d/4 \rceil}$, $R_{x'+\lceil d/4 \rceil, y'-\lceil d/4 \rceil}$, $R_{x'-\lceil d/4 \rceil, y'}$, $R_{x',y'}$, $R_{x'+\lceil d/4 \rceil, y'}$, $R_{x'-\lceil d/4 \rceil, y'+\lceil d/4 \rceil}$, $R_{x',y'+\lceil d/4 \rceil}$, and $R_{x'+\lceil d/4 \rceil, y'+\lceil d/4 \rceil}$. If resolution permits, you continue for another iteration, centering the search around the best matching macroblock so far and dividing the limiting distance of the search in half again, as shown in Figure 7.26. This continues to the limits of resolution. This method reduces the complexity of the algorithm to $O(N^2 \log(d))$ per macroblock in the target frame. This is more reasonable than a full search, but we've only reduced the complexity by a factor of $\frac{O(N^2 \log(d))}{O(d^2 N^2)}$. Since

---

| **ALGORITHM 7.2** | **MOTION ESTIMATION** |
|---|---|

algorithm motion_estimation
/*Input: Two video frames, the target frame $T$ and reference frame $R;$ the origin $(x, y)$
  of a macroblock to be matched
  Output: Motion vector $(p, q)$ */
{
/*Let MAX_NUM be a value larger than any anticipated MAD*/

/*Let $MAD(i, j) = \dfrac{1}{N^2} \sum\limits_{a=0}^{N-1} \sum\limits_{b=0}^{N-1} |T(x + a, y + b) - R(x + i + a, y + j + b)|$*/

 min = MAD(0,0);
 p = 0;
 q = 0;
 for i = −d to d
  for j = −d to d {
   avg = MAD (i,j);
   if (avg < min ) {
    min = avg;
    p = i;
    q = j;
   }
  }
}

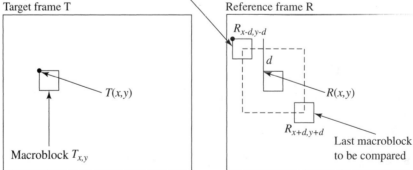

Compare macroblock $T_{x,y}$ to every macroblock $R_{x+i,y+j}$ for $-d \le i \le d$ and $-d \le j \le d$. The dotted line goes through the centers of the most-distant macroblocks to be compared.

**Figure 7.25** Motion estimation, full search

Target frame T

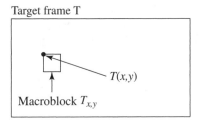

Reference frame R

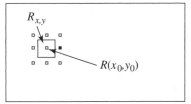

Compare $T_{x,y}$ to 9 macroblocks in R whose centers are spaced evenly around $R(x_0,y_0)$ with limiting distance $d/2$ in both directions. The small squares mark the center points of the macroblocks being compared to $T_{x,y}$. The best match is shaded black (middle of right side).

Reference frame R

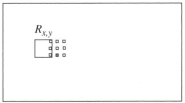

Repeat, centering the search on the best match so far.  Compare $T_{x,y}$ to 9 macroblocks spaced evenly around the best match so far with a limiting distance of $d/4$.

Reference frame R

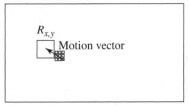

Repeat, with a limiting distance of $d/8$.

Continue to the resolution possible.

**Figure 7.26**  2D logarithmic motion estimation

this operation has to be done $\dfrac{720 * 480}{N^2} * 30$ times per second for MPEG-2 compression, further refinements must be made to make the algorithm more efficient.

There are many variations of motion estimation algorithms that attempt to target the search more effectively while achieving a reasonable computational complexity. A problem with the straightforward logarithmic search is that there is no assurance that the best match will be found. The search will converge to a local minimum but not necessarily to a global minimum relative to the entire frame. To improve the results of the search, more than one candidate for the next step in the search may be considered. A way to improve the efficiency of the search without unduly compromising the results is to consider spatial homogeneity—the fact that the motion vector for one macroblock is often very similar to the motion vector for a neighboring block. The algorithm can also be made more efficient through a hierarchical approach that begins with a lower-resolution estimate of a macroblock and finds the motion vector through increasing levels of resolution.

The range of the motion vector search varies according to the compression standard. For H.261, $d$ is a maximum of 15. For MPEG-1, it is a maximum of 1024. MPEG-1 and MPEG-2 also allow for half-pixel precision in the determination of motion vectors.

### Step 5: For all frames, compress with JPEG compression.

**Motivation:** Compressing a frame of video is just like compressing a still image, and thus JPEG compression can be applied. (See Chapter 3 for more about JPEG compression.) JPEG compression relies on transforming an image from the spatial to the frequency domain. Representing an image in the frequency domain makes it possible to treat high and low frequency components differently, a benefit to compression. The human eye is less sensitive to high frequency components than to low, since they represent areas where colors fluctuate quickly within a very small area. We have limited ability to perceive these small, localized differences, so there is no point representing these very high frequencies at a fine level of detail. Using more coarse-grained quantization levels for high-frequency components than for low frequency provides a savings in the number of bits needed overall to represent the image. Some detail is lost in the compression, but for the most part, it isn't detail that we notice.

**Details:** I frames undergo intraframe compression only. This means that they are subject to JPEG compression in the same way that JPEG compression is used to compress still images, without reference to any other image. The JPEG compression procedure is as outlined in Chapter 3: quantization of the DCT values, a zigzag ordering of values, run-length encoding, and entropy encoding.

P and B frames first undergo motion prediction, as described above. Then the difference between the expected value of a pixel and its actual value is encoded. By "expected value," we mean the value a pixel has in the best matching macroblock from the prediction frame. The differential values are stored in $8 \times 8$ blocks. These are the values that are transformed to the frequency domain by the DCT (Figure 7.27).

Quantization is a process of dividing each DCT coefficient by some integer and rounding. The details of quantization vary greatly from one standard to another, but in general values are not uniformly quantized. Dividing by a larger number amounts to coarser-grained quantization and more loss of information due to the rounding error. Quantization tables are used so that quantizer numbers can vary within a macroblock.

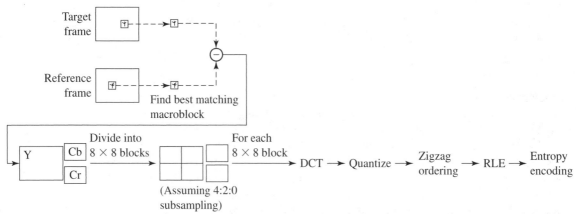

**Figure 7.27** Motion estimation and JPEG compression applied to interframes

# EXERCISES AND PROGRAMS

1. Assume that you are compositing two images that have the following foreground and background colors and foreground alpha level. What will be the resulting pixel color at a point where the images overlap?

   $B = (0, 0, 255)$, $F = (255, 150, 0)$, $\alpha = 0.7$ for foreground

2. Assume that you are compositing three images that have the following foreground and background colors and foreground alpha level. What will be the resulting pixel color at a point where the images overlap? The images are numbered from the bottom up, image 1 being the background.

   Image 1 pixels: $(0, 0, 255)$, $\alpha = 1$
   Image 2 pixels: $(255, 0, 0)$, $\alpha = 0.7$
   Image 3 pixels: $(250, 206, 161)$, $\alpha = 0.6$
   Image 4 pixels: $(0, 255, 0)$, $\alpha = 0.5$

3. What would be the alpha values for the four pixels below, applying the color difference keying method for bluescreening? The pixel values, normalized to the range [0 1], are given above each pixel.

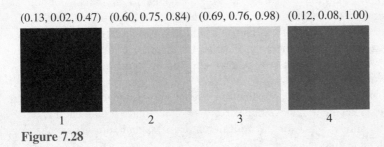

Figure 7.28

4. If you're using drop-frame timecode, and the video is at 00;3;00;00, how many frames have been dropped up to that point?

5. a. If you're using non-drop-frame timecode and the timecode reading at the end of the video says $00:04:00:00$, how long is the video?
   b. If you're using drop-frame timecode and the timecode reading at the end of the video says 00;09;30;00, what would the reading be in nondrop-frame timecode?

6. Say that you have a clip that covers the first 60 seconds of your movie. You want the 90th frame of this clip to appear at exactly the 5th second. You can mark this accordingly. This will cause the first 90 frames to be slowed down so that the 90th frame arrives after 5 seconds rather than after about 3, as it ordinarily would.
   a. Using a variable speed change, what will be the frame rate for the first five seconds of the clip?
   b. Using a variable speed change, what will be the frame rate for the last 55 seconds of the clip?
   c. What happens if you use a constant speed change?

7. Chroma keying programming exercise, online.

# APPLICATIONS

1.  What software do you have or would you like to have for digital video processing on your computer? Do a web search to see what is available for your operating system.
2.  Examine the specifications of the digital video camera that you have (or the one you would like to have). Is one-CCD? Three-CCD camera? Does it use CMOS technology? What storage medium or media does it use? What connection types does it offer to connect to your computer? What special features does it have?
3.  Identify the type and features of the video capture card you have (or the one you would like to have).
4.  Create a one-minute television commercial at your digital video workstation. Shoot a variety of different scenes and composite them in the timeline. Experiment with color correction, timing, special effects, filters, and so forth. Your commercial should include sound. When you've finished sequencing and editing the commerical, compress it to an appropriate file type. Document and justify the steps, including your final compression method, file type, and distribution medium. (As an alternative, you could create a video that illustrates a poem.)

    **Examine the features of your video processing software to see if, where, and try the exercises below with features that are available:**
5.  Capture video footage shot on a digital camera, edit the In and Out points of clips as desired, and sequence them in the timeline, sequence clips in a timeline.
6.  Import other media—for example, sound effects, music, or still images.
7.  Resize clips or have them move across the screen over time.
8.  Make composite scenes by placing clips on different tracks and resizing, applying transparencies, or matting.
9.  Shoot a "talking head" or some other subject against a greenscreen background. Use chroma keying to remove the background and replace it with another.
10. Shoot similar scenes with two different cameras and adjust the color to make them look more alike.
11. Make both variable and constant speed changes.
12. Apply filters and special effects using keyframes.
13. Render and compress to an appropriate format and distribution medium.

# REFERENCES

## Print Publications

*Adobe Premiere Pro CS3 Classroom in a Book*. Berkeley, CA: Adobe Press, 2007.

*Advanced Video Coding for Generic Audio Visual Services. Amendment 1*. ITU-T Recommendation H.264, June 2006.

*Advanced Video Coding for Generic Audio Visual Services*. ITU-T Recommendation H.264, March 2005.

Aronson, Ian. *DV Filmmaking: From Start to Finish*. O'Reilly Media, 2006.

Braverman, Barry. *Video Shooter: Storytelling with DV, HD, and HDV Cameras*. CMP Books, 2006.

Ghanbari, M. "The Cross Search Algorithm for Motion Estimation." *IEEE Transactions on Communications*. Vol. 38, No. 7. pp. 950–953, July 1990.

Lim, Kyoung Won, and Jong Boem Ra. "Improved Hierarchical Search Block Matching Algorithm by Using Multiple Vector Candidates." *Electronic Letters*, Vol. 33, No. 21, pp. 1771–1772, October 1997.

Mishima, Yasushi. "Curved Color Separation Spaces for Blue Screen Matting." SMPTE Technical Conference No. 142, Pasadena, CA, 2001, Vol. 110, No. 3, pp. 131–139.

Nam, Kwon Moon, Joon-Seek Kim, and Rae-Hong Park. "A Fast Hierarchical Motion Vector Estimation Algorithm Using Mean Pyramid." *IEEE Transactions on Circuits and Systems for Video Technology*, Vol. 5, No. 4, pp. 344–351, August 1995.

Nasrabadi, N. M., and R. A. King. "Image Coding Using Vector Quantization: A Review." *IEEE Transactions on Communications*, Vol. 36, pp. 957–971, August 1988.

Po, Lai-Man, and Wing-Chung Ma. "A Novel Four Step Search Algorithm for Fast Bock Motion Estimation." *IEEE Transactions on Circuits and Systems for Video Technology*, Vol. 6, No. 3, pp. 313–317, June 1996.

Porter, T. and T. Duff. "Compositing Digital Images." *Proceedings of SIGGRAPH '84*, Vol. 18, No. 3, pp. 253–259, 1984.

Smith, Alvy Ray, and James F. Blinn. "Blue Screen Matting." *Proceedings of SIGGRAPH '96*, New Orleans, LA, pp. 259–268.

Weynand, Diana. *Apple Pro Training Series: Final Cut Pro 6*. Berkeley, CA: Peachpit Press, 2007.

Wright, Steve. *Digital Composition for Film and Video*, 2nd ed. Burlington, MA: Focal Press, 2006.

## Websites

Cinerella (video editing on Linux)

　　http://heroinewarrior.com/cinelerra.php3

Kino (video editing on Linux)

　　http://www.kinodv.org/

# Multimedia Authoring

*God does not care about our mathematical difficulties. He integrates empirically.*
—Albert Einstein

## OBJECTIVES FOR CHAPTER 8

- Become familiar with current multimedia authoring environments and programming languages, including Director, Flash, Java, Processing, and Max/MSP/Jitter.
- Know the main features of these current multimedia programming environments, including their particular strengths, level of abstraction, extensibility, support for a variety of media, support for concurrency, event handling, and object-oriented programming features.
- Understand the key differences between Director and Flash, and have an overview of these languages that helps you learn them more quickly.

## 8.1 WHAT IS MULTIMEDIA AUTHORING?

Digital photography. Vector graphics. MIDI. Digital audio. Digital video. Pictures, sound, music, motion, and interactivity. This is digital media, a fascinating intersection of technology, mathematics, and algorithms waiting for you to bring it to life with your creativity. Now we add one more tool to put this all together—multimedia authoring.

Multimedia authoring integrates a variety of media, including images, sound, and video along with animation and interactivity. The purposes for working in multimedia authoring range from the commercial to the personal to the purely artistic. The means of distribution vary—CD, DVD, web, email, television, movies. And the languages and environments vary, from all-purpose programming languages like Java to full-featured authoring environments like Adobe Director and Flash with accompanying scripting languages.

In this chapter, we'll consider the issues involved in choosing a multimedia authoring environment or language and compare some current languages. The languages and environments we'll examine—Director, Flash, Java, Processing, and Max/MSP/Jitter—have different features, strengths, and weaknesses, giving you an idea of the possibilities.

The result of multimedia authoring can go by a number of names—*production*, *animation*, *movie*, or even simply *program*, if you're referring to the implementation itself. We'll use all of these names. What does a multimedia production look like? That depends on what you're trying to accomplish and the language you choose. You might use a multimedia authoring environment to create a digital résumé or portfolio, an advertisement, a cartoon animation, a tutorial DVD, a special effects portion of a movie, or an interactive visual poem for personal expression. You may choose to work with vector graphics, bitmap images, or a combination of these. You may include video, digital audio, or MIDI. You may work in 2D or 3D. You may allow user interactivity.

The multimedia authoring environment you choose depends on your purpose. In the next section, we'll consider the important issues involved in choosing an authoring environment or language. We'll then give you an overview of a number of current authoring environments and how to approach them.

# 8.2 CRITERIA FOR EVALUATING MULTIMEDIA AUTHORING ENVIRONMENTS

You're ready to put together a multimedia production, and you need to choose an appropriate language. Where do you begin? Here are some issues to consider as you make your choice:

- *Work process.* What are the main steps when you create an animation or movie in your chosen language or environment? Is it all programming? Will you create pictures, sounds, and movies first and import them into your programming environment, or will you create everything from scratch within the programming environment itself? Do you use drag-and-drop programming with built-in behaviors, or do you program everything from scratch? What elements are already created for you and ready for use? Extensive class libraries? Built-in objects or behaviors? Built-in GUI (graphical user interface) objects like buttons and text boxes? Events that will automatically generate handler calls? (*Behaviors* and *events* will be defined below.)

- *Media supported.* How easy or difficult is it to incorporate the media that are most important to your production? Does your language easily support bitmap images? Vector graphics? Digital sound? MIDI? Digital video? Interactivity? 3D?

- *Ease of programming.* Have you ever used this language before? What is the programming environment for the language? Is there a user-friendly GUI? An IDE (integrated development environment)? Some multimedia languages are based upon a kind of metaphor. For example, Adobe Director has a very visual programming environment, using the metaphor of a stage and cast members. Flash's programming environment resembles a drawing surface, with different pieces of transparent acetate laid one on top of the other. What programming metaphor or environment feels most natural to you?

- *Programming paradigm.* Is this an all-purpose programming language, with full computational power? Is it a scripting language? Does it support object-oriented programming? Is it an event-based language? What is the intent of the language? Is the authoring environment especially designed for a particular purpose—for example, bitmap images, vector graphics, or audio? Is it an education-oriented language—primarily intended to teach you how to program and get you excited about programming—or is it "industrial strength"?

- *Extensibility.* Can you add features to the language or environment with additional third-party plugins or extras? Can you write your own extra components?

- *Efficiency of the language.* Some languages are easy to learn, but they execute inefficiently and do not lend themselves to programs that require heavy-duty computation. Will your chosen language be able to execute fast enough for your purposes? Is it an interpreted or a compiled language? Interpreted languages generally are good for fast prototyping, but they're slower for high-powered computation. Compiled languages can take advantage of compiler optimizations for faster execution. Is it important to you to be able to develop your program quickly? Or is it more important that the final product execute quickly? Does the language give you access at a low enough level of abstraction to allow you to write efficient code?

- *Cost.* Is the language or environment freeware? Shareware? A commercial product? If it's a commercial product, how much does it cost? Can you afford it? Is there a trial version? How long can you keep the trial version, and how much functionality does it have?

- *Language stability.* How stable is the language or environment? Is it standardized? Is it in a constant state of revisions and additions? Will it be around in a year or two?

- *Memory requirements.* How much RAM and disk space are needed to run the programming environment? Can your computer accommodate these requirements?

- *Platform.* What operating system does the language run under?
- *Distribution means.* What options do you have for distributing your multimedia production, in terms of both operating system and distribution media like web, CD, DVD, etc.? Can you distribute the production in a format that will be accessible to your target audience? How large are the resulting files?

The two tables below compare some of the key features in multimedia programming environments of particular interest.

There are three types of languages that you might think of as "multimedia" but that are not covered in this chapter. Because this book focuses on 2D graphics, we don't cover 3D languages such as Maya and 3DSMax. Three-dimensional animation is a big topic covered in depth in many books, along with traditional graphics textbooks that explain the underlying mathematics. We also don't cover the variety of multimedia-oriented introductory

| TABLE 8.1 | Comparison of Some Current Multimedia Authoring Environments, Part 1 | | | |
|---|---|---|---|---|
| **Language** | **Level of Abstraction** | **Style of Programming** | **Media Supported** | **Extensibility** |
| **C/C++ with MFC or X Windows** | low | imperative (C) or object-oriented (C++) | various media supported at a low level of abstraction | can be extended with additional libraries |
| **Director** | high; lower possible with scripting language, Lingo | drag-and-drop environment with built-in behaviors; Lingo offers choice of JavaScript or traditional dot syntax; choice of imperative or object-oriented style | optimized for bitmap images, video; handles digital audio well; can handle MIDI with Xtras; Flash vector graphics can also be included | can be extended with Xtras and new components |
| **Flash** | high; lower possible with scripting language, ActionScript | drag-and-drop environment with built-in behaviors; ActionScript uses JavaScript syntax; choice of imperative or object-oriented style | optimized for vector graphics; handles low-res video and digital audio well; excellent for web-based productions | can be extended with third-party extensions and new components |
| **Java** | medium | object-oriented | AWT and JMF packages facilitate GUI building and inclusion of images, sound, and video | can be extended with new classes, packages, and APIs |
| **Python** | medium | object-oriented | environments like JES facilitate media computation | can be extended with modules for new applications |
| **Processing** | high | object-oriented | designed for artistic experimentation with bitmap images | can be extended with new classes, packages, and APIs |
| **Max/MSP/Jitter** | high; lower possible when interfaced with C, Java, and JavaScript | visual programming environment where built-in components are placed in a Patcher Window and their inputs and outputs linked | Max for MIDI; MSP for digital audio; Jitter for 2D and 3D images and video | C and JavaScript code can be written to create additional components |
| **ChucK** | medium to low | text-based programming environment for real-time synthesis, composition, performance | digital audio and MIDI | ChucK plugins can be written in C/C++ |

| TABLE 8.2 | Comparison of Some Current Multimedia Authoring Environments, Part 2 | | | |
|---|---|---|---|---|
| Language | Platform | Distribution means | Support for Concurrency | Support for Network Communication |
| C++ with MFC or X Windows | Windows, Mac, Unix, Linux | platform-specific executable | low-level threads | sockets and client-server model |
| Director | Windows, Mac; can be played on Linux | DIR is native file format; EXE or OSX is stand-alone executable; DCR is Shockwave format for web | MIAW (Movie in a Window) can run concurrently with main movie | NetLingo for network operations |
| Flash | Windows, Mac, Unix, Linux | FLA is native file format; EXE or HQX is stand-alone executable; SWF is format for web; MOV is a QuickTime movie | movie clip serves as a movie within a movie, having its own internal timeline | NetStream and NetConnection classes |
| Java | Windows, Mac, Linux, and Unix | compiled to bytecode; distributed as an application or applet for web | Thread class, synchronization mechanisms | Client, Server, and Socket classes |
| Python | Windows, Mac, Unix, Linux | compiled to bytecode; run by interactive Python interpreter or distributed as executable file | Thread and Queue class | Socket module |
| Processing | Windows, Mac, Linux, and Unix | compiled to bytecode; distributed as an application or applet for web | Same as Java, though the intent of Processing is to shelter the user from lower-level details | |
| Max/MSP/Jitter | Windows, Mac | platform-specific executable | some inherent concurrency, but not controlled explicitly | Network objects in Jitter |
| ChucK | Windows, Mac, Linux | compiled to bytecode, run by the ChucK Virtual Machine (VM) | VM can run multiple programs in parallel; concurrency through Shreds; events can be broadcast | full OSC support for networking |

programming languages that are emerging, including Alice, Squeak, Scratch, and simplified variants of Java such as JPython. These languages have become quite popular for introductory computer science courses because they allow students to learn programming concepts and constructs without getting bogged down in syntax, and they're marvelous playrooms where students can create colorful 2D and 3D interactive worlds with sound and motion. However, they generally aren't practical languages for implementing large projects, especially of a commercial nature. The third category we don't cover is web-programming languages such as HTML and JavaScript. Although we often associate the web with multimedia, these languages aren't designed to deal with interactive images, sound, and video in a powerful way. HTML is for the creation of basic web pages. It can be multimedia-empowered via Java applets, but HTML alone has little multimedia functionality beyond displaying basic images. JavaScript, when used with web pages, allows you to control the opening, look, size, and position of a web page. It's good for creating interactive web forms, and it allows you to create mouse rollovers—images that change as the mouse cursor moves over an area—but doing complicated multimedia manipulation does not come naturally in JavaScript. (However, JavaScript *does* have a presence in multimedia authoring environments. In particular, Director, Flash, and Max/MSP allow you to write code using JavaScript syntax.)

The representative languages and environments we compare are ***Director***, ***Flash***, ***Java***, ***Processing***, and ***Max/MSP/Jitter***, with the emphasis on Director and Flash since these are full-featured environments especially designed for 2D animations. Before we look at features of these languages, let's consider some of the issues and terminology that give a context to particular comparisons.

We assume in this chapter that you already know how to program in common imperative and object-oriented languages like C, C++, and Java. The purpose of this chapter is to give you an overview of the multimedia languages available to you so that you can choose a language appropriate to your projects. Also, by showing you the essential features, we hope to give you a start on the fastest way to learn your chosen language.

## 8.3 FEATURES OF MULTIMEDIA AUTHORING ENVIRONMENTS AND LANGUAGES

### 8.3.1 Levels of Abstraction

Each programmer has his or her own preferred programming style. Some of you like to "do it yourself" from a low level of abstraction. If this is the case with you, then you may have tried your hand at multimedia or GUI programming using C or C++ as your base language, adding visual elements by means of some type of window and/or sound library. In the Unix or Linux environment, this could be the X Window system, perhaps with an audio toolkit like AudioFile or RPlay. You could also use OpenGL. In the Microsoft Windows environment, you could use the MFC library (Microsoft Foundations Class), DirectSound, and DirectMusic. Working at this level of abstraction gives you a great deal of control over your productions, but it requires that you write quite a bit of code by hand, learning extensive libraries with nonintuitively named functions with parameters that you have to know. Integrated development environments (IDEs) are available to help with GUI-building.

A step up in levels of abstraction would be a language like Java. Java is a full-powered programming language with the added advantage of providing a large library of built-in classes, many of which are useful for building a GUI or working with images and sound. When you work in a language like Java, your first challenge is to get a general picture of the classes available to you so that you don't reinvent something that already exists in the library. A lot of your learning is done by looking at examples. You find a "recipe" for creating something similar to what you'd like, and then you modify the recipe for your own purposes. Visual elements can be added to a Java program by means of the Swing and AWT (Abstract Windows Toolkit) classes, which facilitate the building of GUIs, allow you to work with bitmap images, and allow you to draw geometric objects and shapes dynamically on the display screen. With the sound API, you can write a Java program that can capture, process, and play back digital audio and MIDI, working with AIFF, WAV, AU, and MIDI files. The JMF (Java Media Framework) provides even more facilities for capturing, processing, and delivering time-based media—specifically, sound and video. As with C/C++, IDEs are available to assist with Java GUI-building—for example, Eclipse.

As a multimedia programming language, Java lies at a level of abstraction between C with X Windows and high-level environments like Director or Flash. When you work with Java, you're programming with lines of sequential code, perhaps modularized by classes and Java packages and stored in separate files—but still essentially done through a process of coding. You may have a development environment or Java GUI-builder that allows you to drag and drop buttons, input boxes, and the like onto an interface and then attach call-back routines to these GUI elements. But your media—sounds, video, shapes, and bitmap images—are controlled by lines of code that open files, cause them to be played, draw lines on the screen, move images by changing their *x* and *y* position within a window, and so forth.

In the discussion above, we used the acronym *API*, which stands for *Application Programming Interface*. An API is a specification of a set of classes—usually all related to some specific application area like sound, images, threads, time-based media, and so forth. The API serves as an interface and tells you the classes that are available to you, the methods (*i.e.*, functions and procedures) associated with these classes, the parameters expected in calls to these methods, the actions these methods perform, and the values they return, if any. In keeping with the idea of abstract data types, the interface makes no commitment as to how the methods are implemented. Their specific implementation is actually irrelevant to how you use them. All you need to know is how to call the functions and what to expect in return, in terms of what happens and what values you might get back.

APIs can be added to a language incrementally, as the language develops. Sometimes outside developers will contribute APIs. The programmer's task in working with Java is to find out what APIs exist, download and install them, and learn how to use them. In general, an API brings together related activities, sheltering you from confusing or unnecessary details and giving you ready access to activities you're likely to use repeatedly. Java lends itself to this type of development, and over recent years a number of Java APIs have emerged that simplify Java so that it can be learned more easily by beginning programming students. Processing is an example of this. Although it is often described as a programming language or environment, Processing is actually an API—a group of classes packaged in Java—aimed at digital artists who are interested in increasing their expressive power by learning some computer programming. Processing allows the artist to work with images and sound at a higher level of abstraction than in standard Java, with the emphasis on easy manipulation of bitmap images.

Python is a language that has been gaining popularity as a general-purpose introductory programming languge. It is a particularly palatable language for digital media students because of its English-like syntax and adaptability to for multimedia programming. Python runs on all major platforms and is free, open-source software.

The next step up in levels of abstraction would be languages like Director and Flash, which are specifically designed as multimedia authoring environments. Both of these are visual, user-friendly programming environments that facilitate animations by offering built-in components, behaviors, tweening, and events. You can create an entire animation in these environments with no actual coding. Like video editing environments, Director and Flash productions are built from a frame-by-frame timeline. Each frame shows what the animation looks like at one moment in time. If the frame rate is 12 frames per second—the default in Flash—then that moment in time lasts for 1/12th of a second. The animation is played on a "stage." For each frame, you indicate what you want on the stage and where you want it to be. Both Director and Flash offer built-in *tweening*. (Tweening is introduced in Chapter 7.) With tweening, you indicate the shape, size, color, location, skewing, etc. of an object at one moment in time (*i.e.*, a keyframe), reset any of these properties at another moment in time (a second keyframe), and ask the system to change the object, gradually, from the first state to the second over the intervening frames. This saves you the effort of making the changes by hand, using lines of code that change *x* and *y* positions, colors, angles, and so forth.

Both Director and Flash also have built-in *behaviors*—things that objects on the stage can do, such as spin around, change color, or respond in specific ways to mouse clicks or key presses. The code for these built-in behaviors is already written. All you have to do is drag and drop the behavior out of a library onto an object on the stage. Sometimes you can customize the behavior of an object by setting parameters. Behaviors can also be applied to frames themselves—for example, forcing execution to stop on a frame so that you can wait for the user to click a button.

If you want to define your own behaviors in Director or Flash, you have to learn the *scripting languages*. In Director, the scripting language is called *Lingo*. In Flash, it is called *ActionScript*. So just what is a scripting language, and how does it differ from a regular programming language? This is another of those terms that has different meanings depending on who you ask, and no clear lines to demarcate it. Historically, the term *scripting language* has been associated with interpreted rather than compiled languages. Interpreted languages change lines of code into executable binary format as they execute, line-by-line. This is in contrast to compiled languages that take an entire program, turn it into binary code, optimize the code based on local and global conditions related to how variables change state, and link all modules of the program into one executable file. Compiling and linking a whole project before executing it can be a time-consuming process (for large projects). Thus, scripting languages are good for rapid development and prototyping, allowing you to change small sections of a project without recompiling and relinking the whole thing. The term *scripting language* is also used for languages that exist as part of a larger development environment, which is primarily how Lingo and ActionScript came to be called scripting languages.

ActionScript has evolved considerably since its first version. It now is considered a full-featured language, accommodating object-oriented programming (OOP) and strong typing. Lingo is also a full-powered language that offers object-oriented programming. Both languages allow you to use OOP-style or not, as you prefer. Both ActionScript and Lingo are compiled into platform independent bytecodes, which are translated into platform-specific binary code when the animation is played. (Java is also compiled into bytecodes.) Lingo actually has choices of syntax: either standard Lingo dot syntax (described in a later section) or JavaScript syntax. This can make learning Lingo easier for you if you already know JavaScript. ActionScript has only one syntax—very similar to the syntax of JavaScript and C.

**ASIDE:** *Bytecode* is a binary representation of executable code that is intended to be interpreted by a "virtual machine" rather than executed directly by hardware. Because it is interpreted through software, the bytecode can be standardized across platforms, the assumption being that each platform will have its own version of the bytecode interpreter that will translate the bytecode into the appropriate instruction set for the platform's hardware. This is why languages like Java, which are compiled into bytecode, are called "platform independent."

Max/MSP exemplifies another multimedia programming environment with a visual interface that allows you to work at a high level of abstraction. Max was originally designed for the production of interactive music with MIDI. To this environment, MSP was added for digital audio and Jitter was added for images, video, and 3D graphic objects. Musical objects in Max are created in a Patcher Window, where you can select timers, loops, filters, and so forth and connect the objects' input and output ports. In a similar manner, MSP uses digital audio objects, and Jitter uses image and video objects with transformations defined as matrix operations. Syntax is de-emphasized by the visual nature of the programming environment. However, because Max itself is implemented in C, experienced programmers have the option of writing their own audio or MIDI objects in C and adding these to the environment. Max/MSP also has a scripting language—JavaScript—through which you can manipulate objects by writing actual lines of code. Jitter interfaces with Java by means of the Jitter Java API. A Java class can become the parameter of a Jitter object, allowing the object to execute the Java code.

ChucK is an interesting audio/MIDI manipulation program at a lower level of abstraction. Those who have used it with students report that the students learn ChucK quickly and can go far with it. It has potential for creative exploration in the area of digital sound.

The point of this section is that you can find a multimedia language that suits your preferred level of abstraction. At a lower level of abstraction, you have greater control over efficiency of execution, but the programming can be tedious and the resulting code pretty ugly to look at. At a higher level of abstraction you can work faster, since common activities like event handling are taken care of for you and put in convenient "black boxes." This gives you a chance to focus on the overall design, the media embedded in your production, and the creation of a larger project. If you don't peek into the black boxes, you're forced to accept the implementation given to you by your programming environment, but often you can tweak details by descending into the environment's scripting language.

## 8.3.2 Supported Media

When you choose a multimedia authoring environment, you need to consider the type of production you hope to create. Is your language equipped to handle your media efficiently, whether they be bitmap images, vector graphics, digital audio, MIDI, digital video, or a combination of these?

Some environments particularly lend themselves to certain media—notably, Flash and Director. Flash is designed for the creation of vector graphic images. Since these are generally smaller than bitmaps, Flash is excellent for developing web-based animations. However, vector graphic animations are mostly cartoon-like or poster-like. If photographic realism is what you want, then Director is a better choice, since it is designed to handle bitmap images. Director animations and movies can also be turned into Shockwave format and played on the web. Large Director productions—collections of tutorials or informational pieces—are often distributed via CDs or DVDs.

Although Director is better suited to bitmap graphics and Flash is better suited to vector graphics, you *can* use vector graphics in Director and bitmap images in Flash—it just isn't as natural or seamless, and the media may not be handled optimally. With Flash, you can draw your vector graphic objects directly in the Flash environment—on the "stage," as it is called—or you can import vector graphic objects that were drawn in other environments, like Illustrator. You can also import bitmap images into Flash, and you can leave them as bitmaps in Flash, or even convert them to vector graphics. Director is better equipped to handle bitmap graphics. It also has the nice feature of allowing you to incorporate Flash animations, so you can actually use the two environments together. You can create an animation or button in Flash, export it as an SWF file, and then import it into Director, and thus have both bitmaps and animation in the same environment.

Both Director and Flash handle sound well, allowing you to import, play, and/or stream AIFF, WAV, MP3, and AU sound files. Both handle video well, also, but Director does it on a larger scale than Flash, in the sense that it accommodates more codecs and optimizes the use of larger file sizes. Director allows you to use video compressed as QuickTime, Real-Media, Video for Windows, MPEG-1, and MPEG-4, and with Director's caching optimizations and direct-to-stage mode, it's possible to view video at full screen. Video playback can be controlled by means of buttons that are created in Flash and imported into Director. In contrast, Flash accommodates video in FLV format or with the Sorenson Spark or On2VP6 codecs. Although this video is generally played in small-resolution windows, it is large enough and clear enough for many purposes. Because of the ubiquity of the Flash player (standard in web browsers) and its built-in ability to play Flash video, many commercial companies now use Flash video on their websites.

Java allows you to incorporate images, vector graphics, sound, and video into a project, but without the built-in features for handling the media that Flash and Director provide. You can write a Java program so that it reads an image file and displays it in a graphics context—that is, a window. You can manipulate the data pixel-by-pixel and then redisplay the image. You create the equivalent of vector graphics by dynamically drawing basic shapes into a graphics context and in this way create a picture. You can draw things in a buffer area so that a whole picture can be drawn before you display it. Doing this frame-by-frame can create an animation effect. However, this is much more a "do it by hand" process than in Director and Flash, where tweening can be applied simply by marking keyframes on the timeline, and other actions can be set up by dropping a built-in behavior onto an object on-stage. In Java, you can create a draw or paint program itself and allow the user to do the artwork. You can also open video and sound files and play them. All of these effects are achieved by traditional programming—lines of code that you write using the classes in the Swing, AWT, and JMF packages. The advantage of doing these things in Java is that you can customize your code more tightly, particularly if Java is a language with which you already have a good amount of experience.

Processing is a programming environment initially conceived as an experimental creative playground for "artists, designers, architects, researchers, and hobbyists" (a quote from the project's web page, www.processing.org). Without having to deal with details of ActionListeners and Graphics objects (classes in Java for event handling and updating images), artists can play with pixel colors in dynamic and interactive ways, creating visualizations of cellular automata, eyeballs that follow the mouse, RGB 3D color spaces, and other fanciful images. The emphasis in Processing is on encouraging creativity and demystifying the process of writing programs, primarily in the creation of images and with the possible addition of sound.

Code Segment 8.1 is an example of a simple Processing program—Conway's Game of Life, which causes cellular automata represented as pixels to come to life, live, and expire depending on the number of neighboring pixels. Processing has a PImage class through which you can load existing images or draw an image dynamically by setting pixel colors, as illustrated in the program. Some of the lower-level details of how this is done in Java are hidden in Processing. The main things you need to know in Processing are that *setup* is called when the program begins execution and *draw* is called repeatedly in a loop.

**CODE SEGMENT 8.1   THE GAME OF LIFE IN PROCESSING**

```
/*Conway's Game of Life in Processing*/
int max_x = 360;
int max_y = 240;
float percent_filled_at_start = 0.2;
color cblack = color(0,0,0);
color cred = color(192,0,0); // newly black pixels
color cgreen = color(0,255,128); // newly white pixels
color cwhite = color(255,255,255);

void initialize() {
 loadPixels();
 for(int i = 0; i < max_x*max_y; i++) {
  float r = random(1);
  if(r < percent_filled_at_start) pixels[i] = cwhite;
```

```
     else pixels[i] = cblack;
 }
 updatePixels();
}

void mousePressed() {initialize();}

void setup() { // these statements execute when the program begins
 size(360, 240);
 frameRate(10);
 initialize();
}

void draw() { // main loop of program
 PImage myCopy = get();
 for(int x = 0; x < max_x; x++) {
  for(int y = 0; y < max_y; y++) {
   int neighbours = 0;
   for(int i = -1; i <= 1; i++)
    for(int j = -1; j <= 1; j++) {
     color cxyij = myCopy.get(x+i,y+j); // returns black if out
     if((cxyij == cwhite) || (cxyij == cgreen)) neighbours =
     neighbours+1;
   }
   color cxy = myCopy.get(x,y);
   if((cxy == cwhite) || (cxy == cgreen)) {
    if((neighbours == 3) || (neighbours == 4))
    // it should be 2 or 3, but we counted the center pixel
     set(x,y,cwhite);
    else set(x,y,cred);
   }
   else { // red or black
    if(neighbours == 3) set(x,y,cgreen);
    else set(x,y,cblack);
   }
  } // end for y
 } // end for x
}
```

Max/MSP encourages programmers to exercise their creativity in the realm of sound, combining MIDI and digital audio. MAX programs are written graphically through MIDI objects and functions, numbers, and relational operators that are linked with patch cords.

Figure 8.1 is an example of a MAX program. The dial on the left of the window allows you to change the MIDI patch to a value between 1 and 32, determining what instrument is played. The larger portion on the right performs the following steps (explaining from the top of the figure down):

- Take a note in from the MIDI input device.
- Strip off the *note off* message and process only the *note on* part. (A *note off* message is a note on message with velocity 0.)

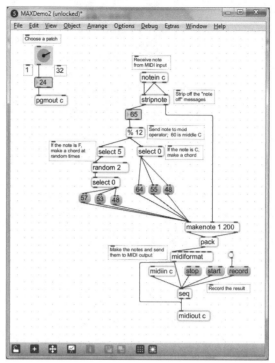

**Figure 8.1** MAX program

- If a C note is played (any octave), add a chord to it.
- If an F note is played (any octave), add a chord to it about half the time, as determined by a random number between 0 and 1.
- Create a note from the result and send it to MIDI output. (*makenote* will make both the note on and note off messages.)
- Optionally, record what is played as MIDI output.

With a program such as this, you can play whatever you want on the MIDI input device and add elements to it, creating and recording a new composition. The elements added in the sample program are simple, but this gives you an idea of the possibilities for algorithmic MIDI music composition in MAX.

MAX can be interfaced with MSP, designed for doing operations on sampled digital audio. MSP is a good environment in which to experiment with digital audio at a low level of abstraction, since it allows you to import audio files or generate waveforms at set frequencies and then add waveforms, filter clips, and implement operations such as phase shift and frequency modulation. You can edit and apply effects to digital audio at the sample level, combining operations in as many ways as you can think of.

Figure 8.2 is an example of an MSP program. This program reads in a digital audio file and applies flange to it. The flanging process adds samples back to the original after a specified delay. The length of the delay is varied sinusoidally, creating a periodic warping of the frequencies.

Jitter, a later addition to MAX/MSP, allows for the manipulation of images, video, and 3D objects. Jitter relies on QuickTime for video and OpenGL for 2D and 3D graphics. An

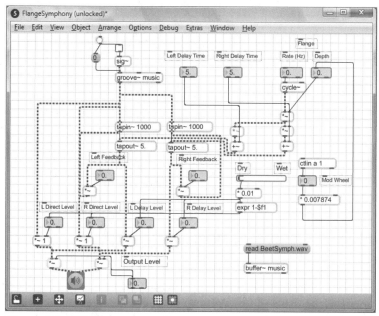

**Figure 8.2** MSP program

example of a Jitter program is given in Figure 8.3. This program implements chroma keying, a method for color extraction described in Chapter 7.

In sum, you should familiarize yourself with the available languages and environments so that you can choose one that lends itself best to what you want to do. We all like to stick with what we know, and you may be inclined to implement something in a language you're

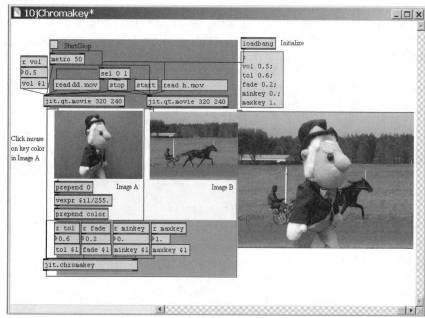

**Figure 8.3** Jitter program (adapted from the Jitter tutorial)

already familiar with. But if you take the time to investigate the possibilities, choose the most suitable language, and learn that language, you may be able to give yourself a new tool with remarkable creative power.

## 8.3.3 Support for Event-Driven Programming

Because they rely on user interaction, multimedia programming languages are essentially event-driven. An *event* is something that happens when the animation is running or a user interacts with a program—the animation starts up, the mouse is clicked or a key is pressed, the playhead enters a frame, a new object is created and placed on stage, a sound is played, and so forth. The Director, Flash, Java, and Processing environments define which events are significant. For these events, procedures are automatically invoked. You have to know which events generate a procedure call, and then you can write an *event handler* to respond to that call, making it do whatever you want it to do—redraw the stage with an object at a new location, change the size of something, open an "alert" window—whatever you want. If you don't want to respond to an event, you simply don't write an event handler for it.

Director, Flash, Java, and Processing allow you to do event-handling from a high level of abstraction, which means that a lot is done for you automatically. You can see this in Code Segment 8.1, the Game of Life program in Processing. The function *setup* is called when program execution begins. Then *draw* is called repeatedly in a loop. As the program loops, it continuously checks for events like *mousePressed*, *mouseReleased*, *mouseDragged*, *keyPressed*, or *keyReleased*. You don't have to do anything to ensure that this happens; event-checking is done for you automatically. You just need to write code for events in the cases when you want something in particular to happen. Convenient global variables are also defined for you, like *mouseX* and *mouseY*, which give the horizontal and vertical position of the cursor when the mouse is pressed.

Code Segment 8.2 shows a partially implemented card-playing program in Processing. In *setup*, the cards are put into an array and shuffled and the first four cards are dealt, like in a game of Blackjack. The *draw* function deals out the hands. In *mousePressed*, the position of the mouse is compared to the position of the buttons and action taken accordingly.

JPEG images are used for the cards, for simplicity named *i.jpg* where *i* is replaced by a number between 1 and 52. To implement the card game fully, you could create a Card class so that each card knows what image it is associated with and what its suit and value are.

| CODE SEGMENT 8.2 | A CARD GAME IN PROCESSING (PARTIAL IMPLEMENTATION) |
|---|---|

```
PImage [] c = new PImage[53];
PImage [] player1Hand = new PImage[8];
PImage [] player2Hand = new PImage[8];
int player1Cards = 0, player2Cards = 0;
int player = 1, handNum;
PImage dealCard, stay;
void setup () {
  PImage temp;
  int j, k;
```

```
  size(720,480);
  for (int i = 0; i < 53; i++)
   c[i] = loadImage(str(i+1) + ".jpg");
  c[52] = loadImage("back.jpg");
  randomSeed(second());
  for (int i = 0; i < 52; i++) {
   j = (int) random(52);
   temp = c[j];
   c[j] = c[i];
   c[i] = temp;
  }
  dealCard = loadImage("Deal.jpg");
  stay = loadImage("Stay.jpg");
  image(dealCard, 210, 10);
  image(stay, 410, 10);
  k = 0;
  player1Hand[0] = c[0]; player2Hand[0] = c[1];
  player1Hand[1] = c[2]; player2Hand[1] = c[3];
  player1Cards = 2; player2Cards = 2;
  handNum = 4;
}

void draw() {
  int cardx = 20, cardy = 30;
  for (int i = 0; i < player1Cards; i++) {
   image(player1Hand[i], cardx, cardy);
   cardx = cardx + 20; cardy = cardy + 30;
  }
  cardx = 600; cardy = 30;
  for (int i = 0; i < player2Cards; i++) {
   image(player2Hand[i], cardx, cardy);
   cardx = cardx - 20; cardy = cardy + 30;
  }
}
void mouseReleased() {
  if (mouseX >= 210 && mouseX <= 310 && mouseY >= 10 &&
  mouseY <= 60) {
   if (player == 1) player1Hand[player1Cards++] =
   c[handNum++];
   else if (player == 2) player2Hand[player2Cards++] =
   c[handNum++];
  }
 else if (mouseX >= 410 && mouseX <= 510 && mouseY >= 10 &&
 mouseY <= 60) {
   if (player == 1) player = 2;
   else if (player == 2) player = 1;
  }
}
```

Director and Flash do event-handling at a similar high level of abstraction, as you'll see in more detail later in this chapter. Java, in contrast, requires that you oversee event-handling a little more closely, in exchange for more control over your objects.

A Java program equivalent to the Processing card game is given in Code Segment 8.3. In Java, you have to specify which objects are listening for events. You do this by adding an ActionListener to an object. A class that needs to respond to events "implements ActionListener," as you can see in the Blackjack class's definition. Then the particular user-interface component that is supposed to listen for the event—in this example, a JButton—has an ActionListener added to it with the *addActionListener(this)* method. There are two buttons on this game interface, both listening for events. In cases like this, each button has a string associated with it. When the button is clicked, the system automatically sends a call to *actionPerformed* with the button's string as a parameter. Then inside *actionPerformed*, *if* statements controlled by the strings determine what actions should be taken, appropriate to the button that was clicked. This approach requires that the programmer pay more attention to detail than in Processing, but provides greater control and greater efficiency, since only objects with ActionListeners receive calls when events occur.

Java still operates as a fairly high level of abstraction, automatically generating calls for redrawing the screen. In the example program, *paintComponent* is called automatically by the system whenever something changes that necessitates a repainting of the display. You can control how the screen is painted by implementing this method.

| CODE SEGMENT 8.3 | A CARD GAME IN JAVA (PARTIAL IMPLEMENTATION) |
| --- | --- |

```java
import java.awt.*;
import java.awt.event.*;
import javax.swing.*;
import java.util.*;

public class Blackjack extends JComponent implements
ActionListener
{
  private Image[] c = new Image[53];
  private Image[] player1Hand = new Image[8];
  private Image[] player2Hand = new Image[8];
  private int player1Cards = 0, player2Cards = 0;
  private int player = 1, handNum;
  private JButton dealCard, stay;
  public Blackjack()
  {
   Graphics g;
   Toolkit toolkit = Toolkit.getDefaultToolkit();
   Image temp;
   int j;
   setLayout(new FlowLayout(FlowLayout.CENTER, 100, 5));
   setSize(720,480);
   Random generator = new Random();
```

```
for (int i = 0; i < 52; i++)
 c[i] = Toolkit.getDefaultToolkit().getImage(String.
 valueOf(i+1) + ".jpg");
c[52] = toolkit.getImage("Back.jpg");
for (int i = 0; i < 52; i++) {
 j = generator.nextInt(52);
 temp = c[j];
 c[j] = c[i];
 c[i] = temp;
 }
dealCard = new JButton("deal card");
stay = new JButton("stay");
dealCard.addActionListener(this);
stay.addActionListener(this);
dealCard.setActionCommand("deal card");
stay.setActionCommand("stay");
add(dealCard);
add(stay);
player1Hand[0] = c[0];  player2Hand[0] = c[1];
player1Hand[1] = c[2];  player2Hand[1] = c[3];
player1Cards = 2; player2Cards = 2;
handNum = 4;
}

public static void main(String args[])
{
 JFrame f = new JFrame("Blackjack");
 f.getContentPane().add(new Blackjack());
 f.setDefaultCloseOperation(JFrame.EXIT_ON_CLOSE);
 f.setSize(720,480);
 f.setVisible(true);
}

public void actionPerformed(ActionEvent e) {
 if ("deal card".equals(e.getActionCommand())) {
  if (player == 1) player1Hand[player1Cards++] =
  c[handNum++];
  else if (player == 2) player2Hand[player2Cards++]=
  c[handNum++];
  repaint();
 }
 else if ("stay".equals(e.getActionCommand())) {
  if (player == 1) player = 2;
  else if (player == 2) player = 1;
 }
}
```

```
public void paintComponent(Graphics g) {
  int cardx = 20, cardy = 30;
  for (int i = 0; i < player1Cards; i++) {
   g.drawImage(player1Hand[i], cardx, cardy, this);
   cardx = cardx + 20; cardy = cardy + 30;
  }
  cardx = 600; cardy = 30;
  for (int i = 0; i < player2Cards; i++) {
   g.drawImage(player2Hand[i], cardx, cardy, this);
   cardx = cardx - 20; cardy = cardy + 30;
  }
 }
}
```

## 8.3.4 Distribution Means

Another important issue in your choice of authoring environment is the format of your end product. What type of file will you have when you're finished, given your choice of programming language? Who are your target end users? What operating system, browsers, players, and plugins are they most likely to have?

If you want your multimedia production to be accessible via the web, then Java, Flash, and Director are good choices. With Java, you have two options: You can write your program as a conventional application program or as an applet. Calls to applets can be embedded in web pages so that when someone accesses the web page and clicks on a button, the applet plays. Java has the additional advantage of being platform independent. Java application programs are compiled into bytecodes. The bytecodes are standard and can be read, interpreted, and executed on any platform. When they are interpreted by a particular platform, they are compiled into machine instructions specific to that environment. Applets are handled similarly, except that they execute via a web browser. (As a Java API, the Processing programming environment yields the same type of distribution file types as for standard Java.)

Director offers a number of distribution formats. If you distribute a Director movie in the Director authoring file format (DIR), it can be played only by those who have the authoring environment on their computers. For distribution, you can publish a Director movie as an executable EXE or OSX or as a web-playable Shockwave file, DCR. EXE and OSX are *executable* formats that are compiled into the instruction set for a particular platform (Windows or Mac). (Another term for *executable* is **stand-alone application**.) In Director, an executable version of the movie is called a **projector**. You can give an executable file to someone, and he or she can play it without having to have the Director development environment (as long as you've given this person the right version for their operating system). To play a Director DCR movie, the web browser needs to have the Shockwave plugin. This feature is becoming standard with web browsers, and if a browser doesn't have the plugin, it is easily installed from the Director website.

Flash offers a similar choice among different distribution formats. The native development format is FLA. Distribution formats are EXE, HQX, SWF, or MOV. EXE and HQX are stand-alone executables. A Flash animation published in the SWF format can be embedded in a web page and played via web browsers. To play a Flash SWF movie, the web browser through which you access the movie needs to have the Flash player plugged in, but this is standard. SWF files can also be integrated into Director. MOVs are QuickTime movie versions of Flash animations.

Max/MSP and Jitter can be distributed as stand-alone applications for Windows or Mac. You may first have to gather your external files into a "collective" that is packaged as an MXF file.

# 8.4 A COMPARISON OF DIRECTOR AND FLASH

## 8.4.1 Why Director and Flash?

We spend more time in this chapter on Director and Flash than on other multimedia environments. The reason is that Director and Flash are full-featured authoring environments, and they give you an opportunity to put to use what you learned in the rest of this book. You can take and edit digital photographs, draw vector graphics, capture video, record and process sound, create MIDI music—in each case, using the best tools and methods available to you. When you've created your media objects, you can import them into Director and Flash and weave them into a complete animation.

In summary, creating an animation in Director or Flash entails the following basic steps. You apply these steps as appropriate to your purposes (which means you don't necessarily do all of these things).

- Create your media outside of Director or Flash. For example, you might take digital photographs, draw some vector graphics, shoot video, and/or record sound. You can create and edit your media in appropriate environments (*i.e.*, Final Cut, Illustrator, Sound Forge, etc.) and then import them into Director or Flash. A note about bitmap images in Director: Make your images the size you want them to be before you import them into Director. Decide on appropriate file types. (For bitmap images, lossless compression is better.) For both Director and Flash, create your sound files with appropriate sampling rate and bit depth. Is your user likely to have high-quality speakers? Does sound quality matter for the type of sound your animation will include? Do you really need stereo? If sound quality is important, fine. Use what you need. But don't force yourself to use high-quality stereo sound if it doesn't really matter for your purposes. It will only make your final production file large.
- Enter the Director or Flash environment. Import the media you created.
- Create other media elements directly in the Director or Flash environment. (They have their own vector graphics and/or paint tools, for example.) You'll probably need text boxes, buttons, etc.
- Put objects on the stage (which equivalently puts them in the timeline).
- Add user-interface components to the stage, *e.g.*, buttons and input boxes.
- Tween objects as needed.
- Set reference points in the timeline as needed. In Director, these are called *markers*. In Flash, they're called *frame labels*.
- Create event handlers and attach them to the appropriate objects and frames.
- Add built-in behaviors to objects.
- Create new behaviors and add them to objects and interface components.
- Synchronize media as needed.
- Embed fonts, plug-ins, and extras as needed for the final product.
- Choose compression options.
- Save for distribution.

The following comparison of the two environments will introduce you to the features available in Director and Flash, tell you what to look for as you delve into details, and in general, give you an idea of what *can* be done so that you'll know where to start and what features to investigate further.

## 8.4.2 A "Quick Start" Tutorial for Director and Lingo

### 8.4.2.1 Get to Know Your Programming Environment

Your first task in learning a new multimedia programming language is to get to know the authoring environment. **Authoring** is the process of creating a multimedia production. Director, as its name implies, is based upon a metaphor of directing a movie. **Cast members** are analogous to classes of objects. Cast members can include bitmap images, text boxes, vector graphics, sound files, Flash animations, movie files, GUI components, and Lingo scripts. If the cast member is a visible object, you can place an example instance of it on the stage, where it is then called a *sprite*.

The three main working windows of the Director authoring environment are the *stage*, the *score*, and the *cast window* (Figure 8.5). The stage displays what is seen in the movie, frame-by-frame. You can set the stage's dimensions to whatever you want, within the limits of the authoring environment. The score has a *timeline* where you can construct your movie with channels where you place the sprites that you want to appear in each frame. The cast window shows your raw material—the images, movies, sounds, and scripts (Lingo code) that you can piece together in your production. You gather this raw material by importing image, sound, and movie files; creating images or text boxes directly in the Director environment; writing scripts; and applying built-in behaviors to sprites. Whenever you import or create a new element, it appears in the cast window and is ready for your use. There are two views of the cast window, as shown in Figure 8.4. You can toggle between them by clicking the list button at the top of the cast window.

The timeline is laid out frame-by-frame in the horizontal direction and channel-by-channel in the vertical direction. The playhead marks the frame you're currently on. When the playhead is on a certain frame in the timeline, you can see what the stage looks like at that moment in time. The default frame rate for playing a Director movie is 30 frames per

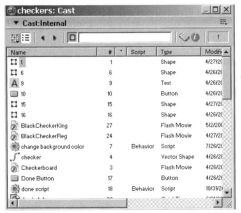
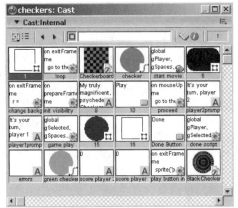

Toggle button, enlarged

**Figure 8.4** Two views of the cast window

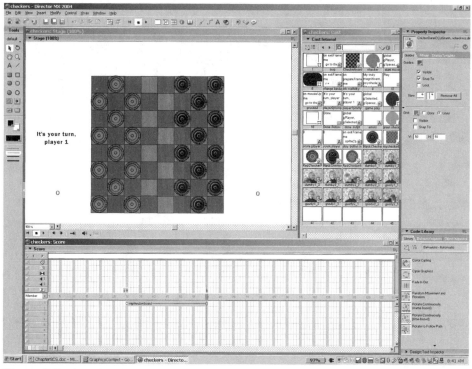

**Figure 8.5**  The Director authoring environment

second. You build a movie by changing the sprites on stage from one moment to the next. The resulting effect is animation.

Arranged vertically down the timeline are a number of *sprite channels*. By default, there are 150 sprite channels, but you can reset the number of viewable channels in the Preferences. Say that the playhead is on frame *j*. If you drag a cast member from the cast member library onto the stage, the sprite that you create is automatically reflected in a channel beneath the timeline, by default spanning frames *j* to *j* + 29, covering one second. Equivalently, if you drag a cast member onto some open channel of the timeline, you'll see it appear on the stage. You can then position the sprite to where you want it on stage. There are also two sound channels. If you drag a sound file cast member into a sound channel, the sound will play during the frames that it covers (or longer, depending on your loop settings and the length of the sound file).

You can have only one sprite per channel on any given frame. The way to get more than one sprite on stage at the same time is to put them on different channels of the same frame. The sprites in the higher-numbered channels appear, on stage, on top of sprites in the lower-numbered channels. Thus if you have a visible sprite on channel 1 of frame 1 and another on channel 2 of frame 1, the sprite in channel 2 will appear on stage on top of the sprite in channel 1 (assuming that they're in the same location on stage).

Frames can be made into keyframes as shown in Figure 8.6. Keyframes mark reference points for how sprites look at a moment in time. You can ask the system to tween key properties of a sprite between two keyframes, and the sprite will gradually change from one state to the next. This is done for you automatically by the system so that you don't have to write the code to make it happen. However, you can accomplish the same thing by means of scripting, as we'll demonstrate later.

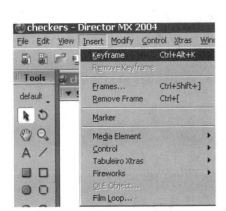

**Figure 8.6** Inserting a keyframe in Director

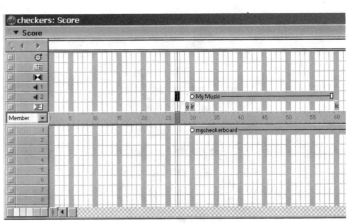

**Figure 8.7** Sound channels in Director

**ASIDE:** If you can't see the sound channels, they may be hiding from you. There's a little "expander" icon on the right side of the score that, when clicked, hides or shows the Effects Channels. Click on this if you can't see the sound channels on the score.

Sound is easily incorporated into Director. Once you've imported a sound into the cast, you can drag an instance of it into one of the two sound channels on the score (Figure 8.7). You can also play sounds by means of Lingo. (See *puppetSound* in Director's Help.)

Other important windows to be aware of are the property inspector (Figure 8.8), the message window, the library palette (or library, for short, Figure 8.9), and the script window. If you can't find one of these windows, you probably need to open it. This can be done by clicking on the appropriate icon on the top task bar or choosing the desired window from the Window menu.

If you've selected a sprite on the stage by clicking on it, the *property inspector* will show you the properties pertaining to that

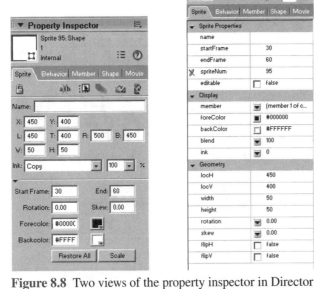

**Figure 8.8** Two views of the property inspector in Director

**Figure 8.9** Library palette in Director

sprite. Properties in Director are similar to data members in C++—the "parts" of an object, like its width, height, color, text, etc. If you click the stage itself, you'll see the property inspector for the stage. This is where you can change the dimensions of the stage and the background color. There are two views for the property inspector, shown in Figure 8.8. You can toggle between them by clicking on the list icon in the upper right corner (indicated by an arrow in the right view).

In your scripts, you can enter messages and debugging statements into the message window with a *put* statement (*e.g.*,

*put ("In initialization function, x = " & x)*

where $x$ is a variable and & is the concatenation operator). Director also has a built in debugger.

The library gives you a selection of built-in behaviors. These are divided into GUI components, animations, navigation, text behaviors, and so forth. You can add a built-in behavior to a sprite by dragging it from the library and dropping it onto a sprite on stage. (If you can't do this, it is probably because the chosen behavior doesn't apply to the type of sprite you're dropping it onto.) For some behaviors, a window may pop up asking you to set parameters of the behavior, customizing it for the sprite to which it is applied. After you've applied a behavior to a sprite, it appears in your cast window also.

You can do a lot using basic tweening and built-in behaviors, without ever having to write any code. But eventually you'll want to apply your programming skills, and to do this you'll need to write some Lingo scripts and attach them to sprites, cast members, frames, and/or the movie itself.

The script window (Figure 8.10) is where you look at and edit code. Scripts are segments of Lingo code. You can flip through all the scripts in your program by clicking the left and right arrows. You can add a new script by clicking the + button.

Director also allows you to create 3D objects. We won't go into this feature of Director in this chapter, but you should look into it yourself. It's not that hard to learn.

An important step in getting to know your environment is exploring the online Help. Try out the tutorials, look at the examples, and find the place in Director's Help where you can look up Lingo methods and properties of objects.

You can run your movie at any time during development by clicking the play button on the top task bar. It's the right-pointing arrow in Figure 8.11. The left-pointing arrow rewinds the movie.

### 8.4.2.2 Basic Lingo Syntax

We need to introduce just a few basic rules of Director syntax so that you'll be able to understand the examples below. Director allows you to choose between Lingo's *dot syntax* and

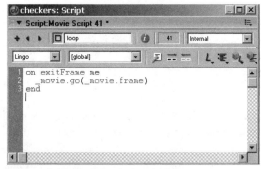

**Figure 8.10** Script window in Director

**Figure 8.11** Play button in Director

JavaScript syntax. JavaScript syntax is a recent addition to the Director environment intended to help new users learn the environment more quickly. In contrast, "traditional" Lingo syntax is basically an object-oriented style, like the syntax C++ and Java. In Lingo dot syntax, you typically have a variable corresponding to an object or sprite, a dot, and then a reference either to a part of the object (like a data member in C++) or some function that can be called through the object (like a member function in C++). Earlier versions of Director had a third syntax, called verbose syntax, which reads more like English phrases. For example, *_movie.go(_movie.frame)* is written in verbose syntax as *go to the frame,* "the frame" being the current frame. Verbose syntax is still mentioned in Director's online help, but apparently it is being phased out.

We will use Lingo syntax in the examples in this chapter.

The essentials of Director's Lingo syntax are given below.

- Lingo syntax is not case-sensitive. Capitalization is used for clarity to help you read the code, but it doesn't matter in the syntax.
- No terminators are required at the ends of lines (*i.e.*, no semi-colons necessary).
- If you need more than one line for a statement, use the line continuation symbol at the end (*i.e.*, \).
- There are three types of variables: *local variables*, *global variables*, and *properties*. Local and global variables are treated in the standard way (as in C, C++, and Java). Properties are defined within behaviors or classes. They're similar to data members in C++ classes. This will be discussed in more detail below.
- User-defined global variables are declared *global*. They are redeclared in each script in which they are used. Many programmers like to begin their global variable names with the letter *g*, to remind them that they are global. For example:

  ```
  global gMaxRuns
  on startMovie
       gMaxRuns = 1000
  end
  ```

- No type declarations are needed.
- Although Lingo is not a strictly typed language, properties of a sprite or cast member can have an inherent data type. If you try to set a property to an inconsistent type, you'll get a run-time error. For example, assuming that *myCastMember* is a cast member, the following produces an error because the *name* property of all cast members can be set only to a string:

  ```
  myCastMember.name = 14
  ```

- Blocks of code end with the word *end*.
- In function definitions, the function name is preceded by *on*. For example

  ```
  on youreInMyWay
       sound.beep()
  end
  ```

- In function definitions, parameters can be defined in one of two ways—either surrounded by parentheses, or not. In either case, multiple parameters are separated by commas.
- Parentheses are required after function names in function calls, even if there are no arguments.

- *for* loops are done as follows:

    *repeat with i = 1 to 10*

    *. . .*

    *end repeat*

- *while* loops are done as follows:

    *repeat while i < 10*

    *. . .*

    *end repeat*

- *if* statements are done as follows:

    *if i < 10 then*

    *. . .*

    *end if*

- *if else* statements are done as follows:

    *if i < 10 then*

    *. . .*

    *else if i =10 then*

    *. . .*

    *end if*

- The basic operators in Lingo are $+, -, *, /, >, <, >=, <=, =, <>$, *not, and, or*, &, and &&. (& is for string concatenation. && is for string concatenation with a line break in between.)
- Test for equality is done with $=$.
- Comments are preceded by --.
- Lists are one of the most useful data structures in Lingo. You can create 1 and 2D lists (or even higher dimensions). You can create a new list with either

    *myList = new list()*

    OR

    *myList = []*

    When you create the list with (), the index starts at 1. When you create it with [], the index starts at 0. You can add new items to the list as follows:

    *myList.add(2)*

    which puts the number 2 at the end of the list. Once the list is created, you can access elements with conventional list/index notation, as in

    *x = myList[1]*

- A number of constants are built into Lingo. Some of the important ones are TRUE and FALSE (both boolean values) and VOID (the value of an object when it is undefined). Constants used in reference to text and keystrokes include EMPTY (used to wipe out the text in a text box), BACKSPACE, ENTER, QUOTE, RETURN, SPACE, and TAB. PI is predefined as the number $\pi$.
- A number of **core objects** are built into Lingo. You can access these from any script. Among the core objects are *_movie, _key, _mouse, _sound*, and *_system*. Through these you can do things like send a movie's execution to a certain location in the timeline, determine what key has been pressed, determine if the mouse has been double-clicked, enable or disable sound, and determine the date. Particular cast members and sprites can be accessed through *member()* and *sprite()*. For example, *member(3)* is cast member 3. *member("myTextbox")* is a cast member that you've named *myTextBox. sprite(3)* is the sprite in the third channel.

With this brief introduction to the syntax, you're almost ready to write some code. The question now is—Where do you put the code to begin with?

### 8.4.2.3 Where Do I Put My Code?

Your first frustration in learning Director, as a programmer, will probably be figuring out where to put your code. It's really not that hard—just different—so if we can get you over this hurdle, you'll be well on your way to learning the environment. You're probably used to sequential programming, where in its simplest form a program can be thought of as existing on one long sheet of paper. Even if you've written modular code or written in object-oriented programming languages, you can still think of your total program as one whole unit, compiled and linked together. It's different in Director, where pieces of code can be attached to different elements in the movie. At first, you may have a feeling that your code is "all over the place."

The terminology related to Director programming can be a little confusing, so let's begin by differentiating among a number of related terms: scripts, handlers, events, messages, event handlers, and behaviors. Because these terms have evolved and changed as Director has gone through different versions, the Director documentation and reference books written about Director don't always use the terms consistently. The issue is further complicated by the fact that you have a choice of syntaxes in Director—either the traditional dot syntax, which has an object-oriented look like C++ or Java, or the JavaScript syntax. We'll try to sort these terms out in a way that will be most useful for you.

A *script* is just a group of procedures and functions in one unit—as if they were all typed onto one sheet of paper or into one file. A script can be attached to a sprite, a cast member, a frame, or the movie itself. We'll return to this issue in a moment.

What you might call a function, procedure, or method in C, C++, or Java is called a *handler* or a *method* in the Director context. A script can contain more than one handler or method, with one calling another in the same script. Thus, just like in other programming languages, you can design your code through functional decomposition, making your code more modular and readable.

While the terms *handler* and *method* are used somewhat interchangeably in Director (depending on who you ask), handler is used most often in association with events. The more specific term is *event handler*. Event handlers are the code that is executed when a significant runtime *event* happens—for example, the movie starting, a mouse click, a keyboard press, the playhead entering a frame, a new sprite being placed on the stage, a sound playing, and so forth. The Director authoring environment has defined certain events that automatically generate calls to event handlers. You need to know what these events are and the calls they generate so that you can write event handlers to respond to the events as needed in your animation. The simplest example is the *exitFrame* event. Each time the playhead exits a frame, an *exitFrame* message is sent to the frame. You can write a simple event handler that tells the playhead to go right back into the frame just exited, effectively creating a loop. This is done by writing the following event handler and attaching it to the frame on which you want the loop.

```
on exitFrame me
  _movie.go(_movie.frame)
end
```

A *behavior* is a script attached to a sprite or a frame. It is called a behavior because the script makes the sprite or frame "act" a certain way. *Built-in behaviors* come with the Director authoring environment. They are organized in the library. To apply a built-in behavior to a frame or sprite, you simply drag it from the library and drop it onto the frame or sprite in question. If the behavior can be individualized by certain properties of the object to which it is applied, you'll be asked to set the properties when you drop the behavior onto the object. (A window will pop up to prompt you to do this.) You can also write your own behaviors, adding them to the behavior library.

So that's the overview, to help you get the lay of the land. Are you ready for more detail? In fact, there are five different types of scripts. We've already talked about the first two types in the discussion above—frame scripts and sprite scripts—both of which are sometimes called *behaviors* in the Director documentation. The complete list is a follows:

A *frame script* is attached to a frame in the timeline. Frame scripts can be used to initialize variables and sprites as you enter a frame, clean things up as you leave a frame, or loop on a frame to wait for user input.

A *sprite script* is attached to a sprite on stage. You can set values when the sprite is prepared for the stage. You can also cause the sprite to react to user input by placing an *on mouseUp* handler or other appropriate event handler on the sprite.

A *cast member script* is attached to a cast member, and it is run via sprites created from that cast member. If you want every instance of a cast member to behave the same way, put the script on the cast member so that you don't have to repeatedly place it on each sprite instance.

A *movie script* is attached to the movie as a whole and is thus more global in nature. You can initialize global variables for the entire movie in the *on startMovie* handler. Also, methods that appear in movie scripts can be called from any other script in the movie. In contrast, methods in non-movie scripts can be called only from within the script in which they appear.

A *parent script* is used to create new instances of a user-defined class, when you're working in an object-oriented programming style. Specifically, they're used to define a *new* method for a class of objects that you're creating. The *new* method is like the *new* function in C++, for dynamic creation of the object. In Director, properties in the *new* method become the data members of the class. We'll look at this more closely in the section on object-oriented programming below.

Execution of a Director movie generally gets rolling by means of events that occur during run-time. As mentioned before, you need to know which events generate which handler calls. Here are the important ones. (There are others.) If no definition is given, you can assume the obvious meaning.

Your natural questions are now—How do I know which type of script to write? And how do the methods get called so that these scripts are executed? Let's start with a simple example.

From Table 8.3, you can see that a *mouseDown* handler can be attached, for example, to a sprite on stage. This sprite might be acting as a button waiting for the user to click it. Clicking the button might initiate the playing of a game, start up an animation, cause a sound or movie to play, and so forth.

So here's a typical scenario for basic interactivity in Director.

- Put a button on the stage with Insert\Control\Push Button. Change the text to something that makes sense (like "Play"). By default, the button will cover the first 30 frames.
- Go to frame 30 of the frame script channel. Double-click to pop open the script editing window. By default, you're given the shell of the *on exitFrame* handler. (You wouldn't have to use this. You can just erase it and type something else if this isn't what you want, but in our example, it *is* what we want.) Use the handler we showed you above for looping on a frame:

  *on exitFrame me*
    *_movie.go(_movie.frame)*
  *end*

| TABLE 8.3 | Some Important Events in Director | | |
|---|---|---|---|
| **Movie Script** | **Frame Script** | **Sprite Script** | **Movie, Frame, Sprite, or Cast Member Script*** |
| *prepareMovie* (called at the beginning of a movie, before the first frame has been prepared) | *prepareFrame* | *beginSprite* | *mouseEnter* |
| *startMovie* (called at the beginning of a movie, right before the first frame begins— after prepareMovie is called) | *enterFrame* | *endSprite* | *mouseUp* |
| *endMovie* | *exitFrame* | | *mouseDown* |
| | | | *keyUp* |
| | | | *keyDown* |

* Handlers in the far right column can be called via a movie, frame, cast member, or sprite. If the handler is attached to a cast member, it can be called through any instance of that cast member. If the handler is attached to the movie, it is called in response to user input anywhere on stage (mouse or keyboard, depending on the handler).

This will cause execution to loop on the frame until something tells the playhead to advance—in our case, the clicking of the button. (*_movie.frame* is the current frame.)

• Select the button on stage. Right-click on the button (Figure 8.12). Select Script from the context menu. By default, you should get the shell of an *on mouseUp* handler. Create a handler that looks like this:

> *on mouseUp me*
> *_movie.go(_movie.frame+1)*
> *end*

Since *_movie.frame+1* is the frame after the current frame, the playhead will advance one frame when the button is pressed.

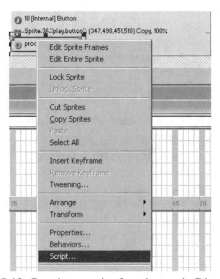

**Figure 8.12** Creating a script for a button in Director

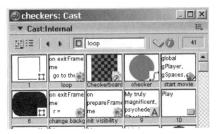

**Figure 8.14** Movie script icon in Director (upper right cast member)

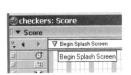

**Figure 8.13** Adding a marker in Director

That's it. The assumption is that things start to happen at frame 31. (Maybe this is where some animation begins, for example, created by tweening.) You could also send the playhead to a different frame, using a marker. You can create a marker by clicking in the white space above all the channels, at the top of the timeline (Figure 8.13). Click at a frame that marks the beginning of some part of the animation's execution. Then give the marker a name—let's say it's "Begin Splash Screen." Then instead of saying _movie.go(_movie. frame+1) you can move the playhead to the marker position by saying _movie.go("Begin Splash Screen").

It's important that your script be the type that you want it to be. You'll know that a movie script is a movie script if it has the little script icon on it in the cast member window. The *startMovie* script in the cast window of Figure 8.14 has this icon. If your script is not the type you want it to be, you can change its type in the property inspector.

At first, your program might seem like it's "all over the place" if you have different scripts attached to different objects. You'll get a better feeling of consolidation if you look at the scripts in the script window, where you can move easily from one to the next with the arrow buttons.

### 8.4.2.4 Director Behaviors: A Step in the Direction of Object-Oriented Programming

Director is an inherently object-oriented programming (OOP) environment, even if you don't choose to do your scripts in an explicitly object-oriented style. Cast members are analogous to classes in C++ or Java. Core objects are globally accessible objects. Sometimes we can call handlers through these core objects, as in _sound.soundEnabled(), sprite(5).visible = FALSE, or member("myTextBox").text = "Hello". Even if you never define a class of your own as you write Lingo scripts, you're still using classes and objects.

As for the code that you write yourself—you can write your own scripts entirely in C-style code, with no user-defined classes or objects. This might be perfectly fine for your application. There are situations, however, where an object-oriented design may be useful. If you're translating to Director a program that you already wrote in an object-oriented language, the translation will be easier if you remain in the OOP style. Another motivation to use OOP is the power it gives you to associate properties with types of objects and to dynamically create objects. Dynamic creation of objects can be cleaner—less brute force—than creating a large number of cast members and sprites that you may or may not need, depending on runtime conditions. So it's good to know the object-oriented features available in Lingo.

There are a couple of ways you can approach object-oriented programming in Lingo. The first way we're going to show you is a step in the direction of OOP, but doesn't go all the way there. To be specific, writing behaviors that have properties takes you a step toward

## CODE SEGMENT 8.4 — A BEHAVIOR WITH PROPERTIES IN DIRECTOR

```
property speed
property direction
property noise
on mouseUp me
  repeat with i = 1 to 100
    puppetSound noise
    sprite(me.spriteNum).locH = sprite(me.spriteNum).locH +
    (direction*speed)
    if sprite(me.spriteNum).locH > 800 then
      sprite(me.spriteNum).locH = 1
    else if sprite(me.spriteNum).locH < 2 then
      sprite(me.spriteNum).locH = 800 − sprite(me.spriteNum)
      .width
    end if
    sprite(me.spriteNum).locV= sprite(me.spriteNum).locV +
    (direction*speed)
    if sprite(me.spriteNum).locV > 600 then
      sprite(me.spriteNum).locV = 1
    else if sprite(me.spriteNum).locV < 2 then
      sprite(me.spriteNum).locV = 600 − sprite(me.spriteNum)
      .height
    end if
    updateStage
  end repeat
end

on getPropertyDescriptionList
 description = [:]
 description[#speed] = \
     [#default: 5, \
     #format:#integer, \
     #comment: "Set speed from 1 to 10:", \
       #range: [#min:1, #max:10] ]
 description[#noise] = \
     [#default:" ", \
     #format: #sound, \
     #comment:"Sound cast member name" ]
 description[#direction] = \
     [#default: 1, \
     #format:#integer, \
     #comment: "Set direction −1 left, and 1 right:", \
       #range: [#min:−1, #max:1] ]
 return description
```

object-oriented programming, though you never actually define a class. To understand how this works, you first need to understand properties and property lists.

A property list is a special kind of list. Each item on a property list has a property name and a value. The property is defined by a symbol, preceded by the # sign. The property is then given a value. Values of different types can be mixed on the same property list. One property might be a string, another an integer, another a sprite, another a sound, and so forth. The property list would look like this:

*spaceship = [#name:"starStreaker", #speed:10, #direction:1, #noise:"squeal"]*

This list defines four properties for the spaceship object.

You can see how this relates to the concept of object-oriented programming, where classes are defined in terms of the data members (*i.e.*, properties) such that each instance of a given class has all the data members defined for that class. Each instance then is individualized by having its own values for the instance variables. Similarly, when properties are used in the definition of a behavior and the behavior is applied to multiple sprites, each sprite can have its own individual values for the properties. Thus, writing a behavior that defines properties for the sprites to which the behavior is applied is a step in the direction of object-oriented programming.

Consider the simple example of a behavior in Code Segment 8.4. This behavior can be applied to different "spaceships"—sprites that you place on the stage (maybe simple bitmaps). Each time you drag this behavior from the cast window (or **behavior inspector**) and drop it onto a sprite on stage, you're prompted to set the properties of speed, direction, and noise (a sound file that will be the spaceship's characteristic noise) for the sprite. Because the behavior is based on a *mouseUp* event, each time you click on a sprite that has this behavior applied, the associated *mouseUp* event handler will be executed, causing the spaceship to make its sound and move in the specified direction for 50 steps. You can follow this recipe for creation of your own behaviors. The *getPropertyDescription* function will be written just as shown, except that you substitute the properties you want for your sprites. This is the function that makes the window pop open when you drop the behavior onto a sprite, prompting you for the properties. (Note that this happens during development of the movie, not when the movie plays for the user. What happens when the movie plays for the user is determined by what's in the *mouseUp* handler.)

Writing behaviors resembles object-oriented programming in that all the sprites to which the behavior is applied become, together, like a class of objects, each instance of which can be individualized by the values of its properties. They all share a behavior, but each sprite executes the behavior in a way that may be partially determined by the values of the properties. However, behaviors are different from object-oriented programming in that you can apply the same behavior to sprites that are of a different nature (*e.g.*, buttons, vector graphics, text boxes), as long as it makes sense for them to do the thing that the behavior implies (like change color, move, rotate, or whatever that may be). Another difference from OOP is that with behaviors, you don't ever actually define a class, nor do you dynamically allocate objects. The behaviors are applied to sprites that are put on stage before run-time.

### 8.4.2.5 Programming a Simple Game in Director

A simple card game program will be used to illustrate the construction of a Director movie. We'll show you the beginning of a Blackjack game—just the dealing of the cards and the users' requests for another card to be dealt. (No gambling permitted!) The dealer and the dealer's opponent (whom we'll call the *player*) are each dealt two cards. The player's cards are both face up. The top of the dealer's two cards is face up. The object is to get as close as possible to a score of 21. Aces are worth 1 or 11 (player's choice), number cards are

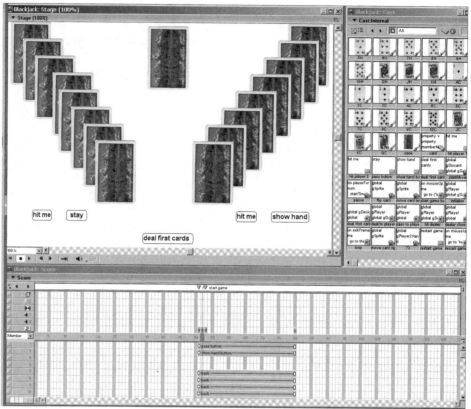

**Figure 8.15** Blackjack in Director

worth their number value, and face cards (king, queen, and jack) are worth 10. The player can repeatedly ask the dealer for another card by clicking the "hit me" button, until he or she decides to "stay." Then the dealer's hidden card is revealed, and the dealer can ask for new cards one at a time. The one closest to 21 without going over wins.

We're going to show you two different implementations for this program—the first using no object-oriented programming, and the second with a little bit of object-oriented programming just to give you the flavor of it.

The layout of the game in Director is shown in Figure 8.15. The player's hand is on the left and the dealer's on the right. You can see eight face-down cards dealt for the player and dealer. This is a trick in the implementation. The cards you see in the figure are just place-holder sprites. When the movie begins playing, these cards will be invisible. (They're made invisible by a line of code in the *prepareFrame* handler that executes on the frame where the cards first appear, as shown in Code Segment 8.5.) You won't see them until they are actually dealt, and then they'll be face up as appropriate and will have a value that is deter-mined randomly. Not all of these placeholders cards will be used. In fact, usually only two to four cards are dealt to a hand before the player asks to "stay," having gotten a score close to or on 21. Having eight placeholders for the hand should be more than enough.

Initialization is often done in a *startMovie* handler, and you might wonder why we don't initialize and shuffle the deck in *startMovie* rather than in a *prepareFrame* handler attached to a particular frame. The reason is that we've put the invisible sprites on stage, and the ini-tialization procedure refers to these sprites. The *startMovie* handler is executed as the

| CODE SEGMENT 8.5 | INITIALIZING A NEW CARD GAME IN LINGO |
|---|---|

```
global gPlayer
global gDeck
global gPlayer1Hand
global gPlayer2Hand
global gSprite
on prepareFrame me
  repeat with i = 8 to 23
    sprite(i).visibility = false
  end repeat
--A holder card for the dealer's "turned over" card; it
will be made visible when the opposing player has asked
to "stay"
  sprite(25).visibility = false
  gPlayer = 1
  gSprite = 8
--Put the hands from the previous game back in the deck
    repeat with i = 1 to gPlayer1Hand.count
      gDeck.add(gPlayer1Hand[i])
    end repeat
    repeat with i = 1 to gPlayer2Hand.count
      gDeck.add(gPlayer2Hand[i])
    end repeat
    gPlayer1Hand = list()
    gPlayer2Hand = list()
--Shuffle the deck
    repeat with i = 1 to 52
      j = random(52)
      temp = gDeck[i]
      gDeck[i] = gDeck[j]
      gDeck[j] = temp
  end repeat
end
```

movie begins, and the sprites don't exist at that point and thus can't be referred to. Also, *prepareFrame* needs to be executed everytime a new game starts—not just once at the beginning of the game session. Each time a game ends (when the dealer clicks his "show hand" button or when one of the two players goes over 21), the playhead is instructed to go to the frame labeled "new game" with the line *_movie.go(_movie ("new game")*.

On the timeline below the stage, you can see the sprites in the channel. The ones labeled "back" are all instances of the card cast member, which is just a bitmap of the back of a card. There are also four button sprites on the stage.

Simple data structures—just lists of integers—are used for the cards and players' hands. The bitmaps that serve as pictures of the cards are cast members 1 through 52. Thus, the numbers 1 through 52 are used to refer to the deck of cards. These numbers are shuffled in *prepareFrame*. The deck of cards and players' hands are initialized in the *startMovie* handler (Code Segment 8.6).

| CODE SEGMENT 8.6 | INITIALIZING A DECK OF CARDS IN LINGO |
|---|---|

```
global gDiscard
global gDeck
global gPlayer1Hand
global gPlayer2Hand

on startMovie me
  gDeck = list()
  repeat with i = 1 to 52
    gDeck.add(i)
  end repeat
  gPlayer1Hand = list()
  gPlayer2Hand = list()
end
```

When the cards are dealt, we show them flipping over, demonstrating "hand tweening"). The code for this is in Code Segment 8.7. A simulation of flipping is achieved by making the card get narrower until it's only four pixels wide, changing the "look" of the card to its face by changing the cast member with which the sprite is associated, and then widening the card again.

| CODE SEGMENT 8.7 | FLIPPING A CARD BY "HAND TWEENING" IN LINGO |
|---|---|

```
global gSprite
on flipCard card
  repeat while sprite(gSprite).width > 5
    sprite(gSprite).width = sprite(gSprite).width - 1
    updateStage
  end repeat
  sprite(gSprite).member = member(card)
  repeat while sprite(gSprite).width < 100
    sprite(gSprite).width = sprite(gSprite).width + 1
    updateStage
  end repeat
end
```

Sliding the card is done similarly, as shown in Code Segment 8.8, by incrementally changing the *x* and *y* location of the card (given by properties *locH* and *locV*).

When the movie enters the frame that marks the beginning of a game, two cards are automatically dealt to the dealer and player, set in motion by an *enterFrame* handler (Code

**CODE SEGMENT 8.8**  **SLIDING A CARD BY "HAND TWEENING" IN LINGO**

```
global gSprite
on moveCardLeft card, x2, y2
  x1 = sprite(gSprite).locH
  y1 = sprite(gSprite).locV
  m = (float(y2-y1))/(x2-x1)
  x = x1 - 1
  repeat while x > x2
    y = y1 - m*(x1 - x)
    sprite(gSprite).locH = x
    sprite(gSprite).locV = y
    x = x - 1
    updateStage
  end repeat
```

Segment 8.10). The scores of the hands are computed with the *getValue* method, which relies on a knowledge of how the cards are arranged in the cast window (Code Segment 8.9). Cards 2 through 9 of spades are at positions 1 through 8; 2 through 9 of diamonds are at positions 9 through 16; 2 through 9 of hearts are at positions 17 through 24; and 2 through 9 of clubs are at positions 25 through 32. Cast members 33 through 48 are the 10s, jacks, queens, and kings, all valued at 10. Cast members 49 through 52 are the aces. This makes it easy to write an algorithm to get the value of the card from the position.

**CODE SEGMENT 8.9**  **GETTING THE VALUE OF A BLACKJACK HAND IN LINGO**

```
on getValue castMemberNum
  if castMemberNum >= 33 and castMemberNum <= 48 then
    return 10
  else if castMemberNum >= 49 and castMemberNum <= 52 then
    return 11
  else
    return ((castMemberNum-1) mod 8) + 2
  end if
end
```

The code for dealing an individual card when the player's "hit me" button is clicked is similar to the *enterFrame* handler and is not shown here. The *pauseFor* method used in the *enterFrame* handler is a user-defined simple method to insert a pause between cards that are dealt. (It isn't a system-defined function.)

This shows you the basic scheme for a simple game program. Now let's look at how you might do this with object-oriented programming.

**CODE SEGMENT 8.10**    **DEALING CARDS AND COMPUTING VALUE OF HAND IN LINGO**

```
global gDeck
global gSprite
global gPlayer
global gScore
global gScore2
global gPlayer1Hand
global gPlayer2Hand

on enterFrame me
 --Deal first card to player 1
 card = gDeck[1]
 gPlayer1Hand.add(card)
 gDeck.deleteAt(1)
 locH = sprite(gSprite).locH
 locV = sprite(gSprite).locV
 sprite(gSprite).locH = 400
 sprite(gSprite).locV = 90
 sprite(gSprite).member = member("back")
 sprite(gSprite).visibility = true
 flipCard(card)
 moveCardLeft(card, locH, locV)
 gSprite = 16
 pauseFor(20)
 --Deal card to player 2 (done similarly, but omitted here)
 --Deal another card to player 1 (done similarly, but omitted
   here)
 --Deal another card to player 2 (done similarly but omitted
   herc)
 --Compute value of player's hand
 gScore = 0
 gScore = getValue(gPlayer1Hand[1]) + getValue(gPlayer1
Hand[2])
 --if there are 2 aces in the hand, make one of them count as 1
   instead of 11
 if gScore > 21 then
   gScore = gScore - 10
 end if
 if gScore = 21 then
   turnOverDealersCard()
   alert("You WIN, Player 1.")
   go to "new game"
   return
 end if
   --Compute value of dealer's hand (done similarly, but
     omitted here)
end
```

### 8.4.2.6 Object-Oriented Programming in Lingo

If you choose to write your production in an object-oriented design, you need to think in terms of classes of objects. For example, to create a card game you might need deck, hand, player, and card classes. What are the data members of each? A deck has a list of cards. A hand has a list of cards and, depending on the game, possibly a value. A player has a hand. A card has a value, a face, and an image to be displayed as its back. How many of these classes you really need depends on your design. If objects need to be created dynamically, as the game is played, then defining them via classes is a good idea. For example, if you're going to allow multiple players but you don't know how many will join the game for a given session, you could create a player class and add new players on the fly. Also, you might allow the players to determine at run time how many decks should be used in a game.

Our Blackjack implementation is a simple example, intended just to show you the basic idea of OOP in Director, so we'll use only one class—a Card class. The idea is to encapsulate the value and the look of a card so that the value doesn't have to be computed at runtime (as it is with the *getValue* method, above).

The main step in object-oriented programming in Director is the definition of a class by means of a parent script, which has in it a *new* method that creates a Card object, to be used in a card game. The parent script for the Card class is shown in Code Segment 8.11. Notice that parent scripts, like behaviors, use properties. These properties become the data members of the class (to use C++ terminology). They can be initialized by arguments that are sent into the method. This script must be saved in the cast and given the name of the class (in this case, Card), and it must be of type parent script (which can be set in the property inspector).

| CODE SEGMENT 8.11 | PARENT SCRIPT TO DEFINE A CARD CLASS IN LINGO |
|---|---|

```
property v
property memberNum
on new me, memNum, num
  v = num
  memberNum = memNum
  return me
end
```

The *new* method is called with a line of code like this:

  *c = new(script "Card", 1, 11)*

This line creates a new instance of the Card class associated with cast member 1 and having a value 11. (The cards in this Blackjack version aren't stored in the same order as they were in the previous version—for no particular reason. They're stored in the order of A through king, suit by suit, in cast member positions 1 through 52.)

This example should give you the idea of OOP in Director. While a consistent OOP design wasn't important to this game program, more complex projects can benefit from OOP design. If you're familiar with the OOP features of Lingo, you'll be able to choose the best design for your project.

**CODE SEGMENT 8.12**  **CREATING CARDS WITH OOP IN DIRECTOR**

```
global gDiscard
global gDeck
global gPlayer1Hand
global gPlayer2Hand
on startMovie me
  gDeck = list()
  c = new(script "Card", 1, 11)
  gDeck.add(c)
  repeat with i = 2 to 9
    c = new(script "Card", i, i)
    gDeck.add(c)
  end repeat
  repeat with i = 10 to 13
    c = new(script "Card", i, 10)
    gDeck.add(c)
  end repeat
  c = new(script "Card", 14, 11)
  gDeck.add(c)
  repeat with i = 15 to 22
    c = new(script "Card", i, i-13)
    gDeck.add(c)
  end repeat
  repeat with i = 23 to 26
    c = new(script "Card", i, 10)
    gDeck.add(c)
  end repeat
  c = new(script "Card"", 27, 11)
  gDeck.add(c)
  repeat with i = 28 to 35
    c = new(script "Card", i, i-26)
    gDeck.add(c)
  end repeat
  repeat with i = 36 to 39
    c = new(script "Card", i, 10)
    gDeck.add(c)
  end repeat
  c = new(script "Card", 40, 11)
  gDeck.add(c)
  repeat with i = 41 to 48
    c = new(script "Card", i, i-39)
    gDeck.add(c)
  end repeat
  repeat with i = 49 to 52
    c = new(script "Card", i, 10)
    gDeck.add(c)
  end repeat
  gPlayer1Hand = list()
  gPlayer2Hand = list()
end
```

#### 8.4.2.7 Optimizing for Distribution

When your sprites and cast members are in place and your code is written, you're ready to prepare your movie for distribution. If you want to distribute it on a CD, you can publish it as an EXE stand-alone application for the desired operating system, Windows or MAC. If you want to publish it on the web, you save it as a DCR file with an accompanying HTML page.

Before publishing, you should be sure that you've made the file as small as possible without compromising the quality of your images or smoothness of your animations. You should choose appropriate settings for compression of images and sound files. For images, it's best to avoid JPEG if you can, since lossy JPEG compression can lead to compression artifacts in the context of Director. Director's own compression method is a better alternative. Remember that you should not have brought in large bitmap images and resized them in Director. Always make them the size you want them to be before you import them into Director in order not to waste space. Also remember that you don't need to overdo the quality of sound files. You may not need stereo sound or a high sampling rate and bit depth if you're using little sound effects that you expect your user will be hearing only on low-quality speakers. Think about your target audience and the needs of the animation.

You might want to check if you have any stray cast members that you haven't actually used—remnants of what you thought you were going to use but didn't, or early versions of the production that later got changed. You can do this by the following steps:

- Go to Edit\Find\Cast member.
- Click the Usage radio button in the window that pops open.
- At the bottom of the Find Cast Member window, you'll see a list of cast members that aren't used.
- Click on one of them.
- Click the Select All button.

In the Cast Member window, all the cast members that are not used in the Score will be highlighted.

Now be careful. You don't necessarily want to delete all these cast members, just because they're not ever used in the score. You may refer to some of these cast members dynamically, in the code. (You'll have to remember which ones are used in the code on your own.) If a cast member is never used in the score nor in the code, you can delete it.

It's good practice to embed fonts in your Director movie. You can do with with Media Element\Insert\Font. When you embed a font, all the necessary font information is saved with the movie so that the font displays properly even if it is not installed in the user's system.

Additional features are available in Director by means of extensions called *Xtras*. These give you the ability to work with 3D, MIDI, XML, Flash animations, and many other extensions of the Director environment. Some Xtras are shipped with Director, and some are available from third-party developers. When you use an Xtra in Director, you need to include it with the published file through Modify\Movie\Xtras.

Once you've cleaned up your production, you can save and compact it and publish it in the desired format.

### 8.4.3 A "Quick Start" Tutorial for Flash and ActionScript

#### 8.4.3.1 Get to Know Your Programming Environment

Director and Flash are just similar enough to make it in some ways easy and in other ways confusing to learn one and then the other. The interfaces look similar, but the metaphors on which the working environments are built aren't quite the same. If, from the outset, you get

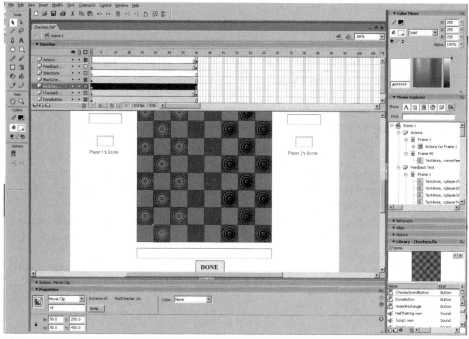

**Figure 8.16** Flash authoring environment

a clear picture of how they differ, you'll be able to move comfortably between the two environments, or at least decide which environment best suits your purposes.

Like Director, Flash has a *stage*, a *timeline*, and a *property inspector* (Figure 8.16). To begin creating an animation, you can draw something directly onto the stage using Flash's built-in vector graphics tools. The *toolbar*, shown to the left of the timeline and stage in Figure 8.16, shows you the tools you have available, including a pen, pencil, and paintbrush; tools to create rectangles and ellipses; a paint bucket; and various selection and transformation tools. You can also draw things in external programs such as Illustrator and import these objects. The Flash *library* is the equivalent of Director's cast member window. This is where reusable objects are stored—which in the case of Flash are called *symbols*. Objects drawn on stage can be converted to symbols. You can also import a picture or sound file into Flash in one of two ways—*import to stage* or *import to library*. If you import something into the library, you can put multiple instances of it onto the stage.

A difference between the two environments is that Flash has layers where Director has channels. A channel in Director can contain only one object at any moment in time (*i.e.*, one sprite per frame). In Flash, a *layer* can contain multiple objects at any moment in time. Also, if an object in Flash is on a higher layer (higher in the physical sense, moving up the screen) then on stage it is visually above objects in a lower layer. It's the opposite in Director. In Flash, two objects that are on the same layer have a depth. You can move an object up or down in depth as you build your animation. You can also include an ActionScript function that swaps the objects' depths if you have the wrong one on top at some point during execution.

The use of layers is illustrated in Figure 8.16, a checkers game implemented in Flash. The checkerboard, red checkers, black checkers, buttons, feedback windows, and actions are on separate layers. The objects don't have to be separated into layers this way, but it helps to keep things organized. It's often convenient to lock a layer so that when you're working on another layer, you don't inadvertently select the layer that you no longer want to edit. You lock a layer by clicking the lock icon.

You can think of Flash layers as sheets of transparent acetate—what teachers used to use as slides for an overhead projector. You can draw something on one layer and something else on the layer on top. The top layer is transparent except for where you drew objects.

You need to familiarize yourself with the drawing tools in Flash. Here are notes to get you started:

- When you draw a shape like a circle or a square, it potentially has a stroke color on the outside edge and a fill color inside. You can set these colors separately (and also delete them). The stroke and the fill are separate objects. If you double-click on the inside of the shape, you'll select both the fill and stroke. A single click will select only the fill or stroke (depending on which one you click on). Before you get used to this, you'll find yourself moving the fill and leaving the stroke behind, or vice versa.
- Shapes can be *grouped* into one object with the menu selection Modify\Group.
- If you draw one shape over another, and then move the one on top, you'll cut a bite out of the one underneath, as shown in Figure 8.17. A way to get around this is to make the one on top a grouped object before you move it over the other one.
- The pen tool is a little hard to get used to, but once you master it you'll find it indispensable for creating curved shapes. (See Chapter 3's discussion of Bézier curves.)
- You can import bitmap images. These don't tween very well, but they're useful for static backgrounds. You can also make a fill pattern from a bitmap.

**Figure 8.17** Drawing in Flash

Like Director, Flash allows you to tween between keyframes (Figure 8.18). When you create a new layer, you automatically get a frame with a blank keyframe. As soon as you draw something on that layer and that frame, it becomes an actual keyframe. You can then set the playhead to a later frame and make the second frame a keyframe (Insert\Timeline\Keyframe or F6). Let's say the first keyframe is frame 1, and you draw an object there. Then you set a keyframe at frame 20. The object you draw on frame 1 is copied onto all frames between 1 and 20 inclusive. Since frame 20 is a keyframe, you can change what the stage looks like at this point and ask that the shapes be tweened in between. You can do this by moving, stretching, and recoloring the object already appearing on frame 20, or by erasing it and completely drawing another object. You then select the object on frame 20, go to the property inspector's Tween drop-down box, and select Shape for the type of tweening. Figure 8.19 shows what it looks like to tween a blue square into a pink circle (showing only five of the frames between 1 and 20).

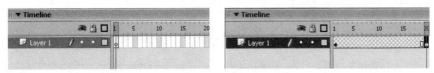

**Figure 8.18** Blank keyframe on left; keyframes at frames 1 and 20 on right

**Figure 8.19** Tweening a blue square into a pink circle in Flash

We've simplified the description of tweening above, and there are lots of details we're leaving out. The type of tweening we've described is called *shape tweening* (a misnomer, since you can change color, positions, and other properties with shape tweening). Shape tweening is applied to shapes that you draw on stage with the drawing tools. It may be the case that you've actually drawn more than one shape—like a stick figure made of lines and circles. All of these shapes could be on the same layer, but if they are, you may get some unexpected results from the tweening. The system is going to try to guess which part corresponds to which between keyframes. But it may incorrectly tween the right arm from the first keyframe into the left arm in the next keyframe, depending on how lines move. Often it's easier to draw each shape—each line and circle—on a separate layer so that the tweening can be better controlled. You can also give the system *shape hints*, telling the system which point to move to which other point, at key places. (This is done through Modify\Shape\Add Shape Hint.) A *motion guide* can be used to define a specific path along which you want a symbol to move.

There are three types of symbols and two types of tweening in Flash. The three types of symbols are graphic symbols, buttons, and movie clips. The two types of tweening are shape tweening and motion tweening. We've already looked at shape tweening and will compare it to motion tweening below. First you need to understand the types of symbols.

A *graphic symbol* is a picture of something, as the name implies. We've already described how you can draw a shape directly onto the stage. A shape is something you draw and use once. It isn't in your library to use again. If you think you're going to want more than one instance of a shape or drawing, you can convert it to a symbol and put it in the library. This is the difference between a shape and a graphic symbol. To convert something to a symbol, you draw it on stage, select the whole thing and go to the menu selection Modify\Convert to Symbol (Figure 8.20). Then a window pops up that asks you to select graphic symbol, button, or movie clip.

Another advantage of making something a graphic symbol (aside from your being able to re-use it) is that you can apply *motion tweening* to it. Motion tweening can be applied only

Convert to symbol
menu selection

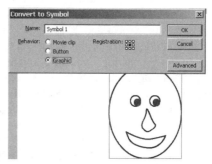

Window pops up asking you what
type of symbol you want.

**Figure 8.20** Converting a graphic to a symbol in Flash

| TABLE 8.4 | A Comparison of Shape Tweening and Motion Tweening in Flash | | | | | | |
|---|---|---|---|---|---|---|---|
| | **Shape** | **Grouped Shape** | **Symbol** | **Broken-Apart Text** | **Text Blocks** | **Properties That Can be Tweened** | **Other** |
| **shape tweening** | yes | no | no | yes | no | shape, color, gradients, position, scale, rotation, skew | shape hints can be inserted to guide tweening |
| **motion tweening** | no | yes | yes | no | yes | motion, alpha (transparency), tint, brightness, position, skew, rotation | a path can be attached to a layer to guide tweening of an object along the path |

to symbols. Motion tweening does more than the name implies. With motion tweening, you can change the shape, color, skew, position, etc. of an object. You can also make the motion follow along a predefined path. (You can't do this with shape tweening.) It takes a while to master the difference between motion and shape tweening and to decide when you should use one and when the other. Table 8.4 gives you an overview of the differences.

Text is easily inserted on stage with the Text Tool. By default, text is treated as a single unit—a "block" of letters. You can motion tween a text block, rotating it or changing its color, for example. If you want to tween the letters individually (so that you can morph one letter into another), you have to break apart the text (using Modify\Break Apart). Then you can apply shape tweening.

Once you've made something into a symbol, you can put multiple instances of it onto the timeline, anywhere you want. If you double-click on a symbol, you get into symbol-editing mode (The red arrow in Figure 8.21 points to the word "car" in the top task bar. This indicates that you're in symbol-editing mode, editing a symbol called "car"). If you change the symbol, your changes will be reflected in all instances of the symbol. If you want to change one instance of a symbol but not others, you have to select the instance on the stage and look at the property inspector. Any properties defined for the instance can be set individually. For example, you can choose the Tint drop-down box and make the instance a different color from the rest.

A significant difference between Director and Flash is that in Flash, objects on stage—if they are converted to symbols—have their own internal timelines. Thus, there is a main timeline, and potentially other timelines nested within it. When you double-click on a graphic symbol to edit it, you'll see the internal timeline. By default, it starts out with one blank keyframe. Sometimes you'll make use of this timeline, and sometimes you won't. A scene of falling snowflakes illustrates one way that you might use the internal timeline of a symbol. Imagine that you create a snowflake as a symbol. Thus, each snowflake has an internal timeline. You can use this timeline to tween each snowflake as it falls to the ground and melts—beginning at full size and ending as a drop of water. To make the scene more interesting, you can individualize the snowflakes through the property inspector, giving them colors that range from shades of icy blue to white. As they are placed at different positions on the stage, the snowflakes create the effect of gently falling snow.

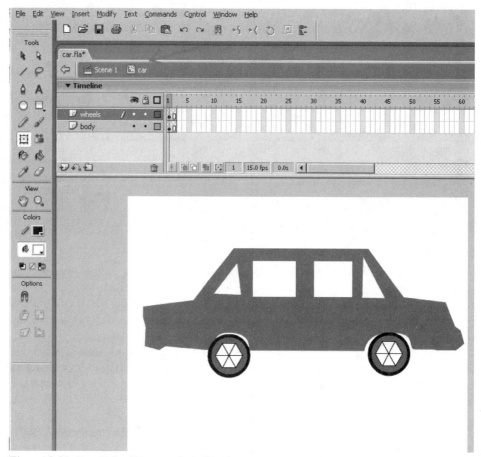

**Figure 8.21** Symbol-editing mode in Flash

A **button symbol** is, of course, a button—set up for you so that you can say what you want it to look like in its *up*, *down*, and *over* states (Figure 8.22). The *up* state is when the button is at rest, the *down* state is when the mouse is clicking on it, and the *over* state is when the mouse cursor is over the button. You might want the button to be one color at rest, another color when the mouse cursor is over it, and a third color when it is being clicked. You define these "looks" for the different states in the button's own internal timeline, which is already set up for you.

To create a button, you do the following:

- Draw a shape on the stage on the frame where you want the button.
- Convert what you've drawn to a button symbol.
- Once you've turned the object into a button symbol, double-click it so that you can edit its internal timeline to specify how you want it to look in the *up*, *down*, and *over* states.
- In symbol-editing mode for the button, click on the frame for the *up* state. Make this a keyframe.
- Change the button to look the way you want it to look in the *up* state. Put text on the shape if you want it.
- Repeat the previous two steps for the *down* and *over* states. If you put text on the *up* state, you can change it in the other two states if you want to.

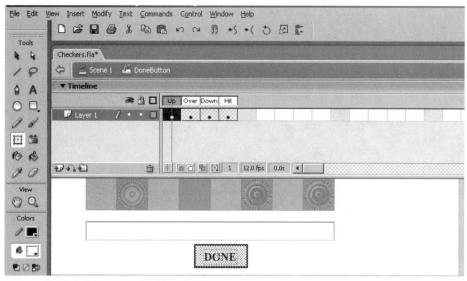

**Figure 8.22** A button symbol in Flash

- If you want the hit area to be larger or smaller than the bounding box of the object you drew, define a different hit area by going to the frame for the hit state of the button's timeline and drawing a rectangle that defines the hot hit area.
- Get out of symbol-editing mode and return to the scene you were editing (in our example, Scene 1). Do this by clicking on the scene name in the top task bar.

You can do even fancier things than this with your buttons, like showing little animations when they are clicked, but this is enough to get you started.

*Movie clips* are the most powerful type of symbols. Like graphic symbols and button symbols, they have their own internal timeline. But a movie clip's timeline can have other movie clips in it, so you have movie clips nested in movie clips. An important difference between movie clip symbols and graphic symbols is that the timeline of a movie clip is independent of the main timeline of the scene it's in. The consequence of this fact is that a graphic symbol's timeline must be at least as long as the main timeline for things to work properly, while this is not the case with a movie clip. By means of movie clips, you can create two separate animations operating independently, or you can even create a movie within a movie. This allows for a much more modular design of your animations, and the result is a very powerful kind of concurrency. Two separate animations can each be "doing its own thing," and you don't have to worry about coordinating them. Or one movie clip can be nested in another, the top-level movie clip can be tweened if you like, and so forth.

A simple example of the use of nested movie clips is an animation of a car driving onto the stage. You could create this animation from the following steps:

- Go to the library window and click the Create New Symbol button (pointed to by the arrow in Figure 8.23). Indicate in the pop-up window that you want to create a movie clip symbol. Call it "wheel." Now you're in symbol-editing mode for the wheel.
- Draw a tire with a hubcap in the middle. Write some word or draw a nonsymmetrical shape on the hubcap so that you can see when it rotates.
- In the tire's internal timeline, tween the tire so that it rotates counterclockwise.

**Figure 8.23** Create New Symbol Button in library in Flash

- Click on the scene name in the top task bar to get out of symbol-editing mode and return to the main timeline.
- Go to library and click the Create New Symbol button to create a second movie clip, this one called "car."
- In symbol-editing mode, draw the body of a car, flat-on from a side view. Leave space for the two tires.
- Insert the two instances of the wheel movie clip, sizing them so that they fit the car.
- Save the car as a movie clip.
- Put an instance of the car movie clip on the timeline.
- Tween the car on the main timeline so that it moves from right to left.

Tweening of vector graphic objects is very powerful and effective because vector graphics are redrawn at full resolution in each frame. For example, if you expand a vector drawing of a dog, making it bigger over time, as if you're moving toward the dog, it never gets blocky or pixelated. Tweening is less effective with bitmap images because as they are enlarged, the pixels are just duplicated (maybe with some interpolation in between), resulting in jagged edges and blocks of the same color.

It's easy to put sounds into Flash. First you have to import the needed sound files so that they're in the library (WAV, AIFF, or MP3). Then you go to the frame where you want the sound to play. In the property inspector for that frame, you click the Sound drop-down box. You'll be shown the sound files that are in the library, and you can choose one to begin playing on that frame. If you set the associated Sync drop-down box to Event, an instance of the sound will begin playing every time you pass this frame. (Thus, if your movie loops, it's possible you could have more than one instance of the sound playing at the same time, and not synchronized.) If you want the sound to begin playing only if there isn't another instance playing, set the Effect drop-down box to Start. If you want it to stream in so that the whole thing doesn't have to be loaded before it begins playing, select Stream. The sound itself can be made to loop or not. If you want multiple different sound files to play at the same time, you have to create a layer for each of them.

There's still more that you can do in Flash without the use of ActionScript code. Like Director, Flash has *built-in behaviors* (although they're not implemented in precisely the same way as in Director, which uses properties in behaviors). You can find these in the *behaviors panel.* Different behaviors are applicable to different types of objects. For example, a movie clip can be told to go to a certain frame and resume playing there with the *gotoAndPlay* behavior. You can also start or stop dragging on a movie clip (allowing the object to be selected and dragged on stage). A sound can be told to play or stop playing. When you select an object on the timeline and click the + button in the behaviors panel, a

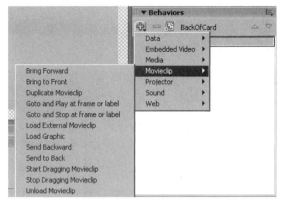

**Figure 8.24** Behaviors panel in Flash

drop down menu will indicate the behaviors available for the type of object, as shown in Figure 8.24.

Flash offers built-in *timeline effects*. You can get to these through Insert\Timeline Effects. Timeline effects can be used for applying transitions (*e.g.*, fade-in), transforms (of color, shape, etc.), blurs, drop shadows, and even "explosions" (the breaking apart of shapes or text).

> **ASIDE:** Behaviors are available in Action-Script 2.0 but not 3.0. In ActionScript 3.0, you can create an *on (release)* method for a button by typing it into the Actions panel yourself, rather than choosing a behavior from the menu as shown in the figure.

The code you write yourself in ActionScript is typed into the actions panel. You can step through all the scripts you've written in this panel. In Figure 8.25, a button is selected in the left pane and the script attached to this button is shown in the right pane. You can automatically check the syntax of your code by clicking the check mark at the top of the code pane.

**Figure 8.25** Actions panel in Flash

The *movie explorer* is helpful for showing you how your movie is organized into scenes, frames, symbols, and scripts. Be sure to open and look at this window. By default, you begin working in scene 1. You can add more scenes if you like, to organize your movie. The movie explore window shows you the objects in each scene as well as associations between frames and objects and scripts (Figure 8.26).

The *history panel* allows you to see your sequence of recent steps and to undo them by sliding a slider up (backward in time) to return to a previous state (Figure 8.27). The output panel is where output statements are printed. You can put debugging print statements into the output panel with the trace function, as in *trace( "I'm in initialization.")* or *trace(x)* where *x* is a variable. Like Director, Flash has an internal debugger. You can test your movie by hitting Enter if the movie just goes across a timeline. If you have scripts and interactivity, you'll have to use Control\Test Movie, which creates an SWF file and allows you to run it.

**Figure 8.26**  Movie explorer in Flash                **Figure 8.27**  History panel in Flash

### 8.4.3.2 Basic ActionScript Syntax

ActionScript uses basic JavaScript syntax. This syntax is very similar to C, C++, and Java. Here are some basic rules of ActionScript syntax:

- ActionScript is case sensitive.
- A semi-colon ends a statement.
- There are a number of built-in classes including Array, Boolean, Button, Color, Date, Math, MovieClip, Sound, String, and TextField. Useful methods are associated with these classes. These methods are called through instances of the classes. For example, through a movie clip you can call the method *gotoAndPlay* or *swapDepths*, you can access the character at some index in a string with *charAt*, and so forth. Some classes allow you to call methods directly through the class object—for example, *Math.ceil*, *Sound.setVolume*, *Key.isDown*, etc. Built-in classes have properties associated with them. You can familiarize yourself with these using Flash's Help.
- Lists are done in Flash by means of the Array class. *var ar = new Array();* creates a new array. Arrays are indexed starting at 0. *ar.push(10)* inserts the value 10 into the front of the array. *x = ar[0]* then places this value into *x*.
- You don't *have to* declare data types, and you can change the type of data assigned to a variable throughout your program.
- You *can* declare the type of a variable. When you do so, automatic type checking is triggered, which may prevent you from making mistakes. A type declaration looks like this, for example:

  *var x: Number = 10;*
  *var c: Date = new Card();*

- An advantage of declaring types is that the system then shows you **code hints** when you type a variable—hints about the data members and member functions that can be accessed through the variable.
- There are four types of variables: local variables, timeline variables, global variables, and properties. **Local variables** are declared within blocks of code which limit their

scope. **Timeline variables** are declared in a script attached to some frame in a timeline and are available to any other script attached to that particular timeline. **Global variables** are accessible in all scripts. **Properties** are like data members in C++ classes.

- Variables are made global by preceding them with _*global*. For example.

  *var_global.maxIterations = 1000;*

- A dot (.) is used to separate an object name from the methods or properties of that object. It is also used to identify the target path of a movie clip, variable, function, or object. A target path takes you through nested scenes and timelines in scenes.
- Blocks of code are set off by curly braces ({ }).
- Functions are defined as follows:

  *function myfunction(name:String, age) {. . .}*

- Parameters in function definitions are placed inside parentheses.
- One line of comments can be set off by //. A block of comments is set off by /* at the beginning and */ at the end.
- Flash operators include +, −, *, /, % (modulo), =, == (testing equality), >, <, >=, <=, != (not equal), && (and), || (or), and ! (not). Bit-level operators (&, |, <<, etc.) and shortcut operators (like ++, −−, +=, etc.) are also available.
- Constants in ActionScript include true, false, BACKSPACE, ENTER, QUOTE, RETURN, SPACE, and TAB.
- Strings are set off by double quotes. + is the concatenation operator.
- In event handler definitions, the handler begins with *on* and then has in parentheses the name of the type of handler. For example, a mouse click is handled by an *on(release)* handler.

  *on (release) {*
     *gotoAndPlay(100);*
  *}*

- User-defined functions look like this:

  *function youreInMyWay(intruder:String, num:Number) {*
     *trace("Hey!" + intruder + "I told you" + num + "times!");*
     *trace("Get out of my way!");*
     *beep();*
  *}*

- Function calls send arguments in parentheses. If there are no arguments, empty parentheses are used.
- *for* loops are done as follows:

  *for (i = 1; i <= 10; i++) {*
     . . .
  *}*

- *while* loops are done as follows:

  *while(i < 10) {*
     . . .
  *}*

- *if* statements are done as follows:

  *if (i < 10) {*
     . . .
  *}*

- *if else* statements are done as follows:

    *if (i < 10)*

    *. . .*

    *else if (i == 10)*

    *. . .*

### 8.4.3.3 Where Do I Put My Code?

The terminology regarding code in Flash is essentially the same as the terminology in Director. A script is one or more procedures grouped together, as if typed as one document. In Flash, a script can be attached to a frame of some timeline or to an object on stage. (We'll also see scripts that define classes of objects, but these are handled differently.) If you attach a script to a frame on the timeline, it is executed when that frame is passed. If you attach a script to an object on stage, the object can respond to some event, like a key press or mouse click. Certain events in Flash automatically generate messages that call event handlers. The code for event handlers is by default undefined—that is, it does nothing. You can define an event handler to do what you want it to do, or leave it undefined.

As with Director, you need to know which events generate which handler calls. Some important events are summarized in Table 8.5. (The list is not exhaustive.) If no definition is given, you can assume the obvious meaning. Notice that the mouse events are specific to the object or movie clip to which they're attached (being activated only when the mouse is on the object). In contrast, mouse-related *movie clip events* are triggered when the mouse is

| TABLE 8.5 | Some Important Events in Flash | | | |
|---|---|---|---|---|
| **Mouse Events** | **Keyboard Events** | **Movie Clip Events for the Mouse** | **Movie Clip Events for the Keyboard** | **Movie Clip Events for Loading Data** |
| *on(press)*—called when mouse is pressed over a button or movie clip | *on(keypress)*—called whenever a key is pressed. You can check to see which key, as in on (keyPress "<Space>") | *onClipEvent (mouseDown)*—called when mouse is pressed anywhere on stage | *onClipEvent (keyDown)*—can be used to create key-combination shortcuts | *onClipEvent(data)*—called when a movie clip is finished loading data from an external source |
| *on(release)*—called when a mouse is released over a button or movie clip | | *onClipEvent (mouseUp)*—called when mouse is released anywhere on stage | *onClipEvent (keyUp)*—can be used to create key-combination shortcuts | *onClipEvent (load)*—called when a movie clip enters a scene |
| *on(releaseOutside)* | | *onClipEvent (enterFrame)*—called every time a movie clip enters a new frame | | *onClipEvent (unload)*—called when a movie clip leaves a scene |
| *on(rollOver)* | | *onClipEvent (mouseMove)* | | |
| *on(rollOut)* | | | | |
| *on(dragOver)* | | | | |
| *on(dragOut)* | | | | |

clicked anywhere on stage. The difference between keyboard events and keyboard-related movie clip events is that keyboard events can check for the pressing of only one key. The keyboard-related movie clip events (*keyUp* and *keyDown*) can check for more than one key at a time, and thus can be used for defining multiple keystrokes.

So here's a simple scenario for basic interactivity in Flash, analogous to the one we gave you in Director for looping on a frame and then going to another frame when a button is pressed.

- Create a button symbol as described earlier.
- Put an instance of the button on stage by dragging it from the library.
- Click on frame 1 in the timeline. Go to the action panel and type

  *stop( );*

- At run-time, this will cause the playhead to stop on frame 1 and wait for you to do something (*i.e.*, click the button).
- Go to frame 30 and insert a keyframe. The button should appear on the stage between frames 1 and 30.
- Click on frame 30 in the timeline. In the property inspector, give the frame a name. We called it "Hi".
- At frame 30, create a textbox that says "Hi!"
- Open the actions panel. At frame 30, attach a script that says *stop( );* by typing it into the actions panel.
- In the left pane of the actions panel, select the button. Then in the right pane, type the script

  *on (release) {*
  *    gotoAndPlay("Hi");*
  *}*

If you test this movie with Control\Test Movie, here's what happens: The playhead stops at frame 1 because you put a *stop( )* there. When you click the button, the playhead is instructed by *gotoAndPlay* to go to the frame labeled "Hi". This will cause the playhead to go to frame 30, and you know you're there because you see the text "Hi!" on the stage. Since there is a *stop( )* script on the frame, the playhead will stop there.

That's enough to get you started on basic interactivity. A couple of things to note: Frame scripts don't have to be surrounded by a function name and braces. You just start declaring variables and listing your lines of code. Whatever is in the frame script will be executed when the playhead enters the frame, and the variables declared in the frame will be accessible from other frame scripts in that timeline. For scripts attached to a button or movie clip, you have to know the name of the event handler you're defining. As with Director, you can have more than one function in a script. One function can call another function as long as the function being called is accessible, which it is, if the called function is defined in the same script.

We've shown you how to define a handler by attaching the handler definition directly to an object—for example, attaching an *on(release)* handler to a button. There's another way to do it, called an **event handler method** (as opposed to **event handler**). Here's an example. Using an event handler method, you can define the handler for a button called *restart_btn* as follows:

  *restart_btn.onRelease {*
  *    gotoAndPlay("init");*
  *}*

The idea is that you put the variable name first—associated with a button or movie clip—then a dot, then the name of the function. These function names can be derived from the list of mouse events in Table 8.5. (*on(press)* becomes *onPress*, *on(release)* becomes *onRelease*, and so forth.) When the handler is defined this way, the function is placed in a frame script. The advantage of using an event handler method rather than an event handler is that you can define the event to be handled one way at one time, and a different way at a later time (with a new event handler method attached to a later frame).

### 8.4.3.4 Programming a Simple Game in Flash: Blackjack

We'll use the same Blackjack game that we used in the previous section to demonstrate the differences between Director and Flash. This game will illustrate the use of ActionScript to implement game logic and move cards around. It doesn't use the type of tweening described above. (Tweening would be useful, however, in creating a splash screen for the game—an opening dynamic sequence that tells the name of the game, gets the players revved up, and ends in a *play* button.) As before, we'll show two implementations of the game, the second using a little OOP.

The layout of the game in Flash is shown in Figure 8.28. The stage is covered by a brown wood table. The buttons, cards, and background are put on separate layers. The red rectangle in the middle of the stage is actually a stack of 52 cards face down, each of which is a movie clip symbol. The hit button is for the player or dealer to request another card. The dealer is on the right.

The actions layer doesn't actually have any visible objects on it. You use the actions layer as a place to keep all the scripts associated with frames. To place a script on a frame, you select a frame on the actions layer, go to the actions panel, and type a script there. In the figure, you can see the script associated with frame one.

There are three named frames in the actions layer shown: *begin*, *init*, and *deal*. A frame script is on each of these frames. The *begin* frame has the movie's initialization script on it

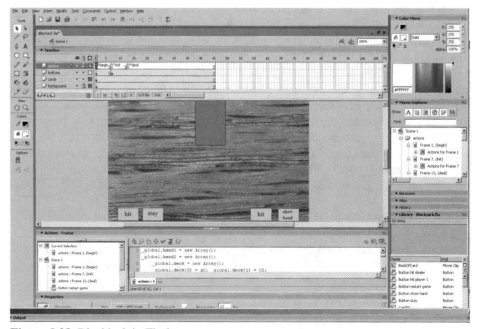

**Figure 8.28** Blackjack in Flash

**CODE SEGMENT 8.13**    **CREATING A DECK OF CARDS IN ACTIONSCRIPT**

```
/*Create deck of cards********************************/
_global.hand1 = new Array();
_global.hand2 = new Array();
_global.deck = new Array();
_global.deck[0] = AC; _global.deck[1] = C2;
_global.deck[2] = C3; _global.deck[3] = C4;
_global.deck[4] = C5; _global.deck[5] = C6;
_global.deck[6] = C7; _global.deck[7] = C8;
_global.deck[8] = C9; _global.deck[9] = C10;
_global.deck[10] = JC; _global.deck[11] = QC;
/*Insert the other three suits into the deck similarly.
Code deleted here, but it's same as above.*/
_global.deck[0].v = 11;
for (i = 1; i <= 9; i++)
    _global.deck[i].v = i++;
for (i = 10; i <= 12; i++)
    _global.deck[i].v = 10;
_global.deck[13].v = 11;
for (i = 14; i <= 22; i++)
    _global.deck[i].v = i-12;
for (i = 23; i <= 25; i++)
    _global.deck[i].v = 10;
_global.deck[26].v = 11;
for (i = 27; i <= 35; i++)
    _global.deck[i].v = i-25;
for (i = 36; i <= 38; i++)
    _global.deck[i].v = 10;
_global.deck[39].v = 11;
for (i = 40; i <= 48; i++)
    _global.deck[i].v = i-38;
for (i = 49; i <= 51; i++)
    _global.deck[i].v = 10;
_global.hand1 = new Array();
_global.hand2 = new Array();
```

(Code Segment 8.13). The *init* frame initializes a new game by putting the previously dealt hands back in the deck and shuffling it (Code Segment 8.14). The *deal* frame deals two cards to each player as a new game begins (Code Segment 8.14).

Each of the 52 cards in the deck is a movie clip, created by drawing a card on the stage and saving it as a movie clip. We need only one instance of each card, so you might wonder why they aren't just graphic symbols. It's because movie clip symbols can be given variable names, which makes it possible for you to refer to them in scripts. (Graphic symbols can't be given names.) Another good reason to make the card a movie clip is because then you can animate the card to go from a *back* to a *front* state—flipping the card. This is done in the movie clip's internal timeline.

**CODE SEGMENT 8.14**    **INITIALIZING A NEW CARD GAME IN ACTIONSCRIPT**

```
//Put the hands from the previous game back in the deck
a = _global.hand1.length;
b = _global.hand2.length;
for (i = 0; i < a; i++) {
    c = _global.hand1.shift();
    _global.deck[_global.deck.length] = c;
}
for (i = 0; i < b; i++) {
    c = _global.hand2.shift();
    _global.deck[_global.deck.length] = c;
}
//Put all cards off the table
for (i = 0; i < 52; i++) {
    _global.deck[i]._x = -125;
    _global.deck[i]._y = -10;
}
back._x = -112;
back._y = 229;
_global.player = 1;
_global.player = 1;
_global.maxDepth = 1;
_global.hand1 = new Array();
_global.hand2 = new Array();
//Shuffle
for (i = 0; i < 52; i++) {
    r = random(52);
    temp = _global.deck[i];
    _global.deck[i] = _global.deck[r];
    _global.deck[r] = temp;
}
```

The deck is created and initialized as an Array of movie clips in the frame script on the *begin* frame, as shown in Code Segment 8.13. The Array class is used in Flash where the list was used in Director. An additional complication is that movie clips for the cards are placed on the stage in a fixed order, which means they have a depth relative to each other, the one on top covering the other. In the *init* frame script, the references to these movie clips on the deck are shuffled. Thus, when a card is dealt from the deck and another is dealt to the same player afterwards, there's no assurance that the second card dealt will appear on stage on top of the first. The depth of the cards must be checked and possibly swapped to put the one most recently dealt on top as they are displayed in a hand.

Like Director, Flash is inherently object-oriented, and you use classes even if you never define one of your own. Movie clips, like all built-in classes, have certain properties, including *_height*, *_name*, *_visible*, *_x*, and *_y* (just to name a few). An interesting thing to note is that a movie clip can be given a new property on the fly. For example, you can give a movie clip called *myMovieClip_mc* a new property called *value* with the statement

    *myMovieClip_mc.value = 10*

Thus, the statement

   *_global.deck[0].v = 11*

in Code Segment 8.15 creates a new property called *v* for the movie clip that is at position 0 of the global deck. This is how the value of a card is stored in the frame script that first creates the deck of cards.

The script shown in Code Segment 8.15 makes use of the card movie clip's internal timeline to flip the card before moving it into position. On its own timeline, the card

---

**CODE SEGMENT 8.15    DEALING CARDS AND COMPUTING VALUE OF HAND IN ACTIONSCRIPT**

```
//Deal the first card to player 1
c = _global.deck.shift();
_global.hand1[0] = c;
c.goToAndPlay("flip");
c._x = 55;
c._y = 70;
//Deal second card to player 1
c = _global.deck.shift();
_global.hand1[1] = c;
c.goToAndPlay("flip");
c._x = 75;
c._y = 90;
if (c.getDepth() < _global.hand1[0].getDepth())
    c.swapDepths(_global.hand1[0]);
//Deal the first card to player 2
//Deal second card to player 2 (done similarly, but omitted here)
//Compute value of player's hand
_global.score = 0;
_global.score = _global.hand1[0].v + _global.hand1[1].v;
if (_global.score > 21)
    _global.score -= 10;
if (_global.score == 21) {
    x = back._x;
    y = back._y;
    back._x = -112;
    back._y = 229;
    _global.hand2[0]._x = x;
    _global.hand2[0]._y = y;
    trace("Player 1 hand = " + _global.score);
    trace("Player 2 hand = " + _global.score2);
    trace("You WIN, Player 1!");
    gotoAndPlay("init");
    return;
}
//Compute value of dealer's hand (done similarly, but omitted
  here)
//Set position for next card to be placed on table
_global.newx = 95;
_global.newy = 110;
stop();
```

movie clip starts by showing the back of the card. The card is tweened so that gets progressively narrower, simulating how it would look to flip the card over if you're looking straight on to the card. When it's sufficiently narrow, the back view of the card is removed and the face of the card put in its place, first narrow and then progressively wider. When the card is completely flipped over, its $\_x$ and $\_y$ properties are changed to move it into place onstage.

This shows you the basic scheme for Blackjack in Flash. Now let's look at how you might do this with a little bit of object-oriented programming.

**ASIDE:** If you want to be able to add more properties to a class at run-time, declare the class as a ***dynamic class***, as in

> *dynamic class Player {*
>
> *. . .*
>
> *}*

All Flash built-in classes are dynamic.

### 8.4.3.5 Object-Oriented Programming in ActionScript

To give you a taste of OOP in Lingo in Director, we showed how you could create a Card class that encapsulates the look and value of each card—associating a bitmap cast member for what the card looks like and an integer for its value. But there isn't really any motivation to do this in ActionScript. In the implementation described above, you use an array of MovieClips for the deck, and we showed you how easy it is to add another property to a MovieClip, the value of the card, simply by writing an assignment statement that has that property on the left-hand side.

So let's consider another improvement to the card game. What if you want to allow more than one player to join the game, in addition to the dealer? (We'd have to redesign the stage to accommodate these new players, but we'll set that issue aside in order to concentrate on the OOP features.) Let's see how you define a class in ActionScript.

Class definitions in ActionScript look a lot like they look in C++ and Java. Here's a definition for the player class.

```
class Player {
    var hand:Array;
    var playerNum:Number;
    function Player(n:Number) {
        playerNum = n;
        hand = new Array();
    }
    function getScore() {
        . . .
    }
}
```

You get a text editor for creating a new class by going to File\New\ActionScript File. When you define a new class in ActionScript, you must save it in a file called *myClass.as* in the same directory as the Flash movie you're authoring, where *myClass* is the name of the class. Thus, our class would be stored in a file called *Player.as*.

Once you've defined the class, you create an instance of it with a call to *new*. In our example, we would begin the game by asking the user how many players there will be. Then we would create as many players as needed with calls like the following. (The players could be put in an array, so we would execute this statement for each *ith* player).

```
var player[i]:Player = new Player(i);
```

Once a player is created, you can access properties as you would expect, through dot notation.

That's the basic idea. There are lots of other features that you may find useful, very similar to OOP in Java and C++. For example, you can use accessor functions public and private members, static data members, inheritance, and packages. ActionScript has evolved to a full-featured OOP language which gives you all the benefits of encapsulation, data protection, and modularity if you want to design your program with these features. We leave it to you now to explore how OOP might work for your purposes.

### 8.4.3.6 Optimizing for Distribution

The options for publishing your movie in Flash are similar to those in Director. A *projector* (stand-alone application) can be made for Windows (EXE) or Mac (HQX). This can be played without the user having the Flash authoring environment or even the player, since the player is embedded into it. If you want to publish it on the web, you save it as a SWF file with an accompanying HTML page.

To prepare your Flash movie for distribution, you need to consider your target audience and think about how to optimize your file size without compromising the quality of the production. Flash allows you to set compression options for imported bitmap images. You can choose to compress them with lossy JPEG compression, setting a quality level. Alternatively, you could choose lossless PNG and GIF compression.

Flash can import and export video using the Sorenson Spark codec. You have a number of compression options for sound, including ADPCM, MP3, and raw (no compression). You can set the compression method globally for all sounds or individually for certain sounds.

The Flash Player has a bandwidth profiler that allows you to test your movie's performance in the context of the download speed you expect the users to have (56 kb/s, DSL, and the like). This will let you know if the download speed can keep up with your movie's frame rate.

## 8.5 NOW THE FUN BEGINS!

You're familiar with the tools for digital media production. You know some of the science and mathematics behind the tools. It's all out there, waiting for you to apply your creativity. Photography, vector graphics, algorithmic art, digital audio, MIDI, digital video, 2D animations—all at your fingertips, ready to be molded by your imagination. You've only scratched the surface here. There's so much more to know, and the field is constantly growing and changing. You need never be bored. Enjoy!

## APPLICATIONS AND PROGRAMS

1. Download and install Processing from www.processing.org. Look at the example programs. Design and implement your own Processing program for creative manipulation of a bitmap. Try adding sound to your program. If you have experience with Java programming, consider how you would have to implement this program in Java, without the Processing API.

2. Download and install a trial version of MAX/MSP and Jitter. Review their tutorials. Write a small program in each of the languages (*e.g.*, an algorithmic music creation program in MAX, a reverb filter in MSP, and a blending mode algorithm in Jitter).

3. Create a Director movie that presents a reading of a poem along with bitmap images that illustrate it. Choose a poem with vivid imagery. ("Pied Beauty" by Gerard Manley Hopkins, "The Wild Geese" by Wendell Berry, or "Dream-Land" by Edgar Allan Poe would work well.) Consider the best format for the images—in file type, compression, and size. Consider the best format for audio. Experiment with different possibilities, analyzing how they affect the movie size and quality. Play the movie on different computers and consider timing issues (related to synchronizing the images with the sound).

4. Create a one-minute web-based advertisement in Director for some hypothetical product or service. Make it dynamic, with sound, motion, and possibly interactivity.

5. Create a one-minute web-based commercial in Flash for some hypothetical product or service. Make it dynamic, with sound, motion, and possibly interactivity.

6. Create an animation in Flash that uses one movie clip within another—for example, a helicopter with a spinning blade, a car with rotating wheels, or a winking eye in a moving face. Tween the top level movie clip. For example, the helicopter could move across the screen, getting smaller as it's moving away from the viewer; the car could drive across the screen; or the head could turn as it's winking.

7. Multimedia language comparison project, online.

# REFERENCES

## Print Publications

*Adobe Flash CS3 Professional Classroom in a Book.* Berkeley, CA: Adobe Press, 2007.

Besley, Kristian, David Powers, Sham Bhangal, and Eric Dolecki. *Foundation ActionScript for Flash 8.* Berkeley, CA: APress (Friends of Ed), 2006.

Blum, Frank. *Digital Interactive Installations: Programming Interactive Installations Using the Software Package MAX/MSP/Jitter.* VDM Verlag, 2007.

English, James. *Macromedia Flash: Training from the Source.* Berkeley, CA: Macromedia Press, 2005.

Flanagan, David. *Java in a Nutshell.* Sebastopol, CA: O'Reilly Media, Inc., 2005.

Greenberg, Ira. *Creative Coding and Computational Art.* Berkeley, CA: Friends of Ed, 2006.

Guzdial, Mark. *Introduction to Computing and Programming in Python: A Multimedia Approach.* Upper Saddle River: Prentice-Hall, 2005.

Liang, Y. Daniel. *Introduction to Java Programming—Comprehensive Edition.* 6th ed. Upper Saddle River: Prentice-Hall, 2006.

Maeda, John. *Creative Code: Aesthetics + Computation.* Thames and Hudson, 2004.

Makar, Job, and Danny Patterson. *Macromedia Flash 8 ActionScript: Training from the Source.* Berkeley, CA: Macromedia Press, 2006.

Mennonah, Dave. *Macromedia Director MX 2004: Training from the Source.* Berkeley, CA: Macromedia Press, 2004.

Moock, Colin. *Essential ActionScript 3.0.* Adobe Developer Library, 2007.

Peters, Keith. *Foundation ActionScript Animation: Making Things Move.* Berkeley, CA: APress (Friends of Ed), 2006.

Reas, Casey, Ben Fry, and John Maeda. *Processing: A Programming Handbook for Visual Designers and Artists.* MIT Press: 2007.

Winkler, Todd. *Composing Interactive Music: Techniques and Ideas Using Max.* Boston: MIT Press, 2001.

Yeung, Rosanna, with Lynda Weinman. *Macromedia Flash MX 2004: Hands-On Training.* Berkeley, CA: Peachpit Press, 2004.

## Websites

ChucK

   http://chuck.cs.princeton.edu/

Director

   http://www.adobe.com/products/director/

Flash

   http://www.adobe.com/products/flash/flashpro/

Java

   http://java.sun.com/

Processing

   http://www.processing.org

Python

   http://www.python.org/

Max/MSP/Jitter

   http://www.cycling74.com/

# Index

# HEALTH PSYCHOLOGY

Biopsychosocial Interactions          Eighth Edition